CW01663890

Dutch Portraits

The Age of Rembrandt and Frans Hals

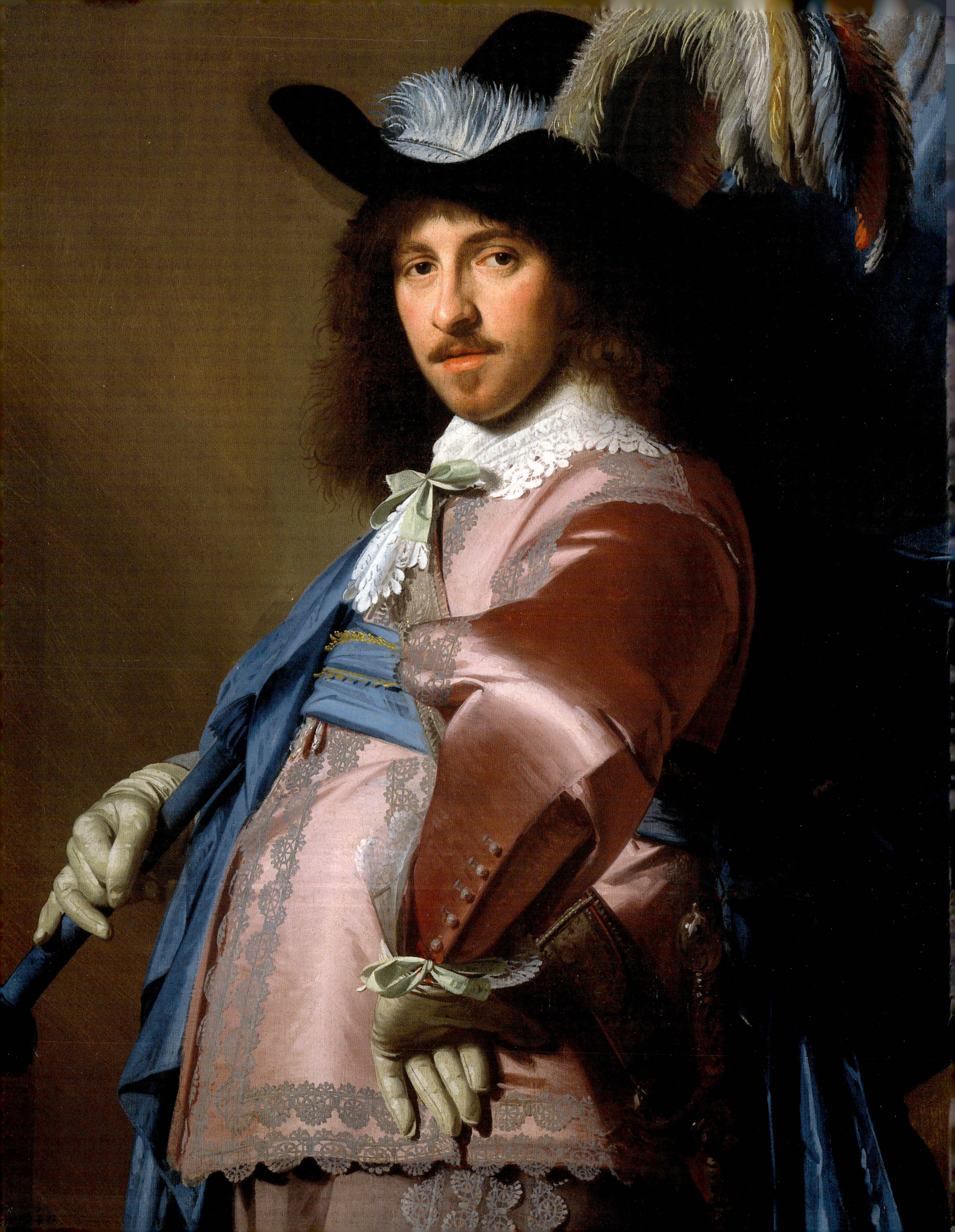

DUTCH PORTRAITS

The Age of Rembrandt and Frans Hals

Rudi Ekkart & Quentin Buvelot

Contributors
Marieke de Winkel, Axel Rüger, Peter van der Ploeg,
Ariane van Suchtelen and Lea van der Vinde

Editor
Quentin Buvelot

Translated from the Dutch by Beverly Jackson

Royal Picture Gallery Mauritshuis, The Hague
National Gallery Company, London
Waanders Publishers, Zwolle

This book was published to accompany the exhibitions

Dutch Portraits:
The Age of Rembrandt and Frans Hals
held at The National Gallery, London
27 June – 16 September 2007

Hollanders in beeld:
Portretten uit de Gouden Eeuw
held at the Royal Picture Gallery
Mauritshuis, The Hague
13 October 2007 – 13 January 2008

Sponsored by
Royal Dutch Shell plc

All measurements give height before width.
Figure numbers followed by a letter refer to comparatives to the catalogue.

Front cover
Rembrandt, *The Anatomy Lesson of Dr Nicolaes Tulp*, 1632 (cat. 53)

Frontispiece
Johannes Verspronck, *Portrait of Andries Stilte as a Standard-Bearer*, 1640 (cat. 64)

Contents

Sponsor's Foreword

One hundred years of Anglo-Dutch partnership in the Royal Dutch/Shell Group and, since 2005, Royal Dutch Shell: this has inspired the exhibition *Dutch Portraits: The Age of Rembrandt and Frans Hals* in the two Shell 'alliance' cities of London and The Hague.

The exhibition highlights Dutch portrait painters of the seventeenth century, the heyday of the merchants, investors, manufacturers, preachers and seafarers of the Dutch Republic. Wind and peat were their energy sources, money their motivator, and painted portraits the symbols of their wealth and status.

Merchants held positions in many political and economic governing bodies and patronised the arts and sciences. In the egalitarian Netherlands, it was not the aristocracy or the Court but primarily 'business people' that placed orders with the portrait-painting industry of that age.

Supremely self-assured they gaze upon us, not without a certain amount of smugness about their prosperity – reflecting the dichotomy between the legacy of Erasmus and the precepts of Calvin remarked upon by the historian Johan Huizinga. And we look back, perhaps sharing Simon Schama's view that here we see 'the moral ambiguity of good fortune'.

One exception is the portrait of Michiel de Ruyter, who made his fortune as a whaling seaman and merchant captain and was brought out of retirement to command the Republic's naval squadrons. He is portrayed in that capacity: a war hero in what would be a notably pacifist country in later centuries. He served in three Anglo-Dutch naval wars. These wars notwithstanding, the two countries became fully reconciled, forming close and friendly ties that are convincingly and proudly epitomised by the 100 years of the Shell Group.

Jeroen van der Veer
Chief Executive, Royal Dutch Shell plc

Directors' Foreword

The portraiture of the Dutch Golden Age is one of the most fascinating phenomena in the history of Western art. It is characterised by a pronounced realism, an enormous diversity and, above all, superb artistic quality. The large output of portraits stemmed directly from the extraordinary economic success of the Dutch Republic, one of the superpowers of seventeenth-century Europe. While in the rest of the continent economic power was concentrated in the hands of the courts and the landed nobility, the Republic's power arose from the success of the fast-growing elite of merchants and entrepreneurs, the so-called regents. Their economic position made it easy for them to obtain high positions in local authorities and civic institutions, thus curtailing the influence of the court and aristocracy in The Hague. The result was a new society of 'burghers' – the emerging middle-classes.

The self-confidence boosted by this new wealth was expressed in numerous portraits. In the new social fabric of the seventeenth-century Dutch Republic, it soon became customary for prosperous burghers to order portraits, resulting in a higher level of production than ever before. Portraits were often commissioned to commemorate important moments in people's lives: engagements and marriages, the birth of a child, or an appointment to high office. These commissions gave artists an opportunity to satisfy their clients by thinking of new themes and compositions for their portraits. The diversity of portraits is unprecedented: aside from small pieces for private homes and larger ones depicting couples and families, monumental group portraits were painted of the administrators of charitable institutions and members of the civic guard.

Remarkably, it is a long time since a special exhibition was last organised on seventeenth-century portraiture of the Northern Netherlands. The last major exhibition on this subject was held in Amsterdam, in the Rijksmuseum, in 1952. Several shows have been held since then on aspects of portraiture – marriage portraits (Haarlem 1986), militia pieces (Haarlem 1988), the œuvre of Frans Hals (Washington, London and Haarlem, 1989–90), Rembrandt's self-portraits (London and The Hague, 1999–2000), children's portraits (Haarlem and Antwerp, 2000–1) and Amsterdam portraits (Amsterdam, 2002–3) – but no one has previously ventured to present a survey. A 1952 exhibition, entitled *Three centuries of portraits in the Netherlands 1500–1800*, included almost 250 portrait paintings, drawings and etchings, many of which were on loan from private collections. The enormous size of that exhibition must have made a visit, however fascinating, a rather exhausting experience. The present exhibition has been conceived on a smaller scale deliberately, and is confined to paintings produced in the seventeenth century. In addition, it was decided to exclude self-portraits and *tronies*. The aim was to produce a balanced survey of about 60 portrait paintings (some of which cannot be exhibited at both venues), focusing primarily on masterpieces. The two great masters of the genre, Rembrandt and Frans Hals, are both represented with their finest works. Portraits from the beginning and end of their careers illustrate the develop-ment of their painting technique magnificently. In addition, the exhibition includes one or more works by 27 other painters. The nucleus of the exhibition is formed by the permanent collections of the National Gallery and the Mauritshuis.

The main theme of the presentation is the development of portraiture, and its range: from works depicting individuals and couples, children and families to group portraits, including militia and regent pieces. In addition to these primary categories of portrait paintings, there are numerous subgenres, such as princely portraits, portrait miniatures and *portraits historiés* – portraits produced in the context of a Biblical, mythological or historical story. Within each of these subgenres, a selection is shown that produces impressive and exciting confrontations. After all, a portrait exhibition works best if the presentation offers a real 'experience'. Some of the portraits have never been seen in the Netherlands or England before, or not for a very long time, so discoveries lie in wait for the visitors. There is also a special reunion: in one case, the companion-pieces of a married couple are reunited, having been separated from each other many years ago (cats 35–6).

The exhibition was produced as a joint effort by the two museums: the idea for the exhibition was conceived and elaborated by Quentin Buvelot, Peter van der Ploeg and Axel Rüger. The leading expert on Northern Netherlandish portraiture, Rudi Ekkart, Director of the Netherlands Institute for Art History in The Hague, advised on the selection of works in the early stages of the project. He also wrote two introductory essays for this catalogue, which together provide a general survey of portraiture in the Golden Age. The third essay, on dress in seventeenth-century Northern Netherlandish portraits, was written by Marieke de Winkel, who has specialised in this subject. The catalogue, which was composed in The Hague, was conceived and elaborated by Buvelot, who also wrote most of the entries and edited the book as a whole. The basic principle was that the catalogue should be accessible to the general reader, but that it should also satisfy the curiosity of those wanting to know more. Van der Ploeg and Rüger supplied a number of catalogue entries, and some of the texts were written by Ariane van Suchtelen and Lea van der Vinde, both of whom work at the Mauritshuis. The writers drew gratefully on De Winkel's descriptions of the dress worn in the paintings. In London we are particularly grateful to Betsy Wieseman, who guided the exhibition and its catalogue to successful completion.

More than anyone else, we are indebted to our lenders – including many private collectors as well as a large number of museums – whose generosity and kind cooperation have helped to make this exhibition possible. In the first place, our thanks are due to Her Royal Highness, Queen Elizabeth II, who made available Rembrandt's fine *Double Portrait of Jan Rijcksen and Griet Jans ('The Shipbuilder and his Wife')* from 1633 (cat. 54). The painting is usually on view at Buckingham Palace. Baron Jan Six, Lord of Hillegom, and his son Jan Six, also deserve a separate mention for their willingness to part with Rembrandt's masterful *Portrait of Jan Six* from 1654 (cat. 57). This unique portrait, which hardly ever leaves its permanent place in the Six Collection, is the jewel in the crown of the exhibition in the Mauritshuis. The bylaws of the foundation that administers the collection do not permit the painting to leave the Netherlands. In London, other loans have been received with particular gratitude, including *'The Meagre Company'* by Frans Hals and Pieter Codde (cat. 21) from the Rijksmuseum. Since this group portrait measures over eight square metres, it was too large to be brought into the Mauritshuis, and is being exhibited only in London.

A major special exhibition such as *Dutch Portraits* can only be held with the financial support of third parties. The Mauritshuis and the National Gallery were most fortunate in the immensely generous support provided by Shell, as the exhibition's exclusive sponsor, in the context of the company's centennial anniversary in 2007. In 1907 the NV Royal Dutch Petroleum Company (The Hague) and Shell Transport and Trading Company Ltd (London) decided to combine their activities. At the beginning of 2005, the two merged into a single enterprise under British law – Royal Dutch Shell plc, with headquarters in The Hague.

An exhibition of portraits from the Dutch Golden Age is also, of course, an exhibition of those depicted, the men and women who shaped this epoch or lived through it. From the young Hugo Grotius, who was immortalised in a most arresting way by Jan van Ravesteyn (cat. 49) in 1599, at the threshold of the new century, to Constantijn Huygens, poet and secretary to the stadholders of Holland (cat. 34), and Michiel de Ruyter (cat. 1), whose likeness by Ferdinand Bol has become almost symbolic of the Dutch Republic's tenacity. This aspect of the exhibition also displays many points in common with seventeenth-century England: rivalry (wars and disputed dominion in the seas), friendship (two English princesses married princes of Orange) and trade relations. We hope that visitors to the exhibition will enjoy the superb paintings and the many stories that lie behind them.

Frederik J. Duparc
Director, Royal Picture Gallery Mauritshuis

Charles Saumarez Smith
Director, The National Gallery

Acknowledgements

In preparing this exhibition and the accompanying catalogue, we received the help of many institutions and individuals. We should like to thank all those who helped to make this exhibition and this catalogue possible. A special word of thanks is due to Frederik J. Duparc, Director of the Mauritshuis. He supported the exhibition enthusiastically from the beginning and contributed a great deal to its success, in particular by securing some crucial loans.

Several of the paintings were restored especially for the exhibition. The portraits of Jacob Olycan and his wife Aletta Hanemans, painted by Frans Hals in 1625 (cats 16–17), were restored in the Mauritshuis by Sabrina Meloni, with the assistance of the intern Alice Tate-Harte and Carol Pottasch. The result was a veritable metamorphosis of the two paintings, in which many details of the couple's dress, for instance, re-emerged into the light of day. The restoration of Nicolaes Pickenoy's *Osteology Lesson of Dr Sebastiaen Egbertsz* from 1619, which belongs to the Amsterdams Historisch Museum (cat. 45), also yielded a spectacular result.

Hals's *Portrait of Willem van Heythuysen* of about 1634–5 was also recently restored. This work was carried out by Martin Bijl, who, together with Pieter Biesboer, curator of the Frans Hals Museum, wrote the catalogue entry on this painting (cat. 20). The text dealing with another of Hals's paintings, '*The Meagre Company*', completed in 1637 by Pieter Codde (cat. 21), was provided by Jonathan Bikker, who was involved as a member of the academic staff in compiling and editing the Rijksmuseum's summary catalogue to be published later this year, in which the monumental group portrait is included.

The research for the exhibition and catalogue relied on a variety of sources. Among those who provided invaluable assistance were the staff of the Netherlands Institute for Art History in The Hague and its Portrait Iconography Collection. Assistant Curator Lea van der Vinde exerted herself with ceaseless dedication in looking up references in a vast volume of literature. She was also responsible for collecting the large number of images required.

The staff of the museums in London and The Hague made indispensable contributions to the organisation of this exhibition. At the National Gallery, our thanks are due particularly to the Director, Charles Saumarez Smith, who supported the project generously and enthusiastically from the outset. Betsy Wieseman, who became Curator of Dutch Paintings in London in December 2006, took care of the installation of the exhibition in London and provided the catalogue's editors with valuable advice.

In the Mauritshuis we are grateful to the Deputy Director, Victor Moussault, the project leader Ariane van Suchtelen, and the registrar André Jordaan. Our thanks are also due to Geert-Jan Borgstein, Simone Hollen, Marianne van der Kruit, Fehmi Pilat, Arjan Rijnsburger, Epco Runia, Mirjam van der Schoot, Pom Verhoeff, Caroline Walta, Pia Westgren and Antia Wiersma. The exhibition in The Hague was installed by Boy van den Hoorn and the staff of his technical service, with Michiel Leijenaar supervising the other general and technical work required for the exhibition. For the insurance of the paintings, indemnity was obtained from the Ministry of Education, Culture and Science by the Netherlands Institute for Cultural Heritage.

The Dutch texts were superbly translated into English by Beverley Jackson, while Dorine Duyster was responsible for copy-editing the Dutch edition. Victor de Leeuw was responsible for the book's attractive design. At Waanders Printers and Publishers in Zwolle, production was supervised by Marloes Waanders, Jan de Ruyter and Loes Hiddink.

This exhibition could not have been mounted without the willingness of the lenders to part temporarily with their precious paintings. This list of acknowledgements would therefore not be complete without the names of those who have helped substantially to make the exhibition a success: Her Majesty Queen Elizabeth II, London; Baron Jan Six, Lord of Hillegom, and his son Jan Six, Amsterdam; Pauline Kruseman, Norbert Middelkoop, Amsterdam; Ronald de Leeuw, Taco Dibbits, Amsterdam; Paul Huvenne, Nico Van Hout, Antwerp; Johan ter Molen, Marieke Spliethoff, Apeldoorn; Bernd Lindemann, Berlin; Daniëlle Lokin, Delft; Peter Schoon, Sander Paarlberg, Dordrecht; Emilie Gordenker, Edinburgh; Antoinette Visser, Marco van Baalen, The Hague; Karel Schampers, Pieter Biesboer, Haarlem; Executive Board, Elizabeth van Thüringen Fund Foundation, Haarlem;

Ruud Spruit, Cees Bakker, Hoorn; Michael Eissenhauer, Gregor Weber, Kassel; Sir Hugh Roberts, Desmond Shawe-Taylor, London; Sandy Nairne, London; Simon Thurley, Sandy Power, London; Richard Green, London; the late Robert Noortman, Eddy Schavemaker, Jeanette Gerritsma, Maastricht; Reinhold Baumstark, Marcus Dekiert, Munich; Konrad Bernheimer, Munich; George Wachter, New York; Mària van Berge-Gerbaud, Hans Buijs, Paris; Henri Loyrette, Vincent Pomarède, Blaise Ducos, Paris; Milan Knížák, Anja Ŝevĉik, Prague; Sjarel Ex, Jeroen Giltaij, Friso Lammertse, Rotterdam; John Buchanan, Robert Futernick, Lynn Federle Orr, San Francisco; Earl A. Powell III, Arthur Wheelock, Washington; Frau Hortense Anda-Bührle, and Lukas Gloor, Zürich, as well as private collectors who wish to remain anonymous. The generosity and cooperation kindly provided by those in charge of private and public collections concerned will be greatly appreciated by the exhibition's visitors.

Quentin Buvelot, *Curator Mauritshuis*
Peter van der Ploeg, *Chief Curator Mauritshuis*
Axel Rüger, *Director Van Gogh Museum, Amsterdam,*
formerly *Curator of Dutch Paintings at the National Gallery*

Curators of the exhibition

Lenders

Her Majesty Queen Elizabeth II
Cats 4 and 54

Private collections
Cats 2, 7, 20, 26, 37 and 52

Amsterdam
Six Collection
Cats 46 and 57

Amsterdam
Amsterdams Historisch Museum
Cats 30, 38 and 45

Amsterdam
Rijksmuseum
Cats 5, 15, 21 and 60

Amsterdam & Rijswijk
Netherlands Institute for Cultural Heritage
Cats 11 and 42

Antwerp
Koninklijk Museum voor Schone Kunsten
Cat. 65

Apeldoorn
Paleis Het Loo Nationaal Museum
Cat. 43

Berlin
Gemäldegalerie, Staatliche Museen
Cats 14, 36, 47 and 48

Delft
Museum Het Prinsenhof
Cat. 39

Dordrecht
Dordrechts Museum
Cat. 11

Edinburgh
National Gallery of Scotland
Cat. 7

The Hague
Haags Historisch Museum
Cats 41 and 50

The Hague
Royal Picture Gallery Mauritshuis
Cats 1, 2, 10, 16, 17, 32, 33, 40, 52, 53, 61 and 62

Haarlem
Frans Hals Museum
Cats 23 and 42

Hoorn
Westfries Museum
Cats 8 and 9

Kassel
Gemäldegalerie Alte Meister, Staatliche Museen
Cats 13 and 56

London
The National Gallery
Cats 3, 12, 22, 34, 44, 55, 58, 59 and 66

London
National Portrait Gallery
Cat. 31

London
English Heritage, Kenwood House
Cat. 19

Munich
Alte Pinakothek, Bayerische Staatsgemäldesammlungen
Cat. 18

Paris
Collection Frits Lugt, Institut Néerlandais
Cat. 49

Paris
Musée du Louvre
Cat. 35

Prague
Národní Galerie
Cat. 25

Rotterdam
Museum Boijmans Van Beuningen
Cats 29 and 63

San Francisco
Fine Arts Museums of San Francisco
Cat. 51

Washington
National Gallery of Art
Cats 6, 24, 28 and 64

Zürich
Stiftung Sammlung E.G. Bührle
Cat. 27

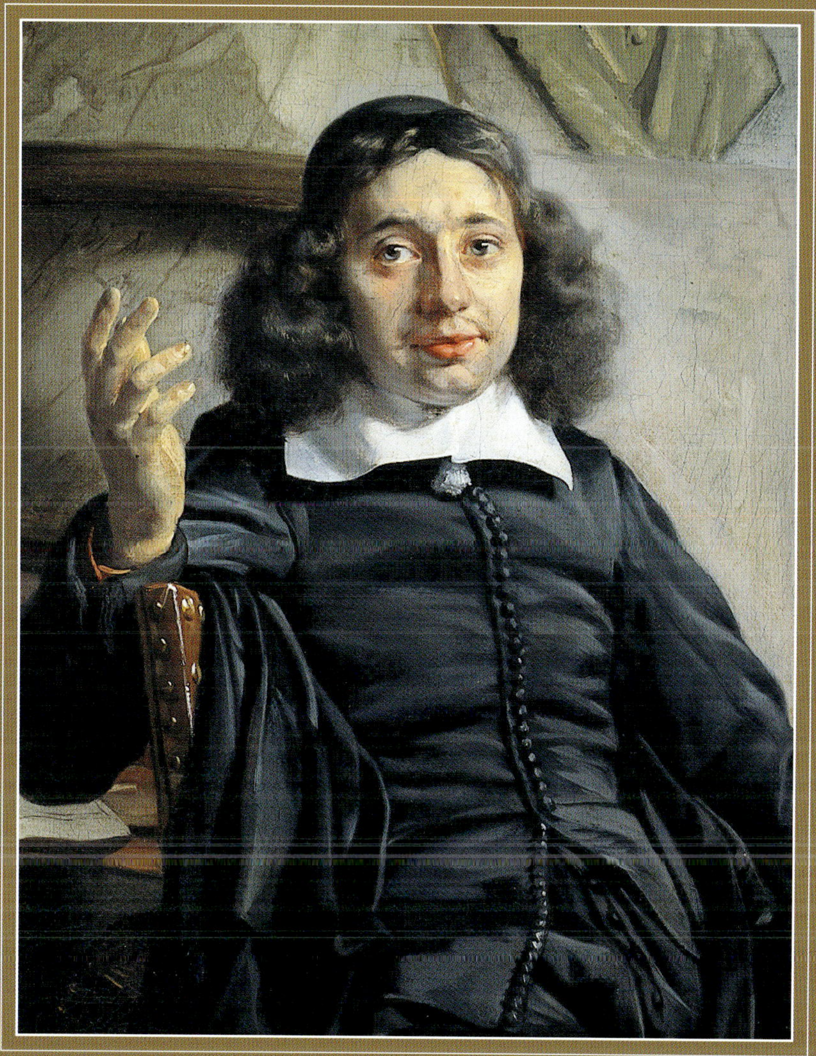

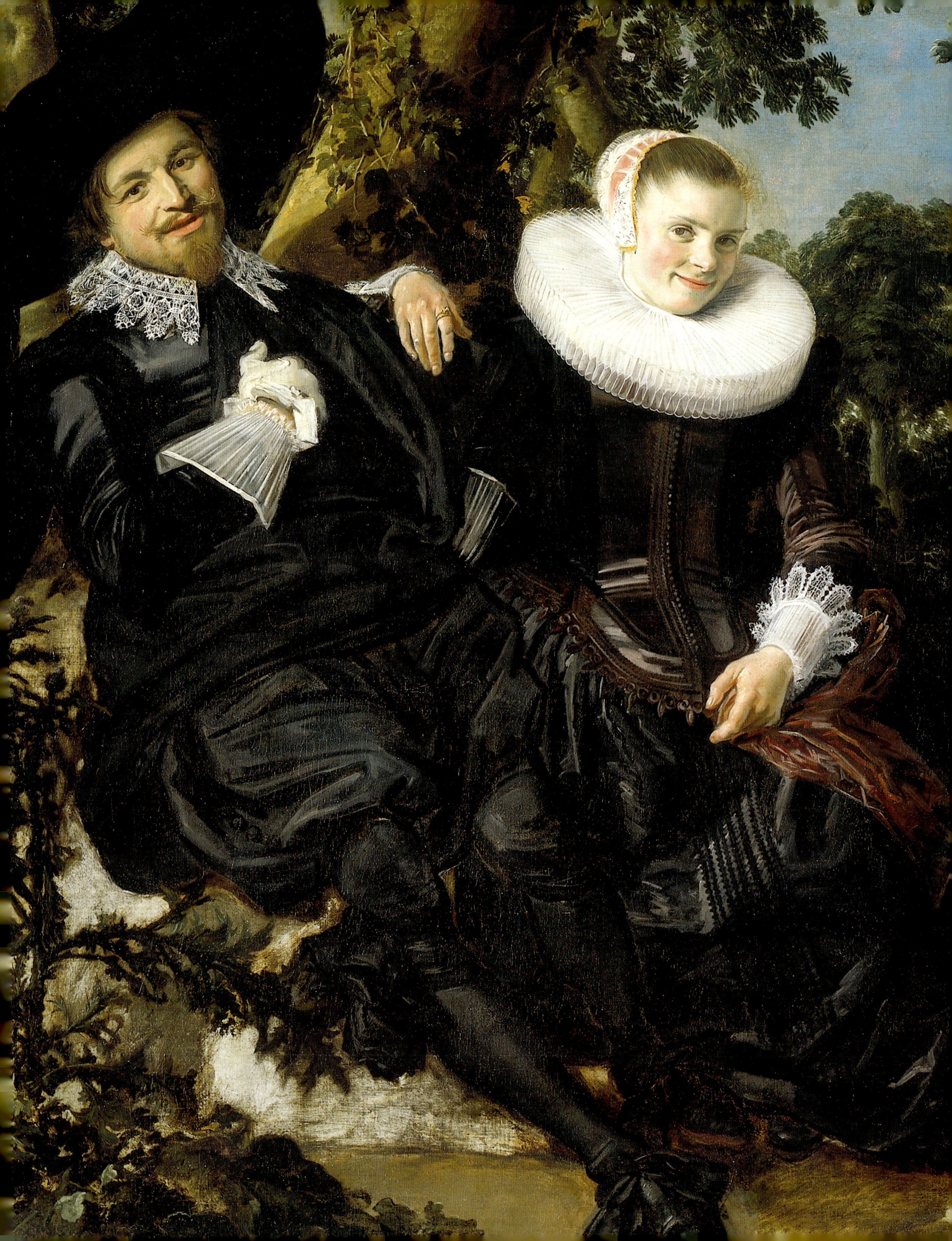

Portraits in the Golden Age

by Rudi Ekkart

One of the most important characteristics of seventeenth-century Dutch painting is the immense interest in the visible world to which it bears witness, expressed in countless landscapes, still lifes and portraits. By even the most conservative of estimates, the number of portraits painted in the Dutch Republic during the so-called 'Golden Age' runs to the hundreds of thousands.[1] A great many have been lost, but tens of thousands remain. The figures for portraits executed in other media pale in comparison to this abundance. After paintings, the largest category is that of portrait prints (p. 116, fig. 19a). Then there is a smaller number of portrait drawings, made either as designs for likenesses to be executed in a different technique (e.g. p. 210, fig. 60a) or as independent works of art. Finally, we must mention portrait sculptures, but these hardly flourished as a genre (fig. 1).[2] This essay will focus specifically on portrait paintings, varying from miniatures with a surface area of some 10 cm^2 (cat. 2) to enormous group portraits measuring almost 15 m^2 (see p. 32, fig. 22). Although portraits, along with landscapes, were produced more than any other types of paintings throughout the seventeenth century, the art critics of the day held this genre in low esteem. In 1604, Karel van Mander (1548–1606) – who had no qualms about producing portraits himself – described portraiture in his *Schilder-Boeck* as a 'side-road of the Arts',[3] to which painters had recourse for profit alone.

The term 'portrait' is used here in the narrowest sense, meaning a more or less accurate likeness of a specific person, produced in order to be recognisable (including cases in which the identity of the person depicted has been lost). This definition excludes studies of heads and other paintings, for which models sat but which were not intended as personal likenesses (fig. 2). Some of the paintings by Rembrandt that have been labelled 'self-portraits', for instance, belong more properly to the category of head studies,[4] sometimes known by the historical term *tronie*, than to portraiture proper.[5] One specific category consists of imaginary portraits of persons who had died long since without leaving any reliable likeness. Those who started their own gallery of family portraits often added ancestors from the fifteenth and sixteenth centuries in the form of imaginary portraits (see p. 50, fig. 46). Even when all such pieces and *tronies* are excluded, the portraiture of the seventeenth-century Northern Netherlands is numerically vast and enormously diverse, certainly in comparison to that of the preceding century. It is one of the pillars on which the fame of paintings from the Golden Age is based (see p. 47).

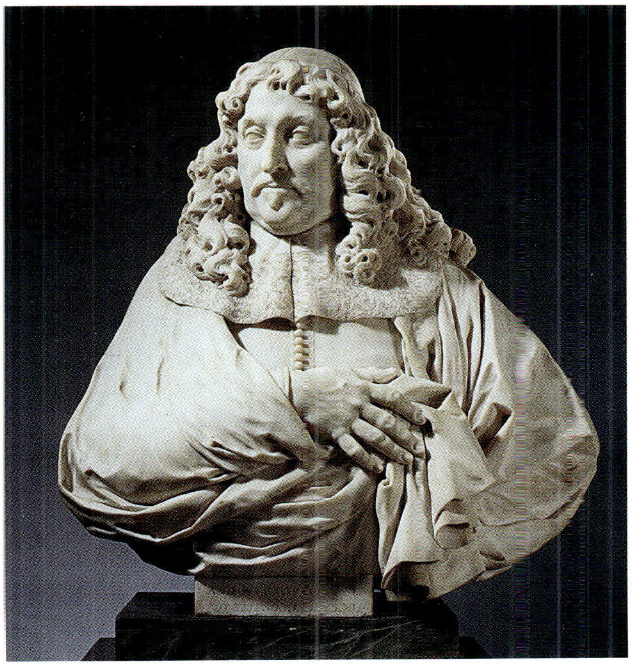

1.
Artus Quellinus,
Portrait of Andries de Graeff, 1661.
Marble, height 75 cm.
Rijksmuseum,
Amsterdam

◂◂
Frans Hals,
Double Portrait of Isaac Massa and Beatrix van der Laen (detail),
about 1622 (cat. 15)

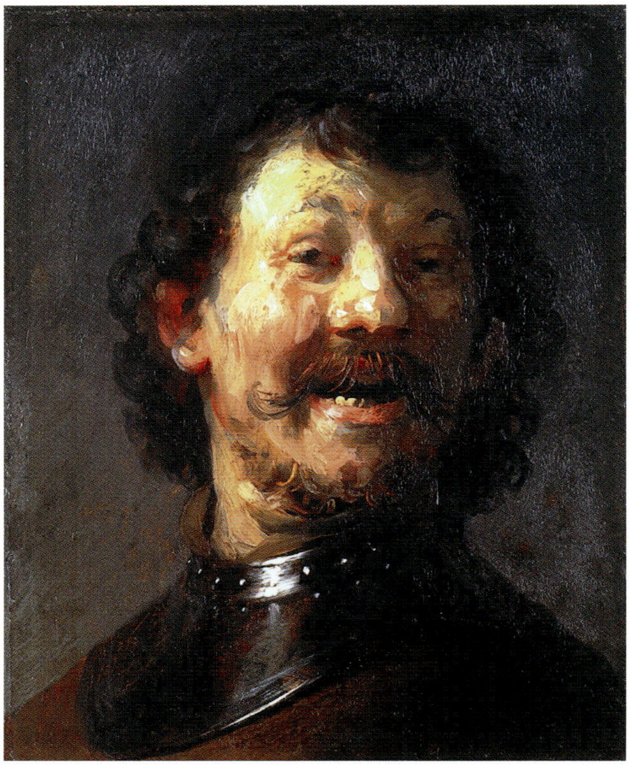

2.
Rembrandt,
The Laughing Man,
about 1629–30.
Oil on copper,
15 x 12 cm.
Mauritshuis,
The Hague

Viewed in this light, it is remarkable that for much of the twentieth century, portraits were thoroughly neglected in studies of seventeenth-century art and culture. While landscapes, genre pieces, still lifes and history paintings attracted rapidly growing interest and a steady stream of studies – and the prices of good paintings in these categories soared to unprecedented heights – scholarly and commercial interest in portraits lagged far behind, with the exception of such artists as Rembrandt (cats 51–61) and Frans Hals (cats 14–27). No general surveys of portraiture or discrete aspects of it were published, and monographs appeared on only a few of the many specialists in this field.[6] For numerous influential artists, the literature was long confined to nineteenth-century studies, brief texts in surveys and entries in encyclopaedic works.[7] Not until the past two decades has there been a reversal of this persistent neglect, as a growing number of exhibitions, books and articles have started to fill up the gaps in our knowledge. The turning-point came with the successful exhibition *Portretten van echt en trouw* held in 1986 in the Frans Hals Museum, Haarlem, focusing on portraits of couples and families.[8] This presentation of a subject that had often been viewed as dull showed the public and art historians alike new facets of portraiture. The upward trend in art historians' interest in portraits is clear, for instance, from a comparison of the survey of Dutch art of the seventeenth and eighteenth centuries by Jakob Rosenberg and Seymour Slive in the 1966 *Pelican History of Art* with Slive's revised version, which appeared in 1995.[9] While in 1966 the chapter on landscape painting was almost five times as long as that on portraiture, the ratio shrank to 2:1 in the 1995 edition. This points to a considerable shift in attitudes regarding the relative significance of these genres – the two genres of painting with the largest output in the seventeenth century.

Background

The development of the visual arts in the Northern Netherlands in the fifteenth and sixteenth centuries cannot be viewed in isolation from the situation in the Southern Netherlands, since there was no political or cultural divide between North and South in those days. Still, even in these early centuries there were regional differences, for instance between Flanders and Antwerp on the one hand, and Holland on the other. We should be wary, however, of equating trends in Holland with those in other parts of the Northern Netherlands. The province of Friesland, for instance, had distinct features of its own, and the cultural development of Gelderland was far more influenced by nearby German territories than by Holland.

Dutch Portraiture until the Eighty Years' War

In the early development of portraiture in the Netherlands – as in many areas of culture – we can still see the dominant influence of certain provinces of the Southern Netherlands, and Flanders in particular. Portraits were initially made primarily for display in churches: on memorial tablets and the wings of altarpieces, depicting patrons – almost exclusively sovereigns, nobles and senior clerics – and their deceased relatives. The oldest extant examples from the Northern Netherlands date from the latter half of the fourteenth century.[10] The earliest secular portraits depict members of these same groups, although in the cities of the Southern Netherlands we find an initial surge of interest in individual portraits of wealthy merchants as early as the fifteenth century. In the North, portraits made for any purpose other than to hang in a church were still extremely rare at that time, and were confined to the highest-ranking members of society. Most of these early portraits, such as that of Countess Jacoba of Bavaria, are known only from later copies. A rare example of an original is the small likeness of Lysbeth van Duvenvoorde made around 1430 (fig. 3), possibly a betrothal portrait; it formed a diptych together with a likeness of her husband Symon van Adrichem, which is no longer known.[11] Portraits on the wings of altarpieces and on memorial tablets were also quite rare in the northern provinces in the fifteenth century.

Not until after 1500 was there a clear increase in numbers of both secular and ecclesiastical applications of portraits; certain developments become discernible for the first time, both in terms of style and form and in an expansion of potential clientele.[12] In the first few decades of the sixteenth century we find major portraitists emerging in several cities: in Haarlem Jan Mostaert (about 1475–about 1556), in Amsterdam Jacob Cornelisz van Oostsanen (before 1470–1533), in Leiden Cornelis Engelbrechtsz (about 1468–1533) and Lucas van Leyden (1494–1533); and Jan Gossaert (1478–1532) from Hainault, who worked in both Middelburg and Utrecht. From about 1520–30 onwards, they were joined – and in part supplanted – by a new generation of gifted portraitists, born in the last decade of the fifteenth century: Jan van Scorel (1495–1562) in Utrecht, Maarten van Heemskerck (1498–1574) in Haarlem, and Dirck Jacobsz (about 1497–1567) in Amsterdam. All these artists made portraits for private homes as well as churches. After around 1530, there was a distinct increase in the number of cities and regions with their own local portraitists, most notably in Friesland. In many cities the clientele still consisted largely of nobles and senior clerics, but it was the changing trends in Amsterdam particularly that set the scene for the flowering of portraiture in the seventeenth century. For in Amsterdam (as earlier in the Flemish town of Bruges) the wealthy upper echelons of the city consisted primarily of burghers, and it was there that portraits became fully subsumed into upper middle-class life. One glance at the œuvre of someone like Dirck Jacobsz, whose father was the painter Jacob Cornelisz van Oostsanen, makes this abundantly clear. Jacobsz's portrait of Pompejus Occo, which was probably painted in 1531 (fig. 4),[13] deserves to be called one of the early milestones in Amsterdam portrait painting. As a banker, Occo had attained the status of 'monied aristocracy', but since he was a burgher by origin, this is a very early example in Holland of a burgher portrait with a princely ethos. Somewhat earlier, in 1529, Jacobsz had produced a work that was of groundbreaking significance to portraiture in Holland: the oldest known militia piece. It depicts 17 members of the civic guard, arranged in two rows, one above the other (fig. 5).[14] This painting inaugurated a tradition of militia pieces in Holland, which became a significant sub-category of burghers' portraits in the Northern Netherlands during the sixteenth and seventeenth centuries. Ten more militia pieces were produced in the following five years, and at least 26 more were painted between 1550 and 1567.[15] Over half of these paintings have been lost, but some are still known from

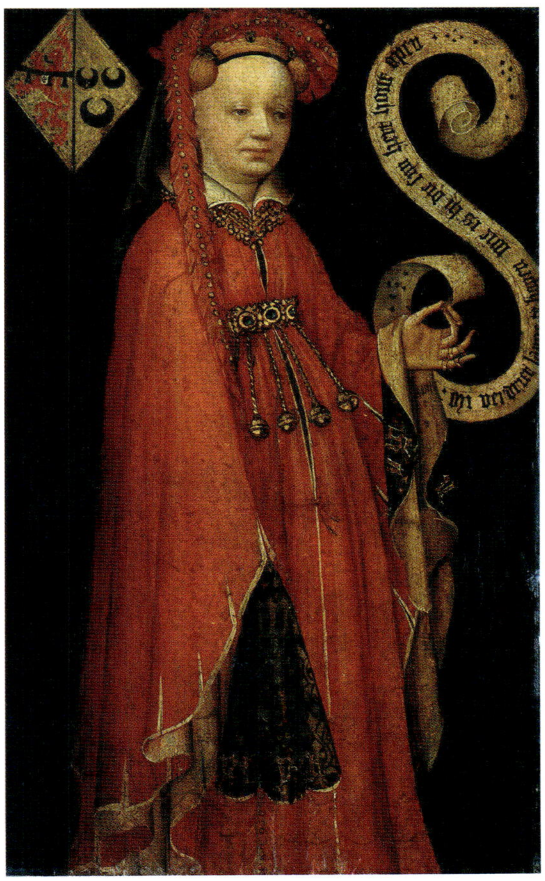

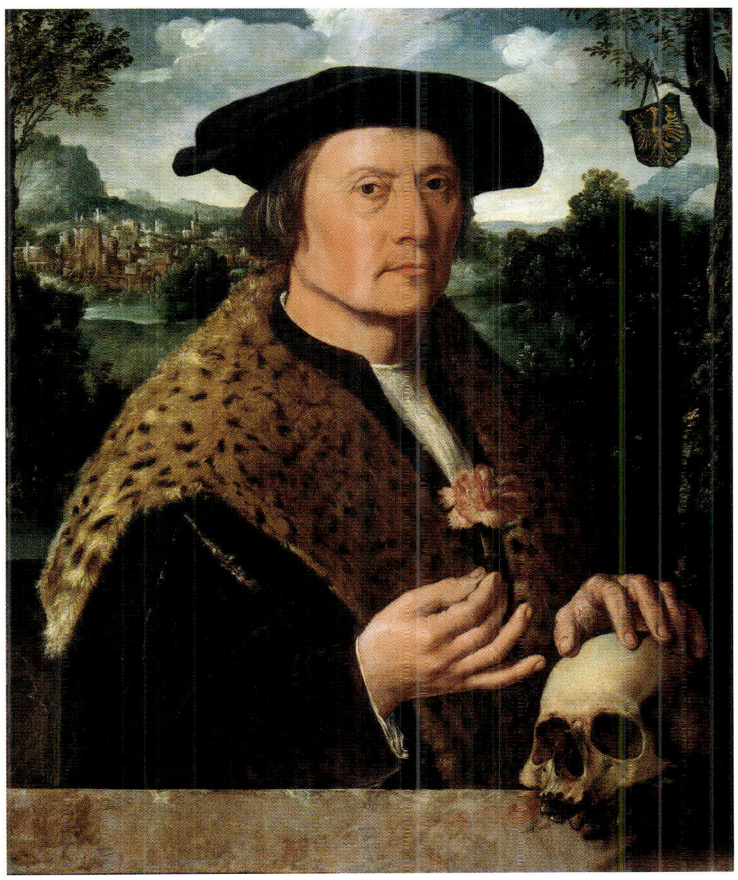

3.
Northern Netherlands, *Portrait of Lysbeth van Duvenvoorde*, about 1430. Vellum, 33 x 21 cm. Mauritshuis, The Hague (on loan to the Rijksmuseum, Amsterdam)

4.
Dirck Jacobsz, *Portrait of Pompejus Occo*, 1531. Oil on panel, 66 x 54 cm. Rijksmuseum, Amsterdam

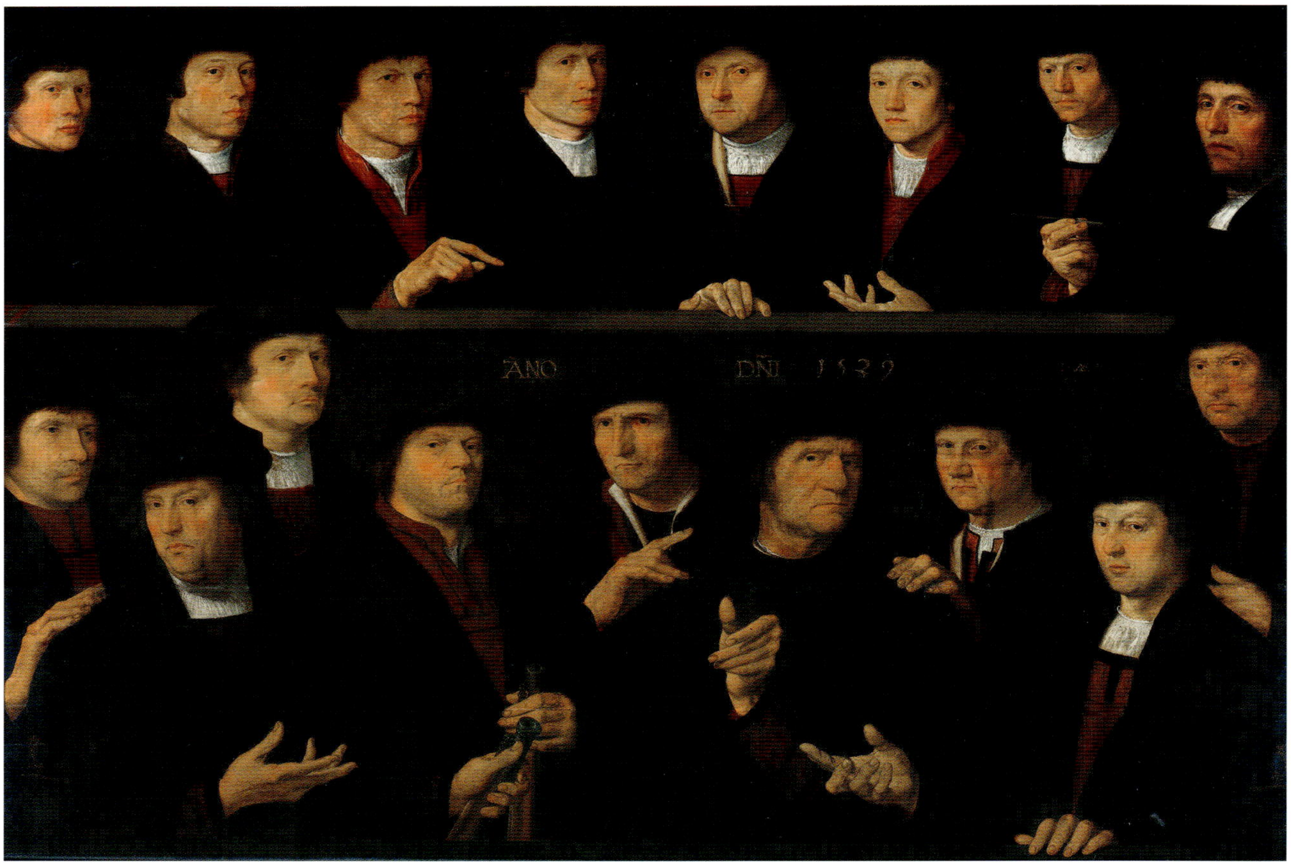

5.
Dirck Jacobsz,
Portrait of a Group of Guardsmen, 1529.
Oil on panel,
122 x 184 cm (with two side panels, not depicted, each measuring 120 x 78 cm).
Rijksmuseum, Amsterdam

drawings made after them. As far as is known, this Amsterdam tradition did not spread to any other city in the years before the outbreak of the Eighty Years' War. Double portraits of married couples and group portraits of families were also made in this period, not only in Amsterdam but also in Haarlem and in the province of Friesland.

Alongside the artists from the generation of Van Scorel, Van Heemskerck and Jacobsz, numerous other portraitists emerged in the period 1540–70, including Pieter Aertsen (about 1508–1575) and Dirck Barendsz (1534–1592) in Amsterdam, Adriaen van Cronenburg (before 1525–in or after 1604) in Friesland, and Anthonis Mor van Dashorst (about 1519–1575/6) in Utrecht, although the latter did much of his work outside the Northern Netherlands.

The Eighty Years' War: Early Period

In some (though not all) respects, the turbulent period from about 1565 to 1580 marks a hiatus in the development of portraiture in the Northern Netherlands – not least because of the almost complete loss of commissions for churches. This did not occur simultaneously in all towns and provinces, however, since political and religious conditions differed from one place to the next. In any case, there was never an absolute break, since the existence of private chapels, and later conventicles, kept the old tradition alive in the late-sixteenth and seventeenth centuries, if sometimes in a revised form. Quite separate from the loss of commissions for churches, there was a general slump in the overall production of portraits from around 1570 to 1580, largely as a result of the unstable political climate. Furthermore, several of the most prolific portraitists died in the 1560s and 1570s, including Jacobsz, Van Scorel and Van Heemskerck, while other painters emigrated to escape from the tumult – such as Cornelis Ketel (1548–1616), a young artist from Gouda who lived in England from 1573 to 1581. In cities and regions where political stability was restored relatively early on, the market for portrait commissions recovered rapidly. In Leiden, for example – as a staunch bastion of the new regime after the Relief of 1574 it was chosen the following year as the seat of a new university – we find an admittedly small but almost uninterrupted production of portraits from the 1560s onwards. Significantly, a 'modern' painter trained in Antwerp started working there in the mid-1560s, Isaac Claesz van Swanenburg (1537–1614), who soon took a strong lead in securing local painting commissions (fig. 6).[16] Since he simply carried on where he had left off after the Relief of Leiden, this was one of the few major cities that did not suffer from a lack of experienced portraitists.

From about 1580 onwards, the gaps on the supply side were rapidly filled in the provinces of Holland and Zeeland as the market gradually recovered, but in some of the other provinces, where the conflict was still raging in the 1580s, this was a far slower process.

The Rise of Portraiture: The 1580s Onwards

In the period from about 1580 up to and including the early years of the seventeenth century, a portrait culture developed that laid the foundations for the great flowering of portraiture in the Golden Age. Although commissions for donors' portraits on altarpieces and memorial tablets had largely evaporated, we see the market widening, primarily because the potential clientele for portraits to be hung in private homes was rapidly growing. Besides the groups that had ordered such works in the past, the nobility and the wealthy urban middle-class, a new administrative elite – including many newcomers – arose within a brief space of time. Commissioning a portrait was one of the ways in which to record newly won status. On the other hand, patricians who had remained Catholic also continued to commission portraits, despite changes in the law that more or less excluded them from government.

A highly eloquent testimony to the rapidly growing self-awareness of the burghers who formed the new upper layer of society can be found in the rise of militia pieces in the provinces of Holland and Zeeland. This genre, which originated in Amsterdam in 1529, had developed rapidly there over the following 40 years, but had ground to a halt in 1567 when Amsterdam's militias were disbanded. Then, after the city shifted its allegiance to the Orangists in 1578, the most prominent Catholic regents were banished and a new city council was formed, after which the militias were reinstated as a civic guard. The old tradition of the militia piece was revived almost immediately, and six are believed to have been painted between then and 1586.[17] More interestingly, however, the tradition now soon spread to other cities of Holland and Zeeland, starting with Haarlem in 1583.[18] The rise of burgher group portraits was not confined to images of civic guardsmen. In the years leading up to the Eighty Years' War, some civic guilds and similar organisations had their own altars in local churches. From around 1600 onwards, we see the introduction and rapid rise of group portraits of administrators of guilds and charitable institutions, as well as professional organisations and government bodies, which were made to hang in the institution concerned. Group portraits of this kind were rare or non-existent before the Revolt, the only exceptions being militia pieces and two paintings of the masters of the mint in Dordrecht, which are known only from passing references.[19] The oldest identifiable example of a regent piece – a tradition that flowered in numerous cities throughout the seventeenth and eighteenth centuries – is the portrait of the six syndics of the clothmakers' guild in Amsterdam (fig. 7), painted in 1599 and attributed to Pieter Pietersz (1540/1–1603).[20] This was soon followed by a group portrait of the officials of Amsterdam's guild of surgeons, who had themselves immortalised in 1601–3 by Aert Pietersz (about 1550–1612), together with

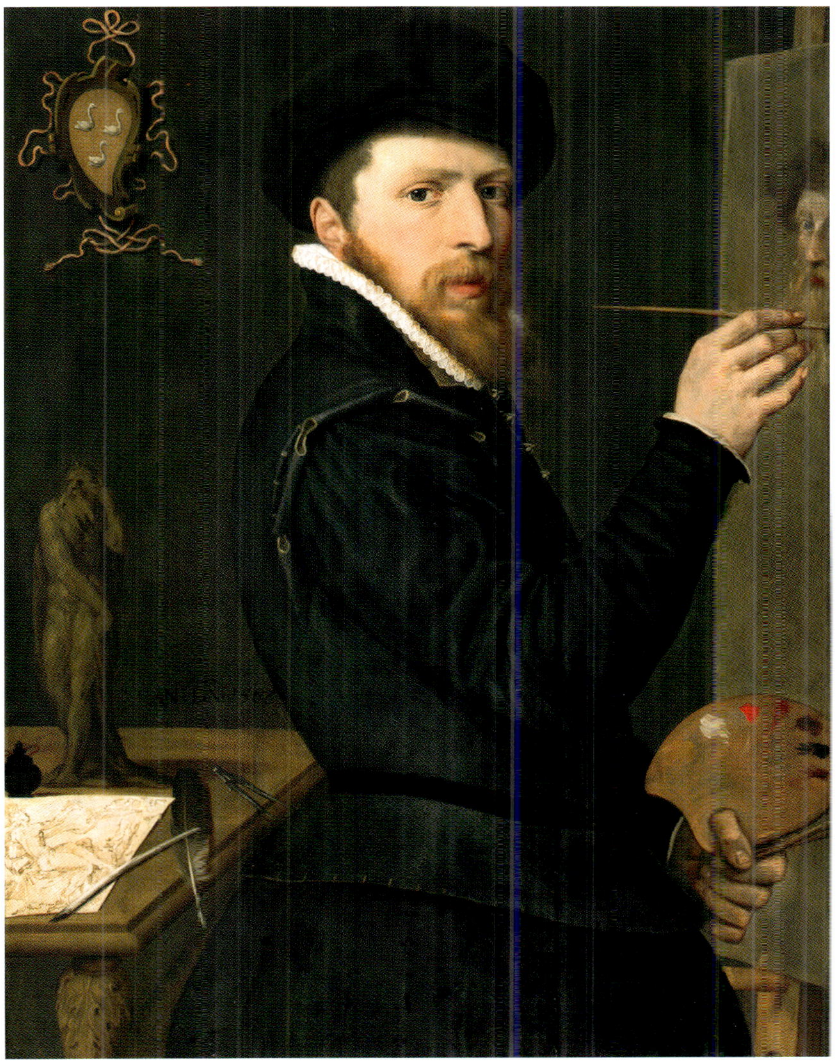

6.
Isaac van Swanenburg,
Self-Portrait, 1568.
Oil on panel,
94 × 72 cm.
Stedelijk Museum
De Lakenhal, Leiden

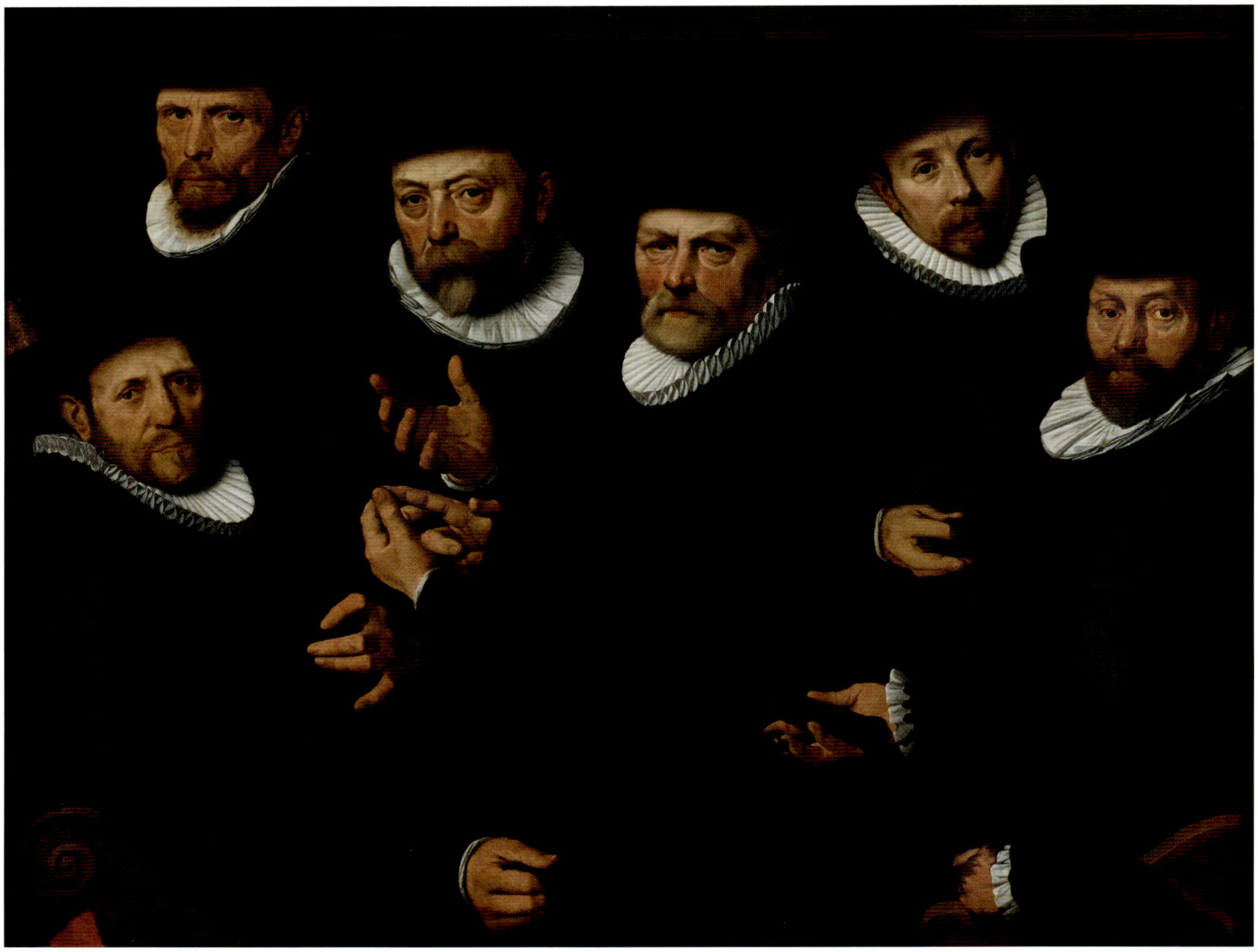

7.
Attributed to Pieter Pietersz, *Portrait of the Six Syndics of the Amsterdam Clothmakers' Guild*, 1599. Oil on panel, 108 x 143 cm. Rijksmuseum, Amsterdam

the praelector Sebastiaen Egbertsz, who is shown presenting an anatomy lesson using a cadaver laid out on a table (p. 172, fig. 45a). With this painting the anatomy painting was born, a genre that was to become a specific tradition within the Northern Netherlandish regent piece (cats 45, 53). The tradition of regent pieces did not spread as rapidly as militia pieces, but after 1615 a growing number of administrative bodies in Amsterdam and elsewhere had their portraits made.

Although militia and regent pieces are among the most striking products of the rage for portraits from the 1580s onwards, their numbers are insignificant in comparison to the flood of portraits of private individuals made to hang in private homes. Most are portraits of adults, frequently likenesses of married couples painted as pendants, but at an early stage we also find portraits of children, and occasionally images of family groups.

Painters 1580–1610

Many of the paintings produced in the late sixteenth and early seventeenth centuries are anonymous, partly for the simple reason that they are unsigned (see also pp. 60–1). But since the person depicted is frequently known, we can often link them to specific cities or regions, establish that certain works from the same city were most probably by the same artist, and in some cases identify this artist using source material or the few signed works. It has thus been established that numerous painters from the Northern Netherlands were making portraits as early as around 1600, and that almost every significant town had at least one local portrait specialist. Amsterdam had the widest choice of painters – and the greatest demand for portraits. The market leaders there, from around 1580 onwards, were the brothers Pieter and Aert Pietersz, whose father was the painter Pieter Aertsen. Although their œuvres are not always easy to tell apart, both were unquestionably trend-setting artists whose influence radiated to other parts of the country. Many of their individual portraits are set against an architectural background with pillars, columns or fireplaces, sometimes with a glimpse of a rear room or the outside world; the backgrounds are closely related to the architectural elements found in their father's history and genre paintings. The figures themselves exhibit various standard poses. Most are depicted to the hips or knees; the men are usually shown standing, while the women tend to be seated, often holding an attribute such as a handkerchief, gloves or a book – frequently a prayerbook. All aspects of each painting are treated with equal care: besides the close attention paid to depicting the sitters' faces, both artists are also generally meticulous in their rendering of clothes, hands, chairs, attributes and background features. Most of their portraits are dated, and they frequently bear age inscriptions and coats of arms; sometimes brief mottoes or other texts are inscribed in the background architecture (fig. 8). Besides portraits of this kind, one family group by Pieter Pietersz is known, dated 1598; it shows the Amsterdam book dealer and publisher Laurens Jacobsz and his family, and incorporates a variety of poses to convey a lively atmosphere (fig. 9).[21]

Dozens of other portraitists were also active in Amsterdam between 1580 and 1610,[22] among which we can identify more than ten individual artists. The leading masters of the older generation included Dirck Barendsz and Cornelis Ketel, who were prominent portraitists, although this was certainly not their main genre. Among the younger generation, we encounter numerous artists who were originally from the Southern Netherlands – most notably Cornelis van der Voort (see pp. 27–8), who became Amsterdam's most influential portraitist. Immigrants from the Southern Netherlands contributed a great deal to the flowering of Dutch culture in the seventeenth century – not only in Amsterdam – and their influence is clearly visible in portraiture.

Amsterdam was unique in its concentration of portraitists in the seventeenth century, but in any large city you could find several artists capable of making your portrait. Of the diverse artists in Haarlem around 1600, for example, not one specialised exclusively in portraiture. Examples include Hendrick Goltzius (1558–1617), who made very few portrait paintings (fig. 10) but who turned out a great many drawings and prints in this area; Cornelis Cornelisz van Haarlem (1562–1638), who, though primarily a history painter, also produced the earliest Haarlem militia paintings; Karel van Mander,

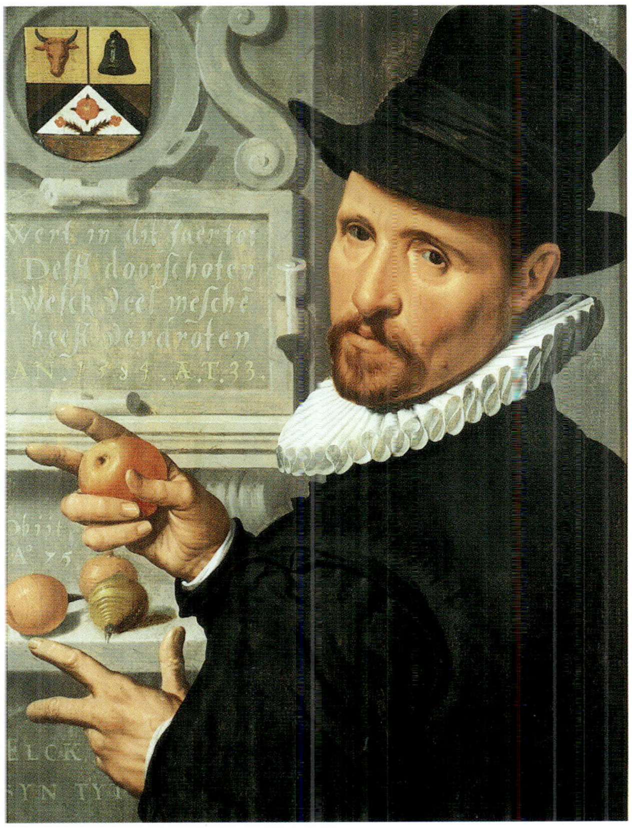

8.
Pieter Pietersz,
Portrait of Cornelis Schellinger, 1584?
Oil on panel,
71 × 54 cm.
Mauritshuis,
The Hague

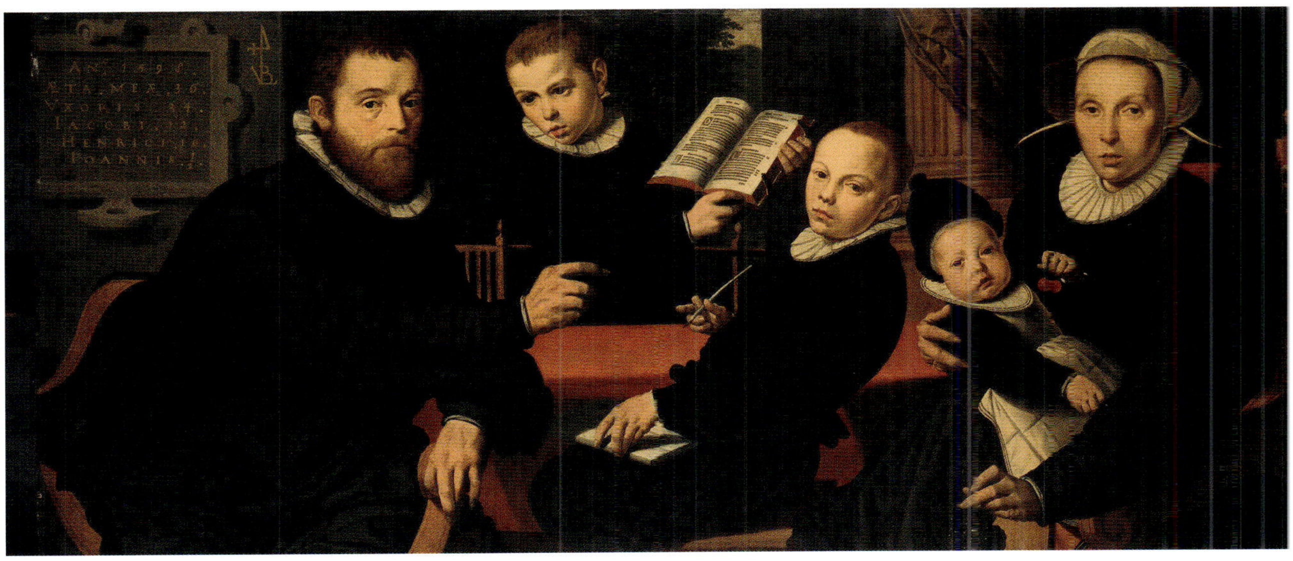

9.
Pieter Pietersz,
Portrait of Laurens Jacobsz and his Family, 1598.
Oil on panel,
73 × 166 cm.
Gemäldegalerie,
Staatliche Museen,
Berlin

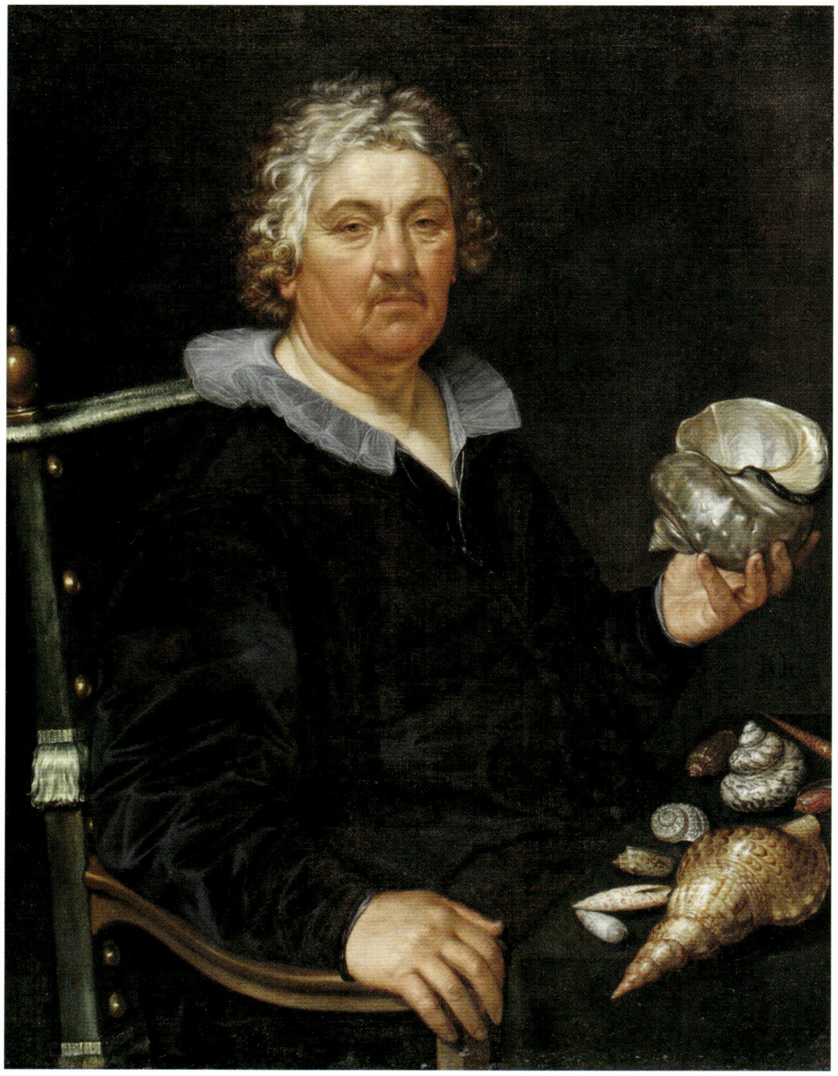

10.
Hendrick Goltzius, *Portrait of Jan van der Aar*, 1603. Oil on canvas, 108 × 83 cm. P. and N. de Boer Foundation, Amsterdam (on loan to Museum Boijmans Van Beuningen, Rotterdam)

who made portraits only incidentally; and Frans Pietersz de Grebber (about 1573–1649) and Cornelis Engelsz (1574/5–1650), whose paintings include several militia pieces and other portraits.[23] Around 1610 Haarlem acquired a real portrait specialist, in the person of Frans Hals (see p. 28).

In the booming and fast-expanding city of Leiden, Isaac van Swanenburg (p. 21, fig. 6) established a very strong position from around 1565. After 1595 there was room for others, such as the Delft-trained Jan Cornelisz van 't Woudt (about 1570–1615).[24] In Delft we find two slightly older masters who are fairly well known, since – unlike most – they often signed their work: Jacob Willemsz Delff the Elder (about 1540–1601) and Herman van der Mast (about 1550–about 1610), and a little later Michiel van Mierevelt (see pp. 25–6).[25] In The Hague, portraiture did not flourish until somewhat later, but there was soon room for more than one master in this area: initially only Daniël van den Queborn (about 1552–about 1605) from the Southern Netherlands, who had previously lived in Middelburg, and later on masters such as Jan and Anthonie van Ravesteyn (see pp. 26–7) and Evert Quirijnsz van der Maes (about 1577–1646/7).[26] The portrait market in Rotterdam, another fast-growing city, was served in this period by at least two painters who hailed from the Southern Netherlands: Gilles Hannuyts (1554–1609) and Adam de Colonia (about 1573–1651).[27] Some of Holland's cities initially had to make do with only one specialist: Enkhuizen had Jan Claesz (cats 8–9), who had probably trained with Pieter Pietersz in Amsterdam, and in Alkmaar there was Frans Menton (about 1550–1615), who had trained in Antwerp.[28]

Portraitists working in the trading cities of Zeeland included Van den Queborn (p. 160, fig. 39a) and Salomon Mesdach (active 1612–1628), but more research is needed on this early period in Zeeland. Utrecht had the painters Roelof van Culemborgh (d. 1596) and Hendrick van Zijll,[29] and before 1600 two superb portraitists set up business there: Joachim Wtewael (1566–1638), most of whose portrait paintings feature his own family,[30] and Paulus Moreelse (1571–1638), who would dominate portraiture in Utrecht in the first few decades of the seventeenth century. As for the provinces of Gelderland, Overijssel and Groningen, we know numerous portraits were made there in the late sixteenth and early seventeenth centuries, including some that are of excellent quality, but most of them remain anonymous.[31] Finally, turning to Friesland, besides the ageing Adriaen van Cronenburg, who was no longer producing his best work, and a number of fairly primitive local painters not known by name, some outstanding portraits were produced there from the 1590s onwards. These are generally attributed to two painters who had moved to Friesland from Flanders, Adriaen van der Linde (d. 1609) and Hans de Clercq (active 1598–about 1613).[32]

Altogether we know the names and works of dozens of portraitists who were active in the Northern Netherlands between about 1580 and 1610. They range from rather humdrum artists to superb portraitists who contributed, each in his own way, to these early developments that presaged the boom in portraiture that began around 1610.

The Boom in Portraits: 1610–1630

Between 1610 and 1620, four men who had played a prominent role as portrait painters in the previous few decades died: Aert Pietersz, Ketel, Goltzius and Van Swanenburg. They can be seen as transitional figures who straddled the sixteenth and seventeenth centuries. Around 1610, the first generation of influential seventeenth-century portraitists reached artistic maturity. They include five masters whose work was crucial to the development of seventeenth-century portraiture in the Northern Netherlands: Cornelis van der Voort in Amsterdam, Frans Hals in Haarlem, Jan van Ravesteyn in The Hague, Michiel van Mierevelt in Delft and Paulus Moreelse in Utrecht.

Portraiture in the Netherlands from 1610 to 1630 is largely characterised by an austere dignity, which sometimes – in the hands of less gifted artists – degenerated into stiffness. This austerity was obviously determined in part by the prevailing fashions, with their emphasis on dark hues. Sober costumes notwithstanding, painters of individual portraits sought not just to depict their subjects as realistically as possible, but also to present them in a more natural way. In group portraits, they faced the additional challenge of devising a presentation that was both varied and natural. The figures had to be arranged so as to create the impression that they were truly gathered in a room together, instead of resembling a static line-up of isolated figures – sometimes even depicted in rows, one above the other – as in the past. In some places we see the first cautious steps towards a wider repertoire, with the introduction of new, unexpected poses and new types of portraits, in which the customary solemn Sunday suits give way to imaginary costumes and – particularly in family groups – a narrative or historicising element is added.

Michiel van Mierevelt

Among the first generation of seventeenth-century portraitists, Michiel Jansz van Mierevelt (1567–1641) was the oldest, and to some extent the artist whose work was most closely related to the late sixteenth-century tradition.[33] Although he was already active in Delft from around 1585, we should probably situate the real beginning of his career as a leading portraitist around 1605. His official portrait of Stadholder Maurits of Nassau (cat. 39), made in 1607 for the Delft town hall, was an important milestone in this respect, since it culminated in his official appointment to the stadholder's court.

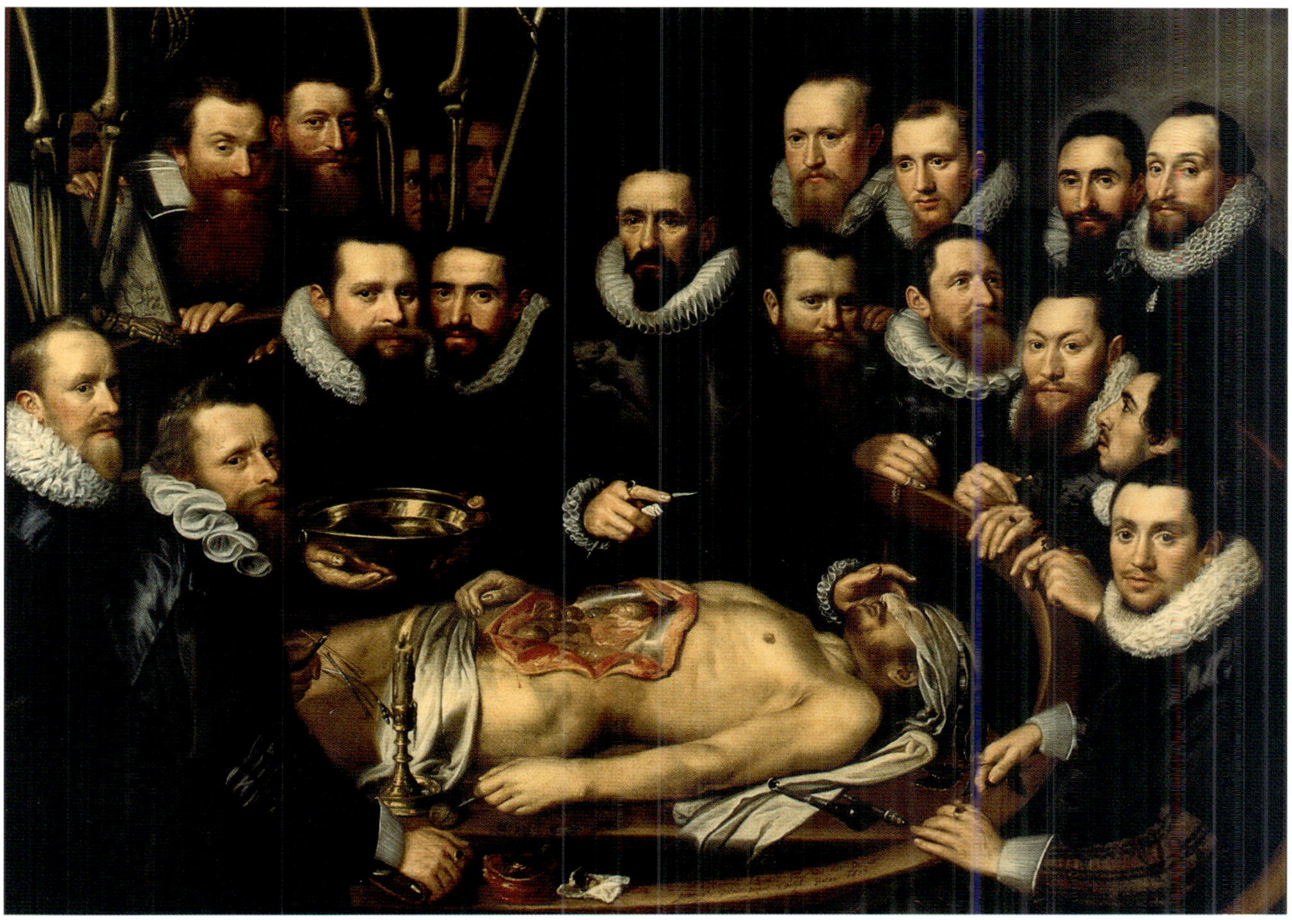

11.
Michiel and Pieter van Mierevelt, *The Anatomy Lesson of Dr Willem van der Meer*, 1617. Oil on canvas, 150 x 225 cm. Museum Het Prinsenhof, Delft

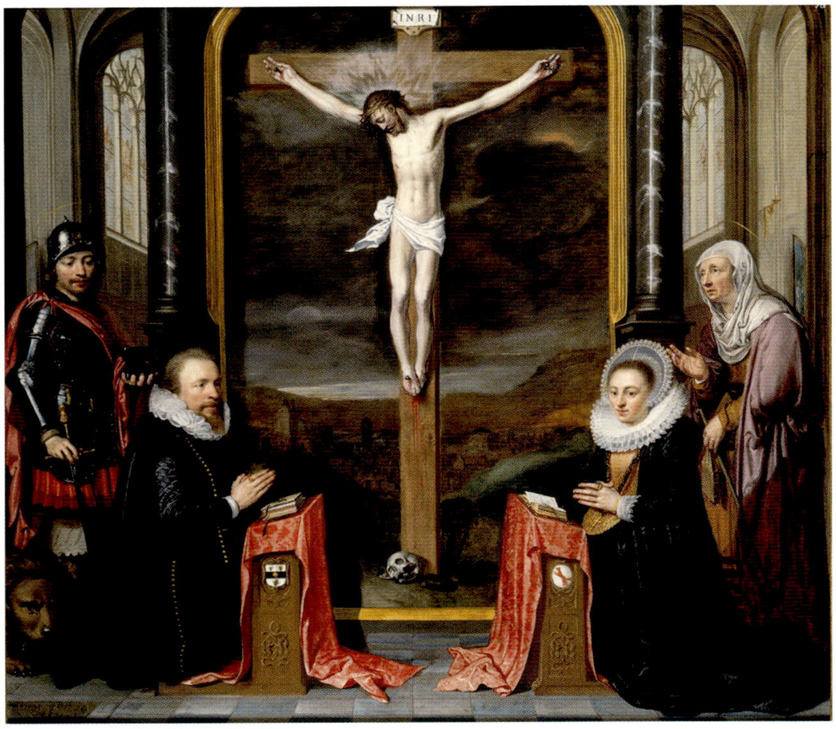

12.
Jan van Ravesteyn, *Memorial Tablet of Adriaen van Maeusyenbroeck and Anna Elant*, 1618. Oil on panel, 128 x 145 cm. Museum Catharijne-convent, Utrecht

Van Mierevelt's dry, precise and rather old-fashioned style of painting brought him enormous success among Delft's prominent citizenry as well as in the courtly circles of The Hague, and he acquired a far wider clientele that included diplomats, senior army and naval officers and government officials who lived in The Hague for varying periods of time. The painter had a large studio from which he could enlist the help of numerous assistants and pupils. Besides hundreds of original portraits, his œuvre includes a great many replicas of his own work, some of which were commissioned while others – those depicting public figures such as stadholders, the Grand Pensionary Johan van Oldenbarnevelt, and the Remonstrant minister Johannes Wttenbogaert – were made for the market. Particularly in the production of these replicas, we may assume that his assistants played a large role. Van Mierevelt's repertoire was limited and his œuvre consists almost exclusively of bust, half-length and knee-length portraits of adults. The men and women in most of these pieces are depicted in standard poses: the figure turns towards the viewer in a three-quarters angle and gazes out of the picture. Group portraits by the artist are extremely rare and not particularly innovative: one militia piece is known, and a painting of an anatomy lesson taught by Willem van der Meer (fig. 11), made in 1617 with his son Pieter van Mierevelt (1596–1623).[34] Van Mierevelt is not known to have produced any family groups, and his childrens portraits are rare; nor does his œuvre contain anything out of the ordinary. The artist was an exceedingly successful exponent of the very solid but rather unimaginative Dutch portrait, in which the likeness was undoubtedly excellent and flattery – contrary to what one would expect of a court painter – was kept to a minimum. With these qualities he became a national and even international celebrity. Although he lost ground at the courts of Frederik Hendrik and the 'Winter King and Queen' in the 1630s to the more fashionable painter Gerrit van Honthorst (see p. 34), who was more inclined to indulge his subjects' vanity, Van Mierevelt retained a large clientele until his death in 1641.

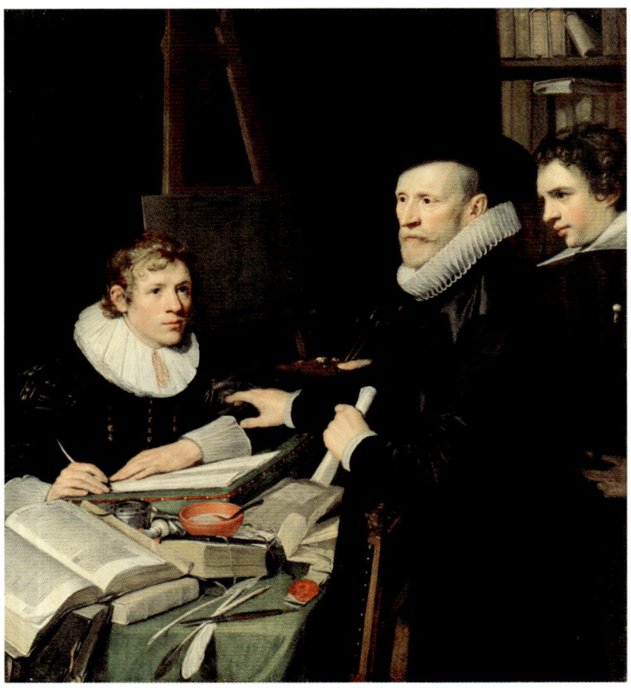

13.
Jan van Ravesteyn, *Portrait of Pieter van Veen with his Son and Secretary*, about 1620–5. Oil on panel, 126 x 115 cm. Musée d'Art et d'Histoire, Geneva

Jan van Ravesteyn

In the first decades of his career, Van Mierevelt's main rival was the somewhat younger Jan Anthonisz van Ravesteyn (about 1572–1657), who was based in The Hague.[35] He is generally described as Van Mierevelt's pupil, though this is probably incorrect. Van Ravesteyn often worked for the prominent citizens of The Hague, but he also took on all the work for the stadholder's court that did not go to Van Mierevelt. Overall his style is so similar to Van Mierevelt's that their works are still frequently confused to this day. Van Ravesteyn's style is less dry, rather more plastic and sometimes more flattering than that of his supposed teacher. Furthermore, his paintings are somewhat variable in quality, while Van Mierevelt is extremely constant. Another major difference is that Van Ravesteyn was more versatile. He had a gift for devising compositions for unusual commissions (cat. 49), as is clear from a number of militia pieces (cat. 50) and his *The Hague Magistracy Receiving the Officers of the St Sebastian Civic Guard* from 1618 (Haags Historisch Museum, The Hague), a complicated commission. His originality is also apparent in other unusual commissions, such as the *Memorial Tablet of Adriaen van Maeusyenbroeck and Anna Elant* from 1618 (fig. 12),[36] and *Portrait of Pieter van Veen with his Son and Secretary* (fig. 13), painted in the 1620s.[37] He also produced a number of children's portraits, which are among his finest work.[38]

Paulus Moreelse

The Utrecht artist Paulus Moreelse (1571–1638) was a pupil of Van Mierevelt. After some years in Italy he returned to his home town around 1595.[39] His portraits reflect a development over the years towards a more fluid style than that of his teacher, although the stately poses of some of his figures are reminiscent of patterns found in Van Mierevelt and Van Ravesteyn. The formal pendant portraits of married couples depicted at knee-length he made in the 1620s are among the highlights of this genre (figs 14–15). But his œuvre also contains more modern variants on traditional portrait formats, which are related to the other genres he practised – pastoral scenes and history paintings. Through these he played an important role in the development of the arcadian portrait, featuring figures dressed as shepherds, and the allegorical group portrait (cat. 43).

Cornelis van der Voort

Cornelis van der Voort (about 1576–1624), who was born in Antwerp but moved to Amsterdam with his parents after 1585, was a great innovator in portraiture.[40] It is not clear who his teacher was – nor is this easy to deduce from his work, since we have only a vague image of his output before 1600. Not until 1614 onwards do we find an uninterrupted series of works continuing until his death, ten years later. In almost every area of portraiture, Van der Voort expanded the work of his predecessors, the Pietersz brothers, to a large extent single-handedly laying the foundations for the development of portraiture in Amsterdam in the rest of the seventeenth century. The compositions of his life-sized, knee-length individual portraits bear some similarity to those of his contemporaries Van Mierevelt, Van Ravesteyn and Moreelse, but they also reflect somewhat greater influence from Flemish masters of the previous generation, such as Adriaen Key (about 1544–after 1589) and Frans Pourbus the Elder (1545–1581). Around 1618, Van der

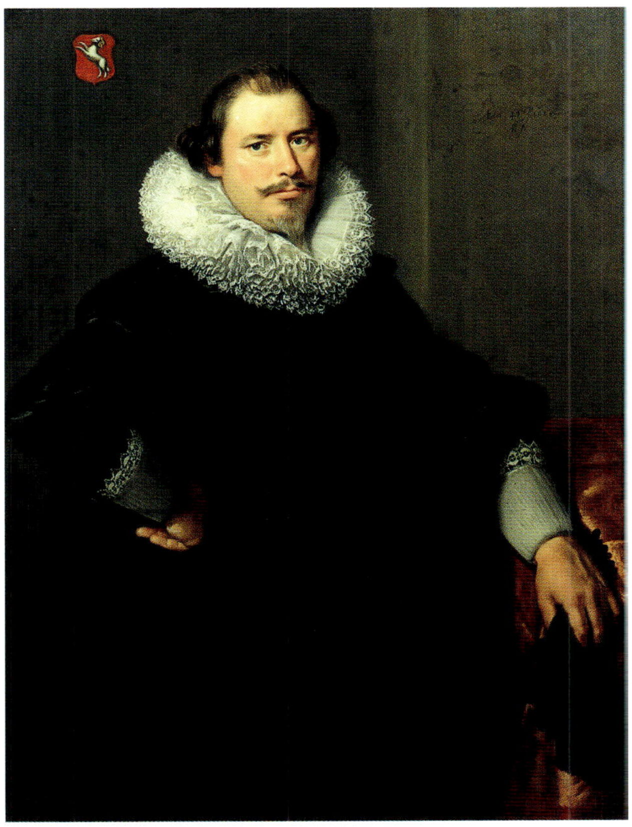

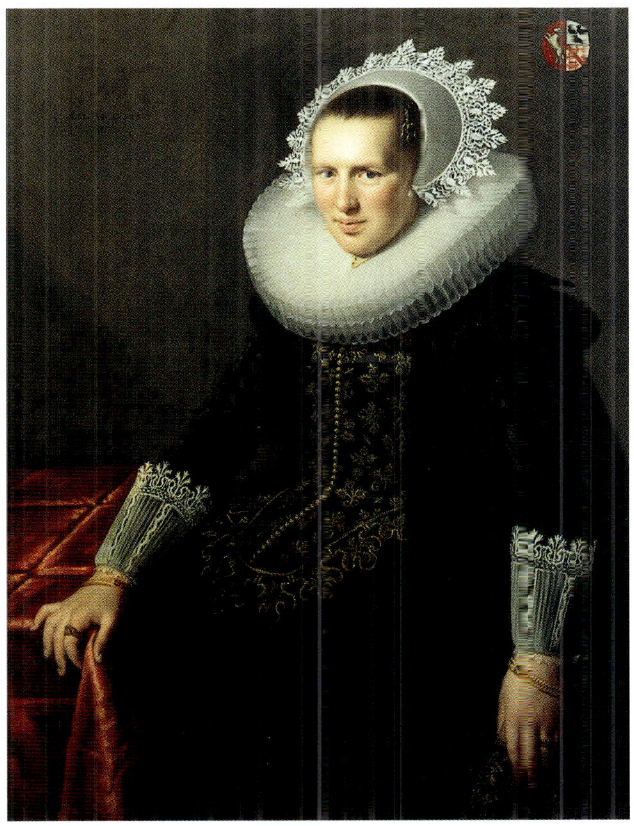

14.
Paulus Moreelse, *Portrait of Philips Ram*, 1625. Oil on canvas, 113 x 85 cm. Centraal Museum, Utrecht (on loan from the Netherlands Institute for Cultural Heritage, Amsterdam/Rijswijk)

15.
Paulus Moreelse, *Portrait of Anna Strick, Wife of Philips Ram*, 1625. Oil on canvas, 113 x 85 cm. Centraal Museum, Utrecht (on loan from the Netherlands Institute for Cultural Heritage, Amsterdam/Rijswijk)

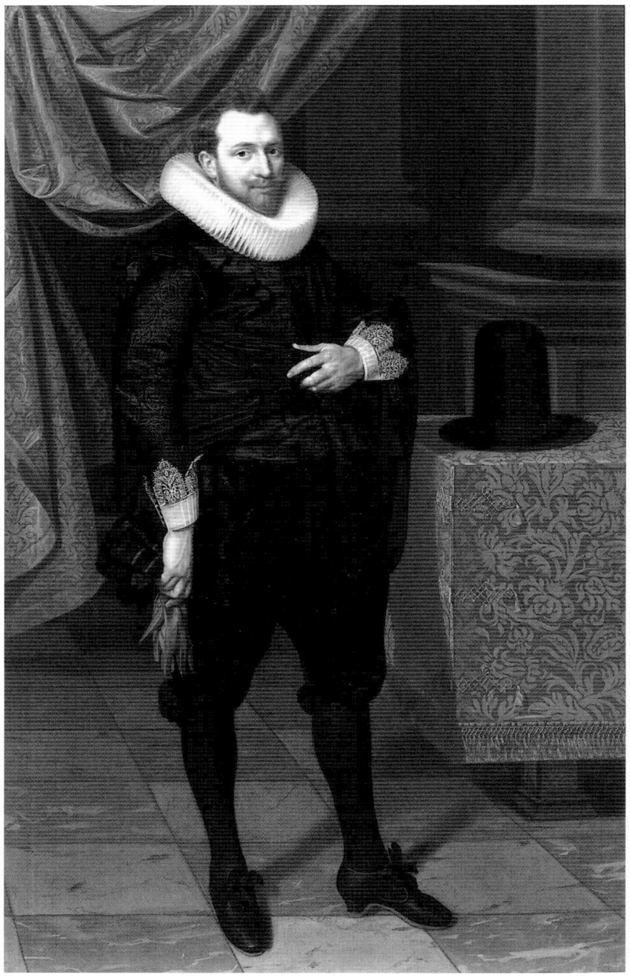

16.
Cornelis van der Voort, *Portrait of Cornelis Bicker van Swieten*, 1618. Oil on canvas, 200 x 127 cm. Formerly Johnny van Haeften, London

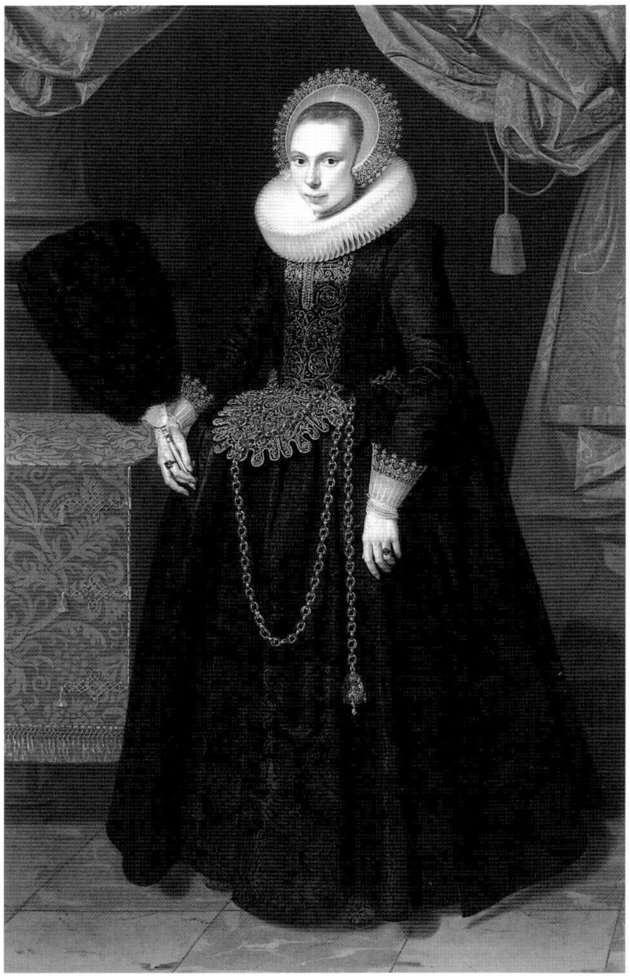

17.
Cornelis van der Voort, *Portrait of Aertgen Witsen*, 1618. Oil on canvas, 200 x 127 cm. Formerly Johnny van Haeften, London

Voort introduced life-sized, full-length likenesses of burghers to the Amsterdam market (figs 16–17),[41] a type of portrait previously reserved mainly for rulers and high-ranking nobles. A family group from 1620 (cat. 65) shows his ability to convey the relationship between his figures – here, a man, a woman and a child – in a natural way. He also played a crucial role in the development of the regent piece: he placed small groups of four to seven figures in a varied arrangement around a table, thus providing the composition with a clear structure (fig. 18).[42] Other artists continued Amsterdam's flourishing tradition of portraiture during Van der Voort's lifetime and took over the market after his death: notably Werner van den Valckert (about 1580/5–in or after 1627), Nicolaes Eliasz Pickenoy (1588–after 1650) and Thomas de Keyser (1596/7–1667).[43] All three fostered significant variation in portrait types by introducing new poses and compositions. De Keyser also played an important role in stimulating the use of smaller formats (cats 35–6). Life-sized images had prevailed hitherto; for smaller portraits, the same or similar compositions were simply reduced in size.

Frans Hals

In Haarlem the presence of a truly remarkable portraitist, another Antwerp-born artist who had arrived in Haarlem at a very young age, Frans Hals (1582/3–1666), provided a completely different impetus for portraiture.[44] Hals started producing portraits around 1610 and continued doing so for over fifty years, making a unique contribution to Dutch portraiture (cats 14–27). After a somewhat hesitant beginning, his œuvre displays loose, varied and often dynamic portraits executed in an extremely vigorous style of painting, in which the figures are depicted with self-assurance, naturalness, and frequently with a degree of humour (figs 19–20). Hals's diverse militia pieces represent one of the pinnacles of his achievement. Notwithstanding the need to respect the iron rules of the officers' hierarchy, he none the less managed to stage his scenes in an apparently casual and uncontrived way, while producing superb portraits of each individual (fig. 21). Although Hals occasionally made portraits of clients from elsewhere, in particular from Amsterdam (cats 14, 21), his influence was almost entirely confined to his own city of Haarlem, and even

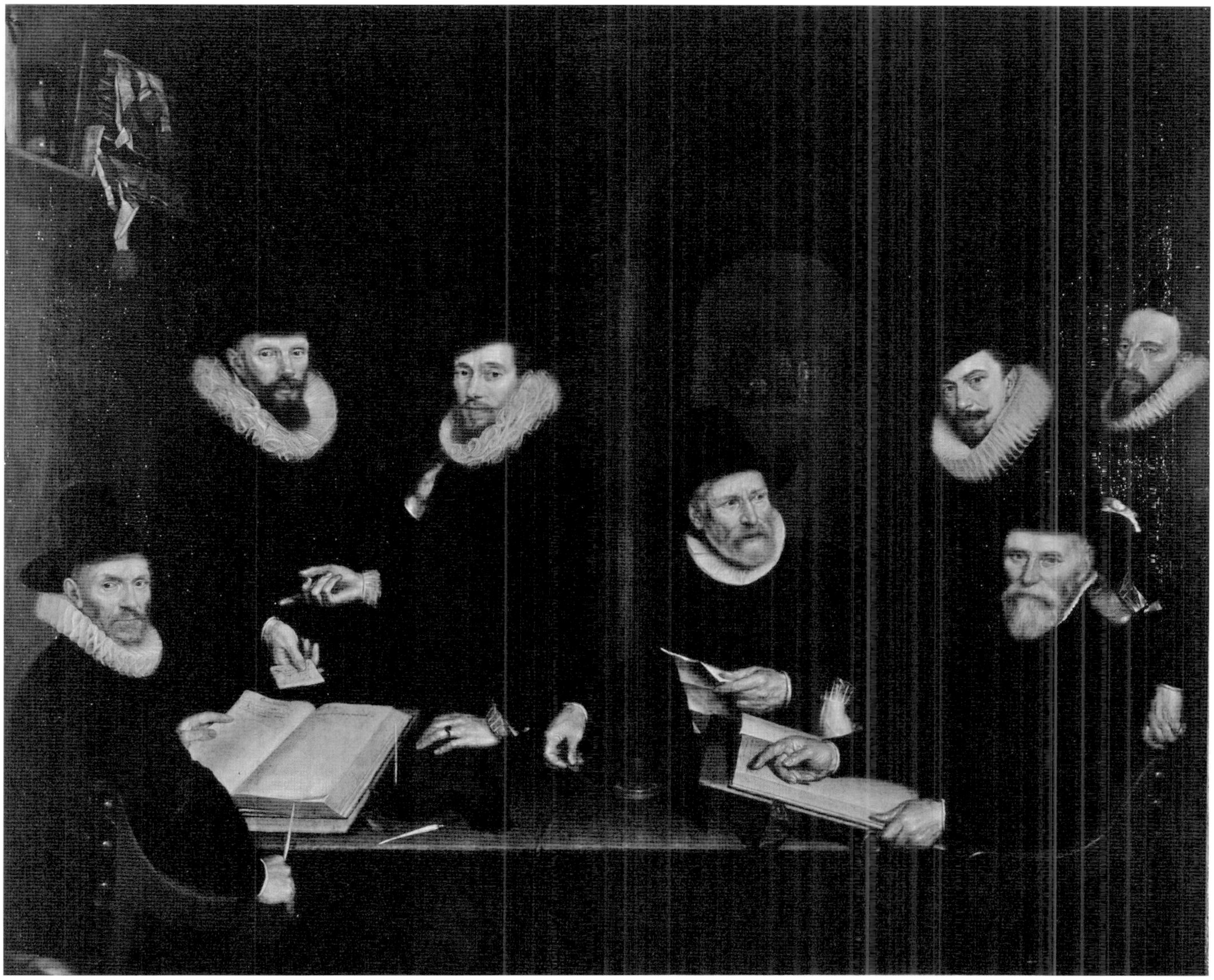

18. Cornelis van der Voort, *The Regents of the Binnengasthuis*, 1617–18. Oil on canvas, 197 × 239 cm. Amsterdams Historisch Museum, Amsterdam

there it was limited, as will become clear. None of the four pioneers of seventeenth-century Northern Netherlandish portraiture who came before Hals remained active after 1641. Accordingly Frans Hals is the only one of their contemporaries whose work continued to shape the genre well after the mid-century mark.

Other Artists

Many excellent artists, besides those discussed above, contributed to the development of portraiture in the Northern Netherlands in the first quarter of the seventeenth century, often working for a local clientele. Examples include Mesdach in Middelburg, David Bailly and Joris van Schooten in Leiden, Jan Daemen Cool in Rotterdam, Jacob Gerritsz Cuyp (cat. 11) in Dordrecht and Wybrand de Geest in Leeuwarden, the last five of whom will be discussed below.

The Period 1630–1660

In the latter half of the 1620s, the stream of portrait commissions became a flood, and we see a sharp increase in the number of artists executing them. Although artists in many other cities had specific qualities that influenced the development of Dutch portraiture, two cities were at the forefront of the main trends after about 1630: the ever-growing metropolis of Amsterdam, and The Hague, seat of the stadholder's court. It was in The Hague that new trends took hold fastest.

The Flowering of Portraiture in Amsterdam: 1630–1640

From the time of Cornelis van der Voort onwards there was a noticeably innovative thrust in portraiture in Amsterdam, evidently answering the needs of a fast-growing clientele of merchants and city magistrates.[45] The regent piece had reached maturity, and most such commissions adhered to Van der Voort's basic formula of a group seated around a table. But for all the innovative efforts of Van der Voort, Van den Valckert, De Keyser and Pickenoy, the militia pieces produced in Amsterdam before about 1640 carried less conviction than those made by Frans Hals in Haarlem. Where individual portraits and family groups were concerned, however, the ongoing trend towards variation produced a wider repertoire. Particularly noteworthy are the group and individual portraits that Thomas de Keyser started producing in the mid-1620s, far smaller than life-sized. They included full-length individual portraits (cat. 33; see also cat. 34) and small, casual group portraits (p. 128, fig. 23a). Artists such as Pickenoy (cats 45–8) with his varied poses and De Keyser with his freer representations of

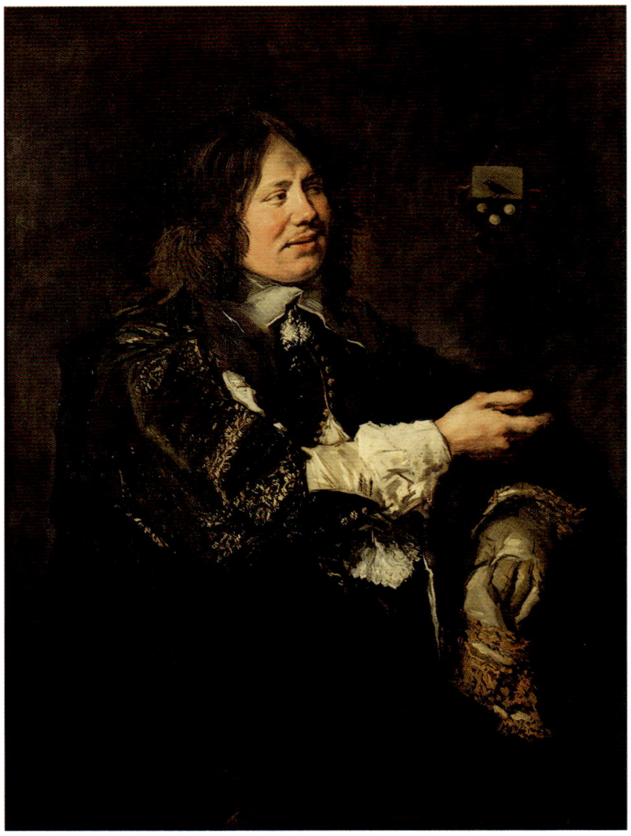

19.
Frans Hals,
Portrait of Stephanus Geraerdts, about 1645.
Oil on canvas,
115 x 87 cm.
Koninklijk Museum voor Schone Kunsten, Antwerp

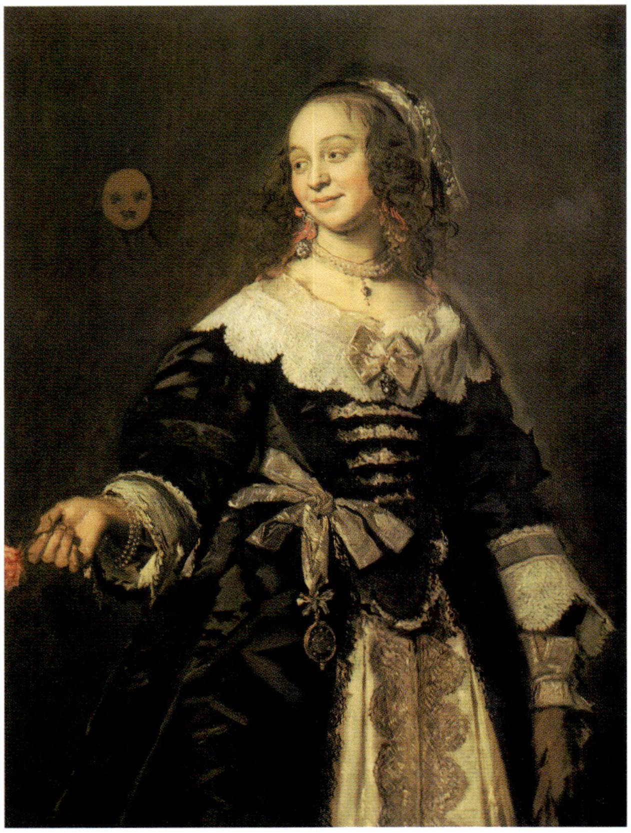

20.
Frans Hals,
Portrait of Isabella Coymans, Wife of Stephanus Geraerdts,
about 1645.
Oil on canvas,
116 x 86 cm.
Private collection

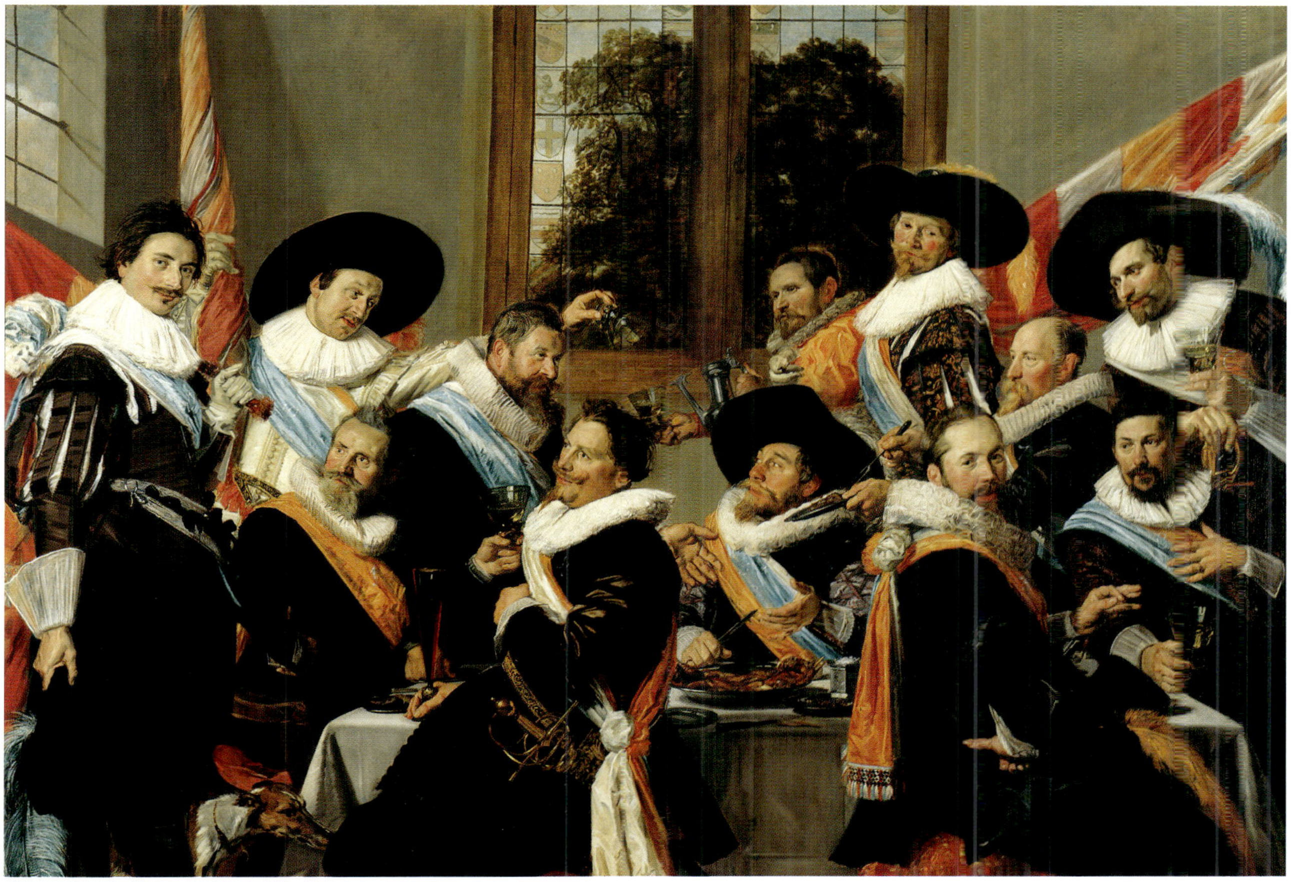

21.
Frans Hals,
Portrait of the Officers of the Kloveniersdoelen,
about 1625.
Oil on canvas,
183 x 267 cm.
Frans Hals Museum,
Haarlem

one or more figures in an interior prepared the ground for the work with which the young Rembrandt (1606–1669) established a dominant position on Amsterdam's portrait market from 1631 onwards. Rembrandt is often regarded as the founder of a new, varied type of portraiture, but in many respects he in fact crowned an existing trend towards originality in pose and composition, with his unparalleled technique and his gift to make his portraits appear wholly natural. We find a similar talent earlier in the century – albeit in a completely different style – in Frans Hals.

From his first appearance on the Amsterdam portrait market in 1631, Rembrandt was enormously successful – so much so that he was briefly able to expand his market as far as The Hague (cat. 51) and Rotterdam (cat. 55). For about five years he was Amsterdam's most fashionable portraitist, but after the mid-1630s his output in portraits declined, probably not because of any decline in popularity but because he preferred to employ his talents in other genres. Still, even after this point we find portraits by Rembrandt which are by no means inferior to his previous work, and which, notwithstanding the artist's versatile powers of invention, adhere fully to the basic conventions of portraiture. Not until *The Night Watch* (fig. 22) did he break with these conventions and produce a work that, aside from the heroic rendering of the main figures, really no longer provided what one was entitled to expect of a group portrait.[46] A group portrait should by definition include fully-fledged portraits of all the figures, even if some are more prominent in the hierarchy than others; in *The Night Watch*, some of those portrayed are demoted to peripheral status, and 'extras', such as the small girl on the left, actually occupy more prominent and more individual places in the composition.

Popular though his portraits were, Rembrandt was certainly not the only successful painter in the genre on the Amsterdam market. Slightly older portraitists such as Pickenoy and De Keyser were still held in high esteem, and numerous more youthful artists came to the fore. Some of the younger generation followed more or less in the steps of Pickenoy, including Dirck Santvoort (1609–1680), who worked as an independent painter from around 1635 onwards, and who displayed a particular flair for children's portraits (fig. 24).[47] Numerous others emulated De Keyser by working in smaller formats; one was Pieter Codde (cat. 10), who also painted genre scenes. Closer to Rembrandt, though by no means dependent on him, was the Frisian painter Jacob Backer, who built up a highly successful practice from 1632 onwards. The late 1630s witnessed the advent of a new star, the Haarlem-

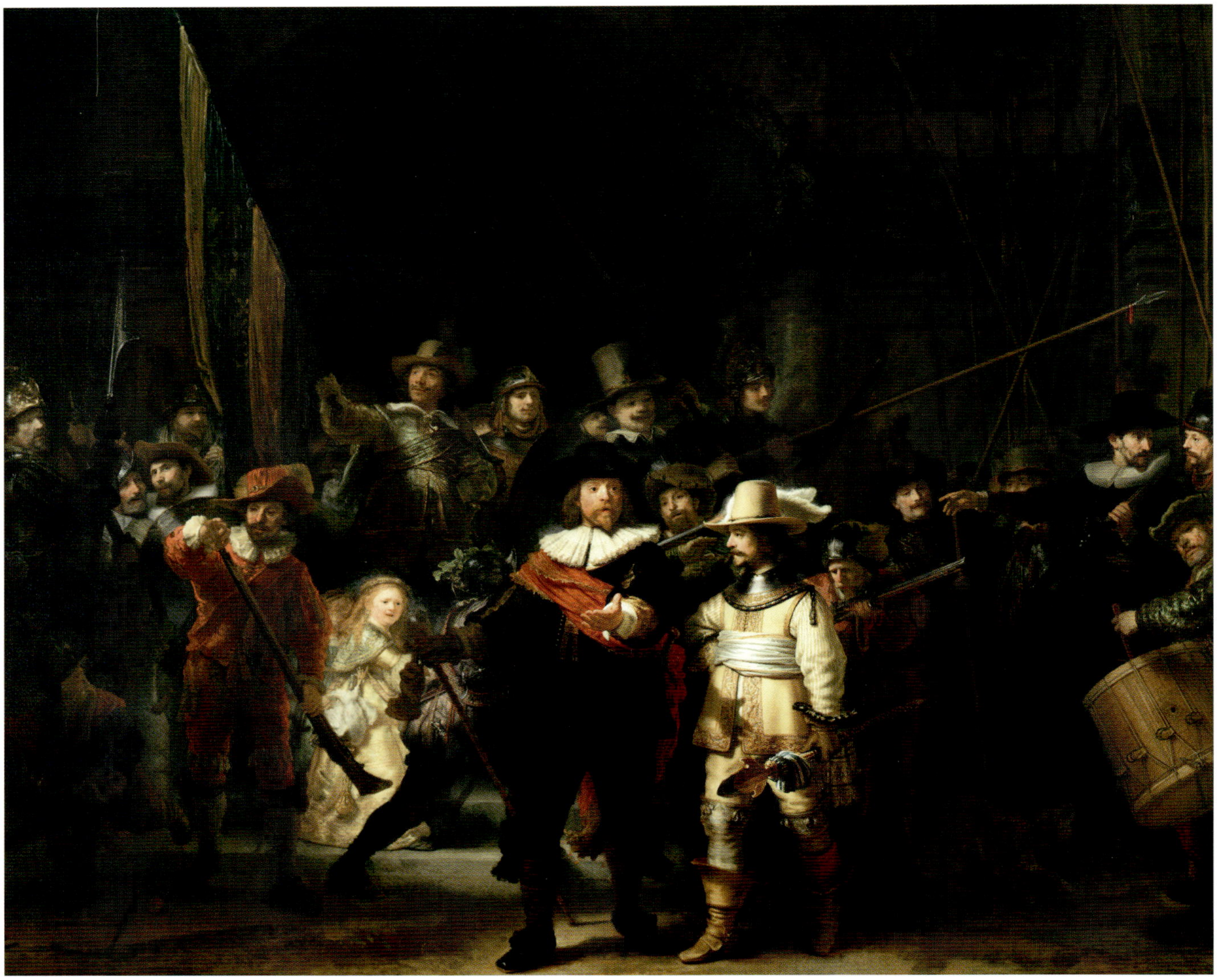

22. Rembrandt, *The Company of Captain Frans Banning Cocq and Lieutenant Willem van Ruytenburgh, known as 'The Night Watch'*, 1642. Oil on canvas, 363 × 437 cm. Rijksmuseum, Amsterdam

born painter Bartholomeus van der Helst, who would be a dominant influence on Amsterdam portraits from 1640 onwards, together with Backer, Govert Flinck and Ferdinand Bol.

Amsterdam 1640–1660

Bartholomeus van der Helst (1613–1670), whose work initially displayed the clear influence of his probable teacher, Pickenoy, soon developed a style of his own, with which he ousted Rembrandt as the public's favourite portraitist.[48] He remained one of Amsterdam's most popular portraitists for over thirty years. In the late 1630s and 1640s his work still displayed a fairly subdued quality, similar to that of his predecessors (fig. 23).[49] But he gradually developed certain distinctive features, such as the somewhat monumental character of many of his portraits, which radiate the marked self-assurance of Amsterdam's regent and merchant elite. Particularly in his group portraits, he displays an ease in arranging figures and producing constant variety that is in some ways reminiscent of Frans Hals, and which gives his works, like Hals's, an almost spontaneous air (cat. 30). Gradually we see in his œuvre a more colourful ambience, greater attention to the depiction of precious fabrics (cat. 29) and eventually, in the course of the 1660s, occasional lapses. Van der Helst's work presents a perfect picture of Holland's regent culture in its seventeenth-century heyday.

Van der Helst did not have a monopoly, however, any more than had Rembrandt; he faced constant strong competition from other highly skilled and successful masters. Jacob Backer (1608–1651) secured a substantial part of the market from the outset, retaining it until his untimely death (figs 25–6). Backer's work includes a considerable variety of portrait types and poses, demonstrating clearly that he was not only a portraitist but a history painter as well.[50] At roughly the same time as Van der Helst, Rembrandt's pupil Govert Flinck (1615–1660) also embarked on a successful career as a portraitist and history painter (figs 27–8; see also cat. 13).[51] Flinck was initially a formidable rival, but after about 1650 he focused mainly on history paintings. By then another of Rembrandt's pupils had started producing portraits for the city's elite: Ferdinand Bol (1616–1680), whose immense popularity in the circles of the powerful Amsterdam Admiralty owed not a little to his family connections (figs 29–30; see also cat. 1).[52] In the 1650s and 1660s, Bol gradually superseded Backer and Flinck as Van der Helst's main rival.

In addition to these major figures Amsterdam supported a legion of other portraitists, including notable masters such as Isaack Luttichuys (1616–1673), Jacob van Loo (1614–1670) and – both for only a few years – Jürgen

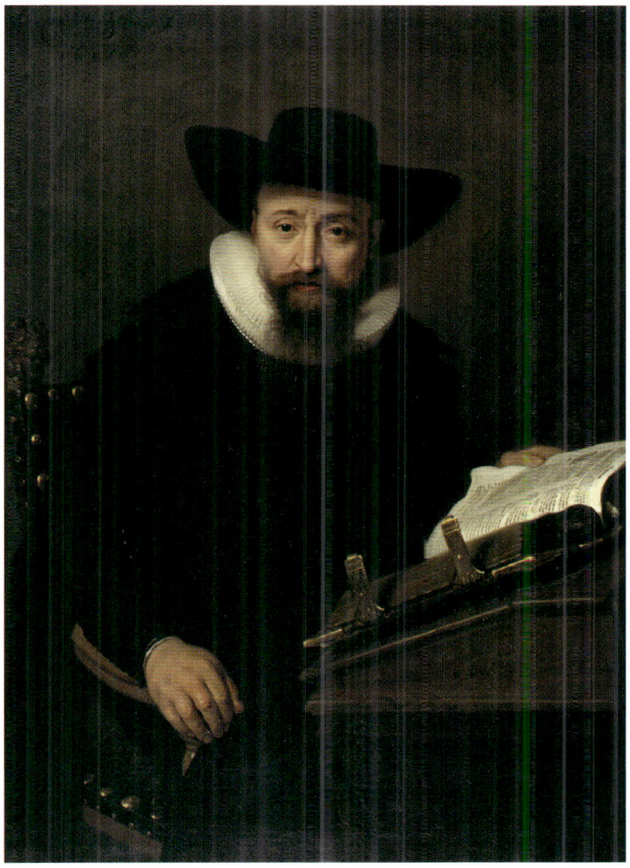

23.
Bartholomeus van der Helst,
Portrait of a Man, 1638.
Oil on canvas,
113 × 81 cm.
Museum Boijmans Van Beuningen, Rotterdam

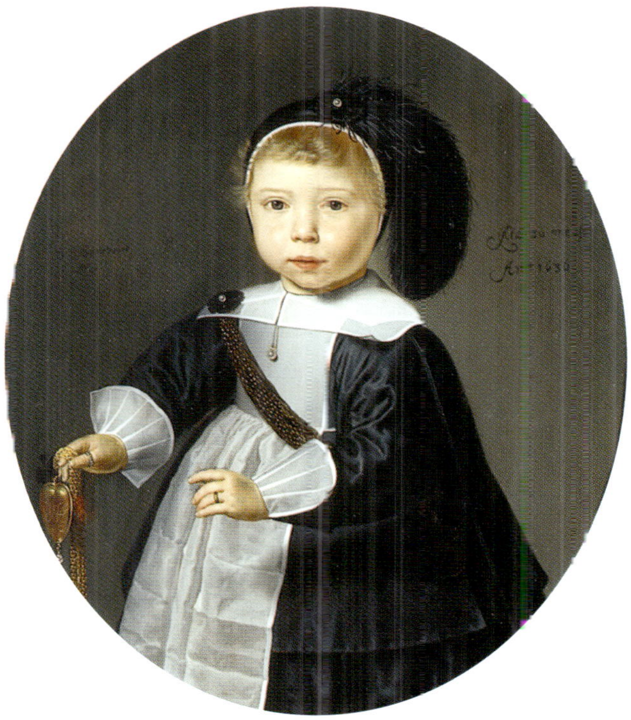

24.
Dirck Santvoort,
Portrait of Willem van Loon, 1636.
Oil on panel (oval),
63 × 52 cm.
Museum Van Loon, Amsterdam

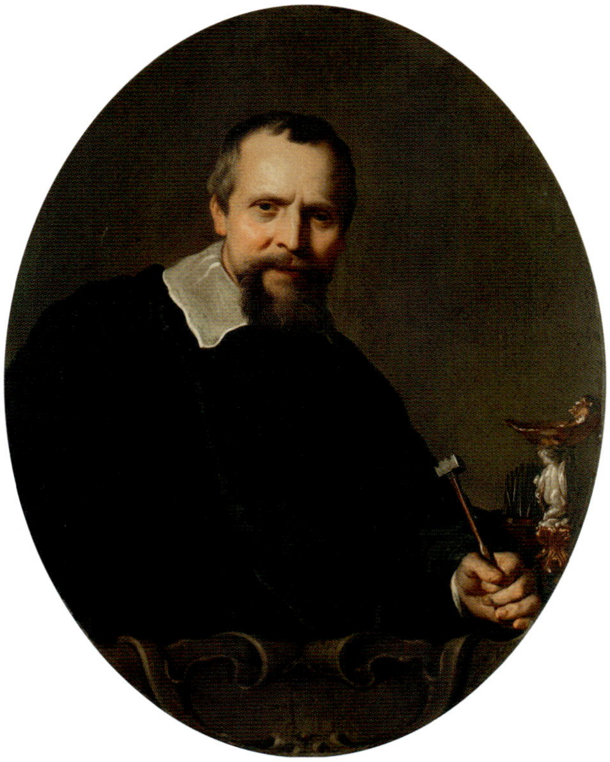

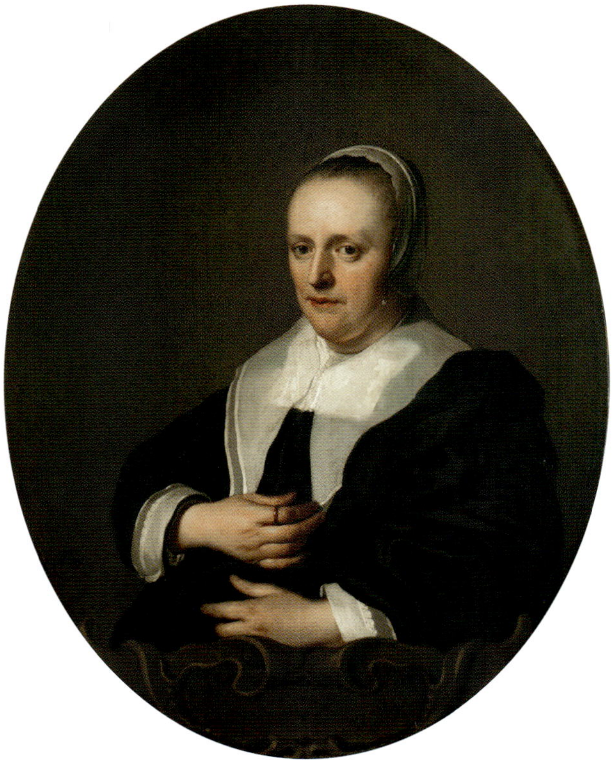

25.
Jacob Backer,
Portrait of Jan Lutma, silversmith, about 1639.
Oil on panel (oval),
91 x 71 cm.
Rijksmuseum,
Amsterdam

26.
Jacob Backer,
Portrait of Sara de Bie, Wife of Jan Lutma,
about 1639.
Oil on panel (oval),
93 x 73 cm.
Rijksmuseum,
Amsterdam

Ovens (1623–1678) from Germany and the English artist Cornelis Jonson van Ceulen (p. 39, fig. 35; p. 132, fig. 25a). Others who made their mark on Amsterdam portraiture in the mid-seventeenth century, either as specialists or generalists, include Gerbrand van den Eeckhout (1621–1674), Jan Victors (1619–1676), Philips Koninck (1619–1688), and Paulus Hennekyn (1612–1672) – as well as De Keyser and Pickenoy.

The Hague 1630–1660

After the death of William of Orange in 1584, The Hague had become the seat of government. It was here that the stadholder resided when he was not away on a military campaign, and it was here that the main executive bodies of the Republic and of the province of Holland held their meetings (p. 53, fig. 49). Prince Maurits hardly presided over what one would call a court culture, however. His first court painter, Van den Queborn, was firmly rooted in the style of the sixteenth century (p. 160, fig. 39a) and his successor was Van Mierevelt, from Delft (discussed above). Alongside these was the Hague artist Van Ravesteyn, who produced portraits for the court, members of government, and senior officials. After Maurits was succeeded by his half-brother Frederik Hendrik in 1625, a true court culture evolved – largely through the work of the stadholder's ambitious wife, Amalia van Solms – in which portraiture featured prominently (cat. 32). This boom was reinforced by the presence of the court in exile of the 'Winter King and Queen', who had sought refuge in The Hague in 1619–20 after their brief adventure as the king and queen of Bohemia. The Winter Queen, Elizabeth, sister of Charles I of England (cat. 31), loved commissioning portraits, and one has the impression that Amalia, her former lady-in-waiting, was an enthusiastic rival. Although the aging court painter Van Mierevelt was still granted plenty of commissions, he was too old-fashioned and unimaginative to completely meet the demands of either court. The gap was filled by the Utrecht artist Gerrit van Honthorst (1592–1656), who owed his introduction as a portraitist at the Hague court to the success he had reaped with King Charles I and his courtiers during his time in London in 1628 (cat. 31).[53] Inspired by his stay in Italy, which left its traces most notably in his Caravaggesque history paintings and genre scenes, and by the innovative tendencies in portraiture that were already noticeable in the work of his older fellow-townsman Moreelse, Van Honthorst created his own sophisticated style of court portraits (fig. 31): elegant and part arcadian, painted in a smooth style, and undoubtedly seen – partly because of the often rather large eyes – as highly flattering. With these works, he dominated portrait commissions in The Hague's courtly circles for two decades and secured a position comparable to that held by Anthony van Dyck (1599–1641) at the English court, from 1632 until his death nine years later. Not until around 1650, the beginning of a

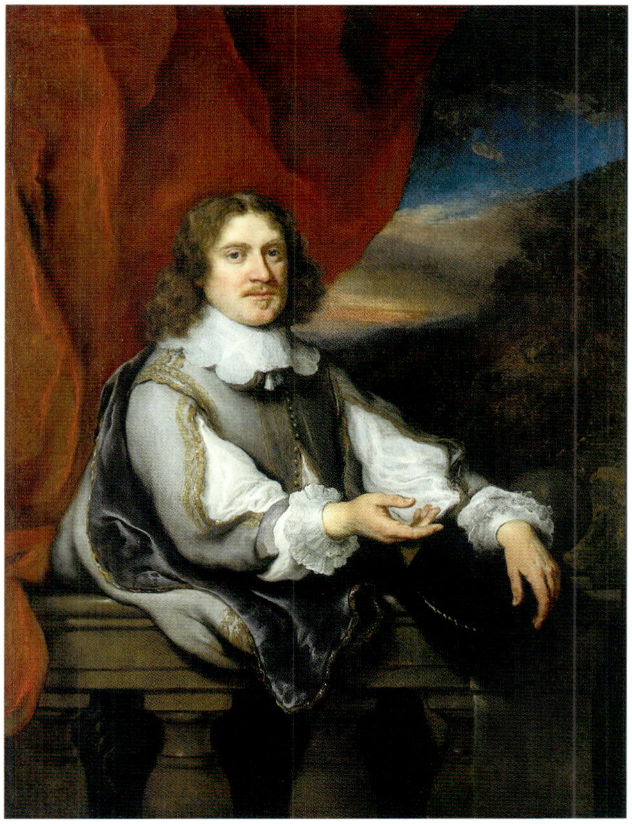

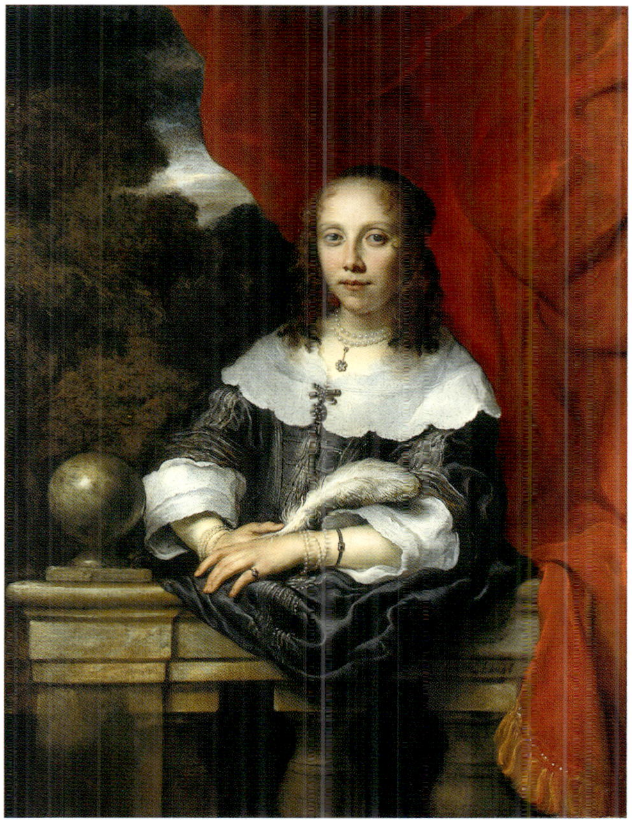

27.
Govert Flinck,
Portrait of a Man,
1646. Oil on canvas,
117 × 88 cm.
North Carolina
Museum of Art,
Raleigh

28.
Govert Flinck,
Portrait of a Woman,
1646. Oil on canvas,
122 × 90 cm.
North Carolina
Museum of Art,
Raleigh

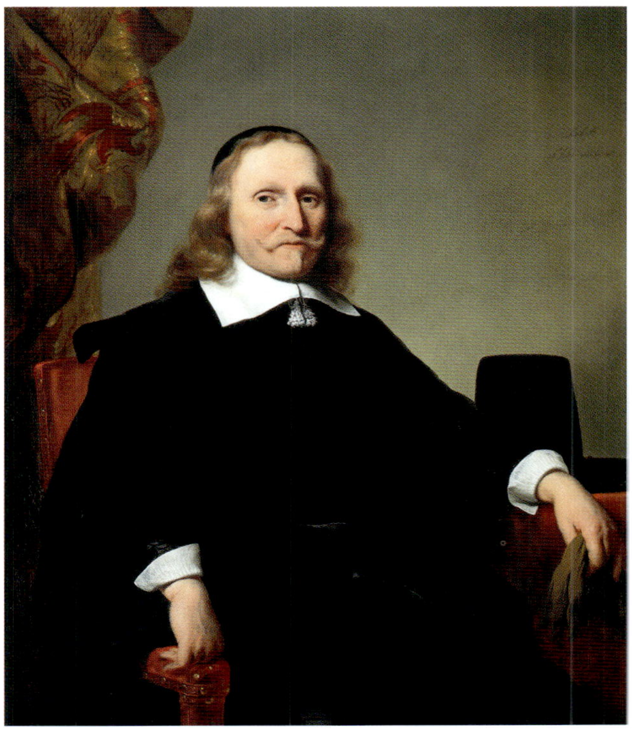

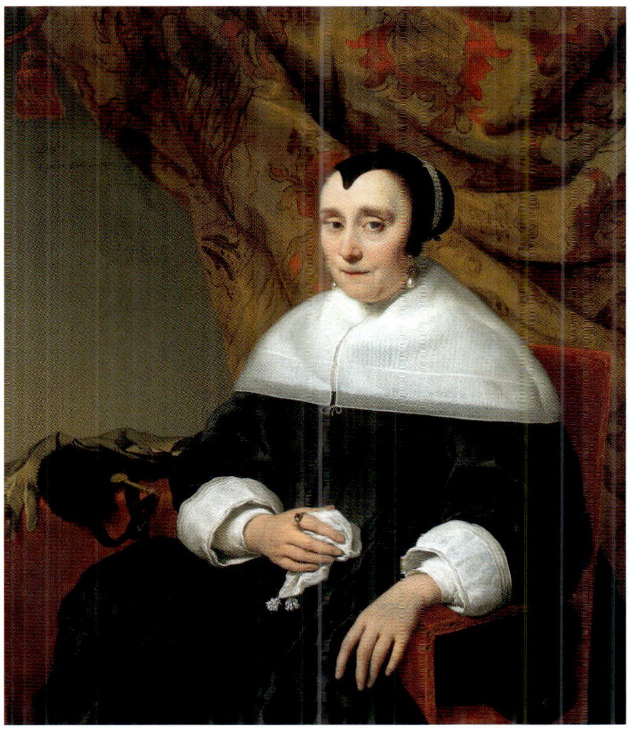

29.
Ferdinand Bol,
Portrait of Elbert Spiegel, 1660.
Oil on canvas,
110 × 92 cm.
Rathaus, Museum
Briner und Kern,
Winterthur

30.
Ferdinand Bol,
Portrait of Elisabeth de Vlaming van Oudtshoorn, Wife of Elbert Spiegel,
1660. Oil on canvas,
110 × 92 cm.
Rathaus, Museum
Briner und Kern,
Winterthur

period without a stadholder, did Van Honthorst's position start to decline. Van Honthorst greatly influenced the paintings produced in the second and third quarters of the seventeenth century – most notably in The Hague, but also further afield, especially in Utrecht, Gelderland and Overijssel. Together with Van Dyck, he placed his stamp on the development of fashionable portraits in the Northern Netherlands.

Van Dyck's direct influence reached The Hague first and foremost through Adriaen Hanneman (about 1604–1671), an artist from The Hague who had worked in close proximity to Van Dyck in London from about 1626 to 1638 and later propagated his style in The Hague (cat. 28).[54] A somewhat younger artist who incorporated stylistic qualities of Van Honthorst and Van Dyck into an idiom of his own was Jan Mijtens (1613/14–1670). Besides superb life-sized individual portraits, this artist also depicted family groups in a smaller format, especially in the 1640s and 1650s (cat. 41).[55] Hanneman and Mijtens were active until around 1670. Pieter Nason (about 1612–1688/90), who went to The Hague from Amsterdam shortly before 1640 and initially depicted primarily members of the Hague burgher classes and officers, also gradually built up a princely clientele.[56] The Hague had numerous other portraitists besides Nason around the mid-seventeenth century – one who stands out is Jan Westerbaen the Elder (1600/2–1686), whose clients consisted primarily of Hague burghers and whose works were less fashionable.[57]

Other Cities in Holland

Although the work produced in Amsterdam and The Hague largely set the trend, artists in many other cities made unique and substantial contributions to seventeenth-century portraiture. Frans Hals in Haarlem went on making portraits in his inimitable style until the 1660s, in the last ten years using even wider brushstrokes than before. His dazzling technique placed him in something of an isolated position, since none of his followers – even his son Jan (about 1620–1654) – could match it. More interesting than these followers are Hals's contemporaries Pieter Soutman (1593/1601–1657) and Hendrick Pot (about 1585–1657): Soutman introduced a distinct Flemish quality into his portraits after his stay in Antwerp, and Pot specialised mainly in smaller portraits, partly inspired by De Keyser's work in Amsterdam.[58] Jan Miense Molenaer (1610/11–1668), who like Pot had been living in both Haarlem and Amsterdam, produced various genre-like family groups and a few formal portraits (cat. 42), but he subsequently appears to have abandoned portraiture.[59] The most important portrait specialist in Haarlem, besides Frans Hals, was Johannes Verspronck (1606/9–1662). Verspronck may have studied with Hals, and in his work from the 1630s he clearly displays the master's influence in his sitters' poses, although he did not try to emulate Hals's loose brushstrokes.[60] Verspronck soon developed a more tranquil type of portrait, in which he attained a balance between light movement and gravitas (fig. 32; see also cat. 64 and pp. 60–61, figs 55–6). After 1650, Jan de Bray gradually took over as Haarlem's leading portraitist, a role that he would fulfil for over 40 years (see p. 43).[61]

Leiden's most influential portraitists up to the mid-century mark were David

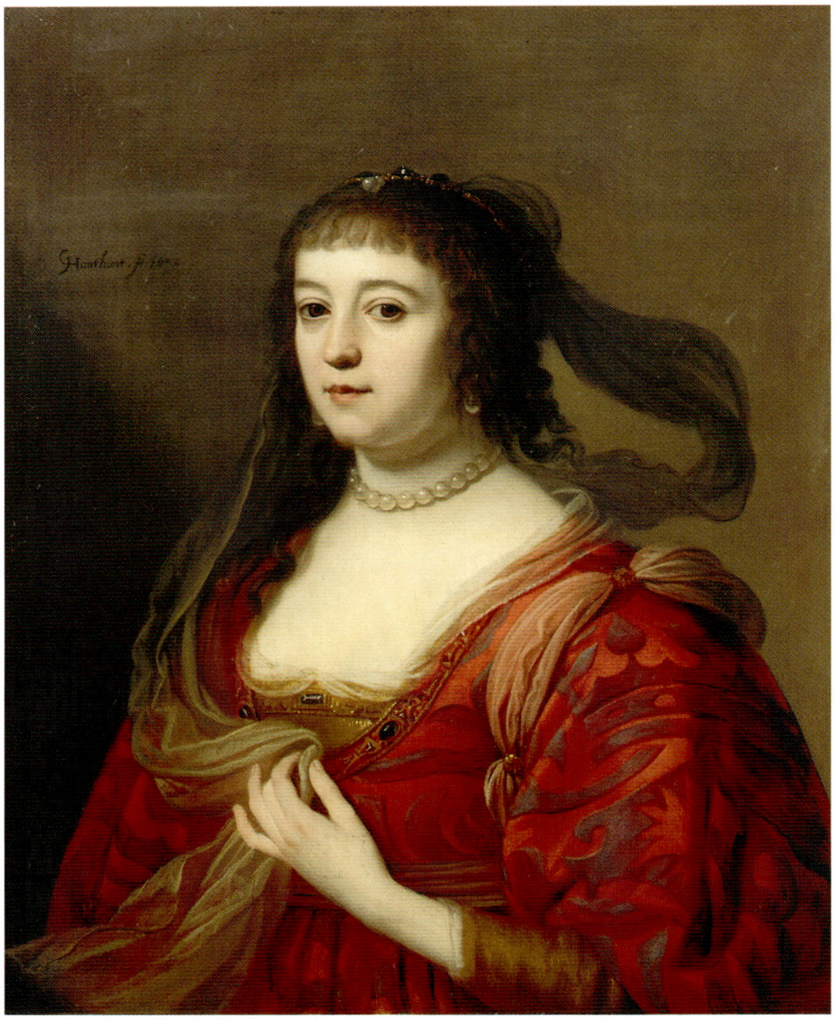

31.
Gerrit van Honthorst, *Portrait of Amalia van Solms*, 1632.
Oil on canvas, 76 x 63 cm.
Centraal Museum, Utrecht

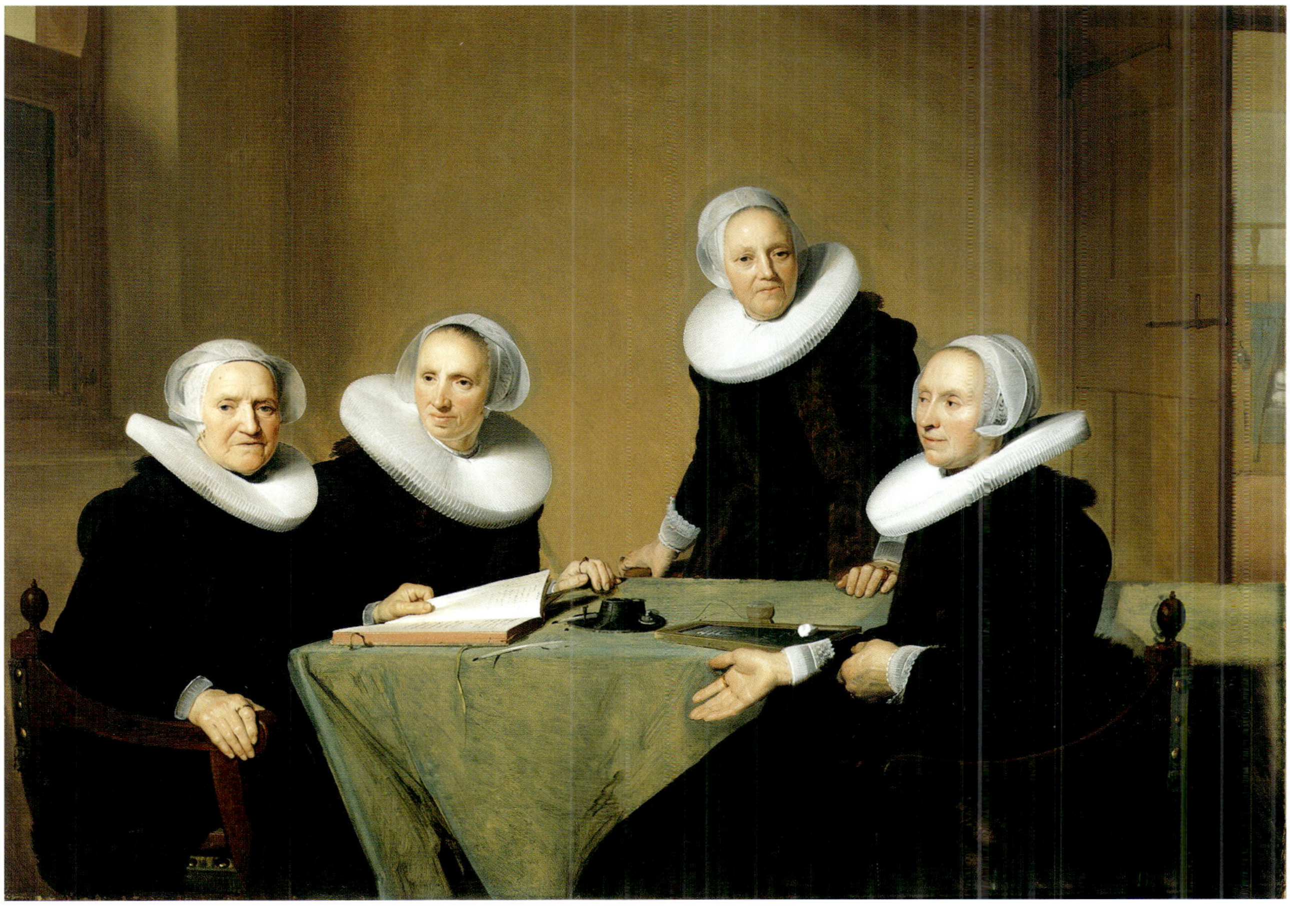

32.
Johannes Verspronck,
The Regentesses of St Elisabeth's Hospital,
1641. Oil on canvas,
152 × 210 cm.
Frans Hals Museum,
Haarlem

Bailly (1584–1657) and Joris van Schooten (about 1587–1652).[62] While the latter focused entirely on life-sized portrait paintings, and made a number of militia pieces, Bailly also produced smaller works, some of them in oil but most in the form of drawings (p. 50, fig. 46). Another portrait specialist working in Leiden was the French painter Pieter Dubordieu (about 1608–after 1678); others produced portraits only incidentally, such as Gerrit Dou (cat. 12), Quirijn van Brekelenkam (after 1622–1669?) and Godaert Kamper (about 1613/14–1679).

Before about 1640, aside from Michiel van Mierevelt (who died in 1641) we see only one professional portraitist of note in the city of Delft: Willem van Vliet (about 1584–1642), who made dozens of superb portraits in the period 1624 to 1642. After Van Mierevelt's death, his business was taken over, though on a greatly reduced scale, by his grandson Jacob Willemsz Delff II (1619–1661). Finally, Anthonie Palamedesz (about 1601–1673) and Hendrik van Vliet (1611/12–1675), who had only made sporadic forays into portraiture in the past, developed into productive portraitists in addition to their other activities.[63]

In Rotterdam, Jan Daemen Cool (about 1589–1660), who had probably trained with Van Mierevelt, was active as a portrait specialist from around 1620 onwards.[64] Besides many individual portraits, he also produced a series of groups, including a regent piece and several families. Abraham de Vries (about 1590–1649/50), who had spent many years travelling around France and the Southern Netherlands, was active in his home city for several years in the 1640s.[65] Around the same time, Ludolf de Jongh (1616–1679) and Hendrick Sorgh (about 1610–1670) came to the fore as portraitists in Rotterdam, although both were more active in the field of genre paintings. While De Jongh, like Cool, made primarily life-sized, formal portraits, Sorgh is best known for his smaller, genre-like portraits.[66]

In Dordrecht, the versatile artist Jacob Gerritsz Cuyp (1594–1652) continued to dominate the portrait market until his death, with images ranging from highly formal likenesses to more or less arcadian portraits.[67] His repertoire embraced single figures as well as groups, and included numerous children's portraits (cat. 11), a genre that brought out Cuyp's talents to best effect. After his death, his studio was initially taken over by his son Aelbert (1620–1691), who had sometimes collaborated with him as well as making his own portraits in his father's style.[68] Aelbert Cuyp also developed a highly

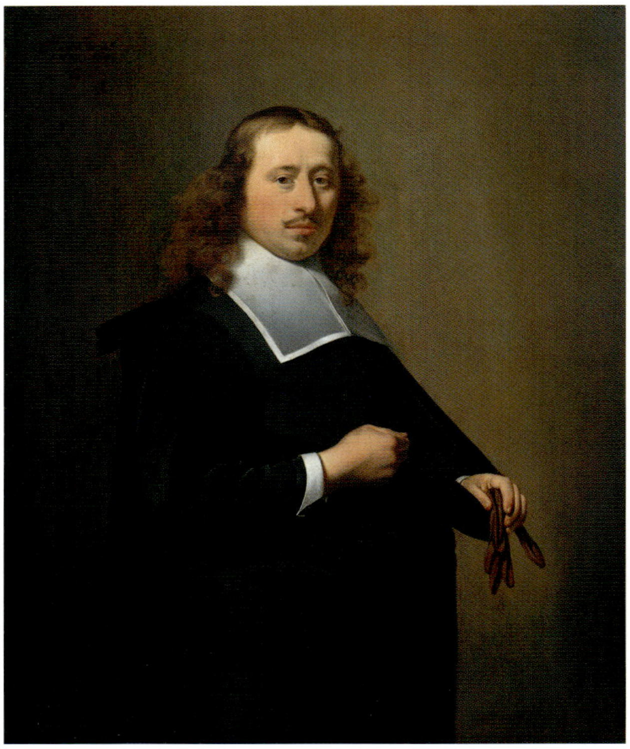

33.
Caesar van Everdingen, *Portrait of Willem Baert*, 1671. Oil on canvas, 110 × 90 cm. Rijksmuseum, Amsterdam

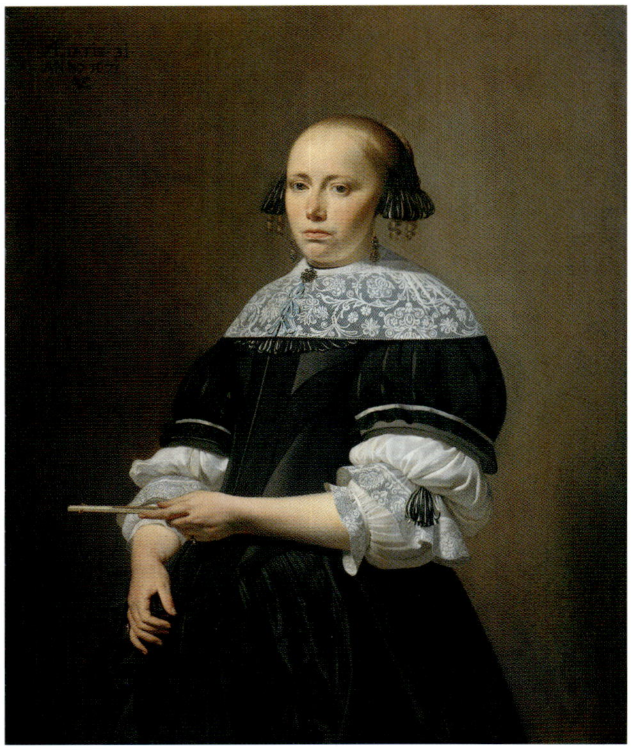

34.
Caesar van Everdingen, *Portrait of Elisabeth Kessel, Wife of Willem Baert*, 1671. Oil on canvas, 109 × 90 cm. Rijksmuseum, Amsterdam

specific genre of his own, equestrian portraits in a landscape (p. 98, fig. 11a), which he continued producing after abandoning regular portrait commissions in 1655. During Jacob Cuyp's lifetime there was little room for competition in Dordrecht, and only Paulus Lesire (1612–after 1654) and (briefly) Jacob van der Merck (about 1610–1664) worked there as portrait painters.[69] After Aelbert Cuyp stopped making portraits, the market was divided among Cornelis Bisschop (1630–1674) and the Rembrandt pupils Maes (see p. 42) and Jacobus Levecq (1634–1675).

In the northern part of Holland, portrait painters were active in the towns of Alkmaar, Enkhuizen and Hoorn. Several artists were active in Alkmaar, but their work was overshadowed to some extent by that of the Utrecht-trained Caesar van Everdingen (1616/17–1678), who regularly accepted commissions from his home town, even while he was working in Haarlem and Amsterdam.[70] The dozens of portraits in his œuvre are quite varied (figs 33–4) and include three militia pieces. The numerous painters working in Enkhuizen from 1620 to 1660 (often for short periods of time) included Gerbrand Ban (1612/13–1652) and Herman Doncker (before 1620–after 1656).[71] Finally, in Hoorn, the older generation of portrait painters was represented by Jacques Waben (active about 1602–1634) and Jan van Teylingen (about 1602–1654). From the mid-seventeenth century onwards, the market was dominated by Abraham Liedts (active about 1652–1660) and the highly skilled artist Jan Albertsz Rotius (1624–1666), who became an excellent portraitist and placed his stamp on the genre in Hoorn.[72]

Other Provinces of the Northern Netherlands

In Utrecht, Van Honthorst was potentially the most serious rival to Paulus Moreelse, who continued to dominate the local market until his death in 1638. Although Van Honthorst concentrated largely on the market in The Hague, he also painted portraits in Utrecht. Moreelse's main natural successors were Hendrick Bloemaert (about 1601–1672) and Jan van Bijlert (1597/8–1671), both of whom were solid portraitists who did not produce anything out of the ordinary.[73] Other painters who made portraits included the brothers-in-law Jan Niwael (about 1595–1673/4) and Jan van Loenen (about 1595–1643), and Bernard Zwaerdecroon (about 1617–1654). From the mid-seventeenth century onwards, Utrecht's portraiture was boosted by the advent of Cornelis Jonson van Ceulen (1593–1661), who had come to the Netherlands from England a few years earlier, and immortalised many of Utrecht's townspeople in his own highly personal style (fig. 35).[74]

In Overijssel, where portraiture seldom rose above a provincial quality in the first half of the seventeenth century, a new development arose around the mid-century mark thanks to Gerard ter Borch (1617–1681), who, having lived in Haarlem and Amsterdam and undertaken several trips abroad, had returned to his home town of Zwolle before moving to the neighbouring city of Deventer in 1654. There he had stayed until his death in 1681, working as a portrait and genre painter and as a member of the city government, except for a brief period in the early 1670s when he lived in Amsterdam. With his bust, half-length and knee-length – and from 1654 onwards sometimes full-length – portraits, all executed in small formats, Ter Borch occupies a unique place in seventeenth-century Dutch portraiture (cats 2–3 and figs 2a, 3a).[75] His works are meticulously painted – each model is rendered with exquisite care – and the overall execution is subdued. Ter Borch generally leaves a large amount of space around his subjects, who thus take up a far smaller proportion of the picture plane than was customary among most of his predecessors and contemporaries (figs 36–7). We see the same feature in his sole regent piece, *The Magistracy of Deventer*, from 1667.[76] Ter Borch's influence extended well beyond Overijssel; one of his pupils was Caspar Netscher (cat. 44), who would later become a prominent artist in The Hague.

35.
Cornelis Jonson van Ceulen, *Portrait of a Woman*, 1650. Oil on canvas, 108 x 80 cm. Centraal Museum, Utrecht

In Friesland, many portrait painters were active around the mid-century mark, of whom Wybrand de Geest (1592–1661/5) was without a doubt the most important (p. 62, fig. 57).[77] His style is reminiscent of the previous generation, most notably of Moreelse. Dozens of works from the period 1621–60, including many made for the court of the Frisian stadholders in Leeuwarden, demonstrate his skill as a portrait painter. Among the other leading representatives of this and the subsequent generation in Friesland are father and son Harmen (active 1632–1644) and Nicolaas Wieringa (died in 1681).[78]

In the province of Groningen, the deaf and dumb painter Jan Jansz de Stomme ('the Mute', about 1615–about 1657) was the most influential master around the middle of the century.[79] In Gelderland, portraitists were active in many towns in the seventeenth century, such as Hendrick Coster (about 1610/20–in or after 1664) from Arnhem. The most important one, however, was Nicolaes van Helt Stocade from Nijmegen (about 1614–1669). He was only based in his home town for a few years, but continued to accept commissions from Nijmegen after moving to Amsterdam around 1652.[80]

Portraiture in Zeeland clearly declined after around 1620, but we can still point to a number of characteristic portraitists there, including Willem Eversdijck (about 1620–1671), Michiel van Limborch (active 1636–1675) and Hendrick Berckman (1629–1679).[81] Even in the newly annexed provinces of Brabant and Limburg, which did not shine, in general, as centres of seventeenth-century painting, we find portraitists in a number of towns. They included painters of surprising ability, such as the Antwerp-trained Theodoor van Thulden (1606–1669), active in Den Bosch, and Harmen de Bye (1600–1683) of Amersfoort, who lived in Venlo (p. 54, fig. 50).[82]

A Later Flowering: 1660–1700

In the older art-historical literature, the period from 1660 or 1670 has often been regarded as a time of decline

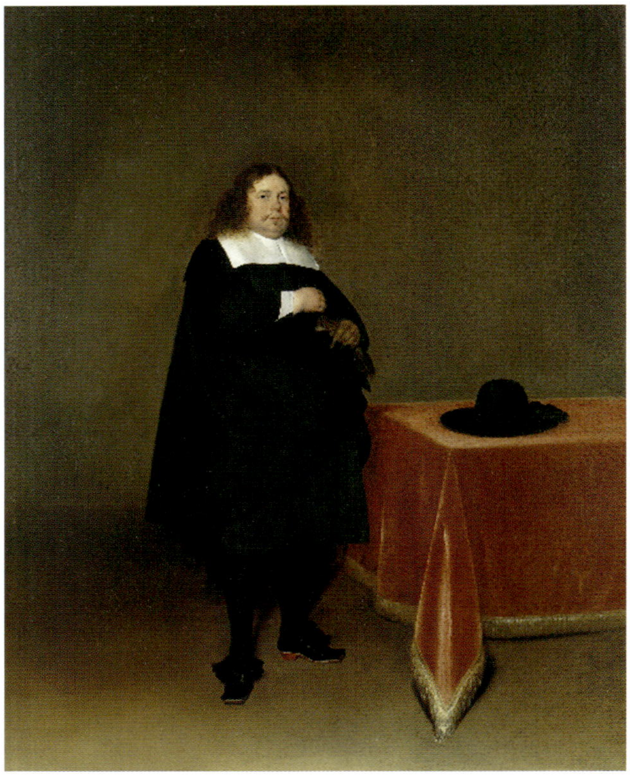

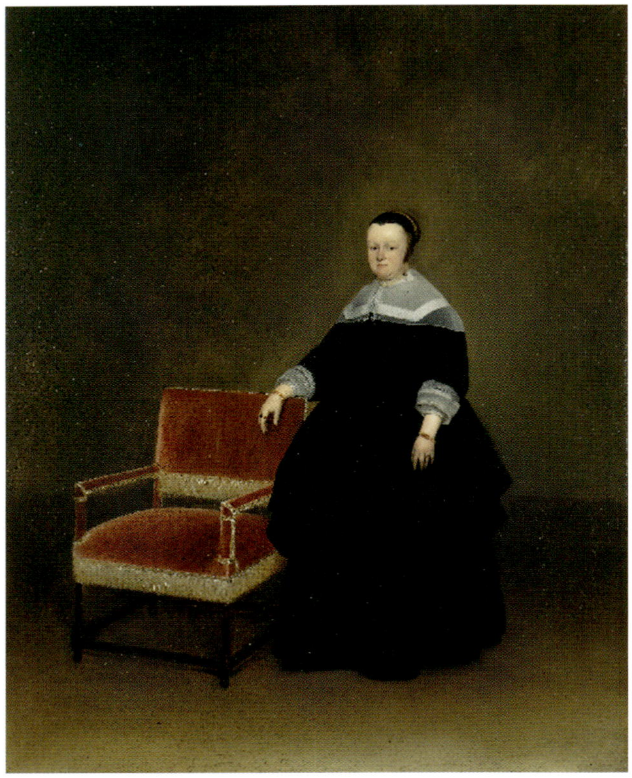

36.
Gerard ter Borch, *Portrait of Jan van Duren*, about 1666–7. Oil on canvas, 82 x 66 cm. Robert Lehman Collection, The Metropolitan Museum of Art, New York

37.
Gerard ter Borch, *Portrait of Margaretha van Haexbergen, Wife of Jan van Duren*, about 1666–7. Oil on canvas, 82 x 65 cm. Robert Lehman Collection, The Metropolitan Museum of Art, New York

or, slightly more positively, as the waning years of the Golden Age. The heading 'later flowering' chosen here is based on an alternate view: that there was in fact no decline at all, but a new development in a different direction, one that had been presaged in the previous years. The far more elegant and international style of the portraiture produced in this period contrasts sharply with the austere, bold style that existed prior to 1650 and is therefore regarded all too often as a form of betrayal of the national character. This negative qualification is wholly unjustified, since the style of the later seventeenth century, like the earlier art at the Hague court, is entirely Dutch in character. Although it reflects influences from beyond the Republic's borders, late seventeenth-century Dutch portraitists themselves contributed to this more international style. Although it must be said that this later period did not produce any new great masters, it was by no means an age of second-rate artists. That this chapter on the later heyday of seventeenth-century portraiture is shorter than those on the earlier periods is not attributable to any lack of quality, but rather to the fact that many of the artists concerned were active before 1660 and have therefore already been discussed.

Amsterdam 1660–1700

Portraiture in the Amsterdam of the 1660s was very much a continuation of the previous period. The most respected painters in this area were Van der Helst and Bol, of whom the latter in fact continued to produce works in exactly the same style and to the same standard as before, whereas Van der Helst's later work exhibits a number of changes that sometimes detract from its strength. Several other artists already mentioned – Van Loo, Luttichuys and Van den Eeckhout – also remained prominent, and the arrival of Abraham van den Tempel (1622/3–1672), who moved from Leiden to Amsterdam in 1660, fortified the ranks of the city's portraitists. Van den Tempel was an outstanding painter of somewhat classical – but certainly not old-fashioned – individual and group portraits (cat. 63; p. 51, fig. 47).[83] Other significant artists in this period include Karel du Jardin (1626–1678) and Wallerant Vaillant (1623–1677).[84]

Around 1660 we also see the surprising return to the market of two painters who had been prominent artists for some time, but had made very few portraits for years. Thomas de Keyser produced a number of portraits again, including his 1660 likeness of Pieter Schout (fig. 38), one of the most successful equestrian portraits in the seventeenth century.[85] Rembrandt, who, after painting *The Night Watch* (p. 32, fig. 22) had executed only a few portrait commissions, including his masterful portrait of Jan Six from 1654 (cat. 57), also began taking on commissions again, and produced a series of late portraits that are among the highlights of his œuvre. This series begins with the likenesses of Jacob Trip and his wife from

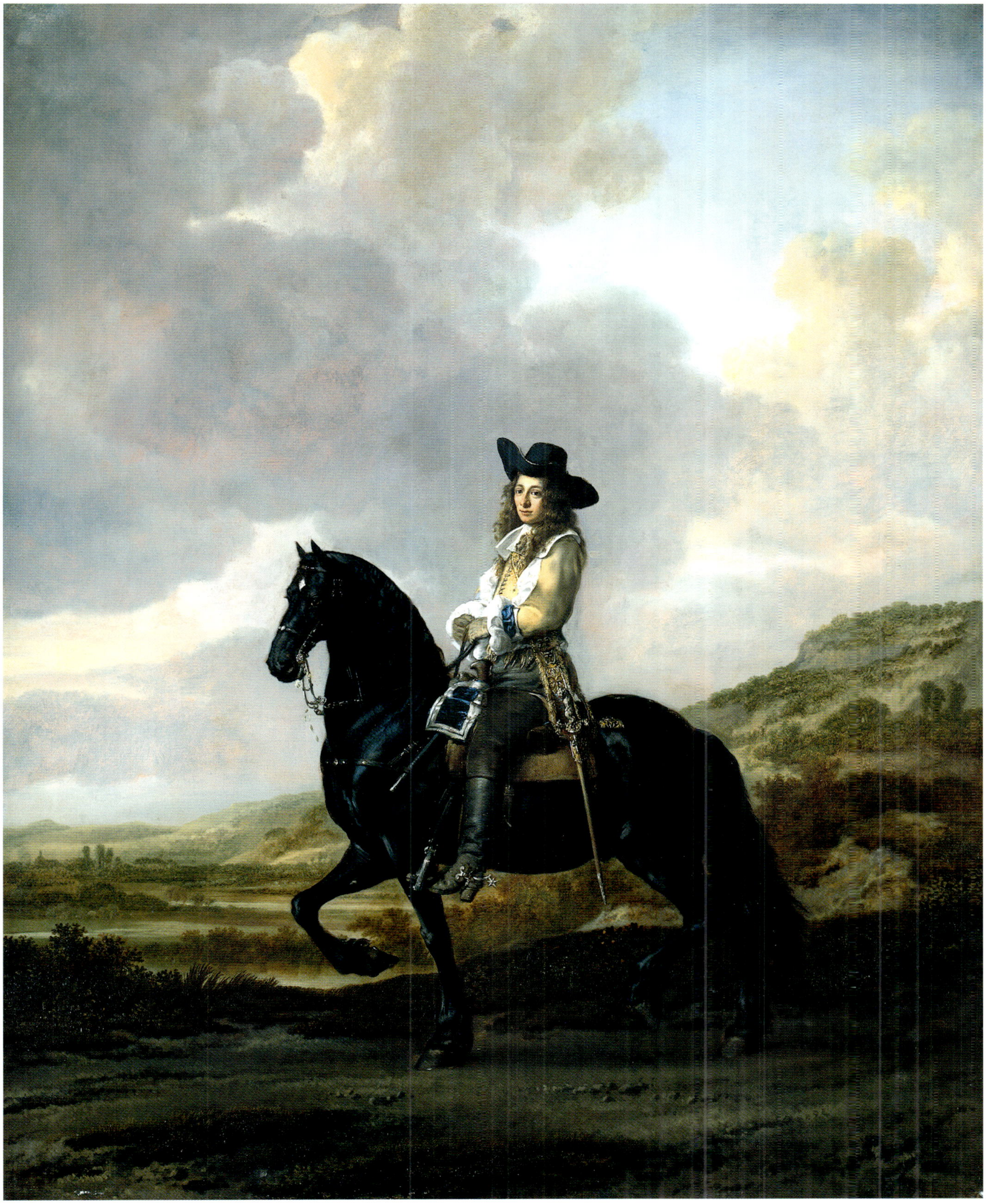

38. Thomas de Keyser, *Equestrian Portrait of Pieter Schout*, 1660. Oil on copper, 86 × 70 cm. Rijksmuseum, Amsterdam

around 1661 (cats 58–9), Jacob probably being depicted posthumously. In 1662 followed *The Syndics of the Clothmakers' Guild* (cat. 60), one of the most classical regents' portraits of the seventeenth century. Then came a number of pieces that were painted quite expansively, many of which surprise the viewer with their unconventional designs, such as *Portrait of an Elderly Man* from 1667 (cat. 61).

In the years around 1670, the ranks of Amsterdam's portraitists were greatly depleted by deaths, departures and retirements. Some painters who were active before 1670, such as Adriaen Backer (1635/6–1684), a cousin of Jacob Backer, Barend Graat (1628–1709) and the Rotterdam-born artist Michiel van Musscher (1645–1705),[86] went on painting for longer and continued to play a prominent role in Amsterdam's portraiture, but the man who became the city's most popular portraitist was Nicolaes Maes (1634–1693), who had come from Dordrecht to Amsterdam in 1673 and had been a pupil of Rembrandt. After a period of concentrating largely on genre paintings, in the 1660s Maes had gravitated towards portraits in his home town, modifying his initially rather conservative approach into a more fashionable style. From around 1670 his work displays growing bravura and a clear suggestion of movement, since he displays his sitters with their heads turned at an angle to their bodies. In Amsterdam this trend continued, while alongside his life-sized portraits he also started producing smaller-scale likenesses (cat. 38). He became truly prolific as an Amsterdam portraitist, producing dozens of paintings a year in his busiest periods (pp. 56-7, figs 52–3 and p. 205, figs 58-9a-b). The nucleus of his work consists of individual portraits of adults – often painted as pendants – and a substantial number of children's portraits, but he also made regent pieces and private group portraits (cat. 37), including several paintings depicting groups of children.[87]

Besides Maes, the artists who made distinctive contributions to Amsterdam portraiture in the final decades of the seventeenth century include Jan Weenix (1640–1719) and Matthijs Naiveu (1647–1726), as well as Michiel van Musscher.[88] Maes died in 1693, and his place as the city's most influential portraitist was taken by Arnold Boonen (1669–1729), also from Dordrecht, most of whose œuvre rightly belongs in a discussion of the eighteenth century.[89]

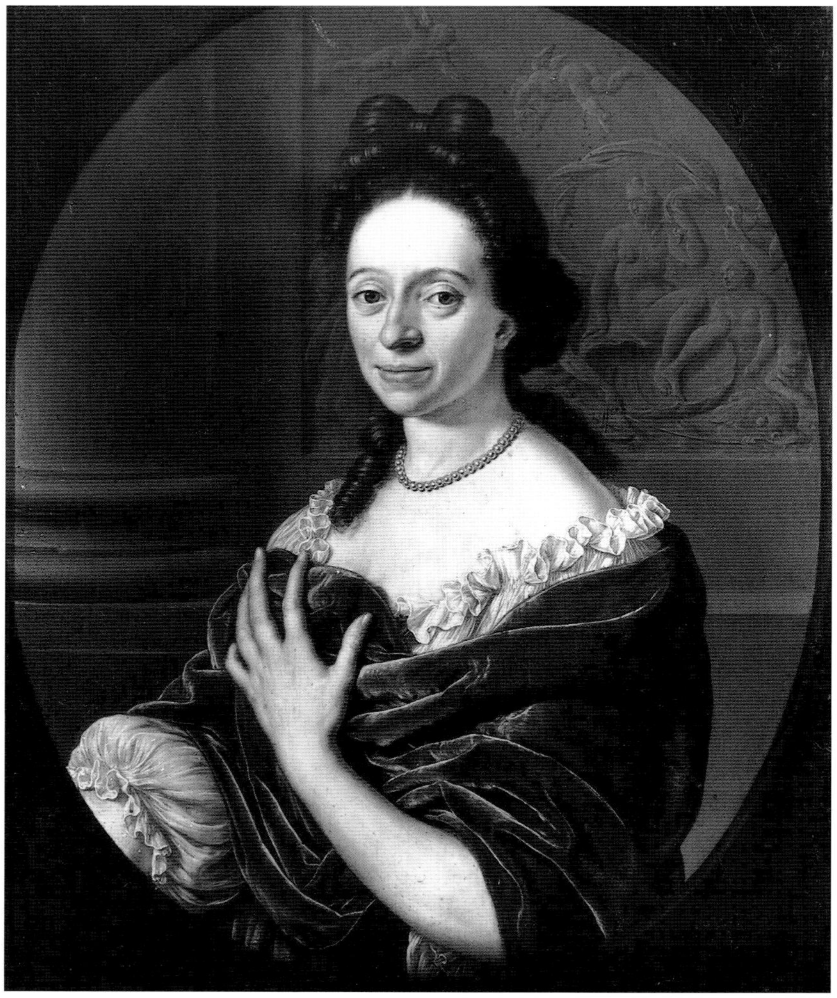

39.
Willem van Mieris, *Portrait of Sara van der Mark*, 1692. Oil on panel, 30 × 24 cm. Private collection

The Hague 1660–1700

The activities of The Hague's leading painters around the middle of the century continued unabated in the 1660s. But the year 1670 witnessed the death of Mijtens, followed a year later by that of Hanneman. Only Nason remained active, though less prolific, after 1670.[90] The city gained two new portraitists in the 1660s, however, who set their stamp on post-1670 trends. Jan de Baen (1633–1702) became the most influential Hague portraitist for life-sized pieces, turning out countless individual likenesses and a handful of group portraits.[91] His style builds on that of artists such as Hanneman and Nason, and often displays a certain air of gentility. Although this quality was attenuated in his later works by a more flamboyant touch, he gradually became less fashionable, as is clear from the virtual absence of work dating from after 1690. His somewhat younger fellow-artist Caspar Netscher (1635/6–1684), a pupil of Ter Borch's in Deventer, set up business in The Hague as a genre and portrait painter in 1662, after spending some years in France.[92]

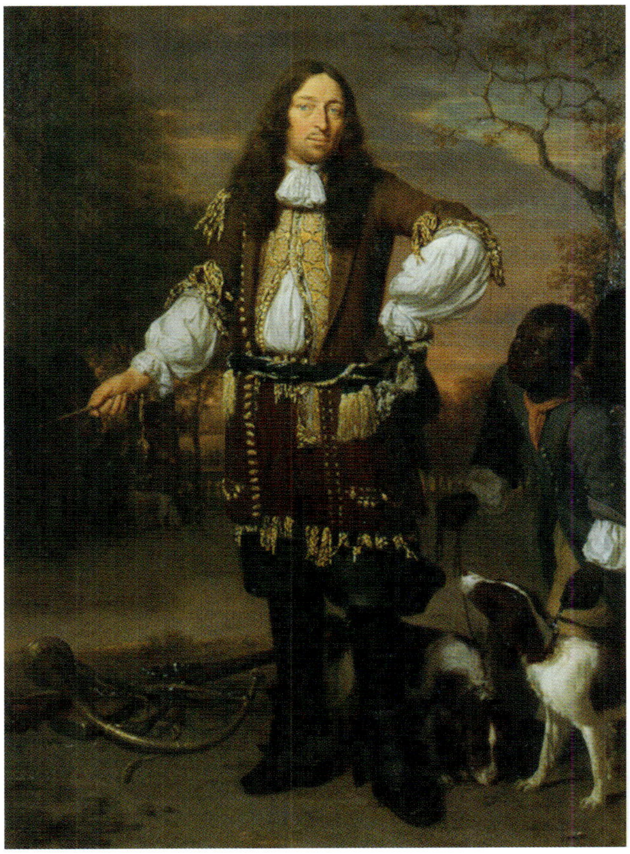

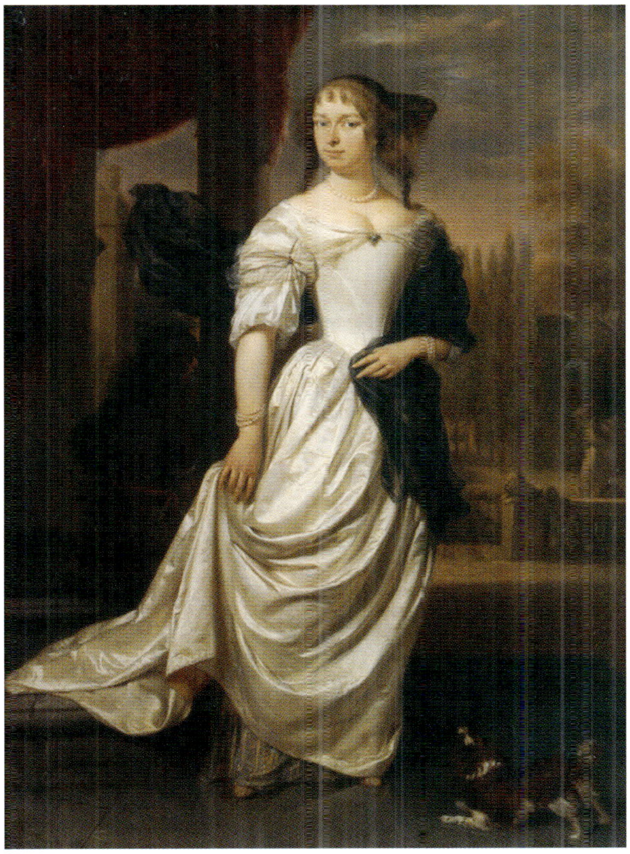

40.
Jan Verkolje,
Portrait of Johan de la Faille, 1674.
Oil on copper,
30 × 41 cm.
The Ella Gallup Sumner and Mary Catlin Sumner Collection Fund, Wadsworth Atheneum, Hartford, Connecticut

41.
Jan Verkolje,
Portrait of Margaretha de la Faille, Wife of Johan de la Faille,
1674. Oil on copper,
30 × 41 cm.
The Ella Gallup Sumner and Mary Catlin Sumner Collection Fund, Wadsworth Atheneum, Hartford, Connecticut

Although he painted a few life-sized portraits early on, he soon switched to smaller formats, partly emulating his former teacher. With his highly meticulous and rather smoothly painted portraits (cat. 44), which also reflect French influence, he became very successful in The Hague's highest circles and attracted many clients from elsewhere. His elegant portraits greatly influenced other masters, including his own son Constantijn Netscher (1668–1723), who continued to paint in his style in the eighteenth century. Other prominent masters in The Hague in this period include Johan van Haensbergen (1642–1705) and Jan Vollevens (1649–1728).[93]

The Hague rather lost its position as a centre of fashionable portraiture from the final decade of the seventeenth century onwards, since it no longer had a court. William III, the stadholder-king, had moved his royal residence to England in 1689 upon ascending the British throne.

Other Towns in Holland: 1660–1700

In the last few decades of the seventeenth century we find rather less differentiation in terms of local portrait styles and artists' personalities throughout the Northern Netherlands. What diversity remains is attributable to the specific characteristics of certain portraitists. Haarlem lost the most prominent portraitists of the previous two generations, Hals and Verspronck, who both died in the 1660s. By then, however, a worthy successor had already stepped into the breach: Jan de Bray (about 1627–1697), by whom a fairly varied œuvre of portraits (cats 4–6 and fig. 4a) and other works is known.[94] As a portraitist he worked in a variety of formats, and besides group portraits of regents, large family groups and life-sized individual portraits, he also left us some works in a small format, which differ widely in execution. In the later seventeenth century his works retain a certain old-fashioned solidity – even, at times, austerity. We also find numerous examples in his œuvre of *portraits historiés* rendering families as Biblical or historical figures (cat. 4 and fig. 4a). Portraits of this type were painted throughout most of the seventeenth century, but they were particularly popular in Amsterdam and Haarlem.[95]

In Leiden too, the production of portraits after 1660 was enormously varied, but the city's greatest contribution to the portraiture of the late seventeenth century was that of the Leiden *fijnschilders*, with their meticulous small works.[96] Frans van Mieris the Elder (1635–1681), who, like Dou before him was first and foremost a genre painter, produced a number of superb, painstakingly executed likenesses (cat. 40) that helped to determine the way this type of painting developed in Leiden in the late seventeenth and eighteenth centuries.[97] In the late

1680s and 1690s his son Willem van Mieris (1662–1747) painted some outstanding portraits in small formats (fig. 39), and his contemporary Karel de Moor (1656–1738) worked in varying sizes. Of the generation of the older Van Mieris we should also mention Pieter van Slingelandt (1640–1691), who distinguished himself in particular with somewhat genre-like portraits (p. 58, fig. 54) and with full-length portraits in medium-sized formats.

In Delft, Jacob Delff II died in 1661, but Palamedesz and Van Vliet continued to work until their deaths in 1673 and 1675, respectively. Palamedesz gradually added a more elegant touch to his fairly dry presentation, while Van Vliet's later work often displays something of a decline in quality. The most important younger portraitist was Jan Verkolje (1650–1693), whose pieces, usually executed in fairly small formats, display an idiosyncratic, often rather genre-like character (figs 40–1).[98]

Portraiture in Dordrecht suffered a severe blow when Nicolaes Maes left for Amsterdam in 1673. His main contemporaries, Levecq, Bisschop and Samuel van Hoogstraten (1627–1678) all died in the 1670s, leaving a distinct gap in the market. In the region of Holland known as 'West Friesland' we also see notably fewer good portraitists around this time. In Alkmaar, Lambert Doomer (1624–1700), a former pupil of Rembrandt's, occasionally produced fine portraits, Enkhuizen had Jan van Neck (1634/5–1714), who also worked in Amsterdam, and Hoorn too was poorly supplied with portraitists after the death of Rotius in 1666, except for the years during which the painter Steven van Duyven (active 1669–1686) made his home there.

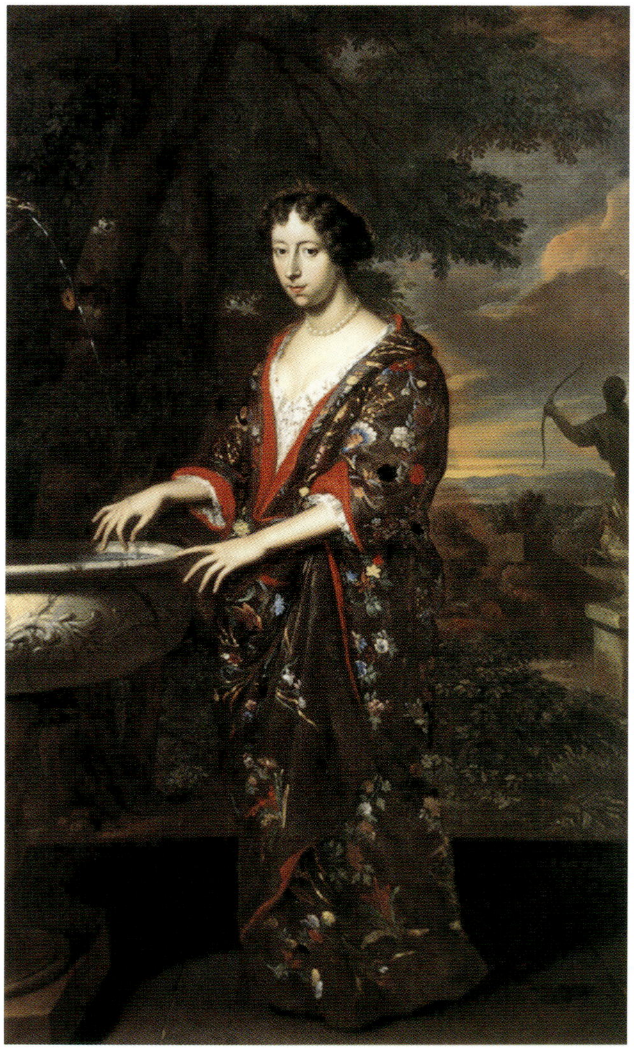

42.
Gerard Hoet,
Portrait of Anna van Reede,
about 1678.
Oil on canvas,
200 × 119 cm.
Slot Zuylen,
Oud-Zuylen

Other Provinces: 1660–1700

Besides the masters from the previous period who continued to work after 1660, such as Ter Borch in Deventer, numerous portrait painters were active in the country's other provinces in the last part of the seventeenth century, but few noteworthy newcomers emerged. In the city of Utrecht we scarcely find any good portraitists by whom more than a few portraits are known after the deaths of Van Bijlert and Bloemaert in 1671 and 1672. Cornelis Jonson van Ceulen the Younger (1634–1715) made some excellent portraits entirely in the style of his father of the same name, who had died in 1661, but his later work displays a decline in quality. The most prominent Utrecht portraitist in the later seventeenth century was Gerard Hoet (1648–1733), who was active there from around 1674 onwards (fig. 42).[99] Gelderland had a number of good local portraitists, in particular Gerrit Alberts (1663–1757) in Nijmegen (fig. 43), who would remain active well into the eighteenth century.[100] In Overijssel, Ter Borch continued to turn out portraits until his death in 1681, and we see a series of younger artists emerging there, including Hendrick ten Oever (1639–1716) and the prolific Roelof Koets (about 1650–1725).[101] In Groningen, Herman Collenius (1650–1723) arrived on the scene.[102] In Friesland, the painter Julius de Geest (about 1639–1699) produced work far inferior to that of his father Wybrand, and the stadholder's court in Leeuwarden instead enlisted the services of the Brussels painter Louis Volders (active about 1700).[103] In Zeeland too we find few younger portraitists of note joining those who had started work before 1660, such as Berckman and Eversdijck.

International Context

The flowering of Northern Netherlandish portraiture in the seventeenth century was related to trends in other European countries. The influence of Southern Netherlandish art – in particular that of Antwerp – in the early decades of the century has already been noted. The Flemish style gradually became less prominent as time went on. Interestingly, Peter Paul Rubens (1577–1640) had less influence on portraiture – far less than on history painting – in the Northern Netherlands than one might expect, given his great renown. That said, we can point to artists who clearly emulated Rubens, in certain cases because they spent some time in Antwerp, often serving as apprentices. Several worked in Zeeland and Brabant. Flemish stylistic features are seen more frequently here than in other parts of the Northern Netherlands, although the Haarlem painter and engraver Soutman is an exception to this rule; he must have worked in Rubens's studio for several years. Far more influential than Rubens was his former assistant Anthony van Dyck. The style he developed at the English court from 1632 onwards was held up as a supreme example by contemporaries and painters of the next generation. As already noted, his work was emulated in the courtly circles of The Hague, after which other artists followed in his footsteps. This enduring influence was still palpable more than twenty years after his death, in portraits made in cities such as The Hague and Amsterdam.

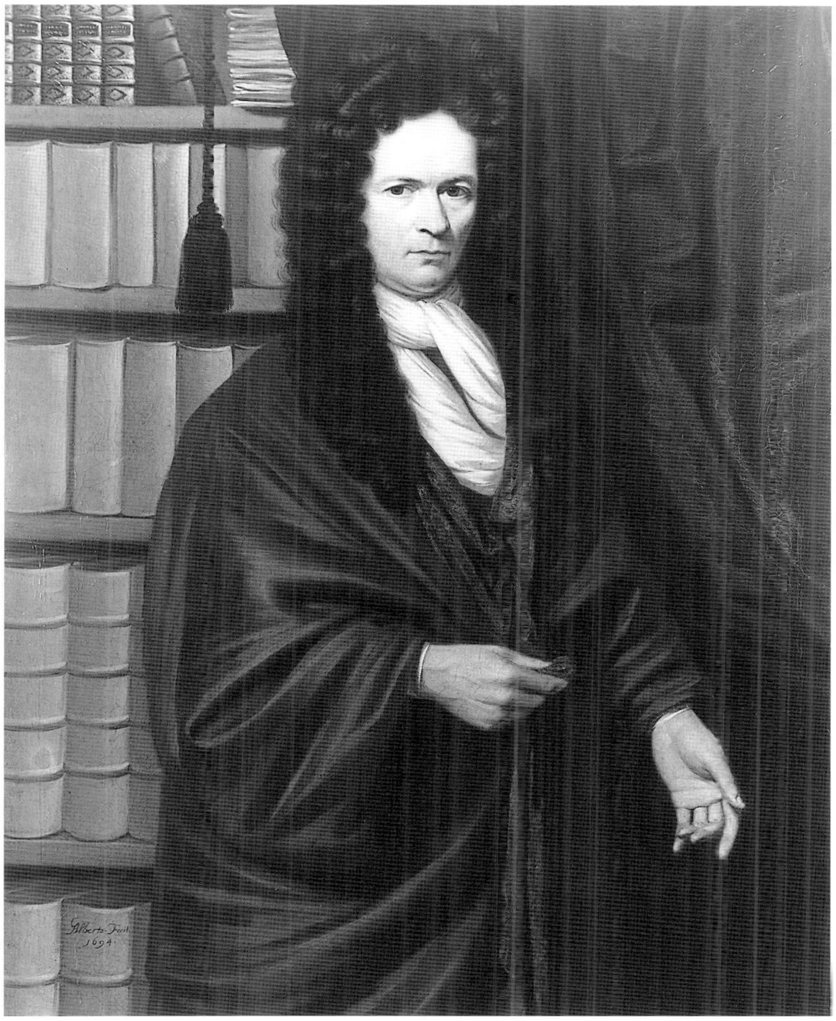

43.
Gerrit Alberts,
Portrait of Cornelis van Eck, 1694.
Oil on canvas,
120 x 94 cm.
Private collection

After 1660, French and international stylistic features dominated portrait painting. The French style extended far beyond portraiture alone, and was most noticeable in fashion. French styles of dress were so fashionable that portraits made in the Northern Netherlands of the late seventeenth century are reminiscent of the work of French artists: not so much because of the style in which they were painted but because of these clothing details. Still, the work of artists such as Nicolaes Maes and Caspar Netscher – who had worked in Bordeaux for a few years before settling in The Hague in 1662 – displays an unmistakeable similarity to that of, say, the portrait painter Pierre Mignard (1612–1695), precisely in the subjects' poses.[104] This does not mean that these Dutch artists should be classified as followers of French examples. Such correspondences are best described as part of the development of an international style of portraiture, incorporating characteristics of artists ranging from Van Dyck to Van Honthorst and Mignard. Artists such as Netscher and Maes – and Peter Lely (1618–1680), who was trained in the Northern Netherlands but was active in England – worked in the context of this international style rather than following a specifically French style of portraiture.[105]

It is worth noting that precisely in the late seventeenth century, Northern Netherlandish artists working in this international style were in great demand abroad. A case in point is Adriaen van der Werff (1659–1722) from Rotterdam, who became renowned as court painter to the Elector Palatine Johann Wilhelm (fig. 44).[106] Leiden's *fijnschilders* were also internationally famous. With their work, the portraiture of the Northern Netherlands, which had been celebrated for decades, reached one of its supreme heights.

Seventeenth-century portraiture of the Northern Netherlands was very influential in Europe,[107] especially in Great Britain, Scandinavia, Germany, Switzerland and Eastern Europe. English portraiture in this period was largely dominated by artists from the Northern and Southern Netherlands and masters who had been trained there,[108] as indeed was portraiture in Scotland and Ireland.[109] In Denmark, painters from Holland – and

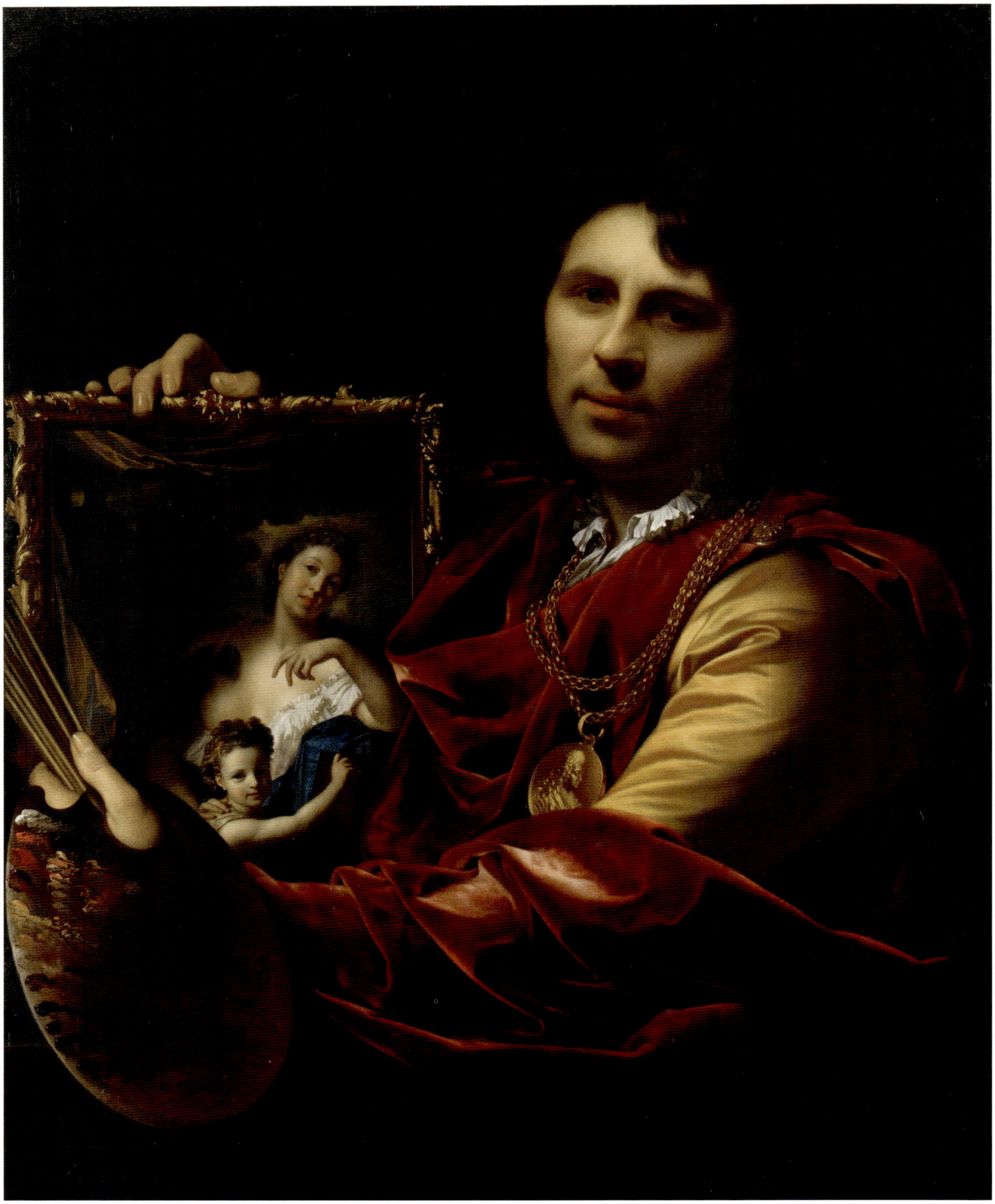

44. Adriaen van der Werff, *Self-Portrait with a Portrait of his Wife, Margaretha van Rees, and their Daughter Maria*, 1699. Oil on canvas, 81 x 66 cm. Rijksmuseum, Amsterdam

to a lesser extent from Flanders – consistently played a leading role in portraiture, and much the same applied in Sweden.[110] Numerous Dutch artists worked in Germany, and many German portraitists did some or all of their training in the Netherlands. Some even worked there for a few years, such as Simon Tilmann (1601–about 1669), Joachim von Sandrart (1606–1688) and Jürgen Ovens.[111] In the late seventeenth and early eighteenth centuries, every self-respecting German ruler wanted a court painter who was either Dutch or had been trained in the Netherlands, such as Van der Werff.[112] In Switzerland, seventeenth-century portraiture was determined to a large extent by artists trained in the Netherlands, and Dutch portraits were also highly influential in Central and Eastern Europe, especially in Poland.[113] Finally, it should be noted that early American portraiture relied heavily on examples from the Northern Netherlands.[114]

This survey – to which numerous examples from other countries could be added – makes it clear that the influence of Northern Netherlandish portraiture extended far beyond the Republic's borders. Furthermore, since Dutch paintings, including countless portraits, became collectable in many countries from the eighteenth century onwards, they continued to exercise an unmistakeable influence on artists for generations to come.

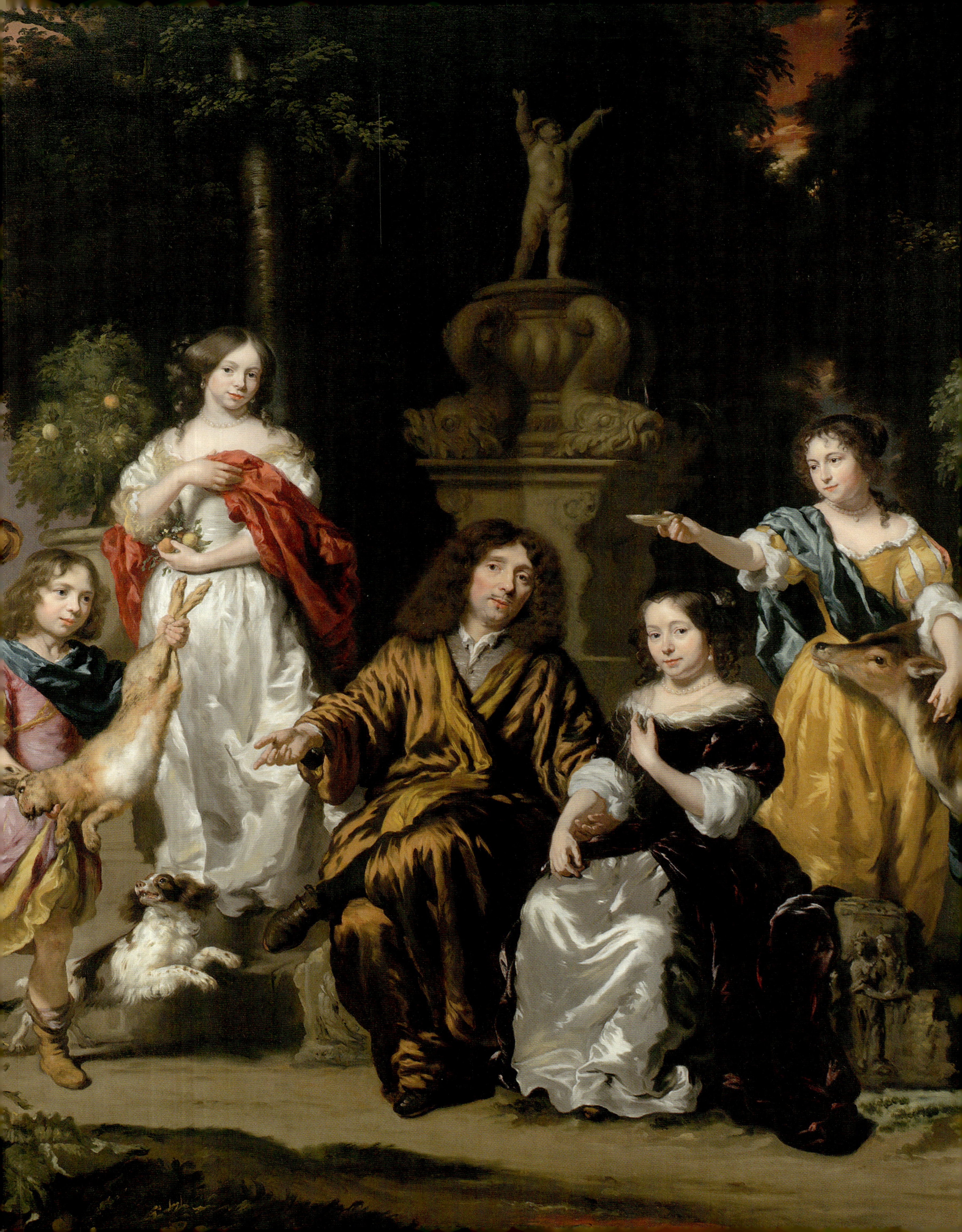

Portraiture in Practice

by Rudi Ekkart

The preceding discussion of seventeenth-century portraits from the Northern Netherlands touched on a variety of practical issues, including the different categories of clients and portraits, the diverse functions of portraits, the geographical distribution of portraitists, and the presence of signatures or inscriptions. This essay will focus in greater detail on these and other important aspects of the working practice of Northern Netherlandish portrait painters in the seventeenth century.

Public and Private Portraits

A large proportion of the portraits made in the seventeenth century have found their way into museums, so we may be in danger of losing sight of their original functions. Broadly speaking, we can divide all portraits into two main categories: those made for a private home, and those made to serve a more or less public purpose. ‘More or less’ is no idle qualification: we should not imagine a situation comparable to today’s art galleries. Public commissions were granted for buildings such as the guild-house of the civic guard, where guardsmen and visitors alike – and others, from time to time – could enjoy the paintings. In other words, a painting produced to serve a ‘public function’ was not made exclusively for the eyes of those depicted and their intimate circle, but to be hung where numerous other viewers would gaze at it.

Portraits made for town halls and other government buildings clearly fall into the category of public commissions. Group portraits of city councils are extremely rare, and are therefore of negligible relevance here. One sub-category worth mentioning, however, comprises the many portraits of stadholders made in the seventeenth century to embellish government buildings (cat. 39 and fig. 39a). Similarly, likenesses of admirals such as Michiel de Ruyter were destined to hang in a variety of admiralty buildings (cat. 1). The portraits in university collections are more difficult to classify, since some of them were originally made for a private home and then donated much later. However, other university portraits, in particular some now displayed in the Senate Hall galleries, were painted to hang there and can therefore be classified as public portraits.[1] The same is true of the occasional portrait series showing the pastors of a particular parish, presumably made to hang in the parsonage.[2]

In terms of numbers, public works account for only a fraction of the total portrait production in the seventeenth century; the vast majority were made for a private

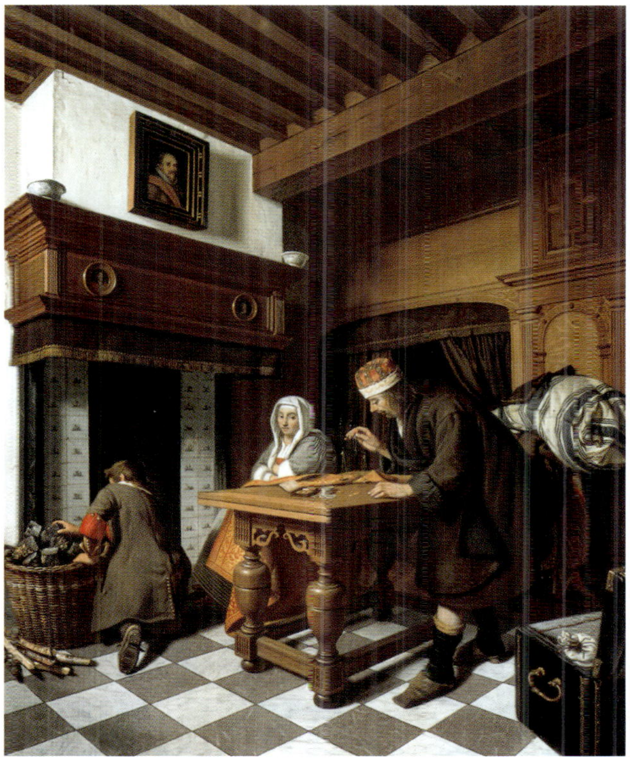

45.
Cornelis de Man,
Gold-Weigher in an Interior with a Portrait of Prince Maurits on the Mantelpiece, after 1672.
Oil on canvas,
82 x 68 cm.
Private collection

◂◂
Nicolaes Maes,
Family Portrait (detail),
about 1676 (cat. 37)

purpose. Many of these can be regarded as family portraits, although some individuals decorated their homes with likenesses of individuals they loved or admired, and of course for some these would have included members of the House of Orange, naval heroes, Church ministers and scholars (fig. 45).

Family Portraits

Hundreds of thousands of family portraits, of all types and sizes, were painted in every part of the Dutch Republic, mostly portraits of individual adult members of the family – busts, half-length, knee-length or sometimes full-length likenesses. It was common for two such pictures to be made as pendants – generally in the case of a married couple, who would commemorate their marriage by commissioning portraits to hang in their new home. Marriage portraits are defined as likenesses of a couple produced within about two years of their wedding (cats 16–17, 35–6, 47–8), and their function is sometimes clarified by the inclusion of special attributes such as wedding gloves (p. 66, figs 59–61).[3] More frequently, however, it can only be inferred by comparing the works' dates to the year of the marriage. If no marriage portraits were made, the couple sometimes rectified the omission by posing for a painter in later years. Occasionally we can link these portraits to a specific event, such as the couple's move to a new home or an appointment to a prestigious new position. Contrary to what one might expect, wedding anniversaries seldom prompted portrait commissions.[4] In companion pieces of spouses, artists almost invariably followed the rule of depicting the man on the left and his wife on the right as seen by the viewer – in other words from the couple's own perspective, the woman stood to the left of her husband.

Marriage was not the sole reason to commission a portrait, of course: numerous likenesses are known of unmarried persons, widows and widowers. Unmarried brothers and sisters were sometimes painted as pendants or in a series of three or more portraits,[5] and there are countless examples of separate likenesses of single people (including cats 18, 20, 55 and 56). The large number of surviving portraits of children makes it clear that many parents or other relatives commissioned paintings to immortalise the new generation (cats 7, 11, 14, 62). From documents we learn that parents frequently decided to have separate portraits made of all their children. Unfortunately, such series have rarely been preserved together, and indeed only a few examples can be fully reconstructed, since they have become dispersed through inheritance and sales, besides which many, of course, have been lost.[6] In some cases additional portraits were commissioned if any children were born after the completion of such a series.[7] Very occasionally, a child born later would even be added to a family group portrait (as in cat. 41).

Family group portraits are enormously diverse, but most frequently we encounter a married couple depicted

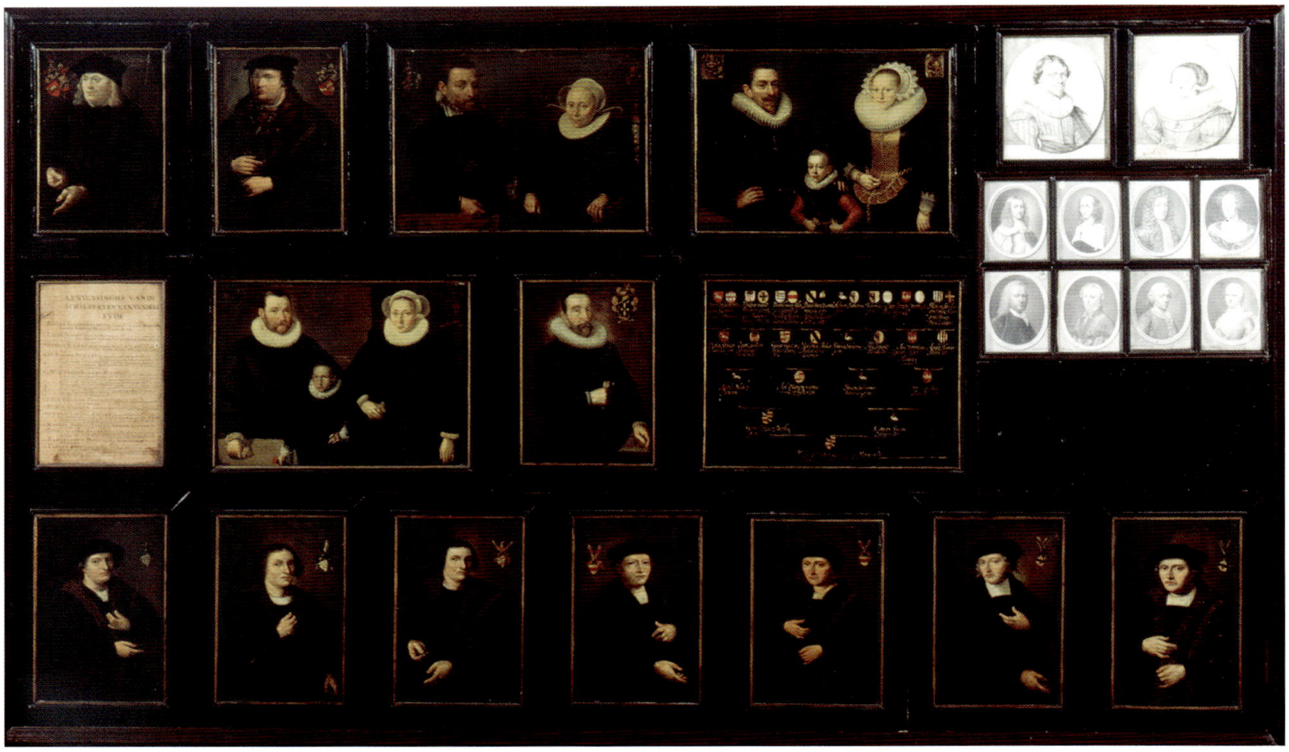

46.
David Bailly, Salomon Mesdach, Jozef Marinkelle and Adriaen Muylkens, *The Ancestors of Gerrit Schaep*, 17th and 18th centuries. Copperplate with small panel paintings and drawings, 84 × 154 cm. Amsterdams Historisch Museum, Amsterdam (on loan from the Backer Foundation)

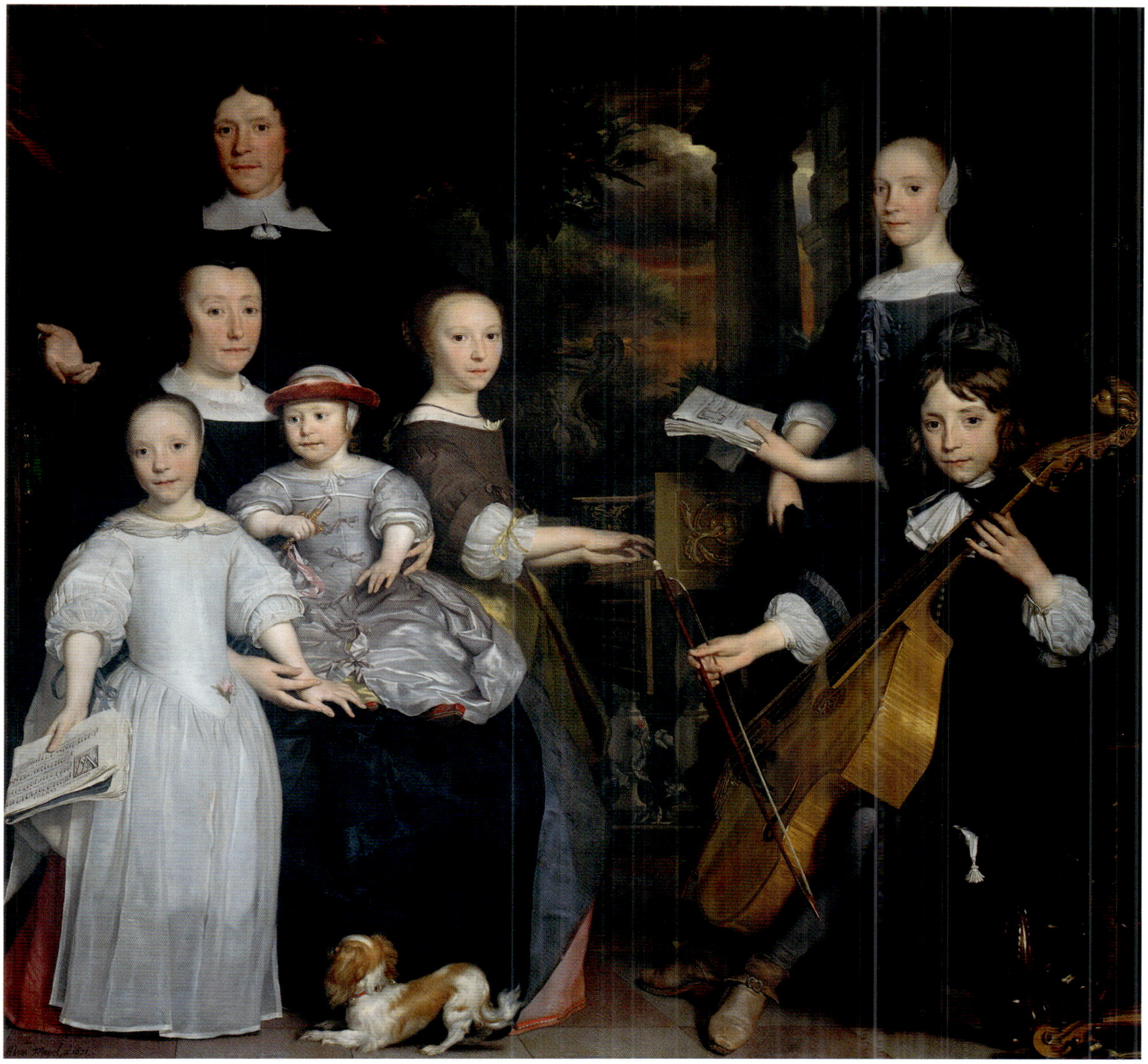

47.
Adriaen van den Tempel, *Portrait of David Leeuw and his Family*, 1671
Oil on canvas, 190 x 200 cm.
Rijksmuseum, Amsterdam

with their children (fig. 47; see also cats 4, 8–9 and 65).[8] The group may include one or more grandparents, or unmarried siblings of one of the spouses. For some clients, portraits of themselves, their immediate family and a few close relations did not go far enough. A number of nobles and burghers decided to build up a gallery of portraits of their deceased ancestors, sometimes only in the male line, but sometimes including that of the mother or grandmother – especially if this line had enjoyed higher social status. If no portraits were available for the artist to copy, he apparently drew on his imagination when illustrating the family tree (fig. 46).[9] The oldest known galleries of ancestors date from the sixteenth century, but from the early seventeenth century they acquired a certain popularity.

This phenomenon, in particular, suggests why so many portraits were commissioned in the seventeenth-century Netherlands; clearly, pride in one's family and its status and prosperity was a prime motive. Still, in many cases such considerations will scarcely have been conscious: once a certain tradition had been established, subsequent generations would order portraits simply to preserve what had come to be seen as a custom within the family. In this respect too, a sense of family is not a negligible factor. One's own portraits and those of one's family undoubtedly symbolised sense of kinship among those who regarded themselves, because of their political and economic standing, as the elite of the Republic.

The death of a relative provided another important reason for commissioning a portrait. In some cases, the

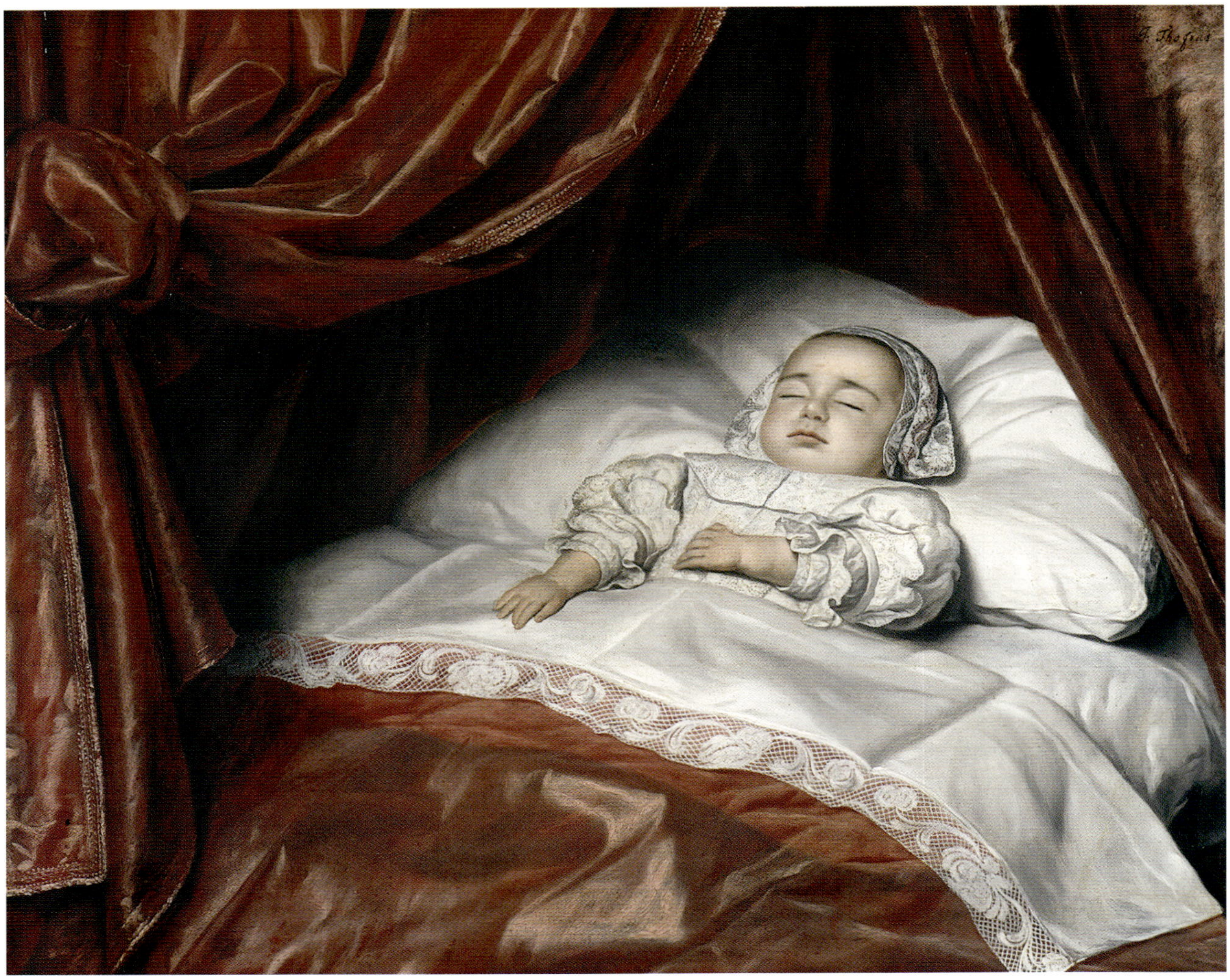

48.
Johannes Thopas,
Girl from the Van Valkenburg Family on her Deathbed,
about 1682.
Oil on panel,
58 x 72 cm.
Van Valkenburg Foundation (on loan to the Mauritshuis, The Hague)

bereaved might order a copy of an earlier portrait hanging in a relative's house, but if someone died without ever having been depicted, relatives might commission a new work. It was possible, evidently on the basis of descriptions provided by relatives or sketches made on the person's deathbed, to produce a sort of reconstructed likeness that was intended to give the impression that it had been painted from life.[10] Alternatively, one might commission a deathbed portrait.[11] This was a very common practice in the seventeenth century, especially when a child had died (fig. 48).[12]

Clientele

Although the potential clientele for family portraits was very large indeed in the seventeenth century, it was still a mere fraction of the total population. For ordinary manual workers, shopkeepers and farmers and the sizeable urban proletariat – whether or not they would have had any interest in having their portraits made – the costs were prohibitive. Only the relatively affluent could afford to have their portraits made, so the market was confined to the upper echelons of society and the *nouveaux riches* who wanted to present themselves as such. The notion that every shopkeeper in the seventeenth-century Northern Netherlands had a portrait made is a complete misconception, fostered by the fact that it was possible at that time to amass great wealth in certain branches of industry, such as the baker's trade – to the extent that some of those concerned were able to rise to the ranks of city government or gentry.

Even taking these limitations into account, the market for portraits was sizable. This derived in large measure from the prosperity that existed in the Republic and the country's tiered system of government. Within this system, everyone involved in the city's government could feel themselves to be an administrator of some importance, since the representatives of city councils played an important role in provincial assemblies, and those of the seven provinces made up the Republic's supreme representative body, the States-General (fig. 49). There were of course great differences in the actual influence of the representatives of Amsterdam and those

of a small town like Schoonhoven, but even Schoonhoven's regents contributed to the provincial, and therefore national, government. The thousands of local regents and their close relatives who formed the local elite, the burghers with their newly acquired wealth – who were eager to join this elite – the old aristocracy, the many affluent citizens who had remained Catholic, who, though excluded from public office, none the less belonged to the upper echelons of society, as well as high-ranking officials and army and navy officers, all made up a large circle of potential clients for portraits. The immortalisation of all those who wanted such portraits made was a branch of industry that generated an income – in some cases a very comfortable income – for hundreds of painters.

Choosing a Painter

Most portraits were painted close to home. Clients tended to choose a painter based in their own town if there was one, or otherwise approach someone nearby. Let us look at a few exceptions to this rule. The most important systematic exception resulted from the fact that numerous prominent public figures had to attend the meetings of the States of Holland, the States-General (see fig. 49) or other high government bodies and were therefore obliged to stay in The Hague, the seat of government, not infrequently accompanied by their families, for weeks or sometimes months at a time. In such cases they might well take the opportunity to have their portraits made by a painter from The Hague. People from a small town where skilled artists were difficult to find would be especially keen to have themselves immortalised by a superior and often more fashionable painter. Then there was the occasional client who deliberately opted for a portraitist from elsewhere, either because the artist had depicted other relatives to everyone's satisfaction in the past or because they enjoyed a popularity beyond the limits of his own city.

The itinerant portraitist is a phenomenon that did not emerge clearly until the eighteenth century. We do find a number of artists in the seventeenth century, however, who served a second market outside their local market, and who would therefore travel to other towns for extended visits, probably with some regularity. We see

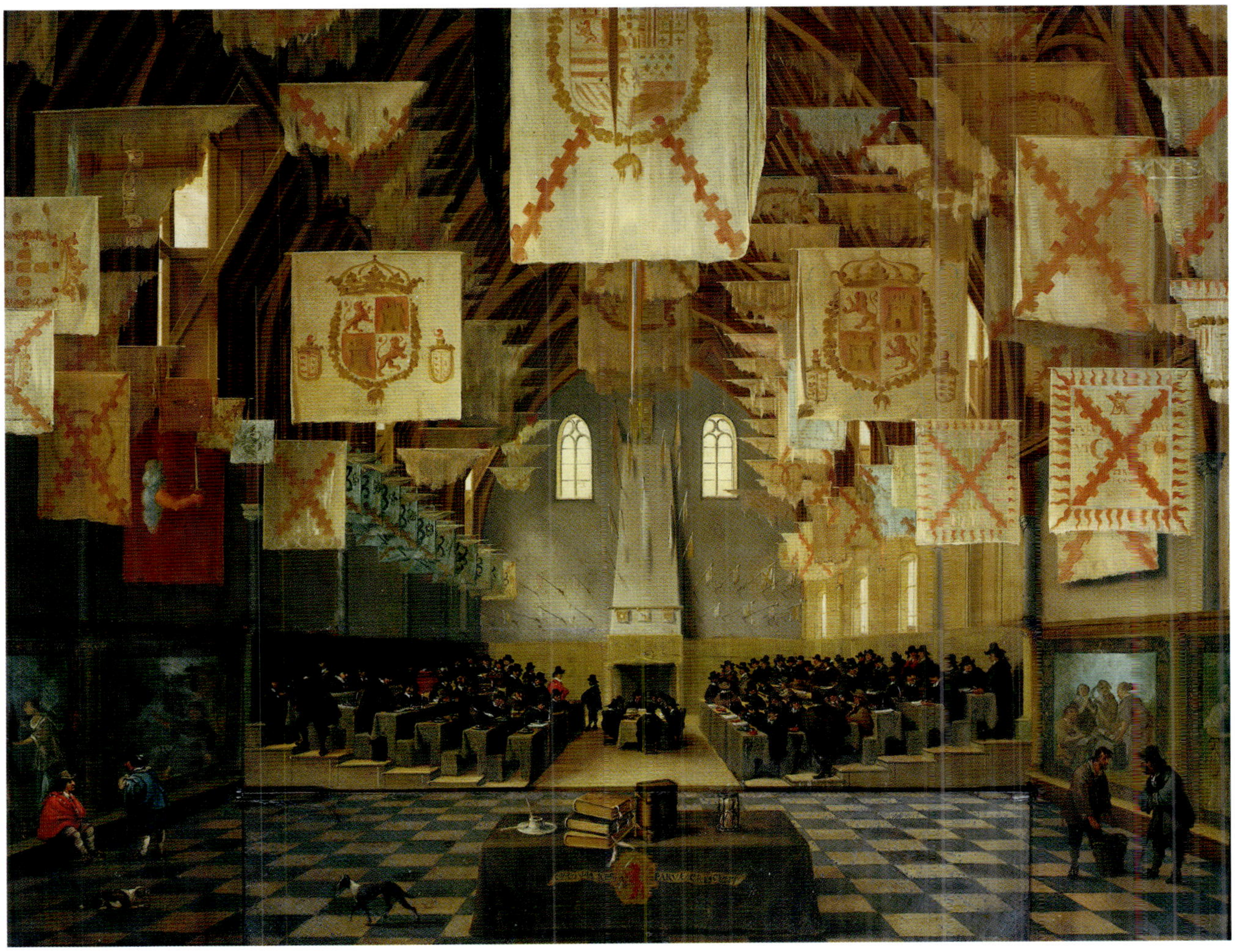

49.
Bartholomeus van Bassen, *Interior of the Great Hall at the Binnenhof in The Hague, during the Great Assembly of the States-General in 1651*, about 1651. Oil on panel, 52 x 66 cm. Mauritshuis, The Hague (on loan to the Rijksmuseum, Amsterdam)

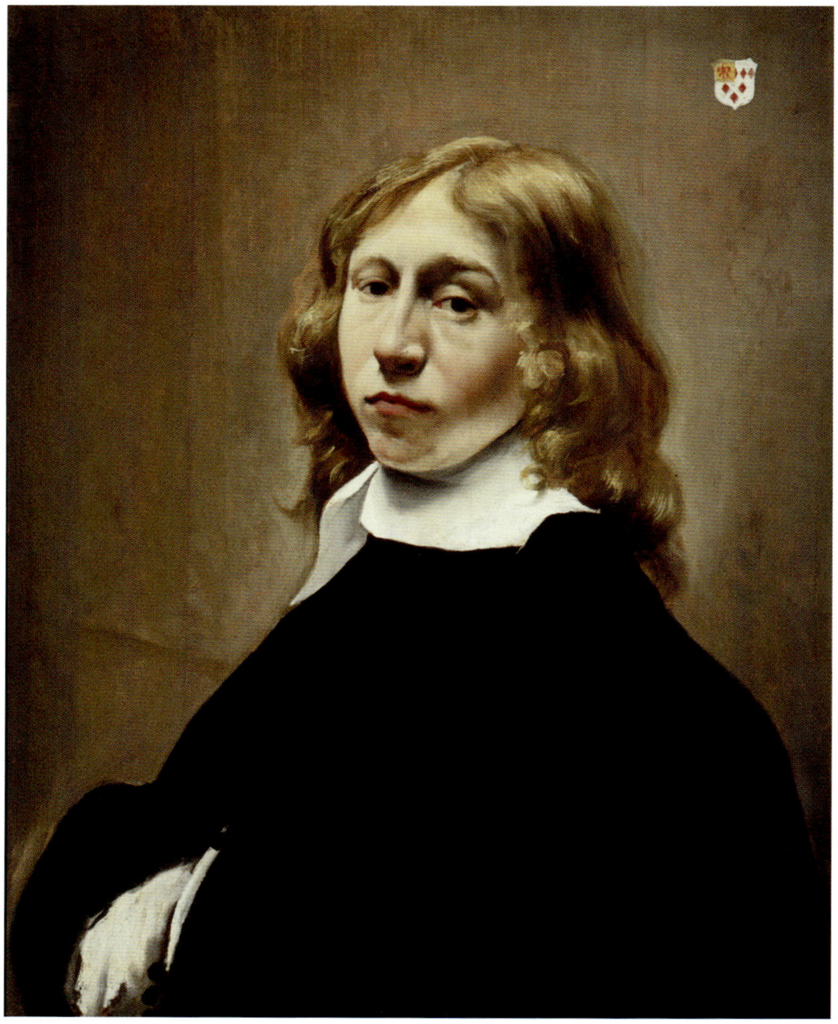

50.
Harmen de Bye,
Portrait of a Boy from the Bor Family,
about 1655.
Oil on panel,
74 × 59 cm.
Museum Boijmans Van Beuningen, Rotterdam

this in Rotterdam, for instance, a city that certainly possessed skilled portraitists of its own, where Rembrandt and Bartholomeus van der Helst, both based in Amsterdam, executed a number of portrait commissions in the 1630s and 1640s, respectively (for example cat. 55).

Portrait Painters

The demand for portraits in every part of the Republic accounts for the geographically dense distribution of portrait painters in the seventeenth century: every district and town of any significance had painters who were capable of producing reasonable and sometimes excellent likenesses. Amsterdam, of course – as in the sixteenth century – had the widest-ranging supply of portraitists, but in other relatively large cities, such as Haarlem, Leiden, Delft and Utrecht, clients searching for portrait specialists and occasional portraitists always had plenty of choice.

Smaller towns were less well endowed, and often supported only one or two painters qualified to accept such commissions. Painters unable to survive the stiff competition in big cities sometimes moved to a smaller town if a gap in the market arose after the local portraitist died or moved away.[13] Whenever such a temporary gap in the market arose, clients tended to find a replacement nearby. In the first decade of the seventeenth century for instance, it seems that there were no skilled portraitists in Hoorn, a gap that boosted the business of the painter Jan Claesz in Enkhuizen (cats 8–9). A few years later the Alkmaar artist Jacob Waben settled in Hoorn, and when Jan van Teylingen also moved there from Dordrecht, the locals no longer had to look further afield for their portraits. After these artists came Abraham Liedts and Jan Rotius, who guaranteed continuity in Hoorn's portrait market for several decades. After the death of Claesz in Enkhuizen, various painters came and went – enough to provide a continuous supply. But in the early 1650s, after the death of Herman Doncker and Gerbrand Ban, it seems that another gap arose: people from Enkhuizen were compelled to rely on the services of Rotius in Hoorn, until Enkhuizen acquired its own portraitist again in the person of Jan van Neck, who also worked partly in Amsterdam.

Although much research remains to be done on the specific subject of portraiture in smaller towns of Holland, Zeeland and Utrecht as well as the other provinces of the Republic before a complete picture emerges, it is clear that portraitists were distributed widely throughout the country. In this respect it is striking that many provincial towns, besides hosting artists whose work can be classified as clearly provincial, also had portraitists who attained a surprisingly high standard. Harmen de Bye, for instance, a painter who was recently 'rediscovered', was based in Venlo for much of the latter half of the seventeenth century, drawing his clientele from the surrounding area as well as from the town itself (fig. 50).[14]

Specialists and Occasional Portraitists

Membership lists kept by the painters' guilds, other archival documents and printed sources tell us of the existence of thousands of painters in the seventeenth-century Netherlands. Remarkably, however, there are many by whom not a single work is known.[15] Looking at

extant works, we can infer that hundreds of these artists made at least one portrait. Although portraiture was not held in high esteem by contemporary theorists (see p. 17), portrait commissions were a far from negligible source of income for painters.

It seems that artists learned to execute portraits as part of their basic training, and besides specialists – those who derived a large part of their income from portraits, for at least part of their career – many made incidental ventures into the field. Some confined themselves to self-portraits or likenesses of close relatives, while others also seem to have taken on commissions: it is quite possible, of course, that some of these masters produced far more portraits, and that many works have been lost or are unsigned and therefore not yet correctly attributed. In most cases, however, we must assume that they were 'occasional' portraitists. A case in point is the still-life painter Willem Heda, by whom one signed family group is known (fig. 51).[16] The genre painters Adriaen van Ostade and Jan Steen (cat. 62) also made portraits from time to time.[17] Certain other artists made portraits at the beginning of their career, but reduced or abandoned this activity as soon as they became more successful in another genre. This seems to apply, for instance, to Jan Miense Molenaer (cat. 42), whose portraits date only from his early period.[18] On the other hand there are artists such as Nicolaes Maes, who specialised in a different genre early on, but in later phases of their career dedicated themselves largely or entirely to portraiture.

Most of the seventeenth-century portraits that have come down to us are by artists who can be regarded as portrait specialists, although some of them also had a second specialist field, such as genre scenes (Gerard ter Borch, Pieter Codde, Frans van Mieris the Elder, Caspar Netscher, Anthonie Palamedesz), history paintings (Jacob Backer, Ferdinand Bol, Jan Victors) or church interiors (Hendrik van Vliet).

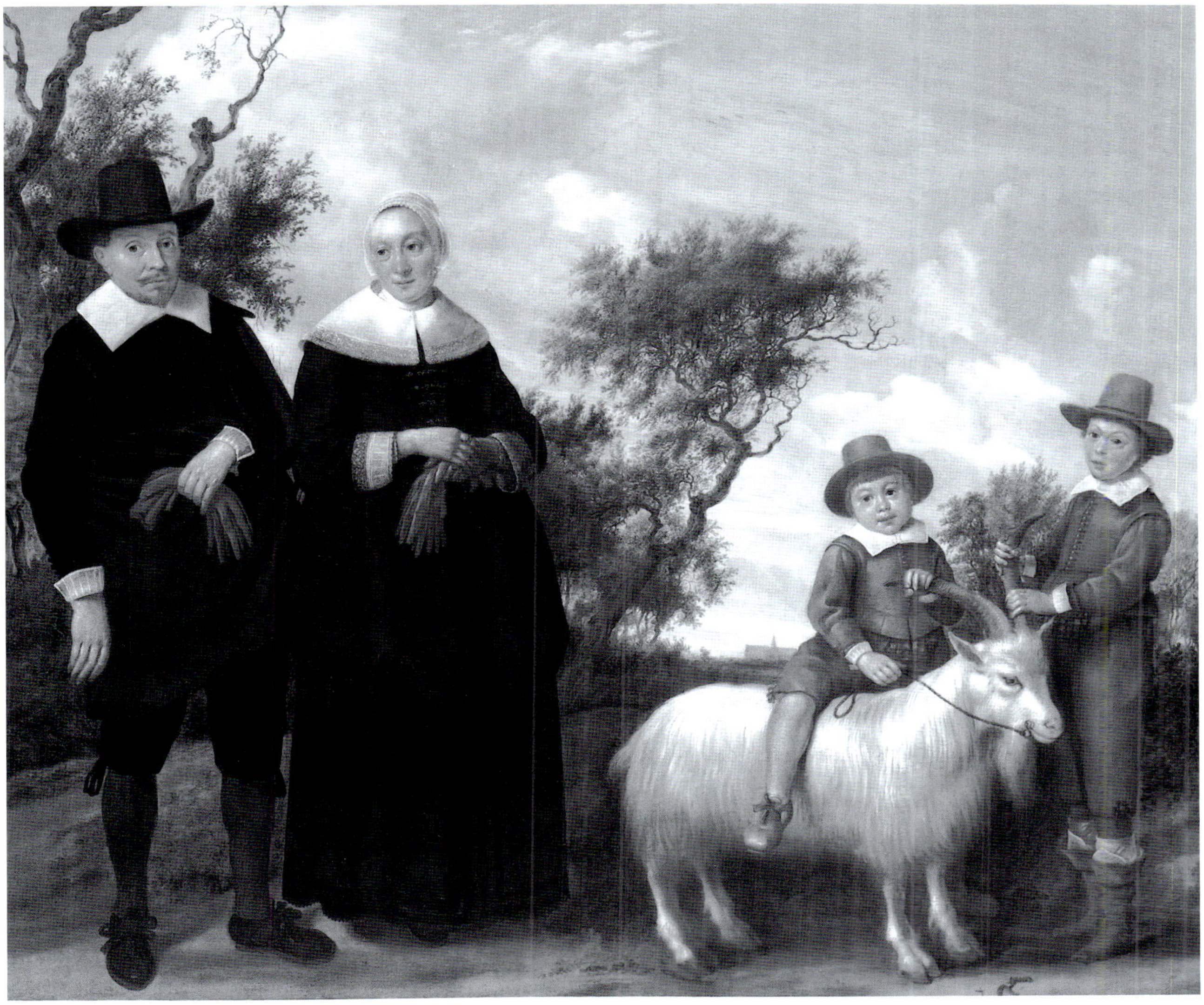

51.
Willem Heda,
Family Group, 1647.
Oil on canvas,
107 × 130 cm.
Private collection

Output

In theory, it was possible for a moderately successful portrait painter to earn a very respectable income, always depending, of course, on his speed and working method. Some portraitists had studios with one or more assistants and several pupils, while others probably worked primarily alone, with at most the occasional assistance of an advanced apprentice. For instance, Nicolaes Eliasz Pickenoy (cats 45–8) had a reputation for being slow to deliver the works ordered from him,[19] but whether he actually worked slowly or just accepted too many commissions is not known.

In the case of painters by whom a great deal of work has been preserved, we can estimate the speed at which they worked on the basis of the number of known works produced in a given period. Nicolaes Maes evidently worked quickly, and we can surmise he worked primarily alone, given the style and execution of his paintings. By studying his extant œuvre and making a conservative estimate of works that no longer exist, or are in any case no longer known, we can conclude that in his most prolific period he must have painted one or two portraits a week (figs 52–3).[20] It should be added, however, that most of these were relatively small, rapidly painted works. Johannes Verspronck (cat. 64), who made life-sized portraits and worked meticulously – and therefore more slowly – also appears to have largely dispensed with the aid of assistants: no fewer than 12 dated portraits are known from his most productive year, 1641, including a group portrait of four regentesses (p. 37, fig. 32).[21] Taking into account the fact that a number of undated works must have been made in the same period, and that other paintings will have been lost, we see that he was evidently turning out at least two portraits a month. Obviously no artist maintained the same output throughout their career, but all this does imply that provided they received enough commissions, a portraitist could produce somewhere between 25 and 100 portraits a year. Today, there are few artists to whom we can attribute more than 100 to 200 works – and these are spread out over careers lasting many decades.

These figures, and what we know about the price of a portrait, make it clear that a sought-after artist could easily attain an annual volume of trade amounting to several thousand guilders. Archival sources none the less reveal that few were able to set aside some of that money, and to amass a reasonable sum in savings from their work.[22]

Prices

In inventories dating from the seventeenth and eighteenth centuries, family portraits – where mentioned at all – were generally priced rather low in comparison to

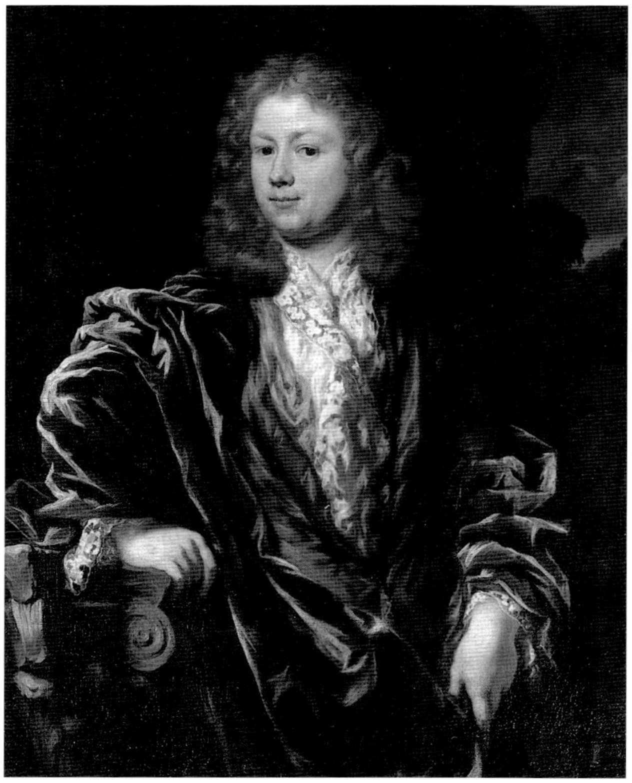

52.
Nicolaes Maes,
Portrait of Cornelis ten Hove, about 1682.
Oil on canvas,
58 × 46 cm.
Mauritshuis,
The Hague

comparable works from other genres. This is solely because of their limited value in trade: there was little demand for family portraits, except for those by artists who were already famous. However, this means that the valuation price cannot be taken as an indication of the artists' selling price. We know little about selling prices. No account-books kept by painters in this period have been preserved, which would enable us to ascertain, as in the case of the nineteenth-century portraitist Jan Adam Kruseman,[23] what each client paid the artist for a particular portrait. Most of the archival documents that refer to the prices of portraits relate to legal proceedings, which were generally instituted because the artist was demanding a far higher sum than the client was willing to pay. For instance, the Meerman family and the painter Pieter van Slingelandt were locked in battle for several years about payment for a group portrait of François Meerman and his family, for which the painter eventually accepted 1,500 guilders (fig. 54).[24]

Still, we do have a few isolated indications of portrait values. Two documents relating to two successive painters at the stadholder's court, Michiel van Mierevelt and Gerrit van Honthorst, are particularly helpful.[25] From other, more incidental references, we learn that these two artists, in spite of their special status as court painters, charged prices roughly similar to those of other established and sought-after portraitists. The details of the commission for Rembrandt's *Night Watch* (p. 32,

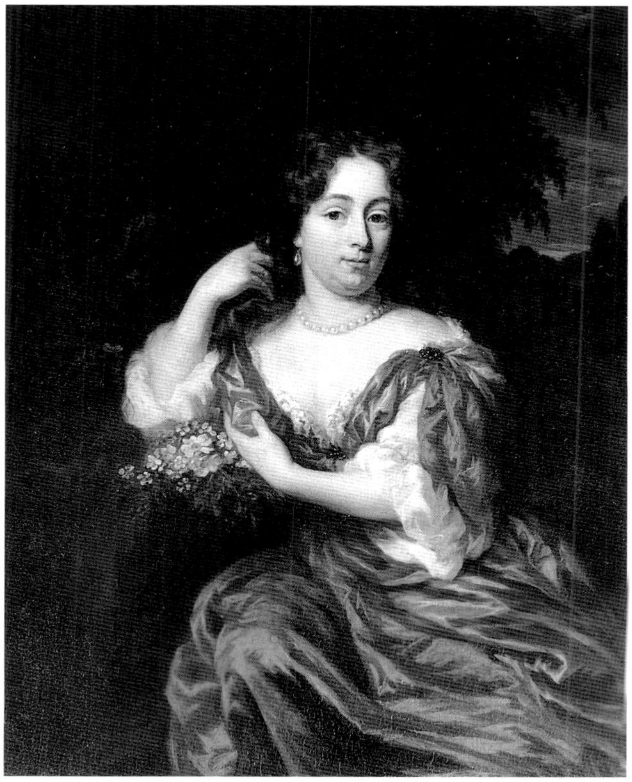

53.
Nicolaes Maes,
Portrait of Catharina Dierquens, Wife of Cornelis ter Hove,
about 1682.
Oil on canvas,
57 × 46 cm
Mauritshuis,
The Hague

fig. 22) also provide good material for comparison in this respect; the guardsmen paid different prices according to the way in which they were depicted, with an average of a hundred guilders each.[26] From the sources we may distil the following approximate prices:

- a life-sized bust portrait: 36 to 40 guilders
- a life-sized half-length portrait: 60 guilders
- a life-sized knee-length portrait: 80 guilders
- a life-sized full-length portrait: 100 to 150 guilders, probably depending on the complexity of the pose and any accessories
- commissions for replicas of existing portraits: 50–75% of the original price
- paintings from the workshop (portraits of celebrities sold from stock), depending on size: 5 to 20 guilders.[27]

So someone wanting an ordinary set of smart pendant paintings (half-figure or knee-length) would have had to pay somewhere between 120 and 160 guilders. Additional portraits of children would boost the price by several hundred guilders, and even a simple group portrait of a family would have cost at least a few hundred guilders. In the case of a sizeable family and the addition of abundant staffage, the price could have easily exceeded 500 guilders.

These prices corroborate the point made above, that commissioning portraits was the prerogative of the well-to-do: an average manual worker earned about 250 guilders, and the numerous ordinary Church ministers and professors, for instance, earned at most twice that sum annually.

Materials and Dimensions

For painted portraits, artists could theoretically choose from three sorts of support: panel, canvas or copper. Until around 1670, the use of copper was confined almost entirely to small works, portrait miniatures and slightly larger works (see cat. 2). A few exceptional miniatures were made on plates of a precious metal. In the last few decades of the century, copper is also regularly found as a support for medium-sized works (40 to 50 cm), especially in the work of *fijnschilders* (see cat. 40).

The choice of panel or canvas was less clearly defined. In the first few decades of the seventeenth century – just as in the sixteenth – panels were used for all but the largest paintings, and even large group portraits were still frequently executed on panels.[28] Although canvas started to be used more in the 1620s, it was not until around 1630 that its popularity soared. It is clear, however, that canvas never ousted panels altogether, and it even appears that panel enjoyed something of a revival after 1650. Further, panels continued to account for a more sizeable share of the whole in small provincial towns than in centres such as Amsterdam and The Hague.[29]

Most portraits were produced in one of a number of standard formats.[30] These dimensions are related to the common types of life-sized likenesses: bust (or extended bust), half-figure and knee-length. In addition, the standard format sizes of the pieces of timber supplied by panel-makers undoubtedly influenced the eventual size of the work.[31] With canvas, the formats corresponded, as a rule, to the customary sizes for panels. For portraits that were less than life-sized, more variations existed. The vast majority of portraits are rectangular, although oval formats were occasionally fashionable, especially in the 1630s, and most notably in Amsterdam (cats 52, 55) and Haarlem.

With the exception of extremely large paintings, canvases were always cut from a single length of linen, just as smaller panels frequently consist of just a single plank of timber. Panels are almost always made of oak; other types of wood are found only sporadically. Most individual portrait paintings on panels consist of three vertical planks, the centre plank generally being wider than the others – sometimes up to twice as wide. This construction was undoubtedly chosen to avoid the join between two panels running through the subject's face.

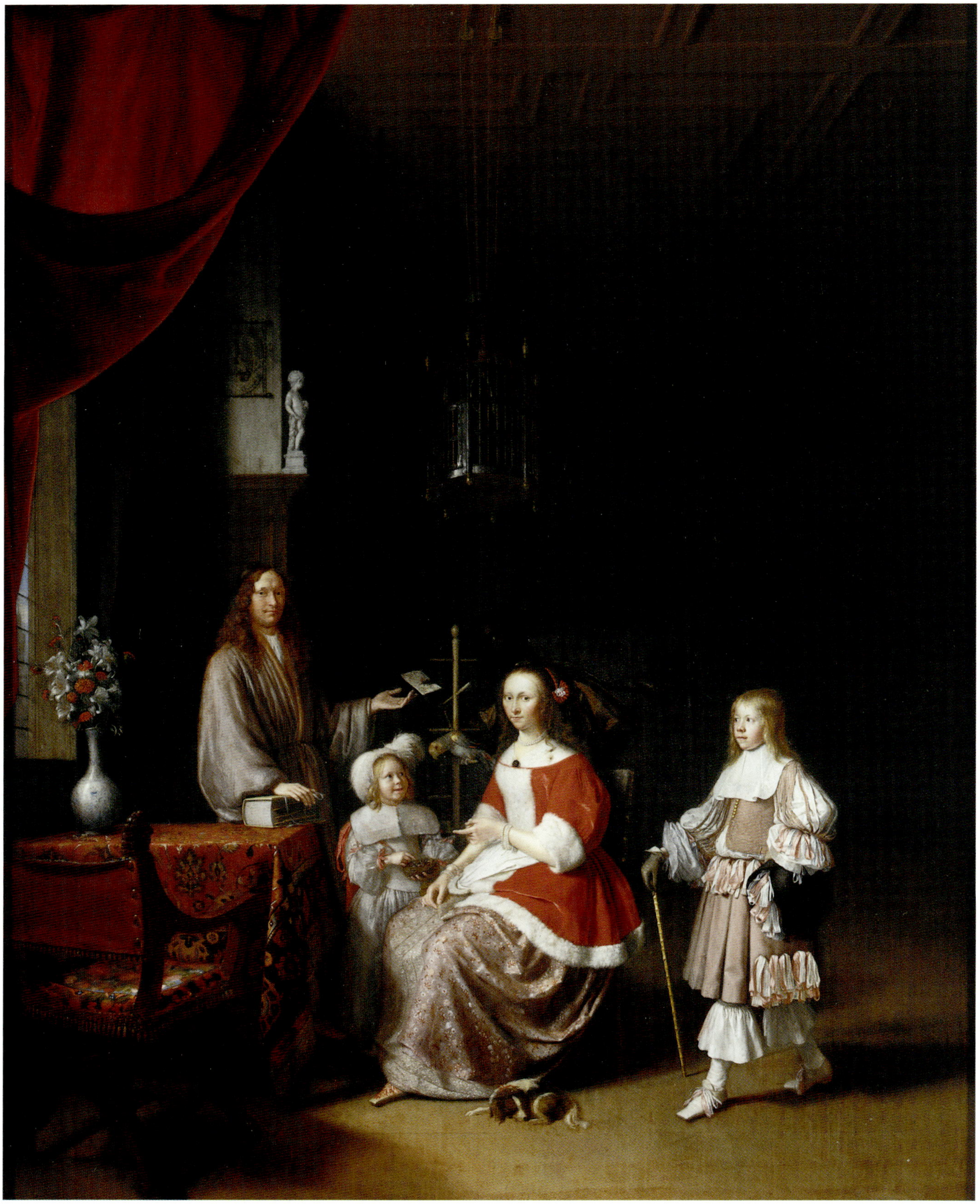

54. Pieter van Slingelandt, *Portrait of François Meerman and his Family*, 1668. Oil on panel, 53 × 45 cm. Musée du Louvre, Paris

Until around 1660, the vast majority of portraits were executed life-size, although smaller dimensions are common in likenesses produced for a series. A far smaller than life-sized format is found occasionally, and from the 1620s more frequently in Amsterdam, where Thomas de Keyser also introduced a distinctive type of small-scale portrait (cats 35–6). From the late 1630s onwards, family groups depicted in these smaller formats also gained popularity in The Hague thanks to the work of Jan Mijtens (cat. 41). These beginnings signalled a trend that spread rapidly from around 1660 to almost every town, with smaller pieces being produced alongside life-sized likenesses. Artists such as Gerard ter Borch and Caspar Netscher made characteristic works in this category (cats 3, 44), and Nicolaes Maes too, for instance, executed smaller than life-sized portraits after his move to Amsterdam (cat. 38).

The movement towards smaller paintings, though partly reflecting burghers' changing tastes regarding their interiors and the decorations they wanted on their walls, may also have been inspired by a wholly practical problem. With portraits having been commissioned for several generations, the walls of many patricians' houses must have been filling up, leaving no space for more life-sized paintings. Those depicted in these existing portraits did not yet belong to such a distant past that their likenesses could be banished to the attic or the basement. The use of smaller formats bore little apparent relation to economic downturns, such as occurred after the 'disaster year' of 1672; smaller, meticulously painted portraits were often actually more expensive.

Frames

In the first half of the seventeenth century, most portraits were framed quite plainly.[32] As a rule, they were given black or brown moulded frames, sometimes with a single gold edge (see the portraits in the background of cat. 42). These are ideally suited to the rather dark palette and generally subdued nature of the portraits made in the period. In the latter half of the century, however, we see somewhat more complex framing, in certain cases even embellished with extensive decorative work: sometimes leaving the wood visible, but often completely gilded (cat. 1). This was unquestionably related to the trend towards a more colourful palette in the paintings themselves, which in turn reflected the new vogue for more colourful clothing. With the more richly executed, carved frames, family coats of arms were sometimes depicted on the mount rather than in the painting (cat. 41). Where such frames were subsequently replaced on account of damage, changes in taste or the need to sell precious frames separately, a vital aid to identifying the sitters was lost.

Originals, Replicas and Copies

Numerous seventeenth-century Dutch portraits are known in two or more very similar versions, especially those depicting well-known public figures (see cat. 39). Sometimes the images are of different lengths: one may depict only a head while another shows the subject to the waist. In addition, two works may differ so strikingly in terms of quality that one sees immediately that one is a mediocre copy made after the other. Obviously, several portraits of the same person were often required, and in the case of prominent public figures, it was more practical to make a copy after an existing portrait than a new work. New versions made by the maker of the original portrait are generally known as replicas, while those produced by others are called copies.

Quite often, however, it is difficult to determine the relationship between the different versions of a portrait. In some known cases, it was already clear when the commission was granted that two or more versions of the portrait were required: in such cases, the artist would supply two or more identical portraits virtually simultaneously, making it exceedingly difficult to establish the order in which they were made, as in two portraits by Verspronck from 1635 (figs 55–6).[33] Sometimes versions were produced with a certain period in between. Splendid examples of this phenomenon are the portraits that Michiel van Mierevelt and his assistants produced of Paulus van Beresteyn, burgomaster of Delft, and his wife, who had their portraits made in 1612. Some of their children were already married by 1612, and it seems that a few extra examples were ordered for them at the same time. In the years that followed, whenever another child was married, another pair of pendants was painted to hang in the newly-weds' home. Since the couple had 11 children, we may assume that the original pendants were repeated ten times; almost all of these paintings are known.[34] In this case, the same studio was able to supply all the repeat orders, but it sometimes happened that the original artist had died or moved elsewhere when a copy was needed. When an inheritance was divided up, several children might want the portraits of their parents that belonged to the estate, in which case it was often decided to have extra copies made.[35] In later years too, family portraits were sometimes copied repeatedly, down to the twentieth century, when descendants wanted to complete their family galleries and found that a member of another branch of the family owned one of the 'missing' portraits.[36]

Signatures

A great many seventeenth-century portraits do not bear the artist's signature. In many cases, signatures were lost because that part of the painting became worn or was

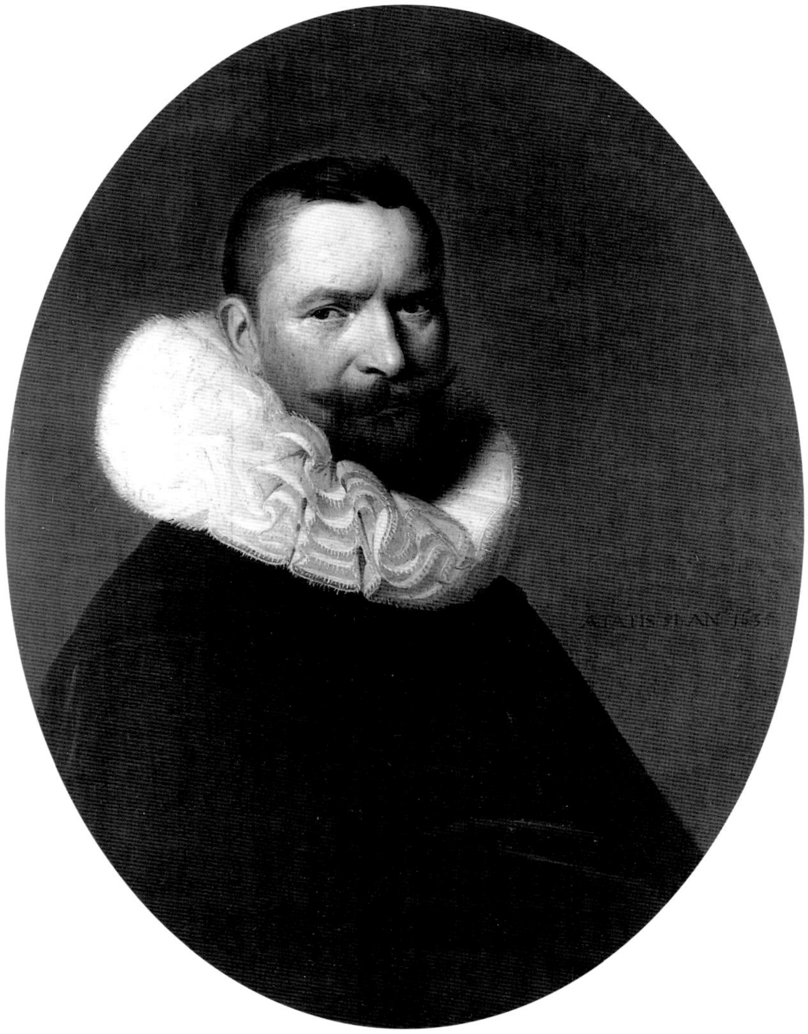

55.
Johannes Verspronck, *Portrait of Josias van Herrewijn*, 1635. Oil on panel, 83 x 65 cm. Hallwylska Museet, Stockholm

cut off; more frequently, the signature of an obscure artist was deliberately removed in order to sell a work under the name of a more famous painter. But many portraits were simply not signed: numerous portraitists neglected to sign their works, or did so only in exceptional cases. Other artists signed only one work in a pair of pendants or a small series, so that if such pieces later became separated (such as cats 35–6), the unsigned specimens were nameless.

Factors influencing the signing or not signing of portraits included local customs as portraits were signed less frequently in the provinces of the Northern Netherlands than was customary in Southern Netherlands, and when we do find them, they are often exceptions in the artist's œuvre.[37] Even influential portraitists such as Dirck Jacobsz, Jan van Scorel and Maerten van Heemskerck signed sporadically. Only Anthonis Mor, who worked primarily in the Southern Netherlands and in other countries, signed a good many of his portraits.[38]

As late as the final decades of the sixteenth century, signing portraits was the exception rather than the rule, even among artists who had been trained elsewhere – in Antwerp, for example. Of the dozens of extant portraits attributable to the Leiden painter Isaac van Swanenburg (p. 21, fig. 6) not one is signed or monogrammed.[39] Delft constitutes a curious exception. In this same period, Delft had two artists, Jacob Delff the Elder and Herman van der Mast, who did generally sign their portraits. Their younger fellow-townsman Michiel van Mierevelt (cat. 39) seldom signed his work before 1607, but after that he frequently inscribed his name. In Amsterdam, an important centre of art, one finds few signatures before about 1620, and it is exceptional to find one on the portraits produced by prominent artists such as Pieter Pietersz, Aert Pietersz and Cornelis van der Voort.[40]

In general, we see that in the period between 1600 and 1625, those most likely to sign their portraits were artists who were leading specialists in their particular field, such as Michiel van Mierevelt in Delft, Jan van

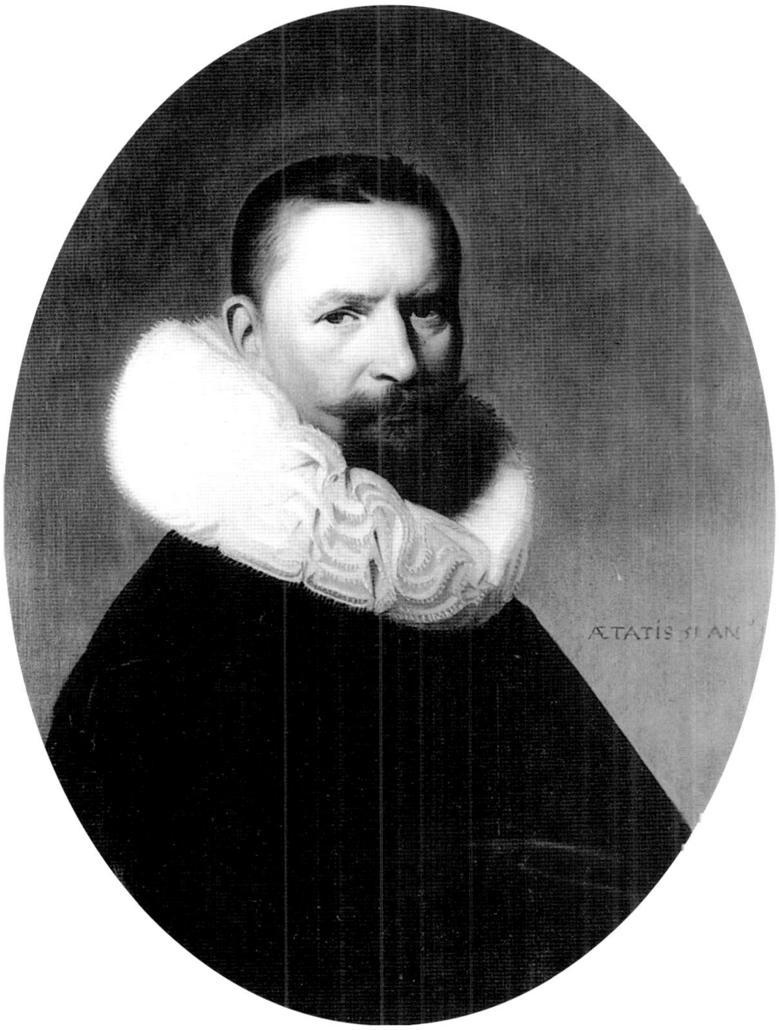

56.
Johannes Verspronck,
Portrait of Josias van Herrewijn, 1635.
Oil on panel,
83 x 65 cm.
Private collection

Ravesteyn in The Hague and Paulus Moreelse in Utrecht; other less renowned portraitists in these and other cities occasionally did so.[41] In the 1620s the number of artists' signatures gradually started to increase, a development that continued over the following two decades as a larger and more competitive market created a need for artists to distinguish their work from one another. A few dozen signing portraitists can be identified in Amsterdam. Still, even in this and later periods, there were probably many portraitists who seldom if ever signed their work, most notably in the provinces and the smaller towns of Holland. The absence of signatures is obviously a major problem in art-historical research: for instance, there are hardly any signed works by artists working in the provinces of Zeeland, Gelderland, Overijssel and Groningen before about 1640. Although there is a sharp increase in the number of signatures after 1650, many works remained unsigned even then, especially in areas and towns where local portraitists had less competition to fear than in the big cities.

Dates, Inscriptions and Coats of Arms

A rather larger proportion of portraits are dated, including many that are unsigned. While in other types of paintings the date is generally part of the signature, in portraits the date has a different function: to indicate the year in which the sitter has been depicted. It is not uncommon for the date to be accompanied by the sitter's age, with the Latin explanation, sometimes abbreviated 'ætatis' (at the age of) or 'ætatis suæ' (at his/her age).[42] Occasionally one finds the words 'ætatis meæ' (at my age), which may lead to the misconception that the image is a self-portrait (see p. 180, fig. 49a). In fact, this inscription is simply allowing the portrait or the sitter to speak directly, as it were. The year is sometimes prefaced by the word 'anno' (in the year) – which may be abbreviated to 'an°' or 'a°' – or 'anno domini' (in the year of our Lord), but frequent spelling mistakes show that not all portraitists were proficient in Latin. Research on the portraits of identified sitters whose dates of birth are known has demonstrated that the age inscriptions are almost always

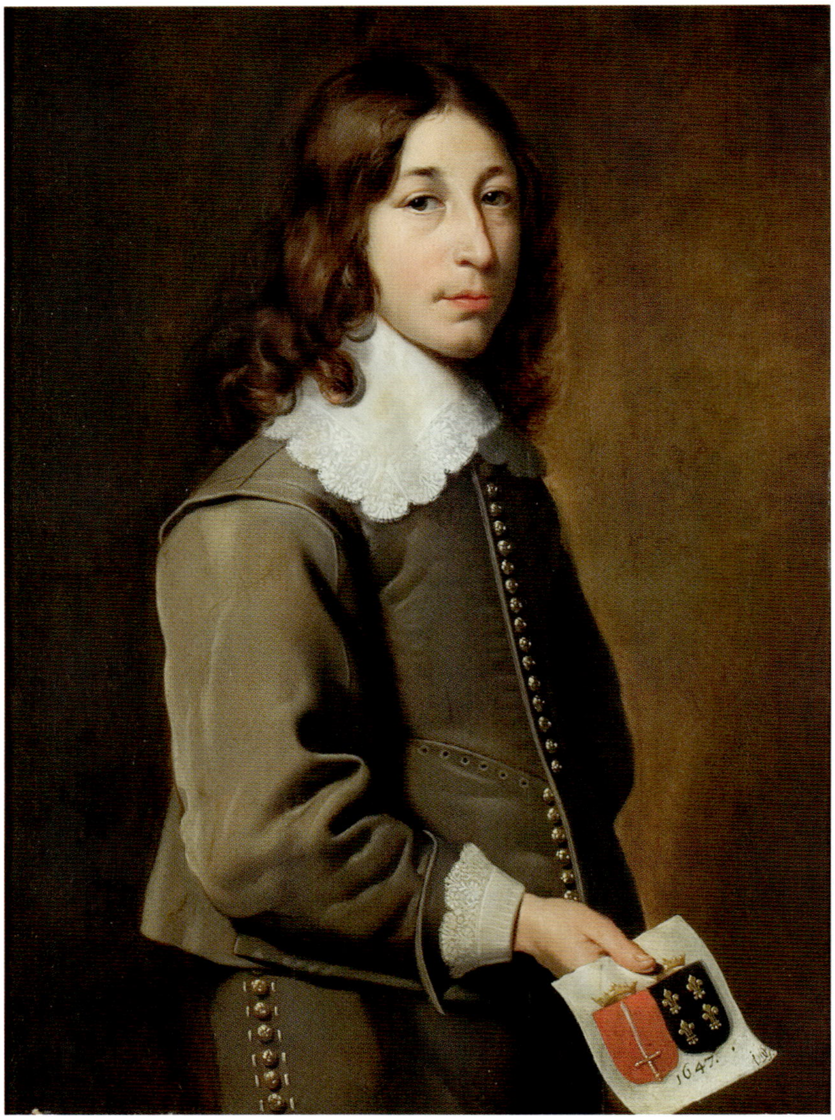

57.
Wybrand de Geest, *Portrait of Barthold van Douma*, 1647. Oil on panel, 83 x 61 cm. Fries Museum, Leeuwarden

accurate, far more so than those encountered in notarial deeds and other archival documents. Seventeenth-century Dutch clients evidently insisted on their portraits being accurate in this respect, and seldom succumbed to the temptation of flattering their age.

Most of the dates and age inscriptions on old portraits were added at the time of painting, but we should bear in mind that faded or damaged figures and letters have sometimes been touched up in later restorations – and not always correctly. In the case of portraits embellished with the sitters' coats of arms, we should be aware that only some of these coats of arms were applied when the portrait was painted; many others were added later (cats 16–17), in some cases not until the nineteenth or twentieth century. Examples exist of entire collections of family portraits that were furnished *en bloc* with coats of arms by the same painter in the late eighteenth or nineteenth century.[43] In the case of such late additions, these coats of arms do not, of course, provide the slightest guarantee regarding the sitter's identity; all they show is that the person who owned the portrait at the time believed that it depicted someone who bore that family coat of arms. In practice, one finds that a great many mistakes were made, sometimes because an erroneous identification of the sitter was consulted, and sometimes because the details of the coat of arms were inaccurate – or indeed because someone ordered entirely the wrong coat of arms.

Portraits occasionally display mottoes, lines of verse or inscribed names; in this respect too, some are original while many others were added in later years. Names inscribed on the image side of a portrait are seldom important indications of the sitter's identity, since they are rarely authentic.[44]

The way in which coats of arms are painted, and sometimes decorated, may display characteristics that the same artist has applied on other occasions, and thus serve as a kind of identifying mark for the painter. Coats of arms and inscriptions are often simply added to the background of the painting, but in some cases they are incorporated into the portrait in an original way, for instance on a piece of paper or a book lying open on the table, or on a sheet of paper in the subject's hand (fig. 57).[45]

Final Remarks

Although many matters relating to the practice of seventeenth-century Dutch portraiture have been discussed here, others have been left unmentioned, such as the social position of portrait painters, the working relationships that existed between portraitists and other artists in painting backgrounds and staffage (see cat. 1) and the organisational structure of studios. Moreover, some of the points touched on in this brief survey merit more detailed consideration in a future study.

It is fitting to close with a few remarks on the verisimilitude of the portraits that have come down to us. The painter's task – that of producing a good likeness of the sitter – was almost entirely confined to rendering the person's face. For the sitter's hands, painters often used existing standard models that would be re-used again and again. When several different portraits of the same individual are available for purposes of comparison, we also notice discrepancies in the rendering of facial features; it becomes clear that portraitists could take certain liberties even in that respect. In addition, there were differences in the way portraitists defined the task at hand: while one artist tended to produce flattering images of those who sat for him, another would scrupulously record every last wrinkle.

Almost nothing is known about seventeenth-century practice in sitting for portraits, but the fragmentary evidence suggests that it was not customary to sit for hours at a time. To what extent subjects posed in the clothes in which they are depicted is hard to say, since the sources do not mention it. It seems likely, however, that in many cases the painter will have completed the clothing in the sitters' absence (see also pp. 68–9). They probably had greater freedom in rendering clothing than the many realistic details in the portraits would suggest. The following essay is devoted entirely to the function of clothing details in seventeenth-century portraiture of the Northern Netherlands.

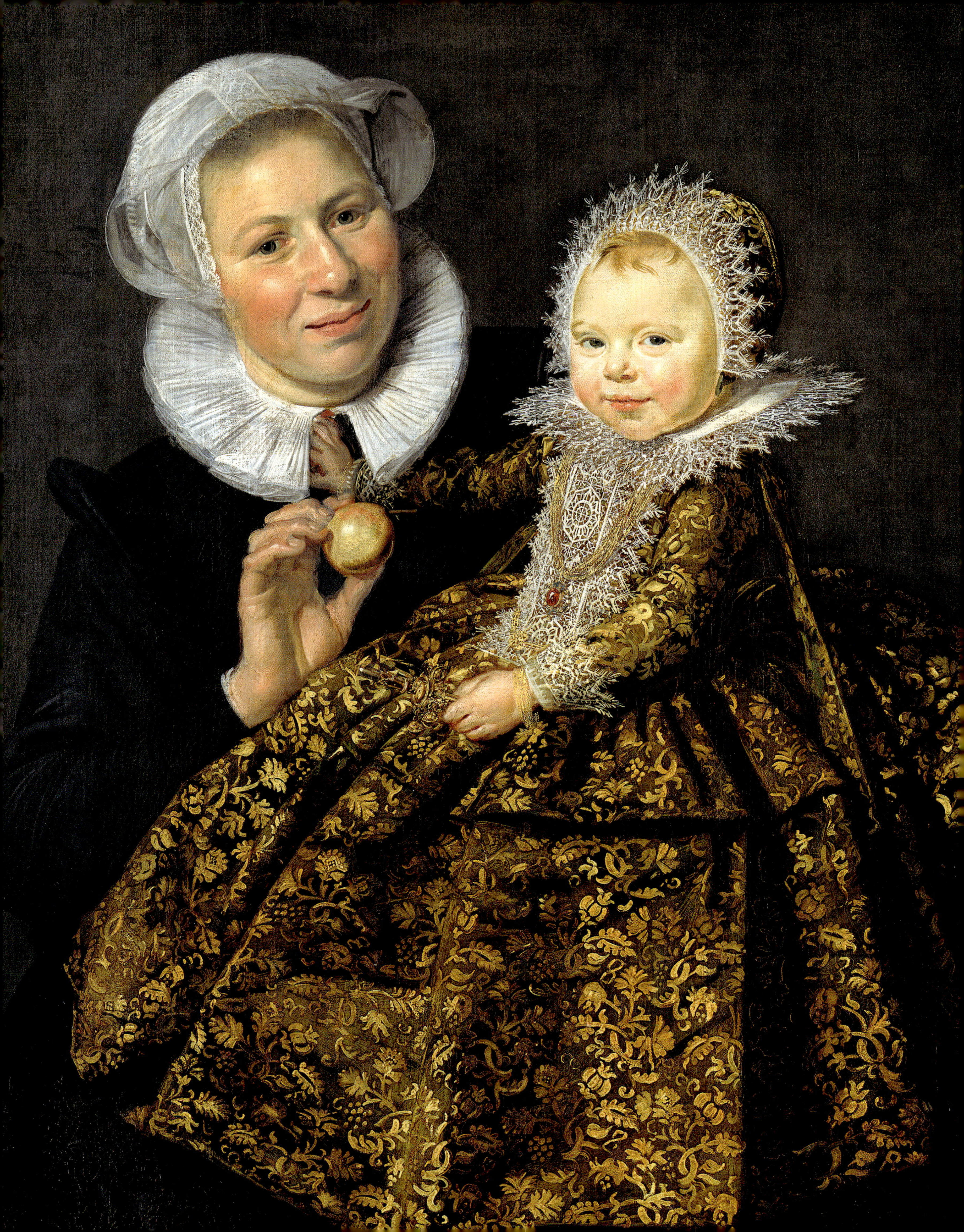

The Artist as Couturier
The 'Portrayal' of Clothing in the Golden Age

by Marieke de Winkel

In a scene from *Batavische Arcadia*, a pastoral novel by Jan van Heemskerck published in 1637, a group of noble youths from The Hague are described looking at a series of portraits in a country house. The hero, curious to hear his lady love's response, asks what strikes her most about these skilfully executed paintings. She answers that it is 'the diversity of costumes in which they were dressed, suggesting that they were not of the same land or time'.[1] The great interest that seventeenth-century citizens took in clothing is obvious from their portraits. Even today we are astonished by the complicated garments and jewels worn, just as we are by the great attention and detail with which painters have depicted them. Quantitatively, dress is often the most important part of a painting, because it takes up so much of the surface area, but in a qualitative sense too, it is frequently one of a painting's highlights. In Rembrandt's *Portrait of Jan Six* from 1654 (cat. 57), the sketchily but extremely effectively rendered cloak and gloves appear to lead a life of their own within the painting (p. 203), and attest to the painter's great virtuosity. Costumes also often feature prominently in the portraits of Gerard ter Borch (cats 2–3) and Bartholomeus van der Helst (cats 29–30); at times, the astonishing brilliance of the satin is so magnificent that the wearer almost pales by comparison.

Fashion influences portraiture more than is often acknowledged, determining key elements such as pose or palette. Yet despite the essential importance of the sitter's dress, remarkably little is known about the process of choice. Who selected the apparel and for what reasons? Did clients expect a literal rendering of the garments' appearance? Did the artist play a role in selecting a particular pose or dress? In short, is the clothing depicted an accurate reflection of reality or is it rather the artist's creation? The following discussion will explore the field of tension between the picture presented by portraits and artistic practice as described in contemporary sources.

Clothes in Documents: Imagination and Fact

The ideal way to determine how accurately clothes were depicted would be to compare them with preserved garments; unfortunately, few seventeenth-century items of clothing have survived to enable such direct comparisons. One noteworthy exception is the portrait, attributed to Nicolaes Eliasz Pickenoy, of Johanna le Maire of

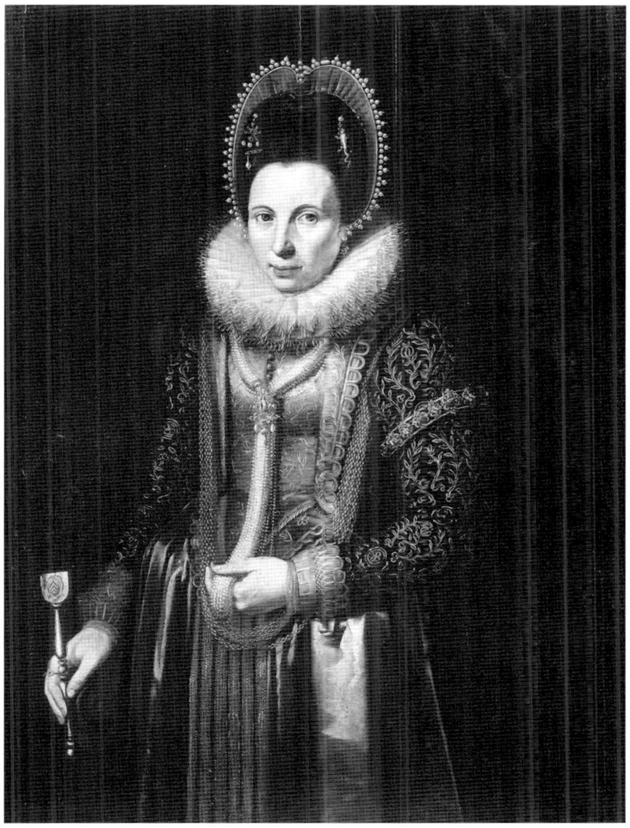

58.
Evert van der Maes,
Portrait of Maria van Voorst 1608.
Oil on panel,
110 x 80 cm.
Duivenvoorde Castle,
Voorschoten

◂◂
Frans Hals,
Portrait of Catharina Hooft and her Nurse
(detail), about 1620
(cat. 14)

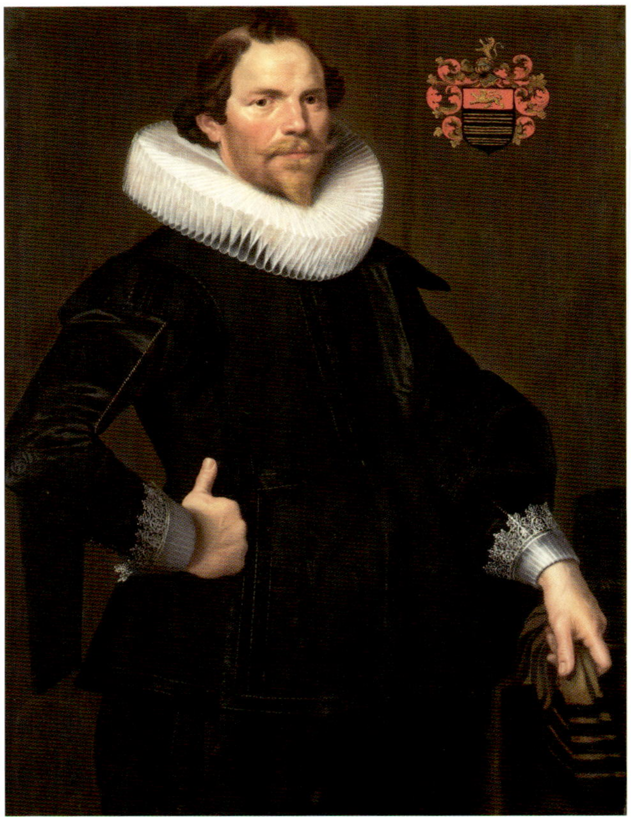

59.
Attributed to Nicolaes Eliasz Pickenoy, *Portrait of Pieter van Son*, about 1622. Oil on panel, 105 x 79 cm. Rijksmuseum, Amsterdam

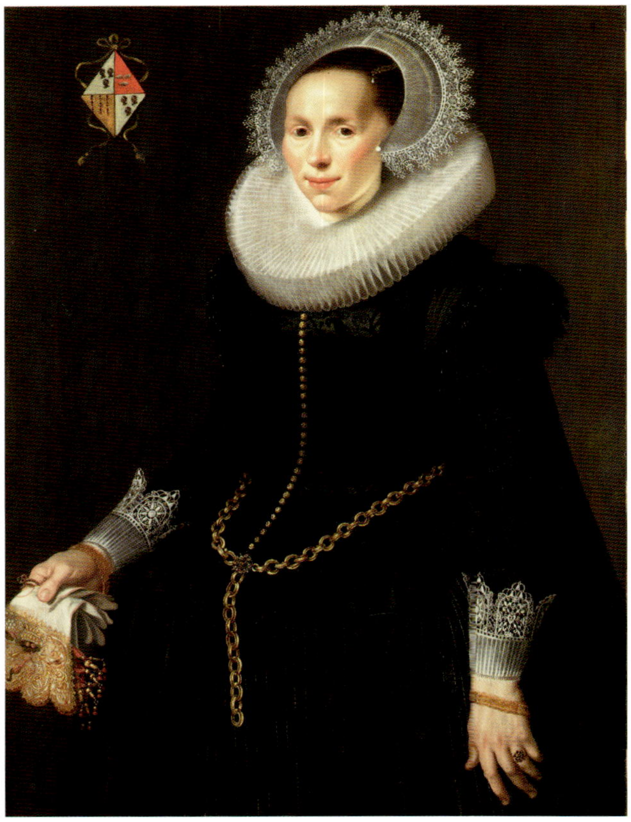

60.
Attributed to Nicolaes Eliasz Pickenoy, *Portrait of Johanna le Maire, Wife of Pieter van Son*, about 1622. Oil on panel, 105 x 78 cm. Rijksmuseum, Amsterdam

Amsterdam, painted to commemorate her marriage to Pieter van Son in 1622 (figs 59–60). By a happy coincidence, the white leather bridal gloves she holds in her right hand have been preserved (fig. 61), enabling us to verify that the embroidered fruit basket, peacock and floral motifs on the cuffs have been transcribed with great precision.[2] Unfortunately, there are no other examples of a garment depicted in a seventeenth-century Dutch portrait actually surviving,[3] so we must consult other sources – such as probate inventories, which frequently included detailed descriptions of clothing. Some of these lists in fact include items recognisable from a

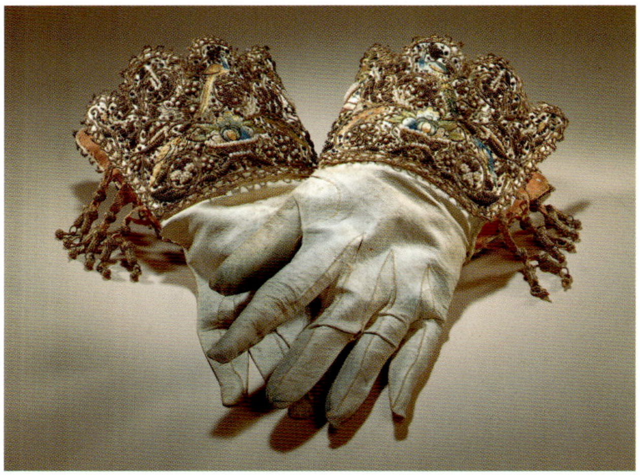

61.
White Leather Bridal Gloves with Embroidered Cuffs Belonging to Johanna le Maire (see fig. 60). Rijksmuseum, Amsterdam

portrait of the person concerned,[4] such as that of the noble Maria van Voerst, whose portrait was made in 1608 by the Hague painter Evert van der Maes (fig. 58).[5] After her death in childbirth only two years later, a list of her clothes and jewels was drawn up which describes the long, black overgown in the portrait as 'a black velvet *cymar* [robe] with gold-embroidered sleeves, trimmed all round with gold braid'.[6] The garments worn underneath it, which appear dark pink in the portrait, are described in the inventory as a 'purple satin skirt trimmed with three gold braid passementeries and a purple satin stomacher embroidered with gold'. Maria's ample selection of linen included 'thirteen Cambric ruffs with lace', 'sixteen pairs of cuffs with lace', and 'Cambric coifs with lace'. The inventory confirms that Maria did in fact own the clothing she wears in the portrait. It also reveals that she had as many as four black overgowns to choose from, which she could combine with six skirts and stomachers of another colour. Understandably, for her portrait she appears to have selected the most opulent combination in her possession. But we also find discrepancies between the clothing described and that in the portrait. The satin skirt and accompanying stomacher are described as 'purple', whereas in the portrait they appear to be pink. This probably has to do with the discolouration of the blue pigment in the painting, but it is also possible that the word 'purple' was used for a different hue in the seventeenth century. These inventories also give the contemporary terms for the garments depicted; however, most of these words ceased to be used when the clothing concerned went out of fashion, and their precise meaning is often extremely difficult to ascertain.[7]

Since many seventeenth-century portraits were made to commemorate a marriage, lists of the bride's trousseau or the bridegroom's outfit are an attractive source. Unfortunately, very few of these lists can be linked to a specific portrait. One fortunate exception is the case of the prosperous Delft burgher Elisabeth van der Aa, who was 20 years old in 1626 when her portrait was painted by Thomas de Keyser (fig. 62).[8] Van der Aa's father had died prematurely, and from Elisabeth's tenth birthday onwards, her mother had to account in detail to the orphans' court for all the money she spent on her daughter.[9] On average, the considerable sum of 130 guilders a year was spent on the young girl's wardrobe, most of it for fabrics. Making the garments up cost considerably less: only 25 guilders of the total sum went to the tailor, Dirck Simonsz. Besides everyday apparel, he made at least one new *bouwen* (gown) with a *keurs* (skirt) for the girl every year. In November 1626 – when the 18-year-old Elisabeth and the Amsterdam merchant Hendrik Verburgh gave notice of their intention to marry – Simonsz's bill for making up the young bride's wardrobe soared to four times the sum of previous years. Among the garments he made for her were three black *vliegers* (mantle-like overgowns), which could be combined with six decorated stomachers and five skirts. The embroidery alone on two of these stomachers cost an impressive 100 guilders. In the portrait, Elisabeth wears the damask *vlieger* with matching sleeves described in the tailor's bill, a satin stomacher with gold embroidery, and a black damask skirt. Three-piece *vlieger* costumes of this kind were standard items of clothing in portraits of the women of the civic elite in the period 1600–40. The *vlieger* was a typically Dutch variant of the Spanish *ropa* and served as a trademark of well-to-do married burgher women. Girls and unmarried women, including beguines, wore a *bouwen* instead: a dress with a fitted bodice and a skirt that was closed all round.[10] This strict distinction between apparel for married and unmarried women is clear not only from inventories and trousseau lists, but also from contemporary sources such as the Dutch-Spanish dictionary published by Juan Rodriguez in 1634. This describes a *bouwen* as a 'ropa de donzella' (overgown worn by a virgin) and a *vlieger* as a 'ropa de casada' (overgown worn by a married woman).[11] In poetry, the two clothing terms are often used as tropes for 'spinster' and 'married woman', respectively, as in a poem from 1624 by Jacob Westerbaen.[12]

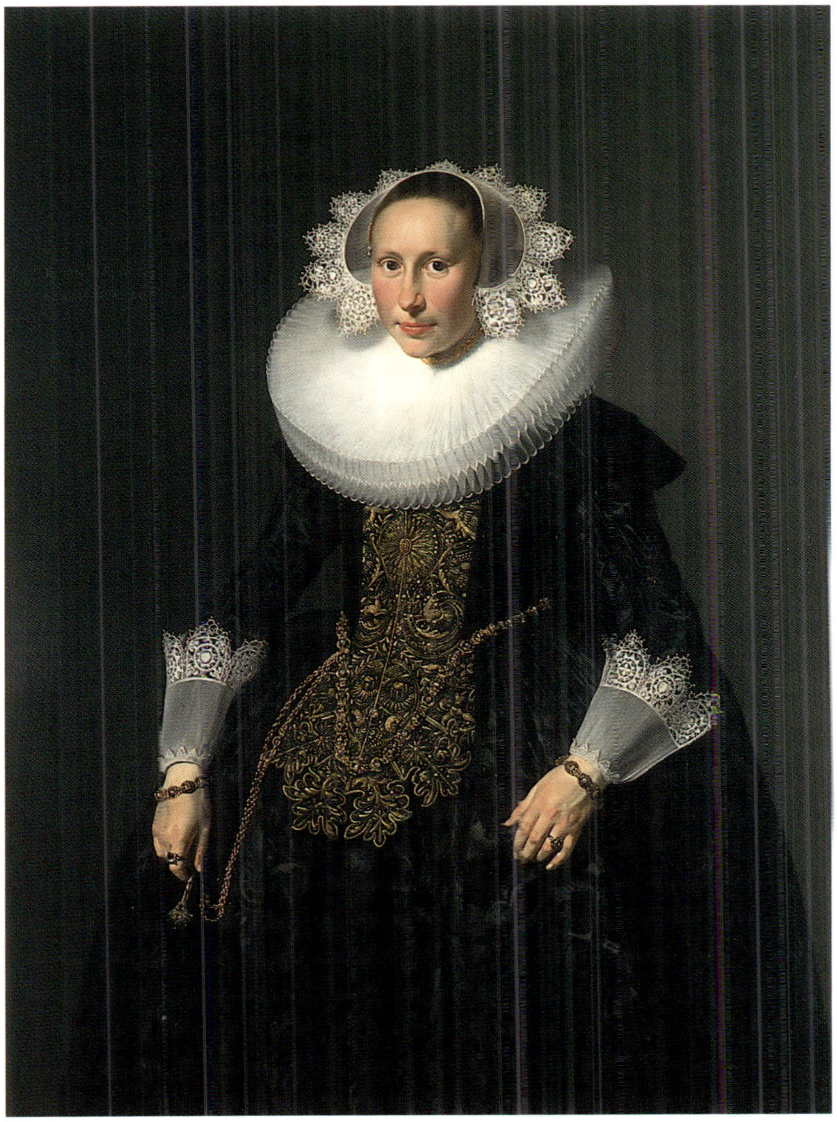

62.
Thomas de Keyser,
Portrait of Elisabeth van der Aa, 1626.
Oil on panel,
122 x 51 cm.
Musée Sandelin et
Musée Henri Dupuis,
Saint-Omer

The distinction between clothes worn by unmarried and married burgher women, as described in written sources, has consequences for the iconography of portraits: clearly, a woman depicted wearing a *vlieger* costume can be regarded as a wife or a widow. On the other hand, it is striking how few women are depicted wearing a *bouwen*, unless they are part of a group, family or children's portrait. Perhaps we can take this as an

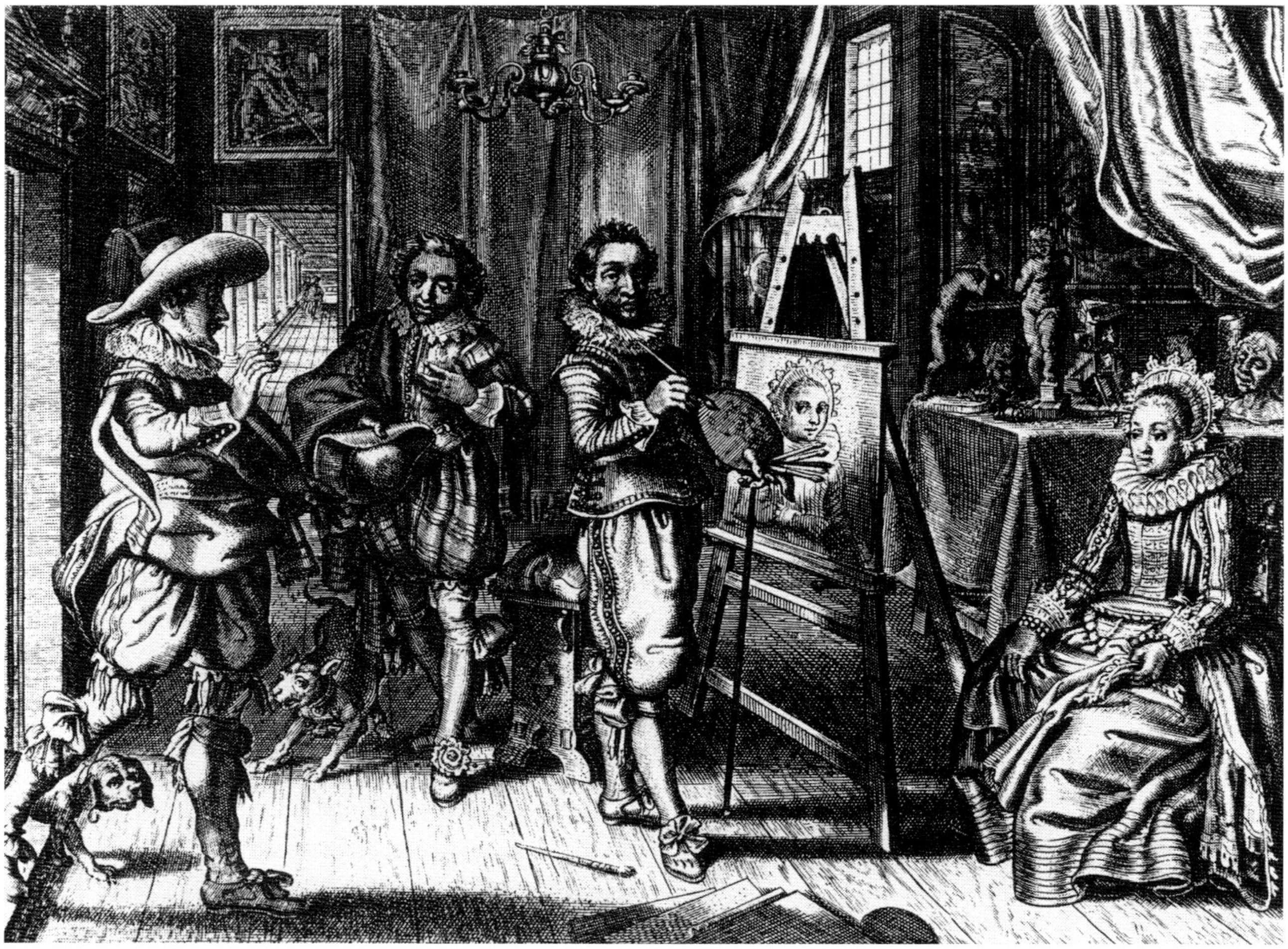

63.
After Adriaen van de Venne, *A Portrait Painter at Work*. Print from Jacob Cats, *Houwelick*, Middelburg 1625

indication that independent portraits of unmarried women were seldom commissioned.[13] This knowledge of contemporary clothing customs, which has never before been applied to portraits, may be helpful in cases such as the portrait of a couple painted by Pieter Codde in 1634 (cat. 10), about which there has been much speculation as to whether the two were engaged or married. The latter appears by far the likelier assumption, given that the young woman is wearing a *vlieger* costume.

Studio Practice

This kind of analysis emphasises the importance of archival sources when we are seeking to determine whether a sitter actually wore a particular garment. The few extant documents bearing on this subject indicate that clients wanted their clothing to be depicted accurately and with this aim in mind, precious garments and jewels were often left at the painter's studio. This is clear, for example, from the testimony given before a notary by the maidservant of Rembrandt's former pupil Isaac de Jouderville (about 1612–1647) in a case involving a ruff belonging to the shoemaker Thomas Coeck, which had gone missing in the studio.[14] Jewels too were copied precisely, as is clear from the 1650 inventory of the property of Gerard Storm, which includes two diamond eardrops with pearls, 'said to be with the painter Santvoort, who is painting the deceased's wife'.[15] The artist concerned was the Amsterdam portraitist Dirck Santvoort (1610–1680), who lived and worked on Antoniebreestraat, not far from Rembrandt.

These documents suggest that garments were sent to the artist to be painted. Although very little is known about the way in which portraits were made in the Netherlands, it may be assumed that during the first session, the painter did no more than set down the sitter's face and pose (fig. 63). The number of sessions required seems to have varied enormously. Sometimes the sitter was only required (or able) to pose for a single session (the well-known Remonstrant theologian Johannes Wttenbogaert, for instance, posed only once for the life-sized portrait that Rembrandt made of him in 1633, according to a note in his diary).[16] Several sessions were probably desirable, but the daughter of the Amsterdam burgomaster Andries de Graeff (for De Graeff, see cat. 56 and p. 17, fig. 1) may have been exaggerating when she said that her father had sat 50 times for his portrait by the Rembrandt pupil Govert Flinck.[17] That the clothing was generally completed at a later stage is clear from the description of a painting found in the studio of Michiel van Mierevelt (1567–1641) after his death: 'A large portrait of the said Jan Michielsz by Michiel van Mierevelt, in which the clothing has however not yet been completed'.[18] It makes sense that to avoid prolonging the posing sessions unnecessarily, clothing was left with the painter, who could arrange it on a lay figure and depict it later. Even the most precious of garments, it seems, were treated in this way. When Anthonis Mor van Dashorst painted a portrait of Philip II in Brussels in 1553, the artist's assistant, Conrad Schot, was responsible for the safe keeping of the king's clothing, chains and jewels.[19]

In the latter case, it was specified that Mor himself should paint the clothes, but in large portrait studios it was not uncommon for this part of the painting to be left to an assistant – frequently someone who specialised in garments. The artists' biographer Karel van Mander relates that Joachim Beuckelaer (about 1533–about 1574), who is better known today for his sumptuous still lifes, hired out his services to Mor 'for clothing in portraits'.[20] From the list of paintings in Van Mierevelt's estate, it is clear that in his own studio, this task fell to his grandson Jacob Delff.[21] According to his biographer, Arnold Houbraken, the young Adriaen van der Werff (1659–1722; p. 46, fig. 44) also painted clothing in the studio of his former master, Eglon van der Neer (about 1634–1703), after completing his apprenticeship.[22] When he himself had become a successful portraitist, he worked according to the following method: 'Van der Werff arranged the garments on the lay figure, then drew them on the panel and had his brother [Pieter van der Werff] paint them; once this had been done, the former painted over it, wet in wet'.[23]

That it was evidently customary for assistants to take over some of the work of depicting clothing does not necessarily imply that this part of the painting was regarded as unimportant: it was always the most advanced, gifted or reliable assistants who were entrusted with this work. In smaller studios and in the case of the most prestigious commissions, the master most probably painted the clothing himself. A good example is the portrait that the stadholder of Friesland, Willem Frederik, commissioned in 1660 from the Hague portraitist Adriaen Hanneman (about 1604–1671). After the artist completed the face, he notified the stadholder that he wanted to complete the portrait, but that a second posing session would be required. Unfortunately, the stadholder had no time. On 25 March 1661 the stadholder sent the completed portrait back because he wanted a sash to be added. Hanneman asked how he wanted the sash: smooth with few folds, twisted or tied in a bow around the waist. He said he would be able to complete the addition within a week. Willem then sent him an orange sash, which was returned to him in good order a month later.[24] From a copy of the portrait produced by Pieter Nason in 1662, it appears that the stadholder wanted the sash twisted and positioned diagonally across his chest (fig. 64).[25] This example indicates the great importance that the client attached to the precise rendering of his attire. One wonders why the trouble was taken to send the stadholder's sash all the way from Leeuwarden, for it to be painted, twisted and scarcely visible, while sashes of this kind were freely available in The Hague; indeed, Hanneman might just as well have used some arbitrary strip of satin. The stadholder evidently considered it essential that his own sash was painted into the portrait.

Clothing made of Paint

There is frequently a certain tension between the painter and the prevailing fashion. On the one hand, the painter wishes to convey his own aesthetic ideas and will try to adjust and manipulate the fashion to that end. On the other hand, he cannot depart too far from the prevailing trends, given the sitter's desire to appear fashionable. In a period that prescribed black – such as most of the sixteenth and seventeenth centuries – painters sought ways of conveying the different nuances and

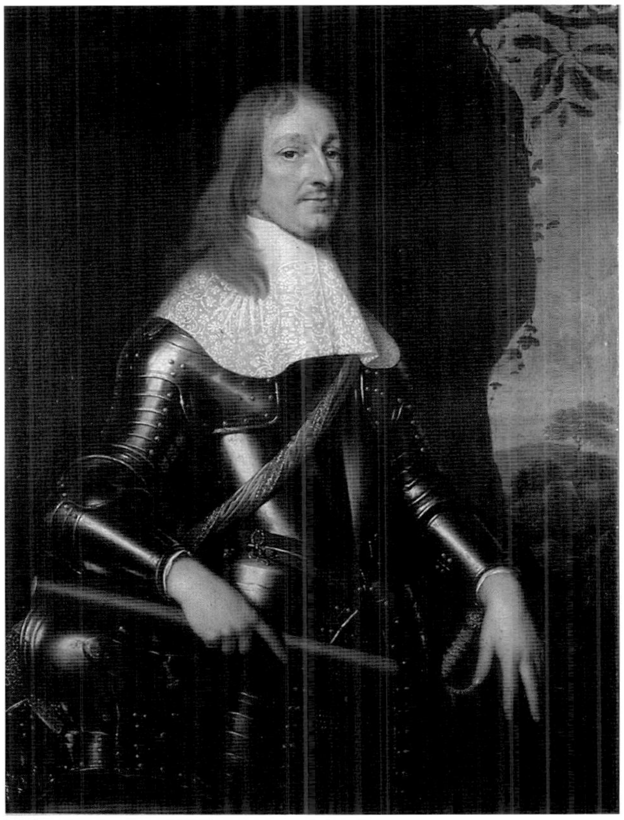

64.
Pieter Nason after Adriaen Hanneman, *Portrait of Stadholder Willem Frederik*, 1662. Oil on canvas, 121 x 94 cm. Mauritshuis, The Hague (on loan to Paleis Het Loo Nationaal Museum, Apeldoorn)

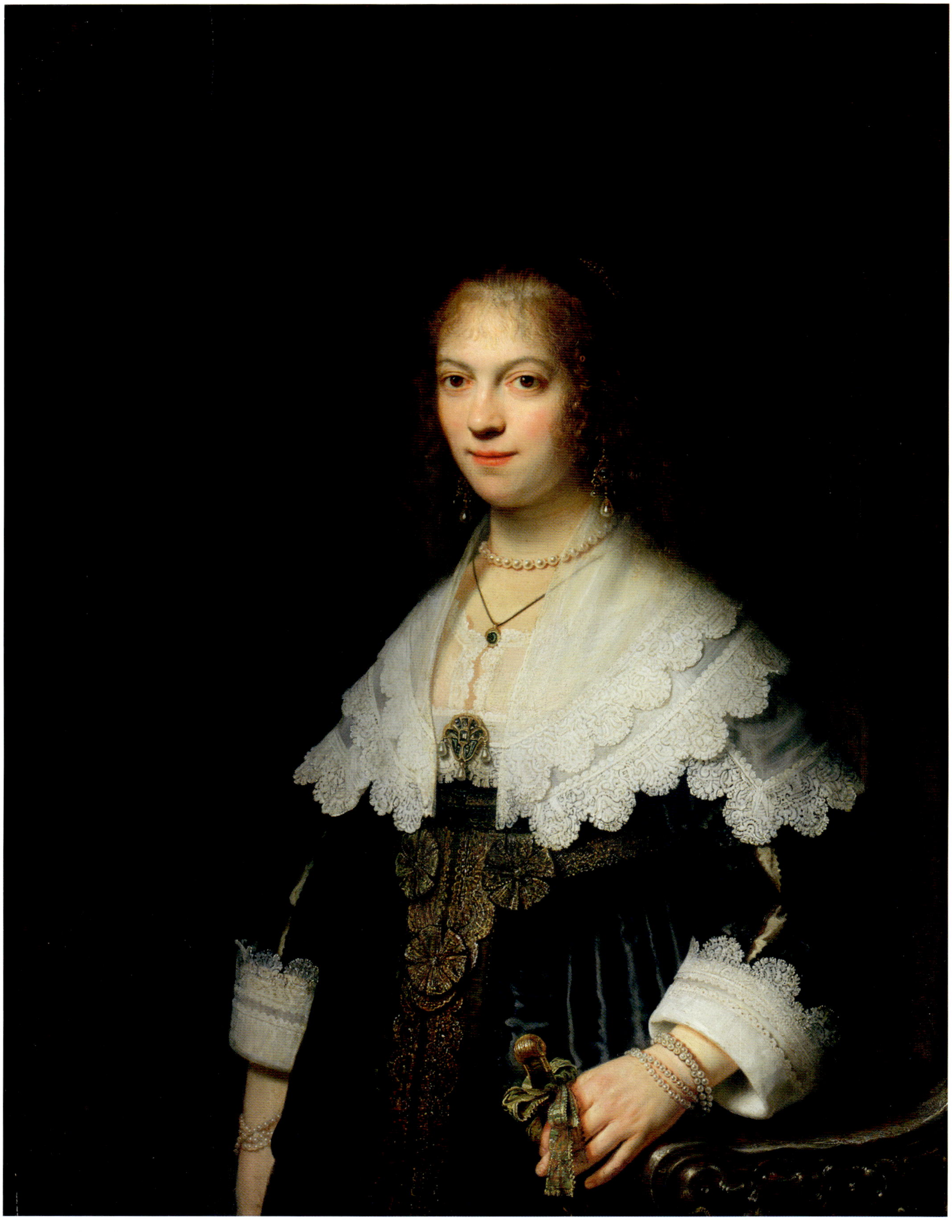

65. Rembrandt, *Portrait of Maria Trip*, 1639. Oil on panel, 107 × 82 cm. Rijksmuseum, Amsterdam (on loan from the Van Weede Family Foundation since 1897)

textures of the black fabrics as convincingly and vividly as possible.[26] In the work of great portraitists such as Frans Hals (cats 14–27) and Rembrandt (cats 51–61), black is never dull; its pictorial potential is utilised to the full. Black is an ideal background against which gold can stand out to dramatic effect, and the contrast with the crisp, white linen, in particular, accentuates the face and hand gestures. This extreme opposition between black and white is both austere and exciting, and is a characteristic feature of the seventeenth-century Dutch portrait.

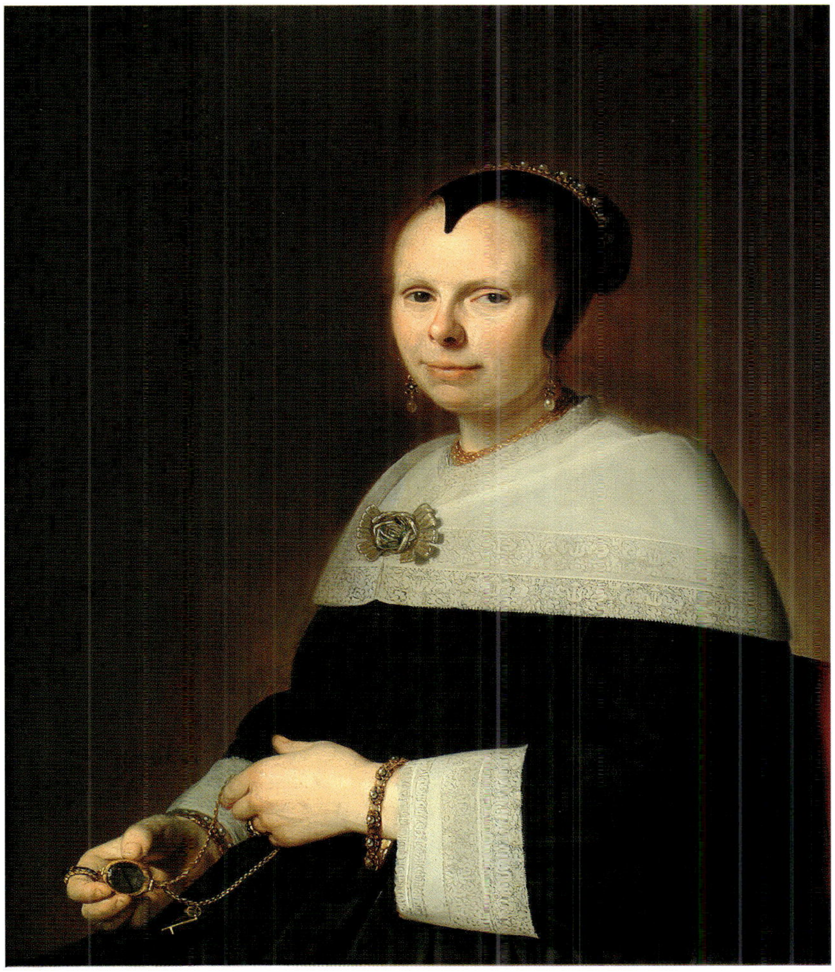

66.
Johannes Verspronck, *Portrait of Eva Vos*, 1654. Oil on canvas, 82 x 65 cm. Frans Hals Museum, Haarlem

Rendering the complex structure and airy transparency of lace was also a special challenge to portraitists. At the beginning of the seventeenth century, lace was still a fairly new invention, and the first laces, made with a needle, displayed geometrical motifs such as pointed stars and shafts or rays, linked by bars.[27] Each section of this pointed, geometrical type of lace, or *reticella*, was literally copied by artists in thin white lines over the completed clothing, a technique employed for the spiky lace that trims the clothing of the little child Catharina Hooft in Frans Hals's portrait, made around 1620 (cat. 14; fig. p. 64). In the 1620s we see a shift away from the stiff Spanish fashion, abounding in gold embroidery, to French styles, with a preference for a more relaxed silhouette and supple, gleaming fabrics in dark, monochrome colour schemes. The looser and more monochrome style of painting that came to the fore around 1630 is part of this general trend towards a different aesthetic ideal. This visual development coincided with the rising popularity of Flemish bobbin lace in the late 1620s. Since large parts of bobbin lace are executed in cloth stitch (which creates a thick weave), its structure is far denser than embroidered, or needle lace, and it was therefore better suited to the new, more voluminous, fashions. Wispy, geometrical *reticella* gave way to more solid floral motifs, while spiky edges were replaced by undulating scallop shapes. The distinctive properties of this kind of lace called for a completely different means of representation, which Rembrandt applied in the portraits he made in the 1630s. Rather than tracing each thread, he indicated the shape of the collar in relatively thick strokes of paint, after which he would paint the contour and pattern of the lace in black dots and short strokes applied with a loose hand (fig. 65).[28] White highlights indicate where the curled edge catches a little more light. To render different layers, the pattern might be selectively painted in brownish strokes rather than black. This reversal of the time-consuming way of depicting lace that had been customary in the past was not just faster but yielded a surprisingly convincing result, and was moreover far truer to the greatly changed nature of the lace itself.[29]

In the 1650s, portraitists were confronted with lace made in an even denser cloth stitch, with a straight edge and small floral motifs between which scarcely any bars can be made out. This *dentelle opaque* is also known as Dutch lace, not because of its provenance (it was in fact Flemish) but because it occurs most frequently in portraits made in the Northern Netherlands. The dense nature of this type of lace was well understood by Johannes Verspronck, who scratched out the detailed floral motifs with the back of his brush in the wet white paint, revealing the black or light ground beneath (fig. 66).[30]

These examples show that to some extent painting technique adapted to changes in fashion, and that artists expressed their creativity within the limits of what fashion dictated. However, if we look more closely at the lace that Rembrandt depicts so extraordinarily convincingly (fig. 65), we discover a different pattern within each scallop: the floral patterns are clearly the master's own design rather than that of the lace worker. An artist who worked in much the same way was the Italian sculptor Gian Lorenzo Bernini (1598–1680), who was so famous that he could dictate what the King of France should wear in his portrait bust (fig. 67). On 17 September 1665, the French art lover Paul Fréart de Chantelou (1609–1694) sent word that Bernini would like the king to pose with a band, or flat collar, instead of the cravat he had worn on previous occasions. He also wished to inspect three such bands from the king's wardrobe to see which pattern best lent itself to being fashioned in marble.[31] Two days later, Louis XIV did indeed pose with the flat collar as the sculptor had requested.[32] Bernini was given five or six collars to choose from, and eventually settled on one made of 'point de Venise', an expensive Venetian needlepoint lace with floral and vine motifs and a thick contour thread. While the bust was being made, De Chantelou asked in surprise why the artist was not following the pattern at all, even though he did look at it now and then. The Italian replied that the pattern was totally lacking in design. 'But what would you expect? It was made by Venetian nuns, who know nothing of beauty'.[33] The next day, Bernini related laughingly that he had never thought he would ever work on anything as tasteless as point de Venise, and that although many had begged him to design a piece of lace, he had never felt the inclination, and yet now he was going further than that by executing it in marble.[34] Like Rembrandt, Bernini declined to slavishly follow the pattern of the lace; instead, he improved and manipulated it to accord with his aesthetic views.

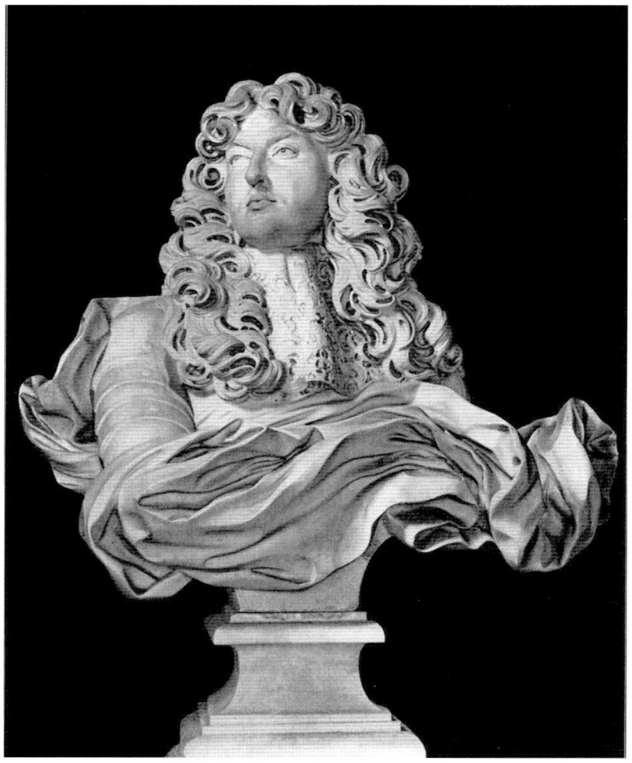

67.
Gian Lorenzo Bernini, *Bust of Louis XIV*, 1665. Marble, height 80 cm. Musée National de Versailles

Portrait painters took certain artistic liberties when rendering clothing, just as they did when depicting the subject's face. In studying seventeenth-century sources on female beauty, we are struck first and foremost by a near-obsessive preoccupation with smooth, white skin,[35] and although contemporary sources testify to the widespread use of beauty spots, one rarely sees them in portraits (but see p. 177, fig. 47–8b).[36] It is also curious that eyelashes are never painted. In reality, few would have had smooth skin in those days, if only because almost everyone suffered a bout of smallpox at some point. Those who survived were frequently scarred for life with deep pockmarks, yet in portraiture all the faces are equally smooth, and pockmarked faces are nowhere to be found. A burlesque entitled *The Painter through Love* (1632) undoubtedly refers to prevailing practice, when the young lady whose portrait is being painted says: 'The original surely merits no great praise; / But the good master will easily erase / The blemishes encountered in the face'.[37]

'Dutch or Roman'

In 1668, Jacob van der Does wrote a poem on the depiction of young ladies from The Hague by the portrait painter Jan Mijtens:

> One he makes Diana of the Hunt, another stands
> beside some flowers or fount;
> or in some other way, clad in elegant attire
> Whether Dutch or Roman, whichever they desire.[38]

The choice between Dutch and Roman refers to a late seventeenth-century custom in Dutch portraiture whereby painters frequently draped their figures in a fantasy costume described as 'picturesque', 'antique' or 'Roman'.[39] Gentlemen had themselves depicted in an antique-looking cuirass or an ample *Japonse rock*, an exotic, Japanese-style chamber gown that was draped around the subject (see cats 37–8 and p. 136, fig. 27a). 'Portrait costumes' of this kind were first introduced in the 1630s by the influential Flemish portraitist Anthony van Dyck (1599–1641). He dressed his aristocratic English sitters in a simplified, romanticised version of the fashions of the day, leaving out fashionable elements such as lace and embroidery and draping his figures in vaguely classical-looking garments with fluttering scarves. This approach was later eagerly adopted by fashionable Dutch portraitists such as Adriaen Hanneman, Nicolaes Maes, Jan

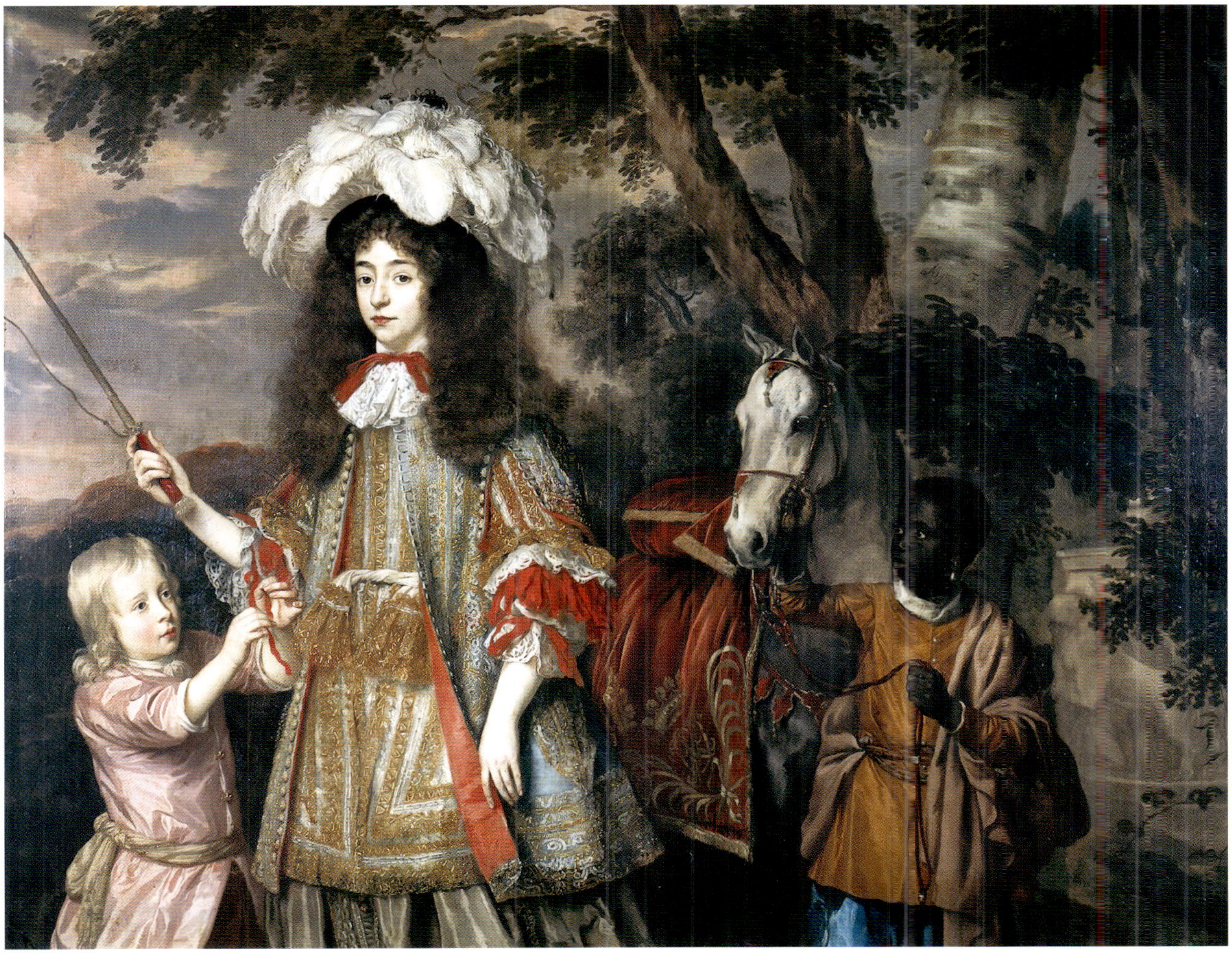

68.
Jan Mijtens,
Portrait of Maria, Princess of Orange, with Hendrik van Zuijlestein and a Servant,
about 1665.
Oil on canvas,
150 x 185 cm.
Mauritshuis,
The Hague

Mijtens and Caspar Netscher (cats 28, 37–8, 41 and 44). These fluttering, imaginary costumes were popular in portraits because fashionable clothes soon looked out of date, while 'Roman' dress was thought to convey a more timeless appearance. Mijtens painted more ladies in 'Roman' than in 'Dutch' dress. An exception is his portrait of Maria, Princess of Orange, whom he depicted around 1665 as a horsewoman in her riding clothes (fig. 68).[40] The bride-to-be had probably expressly asked to be depicted wearing this special costume, which is described at length in her 1666 trousseau.[41] More typical are Mijtens's portraits of ladies wearing unpatterned dresses in brightly coloured satin. These present a distorted picture of reality; they obscure the fact that striped and black fabrics were also worn, as is clear from Princess Maria's trousseau.[42]

'Roman' costumes pose a serious obstacle to studies of the history of dress in the latter half of the seventeenth century. Indeed, De Chantelou displayed considerable foresight in his riposte to the art connoisseurs who criticised the flat lace collar in Bernini's newly completed bust of the King of France: 'The gentlemen would have preferred the bust to be without a lace collar, because an uncovered neck would be "in the manner of the heroes". I told them that French heroes do not have to be portrayed in the Roman or Greek style, and that it was good that the collar had been done in the style of its day, since this is to the benefit of history'.[43]

Ferdinand Bol & Willem van de Velde the Younger

Dordrecht 1616–1680 Amsterdam & Leiden 1633–1707 Greenwich

1

Portrait of Michiel de Ruyter, 1667

Oil on canvas, 157 x 135 cm
To the right of the balustrade: *fBol . fecit. A°. 1667* (fB in ligature);
at lower centre: FLANDRIA
Royal Picture Gallery Mauritshuis, The Hague

This official portrait of Michiel de Ruyter (1607–1676), admiral of the Dutch fleet, was painted in 1667, soon after he had defeated the British navy in the Four Days' Battle of June 1666.[1] To celebrate the victory that secured his fame, Ferdinand Bol depicted the naval hero holding the baton of command and resting his elbow on a celestial globe, while navigational instruments lie on the table beside him. The map showing the coastline of Flanders is an allusion to the scene of the great battle. To the right we see De Ruyter's flagship, *De Zeven Provinciën* (The Seven Provinces) lying at anchor, identified by an escutcheon showing the Dutch lion on a crowned shield, surrounded by the arms of the Republic's seven provinces.

The portrait's original, richly carved and gilded frame is an essential part of the image. The objects on it emphasise that the portrait was intended as a tribute: the carvings depict cannons and a range of firearms, suits of armour, helmets, shields, spears, muskets and at the bottom, a war drum.[2] Blazoned at upper centre is De Ruyter's coat of arms, which King Frederik III of Denmark granted him in 1660. Encircling the coat of arms is the chain of the Order of Saint Michael, presented to De Ruyter by the French ambassador in 1666 on behalf of King Louis XIV; De Ruyter also wears the chain in the portrait.

The general formula for Bol's portrait of De Ruyter derives from the established tradition of heroes' portraits, in which a life-sized figure with attributes is depicted against an appropriate background. Bol painted De Ruyter at knee length, standing before a balustrade and a drapery that has been drawn aside to give us a partial glimpse of his fleet in the distance. While the Leiden artist Jan Lievens portrayed the admiral as a weather-beaten seaman,[3] Bol gave him a smooth face and carefully coiffed hair, more suited to an official portrait of a distinguished naval hero.

After the success of the Four Days' Battle, the governors of all five regional admiralties expressed a desire for a portrait of De Ruyter to hang in their council chambers.[4] It was the first time that an admiral had been publicly honoured in this way. Until then, tributes to maritime heroes had been confined chiefly to laudatory poems and elegies, with their portraits only appearing as prints. The chambers of the five admiralities were located in six cities: Amsterdam (North Holland), Rotterdam (South Holland), Middelburg (Zeeland), Harlingen (Friesland), Enkhuizen and Hoorn (the Northern Quarter). The six portraits were supplied by De Ruyter himself in exchange for various gifts: from Middelburg he received a valuable atlas.[5] Three of the original six portraits are still known,[6] but the Mauritshuis painting, which has been in The Hague since 1894, comes from the building of the Amsterdam admiralty[7] and is the only one to have retained its original frame.

The commission for the six virtually identical portraits went to one of Rembrandt's most gifted pupils, Ferdinand Bol – an obvious choice as Bol, who worked in Amsterdam from 1637 onwards, maintained close ties with the members of Amsterdam's admiralty (p. 35, fig. 29), and had executed commissions for them before.[8] The fleet in the background, however, was painted by the marine painter Willem van de Velde the Younger, who collaborated with Bol on other occasions.[9] Van de Velde based the ships on drawings his father, Willem van de Velde the Elder, had made during the Four Days' Battle at De Ruyter's request.[10] In addition to the original six works, numerous variants of De Ruyter's portrait were produced in Bol's studio between 1667 and 1669. Judging by the difference in quality, assistants must have been involved in their production.[11]

Two preliminary studies clarify the development of the composition.[12] The general design was determined early on: one early study, a rapid sketch, shows De Ruyter standing beside a table with a globe, his right arm resting on a baton.[13] In this sketch, as well as another, more finished drawing, Bol made several corrections to the right arm.[14] He was apparently not able to resolve easily the pose to his satisfaction, as unlike the painting the drawing shows the admiral resting his hand on his baton rather than the globe. QB

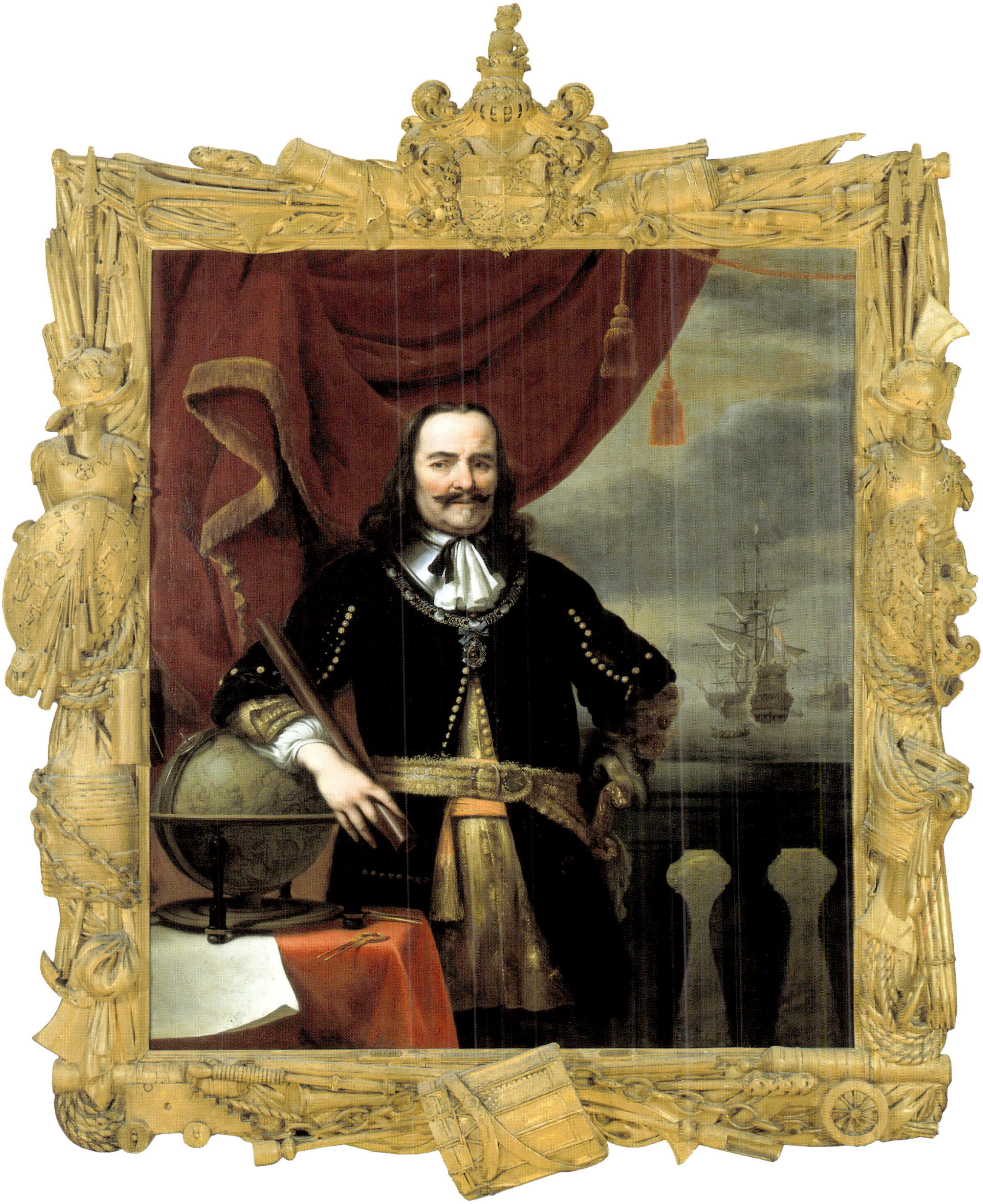

Gerard ter Borch

Zwolle 1617–1681 Deventer

2

Portrait of Caspar van Kinschot, about 1647

Oil on copper (oval), 11 x 8 cm
Private collection (on loan to the Mauritshuis, The Hague)

Gerard ter Borch is known mostly as a painter of stylish genre pieces, which he began painting in the 1650s. These scenes are suffused with luxury and populated with elegant ladies and gentlemen. The meticulously refined rendering of the costly garments in these pictures – especially glistening satin – can be regarded as the artist's trademark,[1] but as well as genre pieces, he also made portraits. The earliest was a chalk drawing from around 1635 of his step-uncle, the engraver Robert van Voerst,[2] which is the only work known to us from the artist's years in London. Then around 1640, Ter Borch started making portrait paintings, full-length depictions of men and women in empty or scantily furnished interiors (cat. 3 and fig. 3a). The artist's standard format for portraits brought him enduring success and wide recognition. Although he settled in Deventer in 1654 and drew most of his clientele from the eastern provinces, he also made portraits for prosperous Amsterdam townspeople around 1670 through the mediation of a relative.[3] Many years before that, probably around 1645, he produced a miniature portrait of Jan Six, one of Amsterdam's most prominent citizens (see also cat. 57).[4] Like the work discussed here, it was executed on a small oval piece of copper.

The *Portrait of Caspar van Kinschot* is one of a group of miniature portraits that Ter Borch painted during the peace negotiations between the Dutch Republic and Spain in Münster (1645–8), where he depicted individual delegates and members of their families.[5] Van Kinschot (1622–1649) was the youngest of the Dutchmen who had their portraits painted there, and here his youth is emphasised by his fashionable long hair, which falls over his shoulders, and the even more fashionable lace-trimmed collar. Only the grey doublet, with slashes at the chest, on the back and in the sleeves, was outdated by this period. Because of the rich clothing details, this is the least formal of the portraits Ter Borch made in Münster. Its informality is enhanced by the fact that the sitter is represented closer to the picture plane, and therefore larger relative to the artist's other miniatures. The soft brushwork and subtle nuances of warm greys and browns are typical of the artist.

The jurist and poet Van Kinschot came from a prominent regent family in The Hague, and was related to Jaspar Schade, whom in 1645 had commissioned a portrait from Frans Hals (cat. 25). While not an official representative Van Kinschot enjoyed a certain standing among the Dutch delegation, but he lived barely long enough to witness their success – not long after returning from the treaty talks he died of tuberculosis in The Hague, at only 27 years of age. The Treaty of Münster was signed on 15 May 1648, formally ending the Eighty Years' War between the Dutch Republic and Spain. By way of commemoration, and on his own initiative, Ter Borch painted a group portrait of the two delegations during the ceremonial event (fig. 2a).[6] Van Kinschot is depicted at the table with documents and seals (as the third man from the left seated at the table). Judging by Van Kinschot's flushed cheeks in the present work, it was probably made slightly earlier: in the group portrait he looks a little older and less blooming with health.[7]

QB

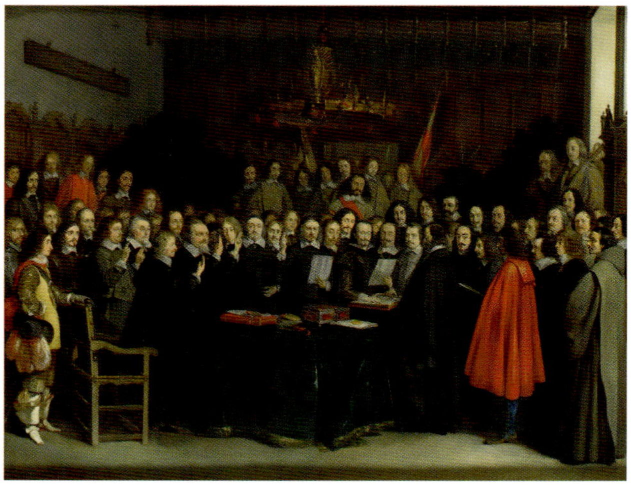

2a. Gerard ter Borch, *The Swearing of the Oath of Ratification of the Treaty of Münster, 15 May 1648*, 1648. Oil on copper, 45 x 59 cm. The National Gallery, London (on loan to the Rijksmuseum, Amsterdam)

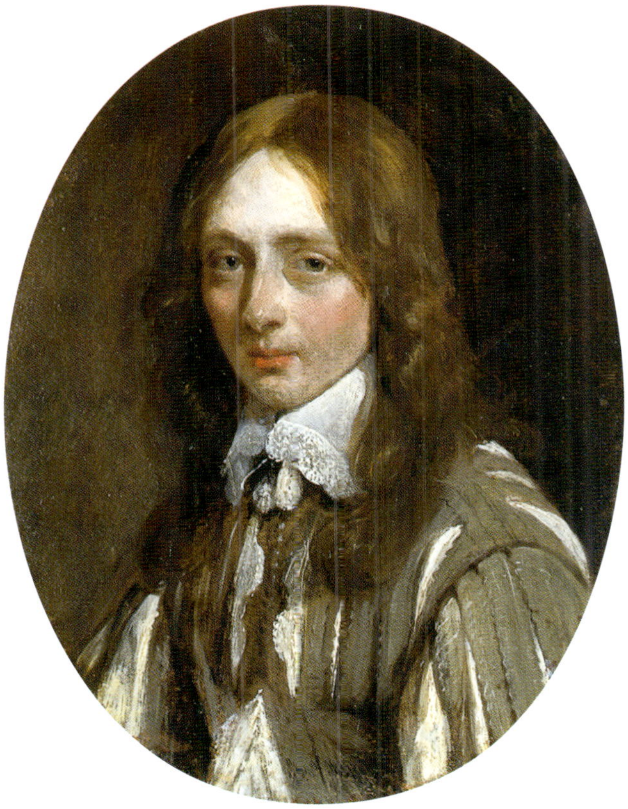

Gerard ter Borch

Zwolle 1617–1681 Deventer

3

Portrait of a Young Man, about 1663

Oil on canvas, 67.3 × 54.3 cm
The National Gallery, London

In the early 1660s, when he was living in Deventer, a wealthy city in the eastern province of Overijssel, Gerard ter Borch turned his attention more fully from genre painting to portraiture. In works from this period, like this *Portrait of a Young Man*, the artist continued his earlier approach of depicting the sitter at full-length in cabinet-size format, in a scarcely defined interior with a minimum of accessories. These understated portrayals of members of the local regent class underscored their individuality and sober character. While in the present picture Ter Borch adhered to that formula – the chair upholstered in red velvet and the table with matching cloth are the only decorative features – the unknown sitter wears remarkably elaborate and luxurious attire that reflects the height of French fashion in the early 1660s.[1] The hat in the distinctive shape of a *suykerbroot*, or sugar cone, in particular, was in fashion between about 1660 and 1663, when it abruptly disappeared, suggesting a clear *terminus ante quem* for the picture. For the rest, the man wears a black silk cloak over a skimpy doublet or 'innocent'. Unbuttoned at the bottom and with open sleeves, the doublet reveals much of the voluminous chemise underneath. The cuffs and broad collar (band or bible-collar) are decorated with lace while the petticoat breeches are richly adorned with ruffles and ribbon loops. The wide overstockings, or canons, are folded over the garters below the knee, creating deep ruffles. Rather than wearing the canons with boots the sitter wears with them with square-toed shoes that are also decorated with ribbons. It is not surprising that such an ostentatious manner of dressing was much criticised at the time:

> not so long ago [one saw] long, loose trousers, being far looser below than above, with baggy material hanging half-way down the shins like women's skirts; likewise the excessively high hats that were worn a few years ago, accompanied by elongated shoes; all such abuses served merely as impediments, besides which the immoderately loose and long garments were redolent of over-abundance and profligacy.[2]

To heighten the sumptuous effect of the materials Ter Borch adds a number of sparkling highlights to various details (note the gleaming shoes). It may seem surprising that a member of the wealthy patrician class, who may also have held some form of public or civic office, had himself – as well as his wife, for her dress in the pendant picture is no less flamboyant (fig. 3a)[3] – represented in this extravagant manner, rather than in more timeless attire. This was not unusual, however, as several other examples in this exhibition reveal (see cats 24–5). Furthermore, despite his almost foppish appearance, the sitter's upright formal pose, his steady gaze and the restrained movement of his body lend the portrait an air of formality and dignity that leaves little doubt about his authority and elevated social position. AR

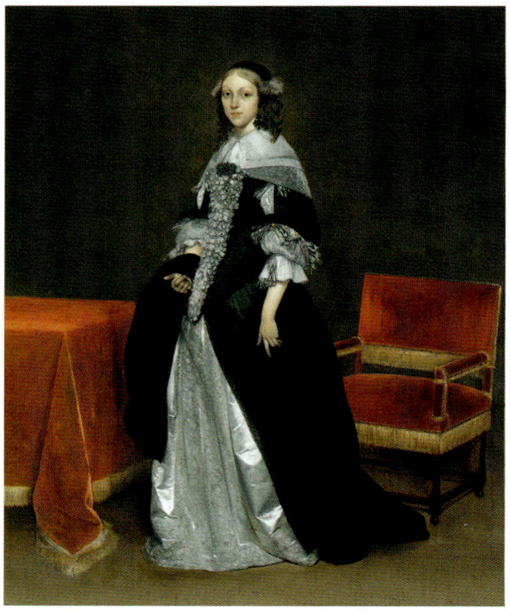

3a.
Gerard ter Borch, *Portrait of a Young Woman*, about 1663. Oil on canvas, 63 × 53 cm. The Elisabeth Severance Prentiss Collection, The Cleveland Museum of Art

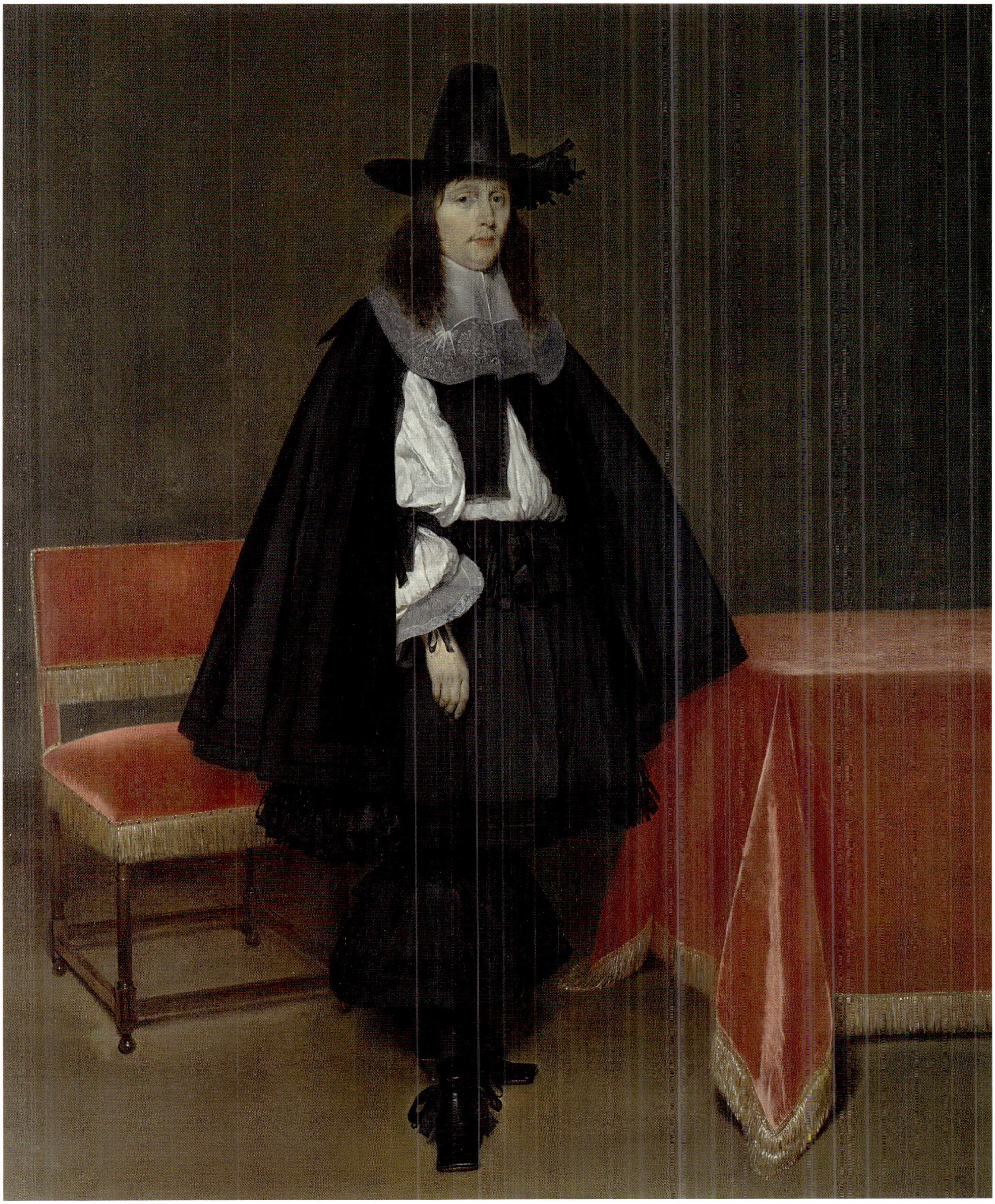

Jan de Bray

Haarlem about 1627 – 1697 Haarlem

4

Banquet of Mark Antony and Cleopatra: Family Portrait with Salomon de Bray and Anna Westerbaen, 1652

Oil on canvas,[1] 170 x 166 cm
On the tablecloth: *JDBray* / 1652 (JDB in ligature); 56
The Royal Collection, London

In this painting from 1652, Jan de Bray has depicted his parents, the painter and poet Salomon de Bray (1597–1664) and Anna Westerbaen (about 1605–1663), in the roles of Cleopatra, Queen of Egypt, and the Roman general Mark Antony at a banquet.[2] At the feast Cleopatra laid a wager with Mark Antony that she could consume a fortune of ten million sesterces.[3] She won the bet by dissolving one of her pearls in a glass of vinegar and drinking the mixture. That the painter should have decided to depict his parents as Cleopatra and her adulterous lover is puzzling, given the queen's far from glowing reputation.[4]

De Bray situated his parents amid some of their many offspring. The protagonists share an intimate gaze, while the woman removes one of her pearl earrings. The small crown on her head identifies her as the queen, but her sumptuous attire is contemporary.[5] Her reddish-orange gown (*tabbaard*) with openwork sleeves is trimmed with gold lace, the fashionable wavy pattern of which enables us to date it to around 1650. The man wears a laurel wreath on his head – the antique attribute of the victorious general, but also a symbol of honour or merit worn by artists and poets.

It is not entirely clear which sons and daughters have been included here. The De Brays had at least ten children, four of whom died young. Since the family was Catholic, the children's names are not included in Haarlem's baptismal registers, so it is impossible to establish the years of their birth. None the less, the soldier with a halberd on the left is sometimes identified as a self portrait of Jan, and the boy with the copper dish in the lower left corner as Jacob, with one of his sisters, Margaretha or Juliana at his side.[6] The two children in the lower right corner may be posthumous portraits of deceased siblings. The facial features of the figure on the left, traditionally accepted as a 'self portrait', are cloaked in shadow and barely recognisable. In fact the young man behind and to the right of Cleopatra – generally identified as the artist's brother Dirck – is more suggestive of a self portrait: he remains somewhat detached from the scene and gazes out at us.[7] This is an age-old way for painters to depict themselves as minor figures amid various participants in a history piece.[8] Further, this figure was evidently added at a relatively late stage, given that no space was reserved for it in the dark background: since the paint has become more transparent over the years, the dark ground now bleeds through the paint surface here.[9]

The number '56' that appears after '1652' – inscribed in the shadow of the white tablecloth – is probably not a second year but Salomon's age: he turned 56 in 1652.[10] The lack of any reference to his wife's age suggests that the couple's eldest son saw the celebrated pater familias, founder of the family business, as the most important figure in the group portrait.

When the painting was first listed in the inventory of the British Royal Collection, in 1688, it was identified as 'The History of Mark Anthony and Cleopatra' by 'John The-Bray'.[11] It must have been this exalted purchase, probably made by King Charles II (1630–1685), that prompted De Bray to paint a second version of the scene in 1669 (fig. 4a).[12] In this replica, which extends the original composition at top and bottom, he added a profile portrait of Maria van Hees, whom he married in 1668, beside his own probable likeness.[13] Since she was dead by the end of 1669, her likeness is probably posthumous, as indeed is that of almost the entire De Bray family in that painting. King Charles must have seen Jan de Bray's history piece as an attractive acquisition, painted as it was in the clear Dutch classicist style of which both De Brays, father and son, were leading exponents from around 1650. The work's value to the new owner was not as a group portrait. To the artist, however, this was undoubtedly its main raison d'être, certainly after almost the entire family had succumbed to the plague in the epidemic of 1663–4; with the second version, he could preserve the memory of his loved ones. AvS

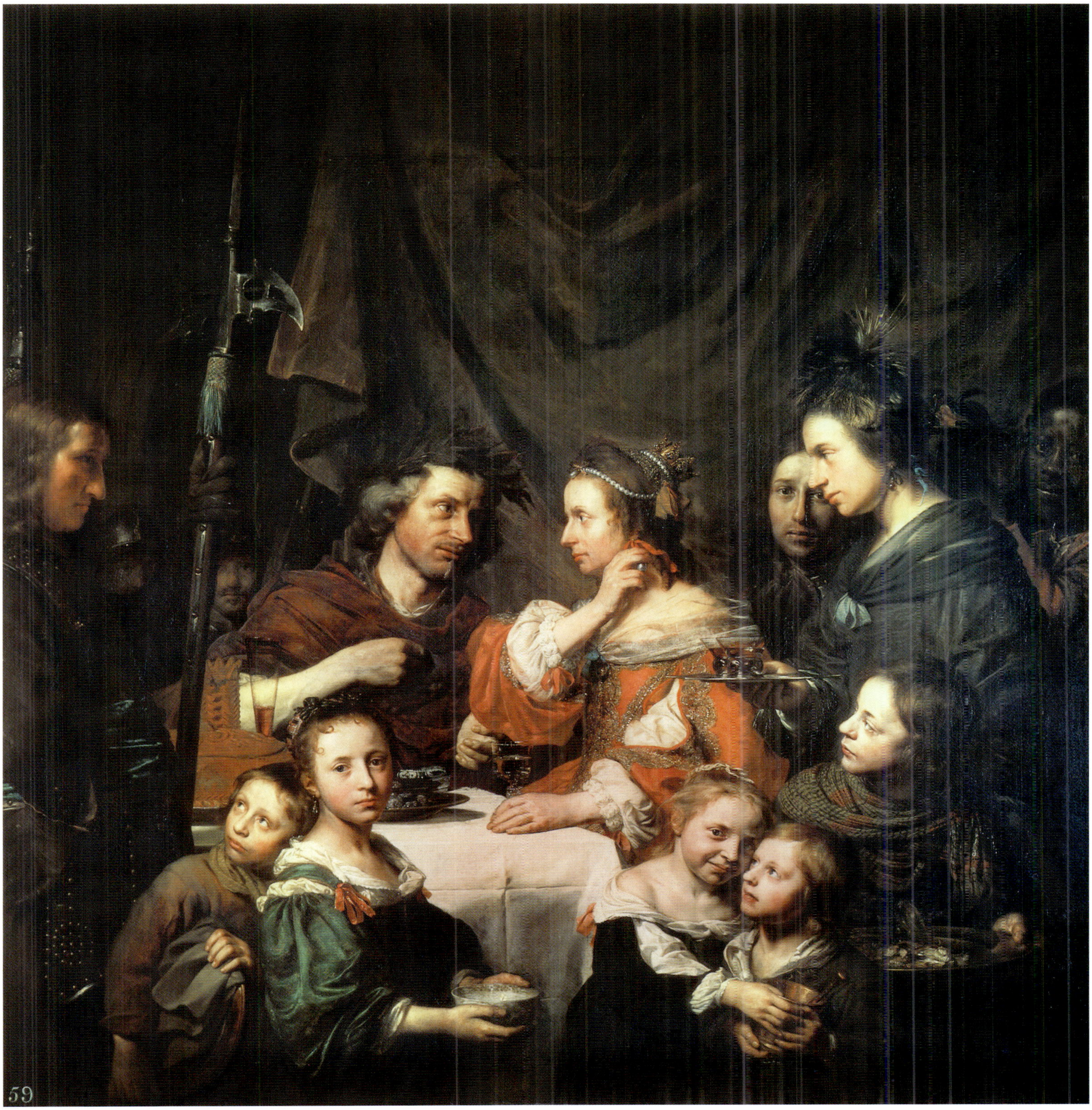

59

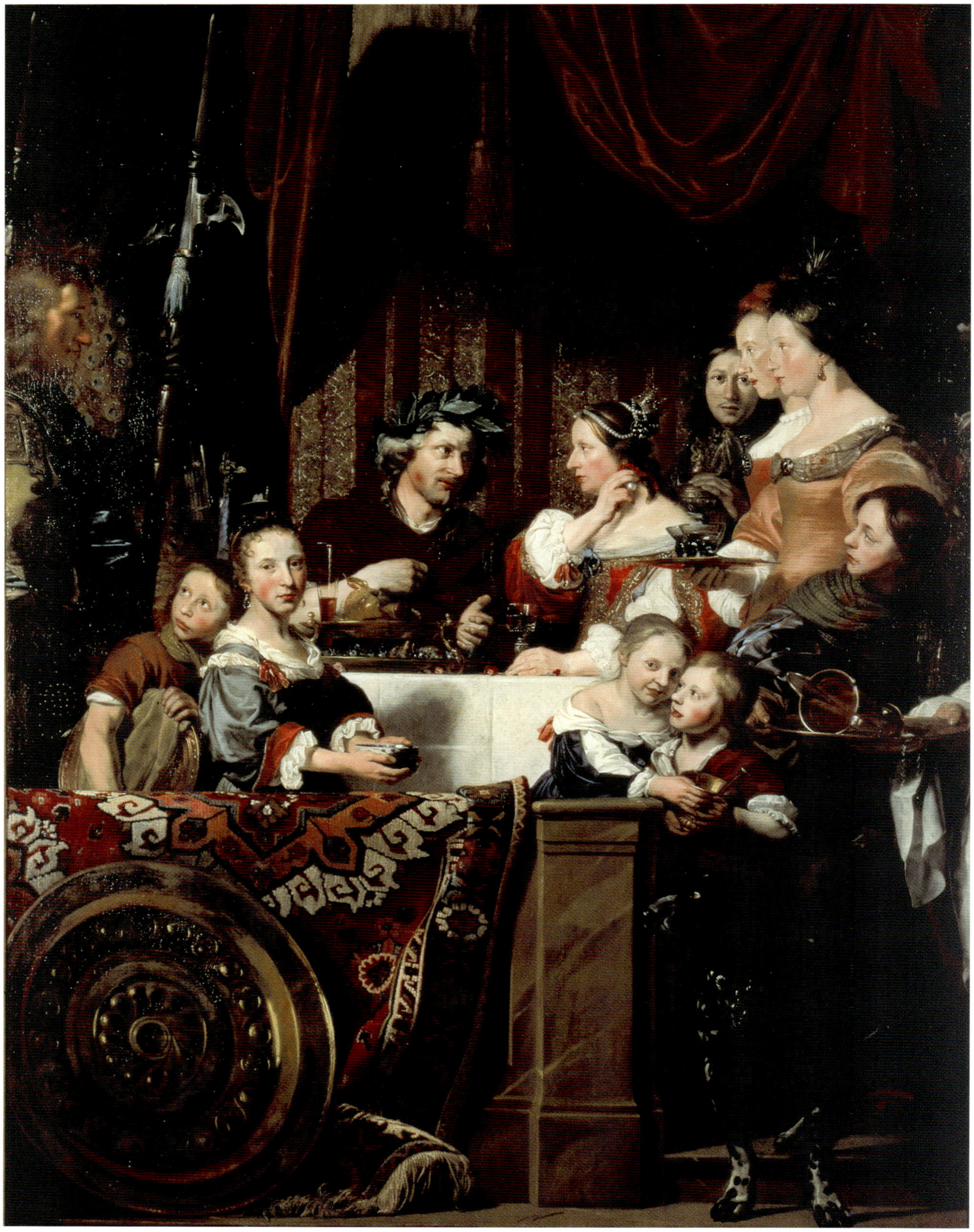

4a.
Jan de Bray,
Banquet of Mark Antony and Cleopatra: Family Portrait with Salomon de Bray and Anna Westerbaen, 1669.
Oil on canvas,
250 x 190 cm.
Currier Museum of Art,
Manchester, New Hampshire

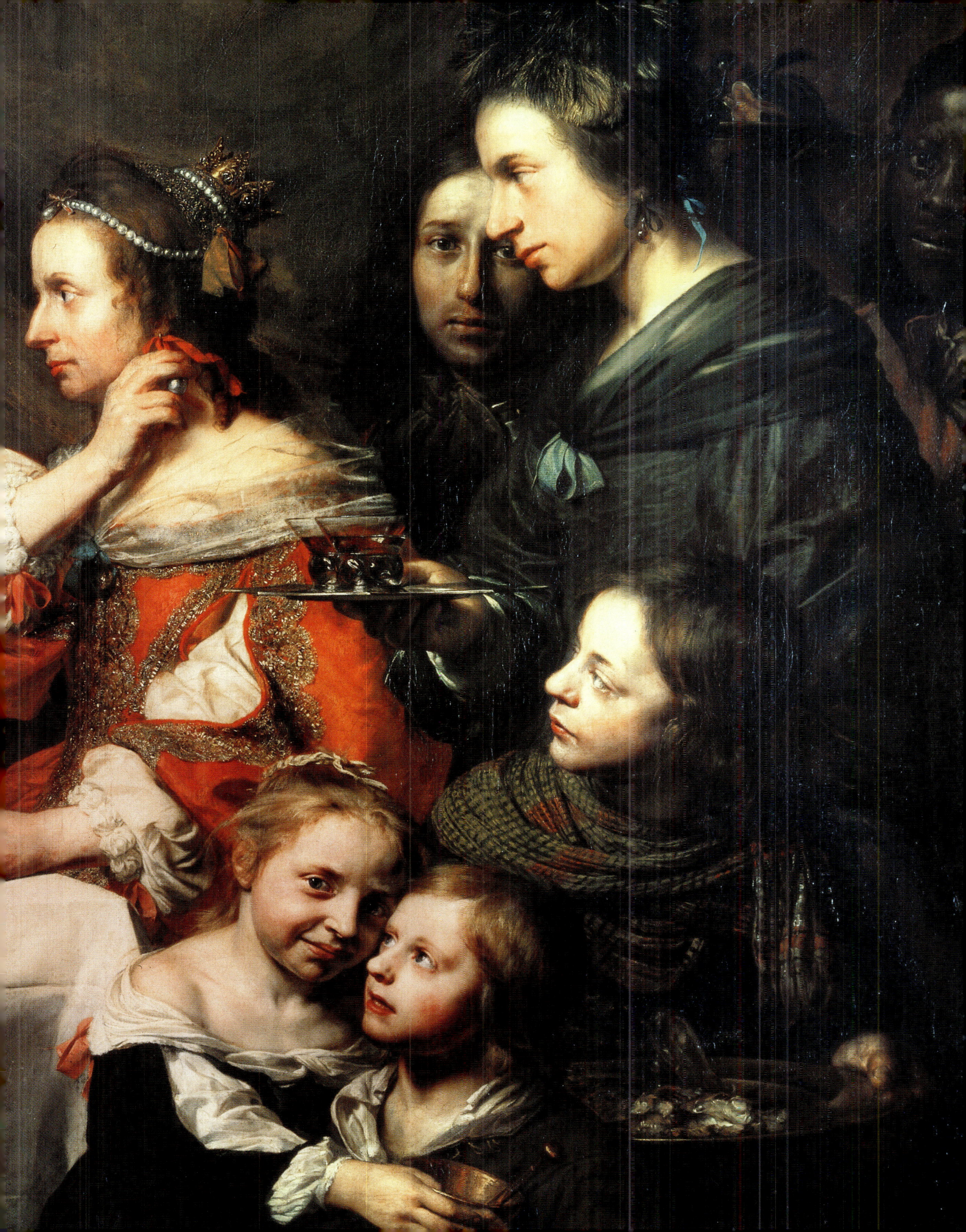

Jan de Bray

Haarlem about 1627–1697 Haarlem

5

Double Portrait of Abraham Casteleijn and Margarieta van Bancken, 1663

Oil on canvas, 83 x 107 cm
At left, on the plinth: *JDBray. 1663.* (JDB in ligature)
Rijksmuseum, Amsterdam

In this double portrait, Jan de Bray has depicted the Haarlem printer and newspaper publisher Abraham Casteleijn (about 1628–1681) and his wife Margarieta van Bancken (died in 1692/3) in a conspicuously casual pose, seated at a table in a space that appears to be half terrace, half study. The gesture with which the couple loosely hold hands and the climbing plant in the right background may be construed as symbols of fidelity and the bond of matrimony.[1] The figures' informal poses and the garden in the background, as well as the vigorous style of painting, all recall Frans Hals's *Double Portrait of Isaac Massa and Beatrix van der Laen*, painted 40 years earlier (cat. 15). The plain clothing, devoid of cuffs, lace or jewellery, reflects the couple's Mennonite faith: the woman's austere white neckerchief was 20 years out of date by 1663, and the man's small collar and the long panels of his coat were likewise old-fashioned.

Even so, this painting, which has been marvellously preserved, expresses much more than Mennonite sobriety. A piece of drapery raised behind Casteleijn reveals a collection of books, a colossal globe and a marble bust on a plinth. The book lying open on the table beside the globe is an atlas. The bust is a likeness of Laurens Jansz Coster (about 1370–about 1440), one of Haarlem's most illustrious citizens, who was still cited in the seventeenth century as the inventor of printing.[2] As a printer, Casteleijn is comparing himself here to his famous fellow-townsman and predecessor. Furthermore, his gesturing right hand, with which he appears to be addressing the viewer, seems to symbolise his role as messenger – bringing the news about the world represented by the globe and atlas behind him.

With his newspapers, Abraham Casteleijn had made informing the public about world events his life's work.[3] He was the youngest son of the printer Vincent Casteleijn, who had been Haarlem's municipal printer since 1642. Abraham succeeded his father in this capacity after Vincent's death in 1658. The first edition of *Weeckelycke Courante van Europa* ('Weekly Newspaper for Europe') had appeared only two years earlier. This periodical was incorporated into the *Oprechte Haerlemse Courant* ('True Newspaper for Haarlem') when Abraham Casteleijn acquired a monopoly on newspaper publication in Haarlem in 1664, winning a competitive struggle over three of his brothers. The *Oprechte Haerlemse Courant* was one of the best-informed newspapers in Europe, and earned Casteleijn the reputation of one of the Netherlands' first newspaper publishers.[4]

On the basis of a drawing showing an expanded version of De Bray's composition (fig. 5a),[5] it was long believed that a large section of the painting had been cut off along the right side. During restoration in 1986, however, the unpainted edges proved to be intact on all sides of the canvas, so we now know for certain that the work was at no time reduced in size.[6] Interestingly, Margarieta van Bancken's outstretched left hand still seems to recall this (presumably earlier) design of the composition, in which she draws attention to two figures approaching from the garden on the right.

When Jan de Bray made these portraits of Casteleijn and his wife in 1663, he was at the height of his career. This was the year of his first official commission: two regent portraits and an overmantel painting for the Poor Children's Home (Arme-Kinderhuis) in Haarlem.[7] As a portrait painter, he vied with his fellow townsman Frans Hals, who would die in 1666. The perfectly balanced bright palette and unusually lively composition make this double portrait one of De Bray's most attractive paintings. AvS

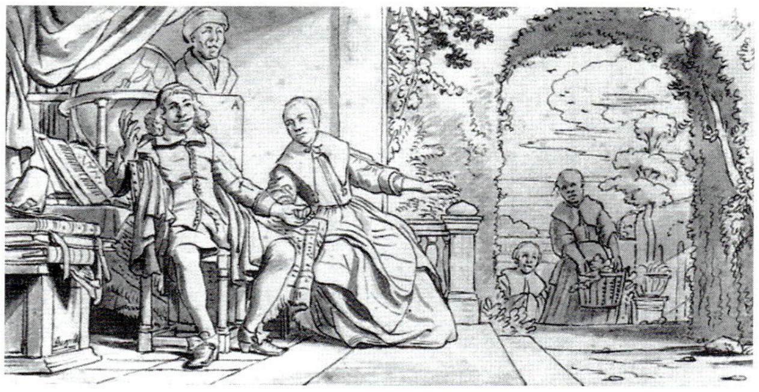

5a.
Jan de Bray,
Double Portrait of Abraham Casteleijn and Margarieta van Bancken,
about 1663. Pen and brush, 10 x 20 cm. Frits Lugt Collection, Institut Néerlandais, Paris

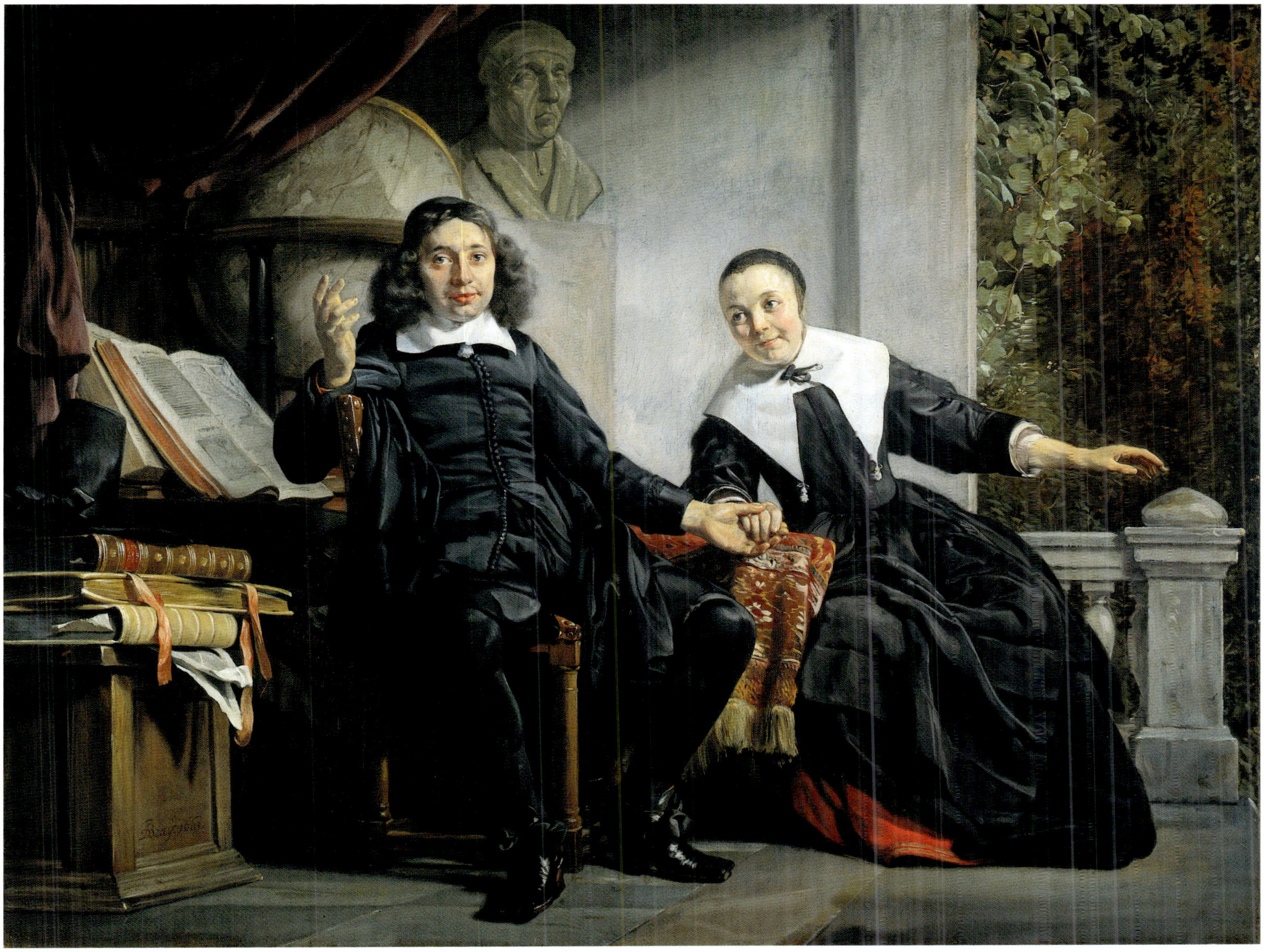

Jan de Bray

Haarlem about 1627 – 1697 Haarlem

6

Double Portrait of Salomon de Bray and Anna Westerbaen, 1664?

Oil on panel, 78.1 x 63.5 cm
National Gallery of Art, Washington (Gift of Joseph F. McCrindle)

In the spring of 1664 Haarlem was ravaged by an epidemic of the plague, and within a short space of time Jan de Bray lost his father Salomon and four of his brothers and sisters (for the De Bray family, see further cat. 4). His mother Anna Westerbaen already lay buried in St Bavo's Church, Haarlem, having died the year before. Shortly after the deaths of almost his entire family, on 17 June 1664, the unmarried Jan de Bray drew up his will, designating his sole surviving brother Dirck his universal heir. To the silversmith Gaeff Fabritius (1602–1666), then burgomaster of Haarlem, he bequeathed a self portrait that is unknown today and a work described as 'the image of his said late father and mother ... painted from the side'. De Bray stipulated that these portraits must become the property of the city of Haarlem following the death of Fabritius, and that it must always remain permissible to make copies of them.[1] Since the painter ended up outliving Fabritius – he did not die until 1697 – the silversmith never actually took possession of these bequests. It is interesting that Jan insisted that the portraits of himself and his parents remain accessible to the public: the portraits evidently served as memorials.

This is not to say that these portraits of Salomon de Bray (1597–1664) and Anna Westerbaen (about 1605–1663) were necessarily made posthumously: although the painting is undated, it is sometimes estimated as around 1660.[2] Even so, the exceptional composition, with a double profile portrait, a black curtain as background, and the couple's somewhat timeless apparel, does seem indicative of posthumous portraiture. Salomon de Bray wears a black velvet cloak, an old-fashioned white collar and a black skullcap – an item of headgear that elderly men often wore indoors in this period. Technical examination has revealed that the rhetorical gesture he makes was probably an afterthought on the painter's part.[3] Anna Westerbaen is wrapped in a black silk robe that bears no relation to the fashion of the day. If this work is indeed posthumous, it must have been painted between 11 May 1664, when Salomon de Bray died, and 17 June that year, when his son drew up his will.

A double portrait of two overlapping profiles is seen sporadically in antique cameos and medallions with – frequently posthumous – effigies of rulers and other important public figures. Peter Paul Rubens undoubtedly took his inspiration from gems of this kind when he painted a double portrait of the emperors Agrippina and Germanicus, around 1615.[4] More important as a precedent for De Bray's painting is the double profile portrait that the Antwerp painter Hendrick van Balen (1575–1632) made of himself and his wife around 1625 (fig. 6a). This can still be viewed today in an Antwerp church, where it crowns a painting of the Resurrection with an epitaph to the Van Balens.[5] Van Balen painted the double portrait especially for that memorial, where it served, in the same way as the double portrait discussed here, to keep the memory of the deceased couple alive. AvS

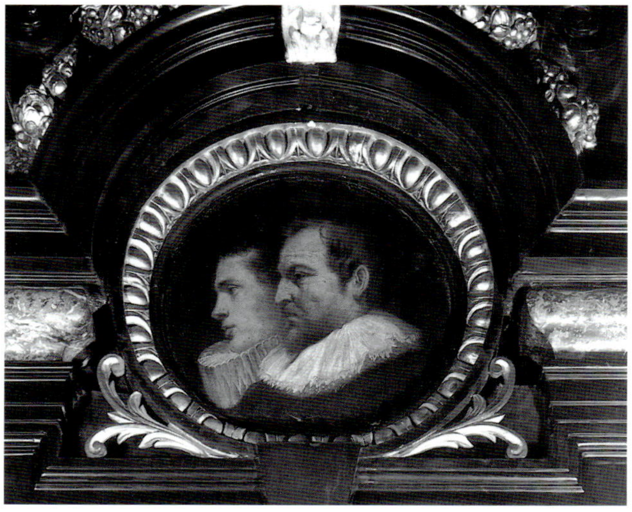

6a.
Hendrick van Balen, *Self-Portrait with his Wife, Margareta Briers*, about 1625. Sint-Jacobskerk, Antwerp (The oval double portrait hangs above a *Resurrection* painted by Van Balen himself)

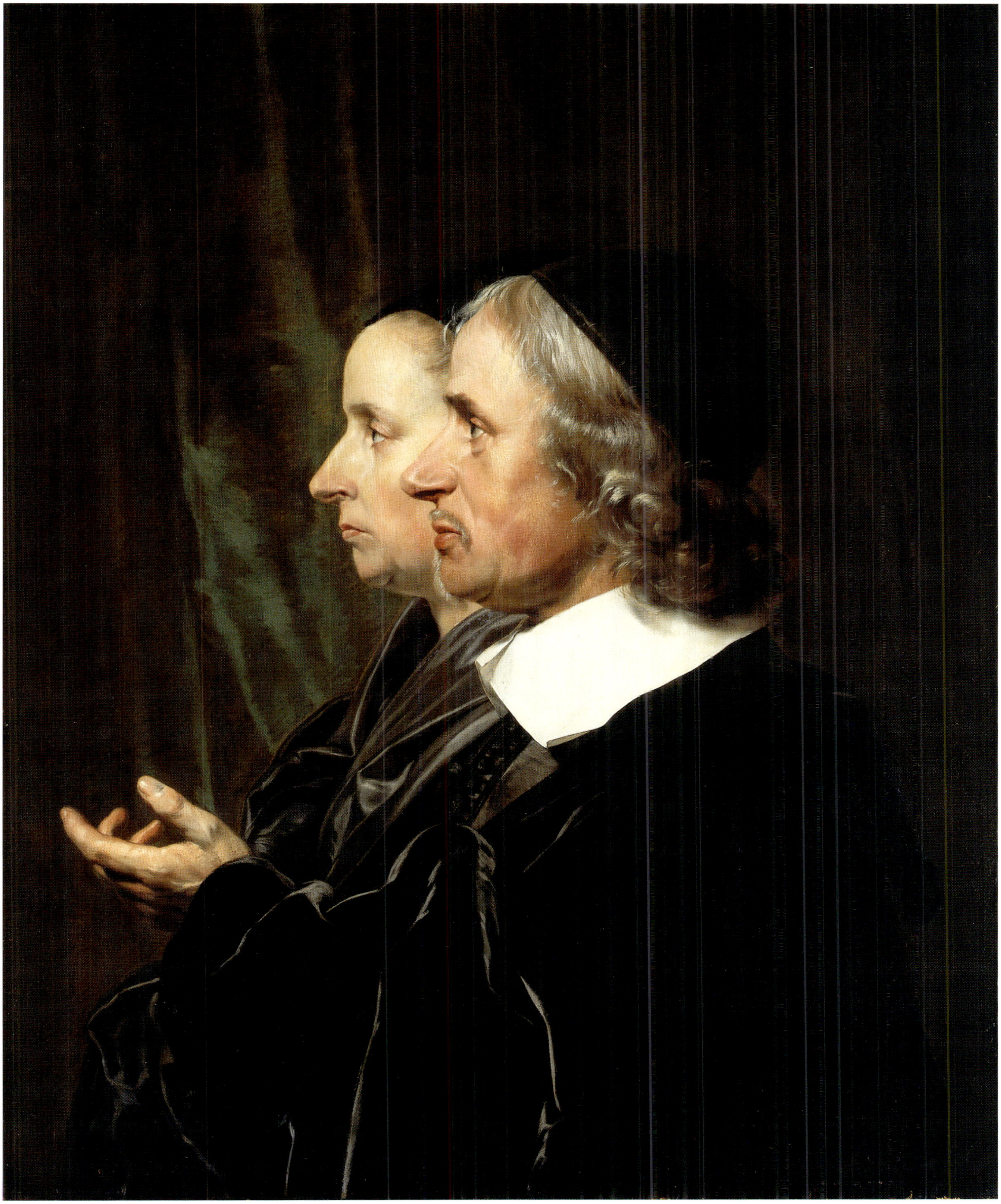

Salomon de Bray

Amsterdam 1597–1663 Haarlem

7

Double Portrait of the Twins Clara and Albert de Bray, about 1646

Oil on canvas, 82.6 x 64.8 cm
Private collection (on loan to the National Gallery of Scotland, Edinburgh)

While posthumous portraits of babies and toddlers were not uncommon in seventeenth-century Dutch painting (p. 52, fig. 48),[1] portraits of living infants were extremely rare.[2] Here we see two babies wrapped in swaddling clothes in a sculpted cradle, which encloses them in the manner of a large gold shell. The crib displays an organic style of shell-shaped or 'auricular' decoration that was popular at the time, and incorporates the torso of a cherub, whose wings merge with the cradle's asymmetrical frame. A green curtain, trimmed with gold embroidery, further envelops the cradle with the babies. The round-faced children with their bright eyes are depicted in a lifelike manner, but they are surrounded by what appears to be a baroque fantasy.

From a preliminary study made in 1646 we know that Salomon de Bray has depicted Clara and Albert de Bray, children of a nephew of the artist (fig. 7a).[3] On 12 August 1646 De Bray sketched the twins sleeping in a wicker crib with handles and a hood, and with great precision he inscribed on the drawing: '1646 8/12 / Neef [nephew] Simon de Braij Symon[szoon] / 2 lingen [twins] / Clara / en Albert'. From the positions of the names on the drawing we can conclude that Clara lies on the left and Albert on the right. The children's father, Simon de Bray, was a Haarlem solicitor who married Grietgen Pauwels of Valkenburg on 11 November 1645.[4] Perhaps the twins immortalised here were not granted long lives: there are records of 'a child born to Sijmen de Braij' being buried in St Bavo's Church, Haarlem, on 21 September 1647 and again on 8 August 1648.[5]

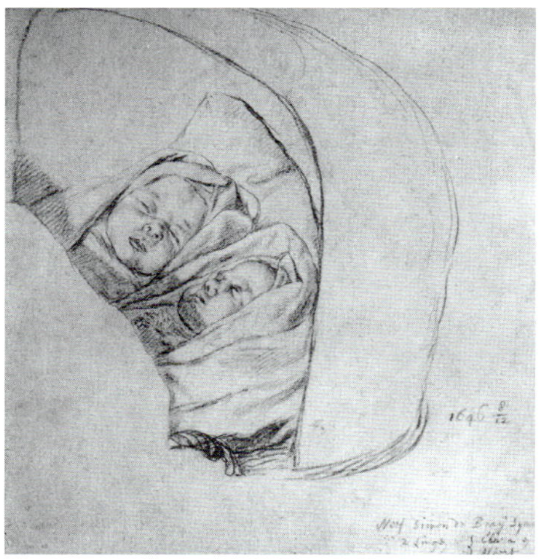

7a.
Salomon de Bray, *Double Portrait of the Twins Clara and Albert de Bray*, 1646.
Red chalk, 16 x 15 cm.
The Morgan Library & Museum, New York

This freely, confidently painted double portrait marks a highpoint in the work of Salomon de Bray, who was a poet, architect and town planner as well as a painter. In 1616 his name was first mentioned in Haarlem, where he studied under the famous masters Cornelis Cornelisz van Haarlem (1562–1638) and Hendrick Goltzius (1558–1617).[6] Like his teachers, De Bray dedicated himself primarily to history painting and made portraits only rarely. As the father of three sons who also became painters – Jan (see cats 4–6), Dirck and Joseph – De Bray appears to have headed a communal studio. In this family business, drawings would have served as important working material – not only as preliminary drawings, but also as precise records produced after paintings – and were often dated exactly.[7] The De Brays frequently used these drawings to produce more than one version of their compositions, and in fact Salomon made a second version of this portrait, depicting the babies asleep as in the preliminary drawing. This work is now lost, however.[8]

Since Clara and Albert are still firmly wrapped in swaddling clothes, we can infer that they were no more than three or four months old.[9] Their great-uncle probably made their portraits to commemorate their baptism,[10] an important milestone for this Catholic family. This is suggested not only by the gold pendants hung around their necks – probably baptismal gifts from their godparents – but also by the shell-shaped cradle, which evokes associations with baptismal fonts: indeed the twins' open eyes may symbolise that their souls have been awakened by baptism.[11] Regardless of any specific reading, this rare portrait of newborns, with its striking portrayals of the flourishing babies, its fine rendering of textures and its marvellous cradle, is a unique painting.
AvS

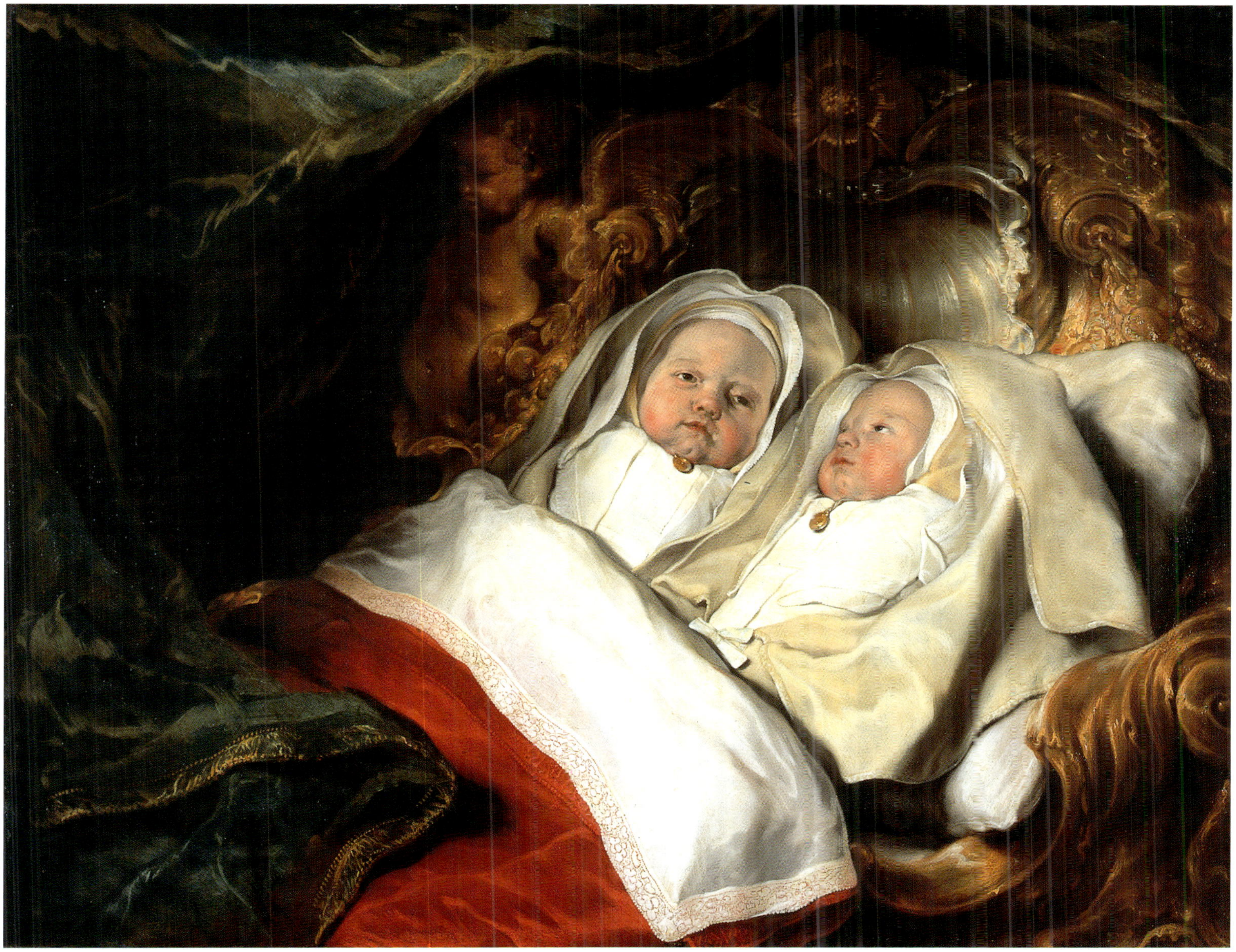

Jan Claesz

Active in Enkhuizen 1593 – 1618

8 | 9

Portrait of Albert Sonck and his Son Frans, 1602

Oil on panel, 104 x 80 cm
At upper right: . *ÆTATIS . SVÆ . 30 . / .* ANNO . *1602*
and . *ÆTATIS . SVÆ . 2 . / .* ANNO . *1602 .*
Westfries Museum, Hoorn

Portrait of Lysbeth Walichsdr and her Daughter Elisabeth, 1602

Oil on panel, 104 x 80 cm
At upper left: . *ÆTATIS . SVÆ . 27 . / .* ANNO . *1602 .*
and on the banderole in the child's hand: *ÆTATIS SVÆ . 4 .*
Westfries Museum, Hoorn

In 1602 the Hoorn merchant and town magistrate Albert Fransz Sonck (1571–1658) commissioned portraits of himself, his wife and their two children. Instead of having all four members of the family depicted together in a family group (see cat. 65), he opted for separate pendant portraits of himself and his wife, Lysbeth Claesz Walichsdr (1574/5–after 1606), each accompanied by one of the children: Albert is depicted with their son Frans (born in 1600), while his wife appears with their daughter Elisabeth (1598–1657).

The 30-year-old Sonck, whose appointment only two years earlier as councillor and town magistrate of the city of Hoorn had been the prelude to an illustrious career in public administration, is depicted standing. His right hand is raised in a gesture associated with speech, as frequently seen in images of Church ministers and professors.[1] With his left arm he embraces the little boy standing at his side, who holds a large silver jingling bell. This precious toy, a kind of rattle, consists of a silver ball with little bells hanging from it, with a whistle at one end and a wolf's tooth mounted in silver at the other. According to popular superstition, this tooth protected the child from evil spirits. In the other painting, Sonck's wife Lysbeth is depicted seated. Like her husband, she has her arm around the child beside her. The little girl is holding a carnation in her right hand; in her left is a banderole giving her age, 'ÆTATIS SVÆ . 4 .'.

The couple are dressed almost entirely in black, aside from white ruffs, bonnet and cuffs. Over Lysbeth's ordinary clothes she wears a *vlieger*, a mantle-like open gown with high shoulder-wings (see cat. 17). The adults' black-and-white apparel is entirely in tune with the fashions of the age, although rather more colour was permissible in children's clothing: besides their red sleeves the children wear white aprons – a common accessory. Boy and girl are dressed almost identically, which was customary up to six years of age; here, only the lace-trimmed rounded cap and the bonnet worn over it differ in shape.[2] More striking is the difference in hairstyle: the girl's hair is combed back, while the boy has a fringe.

The curtains in an upper corner are a characteristic feature of Jan Claesz's œuvre. In the portrait of Sonck, the opposite corner displays his family coat of arms, but evidently his wife did not have any; instead, a window is painted in the corner of her portrait, through which we glimpse a ship at sea. This image undoubtedly refers to Sonck's activities as a merchant, on which the family's prosperity depended. It may also be a biblical allusion, since the Book of Proverbs (31: 14) says of the virtuous woman, 'She is like the merchants' ships; she bringeth her food from afar'.[3]

One might have expected Sonck and his wife to have their portraits made by an artist from their hometown of Hoorn, but it seems that there was no competent painter available locally in the first decade of the seventeenth century, and Hoorn's notables gave their portrait commissions to Jan Claesz, who worked in the neighbouring town of Enkhuizen.[4] Until quite recently this artist was completely unknown, but a cohesive œuvre of about 30 unsigned paintings has now been reconstructed around a group previously described as work by the anonymous 'Master of the Enkhuizen children's portraits'.[5] On the basis of an inscription on an engraving after one of these portraits, the entire group was attributed to the Enkhuizen painter Jan Claesz, about whom very little is known. It is clear from his paintings that he must have been trained in Amsterdam around 1590 by the brothers Pieter Pietersz (p. 180, fig. 49a) and Aert Pietersz (p. 172, fig. 45a), after which he settled in the then very prosperous seaport town of Enkhuizen. There we can follow his trail until 1618, when he probably died. Among his work we find a third double portrait of a parent and child, painted a year earlier, in 1601. In that painting the child sits on the lap of its mother, who, like many of Claesz's sitters, is wearing traditional Enkhuizen costume (fig. 8–9a).[6]

Throughout his career Jan Claesz worked in the somewhat static style of the Pietersz brothers, which is characteristic of the late sixteenth century. Claesz applied this style with an extremely engaging charm, verging on naiveté, a quality ideally suited to children's portraits.[7] About half of his reconstructed œuvre consists of individual images of children and double portraits of a parent and child, suggesting he specialised somewhat in the genre. His success in paintings of this kind greatly influenced portraiture in Enkhuizen over the following decades, in which children's portraits and family groups played a prominent role. RE

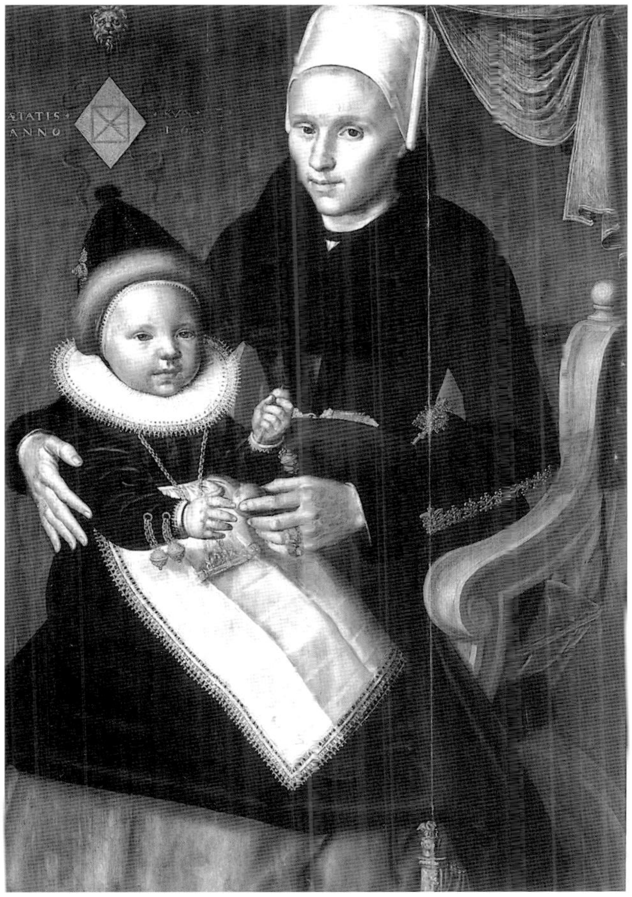

8-9a.
Jan Claesz,
Portrait of a Mother with her Child, 1601. Oil on panel, 107 x 77 cm. Nederlands Openluchtmuseum, Arnhem (on loan from the Rijksmuseum, Amsterdam)

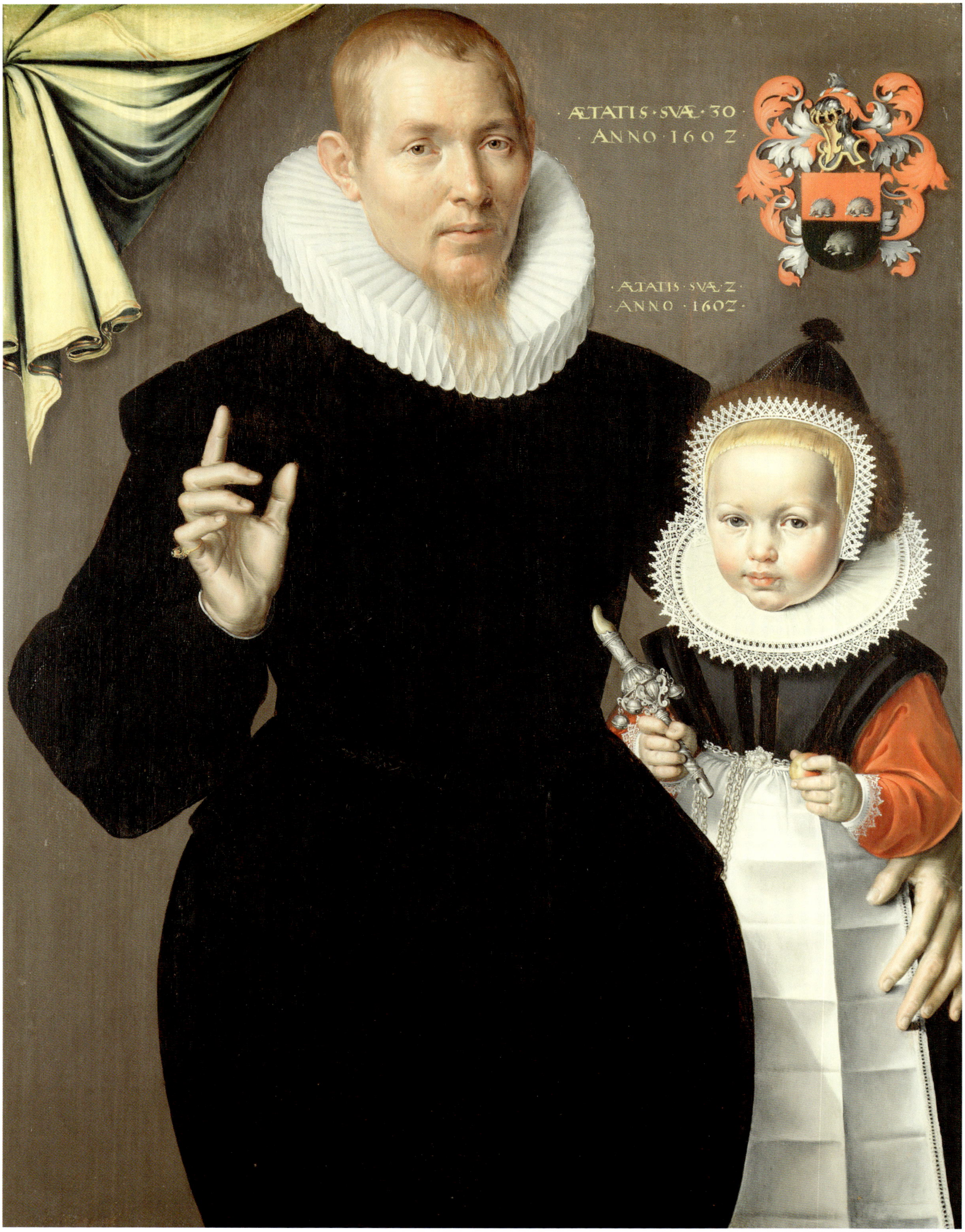
ÆTATIS·SVÆ·30·
·ANNO·1602·
·ÆTATIS·SVÆ·2·
·ANNO·1602·

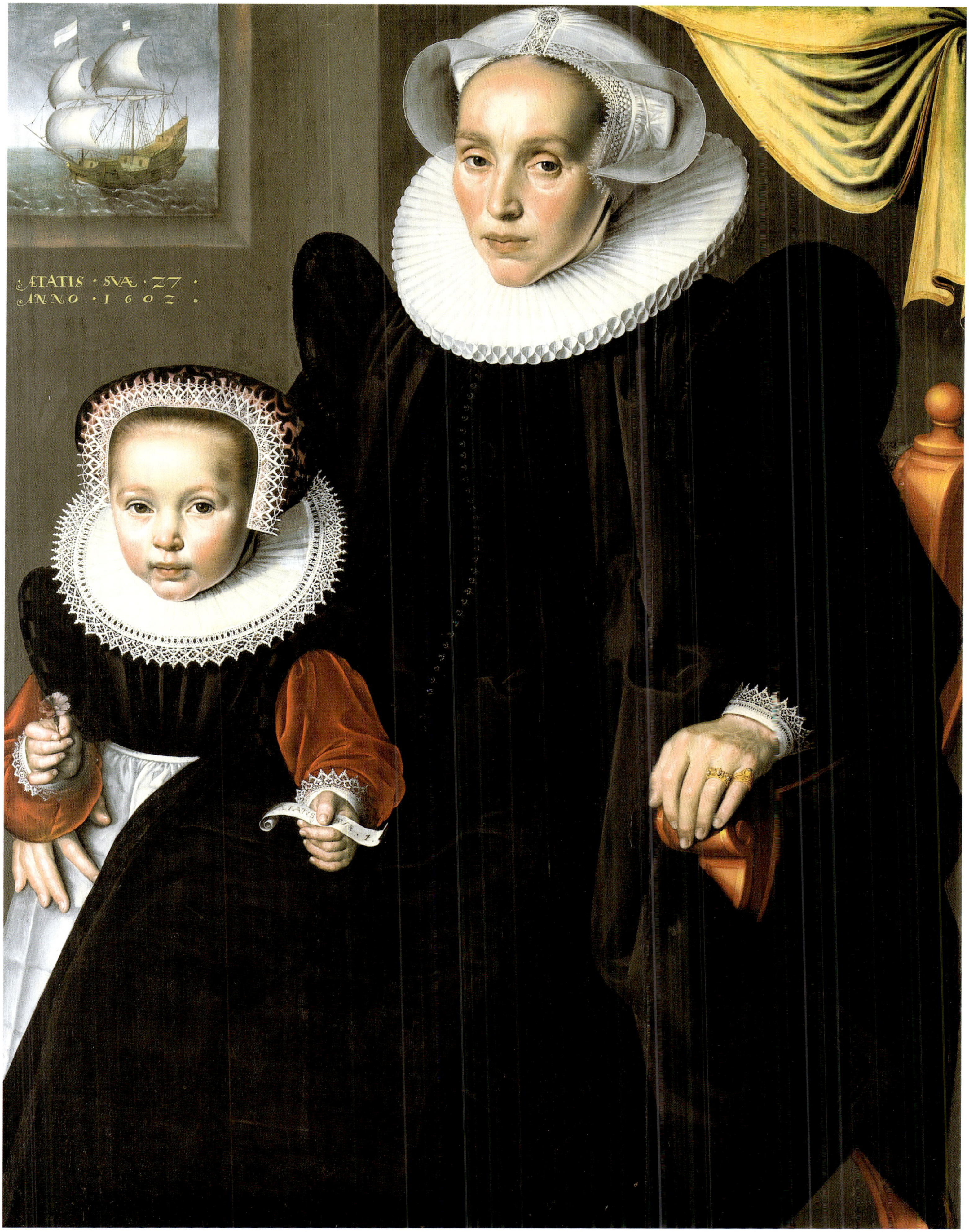
ÆTATIS · SVÆ · 27 ·
ANNO · 1602 ·

Pieter Codde

Amsterdam 1599–1678 Amsterdam

10

Double Portrait of a Married Couple, 1634

Oil on panel, 43 x 35 cm
Above the door: *16* PC *34* (PC in ligature)
Royal Picture Gallery Mauritshuis, The Hague

This attractive portrait by the Amsterdam painter Pieter Codde demonstrates clearly the influence Thomas de Keyser's portraits had on his contemporaries. Codde has painted a full-length portrait on a small panel, a fairly novel combination introduced to Amsterdam almost 15 years earlier by De Keyser (cats 33–6).[1] The modest scale of the present painting, which shows an unknown married couple, is representative of the paintings he made most frequently – 'merry company' scenes. One major exception in Codde's portrait œuvre is his contribution to the monumental *'Meagre Company'* (see cat. 21).

The meticulous rendering of the opulent, fashionable clothing – a stark contrast to the simple and somewhat clumsily depicted interior – reveals Codde's eye for detail. The clothing, based on French fashions, reflects the style favoured by wealthy young people in Holland around 1630–5. The man's black doublet is trimmed with ribbon rosettes and gold decorations; his flat collar and cuffs with bobbin lace. The fashionable nature of the man's apparel is well illustrated by his garters, tied in an extravagant bow. His companion is dressed more conservatively; although the ruff she wears was still seen among Amsterdam women in 1634, it was considered somewhat old-fashioned. Under her black overgown (*vlieger*) she wears a stomacher embroidered with floral motifs in gold thread. The black ostrich-feather fan in her right hand is attached to her clothing by a gold chain. Maerten Soolmans and Oopjen Coppit, an affluent married couple who had commissioned life-sized portraits from Rembrandt in the same year as Codde's *Double Portrait* (p. 177, figs 47–8a-b), wear even more sumptuous clothing.[2] The anonymous couple who posed for Codde undoubtedly had less money to spend than Soolmans and Coppit, however; they too are depicted full-length, but in their case they appear together in a single, much smaller, painting.[3] The man's distinctive pose – one foot forward, the other at right angles to it, one hand on his side – derives from portraits by Anthony van Dyck (1599–1641).[4]

In another painting that surfaced only recently, Codde depicted a couple with their hands intimately entwined as here, in a similar interior. In this work, the man and the woman – again their identity is unknown – have changed places.[5] In accordance with heraldic tradition, a married woman was customarily depicted to her husband's right – as seen by the viewer – in portrait paintings.[6] Curiously, in the current painting, Codde has flouted this convention. That the couple depicted here are indeed married is clear from the woman's *vlieger* overgown, a garment that was worn only by married women (see p. 67).[7] On the index finger of her right hand she wears what is undoubtedly her wedding ring, with a black stone. Her 'bridal gloves' (see cat. 36) lie on the table to the right. The painting is thus a variation on the traditional wedding portrait.[8]

This double portrait, with a ready-made composition in the background, merely needed to be 'filled in', as it were: the setting of Codde's recently discovered double portrait is virtually identical to this one. In both pieces the figures are posed against a plain wall with an open door to the side, and the artist's monogram is incorporated into the moulded crown of the door. Both works include a small table and a simple wooden floor with the same structure. This background adds depth, but perhaps it was also chosen for another reason: the motif of an open door, here creating the impression that the couple have just walked into the painter's studio, may be construed as an allusion to human mortality.[9] Codde also included the motif in an allegorical painting from 1625, where it symbolises vanity and mortality.[10] QB

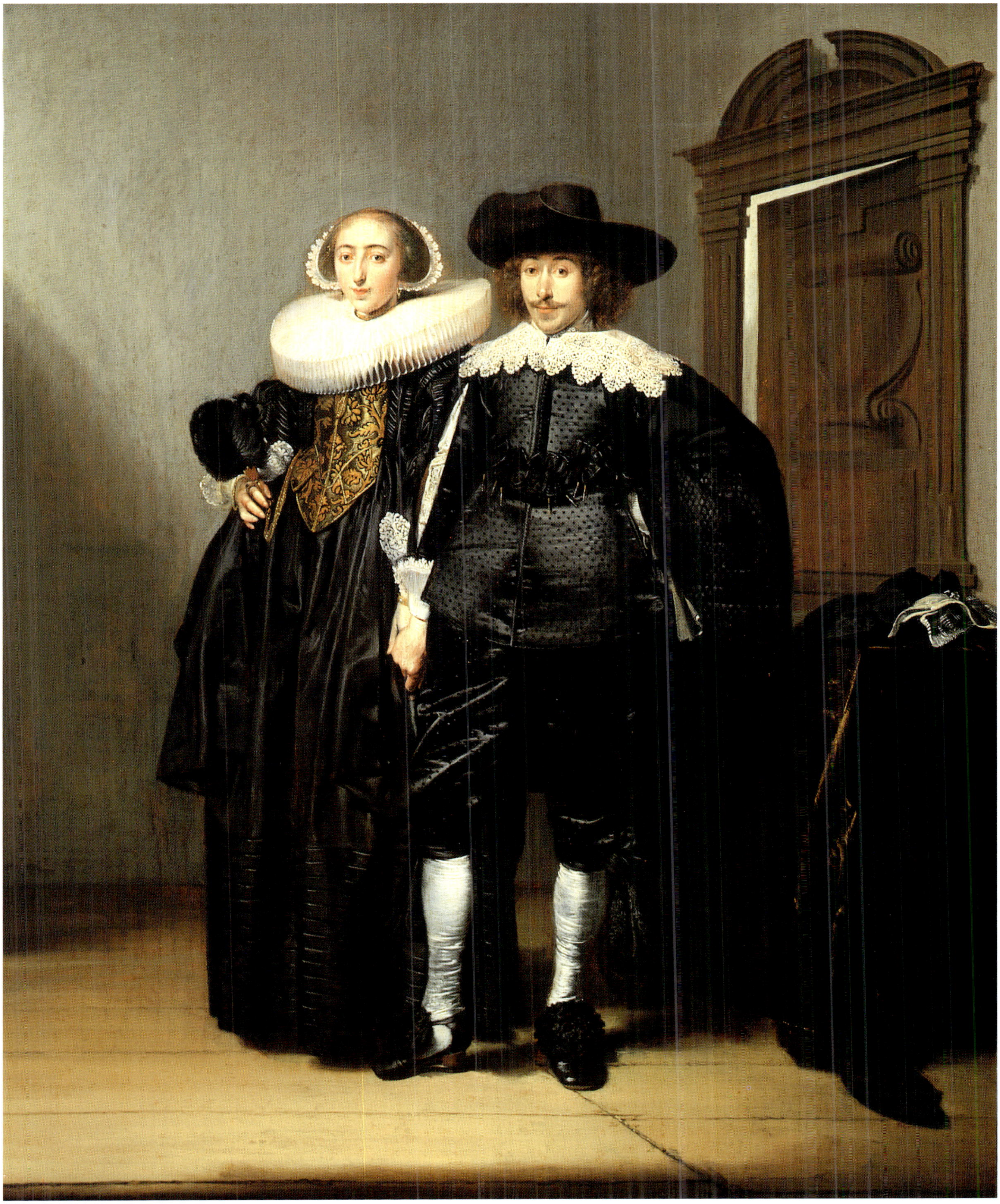

Jacob Gerritsz Cuyp

Dordrecht 1594–1652 Dordrecht

11

Portrait of Michiel Pompe van Slingelandt as a Falconer, 1649

Oil on panel, 106.5 x 77.8 cm
At lower right: *JCūÿp. fecit.* / *A° 1649* (JC in ligature);
between the feet: *Ætatis. 6.* / *1649*
Dordrechts Museum, Dordrecht (on loan from the Netherlands Institute for Cultural Heritage, Amsterdam/Rijswijk)

Though he left behind a highly varied œuvre, Jacob Gerritsz Cuyp specialised chiefly in history pieces and portraits and became the most popular portraitist in Dordrecht in the first half of the seventeenth century. In the past, this painting was wrongly attributed to Jacob's more famous son Aelbert.[1] This confusion is entirely understandable when one realises that the elder Cuyp drew inspiration from his son: one of the latter's drawings inspired the landscape behind the boy, with its small riverside village.[2] Sometimes Aelbert even painted the landscape in his father's portraits.[3]

The child who fills almost the entire picture plane is Michiel Pompe van Slingelandt (1643–1685), a scion of a prominent Dordrecht regent family who later became town magistrate of Dordrecht.[4] The boy's age is inscribed prominently between his feet: '*Ætatis. 6.*' (six years old). He was the eldest son of Matthijs Pompe (1621–1679), a man who attached great importance to his family's social status. The father's noble pretensions are clearly reflected in this portrait: Michiel is shown hunting, an activity that was originally the exclusive prerogative of the nobility. Matthijs Pompe was not of noble birth, but claimed the right to hunt after he purchased the manors of Slingelandt and Capelle. The boy is depicted almost as a young prince – full-length, from a low vantage point. A bird perches on his hand, which is protected by a falconer's glove; with the other hand he points to the partridge dog. It seems that neither painter nor client was entirely familiar with the details of falconry,[5] for the bird depicted here is not a hunting falcon but a kestrel, which only hunts small creatures such as mice. In addition, the bird appears to be spreading its wings, poised to fly away, and yet a hood has just been placed over its head – a device used to keep the bird still; there should also be a bell attached to one of the bird's legs to help the falconer find it after a kill. The unusual clothing is a further sign that this portrait does not depict a real hunting scene: the red coat appears to have been inspired by Turkish fashions. Even the hilt of the boy's sword has a rather exotic appearance, as do his antique-styled sandals and plumed cap.[6] Idealised clothing of this kind (which would have been unsuitable for hunting) is encountered frequently in children's portraits.[7] By way of contrast, not long after this picture was painted, Aelbert Cuyp depicted two of Michiel's cousins in an equestrian portrait that does show an authentic hunting scene (fig. 11a).[8]

Michiel's father evidently loved to commission portraits. In 1644 the Rotterdam painter Hendrick Sorgh (1610/11–1670) depicted Matthijs Pompe and his first wife, Mondina van Beveren, with the one-year-old Michiel on her lap. Separate portraits (by an unknown artist) were made of Matthijs Pompe and his daughter Christina, who was born in 1647. The Hague painter Jan Mijtens produced a second group portrait around 1654, showing Matthijs Pompe with his second wife, Elisabeth, and daughter Christina.[9] Of all these works, the present painting is unquestionably the liveliest. QB

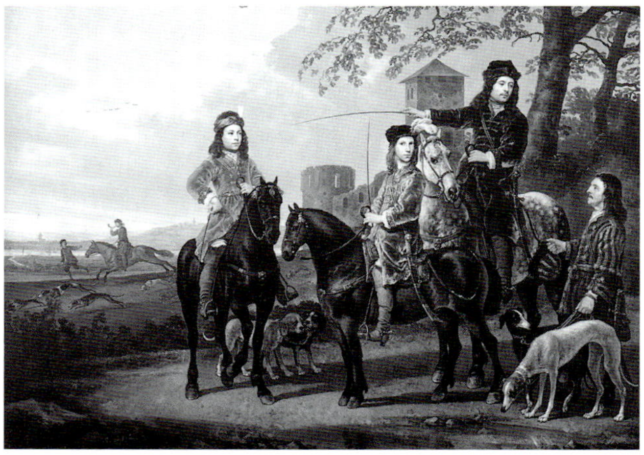

11a. Aelbert Cuyp, *Portrait of Michiel and Cornelis Pompe van Meerdervoort*, about 1652–3. Oil on canvas, 110 x 156 cm. The Metropolitan Museum of Art, New York (bequest of Michael Friedsam, 1914)

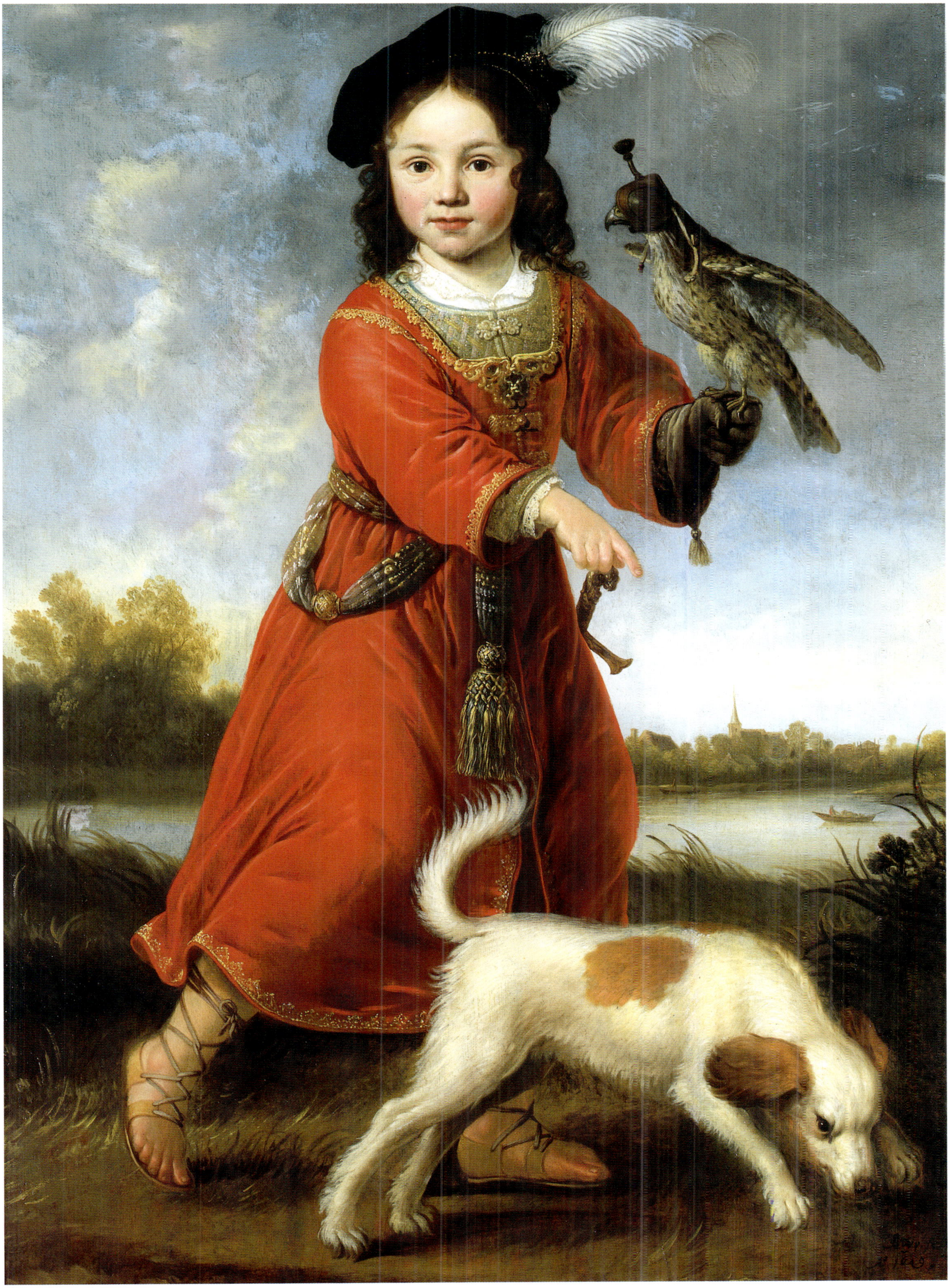

Gerrit Dou

Leiden 1613 – 1675 Leiden

12

Portrait of a Young Woman, about 1655?

Oil on panel (oval), 14.5 x 11.7 cm
Centre left: GDOV (GD in ligature)
The National Gallery, London

Gerrit Dou, the founder of the school of Leiden *fijnschilders*, is most readily associated with exquisite, highly elaborate and detailed genre scenes. Yet this ignores the fact that he spent much of his early career in the 1630s painting portraits and *tronies* (depictions of anonymous 'heads' studies) and single full-length figures. Many of these early portraits are bust-, half- and three-quarter-length images that exclude all narrative detail.[1] The genre scenes that come to mind when we think of Dou really only emerged within his œuvre in the mid-1640s, from which time portraits occupied a less prominent place in his work.

This portrait of an anonymous woman is a small – almost miniaturistic – oval, with a half-length view of the sitter. Her head is turned slightly towards the viewer, whom she fixes with an alert gaze. She wears the sort of noticeably informal everyday dress that one would expect to find in a genre scene rather than in a portrait. Her fur-trimmed green jacket is fastened with a ribbon at the front, and underneath we can see a partlet that serves to cover the décolletage. Her head is covered with a black veil as protection against the sun, a feature also found in other Dutch paintings. The sitter's pearl necklace and earrings add elegance to the intimate depiction. The informality of the dress may suggest that this was not a standard commission, but a more casual portrait of one of Dou's relatives. When the picture entered the National Gallery in 1876, it was described as 'The Painter's Wife', an identification attached to the painting from at least 1823, when it first appeared on the British art market.[2] This identification is impossible, however, since Dou never married.

The dating of the picture has been the subject of ongoing debate. In his catalogue of the Dutch paintings in the National Gallery, Neil MacLaren suggested a date of about 1655–60.[3] Sumowski agreed, relating the painting on stylistic grounds to two other works by the artist.[4] In the revised edition of MacLaren's catalogue, Christopher Brown argued that the paint handling was too loose for a painting of this date, and instead proposed a date of around 1640.[5] More recently, Ronni Baer has pointed out that the particular style of the sitter's costume does not appear in Dou's work until the 1660s.[6] A complicating factor is that Dou seems to have reworked the composition and that the paint handling visible in the X-radiograph of the picture may well date the picture to the late 1630s or early 1640s. In her analysis of the costume, however, Marieke de Winkel argues that a date of 1640 would be too early; it may thus be that MacLaren's original suggestion comes closest to the truth, and that we must assume a date in the 1650s for this charming likeness. AR

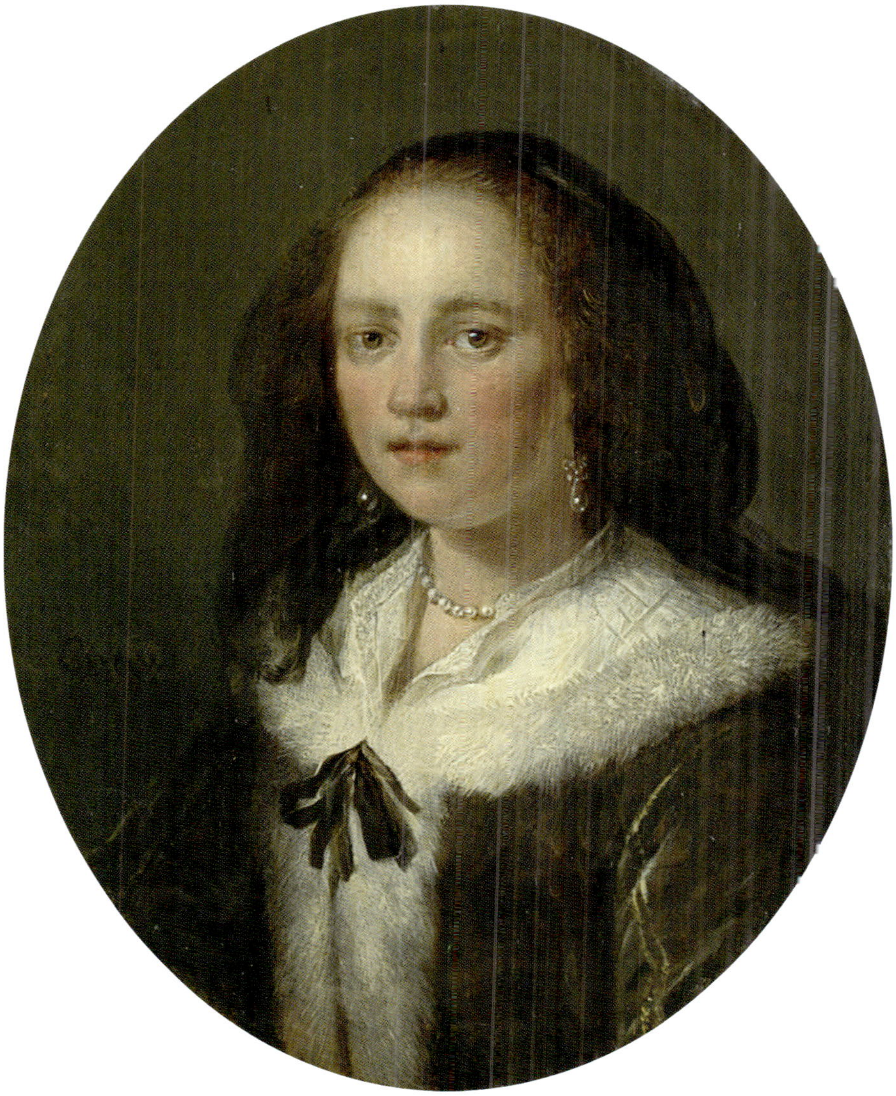

Govert Flinck

Cleves 1615–1660 Amsterdam

13

Portrait of Margaretha Tulp, 1655

Oil on canvas, 138 x 104 cm
At upper right: *G. Flinck f. 1655*
Gemäldegalerie Alte Meister,
Staatliche Museen, Kassel
The Hague only

On 20 July 1655 the marriage of Margaretha Tulp (1634–1709) and Jan Six (1618–1700) took place in Amsterdam. The bride was the daughter of the well-known physician Nicolaes Tulp (see cats 46, 53), while the groom came from a prominent regent family. Govert Flinck's 1655 portrait of Margaretha was probably painted to commemorate the marriage. No portrait was commissioned of the bridegroom, perhaps because Six had been immortalised by Rembrandt the year before (cat. 57). The current portrait does not appear to have been intended as a pendant for that work; not only is Flinck's portrait significantly larger, but it also seems logical to assume that Rembrandt himself would have been approached had an actual pendant been required. Flinck had started as an apprentice with Rembrandt around 1635, and during this period his work resembles his master's style of painting. By 1655, however, when the portrait of Margaretha Tulp was made, little of this resemblance remained. The relatively smooth handling and elegant composition attest to the influence of the Amsterdam portrait painter Bartholomeus van der Helst (cats 29–30), whose portraits of this kind, made from 1640 onwards, were particularly in vogue.

Margaretha is depicted in an imaginary costume loosely based on the fashion of her day. Flinck has left off the lace collar and cuffs, which makes the costume difficult to date. The bodice of the dress is fastened at the front using clasps known as *agraffes*, a delightfully fanciful element. The over-sized pearls she wears attached to bows on her ears also defy reality, since pearls of this size do not occur in the natural world. Her head is draped with a transparent black veil.[1]

Flinck placed his subject in a park-like setting, surrounded by objects that allude to her marital status and her family.[2] The fountain on the right, surmounted by a statue of Amor, god of love, is a traditional feature of the 'garden of love' (see p. 108). In this context the coiled serpent at Amor's feet refers to the boundlessness of love.[3] Margaretha's right hand is in front of her breast, while in her left she holds a sprig of flowers near the fountain; in the traditional iconography of the marriage portrait, this can be construed as a reference to her vow of fidelity.[4] The open tulip in the flower-pot on the parapet seems to be a simple allusion to Margaretha's last name (Tulp meaning tulip).[5] In seventeenth-century portraits of women, pearls often symbolised the sitter's chastity or virginity. Here they may also have been intended as allusions to Margaretha's first name, given that *margarita* is the Latin for pearl.[6] That is precisely how Margaretha usually signed her own name, and it appears with this spelling in the baptismal register.[7]

The marriage of Margaretha Tulp and Jan Six attracted considerable publicity, and the Dutch poet Joost van den Vondel penned a commemorative verse in honour of the occasion.[8] In 1656 he also dedicated a short poem to Margaretha Tulp – which was not published for four years – inspired by the portrait discussed here.[9] In accordance with the literary tradition of his day, his poem plays on the way the painter successfully deceives the viewer in his imitation of nature:

To the lady MARGRIETE TULP
Wife of JOAN SIX
Painted by Govert Flinck

ANIMUM PICTURA PASCIT INANI
[He nourishes his soul with a lifeless painting][10]

A brook's clear waters showed Margrite her face
Alive beneath the surface like a pearl.
Now art with hue and paint her form doth trace,
And true to life, her lineaments unfurl.
When Six beheld this work, his heart caught fire.
He took the charming portrait for the source,
His Tulip, darling Deity of Song.
His blood grew hot, and through his veins did course.
He kissed the image; had it done the same,
The very painting could have quenched his flame.

PP

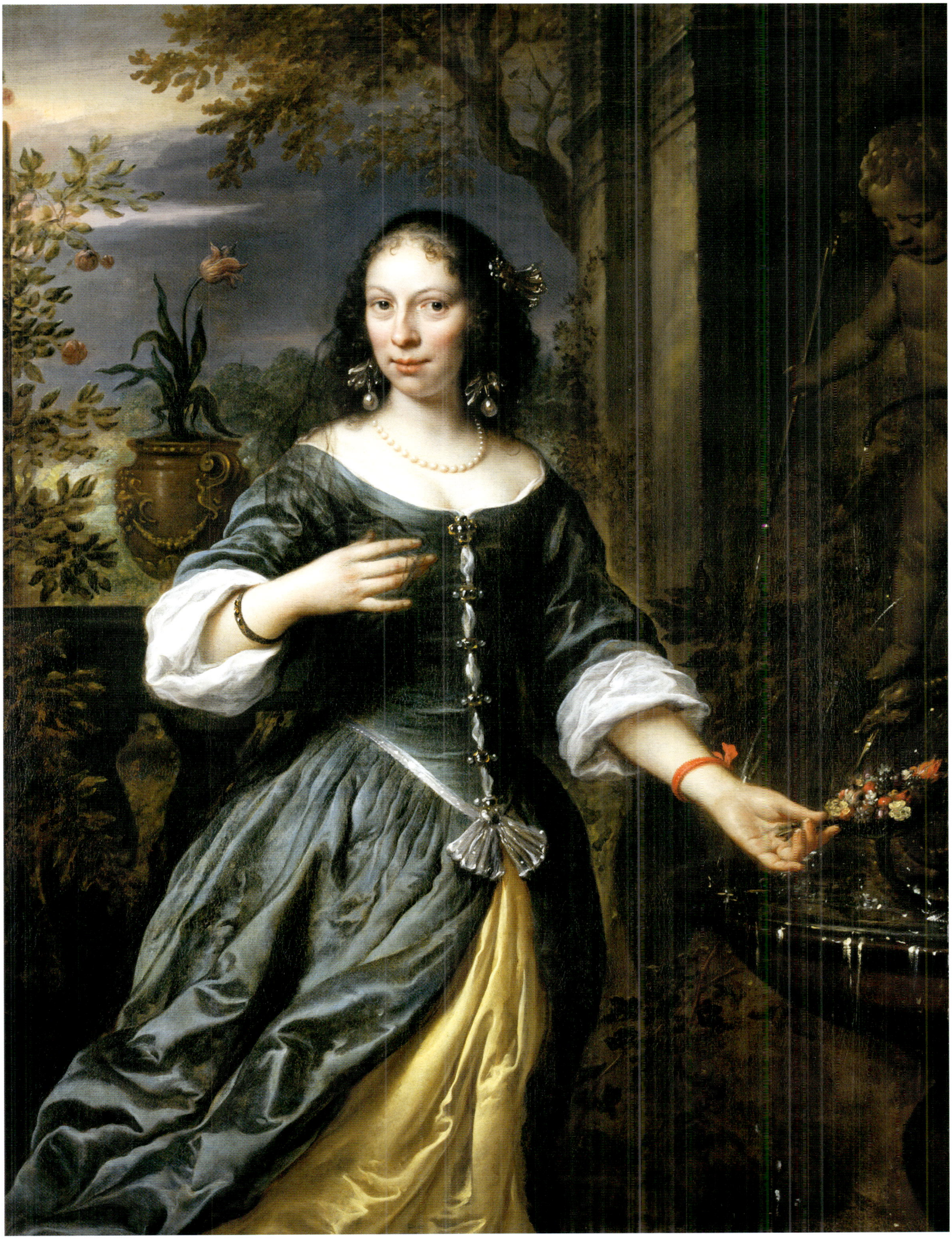

Frans Hals

Antwerp 1582/3 – 1666 Haarlem

14

Portrait of Catharina Hooft and her Nurse, about 1620

Oil on canvas, 92 x 68 cm
Gemäldegalerie, Staatliche Museen, Berlin

In this painting Frans Hals depicted a subject rarely seen in portraiture: a young child with her nurse.[1] The little girl is Catharina Hooft, born in Amsterdam on 28 December 1618, the only child of the lawyer Pieter Hooft and Geertruyd Overlander.[2] Shortly after Catha-rina's baptism, in January 1619, the Hooft family left for Haarlem, where Hals made this portrait. At age 16, Catharina married Cornelis de Graeff, an extremely wealthy man who later became burgomaster of Amsterdam. The couple had their portraits painted by Nicolaes Eliasz Pickenoy in 1636, a year after their marriage (cats 47–8).

Although she appears older than 12 months here, the painting was probably commissioned for Catharina's first birthday and made soon after in 1620. In the seventeenth century, this was the age at which a child parted company with his or her nurse.[3] Nurses temporarily assumed the birth mother's caring role, which often included breast-feeding, creating a strong attachment between child and carer that frequently extended to other family members. This relationship sometimes lasted a lifetime, as is clear from wills that include bequests to children's old nurses.[4] Conversely, the nurse would sometimes leave her savings or a portrait of herself to the children she had cared for.[5] That Hals should have been asked to make this double portrait underscores the special role of the anonymous nurse in the Hooft family's household.

The difference in status between child and adult in this portrait makes it clear that the woman was not the mother.[6] The nurse's black clothing and flat ruff were old-fashioned by 1620, and the same applies to her cap, a style that had been popular 20 years earlier. This modest apparel contrasts sharply with that of the child, who is dressed in sumptuous attire, almost like a princess. The flat collar is in the latest French fashion and is trimmed with expensive lace, which has also been used on her cuffs, cap and *feitel* – a little bib pinned to the child's bodice, which has a largely decorative function here. Catharina's privileged circumstances are reflected in her clothing: the dress, richly decorated with floral and vine motifs; the gold brocade cap; the gold bracelets and necklace, from which is suspended a precious cut stone. The elaborately sculpted gold rattle, an expensive toy that further emphasises the child's high social status,[7] does not immediately catch our eye because it is nearly hidden by the splendid patterns on her dress. From the length of the skirt – this meticulously rendered garment is longer than the child's legs – one may conclude that Catharina was not yet able to walk when this portrait was painted (hanging down her back we see two leading reins – incorporated into her dress – suggesting that this stage was not far away). Toddlers, on the other hand, were dressed in short clothes and their heads were protected from bumps with special caps.[8] Learning to walk was seen in the seventeenth century as a protracted learning process that required a great deal of adult help.

Hals's portraits often create the impression of capturing a brief moment in time, something that certainly applies to this unique double portrait. Child and nurse both gaze towards the viewer, and the nurse appears about to give the child the apple. The prominence given to this fruit is surely no accident: since the late Middle Ages, the presentation of an apple was a recurring motif in paintings of the Virgin and Child. In this Christian context, an apple stands for the original sin of Adam and Eve, from which Christ redeemed humanity.[9] In this child's portrait, the fruit could stand for the transfer of knowledge.[10] Symbolic or not, Hals's exquisite portrait exudes a wonderfully relaxed atmosphere. The smiling nurse has a kindly air, and Catharina's mischievous gaze is very engaging. The way in which she leans her right hand against the nurse emphasises the trusting relationship between the two. QB

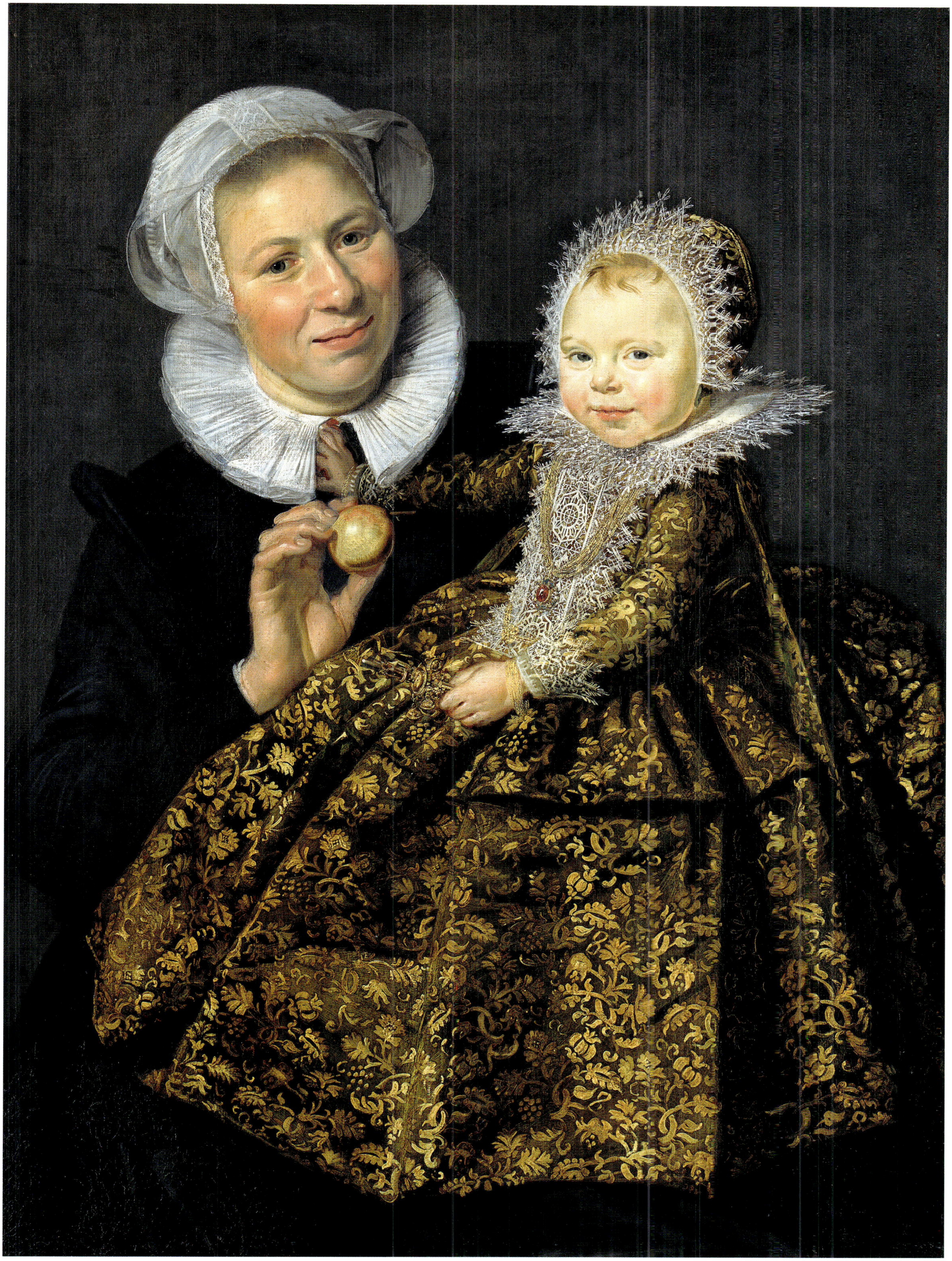

Frans Hals

Antwerp 1582/3 – 1666 Haarlem

15

Double Portrait of Isaac Massa and Beatrix van der Laen, about 1622

Oil on canvas, 140 x 167 cm
Rijksmuseum, Amsterdam

There are not many smiles in seventeenth-century portraits, but here a man and a woman gaze at the viewer from an elevated spot in a landscape, each with a prepossessing grin on their faces (the woman's smile is somewhat warmer than her husband's). Frans Hals always imparted a distinctive quality to his images, and he was one of the few portraitists of the Golden Age to depict his subjects smiling (see also cats 14, 23 and p. 30, fig. 20). The man and woman here have every reason to beam at us, since the portrait was made shortly after their marriage, and almost certainly commemorated it. The couple have been identified as the Haarlem merchant Isaac Massa (1586–1643) and Beatrix van der Laen (1592–1639), whose father was burgomaster of Haarlem;[1] they were married in Haarlem on 25 April 1622. The couple possessed a considerable fortune and belonged to their city's elite. Though undated, a date of 1622 can be proposed on stylistic grounds. As a double portrait, this painting is unique in Hals's œuvre;[2] in other cases he always depicted husband and wife in separate paintings, as in the Olycans' marriage portrait from 1625 (cats 16–17). A decade earlier, around 1610, the Antwerp painter Peter Paul Rubens depicted himself with his new wife, Isabella Brant, in a honeysuckle bower (fig. 15a), a comparable image of a married couple in an idealised garden setting,[3] and Hals may have seen this portrait when he visited Antwerp in 1616.

That this is a marriage portrait can be inferred from, among other things, the woman's clothing and jewellery. On her right hand she wears rings – her engagement and wedding ring – which are conspicuous because the white skin of her hand stands out against the dark clothing. A precious diamond is mounted in the ring on her index finger. Hals rendered the rings with a great eye for detail; he has also devoted meticulous care to the garments, which are painted in vigorous brushstrokes. Massa is dressed in the latest French fashions, exemplified by his understated lace collar and wide-brimmed hat. His loose black breeches have buttons at the sides and his silk garters are tied in a bow below the knee. Van der Laen wears a Spanish-style costume with a large ruff. Her *vlieger* overgown with its shoulder-wings denotes her new status as a married woman, since this garment was not worn before marriage (see p. 67).

The painting is rich with other elements that allude to the couple's recent wedding, carefully chosen to represent interlaced symbolic connotations of a long-lasting union. For example, the realistically rendered vegetation is more than just part of the landscape. Seventeenth-century emblems – prints with accompanying mottoes (see fig. 15b) – tell us that plants could convey covert meanings. The large thistle at lower left, the ivy at lower right, and the vines winding around the tree-trunk between the newly-weds all refer to love, marriage and faithfulness.[4] A tree with a climbing plant wound around it has been associated with these three concepts – and with affection and friendship – since time immemorial. Friendship was equated with marital love in the seventeenth century. The prominence accorded the vegetation twining between the two figures demonstrates the importance attached to this symbol. Like the vine, the ivy at the woman's feet alludes to enduring love. Just as ivy clings to a wall or a tree, it was thought that a woman will cling to her husband. The thistle beside the man was a symbol of male faithfulness in marriage, taken from the plant's popular old German name, 'Männertreu' (man's fidelity). Even the ostensibly casual pose of the figures is not without significance. Massa expresses his love by placing his hand on his heart. His wife rests her hand on his upper arm. This too is no random gesture: just as the leafy vine is upheld by the tree, the woman seeks the support of her husband.[5]

Hals has depicted the figures to the left of centre, quite a daring decision in a marriage portrait. By doing so, he has left ample space for a park-like scene (in his *Portrait of Willem van Heythuysen* it is a mere glimpse; see cat. 18). Since this decorative part of the scene takes up almost half of the painting, it cannot be lacking in significance. Two couples stroll arm in arm past a statue, a fountain, and a building in neo-classical style. Judging

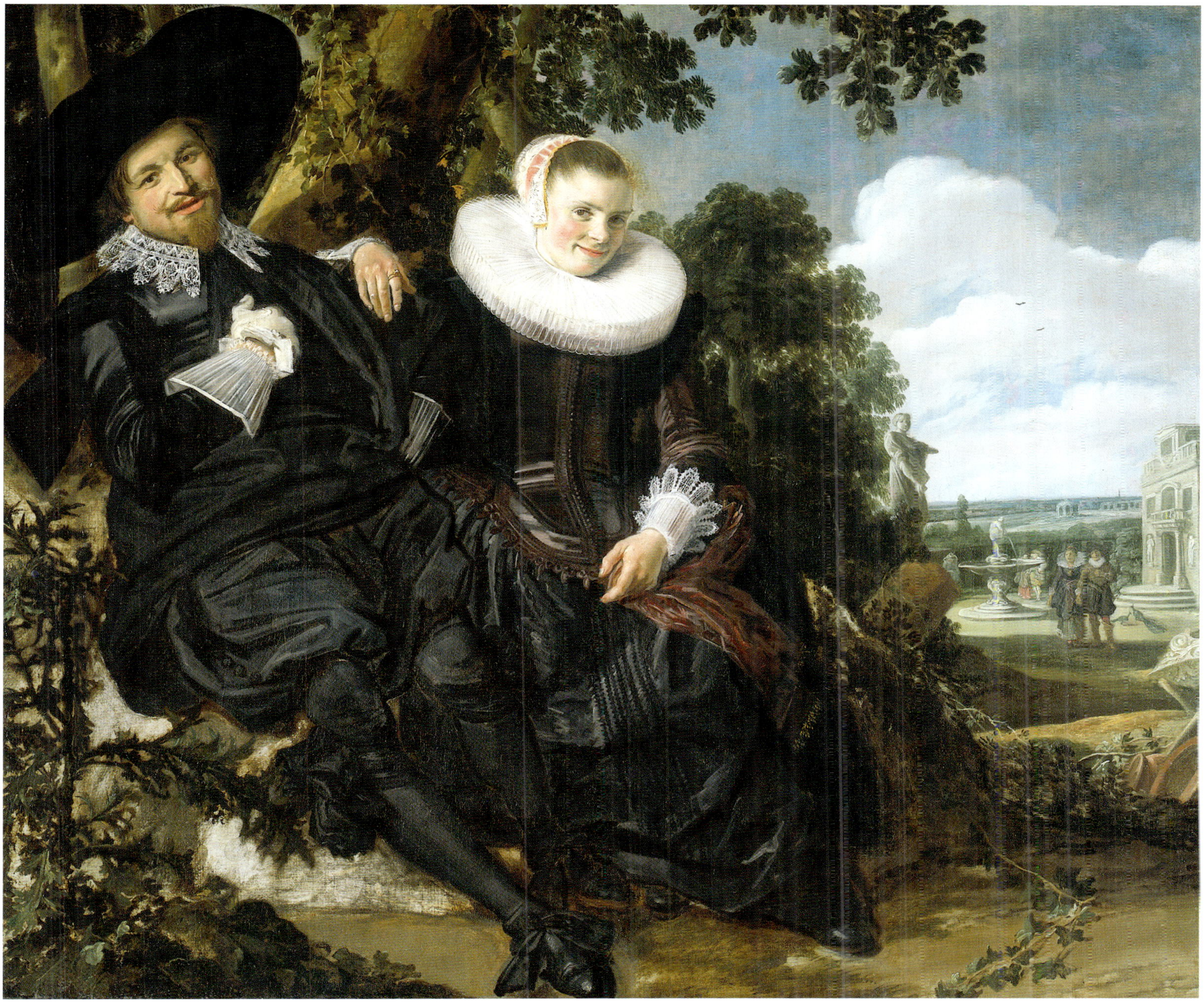

15a.
Peter Paul Rubens,
Self-Portrait with his Wife, Isabella Brant,
about 1609–10.
Canvas on panel,
178 x 137 cm.
Alte Pinakothek,
Munich

15b.
Andrea Alciati,
Amicitia etiam post mortem durans
(Friendship Enduring even beyond Death).
Emblem from Alciati's
Emblematum libellus,
Paris 1534

by the women's clothing – they are not wearing *vliegers* with their characteristic shoulder-wings – these couples are not yet married.[6] Their unmarried status can also be inferred from the position they occupy relative to the men – to their left, as seen by the viewer.[7] Married women were generally depicted to the right of their husbands, as seen here. The peacocks in the garden allude to Juno, the goddess of marriage, who was venerated as the patroness of married women, but whether she can be recognised in the garden statue is uncertain. The garden itself is a wholly idealised creation, derived from the Late Mediaeval concept of the 'Garden of Love' (see also cat. 29), to which love, marriage and fertility are central.

There is a further symbolic detail included with the two terracotta pots in the right foreground and the capital behind them. These elements do not immediately catch the eye, and are indeed partially cut off by the edge of the picture, but together they symbolise the fragility of human life.[8] Although the newly-weds are mortal, their love seems indestructible: in the emblem literature the evergreen ivy (seen here in the foreground) is a symbol of friendship or love that endures beyond death (fig. 15b).[9]

Extensive symbolism such as that described here is rare in the portraits of Frans Hals. In addition, this is the only double portrait that Hals ever made of a married couple. It therefore seems highly likely that the details of the painting were partly inspired by suggestions or instructions by the client, Massa.[10] Massa was an erudite man, who attracted praise for his fine intellect at an early age. He did much to develop diplomatic ties between the Dutch Republic and Russia, where he lived before his marriage. The informal nature of the portrait appears to reflect the good relations that existed between painter and client. Massa was a witness to the baptism of one of the painter's daughters in July 1623 – that is, shortly after the completion of this portrait.[11] In later years he would commission at least two more portraits from Hals.[12] QB

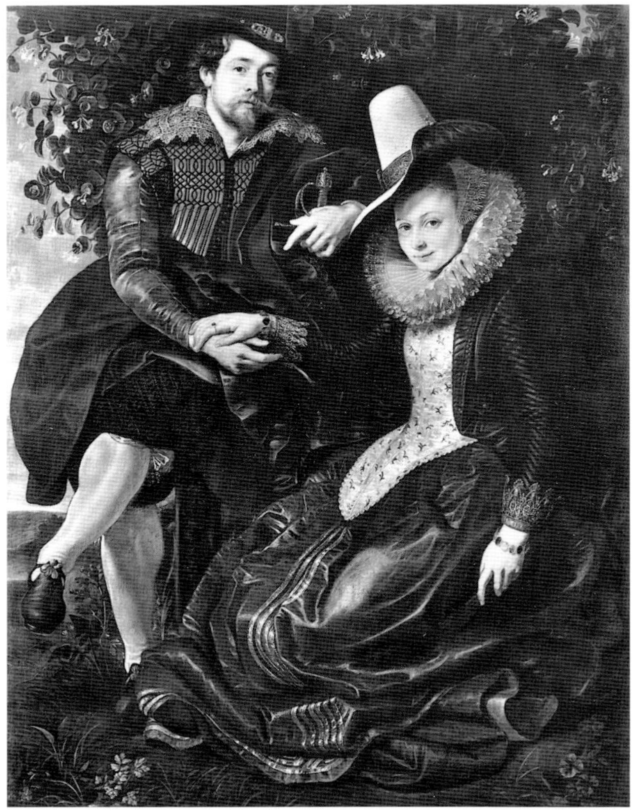

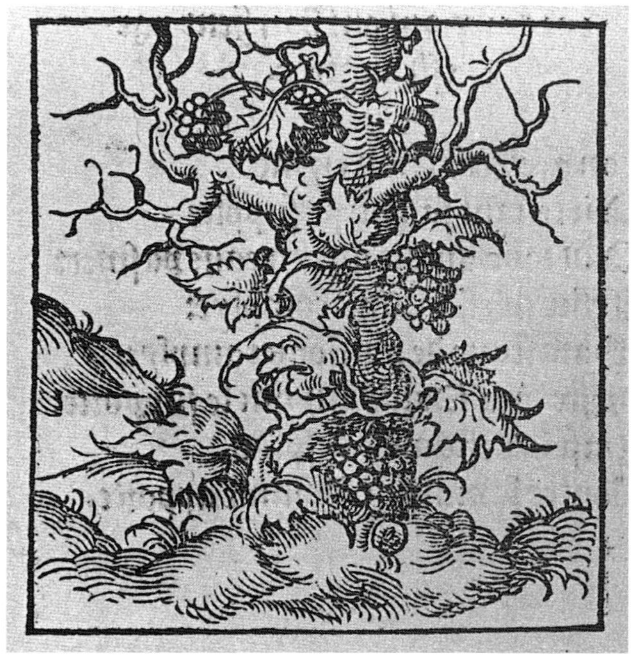

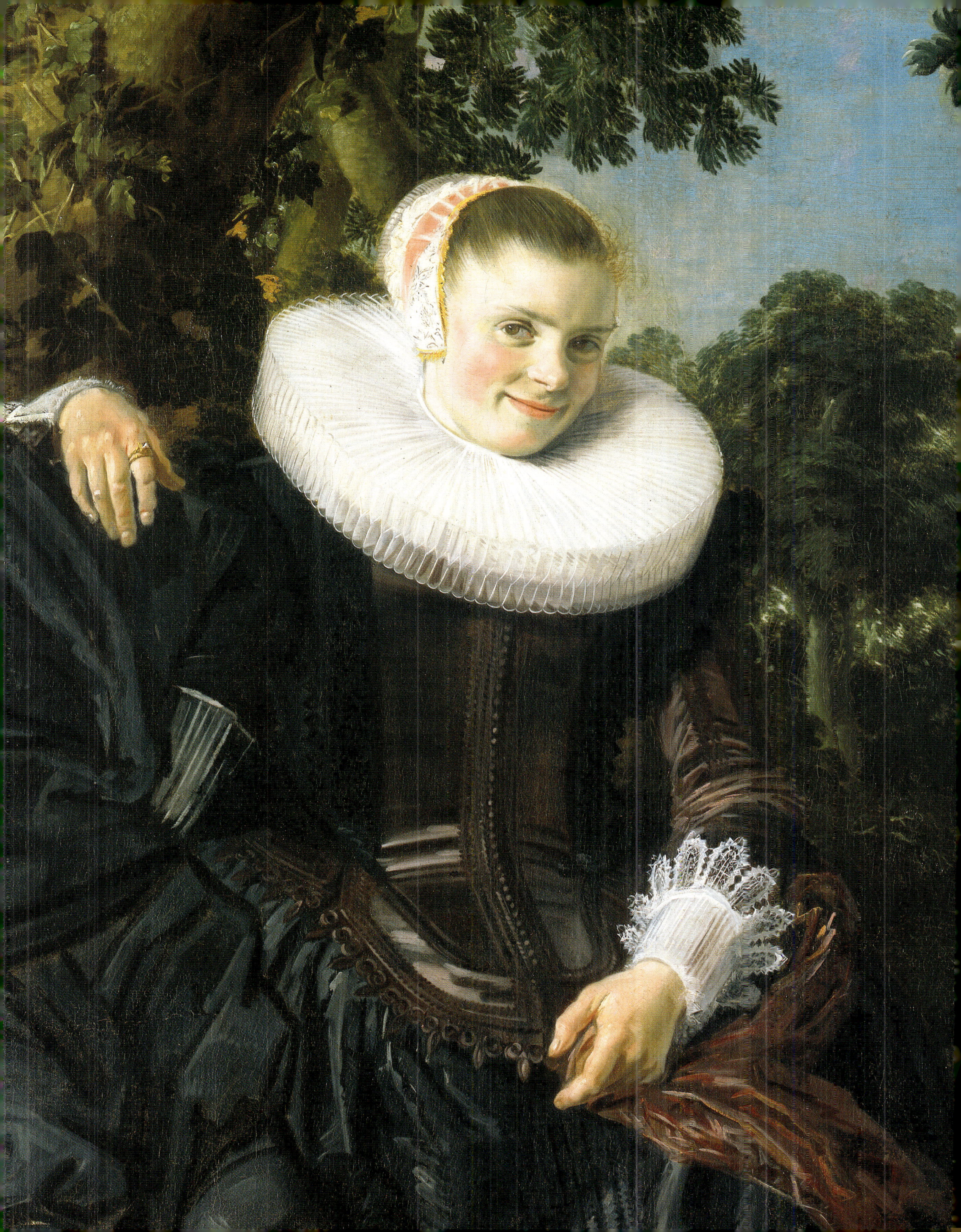

Frans Hals

Antwerp 1582/3 – 1666 Haarlem

16 | 17

Portrait of Jacob Olycan, 1625

Oil on canvas, 125 x 98 cm
At upper right: *ÆTAT SVÆ. 29 / A° 1625*
Royal Picture Gallery Mauritshuis, The Hague

Portrait of Aletta Hanemans, 1625

Oil on canvas, 124 x 98 cm
At upper left: *ÆTAT SVÆ. 19 / AN° 1625*
Royal Picture Gallery Mauritshuis, The Hague

These two portraits of the 29-year-old son of a Haarlem brewer, Jacob Pietersz Olycan (1596–1638) and his 19-year-old wife, Aletta Hanemans (1606–1653), represent a tried and tested compositional form that originated in the late sixteenth century. Frans Hals depicted the man and woman almost frontally, each with one arm bent and the hand at the waist, while the other arms hang close to the body. Olycan is holding a hat, while Hanemans has gloves in her hand. The clients presumably asked the painter to depict them in this traditional, rather old-fashioned, pose.[1] Hals successfully achieved a large measure of plasticity and naturalness here – qualities that are sometimes absent from earlier portraits employing a similar format, such as those by the provincial painter Jan Claesz, dated 1602 (cats 8–9). Details such as Olycan's hat, abruptly cropped by the picture's bottom edge, or the ribbons of Hanemans's embroidered gloves, which also dangle beyond the frame, add a frisson of excitement to Hals's compositions. The splendid portraits were made a few years after the double portrait of Isaac Massa and his wife (cat. 15). Hals continued to produce pendants of a man and woman posed (as here) against a monochrome background, varying the basic pose of the man, which he used here for the first time.[2] Only rarely did he show husband and wife making contact with one another, as in the pendants of Stephanus Geraerdts and Isabella Coymans from about 1645 (p. 30, figs 19–20).[3] Here, Olycan and his wife both gaze at the viewer; the link between the two is indicated by their poses, which mirror one another.[4]

Although Hals is generally known for his extremely loose technique, here his style is quite refined, a feature best seen in the costumes. Thanks to a recent cleaning and restoration, details of the garments can once again be seen clearly, confirming their great importance to costume historians. The couple are dressed in fashionable burgher attire influenced by Spanish fashions,[5] such as the man's *rockgen*, a tight-fitting doublet with shoulder flaps and sleeves that hang down at the back. Hals has rendered the pattern on this garment exquisitely. The undersleeve, trimmed with decorative black bands, is almost tangible. The other sleeve is not visible, since it is hidden by the cloak. The woman wears a black *vlieger* overgown with a floral motif. Where the sleeves are attached to the bodice it has shoulder-wings or *bragoenen* (from the Spanish *brahones*). These large, saucer-shaped shoulder-pieces are decorated with jet beads. The plain black sleeves are decorated with black binding. Her most richly embellished garment is the stomacher, which boasts floral and vine motifs embroidered with gold thread and paillettes.[6] To make the skirt flare more widely, she wears a padded farthingale under it, which also has the effect of making her abdomen appear rather distended. Compared to the other garments, the skirt is painted with strikingly broad strokes. It was originally red or a reddish purple, but the pigments have discoloured with the passage of time.

The two coats of arms shown in the reproductions in the portraits, painted as if they were hanging on a ribbon attached to a nail, were added later. Similar arms are found in the pendant portraits that Hals painted in 1631 of Jacob Olycan's maternal aunt Cornelia Vooght Claesdr and uncle Nicolaas van der Meer.[7] An analysis of the paint revealed that they contain Prussian blue, a pigment not available to painters until about 1720.[8] Indeed, the arms must have been added after 1762, since they do not appear in a drawn copy after the lady's portrait made in that year.[9] During the recent restoration of the portraits, the coats of arms were painted out.[10] They were so prominent as to undermine the sense of depth in the background, but now that they have been covered up, the original effect has been restored.[11]

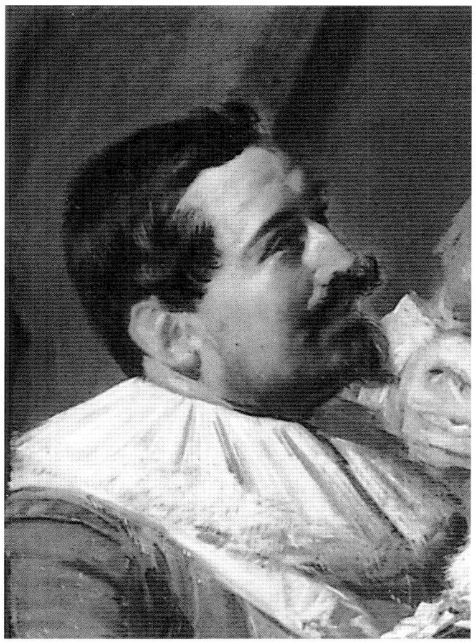

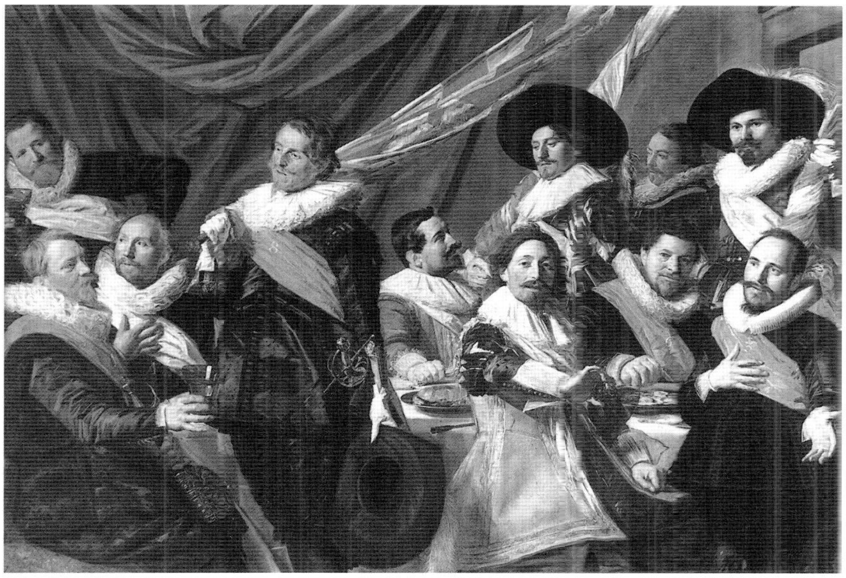

16-17a.
Frans Hals,
The Officers of the St George Civic Guard,
1627. Oil on canvas, 179 x 258 cm. Frans Hals Museum, Haarlem (Olycan is the fifth man from the left)

Although they were added to the paintings at a later date, the coats of arms, together with the original inscriptions giving the respective subjects' ages, were key to identifying the man and woman. The coat of arms on the man's portrait featured an ostrich with a horseshoe in its beak and a jug with two handles. The latter is an allusion to the subject's name 'Olycan' (oil jug), which derives from the name of a house called 'In de Olycan' in Kalverstraat, Amsterdam, where his grandfather had established himself as a merchant. The ostrich alludes to the Haarlem brewery-inn 'De Vogel Struys' (*struisvogel* – ostrich) that belonged to his father Pieter Jacobsz Olycan (1572–1658), and the horseshoe to the latter's second inn in Haarlem, 'Het gecroonde Hoefijser' (*hoefijzer* – horseshoe). After his marriage in 1624 to Aletta Hanemans of Zwolle, Jacob became the proprietor of the latter inn. The hen on the coat of arms in Hanemans' portrait refers to her last name, which translates as 'Henman'.

The couple had a good reason for choosing Frans Hals to make their portraits. The painter depicted many members of the Olycan family between 1615 and 1660, both individually and in group portraits.[12] Together this body of work sheds light on the painter's Haarlem clientele. The pendant portraits of Olycan and Hanemans – the earliest individual pieces in the group – were ordered to commemorate their marriage the previous year. Aletta is depicted in her sumptuous wedding clothes.[13] On the index finger of her right hand she wears a wedding ring, while in the other hand she holds the gloves given to her by her fiancé upon their betrothal (see also cat. 36). Hals depicted Olycan two years later in a large group portrait of the officers of the St George Civic Guard in Haarlem (fig. 16–17a).[14] Olycan is clearly recognisable here by his hair cropped short above his ears, and his pointed moustache and goatee. He is seated in a casual pose, looking up at the standard-bearer beside him. In old documents, Olycan is named as lieutenant of the St George Civic Guard in Haarlem between 1624–7. His father had held prominent official positions in the city, including town magistrate and burgomaster, and was also a delegate in the States-General. Jacob too held a variety of public offices, including regent of St Elisabeth's infirmary (see cat. 23) and lieutenant of the Kloveniersdoelen (see cat. 64). Three years after Olycan's premature death in 1638, his wife remarried. Her new husband, the widower Nicolaes van Loo (1607–1641), also worked as a brewer at 'Het gecroonde Hoefijser' and when he also died suddenly, in 1641, Aletta continued the work there independently. After her death in 1653 an inventory was made of her possessions, which included brief descriptions of the portraits made by Hals. The estate was not settled until 1660, with the paintings remaining in the family. Through Maria van der Horn, the daughter of Jacob Olycan's younger sister, the pendants were handed down in the Van Sypesteyn family in Haarlem. Not until 1880 did descendants sell them to the Dutch government; they were transferred to the Mauritshuis the following year.[15]
QB

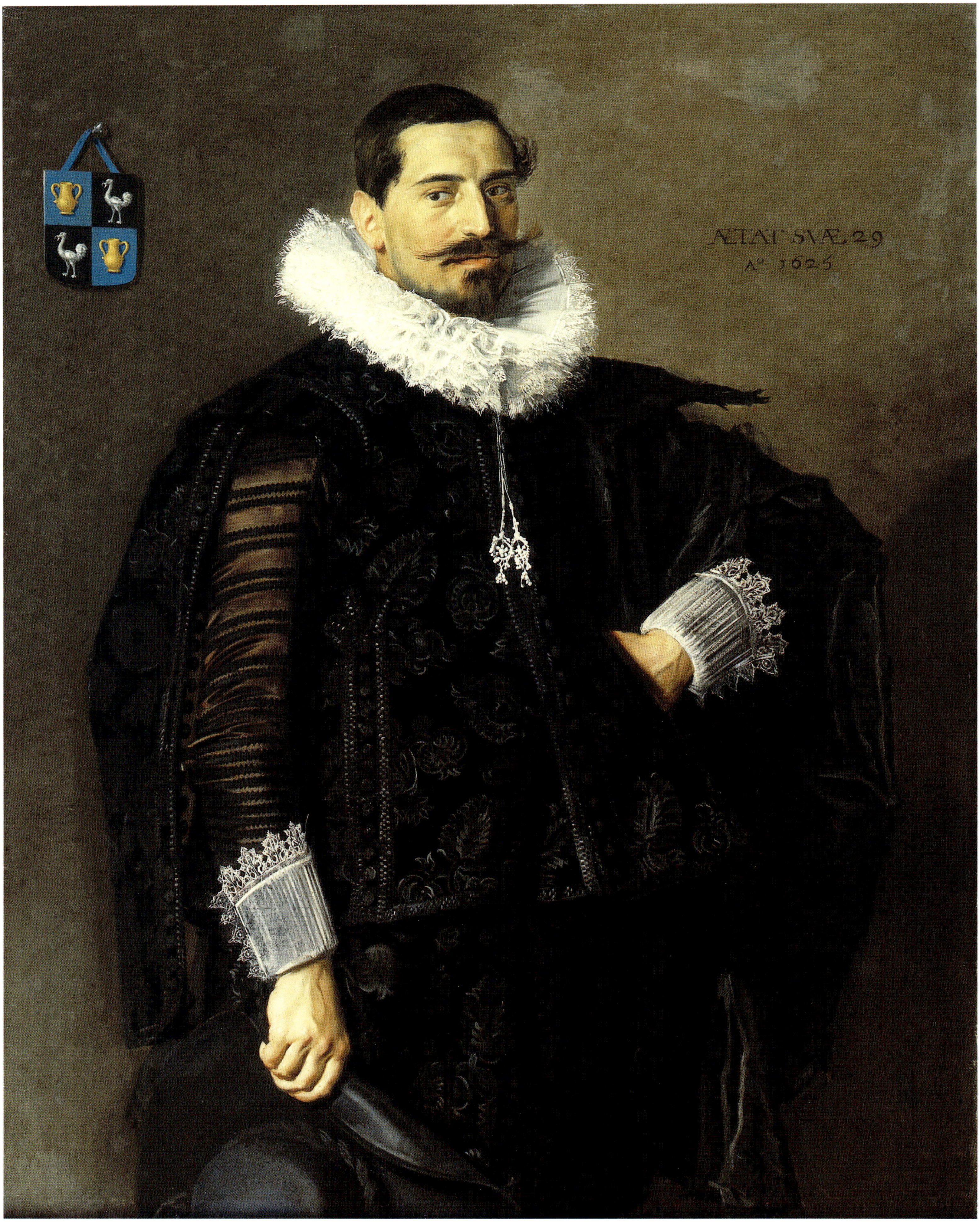

Before restoration

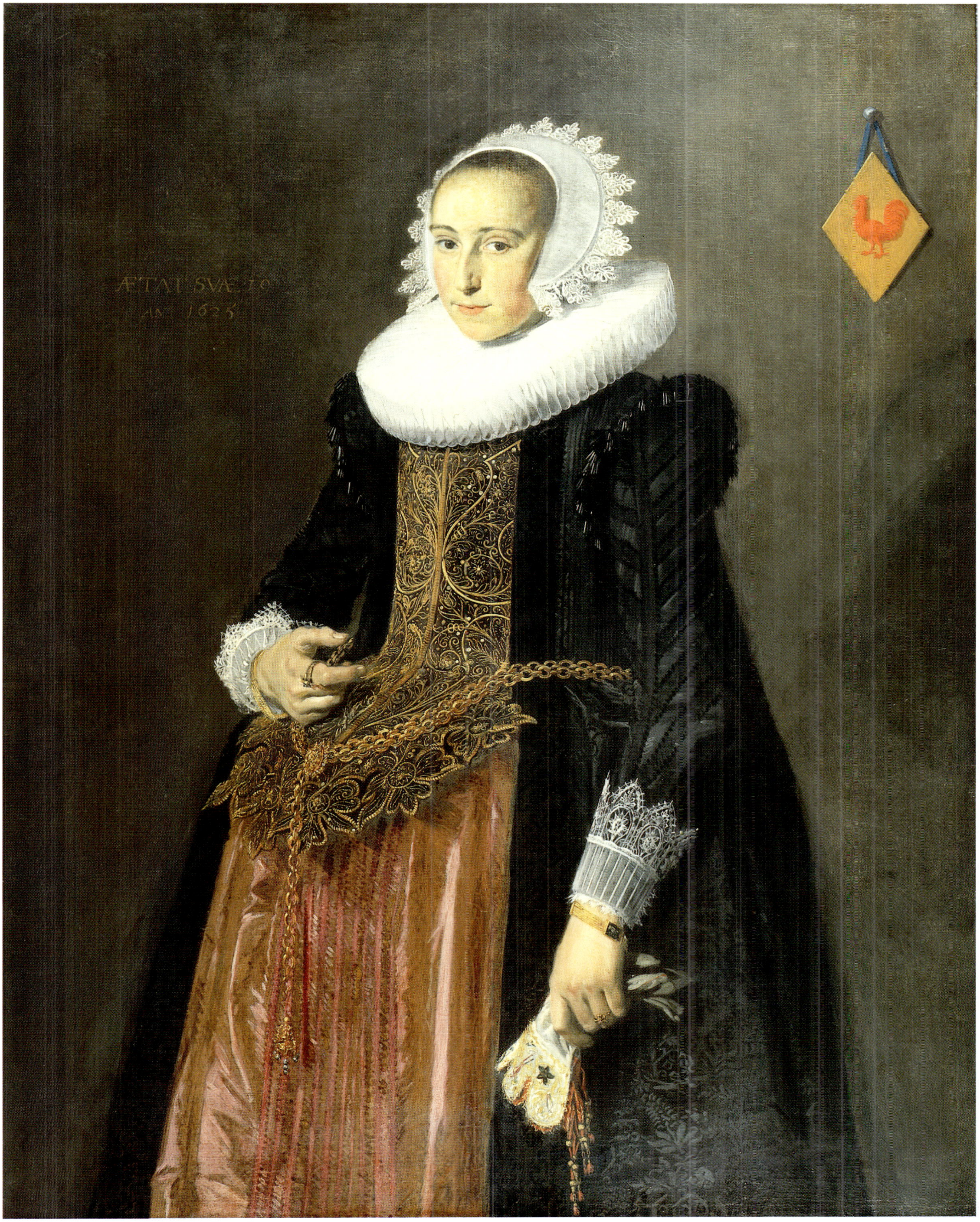

Before restoration

Frans Hals

Antwerp 1582/3 – 1666 Haarlem

18

Portrait of Willem van Heythuysen, about 1625

Oil on canvas, 205 x 135 cm
Alte Pinakothek, Bayerische Staatsgemäldesammlungen, Munich

This imposing work, which embodies the self-assurance so characteristic of burghers in the powerful Dutch Republic, is the only individual portrait Frans Hals made in which the sitter is depicted life-sized and full-length. Official portraits of this kind, originally favoured among the nobility and court dignitaries, were popular from 1615 onwards in prominent Amsterdam regent circles (see p. 28, figs 16–17 and cats 47–8).[1] On stylistic grounds this portrait can be dated around 1625,[2] the year in which Hals also completed, among other paintings, the marriage portraits of Jacob Olycan and his wife (cats 16–17). The sitter Willem van Heythuysen was a Haarlem merchant who amassed a fortune in the textiles trade. Although he never married, he does appear to have been betrothed, many years after this portrait was made, to Alida Roosterman (about 1620–1647), the younger sister of his good friend Tieleman Roosterman,[3] who also commissioned a portrait from Hals.[4] After Alida's unexpected death in 1647, before the couple could be married, Van Heythuysen remained single. When he died, on 6 July 1650, he left countless paintings, as well as precious items of furniture and silverware, to his sister Geertruyt, who shared his home.[5] The portrait described here must be the large portrait ('groot conterfeytsel') mentioned in the inventory of his estate as hanging in the main hall of his house on Haarlem's Oudegracht.[6]

Although we know about his betrothal to Alida Roosterman, it is not known whether Van Heythuysen had looked actively for a wife at an earlier stage of his life. The rose on the floor in the right foreground of this painting is an interesting detail in this context. At left, behind the rosebush, is a garden with a courting couple. A similar glimpse of a garden – a garden of love – appears in the double portrait of newly weds that Hals painted a few years earlier (cat. 15). Is Van Heythuysen presented here as a prospective bridegroom?[7] The roses in his portrait do not necessarily refer to love, however.[8] They also symbolise mortality, and in a contemporary book of moral emblems the poet and lawyer Jacob Cats compares life to the flowering of a rose.[9] The emblem, which was published at virtually the same time as this portrait (1627), is accompanied by the image of a man beside a rosebush holding a sword. The richly decorated sword in Van Heythuysen's hand may depict the one listed in the inventory of his estate,[10] but might also be invested here with some deeper significance. Van Heythuysen poses proudly as a kind of civic guardsman, although sources show that he neither held a military position nor belonged to Haarlem's militia.[11] His activities as a textiles merchant required him to spend much time travelling abroad, thus preventing him from joining the civic guard or holding public office in Haarlem.[12]

Hals conveys Van Heythuysen's affluence in a very distinctive way. We see the merchant from a worm's-eye perspective, so that he towers over us. He poses in front of a wall (perhaps of a garden pavilion?) with a piece of fabric draped over it, a motif familiar from Flemish portrait paintings. Van Heythuysen's proud personality is reinforced by his pose, with jutting elbow and hand on hip. This traditional attitude, used in portraits since the Renaissance, encapsulates the subject's self-assurance and high social standing.[13] The merchant's wealth is also apparent from his extremely expensive clothes, which follow the latest French fashions. Some of these garments – including the black satin suit and the garters with gold lace – are described in the inventory of his estate.[14]

Around 1635, Van Heythuysen commissioned another portrait from Hals. That painting, which is far smaller than this life-sized portrait, is described as hanging in a private chamber.[15] It recently surfaced after having been lost from view for some time (cat. 20). Although the later portrait depicts Van Heythuysen in a far more informal pose, it includes a number of attributes that likewise underscore the subject's high social status. QB

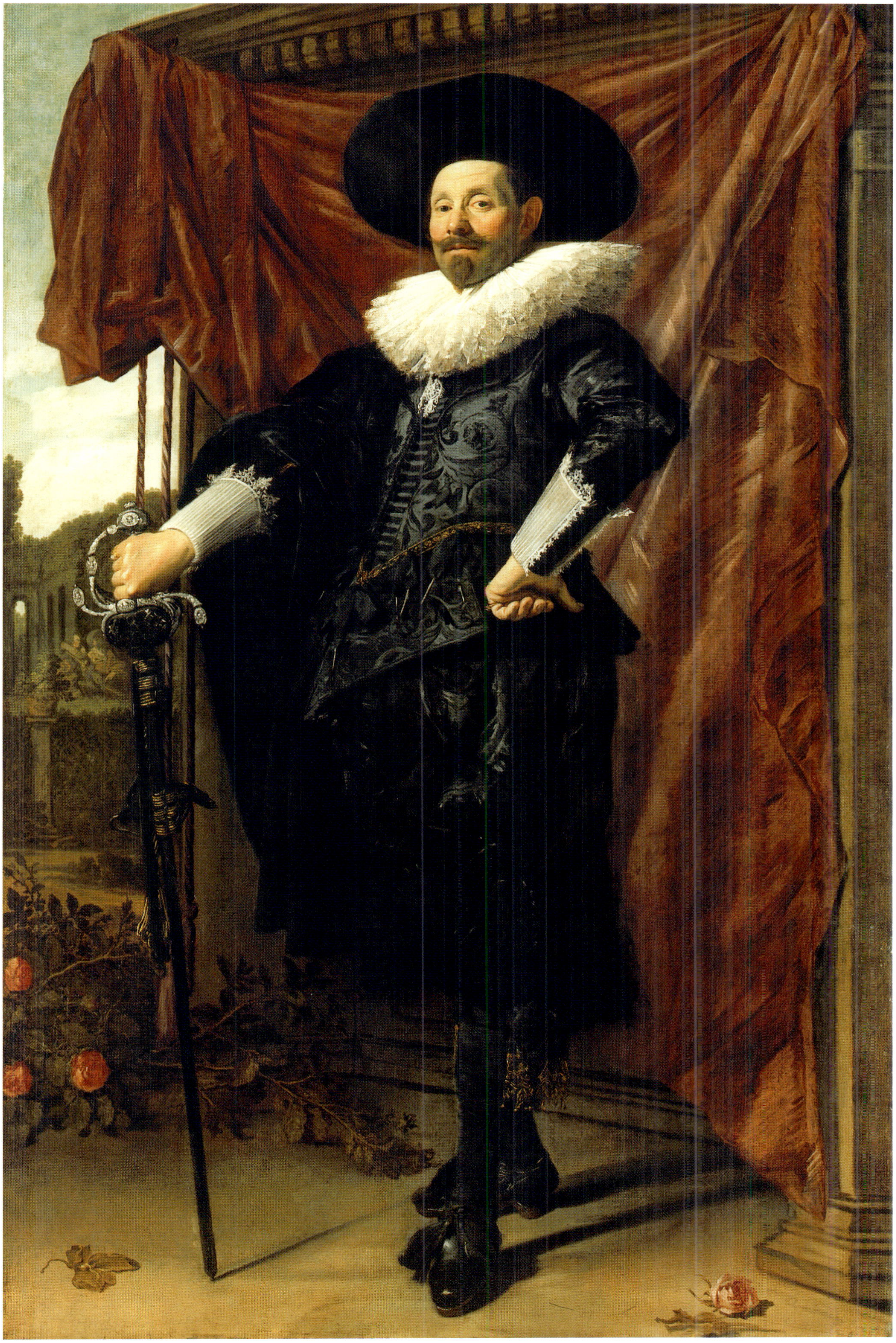

Frans Hals

Antwerp 1582/3–1666 Haarlem

19

Portrait of Pieter van den Broecke, 1633

Oil on canvas, 68.3 x 54.9 cm
Kenwood House, London
English Heritage (The Iveagh Bequest, Kenwood)
London only

Frans Hals's sparkling portrait depicts a man of the world, brimming with self-confidence. Pieter van den Broecke (1585–1640) was a native of Antwerp, his family having fled to the Northern Netherlands to escape Spanish domination – just as Frans Hals's relatives had. In the Dutch Republic Van den Broecke pursued a glittering international career with the Dutch East India Company (VOC), a precursor of today's multinationals. Before joining the VOC in 1613, he had sailed to Africa to find trading partners, sojourning in the Cape Verde islands, Angola and the Congo. In later years, as a senior VOC merchant, Van den Broecke forged ties with traders in countries as distant as Persia and India. The legendary governor-general Jan Pietersz Coen, who played a decisive role in the VOC's conquest of territories in the Indonesian archipelago, enlisted Van den Broecke's help to defend the fortress of Batavia (present-day Jakarta) against English troops. As admiral of the Dutch fleet, Van den Broecke brought Coen's widow back to the Netherlands from the East Indies in 1630. The VOC's directors presented him with a gold chain in June of that year, in gratitude for seventeen years of loyal service. This precious gift, worth 1,200 guilders – as much as a house – is depicted in Hals's portrait, slung from the right shoulder to the left hip. The metal gorget, partially obscured by the fashionable lace collar, and the baton that Van den Broecke leans on, refer to his position as admiral. A few years after this portrait was painted, in 1640, he was killed in the battle for Malacca (Malaysia).

A note on a print made after the painting by Adriaen Matham tells us that the portrait was produced in 1633, when the admiral was 48 years old (fig. 19a).[1] The engraving, which is not reversed, presents Hals's composition within an oval frame. Beneath the frame is a cartouche, decorated with weapons and dolphins and containing four lines of verse extolling Van den Broecke's gift for commerce. Matham also added draperies to the background of the portrait, a motif rare in Hals's work (see p. 118).[2]

In 1634 a smaller version of Matham's engraving was used as the frontispiece of a report published by Van den Broecke on his commercial activities abroad.[3] The merchant emerges from this report, as indeed from other texts, as a frank and energetic man,[4] self-assured and shrewd enough to cope with the cut-throat competition in trade in Africa and South Asia. These characteristics are conveyed in Hals's loosely painted portrait, the composition of which suggests a fleeting moment in time. The man is seated in a chair and rests one hand on his baton, a pose found often in portraits of this period.[5] He is depicted close up, his head turned sharply towards the viewer (see also cats 20, 24). Strands of his rather untidy hair stand out clearly against the bright background. The hand propped at his side is partly cut off by the lower edge of the picture, enhancing the portrait's directness.[6]

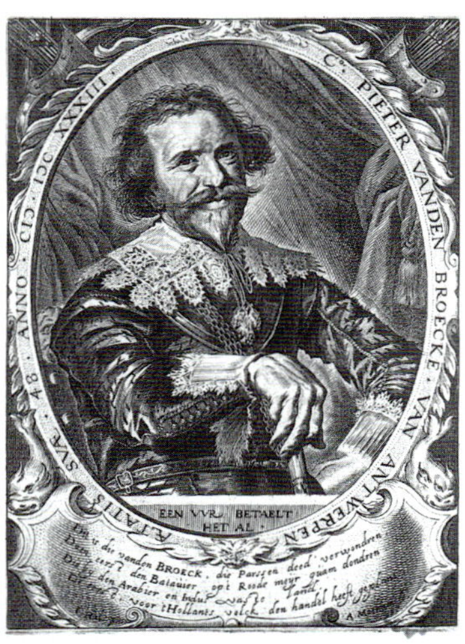

19a.
Adriaen Matham after Frans Hals, *Portrait of Pieter van den Broecke*, 1633.
Engraving, 16 x 12 cm.
Rijksprentenkabinet, Rijksmuseum, Amsterdam

Van den Broecke remained in contact with the painter. About a year after the portrait's completion he acted as a witness at the baptism of Hals's daughter Susanna. Adriaen Matham, the artist who produced the engraving after the painting, was another witness.[7] Evidently the painter, the sitter and the engraver were all well acquainted. QB

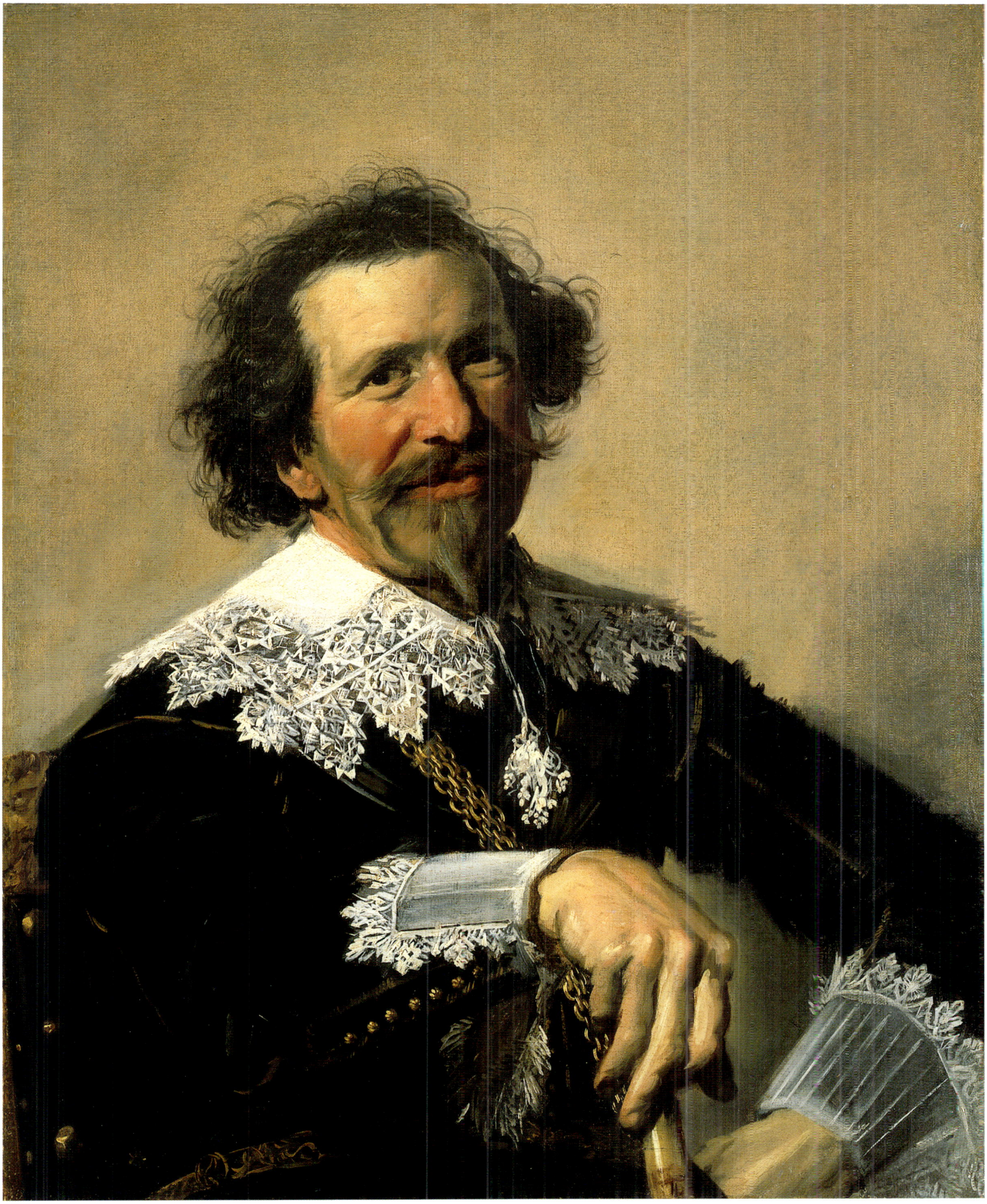

Frans Hals

Antwerp 1582/3 – 1666 Haarlem

20

Portrait of Willem van Heythuysen, about 1634–5

Oil on panel, 47 x 37 cm
At right: FH (in ligature)
Private collection

About ten years after Willem van Heythuysen commissioned his portrait from Frans Hals (cat. 18), he posed again for the artist – but this time the Haarlem merchant ordered a smaller, informal painting. Four versions of the later work now exist, and it has only recently been established that the painting shown here, the whereabouts of which was long unknown, is the original; it had long been assumed that the portrait in Musées Royaux des Beaux-Arts, Brussels, was the first.[1] That painting comes from the regents' room of the Van Heythuysen *hofje* (an almshouse with a central courtyard) that was built in Haarlemmerhout on the land where his manor Middenhout had stood (as directed in Van Heythuysen's will). As such, the Brussels painting was believed to be the portrait described in the inventory of the sitter's canal-side house on Oude Gracht in Haarlem (see p. 114).[2]

The portrait from the *hofje* was sold in 1870, and came into the possession of the museum in Brussels. However, recent research into the architectural history of the almshouse unearthed a payment by Maerten van Sittard, a relative of Van Heythuysen and one of the executors of his will: 'to Frans Hals for the portrait of Van Heythuysen, 36 guilders'.[3] This payment was made in August 1653, more than three years after Van Heythuysen's death, and so the Brussels painting is actually a copy made especially for the regents' room. The date of 1653 fits comfortably with the year – 1647 – in which the tree for the panel was felled.[4] Whether the Brussels painting is a replica by Hals himself, or a copy produced by one of his assistants, is hard to say as the badly discoloured varnish impedes thorough analysis.[5] In any case, the style of painting resembles that of Hals's works from about 1650–1. The two other known copies of the portrait are definitely not painted by Hals, although the one executed on panel certainly dates from the seventeenth century.[6]

The painting shown here, which bears the monogram 'FH', was also long believed to be a copy.[7] It resurfaced only recently, its whereabouts unknown since 1963. After comprehensive technical examination and restoration completed by Martin Bijl in 2006, it proved to be attributable to Hals.[8] The removal of layers of varnish revealed a painting of marvellous quality. Further, a number of *pentimenti* attest to the portrait's authenticity: the hat was moved a little to the left, and one of the hands was also moved. These modifications to the initial design were evidently deemed necessary to render convincingly the tension in the figure's pose. Chemical analysis has shown that all the materials used correspond to Hals's usual technique.[9] However, Hals left the execution of large sections of the background, including the curtain, to an assistant. Even to the naked eye it is apparent that in the painting of the curtain, a dark, preliminary brush drawing was followed meticulously. The painting was dated more precisely through dendrochronological analysis, which showed that the panel could have been available for painting from about 1635, while traces of sawing on the back seem to indicate that it cannot have been made after that year.[10]

Van Heythuysen's nonchalant pose is extremely unusual in Dutch portraiture. He tilts his chair back, flexes his hunting crop and rests his right leg on his left knee. Riding attire, crop and boots with gilded spurs emphasise the sitter's elevated status: hunting and horseriding were the prerogative of the nobility. The portrait's spontaneous, informal character may be explained, perhaps, by the fact that it was intended to be hung in a private chamber, according to the inventory mentioned above. No other portrait from this period is so informal; not even the small works by the Amsterdam painters Pieter Codde and Thomas de Keyser, who depicted their subjects in domestic surroundings (cats 10, 34–6). We do find similar poses in Haarlem genre pieces, however, including paintings by Hals's brother Dirck (1591–1656).[11] MB/PB

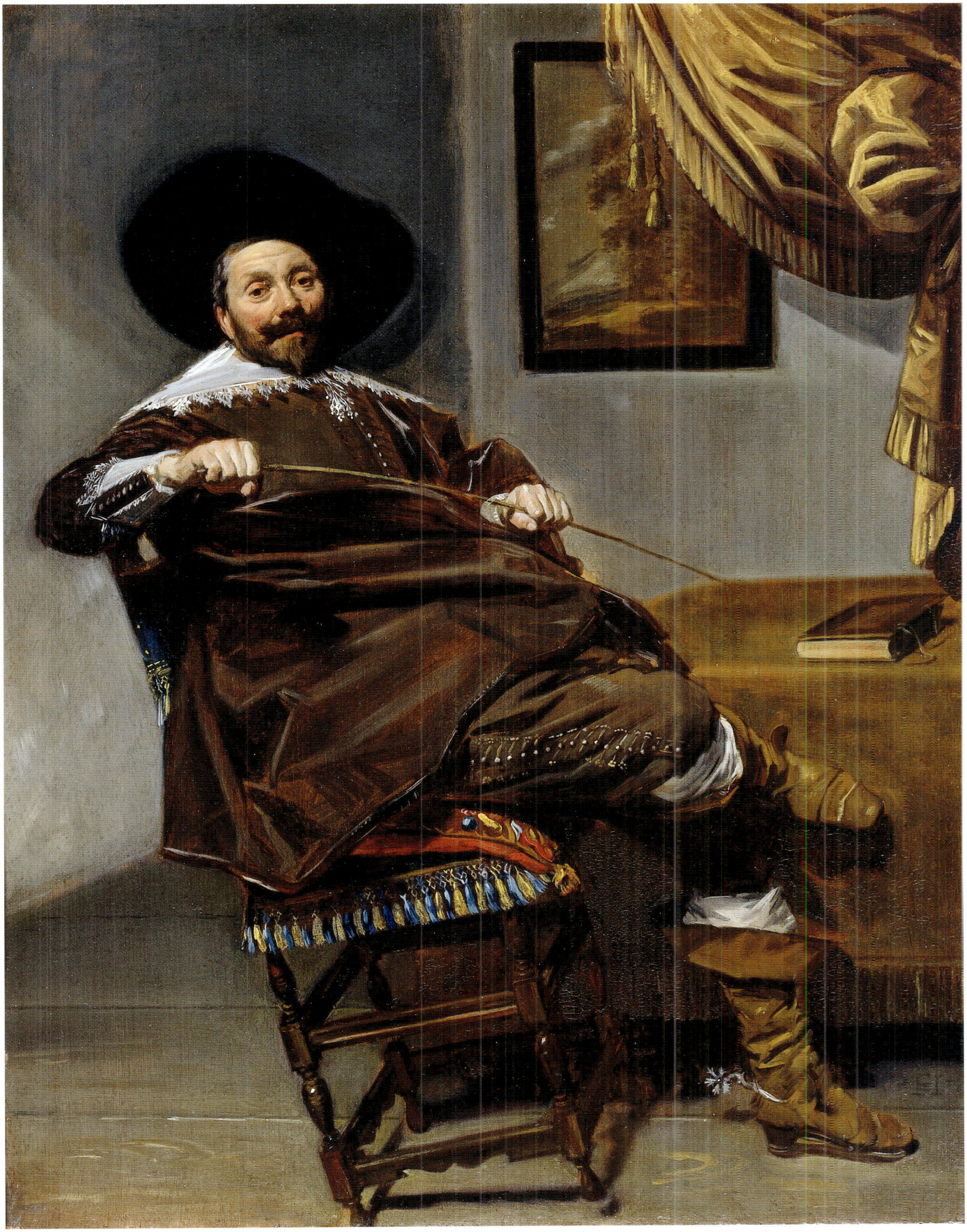

Frans Hals & Pieter Codde

Antwerp 1582/3 – 1666 Haarlem & Amsterdam 1599 – 1678 Amsterdam

21

Officers and Other Guardsmen of the 11th District of Amsterdam under the Command of Captain Reynier Reael and Lieutenant Cornelis Blaeuw, known as 'The Meagre Company', 1633–7

Oil on canvas, 209 x 429 cm
Dated at far right, on the wall: *A° 1637*
Rijksmuseum, Amsterdam
London only

Frans Hals was one of only two artists not resident in Amsterdam to be commissioned to portray one of the city's civic guard companies in the seventeenth century, the other being the Utrecht painter Paulus Moreelse (see cat. 43).[1] The so-called *Meagre Company* shows 16 guardsmen from the Voetboogdoelen (crossbowmen's civic guard) in the eleventh district of Amsterdam, the area around the present-day Waterlooplein, led by Captain Reynier Reael (1588–1648) and Lieutenant Cornelis Blaeuw (1591–1638). Reael, holding a commander's baton, is seated next to the ensign at the far left; Blaeuw is seated to his left, holding a 'partisan'. Both men were merchants living in Jodenbreestraat when the portrait was executed.[2] Reael was made captain in this district in 1626, and in 1630 became one of the governors of the crossbowmen's civic guard. Blaeuw became lieutenant in 1632.[3]

The names of the other guardsmen have not come down to us. In 1974, Isabella van Eeghen proposed two potential candidates for the other sitters from among the prominent citizens resident in the district: Willem Six (1610–1652) and Pieter Ranst (1590–1641).[4] While it is not known whether Ranst served in the civic guard, Willem Six later became a captain.[5] Unfortunately no other portraits of these sitters confirm the identification. More recently, it has been suggested that Nicolaas van Bambeeck (1596–1661) may be the ensign, and Jean Pellicorne (1597–after 1639) the second guardsman from the right.[6] Van Bambeeck also lived in Jodenbreestraat and was a son of the wealthiest man in the eleventh district.[7] Ensigns were required to be from a wealthy family and unmarried, as they had to march in front of the company and could not risk leaving behind a widow and children. Van Bambeeck married in 1638, and would therefore have met this requirement when the painting was executed. A secure portrait of Van Bambeeck by Rembrandt, painted in 1641, shows a man with the same distinctive hooked nose, making the hypothesis quite appealing.[8] However, documented portraits of Jean Pellicorne do not bear a great resemblance to the guardsman second from the right: the eyes, nose and hair colour are all quite different.[9]

From Gerrit Schaep's 1653 list of portraits in the headquarters of Amsterdam's three civic guards, we know that Hals began the portrait and Pieter Codde (see cat. 10) finished it.[10] There are four documents from which the early history of the painting can be surmised.[11] In the earliest, dated 19 March 1636, Reael and Blaeuw testified that Hals had accepted the commission in 1633, but that the painting was still not finished – despite the artist having given his word on 24 June 1635 that he would do so, and despite repeated requests from the patrons. They now demanded that he come to Amsterdam to finish it, and threatened that if he refused to do so, a local painter would be chosen for the job, and that action would be undertaken to recover the money already paid to the artist.

Hals's response is recorded in a second document, written in Haarlem on 20 March 1636. He admitted to having accepted the commission, but with the condition that he would carry it out in Haarlem, not Amsterdam. He wrote further that he had subsequently agreed to go to Amsterdam to work on the heads, which he had planned and already begun to finish in Haarlem, but that it proved impossible to get the guardsmen together and his stay in Amsterdam was costly. He now promised to finish the painting quickly, provided the guardsmen came to Haarlem. In the third document, dated 29 April 1636, Reael and Blaeuw took issue with Hals's version of the story. The initial agreement, according to them, was that he would receive 60 guilders per head, which he would work up in Amsterdam and complete in Haarlem. Later, it was agreed that he would receive an extra 6 guilders from each guardsman if he would fully paint not only the heads in Amsterdam but the entire figures, which he had already begun to do with some of them

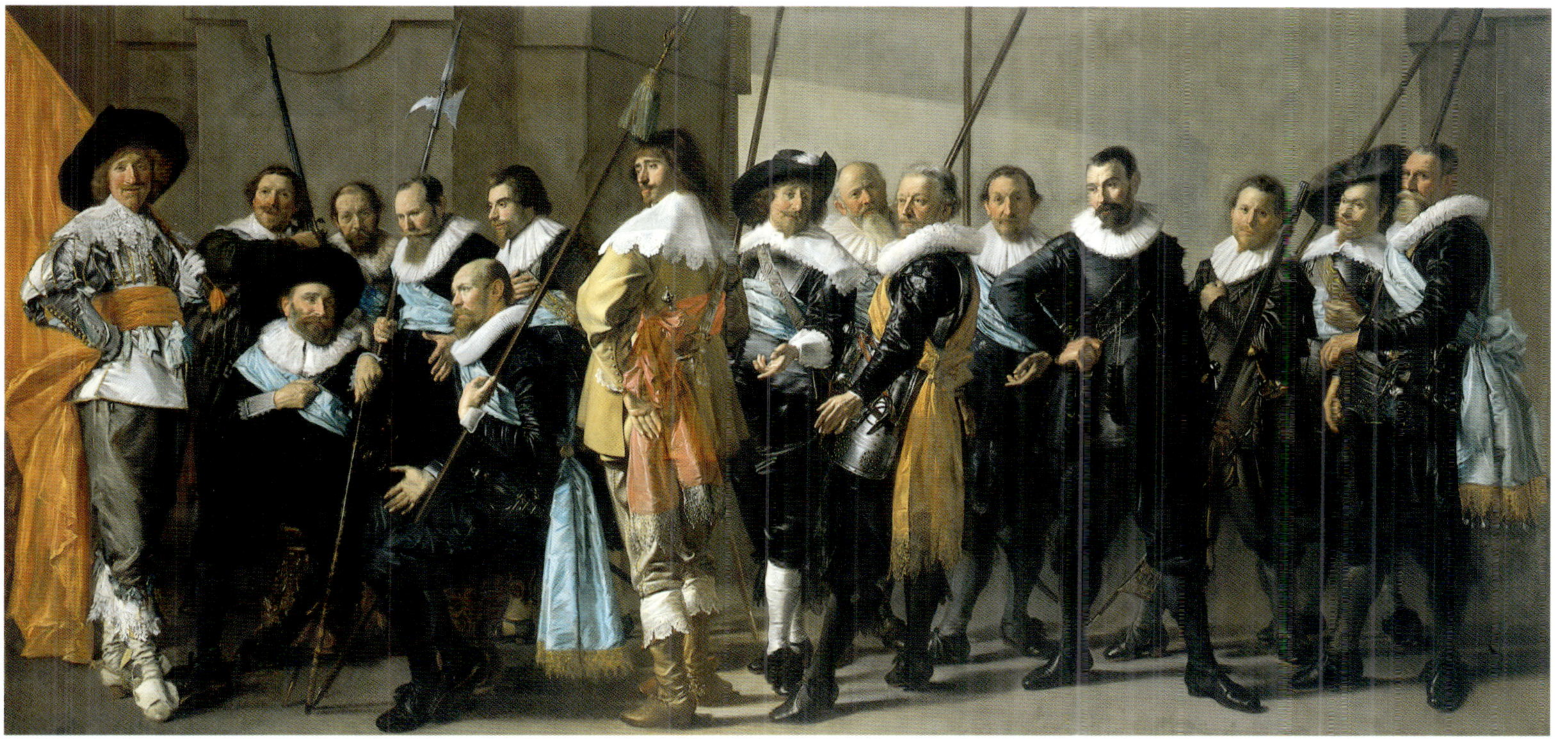

there. This time, Hals was given ten days to come to Amsterdam to resume work on the painting.

For some reason this document only became known to Hals three months after it had been written. In his second response, dated 26 July 1636, he proposed to have the painting brought to Haarlem, where he would complete the unfinished parts of the clothing. The guardsmen would also come to Haarlem so that he could finish painting the heads. However, should six or seven of the men decline to come, he would have the canvas – by then completed to all intents and purposes – transported to Amsterdam where he would paint the remaining heads. The guardsmen did not take Hals up on his offer, but instead had Codde complete the painting in 1637.

The presence of cursory underdrawing in oils by Hals's hand indicates that the entire composition was his invention.[12] He followed the Amsterdam tradition for civic guard portraiture by showing the men at full length (in Haarlem there was a preference for knee-length civic guard portraits, a preference that Hals adhered to in the pieces he executed for that town). By the time he began *The Meagre Company*, he had painted three civic guard portraits in Haarlem (p. 31, fig. 21; p. 111, fig. 16–17a), and was probably putting the final touches to a fourth, *The Officers and Sergeants of the Calivermen Civic Guard Company*.[13] There are especially strong compositional similarities between *The Meagre Company* and the latter picture, which is generally dated around 1633. In both paintings there is less movement than in Hals's earlier work in the genre, primarily because the emphatic diagonals have been replaced by more horizontal compositions.[14] The left side of *The Meagre Company*, in particular, where the captain and lieutenant are shown seated and flanked by two flamboyant standing figures, recalls Hals's Haarlem composition. As in that painting, Hals may have intended to show the Amsterdam guardsmen out of doors, for scientific examination of the painting has revealed that a building in the right background was painted over.[15]

The implication of Hals's second statement, that he still needed to paint as many as seven of the heads, was confirmed by technical examination in 1988. The seven figures on the right side of the canvas are the work of Pieter Codde, who did his best to suppress his usual smooth, almost invisible brushwork in favour of an imitation of Hals's much broader touch.[16] Codde apparently also changed the central figure standing with his back to the viewer.[17] The X-radiographs reveal that originally even more of this figure's back was visible, and that his left hand was placed on his chest. The figure also initially wore a bandolier with powder charges instead of the present sash, and he may also have been equipped with a sword. Codde was also responsible for putting the finishing touches to several figures that had already been largely completed by Hals. Van Eeghen suggested that the guardsmen may have chosen Codde to complete the picture because he was one of the few artists living in the eleventh district at the time.[18] Her hypothesis that Codde may also have been a member of Captain Reael's company cannot, unfortunately, be substantiated with documentary evidence.[19]

The painting's unusual nickname, *The Meagre Company*, can be traced back to Jan van Dyk's 1758 list of paintings in Amsterdam's town hall.[20] Van Dyk remarked that the guardsmen here 'are so withered and slender that one justifiably can call them the meagre company'.[21] JB

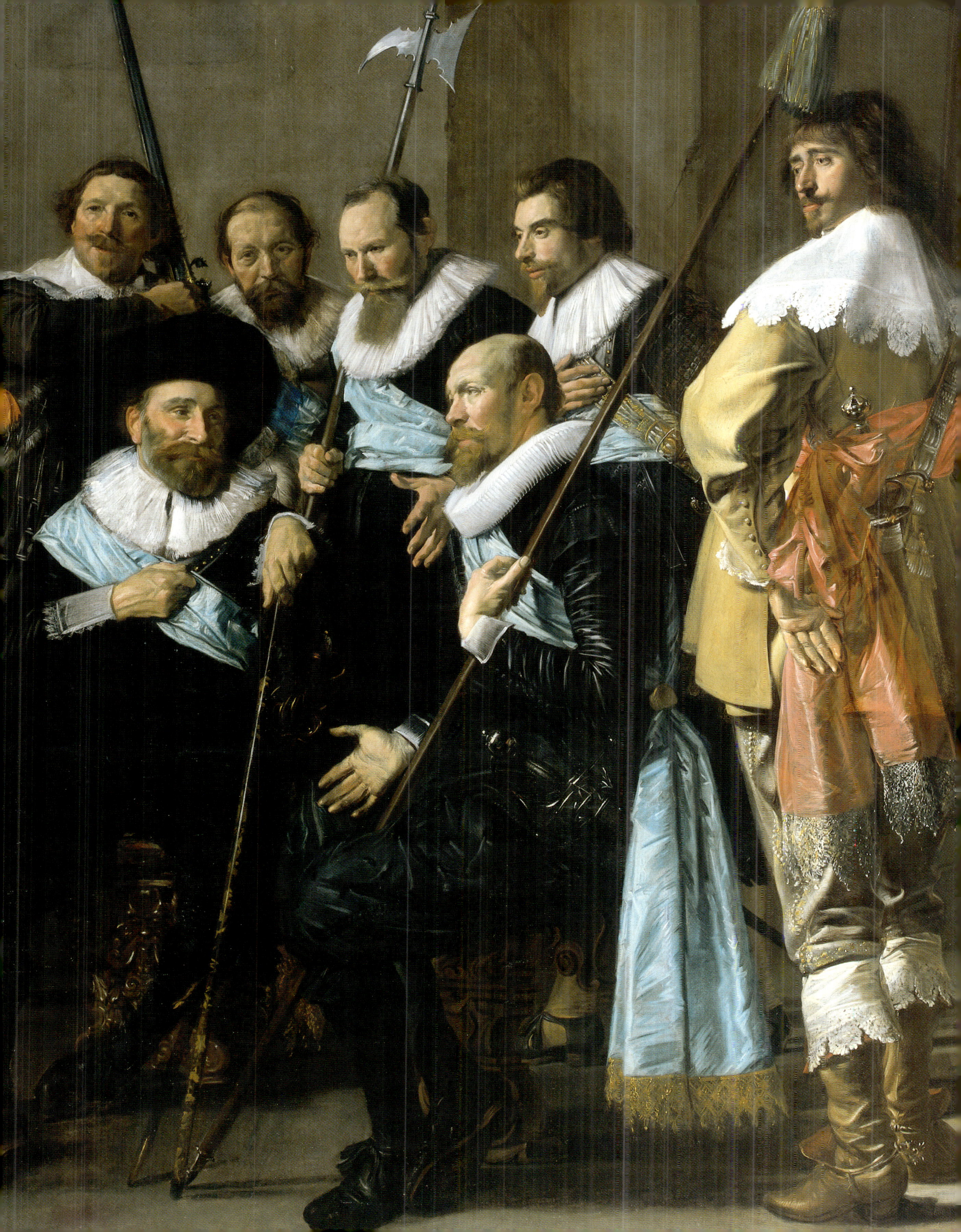

Frans Hals

Antwerp 1582/3 – 1666 Haarlem

22

Portrait of Jean de la Chambre, about 1638

Oil on panel, 20.6 x 16.8 cm
Upper left: 1638. / aet 33.
The National Gallery, London

Almost all the paintings by Frans Hals featured in this exhibition are large-scale portraits of members of the regent classes in Haarlem and Amsterdam (with the exception of cats 19 and 26). Despite the apparent informality of some of them (for example cat. 15) they were ambitious and expensive commissions that underscored the sitters' power, influence and elevated social position. This portrait of the calligrapher Jean de la Chambre (1605/6–1668), on the other hand, belongs to a group of small and relatively unassuming works that were conceived as *modelli* for engravings by Jonas Suyderhoef (about 1613–1686).[1]

The composition of this half-length portrait is extremely simple. It shows the sitter silhouetted against a plain brownish-beige background that is only a subtle variation on the colour of De la Chambre's skin. The black and white costume – De la Chambre's narrow-sleeved doublet and falling ruff, dating from the 1620s and early 1630s respectively and thus remarkably old-fashioned – add to the unassuming nature of the image. Yet Hals uses the sitter's pose and his own characteristic loose brushwork to give the portrait an air of movement and spontaneity. De la Chambre's quill is poised and his head is turned towards the viewer, creating the impression that he has just been interrupted at his work and is looking at us, the source of the disturbance. Hals cleverly keeps the sitter's left eye in the light even though that half of his face is engulfed by shadow. This emphasises the expectant, even gaze with which he fixes the viewer, waiting for an explanation of the interruption.

Jean de la Chambre was the Master of the French School in Haarlem, as well as an accomplished calligrapher.[2] The engraving after this painting (fig. 22a) was used as the frontispiece for a book, written by De la Chambre, containing six engraved plates of examples of his calligraphy (fig. 22b).[3] Suyderhoef's print gives the title of this book as well as the date 1638, and records that it was engraved after a painting by Hals.[4] AR

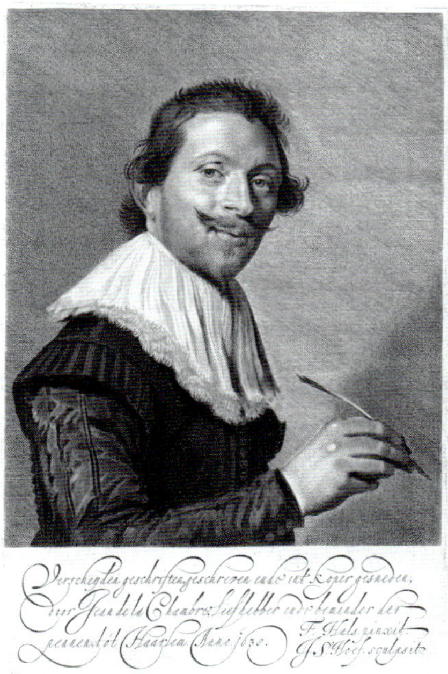

22a.
Jonas Suyderhoef after Frans Hals, *Portrait of Jean de la Chambre*, 1638. Engraving, 26 x 18 cm. From J. de la Chambre, *Verscheyden geschriften*, Haarlem 1638

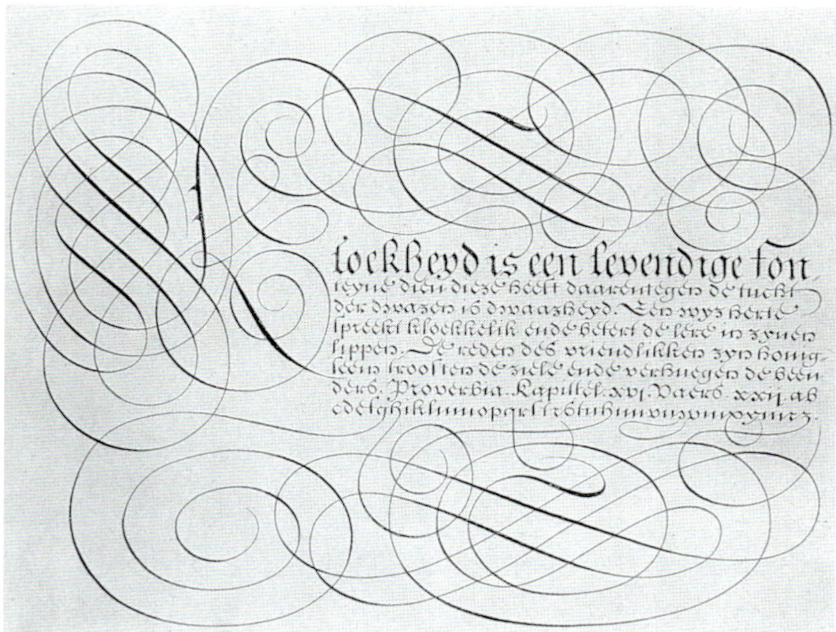

22b.
'*Kloekheyd is een levendige fonteyne …*' (Proverbs 16: 22). From J. de la Chambre, *Verscheyden geschriften*, Haarlem 1638

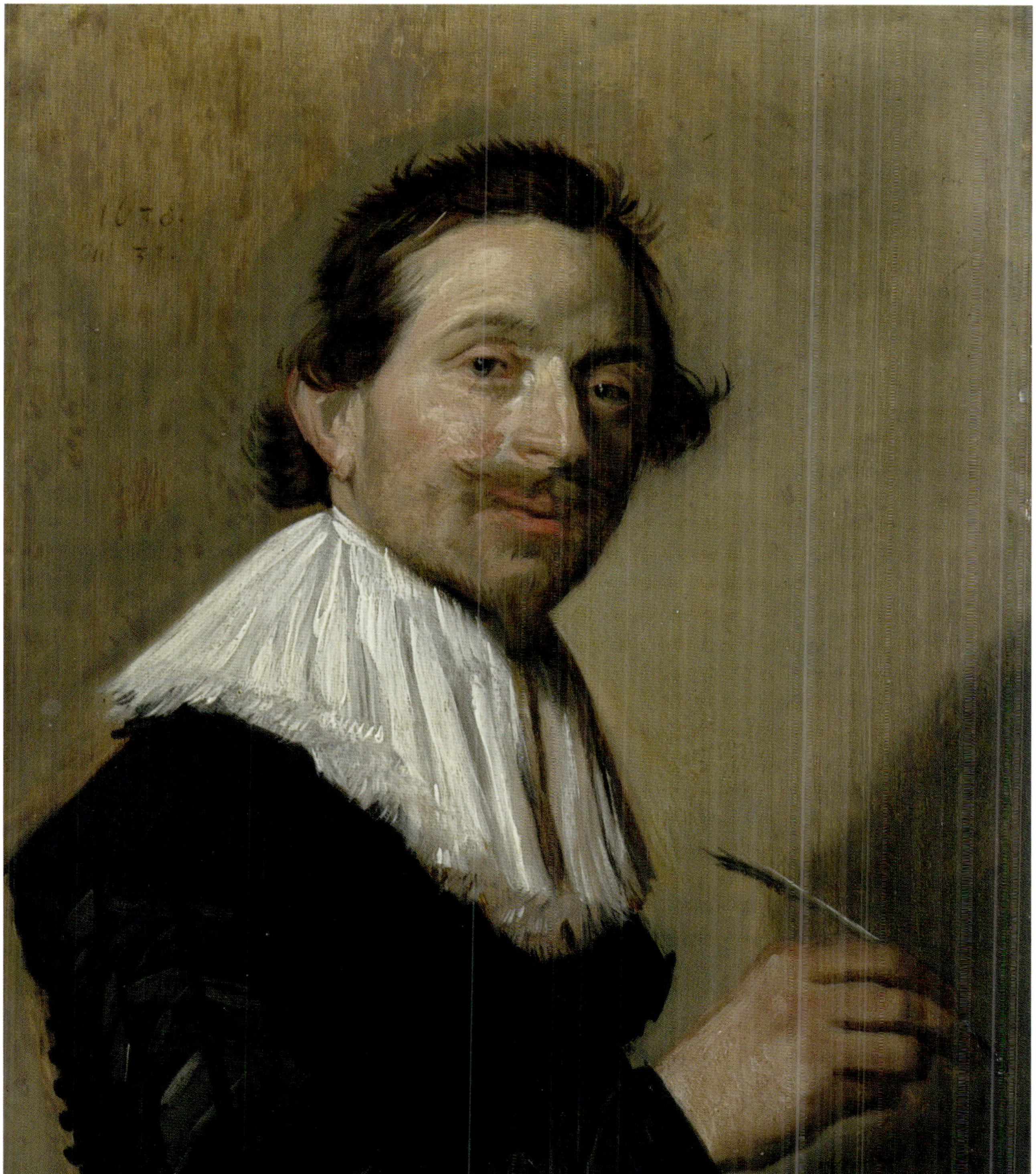

Frans Hals

Antwerp 1582/3 – 1666 Haarlem

23

The Regents of St Elisabeth's Hospital, 1641

Oil on canvas, 153 x 252 cm
Frans Hals Museum, Haarlem (on loan from the Elizabeth van Thüringen Fund Foundation)

This dynamic group portrait of the regents of Haarlem's St Elisabeth's Hospital is one of the earliest examples of the genre painted in the city. Still in its original frame,[1] it is traditionally dated 1641. In that year, the following men are listed as regents, or governors, of the institution, which was dedicated to the care of the sick and needy: Siewert Warmont (born 1614), Salomon Cousaert (1608–1655), Johan van Clarenbeeck (1601–1642), Dirck Del (died after 1646) and François Wouters (1600–1661).[2] Since four of these are also depicted in other group portraits, all the men shown here can be identified (from the left, we see them in the above order).[3] As the regents were appointed for a one-year term of office, we can presume that the painting was indeed produced in 1641.

Hals may have received this prestigious commission through Wouters,[4] who, as a lieutenant, had posed for the painter two years previously in the portrait of the officers (and non-commissioned officers) of the Haarlem's St George Civic Guard.[5] However, family matters had brought Hals into contact with the regents of the hospital before: one of his children, Pieter, was considered mentally challenged. In 1637, Haarlem's burgomasters had ordered the hospital to contribute 50 guilders a year to his maintenance in a workhouse outside the city. Pieter was subsidised in this way until his death in 1667.[6]

Hals clearly endeavoured to make his portrait as lively and natural as possible. He placed the men around a table in the regents' hall, a suitable place for them to be depicted in their official capacity, but the walls are only vaguely defined. Rays of light stream through an invisible window onto an unidentified map, which may refer to the estates owned by the hospital.[7] The regents administered the hospital's property, using the proceeds to pay for the hospital's programme. On the table we see a number of objects alluding to this aspect of their work: writing implements, a ledger or records book, and coins.

These dignified gentlemen are dressed more or less in accordance with the fashions around 1641: entirely in black, including their hats, which they have kept on even indoors. Their subdued dress contrasts quite sharply with the more colourful apparel worn by the men in the spectacular militia pieces Hals painted for Haarlem's civic guardsmen (p. 31, fig. 21 and p. 111, fig. 16-17a). The regent on the far left, Warmont, is the most fashionably dressed of this group: he has the smallest collar. His open sleeves, slashed to reveal his white shirt, and his long hair and smaller hat, are also decidedly *à la mode*.

Four of the men are seated at the table, one on each side. The fifth figure, Cousaert, stands behind them, and is probably the lowest in rank (he also wears the most subdued attire). He is looking at the man in the foreground, Del, whose face is the only one to be rendered in profile, bathed in sunlight. Del must be the chairman, since three of the others look at him attentively (Wouters, the treasurer on the far right, appears lost in contemplation). The three men all appear to be moving their hands, as though they are reacting to what Del has just said. His self-assured glance and the relaxed pose of his outstretched hand – note the subtly observed little finger, which slips casually off the side of the table – underscore his natural authority.

Hals devoted a great deal of attention to the figures' individual expressions: each of the five faces reflects a distinct personality. The different positions of the hands, which are elaborated with a striking degree of care, also underscore the figures' individuality. Hals's seeming insight into the character of his sitters accounts for much of this portrait's appeal. Unusually for Hals, none of the sitters look at the viewer.

A portrait was made of the regentesses of the hospital in the same year, not by Hals but by Johannes Verspronck (see p. 37, fig. 32).[8] Like Hals's group portrait – it is not known which of the two was made first – this work has long been exhibited in the Frans Hals Museum, on loan from St Elisabeth's hospital, which until 1971 stood directly opposite the museum. Given its subject, and the fact that it is signed and dated 1641, Verspronck's painting has been seen as a kind of counterpart to that of Hals. The two portraits are of different sizes, however, a factor usually attributed to the different number of figures depicted:

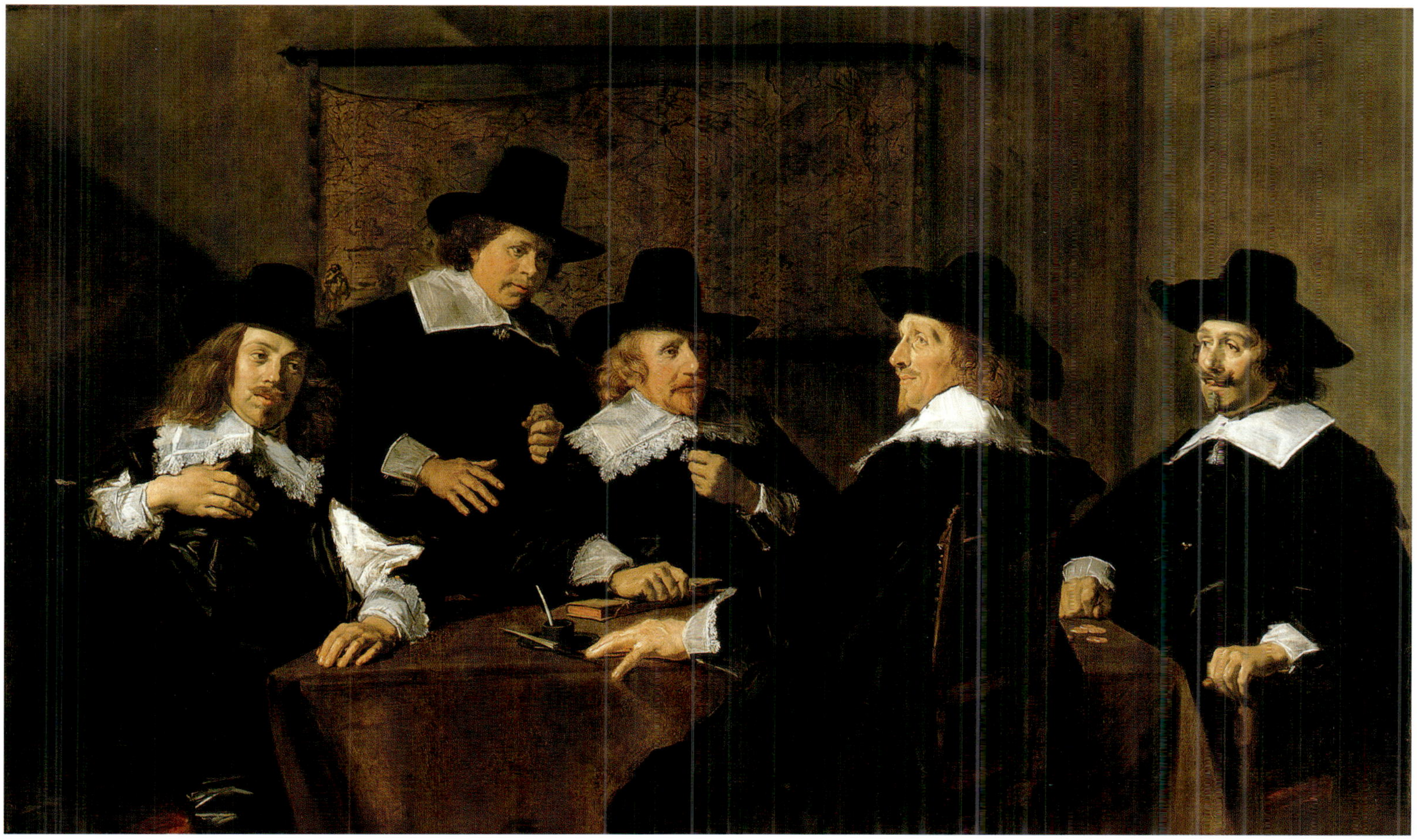

the hospital was administered by five regents and four regentesses. The relative sizes of the portraits could also be explained by the fact that the men and women had separate meeting-rooms within the hospital. The portraits also display a different finish: Verspronck's brushwork is more controlled than that of Hals, whose loose technique is particularly evident in the men's hair, and in their sparkling white collars and cuffs.

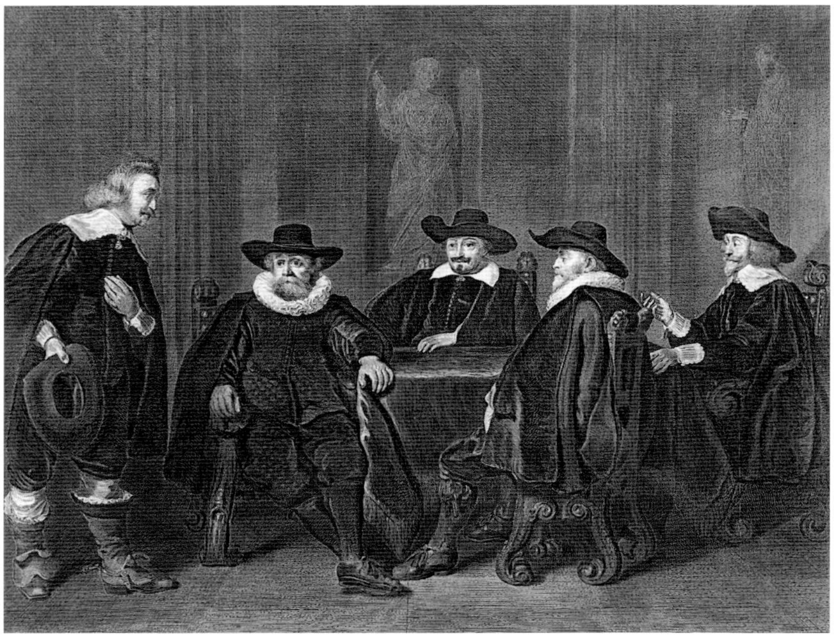

23a. Jonas Suyderhoef after Thomas de Keyser, *The Four Burgomasters of Amsterdam Being Informed of the Arrival of Maria de' Medici*, 1638. Engraving, 32 x 38 cm. Rijksprentenkabinet, Rijksmuseum, Amsterdam

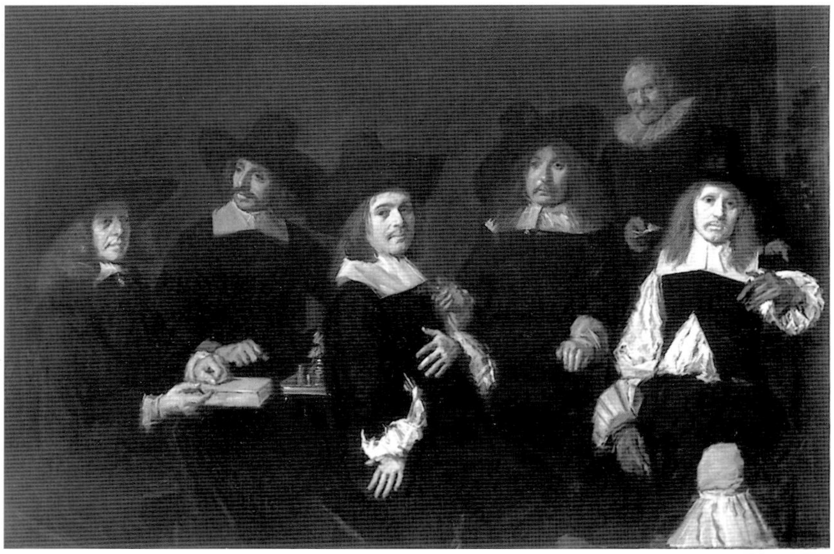

23b. Frans Hals, *The Regents of the Old Men's Home*, about 1664. Oil on canvas, 173 x 256 cm. Frans Hals Museum, Haarlem

The composition of the paintings by Hals and Verspronck derives from older examples of regents' portraits produced in cities other than Haarlem. As a genre, regent pieces were most popular in Amsterdam, where the Haarlem-born artist Pieter Pietersz made the earliest known portrait of the administrators of an institution (p. 22, fig. 7). A few years later, around 1617–18, the Amsterdam painter Cornelis van der Voort introduced a new compositional form by arranging a small group of regents around a table covered with a rug, some sitting and some standing (see. p. 29, fig. 18). This scheme was adopted by numerous artists, including Hals and Verspronck, and would be the point of departure for Rembrandt's famous group portrait of the syndics of the Clothmakers' Guild (cat. 60).

There is a specific source of inspiration for this picture. The composition and poses of the figures appear to have been based on a small oil sketch by Thomas de Keyser, which represents the only group portrait of Amsterdam's burgomasters. This sketch was made as the *modello* for a print dated 1638 by Jonas Suyderhoef, whom Hals knew well (fig. 23a).[9] The positioning of the men around the table, with the figure in the foreground viewed from behind, occurs in both images. Like De Keyser, Hals has portrayed the latter's face in profile, a device rarely seen in his work.[10] Instead of depicting the figures at full-length, however, Hals shows them to the knee, which draws the protagonists closer to the picture plane and consequently emphasises their different facial expressions.

Over 20 years would pass before Hals was again asked to make a group portrait of administrative officials. In two portraits from around 1664 depicting the regents (fig. 23b) and regentesses of the Old Men's Home in Haarlem, the aged painter depicted his subjects in highly informal and spontaneous compositions.[11] QB

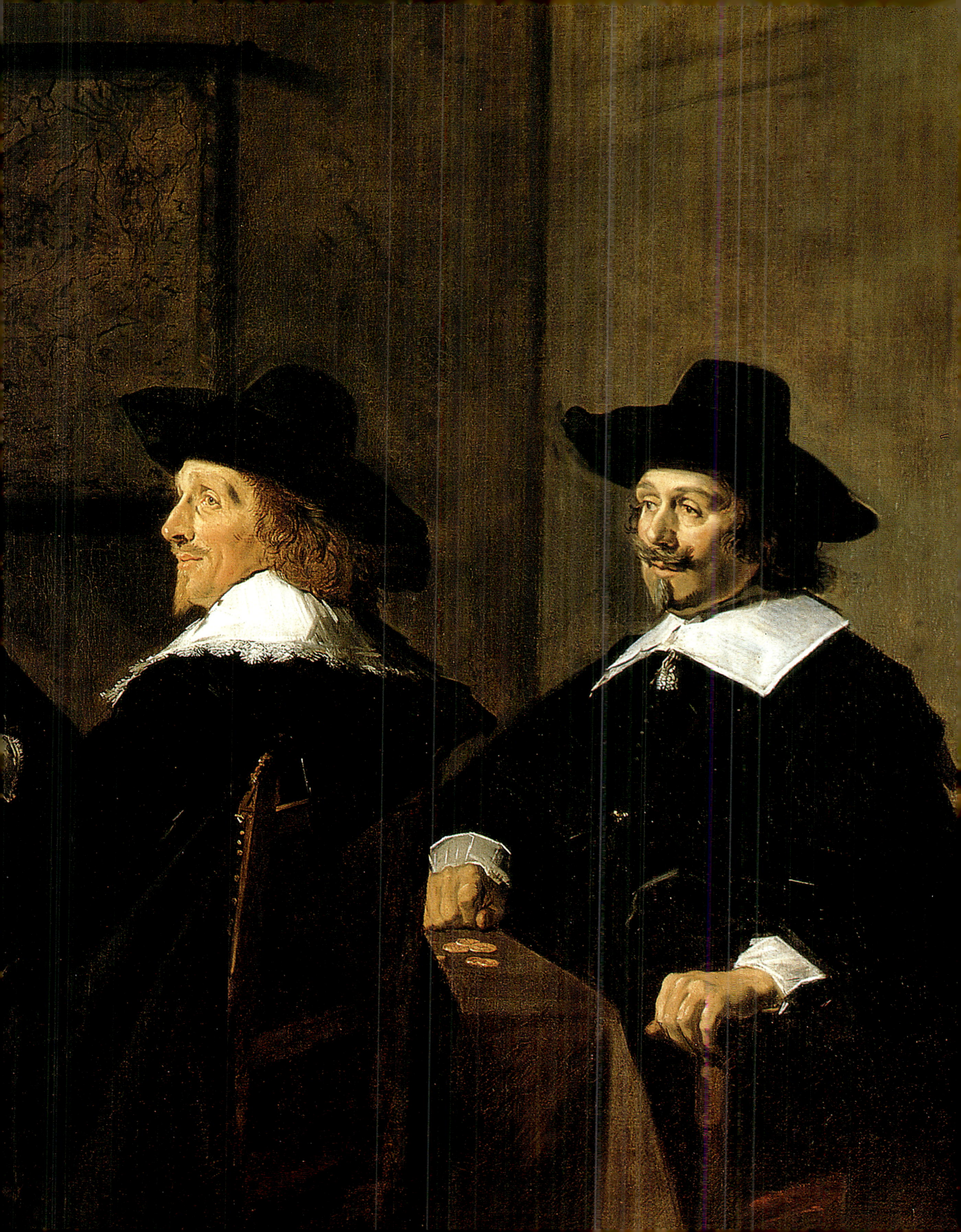

Frans Hals

Antwerp 1582/3 – 1666 Haarlem

24

Portrait of Willem Coymans, 1645

Oil on canvas, 77 x 64 cm
To the right of centre: ÆTA SUÆ. 22 [later changed to 6] / 1645
National Gallery of Art, Washington
(Andrew W. Mellon Collection)

This portrait of Willem Coymans (1623–1678) provides not only a superb example of Hals's loose style of painting, but also a unique insight into the painter's clientele. Hals enjoyed extensive contact with a range of families, including the Olycan (see cats 16–17) and Coymans families.[1] Just one year before the artist completed this portrait of Willem Coymans, he depicted Josephus Coymans and his wife, Dorothea Berck. Hals also produced brilliant pendant portraits of their daughter Isabella Coymans and her husband Stephanus Geraerdts shortly after their marriage, which was consecrated at the end of 1644 (p. 30, figs 19-20).[2] Thus within a short span of time Hals made portraits of at least five members of the Coymans family. Sadly these paintings have all since been dispersed to different collections.

It was once believed that the man depicted here was a famous scion of the family, Isabella's brother Balthasar Coymans (1618–1690)[3] who, together with his brothers, presided over the successful family business in Amsterdam.[4] Accordingly, around 1900 the age inscribed beneath the coat of arms with the three oxheads was changed from 22 to 26: Balthasar was born in 1618, and would not have been 22 in 1645. In 1970, however, the sitter was convincingly identified as the five-years-younger Willem, who belonged to a different branch of this highly affluent and influential family.[5] Willem was the son of Coenraet Coymans, who emigrated from Antwerp to Amsterdam, probably to join the family business.

Only fragments of his life story have come down to us, although we know he maintained contact with Hals after the completion of this portrait in 1645. In 1660, at the request of Willem and his brother-in-law Johan Fabry, Hals and Pieter Molijn (a landscape painter) valued paintings included in the estate of Willem's father.[6] Willem's name appears with that of Fabry in other documents from Haarlem and Amsterdam that imply he was a merchant of some sort. The garments Coymans wears in this portrait would certainly suggest that business was flourishing.

Coymans wears a French suit in the latest fashion. The sleeve is casually unbuttoned and turned back at the wrist to reveal the white shirt underneath. Like the suit, the rakishly cocked hat and its pom-pom is typical of the fashions of 1645 (see also cat. 25). The loosely curled long hair enhances the elegant nonchalance of fashions worn by the younger generation at this time. Hals conveys the impression of having painted the clothing with great ease: the gold embroidery on the sleeve of the doublet is rendered in extremely bold brushstrokes and the artist has ingeniously left areas of the brown ground visible here. The pleated white sleeve is the element of the portrait painted most loosely – here, with opaque white strokes over grey layers of paint, Hals convincingly expresses the fabric's transparency.

The technique accords perfectly with the sitter's casual pose. Coymans twists in his chair to face the viewer, whose gaze he meets with absolute self-confidence. He rests his arm in a relaxed fashion on the back of the chair, a pose seen in Hals's paintings from 1625 through to the very end of his career.[7] Earlier artists had incorporated the pose into group portraits, but Hals was the first to use it in individual portraits. The back of the chair becomes a perfect vehicle for injecting a lively informality into a portrait (see cat. 61). Hals had already applied this idea to superb effect in his portrait of Willem van Heythuysen, whom he painted tilting his chair backwards (cat. 20), and like the earlier painting, Hals's portrait of Coymans is intended to capture a fleeting moment in time. QB

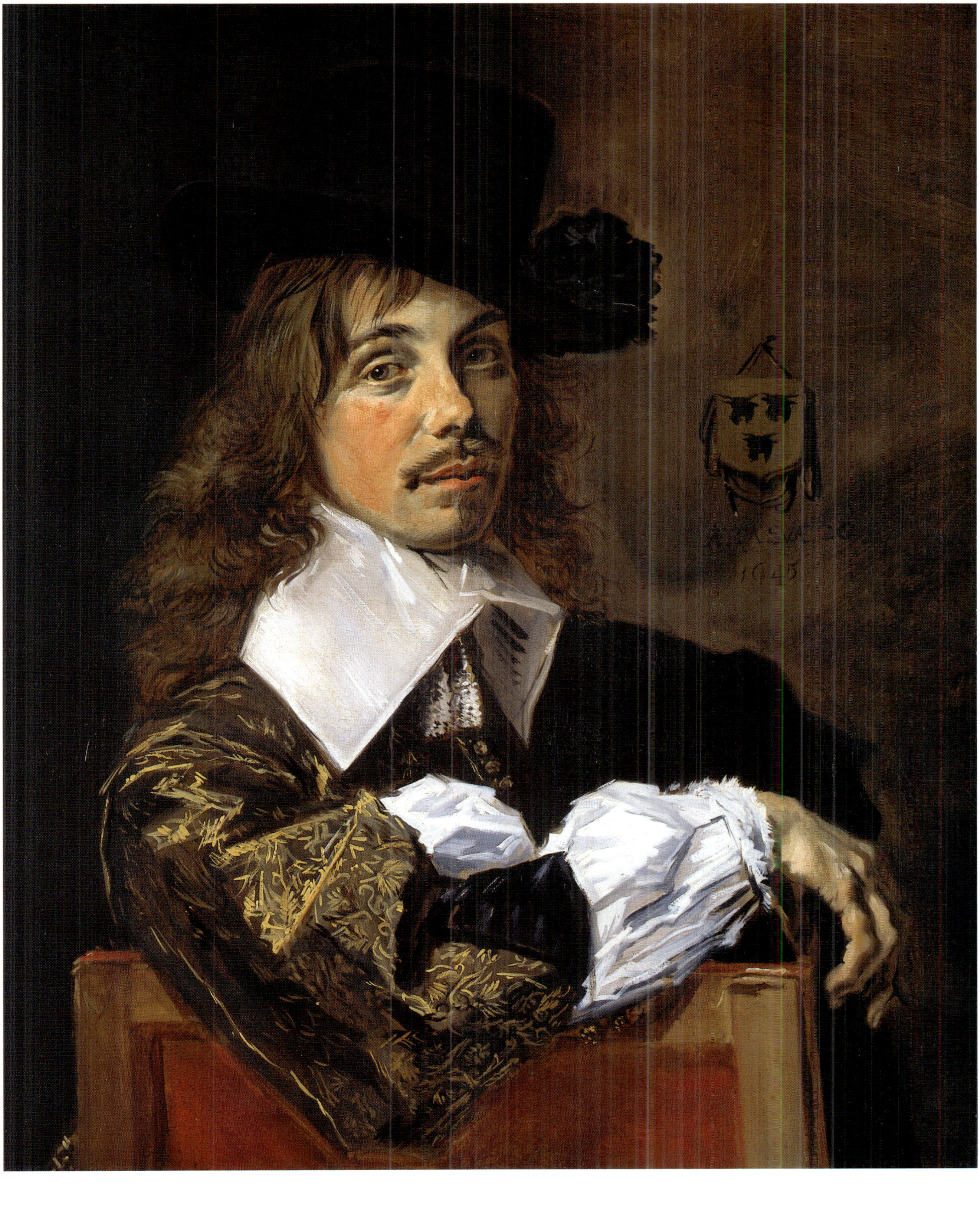

Frans Hals

Antwerp 1582/3 – 1666 Haarlem

25

Portrait of Jaspar Schade, about 1645

Oil on canvas, 80 x 68 cm
Národní Galerie, Prague

This remarkable painting confirms Hals's prodigious talents as a portraitist. A self-assured, almost arrogant-looking young man looks down at the viewer with a certain aloofness. The subject, Jaspar Schade (1623–1692), is dressed according to the latest French fashion. He wears a suit of black and gold brocade, the sleeves of which have been left open along the upper seam. His doublet is unbuttoned at the bottom to reveal his white chemise. The hat, with its cylindrical crown (an accessory fashionable briefly around 1645), is decorated with two gold-coloured bows. Schade's exuberant attire and voluptuous locks contrast sharply with the subdued black garments of the far older regents whose portraits Hals painted just a few years earlier (cat. 23). A particularly revealing comment on Schade's clothes has been preserved, dating from the year of this portrait: a relative of his received a letter while he was staying in Paris, warning him not to spend as much money on his wardrobe as his cousin Jaspar, who had run up enormous bills at the tailor's![1]

Schade was not a burgher who had made his own fortune; he came from a prominent patrician family.[2] Destined to be overlord of the district known as 'Tull en 't Wael', he became a canon in 1642 and dean of the chapter of Oudmunster, Utrecht, in 1666. This Protestant board had executive powers in the see of Utrecht. In 1672, Schade took up a seat in the States-General in The Hague as a deputy for Utrecht, and in 1681 he became president of the Court of Utrecht. How this Utrecht native commissioned his portrait from Hals, who lived and worked in Haarlem, is not known. Schade was only 22 years old when this portrait was made. On the basis of his fashionable clothing and the year inscribed on the painting's current frame – the coats of arms on it must have been copied from the original frame[3] – the work can be dated to 1645. The style of the painting corresponds closely to that of documented works by Hals from that year, such as the portrait of Willem Coymans (cat. 24). A few years after it was made, Hals's portrait was built into a wall of the reception hall of Schade's country home, Zandbergen, near Utrecht, where it hung until the late nineteenth century.[4]

In 1654, Schade commissioned another portrait of himself (fig. 25a), this time with his wife, Cornelia Strick van Linschoten, whom he had married in 1649.[5] For these pendants he approached not Hals but the portrait painter Cornelis Jonson van Ceulen (1593–1661), who was then based in Utrecht after having worked in London until 1643. Van Ceulen showed Schade in the same pose as Hals, though he opted for a three-quarter-length view and made both hands visible. The work's refined finish recalls the portraits of Anthony van Dyck (1599–1641), whose style was extremely popular in the Northern Netherlands after 1650. Van Ceulen's composition, in which Schade's hand dangles carelessly, also lacks originality. Hals's portrait, completed less than ten years earlier, displays this artist's keen sense of composition. It is painted loosely and idiosyncratically, conveying the play of light on the gleaming sleeve with great effect. This particular detail is a feast for the eyes, a maze of zigzag lines painted with remarkable accuracy. The same pattern is visible on the front of the doublet, although it is less conspicuous here. The close framing of the image – the sleeve is actually cut off above the hands – gives the subject an air of strength. Van Ceulen was skilled at his trade, but Hals was one of the greatest portrait painters of all time.[6] QB

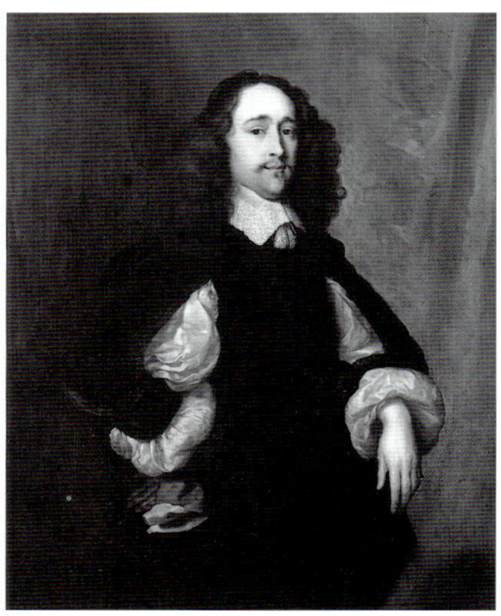

25a. Cornelis Jonson van Ceulen, *Portrait of Jaspar Schade*, 1654. Oil on canvas, 113 x 90 cm. Rijksmuseum Twenthe, Enschede

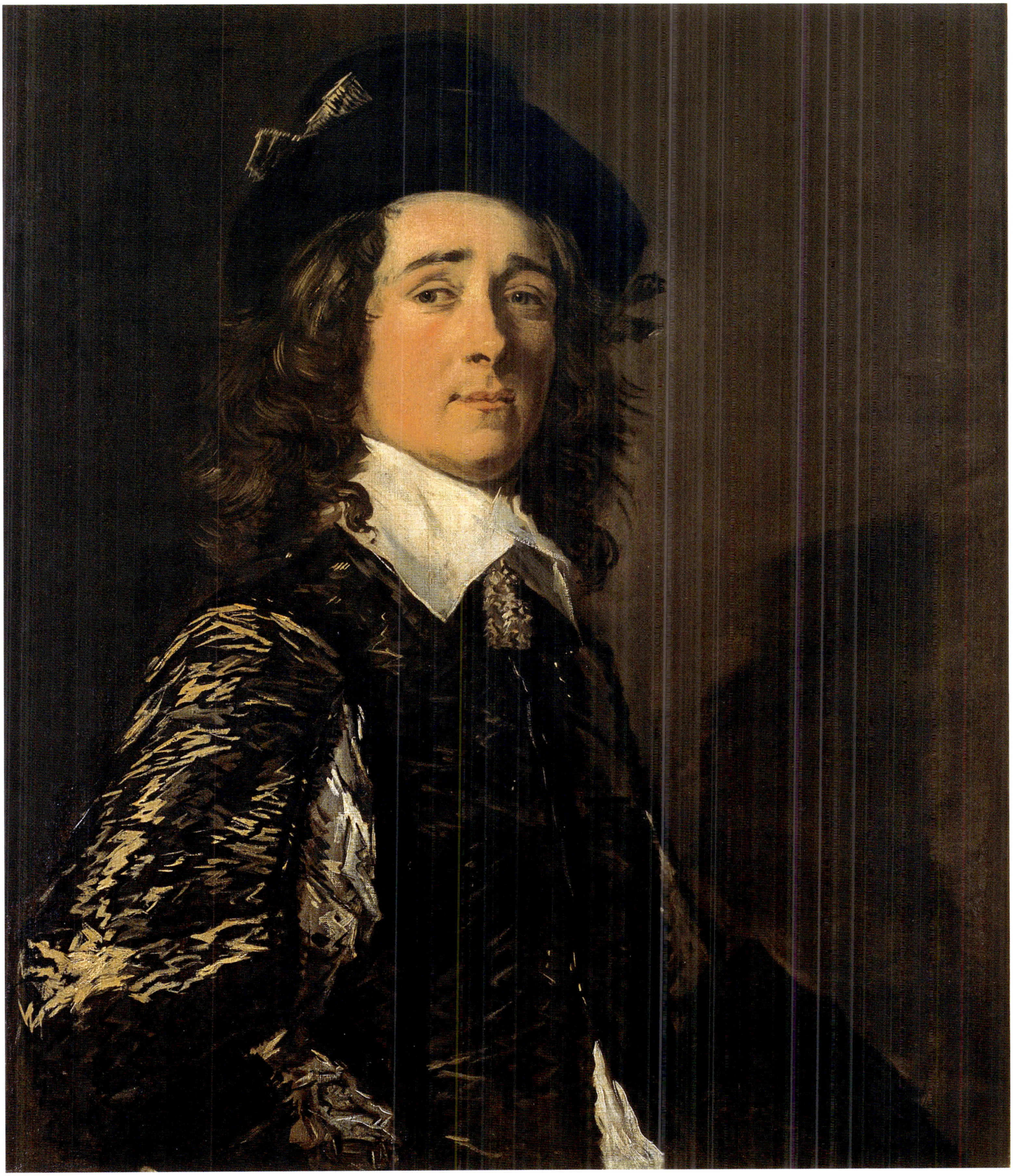

Frans Hals

Antwerp 1582/3 – 1666 Haarlem

26

Portrait of a Preacher, about 1660

Oil on panel, 36 x 30 cm
At lower right: FH (in ligature)
Private collection

For all its simplicity and modest size, this portrait by Frans Hals is an impressive work. It shows the half-length figure of a man set against a plain background. He wears a simple black doublet cut in a conservative style, with an unassuming white collar. His skull-cap has led to the traditional assumption that he was a preacher, but other professions wore similar headgear in the seventeenth-century Republic (see cat. 5).[1] Still, the man's short hair and austere clothing make it reasonable to conclude that he was indeed a minister. He holds a small book, presumably a Bible, in one hand, while the other is concealed behind his black cloak. This pose is characteristic of Hals's other portraits of preachers, such as that of the influential Church minister Herman Langelius of Amsterdam, which was also painted around 1660.[2]

At the same time as the portrait discussed here, Hals produced two other likenesses of austerely dressed men, one of which is painted on a somewhat smaller panel (fig. 26a).[3] The collar of the man in that portrait is embellished with small tassels, a rather unusual adornment for a preacher; neither does he wear a skull-cap. To date, none of the men depicted in these small portraits has been convincingly identified. In 1680, Arnold Moonen wrote a poem about Hals's portrait of the Haarlem minister Jan Ruyll,[4] but the text of this poem does not provide any details about this image. Moonen emphasised, in his rather pedestrian verse, that Hals could convey the man's appearance, but not the wise lessons from his 'golden mouth'. In the past, the poem has been linked – probably incorrectly – to the portrait described here.[5]

The expressive character of the portrait and the intense observation of the sitter are comparable to the large regent pieces Hals painted around 1664 (p. 128, fig. 23b). The freedom with which this small portrait is painted also corresponds to that of the more famous works. The portrait was probably made around 1660, when Hals was in his late seventies but still in full command of his powers; the loose brushwork of the man's face and hand is especially characteristic of the Haarlem painter's late work. The man's facial expression has been captured with extraordinary skill, and the deliberately plain background further emphasises the face. Hals painted the background quickly, making ingenious use of the lighter ground that glimmers through the paint. While the doublet is also painted very thinly in places, the face is so meticulously worked up that – despite the apparently loose brushwork – it must have required more than one session.[6] The richly varied flesh tints stand out superbly against the dark background.
QB

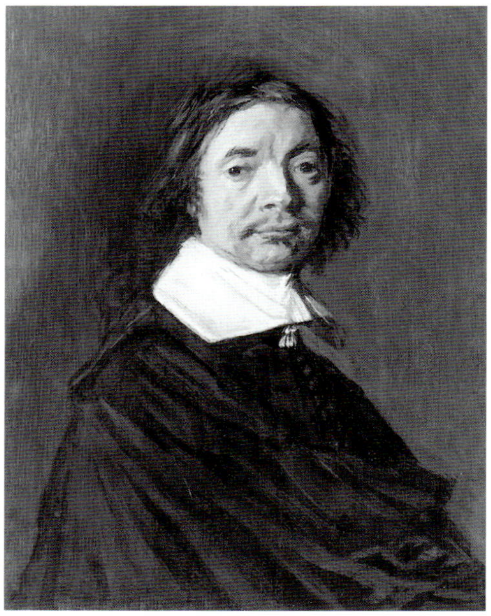

26a.
Frans Hals,
Portrait of a Man, about 1660.
Oil on panel, 31 x 26 cm.
Mauritshuis,
The Hague

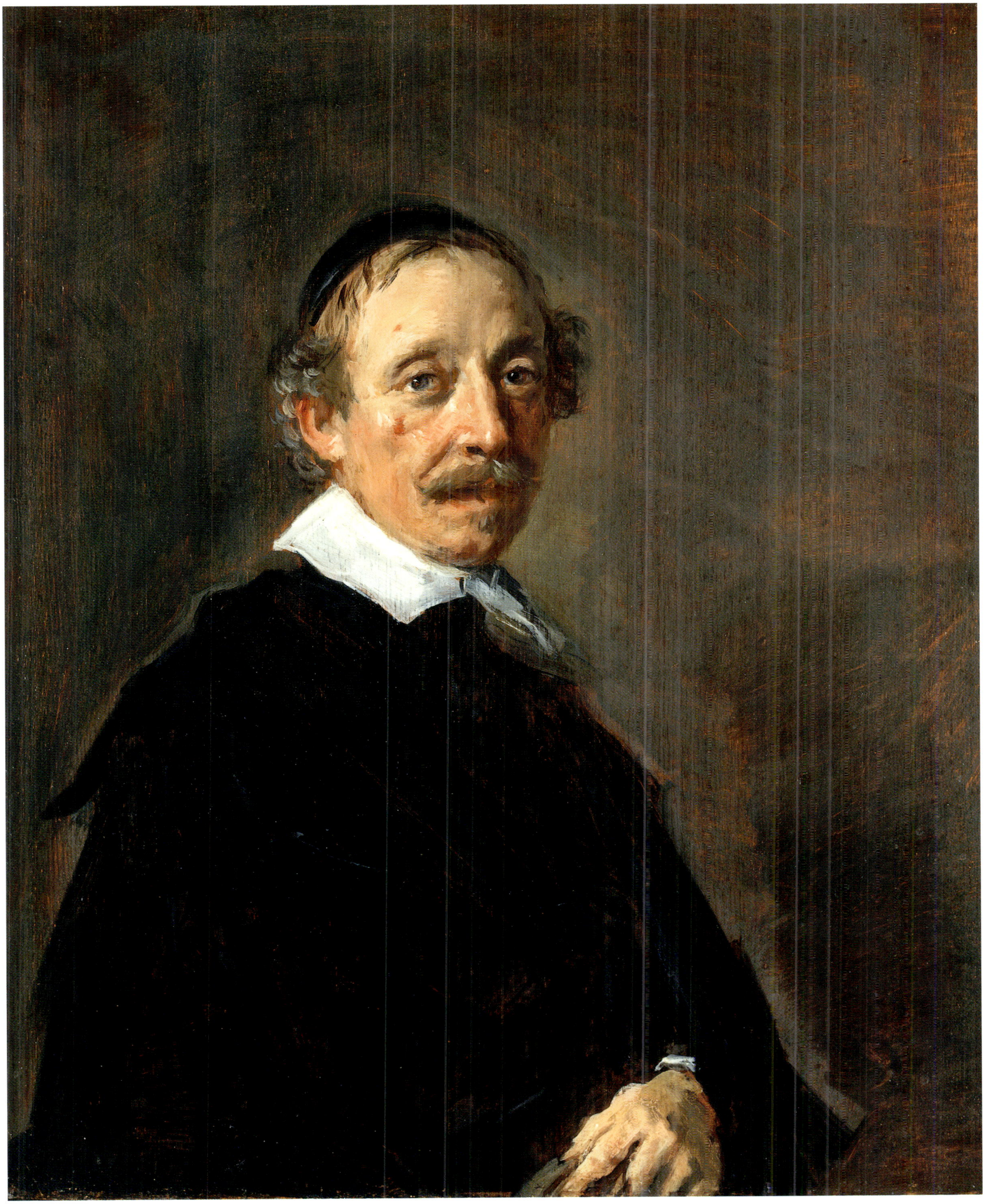

Frans Hals

Antwerp 1582/3 – 1666 Haarlem

27

Portrait of a Man, about 1660–5

Oil on canvas, 71 x 59 cm
Stiftung Sammlung E.G. Bührle, Zürich
The Hague only

This painting is one of a very small number of portraits that Frans Hals produced at the end of his life.[1] He executed these works with an extremely loose and boisterous technique (see p. 128, fig. 23b), and a directness that rivals that of Rembrandt's late portraits (cats 58–61), but by the 1660s, most clients preferred a more carefully finished portrait (such as cats 1, 3 and 40). The smiling man in this portrait, which, judging by the loose style of painting, must have been executed between 1660 and 1666,[2] evidently liked Hals's more idiosyncratic approach. We know nothing about the sitter: the portrait does not contain any clues to his identity, such as a family coat of arms or an inscription with a reference to his age.[3]

At roughly the same time as this work, Hals produced another portrait, now in Boston, of a man seen at half-length against a barely defined background (fig. 27a).[4] In both pieces, Hals concentrated far more energy on the face – only half of which is illuminated – than on the hands (it is worth contrasting this approach with that Hals took in earlier works, such as cat. 23). Here, we can see only the right hand – his other hand is probably on his side – while the man in the Boston portrait clasps his hands together. In both paintings the sitter's elbow is cut off by the picture-edge, although the man in the present portrait is shown closer to the picture plane. He is dressed far more simply than the sitter for the Boston painting, who is shown in an expensive Japanese-style chamber gown (*Japonse rock*) – a garment that was all the rage a decade later (see cat. 38) – and, possibly, an expensive wig.[5] The sitter here wears a plain black doublet over a white shirt, the collar of which is open, leaving the tasselled cords, or *akers*, dangling. This quasi-nonchalant mode of dress was fashionable around 1655;[6] we can probably assume that the man depicted by Hals five to ten years later took little interest in fashion. The man's open collar and long unruly curls lend the portrait an air of informality. Just as in Rembrandt's *Portrait of an Elderly Man* from 1667 (cat. 61), the collar and cuffs provide light accents in an image dominated by brown and black hues.

Hals produced this remarkable portrait at about 80 years of age, proof that he did not suffer an artistic decline at the end of his long career. Indeed, his technique appears to have become all the more powerful with the passage of time. The face, composed of numerous small dabs of paint, appears almost to have been modelled in clay.[7] Collar, hand and cuff are constructed with strikingly vigorous brushstrokes applied *alla prima*; the *akers* with strokes of white paint of varying thickness that are highly convincing from a distance. Small accents of red in the corner of one eye, in the face and the thumbnail bring the figure to life.[8] It was paintings like this that had such a great impact on the French Impressionists in the nineteenth century. QB

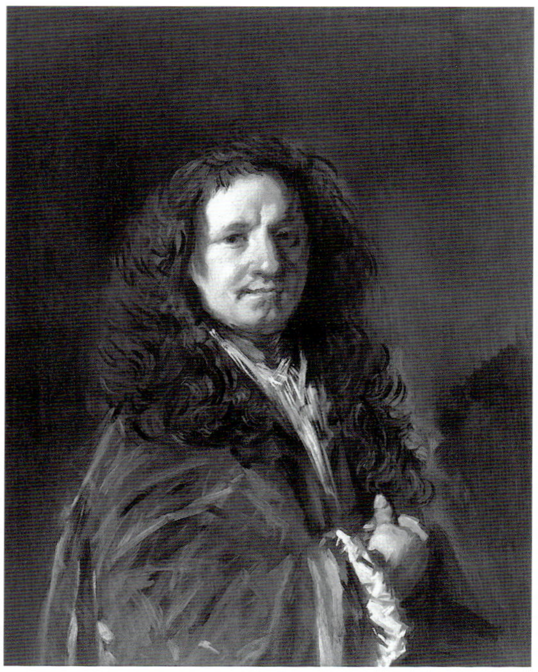

27a. Frans Hals, *Portrait of a Man*, about 1660–5. Oil on canvas, 86 x 67 cm. Museum of Fine Arts, Boston (Gift of Mrs Antonie Lilienfeld in memory of Dr Leon Lilienfeld, 1966)

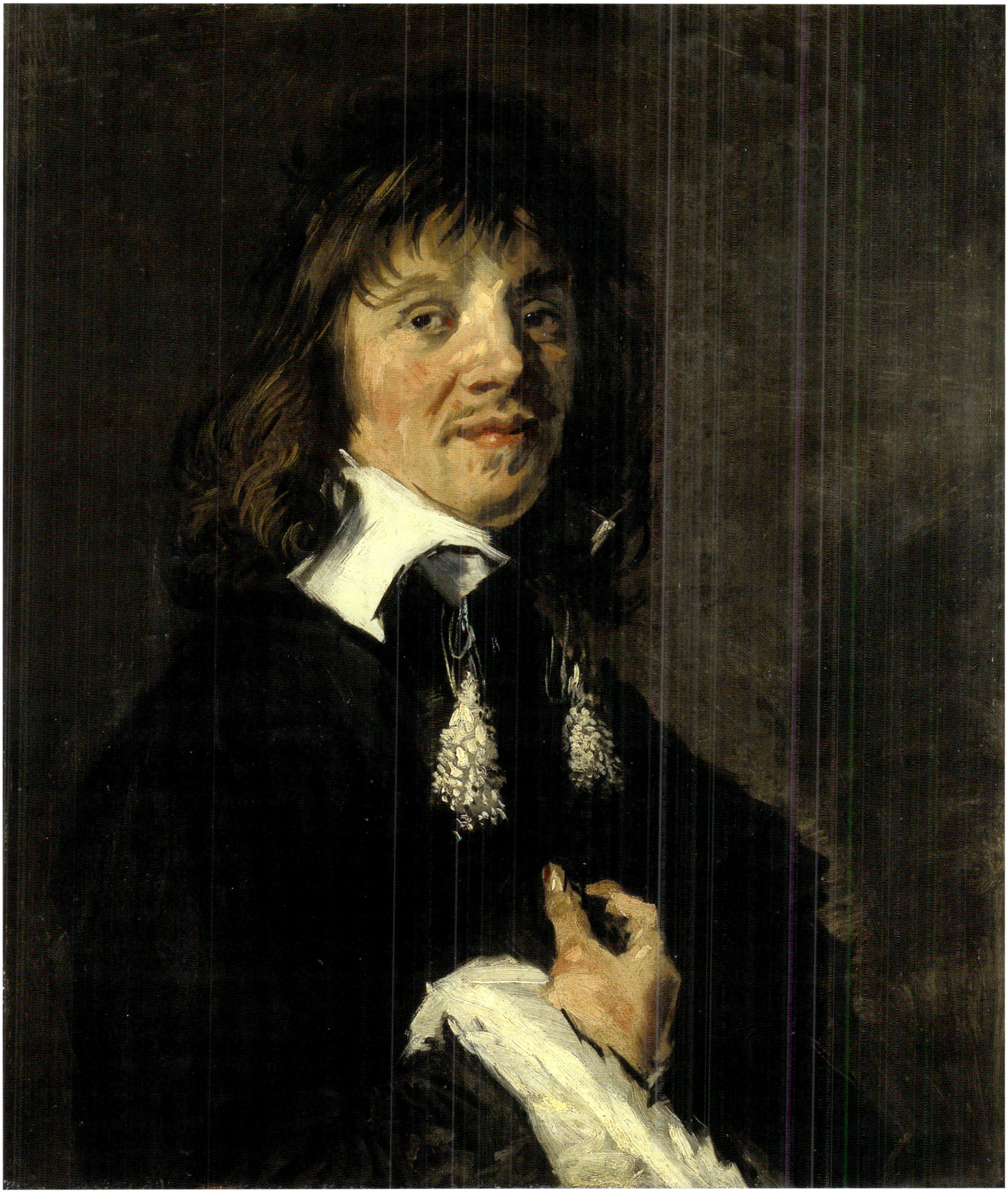

Adriaen Hanneman

The Hague about 1604–1671 The Hague

28

Portrait of Henry, Duke of Gloucester, about 1653

Oil on canvas, 105 x 87 cm
National Gallery of Art, Washington
(Andrew W. Mellon Collection)

Portrait painters working in the Northern Netherlands occasionally received commissions from foreigners residing in (or travelling through) the Republic. Adriaen Hanneman, a Hague-born painter who returned home in around 1638 after several years in London, occupies a unique position in this regard: a large proportion of the portraits he made in the Republic were commissioned by English clients.[1] Civil War broke out in England in 1642, and there was a significant exodus – largely of those on the royalist or 'Cavalier' side – to continental Europe in the years that followed. Many settled in The Hague, where they were received warmly at the court of the 'Winter Queen' Elizabeth Stuart, sister of King Charles I (1600–1649). Here, Hanneman depicts Henry, Duke of Gloucester (1640–1660), the third son of Charles I and Henrietta Maria (1609–1669),[2] who, as the son of the king, had been a virtual prisoner of the English Parliament from an early age. He was given permission to travel to the Dutch Republic in 1652, and Hanneman, who had already painted Henry's elder brother Charles (King Charles II from 1660),[3] executed this portrait about a year later.

That both brothers had their portraits painted by Hanneman, The Hague's foremost portraitist at the time, was undoubtedly partly due to the fondness their sister, Maria Henrietta Stuart (widow of Stadholder Willem II of Orange) had for the artist's work. Additionally, Hanneman worked in the style of Anthony van Dyck who, as court painter to Charles I, had produced official portraits in London of the heir to the throne. Perhaps to emphasise the continuity of the Stuart dynasty, it was deemed desirable to depict the young Henry in a comparably 'Van Dyckian' pose and style.[4] In the Republic, there was no one better suited to this task than Hanneman; during his years in London he had been strongly influenced by Van Dyck, and indeed probably worked in his studio. He adopted the Flemish master's characteristically elegant poses, bold brushstrokes, and convincing rendering of garments in his own portraits, and imported this innovative style to The Hague (see also cat. 41). This superbly preserved portrait of Henry, which echoes a 1641 Van Dyck portrait of Charles II,[5] is often regarded as Hanneman's finest painting.[6] Indeed, it is of such high quality that for many years it was attributed to Van Dyck himself.[7] A curious feature typical of many of Hanneman's portraits is the 'halo' of light around the head, caused by the light-coloured, brownish-grey ground that was left visible during the painting of the rock in the background.[8] The background was only filled in after the figure was completed.

The choice of garments and accessories confirm that Henry is represented as an army officer: he wears a breastplate over his buff-coloured doublet, and in his right hand he holds the baton with which generals were traditionally depicted (see cats 1, 32, 39). With a graceful gesture he grasps a gilded sword in his left hand. The bands of gold braid trimming the doublet and trousers are painted with remarkably loose, yet bold, strokes. The small, simple collar, with ties ending in decorative tassels, corresponds precisely to the fashion of 1653. On 4 May that year, Henry's brother made him a knight of the Order of the Garter, and the blue sash draped over the young man's shoulder is one of the Order's insignia.[9] Shortly after receiving this distinction, Henry joined his mother in Paris. After the House of Stuart was restored to the throne in 1660, he returned to London with his brother. There he contracted smallpox and died that same year, at only 20 years of age. QB

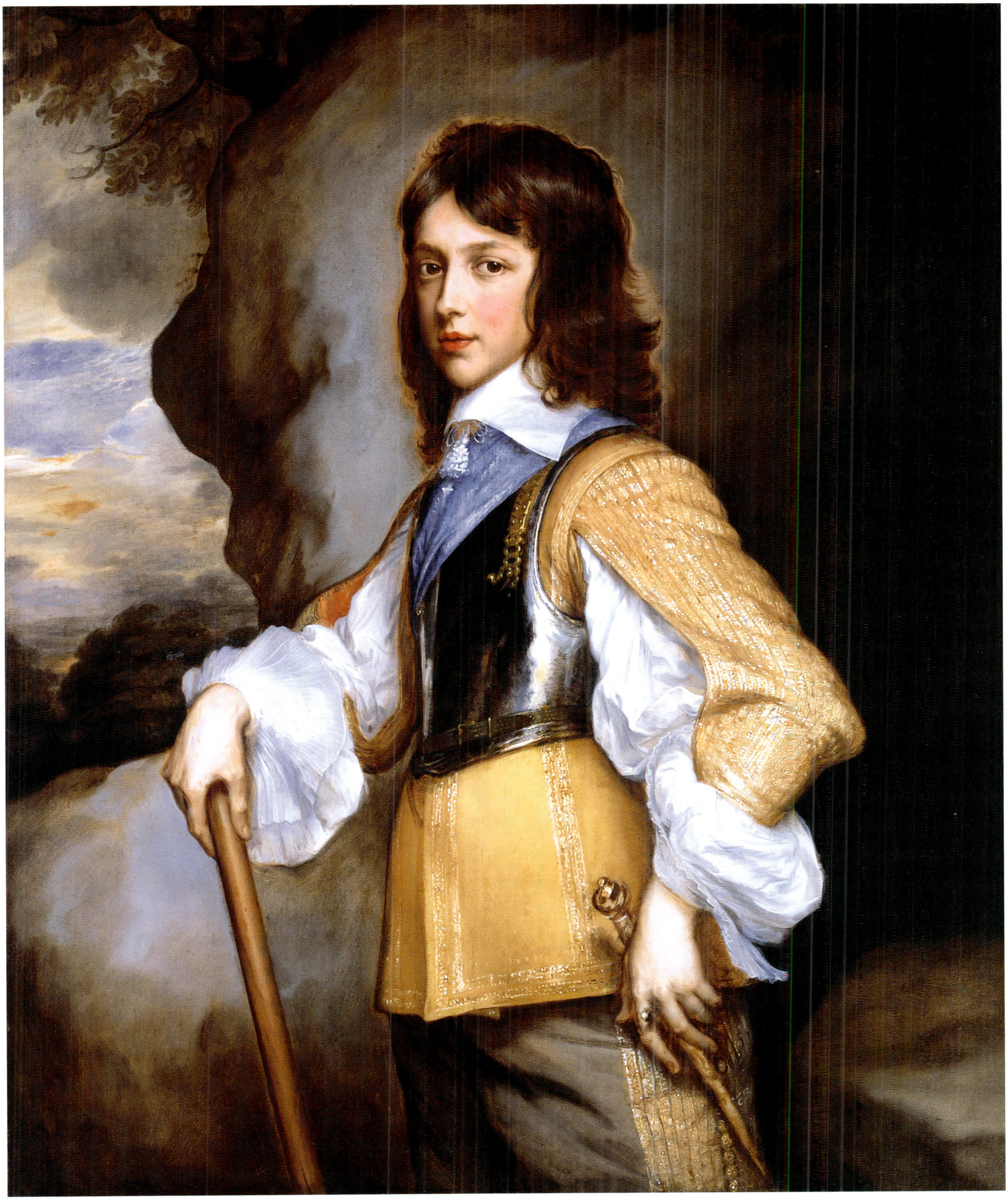

Bartholomeus van der Helst

Haarlem about 1613 – 1670 Amsterdam

29

Double Portrait of Abraham del Court and Maria de Kaersgieter, 1654

Oil on canvas, 172 x 146.5 cm
At left, on the bench: B. *van der. helst. fec. / 1654.*
Museum Boijmans Van Beuningen, Rotterdam

This monumental double portrait shows why Bartholomeus van der Helst was so much in demand as a portraitist, perfectly illustrating his immense skill at rendering faces and materials. He devoted extraordinary care to the fabric of the sitters' clothing; almost half of this painting is taken up by the splendid satin gown of the woman, Maria de Kaersgieter (1631–1660).[1] The shimmering, silver-grey fabric is painted in minute detail, as are the silver lace on the dress and the bands of white bobbin-lace that form the shawl collar and cuffs. Van der Helst's smooth technique superbly conveys the play of light on the satin.

The emphasis on fabrics is related directly to the occupation of De Kaersgieter's husband, Abraham del Court (1623–after 1663), who was a cloth merchant in Amsterdam's Kalverstraat and a connoisseur of textiles. Four years after the completion of this portrait, which is dated 1654, Del Court was appointed a syndic of the guild,[2] an honorary position that involved inspecting the quality of fabrics (for this position, see also cat. 60). Del Court's black silk apparel – an outfit just as expensive as his wife's – contrasts with the silver-grey of her dress. The opulence of the couple's *à la mode* garments is underscored by the woman's precious jewellery. She wears ropes of pearls in her hair and around her neck and wrists, as well as a diamond brooch at her breast and a diamond ring on her hand.

Although this portrait was painted a few years after the couple's marriage, the love between them is central to the image. The woman is depicted to the right of her husband, according to custom. While the man makes contact with his wife by bending solicitously towards her, she engages the viewer's gaze. Her left hand holds a rose, key to the symbolism of this painting: an allusion to the joy and pain of love.[3] The man's eyes focus on this bloom, and the woman's other hand is at the centre of the image. Her husband gently supports her wrist, emphasising the wedding ring on her thumb. Their gesture is a variation on the traditional *dextrarum iunctio*, two entwined right hands that symbolise fidelity and the matrimonial bond.[4]

The park-like surroundings are also part of the matrimonial symbolism of the portrait. The 'garden of love' in which the couple is depicted recalls earlier double portraits of lovers amid a wealth of greenery. Peter Paul Rubens made a famous painting of himself with his wife Isabella Brant in a garden around 1610 (p. 108, fig. 15a), and a dozen years later Frans Hals used the motif in a double portrait of a newly married couple (cat. 15). The fountain playing behind Maria de Kaersgieter is entirely appropriate to this setting: the 'fountain of marriage' was a commonplace in the seventeenth century, referring to the purity of the relationship between man and wife.[5]

When Del Court and De Kaersgieter had their portraits made by Van der Helst, the painter was at the peak of his fame, and he remained the most influential portrait painter of the Amsterdam elite until his death in 1670. He also produced a number of regent pieces in this period (see cat. 30). Although the matchless rendering of fabrics was one of his trademarks, Van der Helst did not confine himself to superficial appearances in this portrait, paying considerable attention to the composition and its many eloquent details. The figures' demonstrative gestures – the man holds his hat, the woman a rose, and with their other hands they make contact – add a dynamic quality to the painting. The sitters' self-assured, confident poses are particularly characteristic of Van der Helst's work. QB

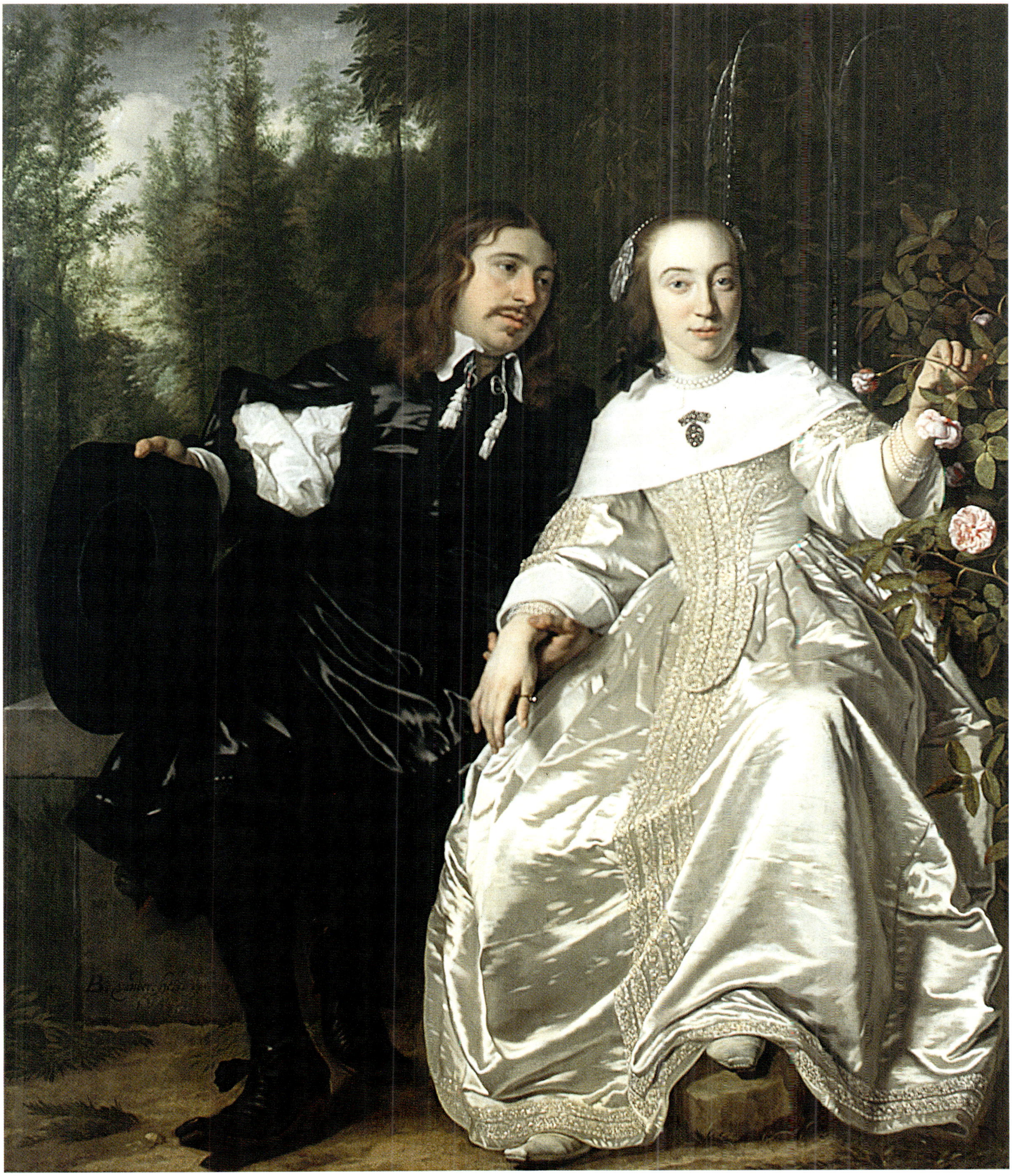

Bartholomeus van der Helst

Haarlem about 1613 – 1670 Amsterdam

30

Portrait of the Regents of the Voetboogdoelen, 1656

Oil on canvas, 183 x 254 cm
At lower right: B. *vander. helst. fecit 1656*
Amsterdams Historisch Museum, Amsterdam

This monumental group portrait of four prominent regents of Amsterdam marks the end of a long tradition of civic guard portraits (*schutterstukken*) commissioned by the Amsterdam militia guilds (see cat. 21). The civic militias were organised into three different companies: the Handboogdoelen, the Kloveniersdoelen and the Voetboogdoelen (companies of longbowmen, arquebusiers and crossbowmen, respectively). The regents, or governors, of the three boards that oversaw the companies' headquarters all commissioned their portraits from Van der Helst in the period 1653–6.[1] The portrait of the regents of the Voetboogdoelen – also known as St George's Hall (Sint-Jorisdoelen) – was the last of the three. During the seventeenth century, the Voetboogdoelen and other guardsmen's halls gradually lost their original purpose, as the 1648 Treaty of Münster marked the end of the Eighty Years' War between Spain and the Dutch Republic (p. 78, fig. 2a) and eliminated the need for an active militia to guard the city. No longer used as practice grounds, the shooting ranges at the civic guard's headquarters were filled in with new buildings, and the main buildings were converted into gentlemen's clubs for meetings and social gatherings. The position of regent of one of the militia companies was much coveted, since it brought with it a share of the profits gained from the buildings, which were also used as inns. Even so, we know from a book by one of these regents' contemporaries that they did not pay for the portrait discussed here out of their own pockets, but from the militia hall's general treasury.[2]

The regents of the Voetboogdoelen were appointed for life in 1653. One of them, Frans van der Meer, died shortly after his appointment and was succeeded by either Gerard Hasselaer (1620–1673) or Frans Reael (1618–1669). One of these two men must be depicted at far left, since the other three men can be identified with certainty. From left to right, they are Joris Backer (1607–1666), Hendrick Spiegel (1598–1667) and Joan Huydecoper (1599–1661).[3] In 1656, the year of this portrait, Spiegel and Huydecoper were also serving as burgomasters of Amsterdam.

The painting is quite static in feel as Van der Helst depicted the gentlemen seated around a table, as was customary in the case of regent pieces (see cat. 23). Two of the men look obliquely out of the picture, while the other two look straight at the viewer. The men's heads are all level with the same imaginary horizontal line. Standing just behind the four regents is the Voetboogdoelen's innkeeper, Christoffel Pook (1603–1661). On the right, a servant carries a ceremonial silver drinking horn to the table, a reminder of the militia's long history.[4] The horn, crafted in 1566, bears an effigy of Saint George, the patron saint of the archers of the guild.[5] The horn's survival was due partly to the good offices of the regents, who, as administrators of the guardsmen's hall, were also in charge of its rich holdings of paintings and silver. The finely decorated horn is depicted prominently in the foreground of an earlier group portrait Van der Helst made for the Voetboogdoelen, his famous 1648 militia banquet, which shows the regents of the militia as well as the guardsmen themselves.[6]

Here, the innkeeper – who is also depicted in the 1648 painting – actually plays a part in the action. Instead of pouring drinks, as in the earlier painting, he brings the men an inkpot, and looks directly at the viewer. That his name is explicitly inscribed on the inkpot is related to an event that was topical at the time. In June 1656, the year in which the portrait was completed, the regents won a lawsuit against Amsterdam city council: the innkeeper was no longer required to make annual payments to the regents of the Almoners' Home on behalf of the Voetboogdoelen.[7] The document Spiegel is holding in one hand – and pointing at emphatically with his other – must be related to this lawsuit. The folded sheet of paper is presumably about to be addressed or signed, since Pook is bringing the inkpot and quill to the table. The regents – two of whom were burgomasters of the city – seem delighted with the outcome of the lawsuit: perhaps the drinking horn has been brought in for a celebratory drink?[8] QB

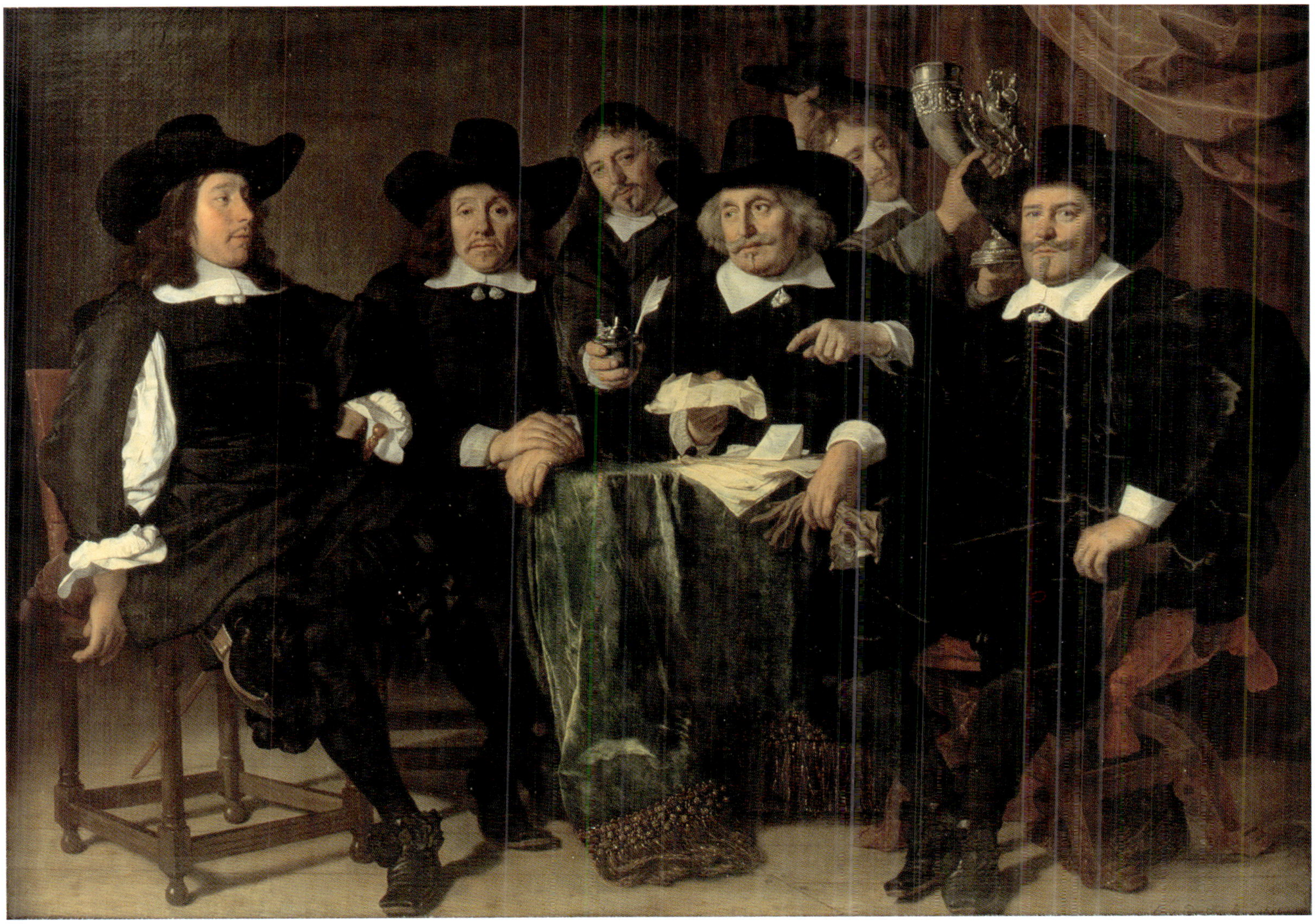

Gerrit van Honthorst

Utrecht 1592 – 1656 Utrecht

31

Portrait of King Charles I with a Letter in his Hand, 1628

Oil on canvas, 76.2 x 64.1 cm
National Portrait Gallery, London

In the late spring of 1628, Gerrit van Honthorst travelled to London at the invitation of King Charles I (1600–1649; reigned 1625–49), evidently to execute a commission for a monumental history painting of the twins *Apollo and Diana* (fig. 31a).[1] This daring composition shows the seven Liberal Arts paying homage to these gods, who are seated on the clouds in the upper left corner of the picture. The procession is led by Mercury, identifiable by his winged helmet. Interestingly, several of the main characters bear the features of real people. In Mercury and Grammar, the woman kneeling beside him, we recognise the Duke and Duchess of Buckingham; Charles I and his wife, Henrietta Maria (1609–1669) are cast as Apollo and Diana respectively.[2]

One can scarcely conceive of a greater contrast to these formal, allegorical, courtly portraits than this intimate painting of Charles I that Van Honthorst made at about the same time. The king is shown here so intimately and so informally, momentarily looking up while reading a letter, that the portrait must have been made from life.[3] The king's pose is strikingly similar to that in *Apollo and Diana*, and it has been assumed that the portrait was taken as the basis for the sovereign's likeness in the allegory.[4] Whatever the case may be, this remarkable painting is one of Van Honthorst's most convincing and accessible portraits.

The painter rendered the monarch's apparel with great care. The falling ruff and the cuffs are trimmed with lace patterned with geometrical motifs. The supple fit of the doublet gives the impression of an informal garment. The deep slashes in the sleeves and body are typical of the latest French fashion, as is the king's hairstyle, with its 'lovelock' or cadenette cascading to his left shoulder.[5] The striking red and green colours reflect the king's personal preference. In the Royal Wardrobe accounts we find a note as early as 1618–22 that most of the king's clothes were made in a 'greene, sea-greene or willow collour', frequently trimmed with another shade of green or 'scarlet, crimson or carnation'.[6]

In December 1628 Van Honthorst returned to The Hague. His luggage contained replicas of the portraits he had made of the king and queen of England, a gift from the king to Frederik V, the 'Winter King', who lived in The Hague (Frederik's wife, Elizabeth Stuart, was Charles I's sister). Commissions from the latter court and from the stadholder and his wife, Frederik Hendrik and Amalia van Solms, followed soon after Van Honthorst's return (cat. 32). In retrospect, his short stay at the English court proved to be a turning-point in his career. Until 1628 he was known chiefly as a gifted purveyor of history paintings and genre scenes; later he developed into a prominent and sought-after portraitist who specialised in depicting rulers.[7] PP

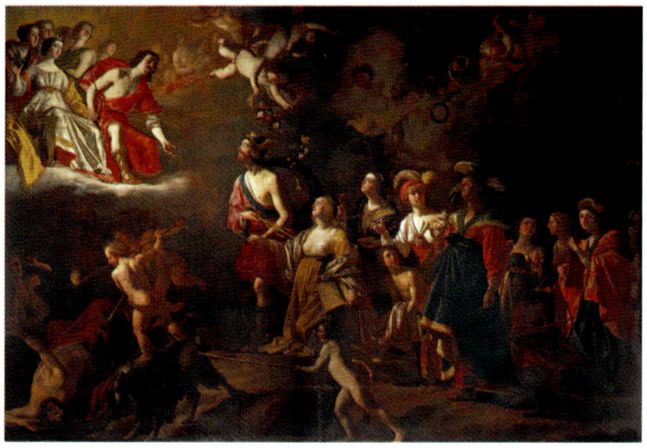

31a.
Gerrit van Honthorst,
Apollo and Diana, 1628.
Oil on canvas,
357 x 640 cm.
The Royal Collection,
Hampton Court Palace

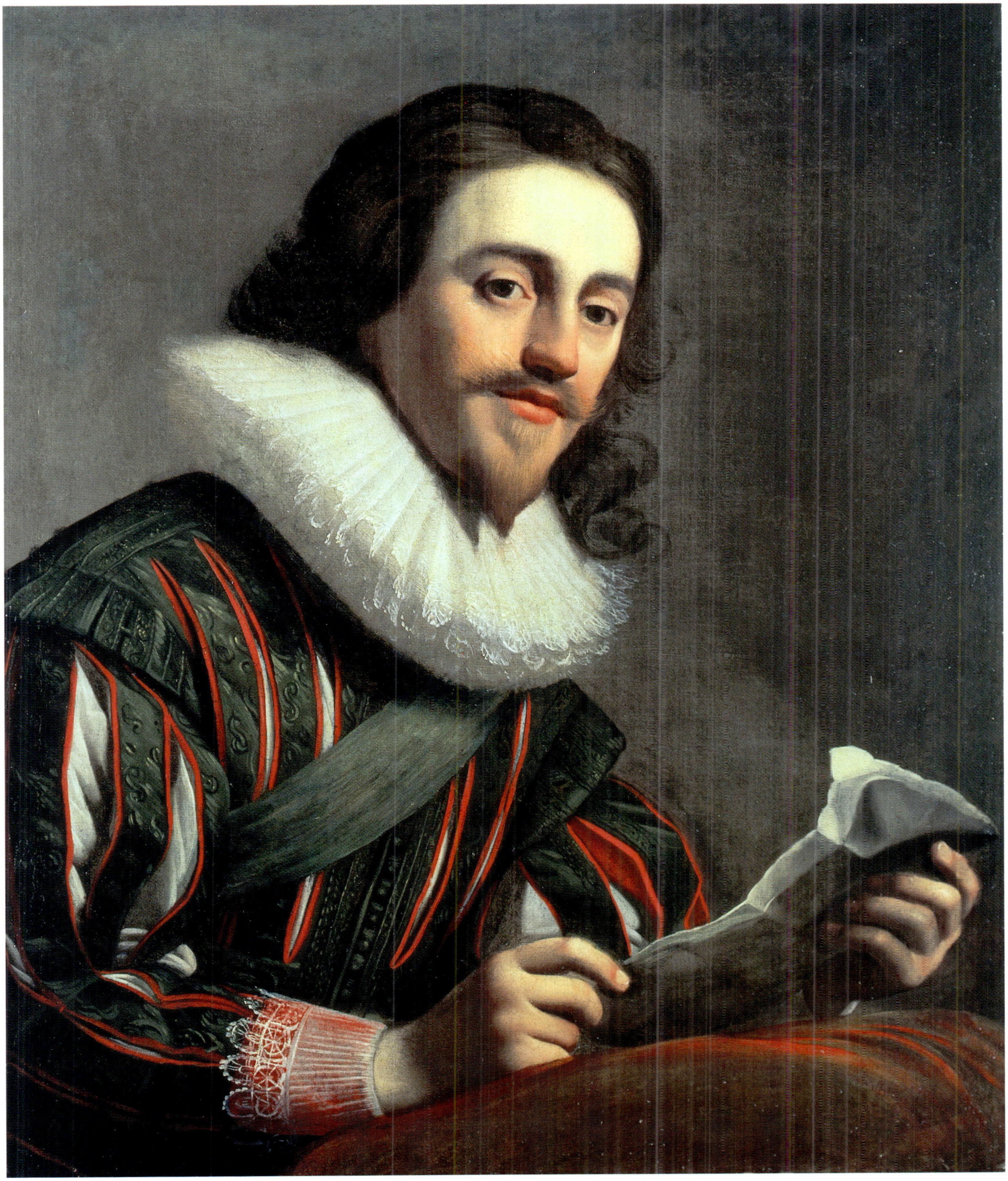

Gerrit van Honthorst

Utrecht 1592 – 1656 Utrecht

32

Double Portrait of Frederik Hendrik and Amalia van Solms, 1637–8

Oil on canvas, 213 x 202 cm
Royal Picture Gallery Mauritshuis, The Hague
The Hague only

Not all portraits made in the Republic were produced for burghers. Members of the ruling House of Orange ordered a great many portraits for their palaces, and their relatives and entourage also granted numerous commissions. This official portrait by Gerrit van Honthorst represents the Stadholder and Prince of Orange Frederik Hendrik (1584–1647) and his wife, Amalia van Solms (1602–1675). The stadholder is depicted as a general in a suit of armour. His pose, with one hand holding his baton and the other on his side, above his sword, radiates dignity and authority. Around his neck he wears the prestigious Order of the Garter, presented to him by the king of England. The ceremonial helmet with its orange plume and the orange sash are allusions to the House of Orange. Amalia is dressed formally in black and adorned with copious quantities of pearls, entirely in accordance with the fashion in 1637. Strands of pearls are everywhere: around her neck, décolleté, waist, arms and wrists. Pearls have even been woven into her hair and incorporated into her earrings. The large freshwater pearls around her neck were purchased for her in 1635 by her husband, who paid a phenomenal sum for them.[1]

Van Honthorst painted this life-sized double portrait after the prince achieved one of his greatest military triumphs over the Spanish troops. This victory, the taking of Breda (1637), is represented behind the couple, where the curtain is raised to reveal a landscape with a military encampment. Van Honthorst's consummate skill is revealed in the striking likeness of the figures – their features are known from many other paintings – and beautiful rendering of the fabrics in this fluidly painted work.

The regal ambiance of the composition draws upon the international tradition of rulers' portraits. There are also distinct resemblances to Michiel van Mierevelt's full-length portrait of Prince Maurits, which was made about 20 years earlier (see also cat. 39). The stadholder's apparel and pose are virtually identical in these two paintings, as are such accessories as the curtain and the plumed ceremonial helmet.[2]

The Utrecht-born Van Honthorst was active in courtly circles in The Hague from 1630 onwards. He received his first commissions there from the Elector Palatine Frederik V and Elizabeth Stuart, known as the 'Winter' King and Queen of Bohemia, who were introduced to Van Honthorst's portraits through Elizabeth's brother, King Charles I of England (see cat. 31). Van Honthorst's talent for depicting his subjects in an idealised manner, evenly lit and elegantly posed, was greatly admired by his clientele. In 1631 he painted his first official portraits of Frederik Hendrik and Amalia.[3] The double portrait discussed here, painted about 1637, marks Van Honthorst's breakthrough as court painter to the stadholder and his wife. In this capacity he succeeded Van Mierevelt (see cat. 39),[4] whose style was deemed old-fashioned. This work became the prototype for the artist's later portraits of Frederik Hendrik, although he modified the facial features to reflect the stadholder's age. Replicas of the double portrait exist in various forms: some are bust or three-quarter length, and some depict the couple separately instead of together.[5]

This work is an autograph replica of a painting made for the Huis ter Nieuburg, Frederik and Amalia's country house near Rijswijk. The original, today known only from a print, hung above the mantle in the Great Hall of the house's central pavilion.[6] The portrait's prominent location underscores the couple's dynastic ambitions. It was surrounded by portraits of the 28 most important European sovereigns and their wives, which were displayed in galleries linking the central pavilion with Frederik Hendrik and Amalia's apartments.[7] The men's portraits hung in the eastern gallery, which Frederik Hendrik passed on his way to his rooms, while the women's portraits were in the western wing, along Amalia's route to her part of the house.

This version of the portrait is described in a letter that the painter wrote in 1637 to his client, Constantijn Huygens, the stadholder's secretary (see cat. 34).[8] Completed in late 1637 or early 1638, it was made to hang in Huygens's residence at Haagse Plein. It was transferred to the adjoining Mauritshuis in 1829. QB

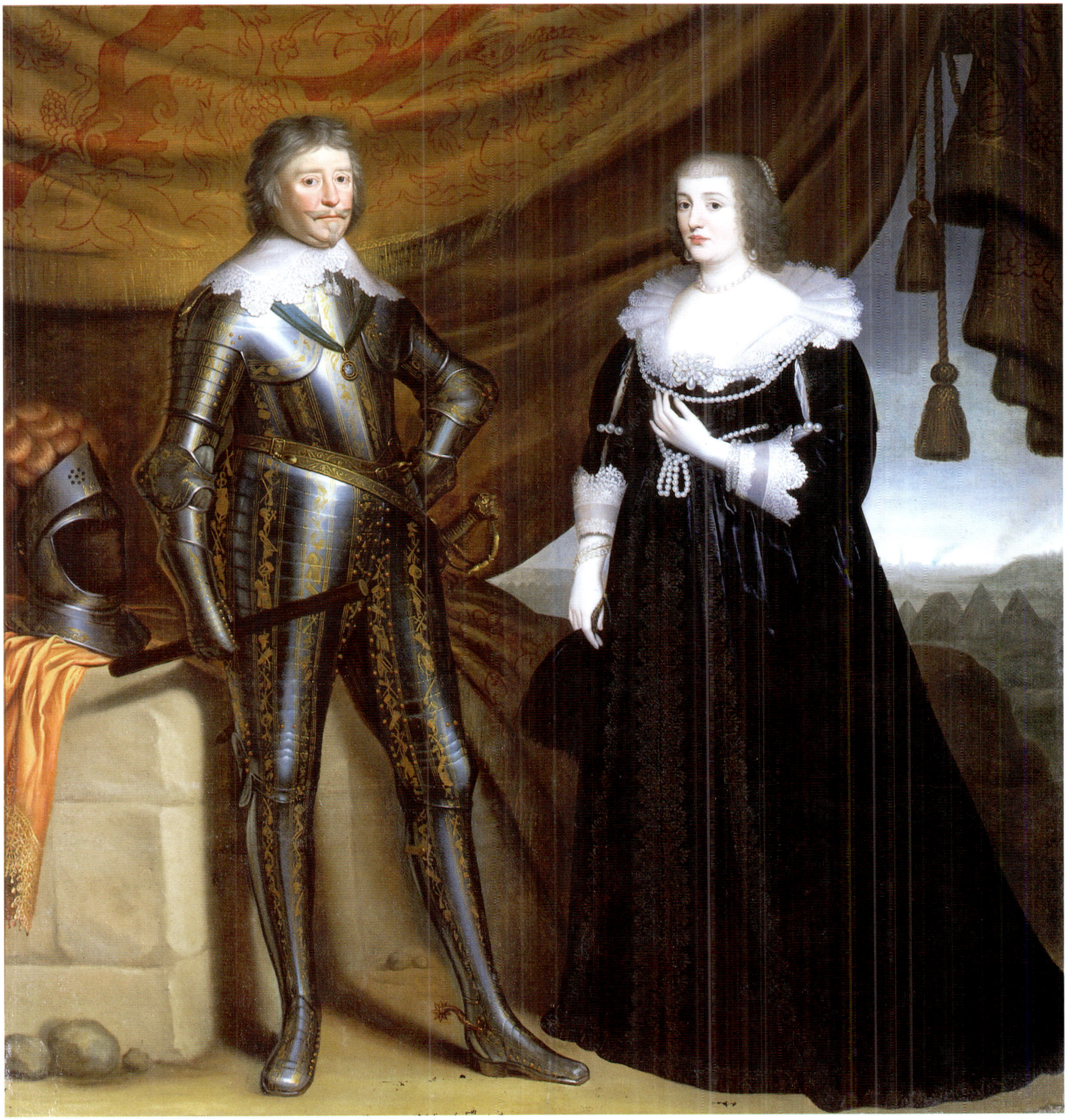

Thomas de Keyser

Amsterdam 1596/7 – 1667 Amsterdam

33

Portrait of Loef Vredericx as a Standard-Bearer, 1626

Oil on panel, *92 x 70 cm*
Above the door: ANNO TDK *1626* (TDK in ligature)
Royal Picture Gallery Mauritshuis, The Hague

This painting is a characteristic example of a new type of portrait that Thomas de Keyser had been developing since 1620: small, full-length portraits were an innovation in Amsterdam portraiture. As in his 1627 portrait of Constantijn Huygens (cat. 34), De Keyser represents the sitter in a specific function, namely as a standard-bearer, developing the portrait as an iconic expression of pride and resolve. Loef Vredericx (1590–1668) stands in a confident pose, gripping a rapier with a firm hand sheathed in a white leather glove. This figure is neatly framed by the raised tiled floor and columns. Indeed, the painter devoted considerable attention to creating a neo-classical space, which was meticulously prepared with a detailed underdrawing.[1] Surmounting the door frame is the coat of arms of Amsterdam, the city in which the subject lived and worked at the time. Shadows cast on the floor and wall enhance the portrait's three-dimensionality.

The composition of De Keyser's portrait of Vredericx is representative of its type. Standard-bearers were generally depicted not as individuals, but as part of life-sized militia pieces made for the premises of the groups' shooting galleries (*doelen*) (cat. 21). However, individual members sometimes ordered smaller portraits of themselves in full regalia for domestic display, as in the case of this painting, or Johannes Verspronck's portrait of Andries Stilte (cat. 64).[2] The paintings by Evert van der Maes (1617) and Joachim van Houckgeest (1621) are among the earliest examples of the type.[3] The commission for this striking portrait by Thomas de Keyser – who subsequently painted group portraits of Amsterdam's militia companies – was probably prompted by Vredericx's initial appointment as a standard-bearer. This took place on 15 August 1626, the year in which the portrait was painted, and there is an old inscription on the back of the panel that gives this date.[4]

Loef Vredericx's life is well documented.[5] As a silversmith, he presided over Amsterdam's guild of gold- and silversmiths a full seven times. Like two of his brothers, Vredericx chose the profession of his father, the prominent goldsmith Frederik Jansz (1534–1595; see fig. 30a). He is first mentioned as a silversmith in 1616, and is known to have produced silver goblets, dishes and salts. In this painting, however, he has been immortalised (aged 36) not as a silversmith, but as a member of Amsterdam's civic guard. His fashionable guardsman's attire is rendered in all its sumptuous detail: he wears a satin doublet under a protective buff leather jerkin, the yellow of which contrasts with his grey breeches and silk stockings. His guardsman's kit consists of a green sash around his waist trimmed with gold lace, a long rapier attached to a carrying belt, an iron gorget beneath a lace ruff, and a wide-brimmed hat with a white plume. On the tricoloured standard that he proudly holds aloft – the symbol of the civic guard – we see the Dutch lion and the text 'PR[O] [P]A[TRIA]' (For the fatherland). Standard-bearers had to be of good birth and unmarried (see cat. 21); marriage entailed automatic discharge from their position. Given the weight of the standard, they also had to be strong. The role, which entailed both holding and preserving the standard, occupied a special position within the officers' corps: together with the captain and lieutenant, the standard-bearer was one of the field officers who commanded a company of infantrymen. Vredericx remained a bachelor, and he was still a member of Amsterdam's civic guard when he died in Utrecht.

De Keyser executed a second portrait of Vredericx: in 1627 he completed a group portrait of the leaders of Amsterdam's goldsmiths' guild,[6] in which Vredericx is shown as a silversmith. On the basis of these two portraits – and several other paintings he made – it can be concluded that the Amsterdam portraitist was on good terms with goldsmiths and silversmiths working in the city.[7] Indeed, Vredericx and De Keyser not only had a business relationship, they were related. When the painter married in 1626 – the year he produced this one-man militia piece – Vredericx was one of the witnesses for the bride, his niece Machtelt Andries.[8] QB

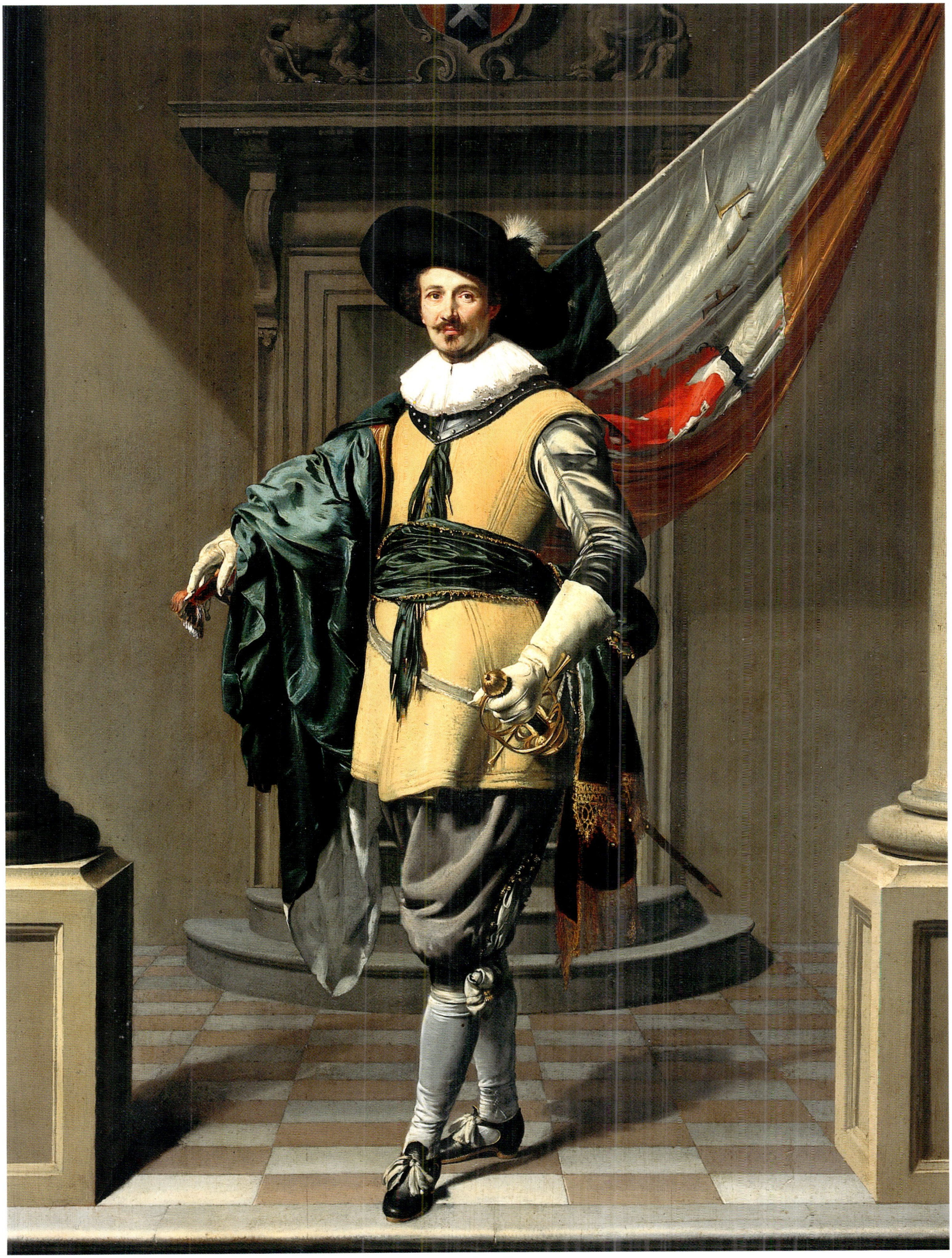

Thomas de Keyser

Amsterdam 1596/7 – 1667 Amsterdam

34

Portrait of Constantijn Huygens and his (?) Clerk, 1627

Oil on oak, 92.4 x 69.3 cm
On the mantelpiece: TDK AN 1627 (TDK in ligature)
The National Gallery, London

In 1627 Thomas de Keyser painted this fine portrait of Constantijn Huygens (1596–1687), whose face is familiar from the unusually large number of portraits Huygens had made of himself.[1] None of the other portraits depict him full-length, as here. As secretary to Stadholder Frederik Hendrik, the most influential man in the seventeenth-century Republic (see cat. 32), Huygens was at the heart of the political and cultural life of his day. From 1630 onwards he also served on a committee that administered the stadholder's property, in which capacity he greatly influenced the execution of paintings and buildings for the stadholder. Huygens, who had commended Rembrandt (among others) to the stadholder after visiting the painter's studio,[2] undoubtedly placed his stamp on the exquisite collection of paintings built up by Frederik Hendrik and his wife, Amalia van Solms.[3] He had an impressive knowledge of architecture and painting, and was an active musician, poet and translator. Huygens supervised the building of the Mauritshuis (1633–44) in The Hague while Johan Maurits of Nassau-Siegen was out of the country. Next to this city palace – now an art gallery – he built his own mansion, which is no longer standing today.

De Keyser allows us an apparently impromptu glimpse of Huygens, seated at a table covered with an expensive Turkish rug – a common compositional motif for the painter (cat. 35)[4] – and receiving a letter from a messenger or clerk.[5] As a sign of deference the boy has doffed his hat and removed his glove from the hand tendering the letter. Huygens, on the other hand, has kept his hat on, and accepts the letter with his gloved right hand. The clerk's specific action is a reference to Huygens's work as secretary (in which post he succeeded his father in 1625), which involved handling the stadholder's incoming and outgoing correspondence. On average, Huygens wrote between 100 and 120 letters a month,[6] employing a clerk to produce neat copies of his initial drafts. His close relationship with the stadholder brought considerable power with the passage of time.[7] The drawing of a floorplan also refers to his position: it is probably a design for the renovation of one of the stadholder's palaces.[8] Lying on the table are a pair of compasses and a chronometer, next to which we see a small inkpot and some books. The terrestrial and celestial globes have been regarded as allusions to Huygens's international ties and his interest in astronomy.[9] The lute denotes his love of music.

On 6 April 1627 Huygens married Suzanna van Baerle (1599–1637) in Amsterdam. The portrait discussed here was painted shortly before their marriage, as is clear from poems that Huygens sent his bride in August 1627 from Groenlo army camp, where he was on a summer campaign with the stadholder. In these witty protestations of love, Huygens mentions a portrait of himself made 'shortly before my wedding'.[10] The painting must have been made before April 1627, and Huygens may well have posed for it several months earlier.[11] He appears to be wearing the *kazak*, the riding outfit he wore when visiting the painter's studio. The conventional colours for riding clothes were brown or grey, colours less likely to show the mud and other dirt splashing up from the road.[12] Huygens travelled a great deal in the winter of 1626–7, partly in connection with his work for the stadholder and partly because he was courting Van Baerle, who lived in Amsterdam.[13] His decision to be portrayed in his riding outfit, with its characteristic hanging sleeves and boots, stems from the exclusivity of this mode of dress: riding suits were worn only by troop captains or burghers wealthy enough to afford them (see cat. 20). This practical but costly attire, which Huygens may have purchased shortly before commissioning the portrait, can therefore be regarded as a status symbol. Many years later, in 1654, Amsterdam's burgomaster Jan Six also had himself depicted in his riding outfit (cat. 57).[14] QB

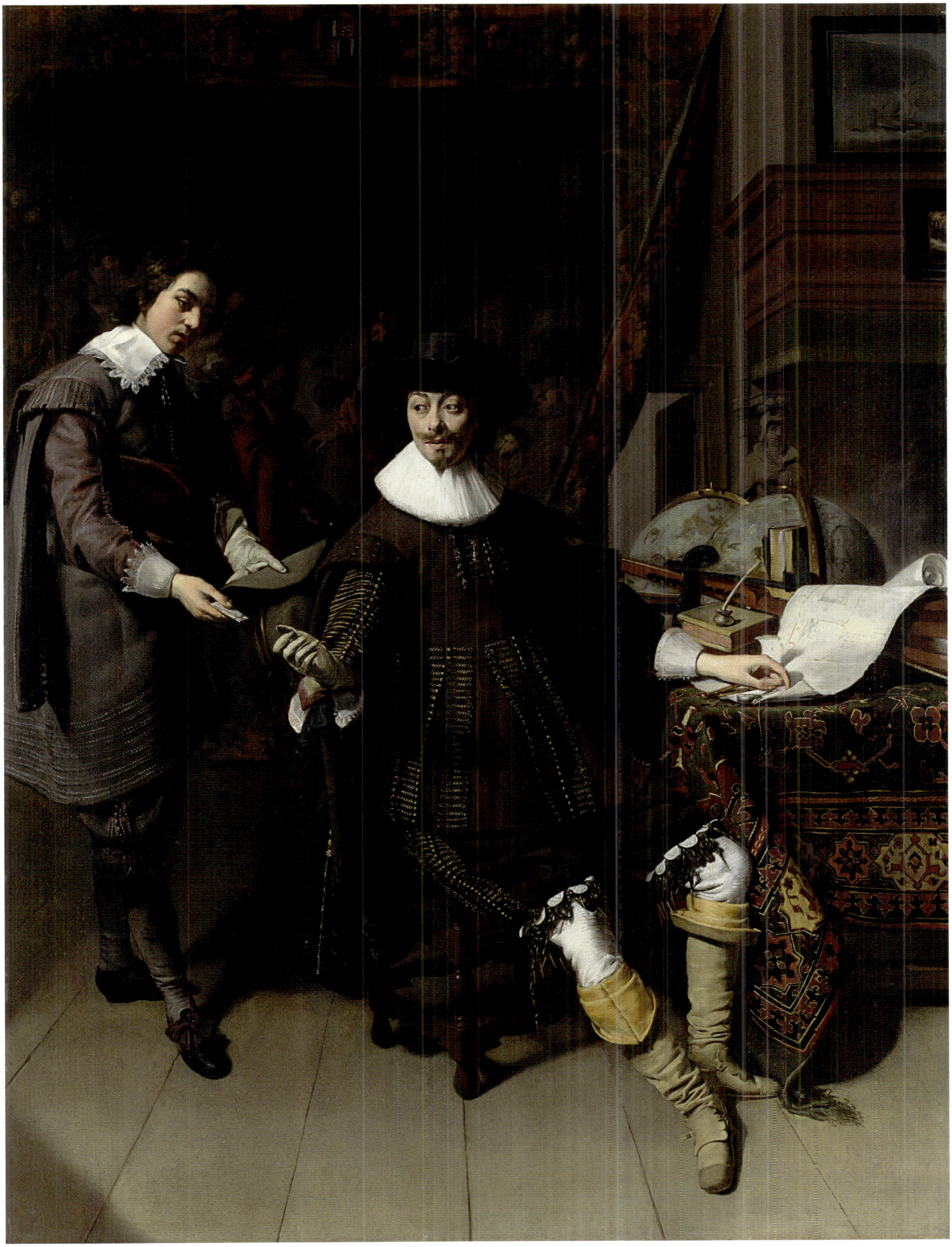

Thomas de Keyser

Amsterdam 1596/7 – 1667 Amsterdam

35 | 36

Portrait of a Gentleman, 1632

Oil on panel, 79 x 53 cm
Musée du Louvre, Paris

Portrait of a Lady, 1632

Oil on panel, 79 x 53 cm
On the door: TDK 1632 (TDK in ligature)
Gemäldegalerie, Staatliche Museen, Berlin

These polished and elegant portraits, which make a powerful impact despite their relatively small size, are among the highlights of Thomas de Keyser's œuvre and help to explain his great success in Amsterdam. De Keyser took as his point of departure the traditional formula of depicting husband and wife in separate portraits. In companion pieces of this kind, painters usually depicted their subjects life-sized, at three-quarter length (see cats 16–17). Here, however, De Keyser opted for a full-length portrayal in small format, a type of portrait that he himself introduced (see cat. 33). The monumental effect of the pendants described here is determined in part by the empty space surrounding the figures, each sitting at a table. With the exception of the mantelpiece behind the man, and the door with its finely carved frame behind the woman, the background consists solely of the room's plain walls. The meticulous rendering of the doorframe reminds us that De Keyser had initially been trained as an architect by his father, the gifted sculptor and architect Hendrick de Keyser.

De Keyser had depicted figures in an interior with just a few items of furniture before, for example in a portrait from 1631 (fig. 35–6a).[1] Close formal similarities with the portraits discussed here indicate that the painter worked according to a standard compositional formula. In both cases, the men's poses seem to suggest that the viewer has distracted them from their work. Similarly, in both the earlier portrait of a man and the current paintings, the illusion of depth is determined by the pattern of the floor, with its multi-coloured marble tiles. The illusion is enhanced by the shadow cast by the woman. The two pendants are linked by the uniform floor and the table, which is covered by a beautifully patterned Turkish rug.[2]

Husband and wife wear conspicuously extravagant attire which, like the rug, is visual confirmation of their wealth. The man is dressed in a black suit cut in the French style and corresponding to the fashion around 1630. The suit is made of precious silk patterned with polka dots. A white shirt is visible through the ubiquitous slashes in the chest and sleeves, and the white lace collar and cuffs provide a subtle transition between the dark fabric of his clothing and the warm flesh of his face and hands. Other eye-catching elements of his elegant costume are the grey silk stockings, the shoes decorated with rosettes, and the particularly wide up-turned brim of his hat. The woman is also expensively dressed in the latest French style. Her fashionably pinned-up hair is encircled by a small cap with a flared brim. This cap and the splendid, slightly raised lace collar frame her face, which is fully illuminated. The delicate pearls trimming the edges of the cap allow her hair to stand out against the dark background.[3] The design of her costume, with its double sleeves, is highly unusual: beneath open sleeves of black silk, we see dark under-sleeves fastened with bows against a billowing white fabric. Gold necklaces, rings and earrings further emphasise the woman's affluence.

The woman's attire indicates that she was married, since the *vlieger* (overgown) was worn by Dutch women only after marriage (see p. 67). It is likely that De Keyser's portraits, one of which bears the date 1632,[4] were made to commemorate the couple's wedding; in well-to-do circles it was customary to commission a portrait before or after the wedding day (see p. 50). Assuming this is correct, the ceremony probably took place in the winter, judging by the foot-warmer the woman uses. Before the wedding, when the marriage settlement was signed at the notary's office, the engaged couple would exchange not only a marriage medallion and ring – the ring mounted with a stone on the woman's index finger is probably her wedding ring – but also luxurious clothing accessories, such as gloves, lace collars and cuffs, handkerchiefs or a fan.[5] The fine gloves placed so conspicuously on the table beside the woman are presumably her bridal gloves, which she would have received from her fiancé during the engagement (see also cat. 17). The feather fan hanging from her waistband may be another gift. It seems highly probable that the couple asked De Keyser to make their portraits in their wedding clothes to commemorate this important event. The bride's wedding dress was always paid for by her parents, while the bridegroom paid for his own new wardrobe.

We know nothing about this couple apart from their apparent wealth. The few accessories in the man's portrait – books, documents, a lectern and writing implements – are unfortunately too general to enable us to draw any conclusions as to his occupation. The couple may have belonged to the network of De Keyser's brothers Pieter and Willem, who worked as architects and through whom the artist received a number of commissions.[6]

The husband and wife have had separate permanent homes for over 100 years, as the man's portrait belongs to the collection of the Musée du Louvre in Paris, while its pendant hangs in the Gemäldegalerie, Berlin. They were last in the same collection when owned by Rodolphe Kann, who left the man's portrait to the Louvre at his death in 1905. Its pendant was auctioned, and after changing hands a few times ended up in Berlin in 198[illegible]. The paintings of husband and wife are now on show together for the first time in over 50 years.[7] QB

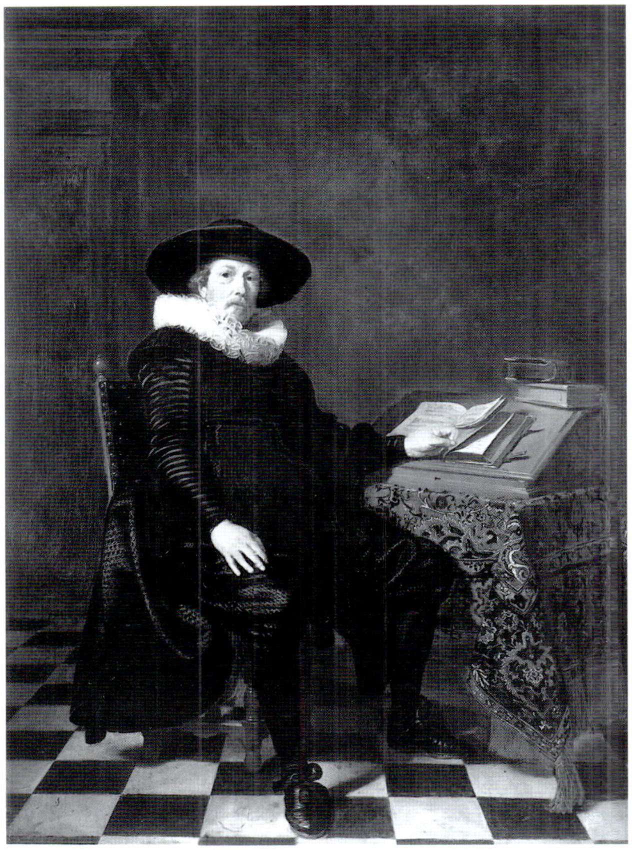

35–36a.
Thomas de Keyser
Portrait of a Gentleman, 16[illegible]1.
Oil on panel, 83 × [illegible]1 cm.
Mauritshuis, The Hague

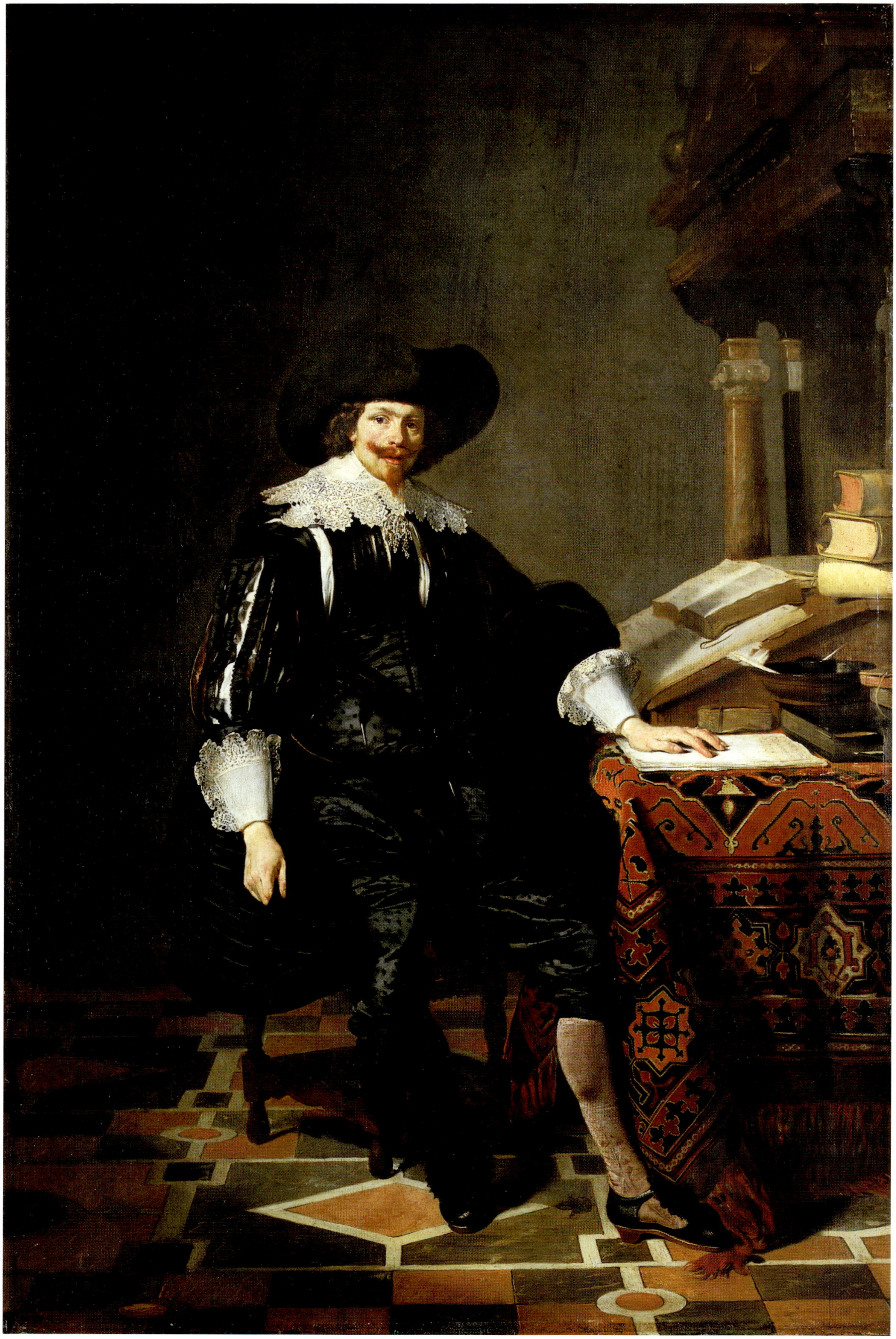

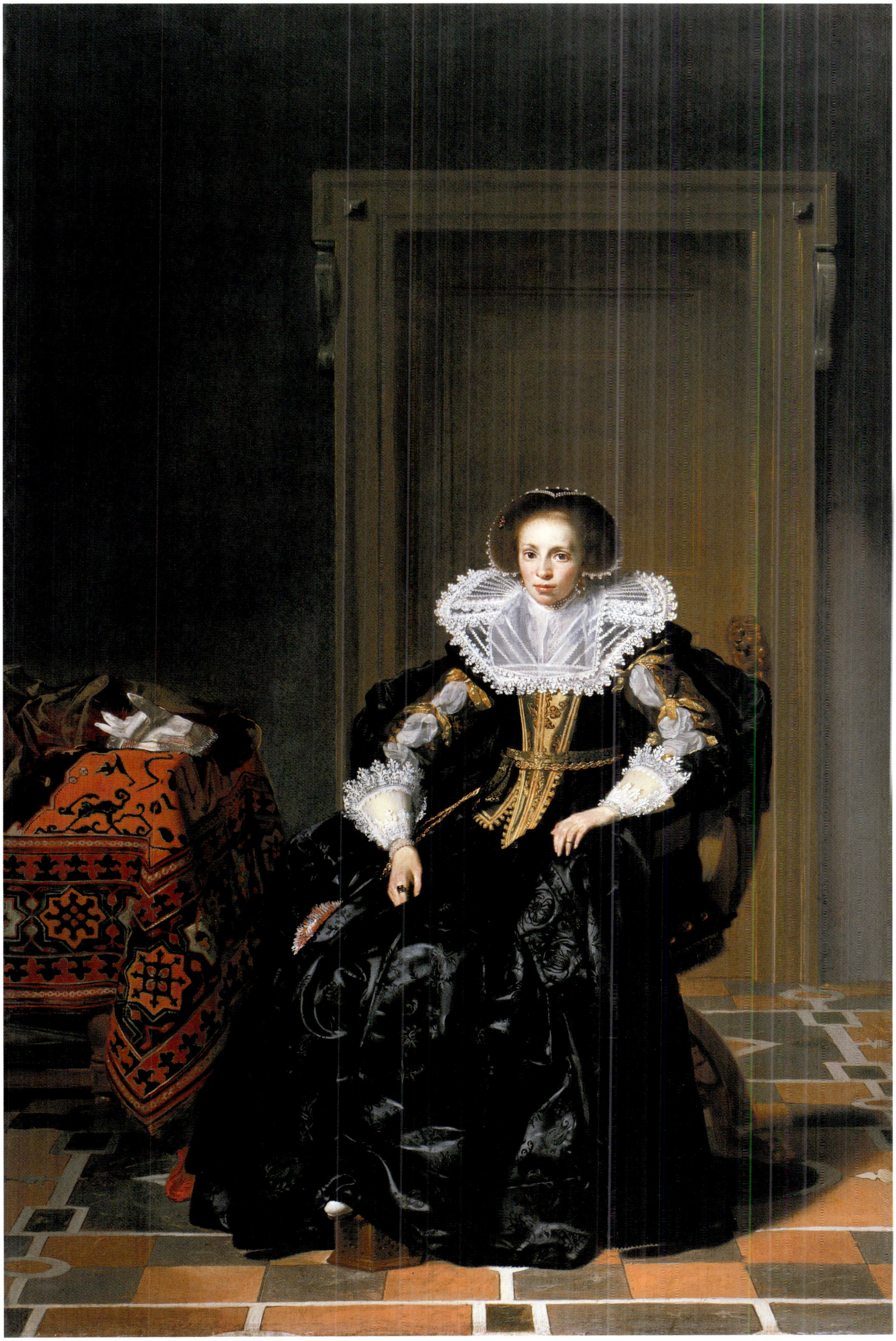

Nicolaes Maes

Dordrecht 1634–1693 Amsterdam

37

Family Portrait, about 1676

Oil on canvas, 153.1 x 170.2 cm
Courtesy of Konrad O. Bernheimer of P. & D. Colnaghi, London, and Richard Green, London

Nicolaes Maes was a gifted and prolific portrait painter. He began painting portraits in 1655, and after 1660 applied himself to the genre exclusively. He received commissions from wealthy citizens in his hometown of Dordrecht, including the fabulously rich merchant Jacob Trip and his wife, Margaretha de Geer (p. 205, figs 58–9a–b), whose portraits were also painted by Rembrandt (cats 58–9). In 1673, Maes set up business in Amsterdam, where he received hundreds of commissions over the next two decades (cat. 38). He achieved unprecedented popularity, in part because Bartholomeus van der Helst and Abraham van den Tempel, two of Amsterdam's most prominent portraitists (cats 29–30, 63), died just before he arrived. In his biography of the painter, Arnold Houbraken records that it was considered a privilege to have one's portrait painted by Maes.[1] Throughout his career he devoted himself mainly to pendant portraits of married couples (pp. 56–7, figs 9–10), but he also produced a number of group portraits of children and families.

The painting discussed here, formerly in the famous Cook collection, depicts a family in a park-like landscape, the four children standing and the parents seated.[2] The youngest son, second from the left, is clad in imaginary 'Roman' attire (see p. 72). Both his garments and the flowing scarves worn by his three siblings were intended to give a timeless 'classical' look to the scene. The vivid colours of the children's garments further enhance the appeal of the image. Just as striking as the clothing are the diverse actions and elegant gestures of the figures: the eldest son approaches from the left holding a hunting spear and accompanied by two dogs, one of which is on a leash; the younger boy shows his parents a hare, which attracts the attention of another small dog. One of the boy's sisters, dressed in white satin, holds some fruit she has just picked from the little tree beside her; the other uses a shell to collect water from the fountain as a deer gently nuzzles her waist. Both parents, and two of their children, meet the viewer's gaze. The way in which the man, who is dressed in a fashionable Japanese-style chamber gown (*Japonse rock*) supports his wife's arm can be construed as a sign of marital fidelity and the bond of matrimony (see also cats 5, 29). With his right arm he appears to be making a gesture of speech. There is nothing coincidental about the placement of a fountain behind the parents: it alludes to a well-known concept in the seventeenth century, 'the fountain of marriage' (see also cat. 29).[3]

We know nothing about the identity of this family, although they presumably came from Amsterdam. Nothing is known about the earliest provenance of the painting, nor does the canvas bear any inscriptions or coats of arms that could provide further information. Efforts to identify the family on the basis of the ostentatiously displayed hare – 'De Haes' (the hare) was a common surname in the seventeenth century – have proved unsuccessful.[4] The painting's other motifs are also too general for positive identification. That the family attached importance to social status is clear from the allusions to hunting, since the right to hunt was restricted and was therefore a status symbol (see cat. 11).

This impressive group portrait, which must have been an important and expensive commission, is one of Maes's largest paintings.[5] Its composition is quite ambitious: while Maes's many pendant portraits eventually became quite formulaic, the figures in this painting are distributed through the landscape in diverse poses that appear to express a coherent narrative. In that respect, this portrait has been designed almost as a history painting, a genre in which Maes was trained and which in the seventeenth century was held in higher esteem than the art of portraiture.[6] The composition reflects the considerable artistic development within Maes's œuvre: while his portrait of a Dordrecht family from 1659 is quite stiffly posed,[7] this later work incorporates more natural poses and a greater sense of movement. On the basis of the style and the fashionable coiffures, it can be dated to about 1676.[8] The portrait reflects an international trend towards greater elegance and refinement (see also cat. 44), a clear contrast with the more austere portraits produced in the Northern Netherlands before 1650 (see p. 42). QB

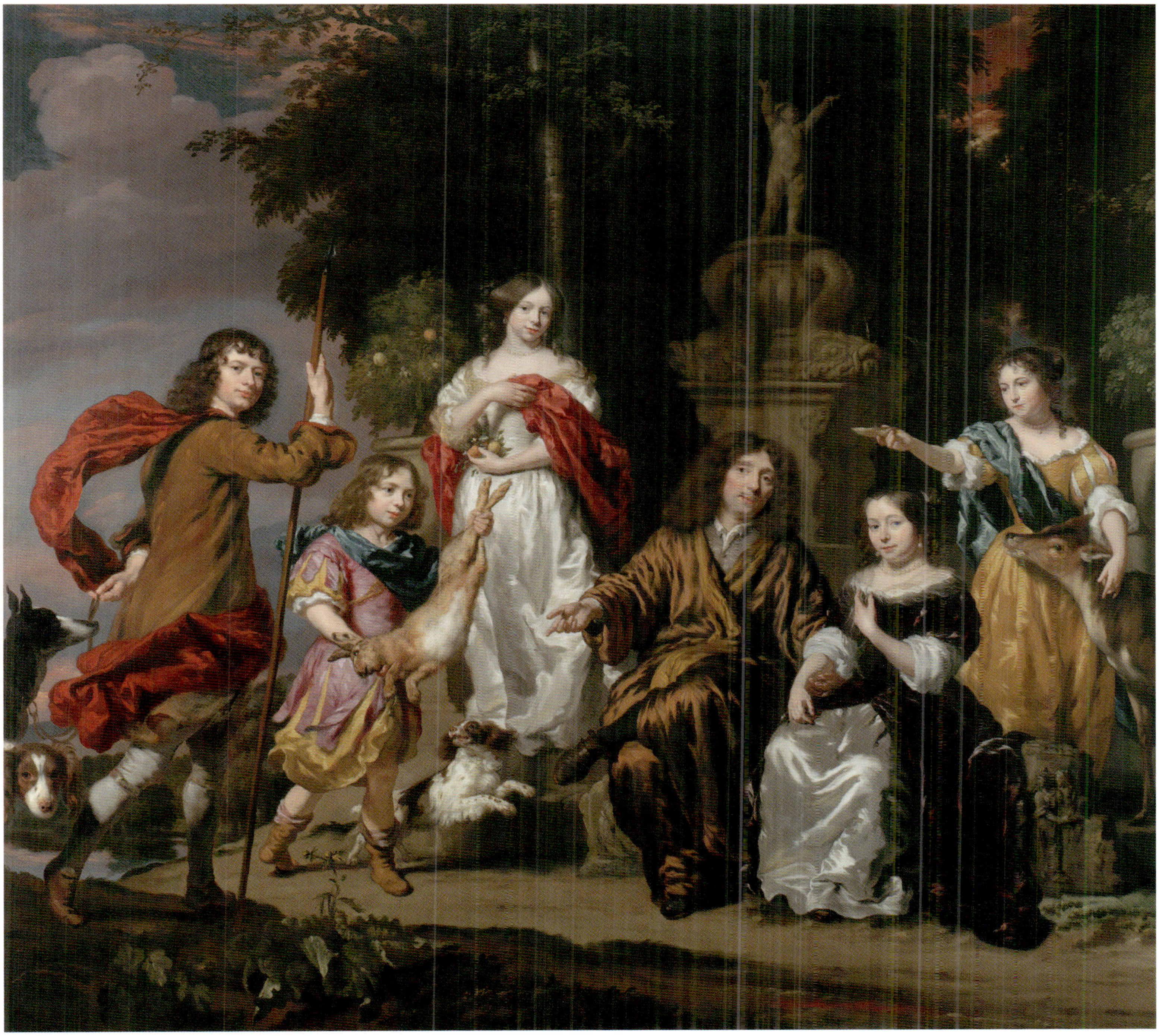

Nicolaes Maes

Dordrecht 1634–1693 Amsterdam

38

Portrait of Cornelis Munter, 1679

Oil on canvas, 56 x 48 cm
On the edge of the pedestal: *Maes 1679*
Amsterdams Historisch Museum, Amsterdam

Around 1680, there was a vogue in Amsterdam for stylish portraits in which the subjects were depicted in extremely graceful poses, with clothing and accessories rendered in refined detail. This portrait by Nicolaes Maes is a good example of this elegant mode of portraiture. Besides Maes, painters in The Hague, such as Caspar Netscher (cat. 44), were also very successful with portraits of this kind.[1] The building in the background of this portrait is the Amsterdam's town hall at Dam Square (now the Royal Palace). This monumental structure, with its easily recognisable dome, may be regarded – together with the Mauritshuis in The Hague – as a textbook example of neo-classical architecture in the Northern Netherlands.[2] Because of this prominent view of the building, in the past this painting has been taken for a portrait of Jacob van Campen (1596–1657), the town hall's famous architect.[3] But Van Campen had been dead for many years when the painting was made.

The accessories surrounding the figure make it clear that the man was connected with the town hall in some professional capacity. He is leaning on a folio volume that he opens with a graceful gesture. A second book is depicted behind him, and in the foreground is a folded document with seals. In a nineteenth-century account of the paintings in Amsterdam's town hall, where this work was then hanging, it was described as a portrait of Cornelis Munter (1652–1708),[4] who was employed as town clerk in 1679. This identification is confirmed by the painting's provenance,[5] and by the relief on the pedestal at lower left, which depicts a recumbent figure and a barking dog. This motif derives from a relief by Artus Quellinus that can still be seen above the door of the former town clerk's office in the Royal Palace. According to a late seventeenth-century source, it depicts canine faithfulness: the dog stands guard over the body of its slain master.[6]

Munter was appointed town clerk in 1676, three years before Maes painted this portrait. In 1692 he was appointed town magistrate, in 1701 town councillor, and in 1706 he became burgomaster, an office that his grandfather, Jan Geelvinck, had also held. In addition, Munter was for many years one of the directors of the Dutch West India Company. Whether he commissioned another portrait after 17 October 1679, the date of his marriage to Maria Piso, is unknown. One would have expected him to order two portrait paintings of himself and his wife to commemorate their marriage.[7] The painting discussed here appears to stand alone, although it is not inconceivable that it once had a pendant. The composition, in which the man rests his right arm on a pedestal corresponds wholly to the format of Maes's paired portraits, which draw from a finite repertoire of standard poses.[8] The general composition of this painting, in which the figure stands in the open air in a *contrapposto* pose beside a parapet or column, derives from the elegant portraiture of Anthony van Dyck (see cat. 40).

Munter's distinguished social status can be inferred from his fashionable wig of long curly hair. He is dressed in the latest fashion, a Japanese-style chamber gown (*Japonse rock*), which was sometimes worn by men with a sedentary occupation as its padding kept the wearer warm in cold weather. Maes has depicted this garment with characteristic bravura, with loose brushstrokes applied wet-in-wet. Indeed, the coat has been painted with such verve that it almost looks like an outlandish fabrication. The flamboyant brushwork creates the impression that the portrait was dashed off in a very short time, but in reality he has taken extraordinary pains to make individual brushstrokes invisible by thinly applying successive layers of paint to the surface.[9] This virtuoso effort to conceal brushwork was one of the primary characteristics of paintings by the Leiden *fijnschilders*, although their painstaking approach was quite different from Maes's showy flourishes (cats 12, 40). QB

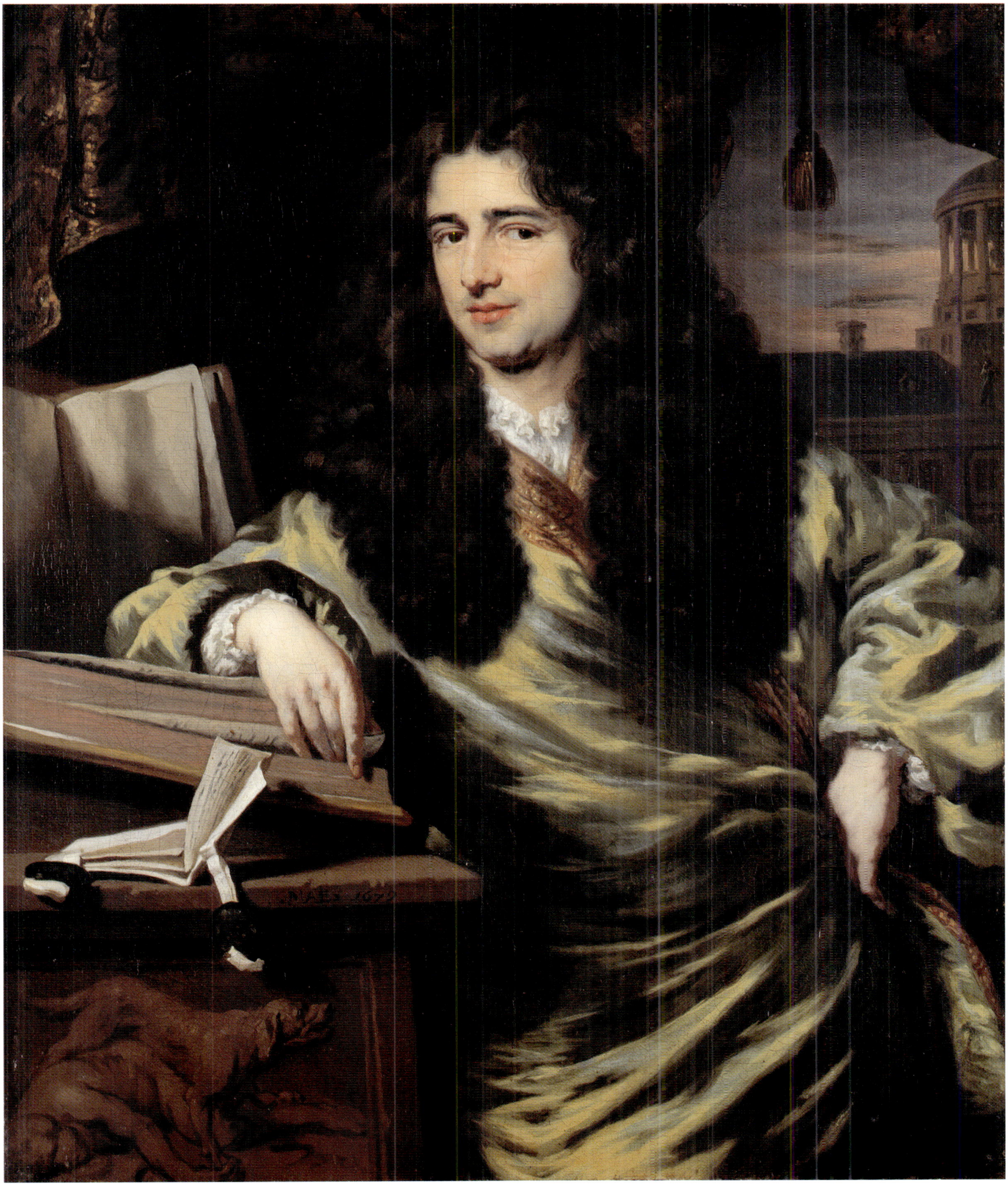

Michiel van Mierevelt

Delft 1567–1641 Delft

39

Portrait of Maurits, Prince of Orange-Nassau, 1607

Oil on panel, 110 x 82 cm
At lower left: *Ætatis Suæ 40. 1607*; at upper right:
Cum venia principis et Ord. Fed. Privilegio sex. Current. ann.
Museum Het Prinsenhof, Delft

In 1607, or shortly before, the Delft city council decided to commission a portrait of the Stadholder of Holland, Maurits of Nassau (1567–1625), for the town hall. Since Daniël van den Queborn, who had painted official portraits of the stadholder in the past, had died a few years before, a new portraitist had to be found. The choice fell on the influential local master Michiel van Mierevelt, who duly became the new court painter. Nothing is known of the commission itself or the circumstances surrounding it. A receipt from 1608 reveals that Van Mierevelt received the significant sum of 200 guilders for this painting, which was completed in 1607; the amount undoubtedly included the costs of the panel and frame.[1] On 14 May 1607, the States-General granted the artist a six-year patent on reproductions of the portrait in the form of copperplate engravings.[2] This must have been of prime importance to Van Mierevelt, since it is mentioned explicitly in the inscription at upper right: 'Cum venia principis et Ord. Fed. Privilegio sex. Current. ann.' (with a patent from the prince and the States-General for the period of six years).

Maurits, who was appointed stadholder after the murder of his father, William of Orange, in 1584, is depicted at almost three-quarter length, wearing a richly decorated gold-coloured suit of armour. The orange-red of his sash and the plume on the helmet lying on the table allude to the House of Orange. His gloved left hand rests on the table and in his bared right hand he holds a baton – a reference to his position as captain-general of the States army. The medallion of the Order of the Garter hangs from a ribbon on his chest, a detail that was not added until after 1613, when Maurits was awarded the distinction.

Van Mierevelt depicted the stadholder in a very natural pose and rendered details of the composition with utmost believability. The scene therefore makes a sharp contrast with the rather stiff portrait that Van den Queborn produced about nine years earlier (fig. 39a).[3] Van Mierevelt's portrait was extremely successful: as early as 1607, the year of its completion, at least one replica was painted, for the States-General.[4] In 1608 Jan Muller's print of the painting appeared, for which Van Mierevelt had been granted a patent in 1607.[5] Dozens of other portraits of Maurits from Van Mierevelt's studio – busts, three-quarter and full-length likenesses – show that the painter and his assistants probably turned out hundreds of versions in the ensuing decades, for which they may well have used cartoon drawings.[6] The basic concept remained the same throughout, although the facial features were sometimes modified to reflect Maurits's advancing years; the stadholder probably did not pose for the painter again after 1607.

After Delft built a new town hall in 1620, Van Mierevelt was commissioned to furnish it with four equally large portraits of Maurits's father, his two brothers and his nephew.[7] In 1624 he supplied another three works for the town hall,[8] making a series of eight portraits in all. These paintings probably served as an example for similar portrait galleries elsewhere, such as the one in Kampen. The artist produced five full-length portraits of the stadholder for this city's town hall in 1625.[9] RE

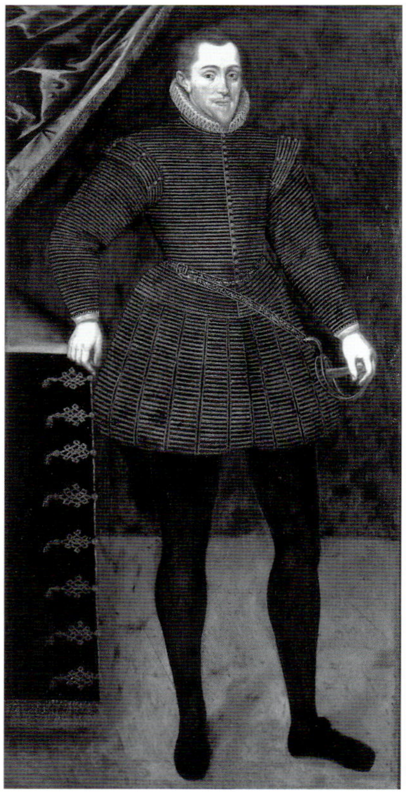

39a. Daniël van den Queborn, *Portrait of Maurits, Prince of Orange-Nassau*, about 1597. Oil on canvas, 190 x 100 cm. University Library, Leiden

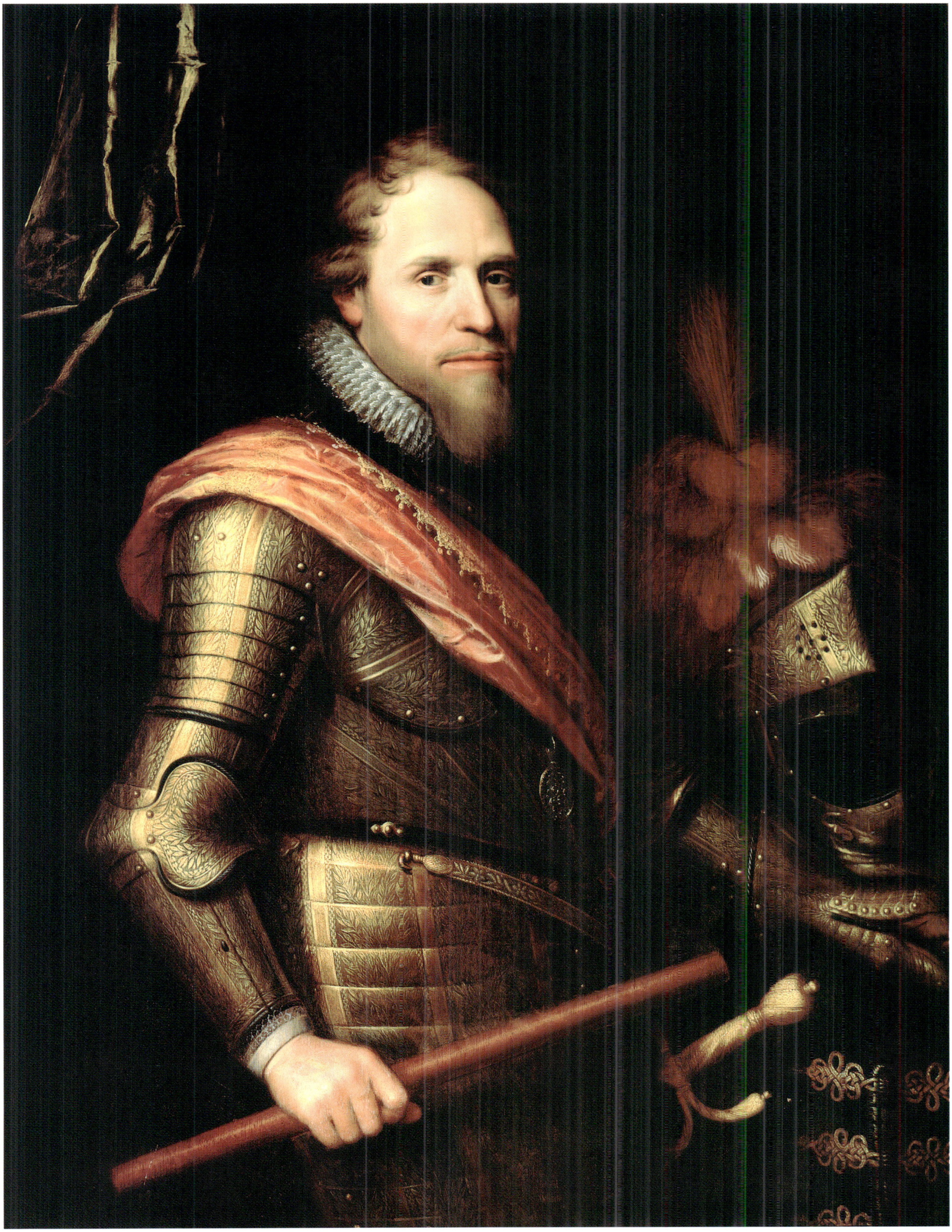

Frans van Mieris the Elder

Leiden 1635 – 1681 Leiden

40

Portrait of Florentius Schuyl, 1666

Oil on copper, 21 x 17 cm
On the parapet: *F. van Mieris. fe. A° 1666*
Royal Picture Gallery Mauritshuis, The Hague

Frans van Mieris, arguably the most accomplished of the Leiden *fijnschilders*, is mainly known today for his cheerful genre scenes, but he also painted self-portraits and portraits of well-to-do burghers. Like his genre pieces, these portraits were executed in a small format and with meticulous care, and are among the best produced in Leiden. Of the 20 extant portraits that he made on commission, only five have been identified, including this portrait of the Leiden professor Florentius Schuyl (1619–1669).[1] Schuyl, who granted only this one commission to Van Mieris, was appointed professor of philosophy in Den Bosch at 24 years of age after establishing his academic reputation with a Latin edition of Descartes's *Traité de l'homme* (*De Homine*, 1662).

In 1664 Schuyl abandoned philosophy for medicine, earning his doctorate under the Leiden professor Franciscus Sylvius (1614–1672). Sylvius was one of Van Mieris's most faithful clients, and is believed to have introduced his student to the portraitist. Schuyl was appointed professor of medical science in Leiden only a few months after acquiring his doctorate but his interests were not restricted to that field. The plant in the left foreground (mullein) has led to this portrait of Schuyl becoming known as the 'botany professor'.[2] In 1666, the year in which the work was completed, Schuyl did in fact receive permission to teach at Leiden's botanical gardens, after which he was appointed professor of botany. Van Mieris's commission probably followed in the wake of Schuyl's appointment that same year as rector of the University of Leiden, the crowning achievement of a highly successful career.[3]

Van Mieris depicts Schuyl against a sunlit hilly landscape. At left we see statues of two unidentified 'philosophers' – allusions to the sitter's former career. The corpulent Schuyl tucks his left arm behind his back and rests his right on the parapet: a pose that draws attention to the artist's flamboyant signature, illusionistically 'carved' into the parapet. Van Mieris derived this compositional form, in which the sitter stands in the open air, leaning on a parapet or the base of a column, from the fashionable portraits of Anthony van Dyck (1599–1641).[4] A clear resemblance can also be seen with Van Dyck's *Iconography*, a celebrated series of engraved portraits of prominent men. Van Mieris was among the first Dutch artists to paint this type of portrait, which was based in part on examples by Raphael (1483–1520) and Titian (d. 1576), in a small format.

The sitter's clothing must have struck his contemporaries as old-fashioned: this type of white collar with tied tasselled bandstrings had been fashionable around 1655, but perhaps as a man of science Schuyl disdained fashion. Over his black doublet he wears a cloak draped over his shoulder and abdomen; the velvet facings display Van Mieris's gift for rendering fabrics with tactile realism. Schuyl's shoulder-length hair recalls a curious polemic. In 1643, the Reformed minister Godefridus Udemans had fulminated against men who allowed their hair to fall over their shoulders in long tresses. Schuyl responded by dashing off a pamphlet in 1644 in defence of his long-haired compatriots.[5] By 1666, when this portrait was made, long hair had become generally accepted.

The little portrait is painted on a copper plate, an ultra-smooth support suited ideally to Van Mieris's refined and meticulous technique. Interestingly, the artist, who had spent a short time training as a goldsmith, applied a layer of gold leaf over the ground. Rembrandt had done the same around 1629–30, in his *Laughing Soldier* (p. 18, fig. 2).[6] But while Rembrandt allowed the gold to glint through the surface of the paint, Van Mieris covered it up with two preparatory layers of brown paint. He probably wanted to protect the painting from the ravages of time: the gold shields the paint from the copper's oxidation. This helps to explain the painting's outstanding condition. QB

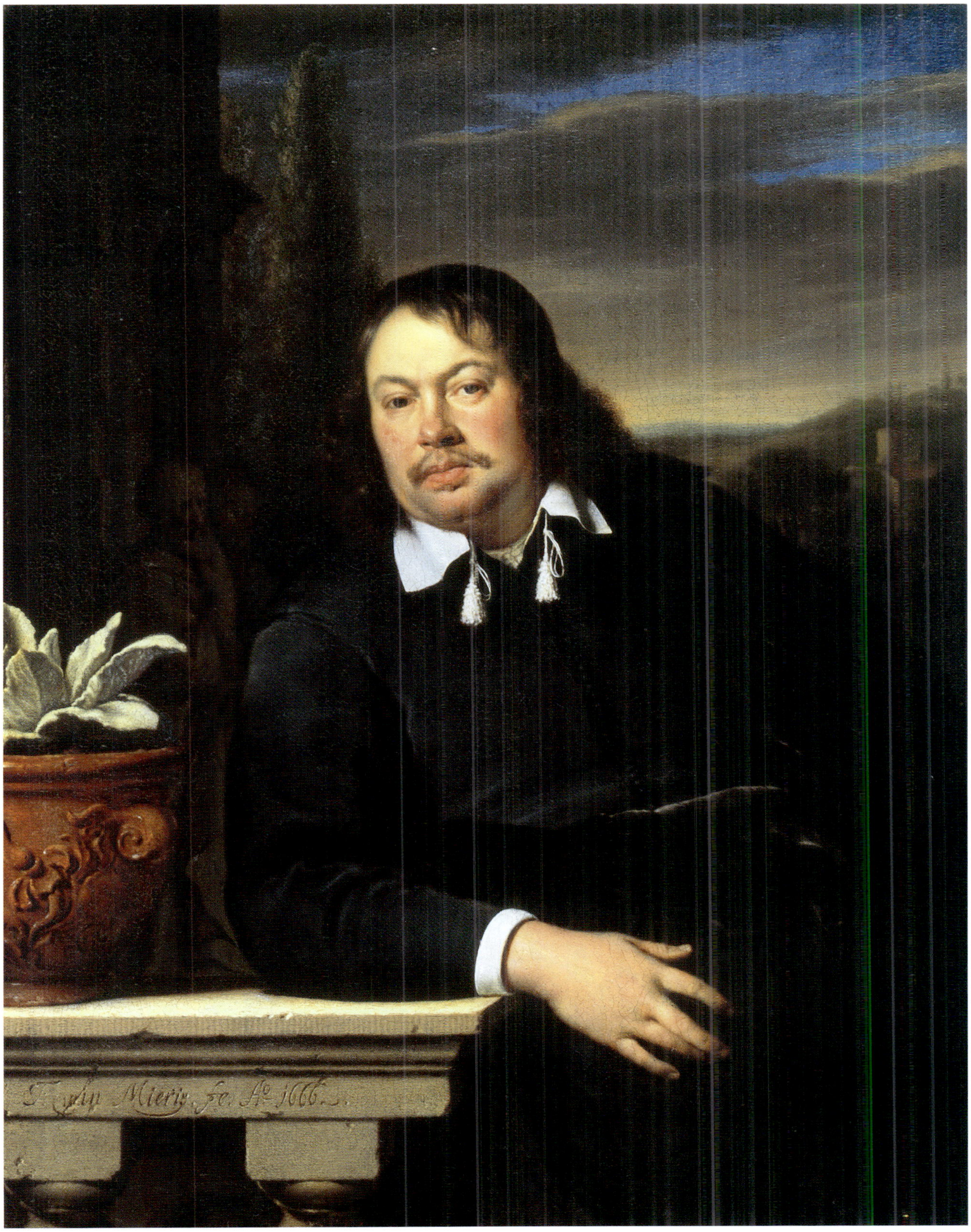

Jan Mijtens

The Hague 1613/14–1670 The Hague

41

Portrait of Willem van den Kerckhoven and his Family, 1652 and 1655

Oil on canvas, 134 x 182 cm
At lower centre: *Joan Mijtens pinx. 1652;*
on the leading reins of the youngest child: *1655*
Haags Historisch Museum, The Hague

The Hague painter Jan Mijtens excelled in rendering family portraits set against a lush landscape background. His deft blend of elegant poses, a park-like setting, and meticulously recorded garments, all executed in a very refined technique, emulates the work of his predecessors in The Hague, Gerrit van Honthorst and Adriaen Hanneman (cats 28, 31–2). They in turn had been influenced by the portraiture of Anthony van Dyck. Elegant portraits of this kind were in great demand in The Hague, both at the stadholder's court and among the upper middle classes.[1] Mijtens's family portraits are generally executed in a small format; this painting, incorporating an astonishing crowd of figures, is the largest he produced in this category.

The painting represents the jurist Willem van den Kerckhoven (1607–1680), his wife Rijnburgh Sebastiaensdr de Jonge (1609–1679) and their ten children. Van den Kerckhoven had served as a justice at the Court of Holland in The Hague since 1639, and in 1652, the year in which this painting was made, he also became councillor to Amalia van Solms (cat. 32) and Mary Stuart (p. 170, fig. 44a), widows of Frederik Hendrik and William II, Prince of Orange, respectively.[2] Kerckhoven and his wife dominate the left side of the image, surrounded by seven children. Their eldest son Melchior stands at right, beside two daughters. The five cherubs hovering in the air represent children who died before 1652. The couple's youngest child, Pellegrom, had not yet been born in 1652; three years later Mijtens added him to the picture. He stands at the centre of the composition, leaning against his father's knee. His leading-reins, which are decorated with pink bows, display the year 1655. The enormous prosperity of the family can be inferred not only from their precious garments but also from the small black boy walking towards them, leading a horse by its reins. Moorish pages are regularly included in portrait groups from about 1650, in most cases apparently to emphasise the sitters' high social status (see also p. 73, fig. 68).[3] The painting's possibly original frame is surmounted by the Van den Kerckhoven and De Jonge families' coats of arms.[4]

Mijtens has given each of the children an individual attribute. Adriaen, the boy standing directly behind the mother, is holding a bunch of grapes by its stem, while his brother Egbert holds a tray with bunches of grapes. The girl standing on the far left, Margaretha, holds a string of pearls in her hand, which she rests lightly on the nautilus shell that her brother Sebastiaan raises. He expressly emphasises this attribute by pointing at it. The girl standing on the far right, Elisabeth, offers the viewer a rose from the rosebush, while her younger sister Rijnburgh weaves flowers into a maiden's wreath. The boy in the yellow suit, Willem, has his hand near the myrtle branch that his mother holds, while in the centre foreground his brother Cornelis embraces a little dog. Finally, Pellegrom holds a little branch bearing a peach. Several of these elements may have a symbolic meaning based on the traditional emblematic literature. The image of someone holding a bunch of grapes by the stem, for instance, is mentioned by the poet Jacob Cats as an emblem for female chastity. The pearls may have the same significance, but here they undoubtedly also refer to Margaretha's name: 'margarita' is the Latin word for pearl (see cat. 13). It is tempting to conjecture that Mijtens may have intended all these elements to convey specific meanings in the manner of a complex 'puzzle', and the painting has indeed been interpreted along these lines.[5] In portraits of families and children, however, fruit and flowers were primarily used to express a more general significance. Countless poems associate fruit with large families and in particular with a woman's fertility. Fruit and flowers are also used as metaphors for children: just as crops flourish only if cultivated with care, children will thrive only if they are raised well.[6] If the painter and his client did indeed have this significance in mind, the portrait is an expression of a couple's pride not only in their wealth and social standing, but also in the successful nurturing of their children. PP

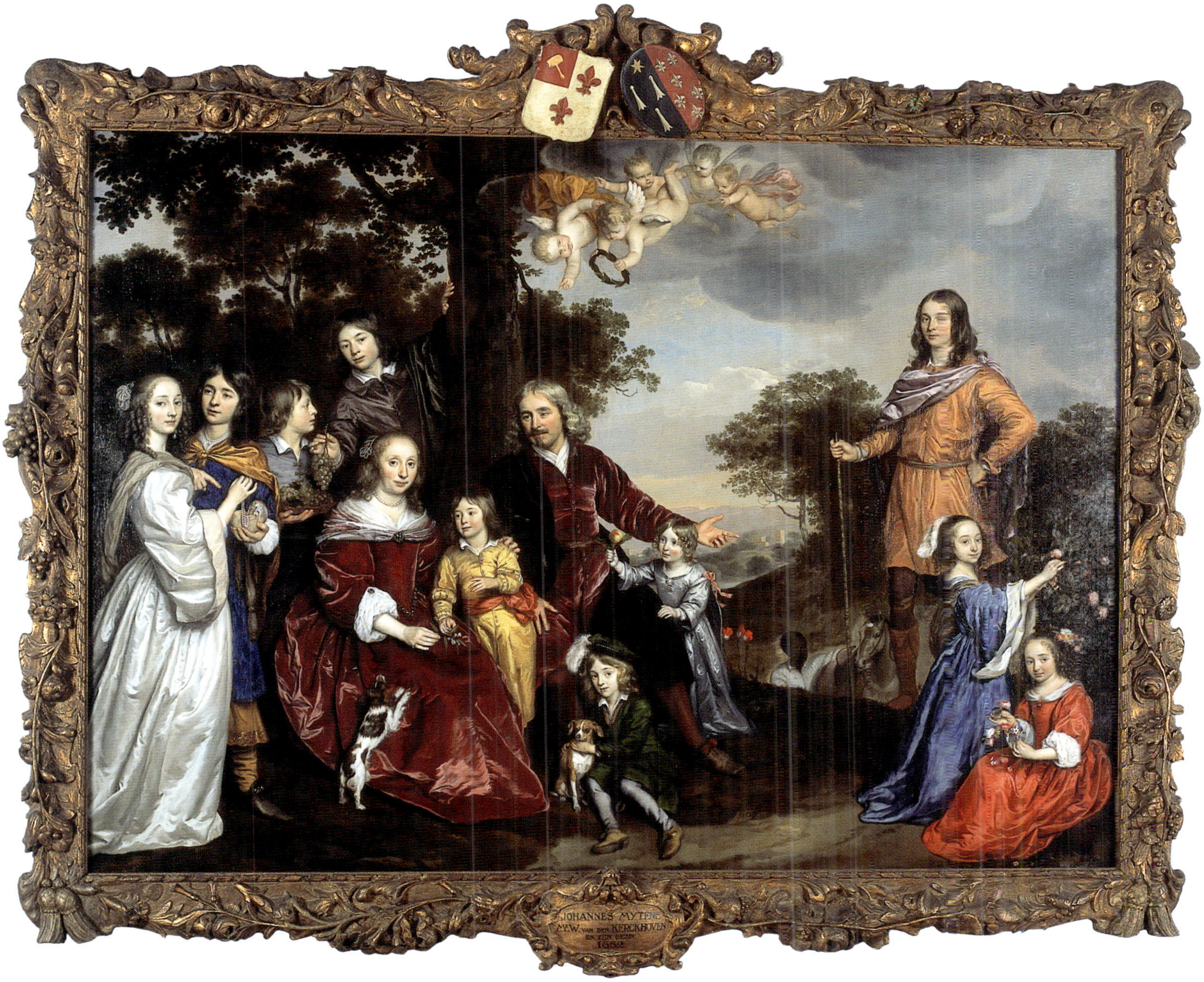
JOHANNES MYTENS
Mr W. VAN DEN KERCKHOVEN
1652

Jan Miense Molenaer

Haarlem 1609/10 – 1668 Haarlem

42

Portrait of the Painter's Family, about 1635

Oil on panel, 62.3 x 81.3 cm
Inscriptions: on the booklets under the cello: TNOR (tenor) / *BASSVS* (bass); on the songbook: *superius* (soprano)
Frans Hals Museum, Haarlem (on loan from the Netherlands Institute for Cultural Heritage, Amsterdam/Rijswijk)

This family portrait by Jan Miense Molenaer is one of the first Dutch paintings to depict a family group making music together.[1] It also provides important information about the presentation of portraits in the seventeenth century: in addition to the ten figures in the interior, we see pendant portraits of a man and a woman hanging on the wall, and below, a series of eight small portraits, some with family coats of arms. The elegantly dressed figures in the foreground have been convincingly identified as members of Molenaer's family,[2] with the painter himself surrounded by his seven brothers and sisters. From left to right, we see Geertruijt (with sistrum), Bartholomeus (violin), Adriaen (lute), Maria (songbook), Anthonij (cello), and beside the painter his younger brother Nicolaes and sister Lucia. The men in particular are strikingly fashionably dressed. In fact the lute-player's fashionable collar, made of precious lace, enables us to date the painting to around 1635. The expensive garments of the painter – he wears a black velvet suit and has lace rosettes on his high-heeled shoes – are also in the latest French fashion. Like the other men in the painting, he has kept his hat on.

The painter's stylish outfit makes something of a contrast with the old-fashioned apparel of the older men in the left background, who are dressed according to the fashion of 1620. These two figures – the painter's half-brothers, Meijndert and Cornelis – are subtly segregated from the other members of the family by the placement of the virginal. The little painting one of them holds is a portrait of their mother, Cornelia Jans. After her death, Jan Mientsen, the painter's father, took a second wife, Grietje Adriaens. It is this couple (Jan and Grietje) that is depicted in the pendant portraits hung at the back of the room. Father and mother, who survey their children from this honoured position, are each holding a Bible (or prayerbook). Judging by their clothes, their portraits were probably painted around 1610, the year of their marriage.[3] The symbolic objects in their portraits – the skull in the man's portrait and the hourglass in the woman's – recall the transience of human life.

The everyday actions of the various family members also convey a deeper significance. North of the Alps, the motif of a family group making music together is first seen in sixteenth-century Flemish portrait painting. On the original frame of a family portrait from 1561 by the Flemish artist Frans Floris (1519/20–1570) is a Latin inscription referring to harmony within marriage and in the family.[4] Musical harmony was regarded as a metaphor for the harmony between man and wife and among the different members of a family. It is this imagery that underlies Molenaer's group portrait. The woman singing at the centre of the scene is keeping time with her hand. It is fair to assume that her actions can be applied symbollically to life, in which one must preserve rhythm (or moderation: the Dutch word for rhythm, *maat*, also means moderation) to attain harmony.[5] We should not overlook the clock on the wall in this context, since this is one of the standard attributes of the personification of Moderation.[6]

Other details in the image likewise convey a deeper meaning. The little dog on the cushion in front of the woman playing a sistrum is a common symbol of fidelity. The decorative motif on the virginal's hinged lid – two entwined hands over a burning heart pierced with arrows – stands for love and unity.[7] The clock is not solely an attribute of Moderation; by virtue of its position between portraits of the painter's parents it also emphasises the passage of time and the brevity of human life.[8] The boy blowing bubbles in the right foreground reminds the viewer again that life is ephemeral, like a soap-bubble. The sculpted figure on the plinth behind him continues the *vanitas* theme. She is Justice, whose scales and sword refer to the Last Judgement.[9] The relief is rather conspicuous amid what is otherwise a scene from everyday life, but emphasises the devoutness of the painter and his family.[10] The most important message the painter conveys is that one must seek to preserve harmonious relations within one's family. QB

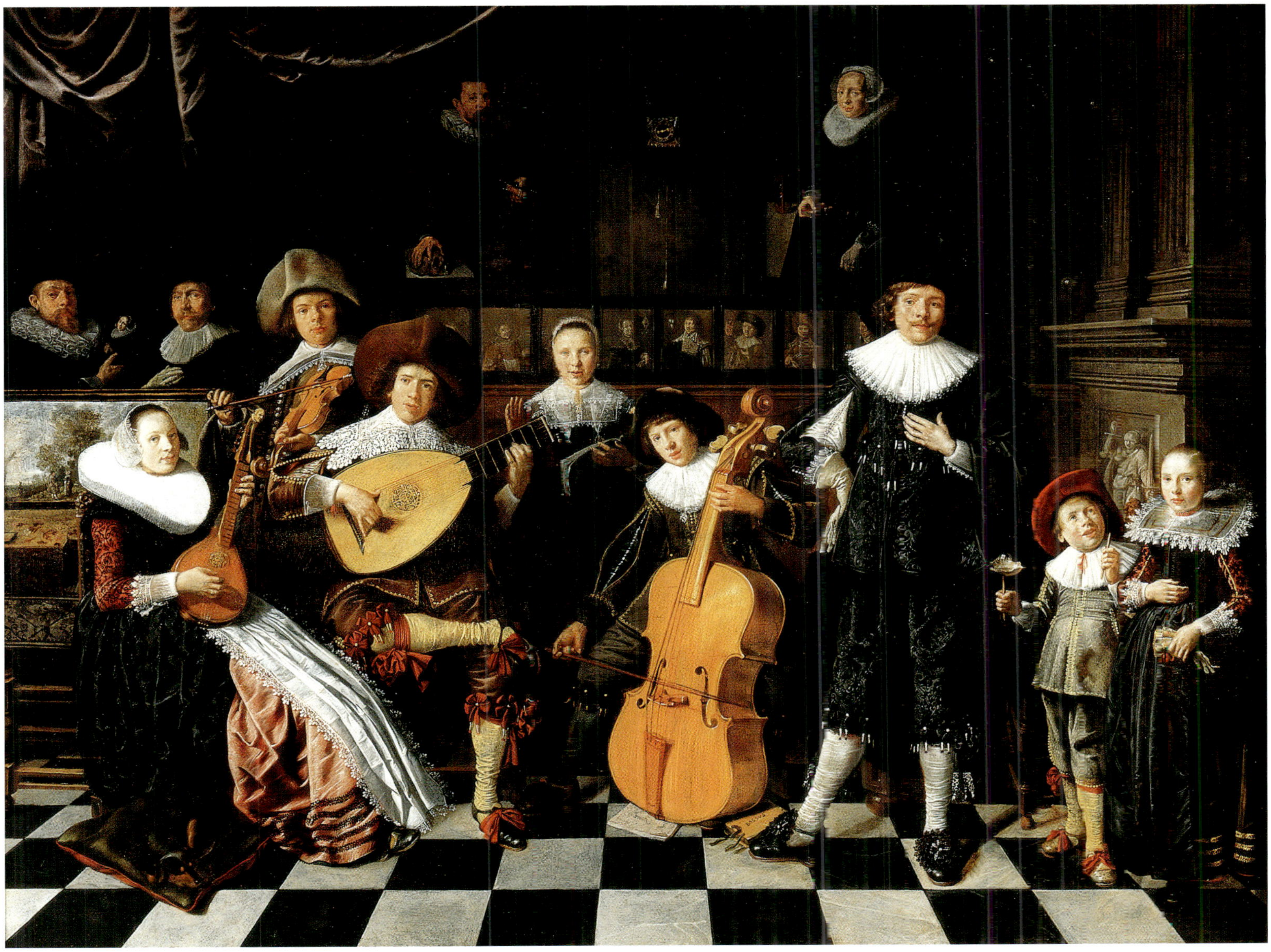

Paulus Moreelse

Utrecht 1571 – 1638 Utrecht

43

Portrait of Sophia Hedwig, Countess of Nassau-Dietz, as Charity, with her children, 1621

Oil on canvas, 136.5 x 119.5 cm
On the base of the column: *PMoreelse / 1621* (PM in ligature)
Paleis Het Loo Nationaal Museum, Apeldoorn

For much of the seventeenth century the stadholder of the Republic's three northernmost provinces came from the Frisian branch of the House of Nassau, the counts of Nassau-Dietz. In 1607, Count Ernst Casimir of Nassau-Dietz (1573–1632) married Sophia Hedwig of Brunswick-Wolffenbüttel (1592–1642). Of this marriage six children were born, but only the two eldest sons survived to adulthood. Ernst Casimir was appointed stadholder of Friesland in 1620, followed by Groningen and Drenthe five years later. He was killed during the conquest of Roermond in 1632. His eldest son, Hendrik Casimir I (1612–1640), succeeded him but was killed eight years later in the siege of Hulst. The second son, Willem Frederik (1613–1664), became the new stadholder. In 1652 he married Albertine Agnes, a daughter of Frederik Hendrik and Amalia van Solms (see cat. 32), becoming the forefather of the Netherlands' Royal House of Orange.[1]

Paulus Moreelse's vibrant family portrait depicts Sophia Hedwig with three of her sons. Standing behind her on the left is Hendrik Casimir I, the boy in the right foreground with a bowl of fruit is Willem Frederik, and seated on the cushion is the youngest son, Maurits (1619–1628). Standing in front of the entrance to a large building in the background is a young woman with a baby in her arms. This infant is most probably the youngest daughter, Elisabeth (1620–1628). She was born in November 1620, a month after Ernst Casimir had moved from Utrecht to Leeuwarden, together with his family, to take up the office of stadholder.

The Utrecht artist Moreelse had executed portraits for the family before, but most of them are fairly conventional.[2] The painting discussed here is one of his most noteworthy works because of its iconography. On the back of the canvas is an old inscription that came to light when the painting was restored in 1977. It begins: 'CHARITAS no. 154 Sophia Hedwich'.[3] The portrait is also described as 'Charity' (*Caritas*) in the inventory of the property of the stadholder's court in Leeuwarden, drawn up in 1633 after the death of Ernst Casimir: 'A Charity of H.F.G.'[4] Charity had been defined since early Christian theology as the most important of the three heavenly graces – faith, hope and love. A distinction was made between the love of God, *amor dei*, and the love of one's fellow human beings, *amor proximi* or charity, which in the seventeenth century was generally represented by images of motherhood. Such pictures showed a woman surrounded by her children, and frequently emphasised her loving care in nurturing them.[5] Moreelse's portrayal of Sophia Hedwig surrounded by her children and with one breast bared, against which she presses two fingers as if about to feed an infant, belongs to this tradition. Even the striking red colour of Sophia Hedwig's robe may be taken as an allusion to love.[6] Seventeenth-century Dutch theologians and poets went one step further: in their writings they explicitly linked the concept of charity to the love between husband and wife. If this connection applies to the painting exhibited here, the absent husband plays a spiritual role in the scene.[7]

By draping the figures in timeless, imaginary dress, Moreelse emphasised the allegorical nature of this portrait. Sophia Hedwig wears a pointed headdress, the tip of which is bent forwards – supposedly a Persian accessory. Her veil, made of some transparent stripy material, appears oriental. The two eldest boys wear quasi-Roman tunics with strips of leather hanging from the shoulders. Only the old-fashioned attire of the children's nursemaid (see also cat. 14), with its high *bragoenen* (stuffed shoulder-rolls) attached to the bodice, identifies the setting as the Leeuwarden of the early seventeenth century. PP

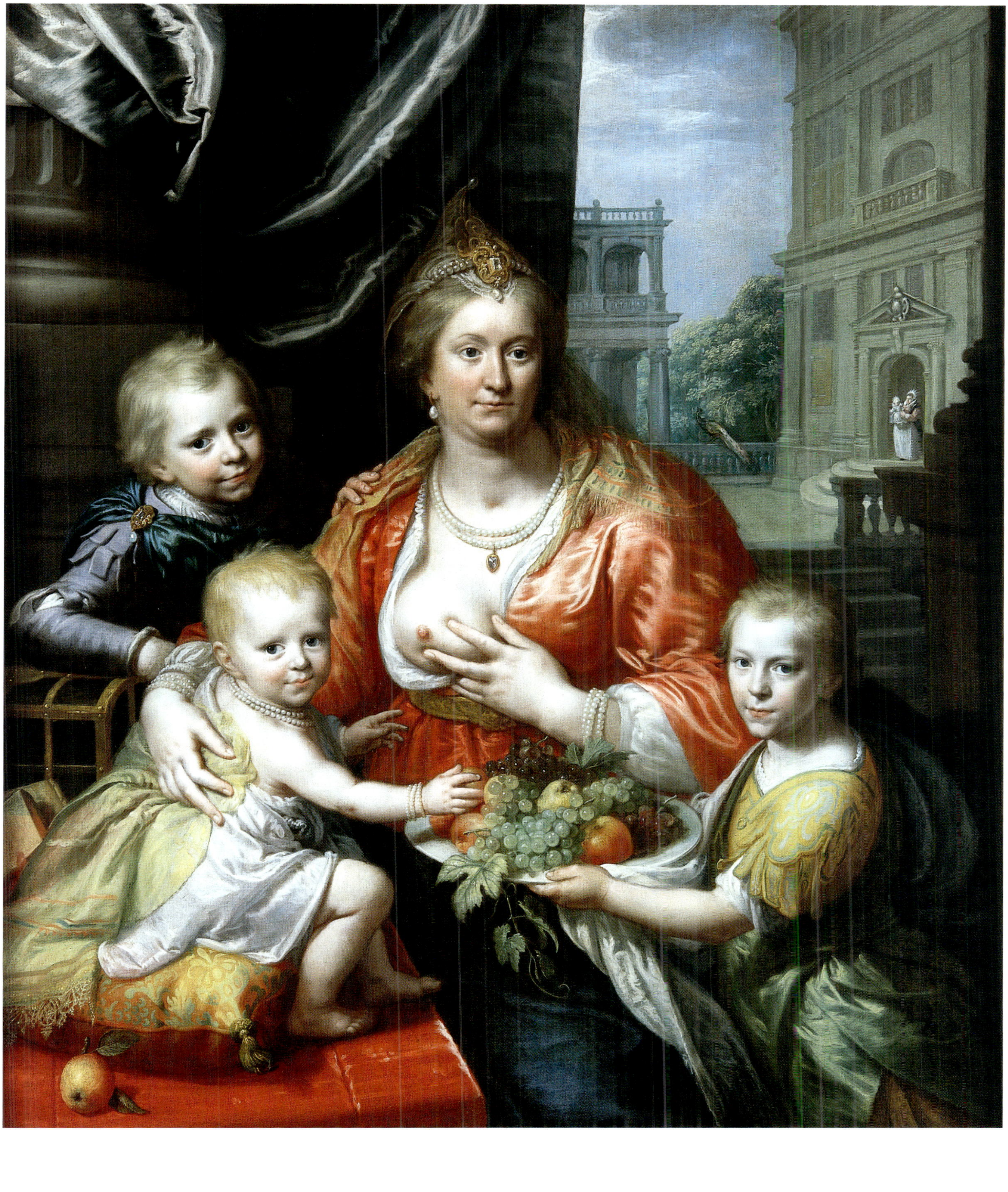

Caspar Netscher

Heidelberg (?) 1635/6 – 1684 The Hague

44

Portrait of a Lady, 1683

Oil on canvas, 78.5 x 62 cm
At the bottom of the stonework: *CNetscher. Fec. / 1683.* (CN in ligature)
The National Gallery, London

From about 1670 onwards, Caspar Netscher was the most sought-after portrait painter in The Hague, where he had settled around 1662. During the early part of his career he concentrated on elegant genre scenes in the tradition of his teacher Gerard ter Borch, but after about 1667 he turned his attention increasingly towards portraiture. Here he followed the refined style of artists such as Adriaen Hanneman (cat. 28), Jan Mijtens (cat. 41) and Jan de Baen (1633–1702) that was so popular with courtly and aristocratic patrons in The Hague. The portrait style of each of these artists, including Netscher, was based on the tradition of Anthony van Dyck.

Yet unlike his colleagues, Netscher never aspired to produce large-scale, life-size depictions, and instead concentrated on finely executed cabinet pictures. The present work epitomises this approach, and is a characteristic example of the artist's many small-scale portraits painted in The Hague in the 1670s and early 1680s. By the time it was painted, 1683, the realist tradition that characterised the so-called 'Golden Age' of Dutch painting had given way to the more idealised and decorative style of academic classicism. The sitter of this portrait thus reflects little of the psychological scrutiny and insightfulness that characterised much of Dutch portraiture of the previous decades. The sitter is shown full length, seated on a stone bench in a garden. The setting is decorated with the usual accoutrements such as the pedestal she is leaning on, embellished with a bas-relief showing two embracing putti,[1] the sculpted fountain in the shape of a putto holding up a ewer behind her, and the draperies. In the background we may glimpse some trees. Typically for the period and for this type of portraiture, the sitter does not wear contemporary fashion, but is instead dressed in decorative imaginary costume which was often referred to at the time as 'antique' or 'Roman'. Her hair, on the other hand, is arranged and curled according to the fashion of the day. It is not clear whether the orange blossom she is holding in her hand is to be interpreted as a symbol (of love or chastity) or as a purely decorative item. Equally, we cannot be sure whether the picture was a pendant to a male portrait – in which case the connotation of the blossom would be evident – or whether it was conceived as an independent work.

When the picture entered the collection of the National Gallery in 1935 the sitter was identified as Mary Stuart (1662–1694), the daughter of King James II, who married William III, Prince of Orange in 1677 and who in 1689 became Queen Mary II. This identification was partly based on the orange blossom in the woman's hands, which was seen as a reference to the House of Orange. When comparing this picture with securely identifiable portraits of Mary, however, including one by Netscher from the same year (fig. 44a),[2] there can be no doubt that this identification is erroneous.[3]
AR

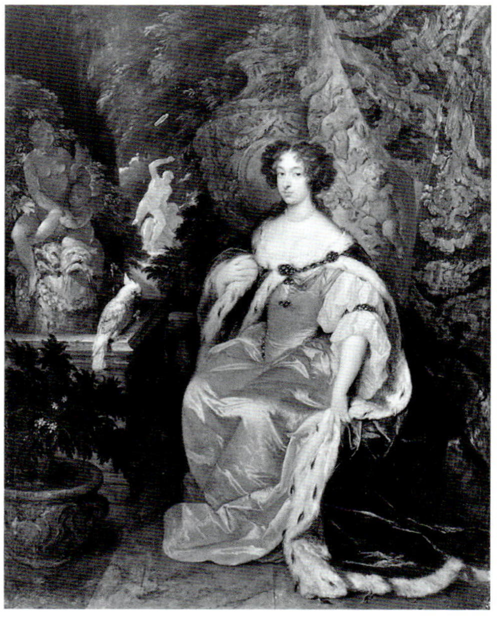

44a.
Caspar Netscher, *Portrait of Mary Stuart II*, 1683. Canvas (transferred from panel), 81 x 64 cm. State Hermitage Museum, St Petersburg

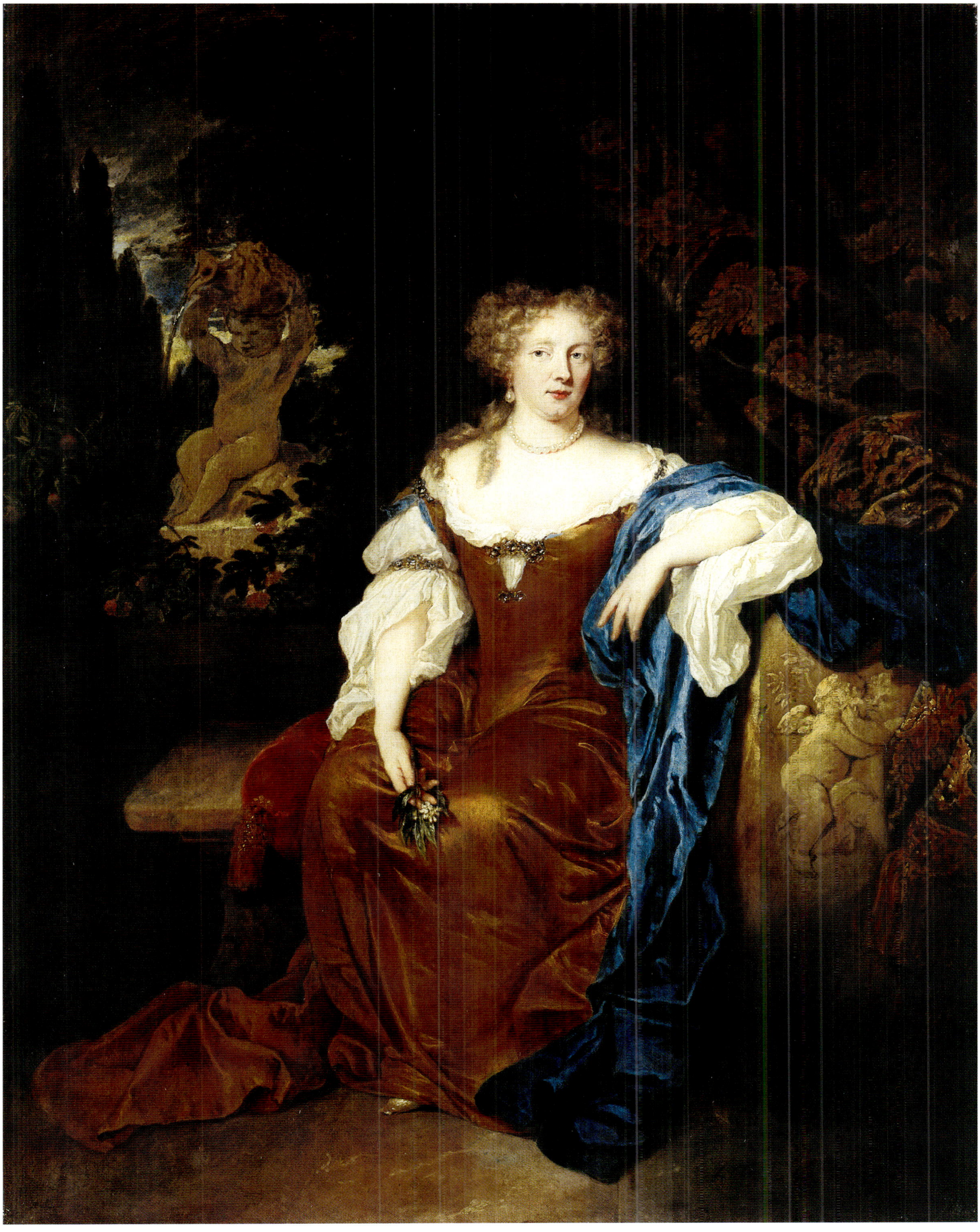

Nicolaes Eliasz Pickenoy

Amsterdam 1588–after 1650 Amsterdam

45

The Osteology Lesson of Dr Sebastiaen Egbertsz, 1619

Oil on canvas, 135 x 186 cm
Amsterdams Historisch Museum, Amsterdam

The new guild-hall of Amsterdam's surgeons' guild, in the former weighing-house known as Sint-Anthoniswaag (p. 190, fig. 53b), was opened in 1619, and it seems likely that this painting was commissioned to mark the occasion. It was commissioned by several members of the guild, and hung above the mantelpiece there for many years. Several years earlier, in 1601, the guild members had asked the painter Aert Pietersz to make a group portrait of them together with their *praelector*, Dr Sebastiaen Egbertsz (fig. 45a).[1] This commission initiated an Amsterdam tradition that endured through much of the eighteenth century, and was emulated elsewhere throughout the Republic (see p. 25, fig. 11).[2]

Egbertsz is depicted in both works, in the one by Pietersz performing an anatomy lesson, and in that by Nicolaes Pickenoy during an osteology lesson – a lesson on the structure of the skeleton, rather than a dissection. Pickenoy's composition is completely different from that of Pietersz, in part because it depicts only the five headmen serving in 1619 and the *praelector*, and not all 28 guild members. The subject of the lesson is no longer a cadaver lying horizontally on the table, but a skeleton placed vertically at the centre of the composition. The skeleton is probably that of an English pirate executed in 1615 (this skeleton is mentioned in a number of guild inventories).[3]

The painting depicts, from left to right: Lambert Jacobsz (about 1583–1635), Anthoni Jansz Uytdenhooven (about 1582–1630), the *praelector*, Dr Sebastiaen Egbertsz (1563–1621), Hendrick Claesz Koolvelt (about 1577–1645), Jan Arentsz de Wees (guild headman from about 1618–21) and Gerrit Indies (about 1577–1622).[4] The figures are grouped symmetrically on either side of the skeleton, yielding a balanced composition that affords equal attention to each figure. The men's heads are all held at different angles and facing in different directions, adding to the scene's vitality. Only two figures engage the viewer's gaze; the other four are intent on the demonstration. Unlike the majority of anatomy pieces, the praelector does not occupy the most prominent position here. He is, however, the only man to be depicted wearing a hat (see cat. 53). A recent restoration has uncovered many exquisite details throughout the painting, especially in the superbly rendered black garments.

From 1750 to 1993, the painting was invariably attributed to Thomas de Keyser. The attribution to Pickenoy in 1993, which was initially treated with some scepticism, has since won universal acceptance.[5] Highly ambitious, the painting is the earliest known work by this painter, and constitutes a major contribution to the development of the Dutch group portrait. In 1625 Pickenoy was given another commission for a group portrait of the surgeons' guild, this time with its new *praelector*, Dr Johan Fonteijn.[6] Seven years later, in 1632, the members of the guild would have their portraits painted by Rembrandt (cat. 53). RE

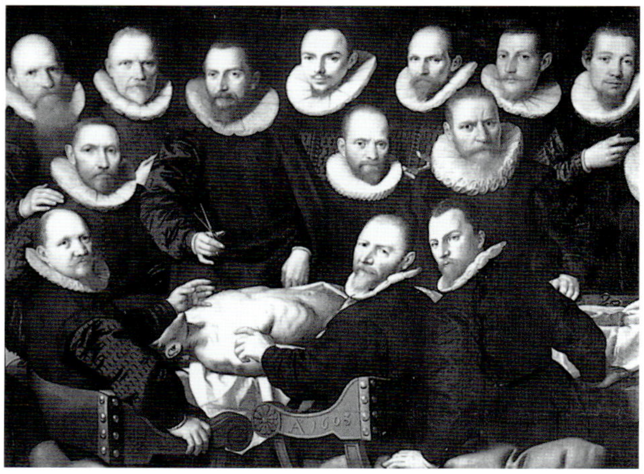

45a
Aert Pietersz,
The Anatomy Lesson of Dr Sebastiaen Egbertsz (detail), 1601–3.
Oil on canvas,
147 x 392 cm.
Amsterdams Historisch Museum, Amsterdam

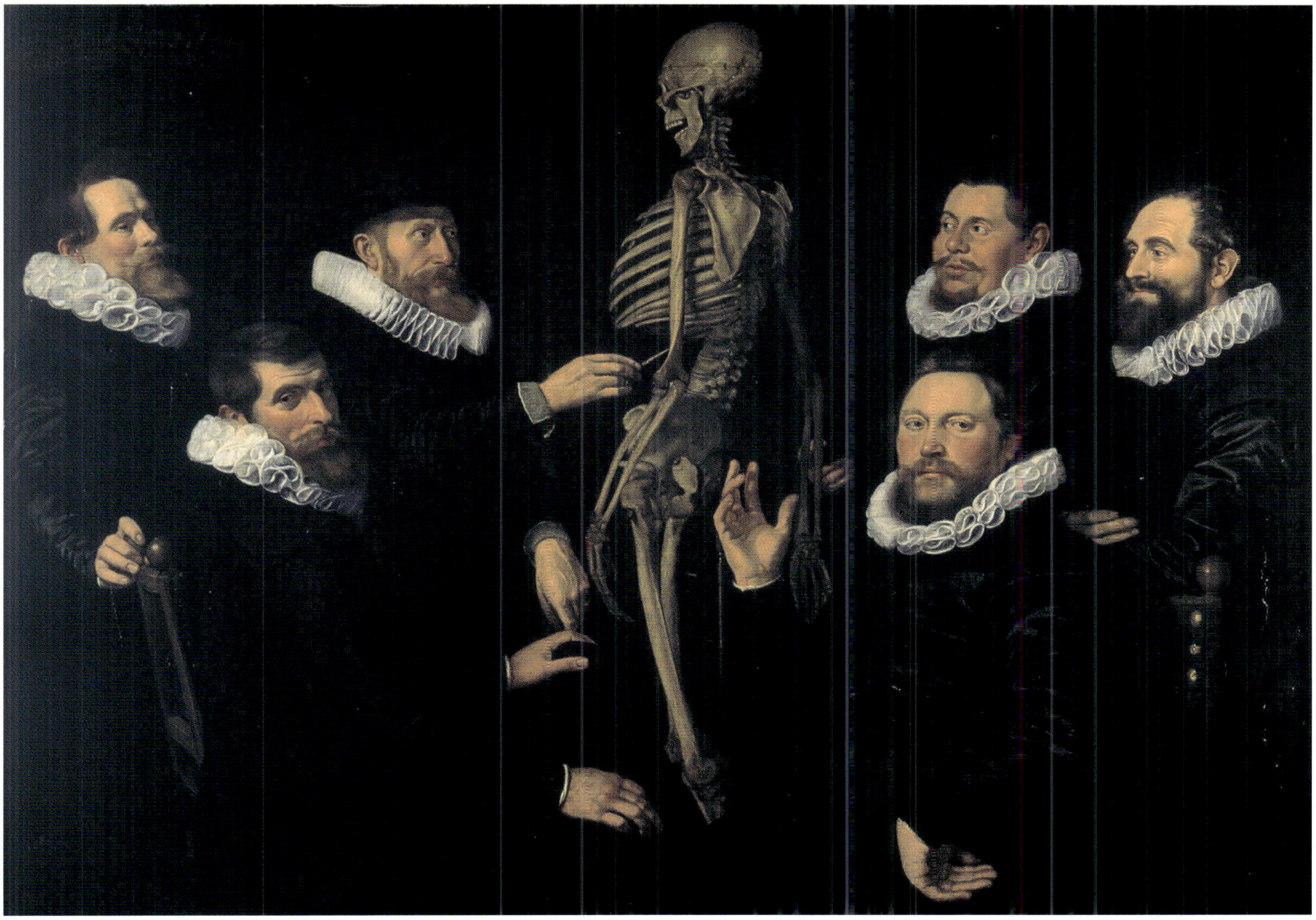

Before restoration

Nicolaes Eliasz Pickenoy

Amsterdam 1588–after 1650 Amsterdam

46

Portrait of Dr Nicolaes Tulp, about 1633–4

Oil on panel, 39 x 30 cm
At left and right on the parapet: NICOLAVS / TVLPIVS;
in the cartouche at lower centre: ALIIS INSERVIENDO / CONSVMOR;
on the back *'Aetatis 40'*[1]
Six Collection, Amsterdam
The Hague only

Nicolaes Tulp (1593–1674) became a world celebrity with his portrait in Rembrandt's 1632 anatomy piece in the Mauritshuis (cat. 53). The eminent doctor subsequently commissioned portraits from several other artists,[2] including the Amsterdam painter Nicolaes Eliasz Pickenoy, who produced this portrait in 1633 or 1634.[3] The painter had previously executed commissions for the surgeons' guild where Tulp worked from 1628 to 1650 as *prælector anatomiæ* (reader in anatomy): in 1619 he completed a group portrait of Dr Sebastiaen Egbertsz and five officers of the guild during an osteology lesson (cat. 45), and in 1625 the guild enlisted his services for a group portrait of Dr Johan Fonteijn and six of the guild's officers.[4] Tulp must have known Pickenoy, since the artist's daughter was one of his patients.[5] It is possible that the artist made the portrait described here, which belonged to the physician's private collection, in gratitude for Tulp's care.[6] Several art objects and manuscripts belonging to him, including this portrait, have been in the Six Collection in Amsterdam since the eighteenth century.[7] Tulp's estate would end up in this famous collection by way of a descendant of his son Diederick. There was already a connection between the two families, since Tulp's daughter Margaretha (see cat. 13) married Jan Six (see cat. 57) in 1655.[8]

This portrait shows Tulp behind a parapet on which his name is inscribed in Latin. Aside from being bare-headed, he wears precisely the same clothes as in Rembrandt's group portrait, made one or two years earlier. The physician gazes at the viewer, while his right hand draws attention to a burning candle. The significance of this striking gesture and attribute is clarified by the Latin motto in the cartouche in the lower centre: 'ALIIS INSERVIENDO / CONSVMOR' (consumed in the service of others).[9] The combination of this motto with a burning candle is known from seventeenth-century emblem-books such as Gabriel Rollenhagen's *Nucleus emblematum selectorum* from 1613 (fig. 46a).[10] Other physicians also used burning candles to symbolise their dedication to their profession, but none as expressively as in this portrait.[11] Just as the candle slowly melts to give light, Tulp dedicated his entire life to medicine. He conducted innovative research on diverse cases of disease, and occasionally performed autopsies on deceased patients. His three-volume *Observationes Medicae* (1641) contains descriptions of no fewer than 231 syndromes.[12]

Burning candles were often used in seventeenth-century art to symbolise mortality, and the skull on the cartouche with the motto reinforces this reading. Tulp's work brought him face-to-face with the reality of mortality. Further, candles were among the accessories required for dissections, and they are frequently depicted in paintings of anatomy lessons (see p. 25, fig. 11).[13] Besides illuminating the room, fragrant candles were also used to mask the unavoidable smell that accompanied a dissection.[14] These added characteristics make burning candles particularly appropriate as an emblem for a physician such as Tulp. The iconography of this portrait is extremely unusual: there is no other work in this exhibition with such explicit symbolism. LvdV

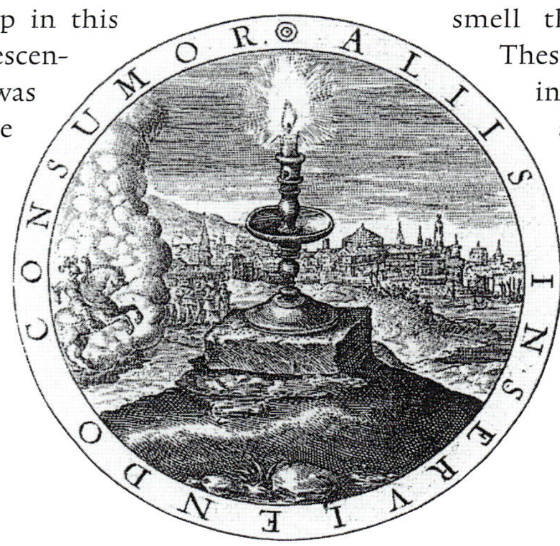

46a.
Crispijn van de Passe the Elder, *Aliis inserviendo consumor*. From Gabriël Rollenhagen, *Nucleus emblematum selectorum*, Utrecht 1613

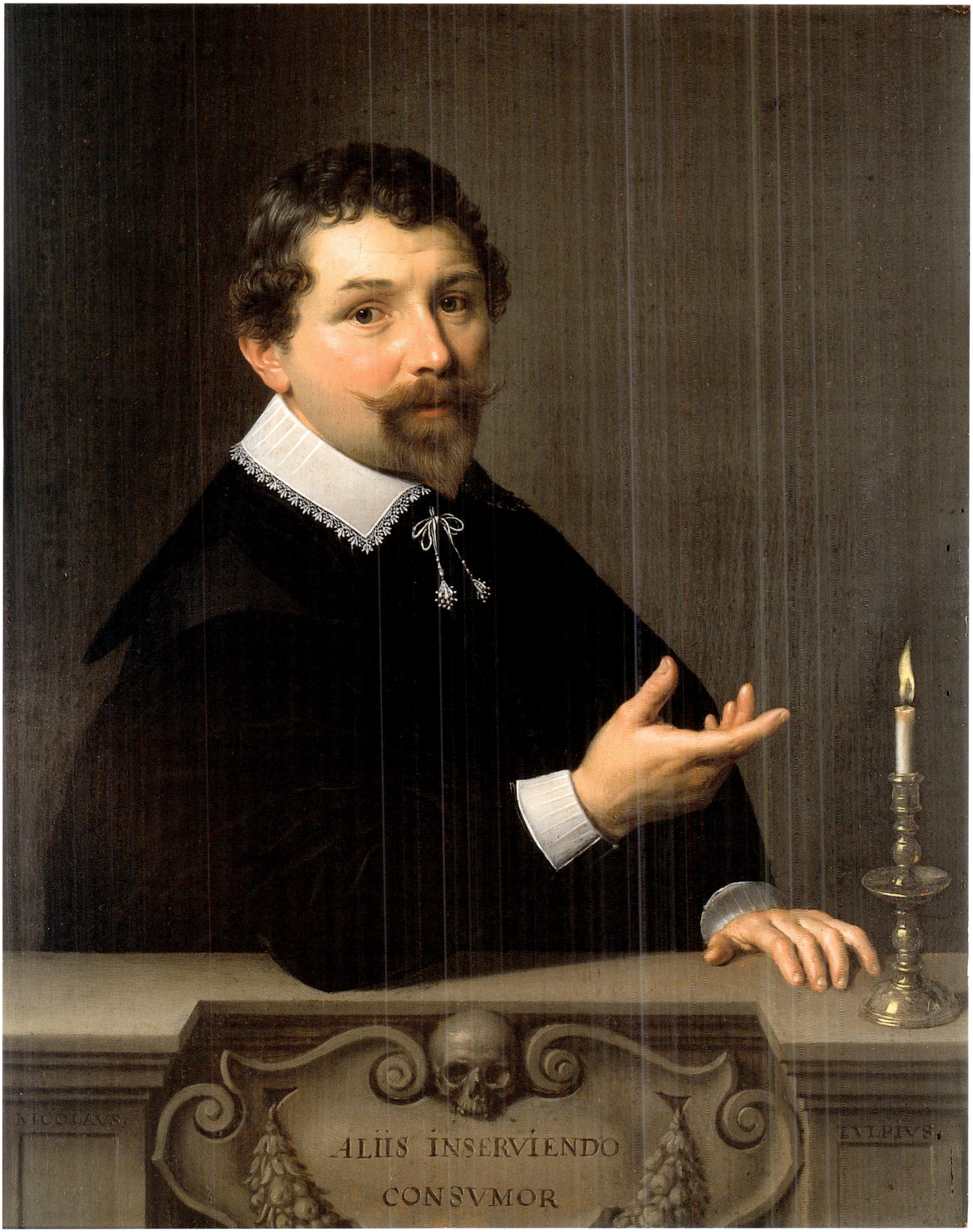
NICOLAVS
ALIIS INSERVIENDO
CONSVMOR
TVLPIVS

Nicolaes Eliasz Pickenoy

Amsterdam 1588–after 1650 Amsterdam

47 | 48

Portrait of Cornelis de Graeff, 1636

Oil on canvas, 185 x 105 cm
Gemäldegalerie, Staatliche Museen, Berlin
London only

Portrait of Catharina Hooft, 1636

Oil on canvas, 185 x 105 cm
Gemäldegalerie, Staatliche Museen, Berlin
London only

These two life-sized, full-length portraits represent the pinnacle of the genre in Amsterdam. On 14 August 1635, the 35-year-old widower Cornelis de Graeff (1599–1664), a scion of an Amsterdam regent family and later a prominent long-time burgomaster of Amsterdam, married the 16-year-old Catharina Hooft (1618–1691). She was related to his first wife, Geertruid Overlander (1608–1634), who died only two months after their marriage in November 1633. In 1633 De Graeff had ordered wedding portraits of himself and his first bride from Nicolaes Pickenoy. In these paintings, the subjects were depicted at knee-length.[1] Shortly after his second marriage, De Graeff commissioned the same artist to make the two wedding portraits discussed here, which unlike the earlier pendants, showed their subjects at full-length.[2] This ambitious choice was not entirely surprising, since around 1620 Catharina Hooft's parents, Pieter Hooft and Geertruyd Overlander, had full-length portraits executed by an as yet unidentified artist.[3] Evidently both the De Graeff and Hooft families took a keen interest in commissioning expensive portraits. The many portrayals of these families include one of Catharina with her nurse, painted by Frans Hals in about 1620 (cat. 14).

Life-sized, full-length portraits became popular among prominent Amsterdam regent families around 1615, and remained so for decades.[4] When the fashion first took hold, Cornelis van der Voort (see cat. 65) produced several works in the genre, and after his death such artists as Pickenoy and Rembrandt continued the tradition. These paintings' immense popularity in successive generations of the De Graeff and Hooft families is apparent from the 1709 inventory of the estate at Huis Ilpenstein left by their son Pieter de Graeff (1638–1707), which describes an entire gallery of large, full-length portraits.[5] Besides the likenesses discussed here, these included the portraits of Catharina's parents, mentioned above, and life-sized portraits of Volkert Overlander and Geertruyd Hooft, their daughter Maria Overlander and her husband Frans Banning Cocq (see p. 32, fig. 22), the parents, sister and brother-in-law, respectively, of De Graeff's first wife.[6] Volkert and Geertruyd were painted by Van der Voort, while the artist who executed the portrait of their daughter and her husband is not known. Among other Amsterdam citizens immortalised in this way were De Graeff's brothers, Andries and Dirck. Andries de Graeff had his portrait painted by Rembrandt in 1639 (cat. 56).[7] Dirck de Graeff commissioned portraits of himself and his bride Eva Bicker somewhat earlier, around 1630, from an anonymous artist.[8] His mother's cousin, Cornelis Bicker van Swieten, had also ordered life-sized portraits of himself with his bride Aertgen Witsen in 1618, from Van der Voort (p. 28, figs 16–17).[9]

Pickenoy depicted the newly-weds standing on a tiled floor before an architectural background. The man is dressed in black, the woman in a black overgown opened to reveal a gown of pearl-grey satin trimmed with silver lace, surprisingly ostentatious in an age in which women too were usually dressed entirely in black. As one would expect in a formal portrait of this kind, the poses are rather stately, with little dynamism. Our eyes are drawn to Cornelis de Graeff's short, rather stiffly hanging left arm. This detail is not a shortcoming on the painter's part, but rather reflects the considerable (and not always flattering) realism that we often encounter in portraiture of the period. De Graeff suffered a fall in childhood, and the growth of his left arm was stunted as a result.[10] Pickenoy did not endow his subject with an expressive hand gesture, like that devised by Rembrandt in his life-sized, full-length portrait of Maerten Soolmans, dated 1634 (fig. 47–8a). In the pendant to that painting (fig. 47–8b), Rembrandt suggests movement by depicting Sool-

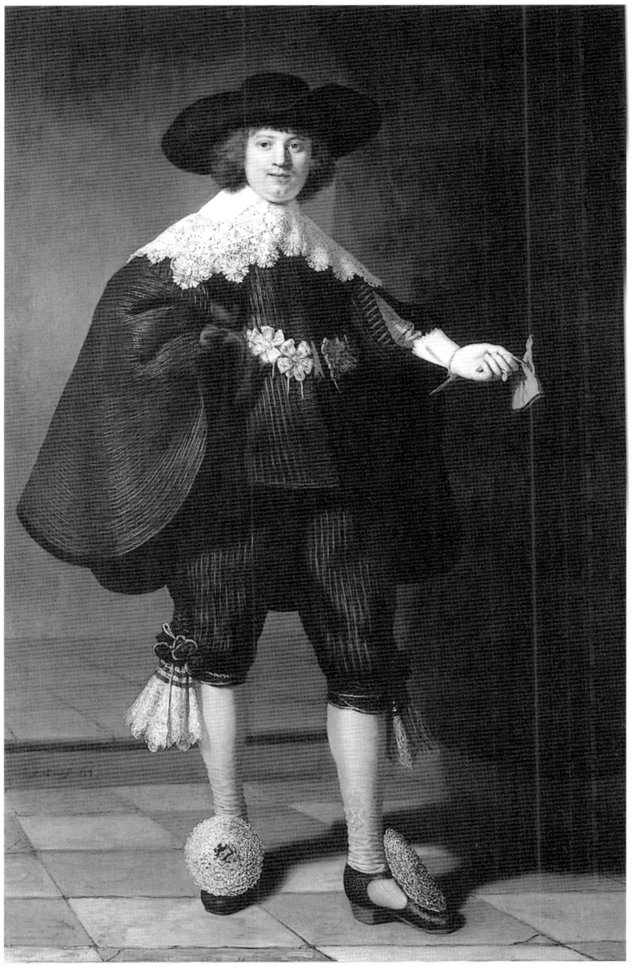

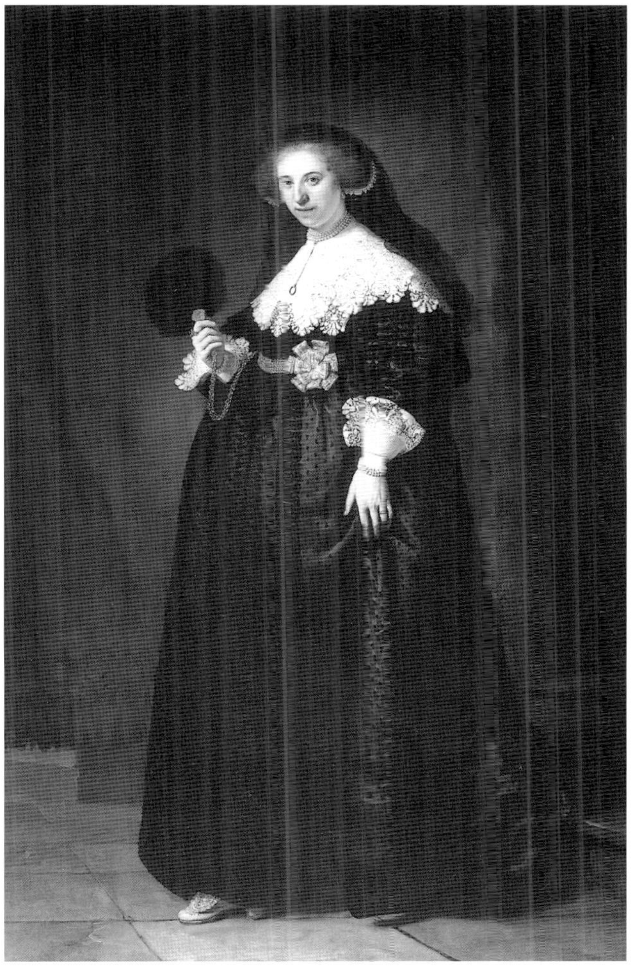

47–48a.
Rembrandt,
Portrait of Maerten Soolmans, 1634.
Oil on canvas, 210 x 135 cm. Private collection, France

47–48b.
Rembrandt,
Portrait of Oopjen Coppit, 1634.
Oil on canvas, 210 x 135 cm. Private collection, France

mans's bride Oopjen Coppit walking. Soolmans's gesture emphasises the link between the two pendants.[11] No such explicit link is made in the case of Pickenoy, with the possible exception of Catharina's subtle use of the fan held in her right hand.

Completed in 1636, these paintings exemplify Pickenoy's qualities as a portraitist. His earliest known work, an ambitious group portrait of members of the surgeons' guild in Amsterdam, dates from 1619 (cat. 45). After the death in 1624 of Cornelis van der Voort – who was probably his teacher – Pickenoy, with Thomas de Keyser, became one of Amsterdam's most influential portraitists. Although Pickenoy had stronger competition to contend with in the 1630s, he remained successful throughout the decade. Not until the 1640s do we see a certain decline in his output. RE

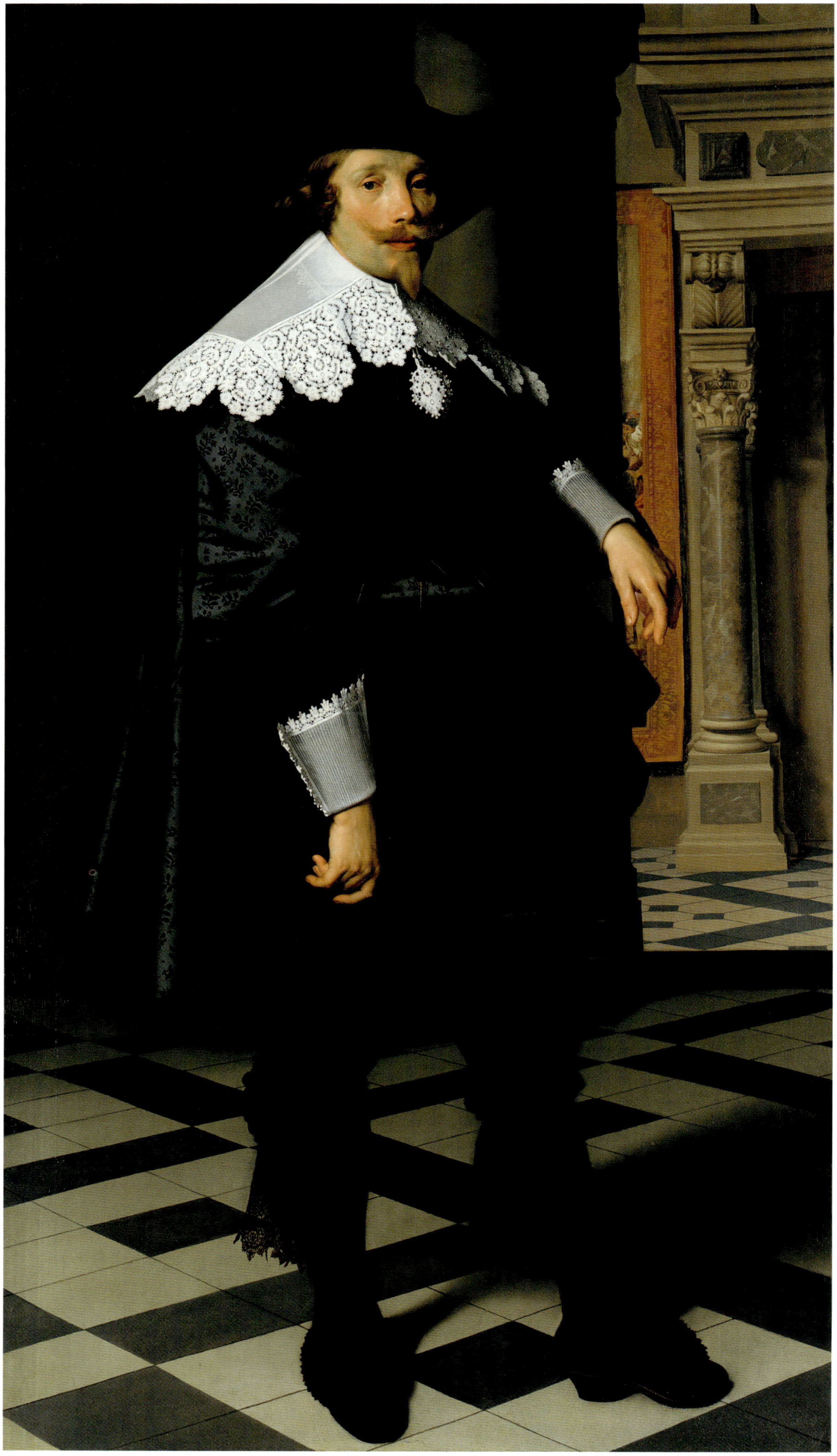

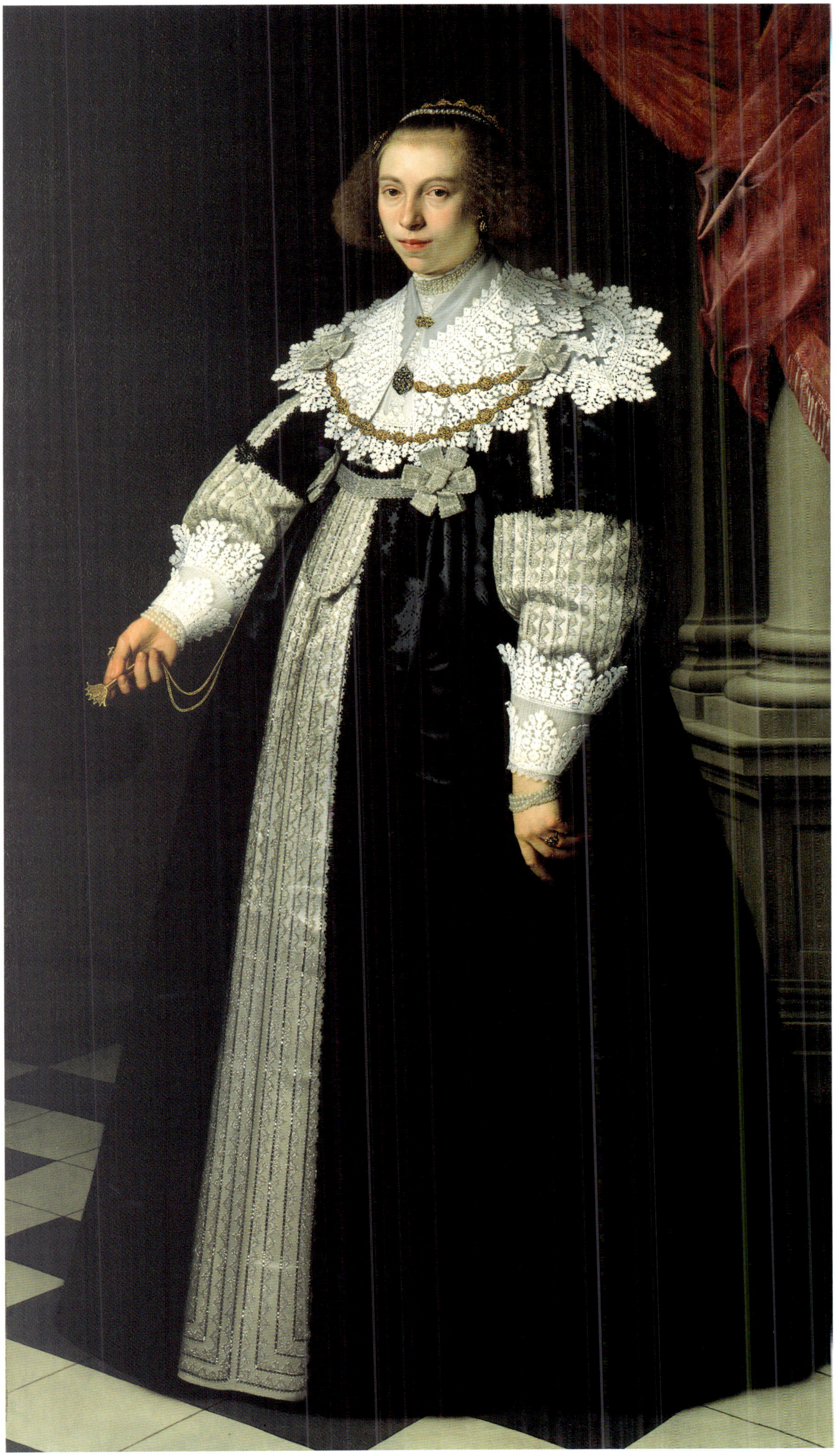

Jan van Ravesteyn

The Hague (?) about 1572–1657 The Hague

49

Portrait of Hugo Grotius, 1599

Oil on panel (circular), diameter 31 cm
At left: *Jo: a. Ravesteÿn Pinxit. An°. 1599;*
at right: *Æta. meæ. 16*; below: *Hugo de Groot.*
Frits Lugt Collection, Institut Néerlandais, Paris

Dating from 1599, a period dubbed the 'Dawn of the Golden Age',[1] this portrait of Hugo Grotius (1583–1645) is the earliest painting in the exhibition. Between 1580 and 1620 diverse types of portraiture developed (see pp. 16–47), but this portrait of Grotius by Jan van Ravesteyn is distinctive among them. The compelling likeness arrests and holds our gaze not only because of its unusual circular shape, but also because of the manner in which the sitter has been portrayed. The image is restricted to the head and shoulders, and the subject is depicted at very close range. His face and stiff white ruff project sharply against the dark background. The large eyes and incisive gaze (which is not directed at the viewer) lend the portrait an informal and quite idiosyncratic air. About four years later, Grotius ordered another portrait of himself from Van Ravesteyn – a more traditional one, in which he does meet the viewer's eye. The whereabouts of this portrait is no longer known, but it became widely known via an engraving published in 1614.[2]

The style of the current painting has much in common with contemporary portraits by Amsterdam artists. It has even been posited that Van Ravesteyn was trained by the Amsterdam portrait painter Pieter Pietersz (1540/1–1603). The schematic manner of painting and the stylised rendering of elements such as eyelids and eyelashes strongly recall Pietersz's work.[3] The placement and wording of the inscriptions correspond to those in portraits by Pietersz, who made a set of circular portraits in 1597, two years before this painting was executed (fig. 49a).[4] The circular shape of these paintings and their inscriptions are reminiscent of portrait medallions or miniatures, albeit on a larger scale. The informal quality of Van Ravesteyn's portrait also recalls the work of Cornelis Ketel (1548–1616) who, like Pietersz, worked in Amsterdam. In his portraits, Ketel – again like Pietersz – depicted his sitter very close to the picture plane, from an unusual angle and cropped closely by the frame.[5]

The young Hugo Grotius is depicted here in the year in which he settled in The Hague. He was installed there as a lawyer in December 1599, at only 16 years of age. A year earlier, after completing his studies in Leiden, he had accompanied a Dutch diplomatic mission to King Henry IV in France.[6] While there, Grotius was awarded a doctorate in Orléans. In academic and administrative circles he was seen as a young man of great promise – so it is not surprising that another portrait was made of him during this period. Shortly before the work described here, Jacques De Gheyn II made a small drawing that was engraved and reproduced in one of Grotius's books in 1599.[7] Grotius went on to realise his potential, becoming an ambassador and a renowned jurist in his maturity.

Jan van Ravesteyn was the most important portraitist in The Hague for several decades. From about 1610 onwards, he sought inspiration in the work of Jacob Delff (about 1540/1–1601) and Michiel van Mierevelt (cat. 39), both of whom worked in nearby Delft; from them he adopted a more down-to-earth rendering of his subjects. Among Van Ravesteyn's most important works is a series of 25 portrayals of officers from the years 1611–24 – probably commissioned by Prince Maurits (1567–1625) – and five militia company portraits painted between 1616 and 1638 (see cat. 50).[8] Although Van Ravesteyn had no immediate followers, a later generation of the Hague elite commissioned their portraits from Adriaen Hanneman (cat. 28), a pupil of Jan's brother Anthonie van Ravesteyn.
QB

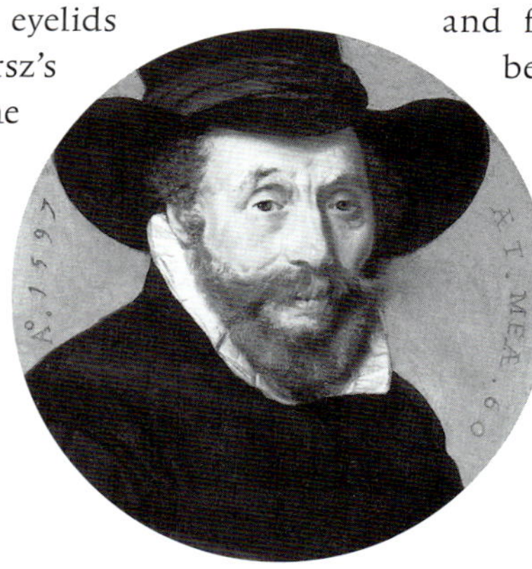

49a.
Pieter Pietersz,
Portrait of a Man,
1597. Oil on panel
(circular),
diameter 42 cm.
Mauritshuis,
The Hague

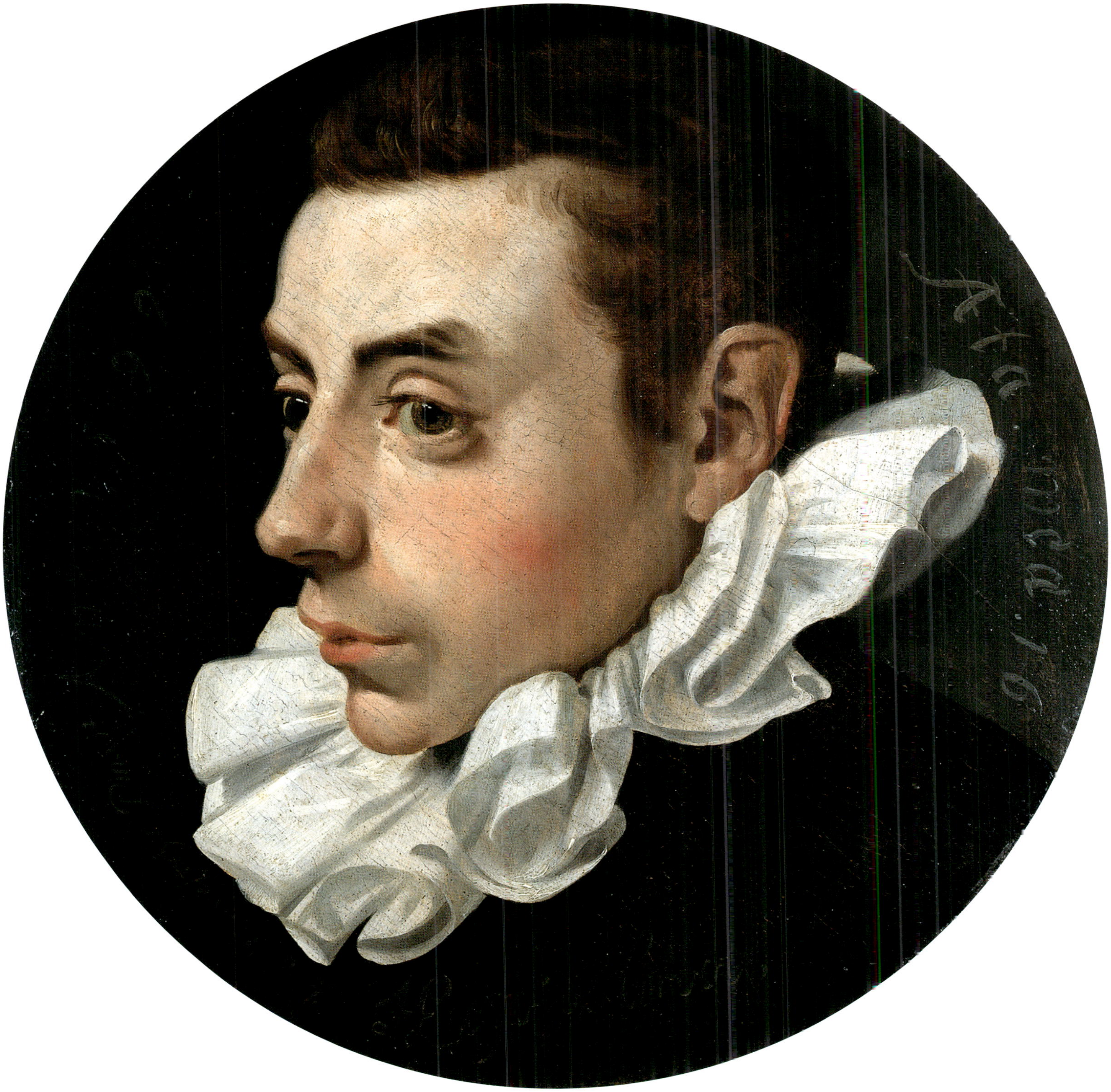

Jan van Ravesteyn

The Hague (?) about 1572–1657 The Hague

50

The Officers and Guardsmen of the Orange Company of The Hague on the Steps of the Town Hall, 1616

Oil on panel, 204 x 180 cm
On the base of the column: *ANNO. 1616 / vRaüesteijn. F* (vR in ligature)
Haags Historisch Museum, The Hague
The Hague only

Although militia pieces flourished mainly in Amsterdam and Haarlem, Jan van Ravesteyn made a significant and influential contribution to the genre with his group portrait of The Hague's Orange Company. This company was part of the St Sebastian Civic Guard, which consisted of merchants and shopkeepers, with regents holding most of the top positions (see cat. 51). Sint-Sebastiaansdoelen, the civic guardsmen's guild-house, stood near the Mauritshuis overlooking the lake known as the Hofvijver.[1] Today it houses the historical museum of The Hague (Haags Historisch Museum).

Every male burgher with sufficient means to purchase his own military equipment was more or less obliged to join the civic guard. Even artists became guardsmen, including Jan van Ravesteyn himself. In 1618 he was excused from all further duties such as taking part in processions and keeping guard.[2] He remained an 'associate' member, however, and the civic guard granted him three major commissions between 1618 and 1638.[3] There is good reason to believe that Van Ravesteyn included a likeness of himself in this group portrait from 1616.[4] The painter – who was then about 44 years of age – is probably the figure shown almost in profile among the upper tier of guardsmen (seventh from the left), behind the man resting the barrel of his musket against the parapet.[5] This identification is based on the similarity to a self-portrait included in a group portrait he produced two years later, which depicts the Hague magistracy receiving the officers of the St Sebastian Civic Guard. This likeness is documented by the list of names preserved with that painting.[6]

The St Sebastian Civic Guard had close organisational ties with The Hague's magistracy, whose offices were in the town hall at Groenmarkt. In this portrait, Van Ravesteyn posed the guardsmen of the Orange Company, identifiable by their orange sashes, on the steps of the town hall.[7] By arranging the 25 men in two levels, the artist created a dynamic composition while ensuring that each individual portrait remains clearly recognisable. Placing some figures in the foreground and others behind the parapet was a tried and tested solution for large militia pieces. Initially such arrangements consisted of static rows of men standing side-by-side, but in the early seventeenth century artists started creating more active presentations. This new dynamism is strongly in evidence here: the wavy lines of the numerous heads and the diverse poses make an almost chaotic first impression. The casualness of the figures is particularly innovative. The viewer is struck by the lively gestures of the officers in the foreground, for instance, and by the two guardsmen who have slung a friendly arm over each other's shoulders behind the parapet on the left. The poses of these two men undoubtedly derive from a group portrait of the Delft civic guard that Michiel van Mierevelt had produced in 1611.[8] Unlike Van Mierevelt and other artists, Van Ravesteyn opted for a vertical, almost square format, and as a result the picture plane is almost entirely filled with portraits. This choice of format was inspired by the painting's destined location – above the mantle in the dining room of the civic guard's guild-house.[9]

Besides Van Ravesteyn himself, only one of the guardsmen portrayed here can be identified. Cornelis Jacobsz van Wouw, captain of the Orange Company, is descending the steps on the right.[10] There is a striking lack of hierarchy in the positioning of the figures. In most militia pieces, the captain and chief officers are at the centre, but here some are in the foreground and others towards the back. Their ranks are indicated by their headgear and the decorative weapons they bear. The officers and non-commissioned officers all wear plumed hats and hold 'partisans' or halberds. The man in the right foreground is holding his hat in his hand, and from his characteristic pose we can infer that he must be the ensign.[11] To have depicted him actually holding the standard, however, would not have been appropriate in this densely packed composition (see cats 21, 33, 64). The forest of lances in the right background is a reflection of the large size of the Orange Company. By including them, Van Ravesteyn has ensured that even those guardsmen who lacked the rank or the means to have their portraits made were given a place of sorts in this spectacular painting. LvdV

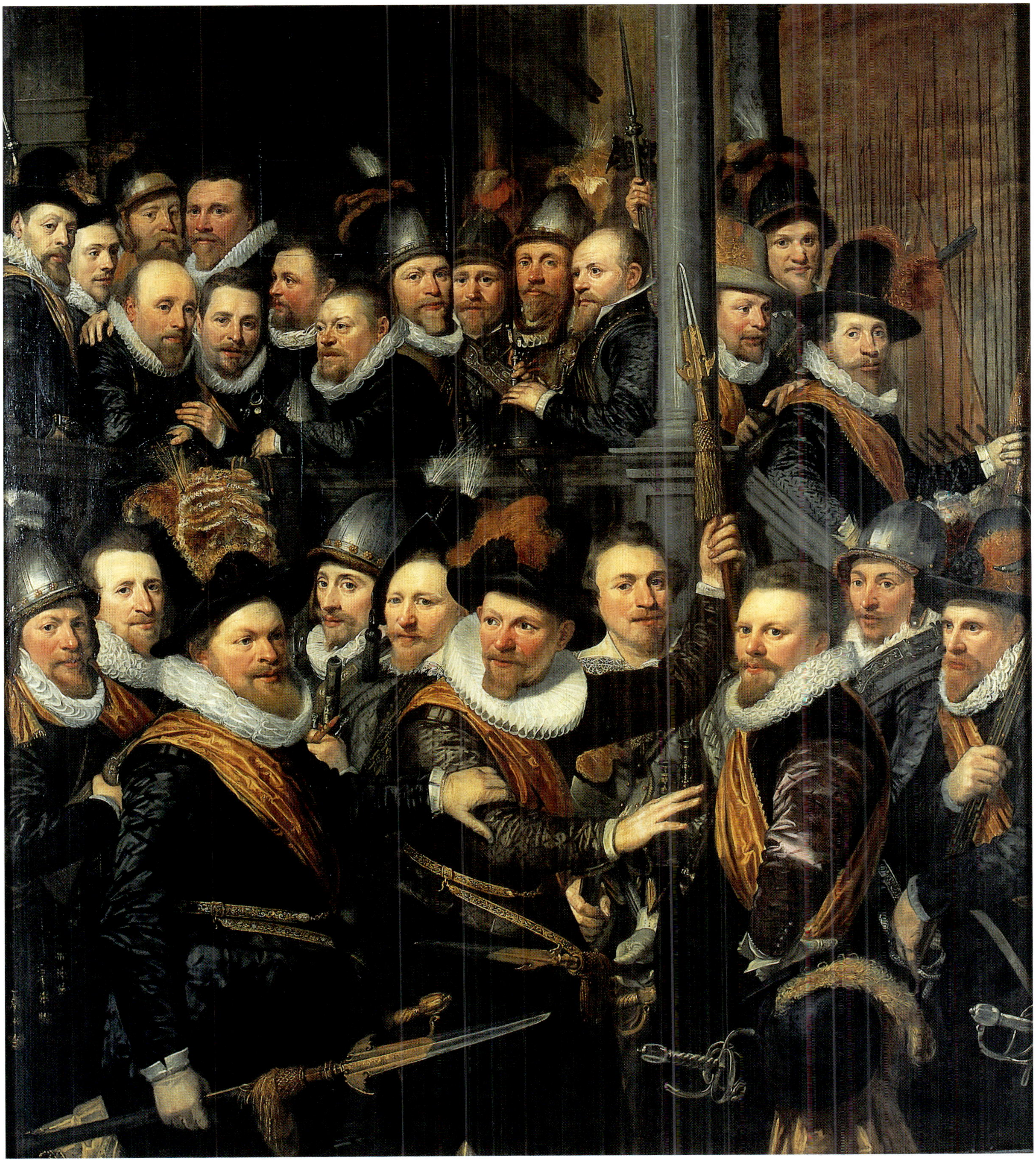

Rembrandt

Leiden 1606–1669 Amsterdam

51

Portrait of Joris de Caulerij, 1632

Oil on canvas mounted on panel, 102.4 x 84.3 cm
At right: RHL. *van Ryn* / *1632* (RHL in ligature)
Fine Arts Museums of San Francisco
(Roscoe and Margaret Oakes Collection)

In 1632 Rembrandt made numerous portraits of prominent Amsterdam burghers, including the members of the local surgeons' guild (cat. 53). At the time, the Leiden-born artist was working as a portrait painter in the Amsterdam studio of Hendrick Uylenburgh, in whose home he had taken lodgings. The city's economy was booming, and many newly wealthy townspeople wanted their portraits made to memorialise their success. This portrait depicts Joris de Caulerij (died in or after 1661), a client from The Hague. It was probably made not in Amsterdam but in Leiden, where the young painter retained the use of his old studio. He did not make his permanent home in Amsterdam until 1633.[1]

Rembrandt depicted De Caulerij life-sized, as a member of the civic guard. His yellow tunic identifies him specifically as a lieutenant of The Hague's guild of arquebusiers. He wears an iron gorget that his scarf partially covers. Only the hilt of his sword is visible, hanging from a superb bandolier embroidered with gold thread. The second weapon in his arsenal – a small musket known as a *roer* or *klover* – underscores De Caulerij's position as a guardsman. The firearm is accentuated by the light reflected along the barrel. As lieutenant of St Sebastian's Civic Guard, De Caulerij witnessed the building of the Mauritshuis (1634–44) less than 100 yards from its headquarters (the building today houses the historical museum of The Hague). His later military career as a sea-captain in the service of the Republic was distinguished by deeds of heroism during the First Anglo-Dutch War (1652–4) and the later naval war with Sweden (1658–9).[2] In 1654 De Caulerij had a legal document drafted (in connection with his debts) in which this painting is described as the 'Portrait of [Joris de Caulerij] with a *roer* in his hand'.[3] The naval hero drew up his will in August 1661 and died soon after in Denmark, probably while commanding a ship. Under the terms of his will, the portrait by Rembrandt went to De Caulerij's daughter Josina, and passed down in the family until 1750. It also appears from the will that De Caulerij and his wife Maria de la Samme had their portraits made by numerous other artists, including Moyses van Uyttenbrouck, Jan Lievens and Anthony van Dyck,[4] although these can no longer be identified today.[5] The same applies to a portrait that Rembrandt made of De Caulerij's son Johan between 1654 and 1661.[6]

How Joris de Caulerij met Rembrandt is unknown. The painter spent some time in The Hague in 1632, working on a commission for Frederik Hendrik.[7] Since De Caulerij owned an inn in this city at the time, it has been suggested that Rembrandt may have stayed there while he was in The Hague.[8] Perhaps De Caulerij met Lievens and Van Dyck in the same way; they were working for the stadholder's court at the same time as Rembrandt.[9]

De Caulerij's confident pose, with his left hand propped at his hip and the firearm held in his right, resembles those of other civic guardsmen who commissioned individual portraits in cities such as The Hague, Haarlem and Amsterdam (cat. 33). Verspronck's *Portrait of Andries Stilte* (cat. 64) is similarly composed. These paintings for the most part draw on poses seen in large group portraits of entire militia companies (cats 21, 49). The dramatic chiaroscuro of Rembrandt's painting, characteristic of many of his early paintings,[10] distinguishes it from these larger works and to a large extent creates the composition's feeling of depth.[11] The illusion is enhanced by the fact that De Caulerij is gazing at the viewer over his shoulder, his arm strongly foreshortened. His silhouette emerges powerfully from the light-coloured background, and only his head and part of his torso catch the light that falls from the upper left – but Rembrandt has paid minute attention to the suggestion of reflected light on the hard metal of the gorget and the soft leather of the tunic. This portrait makes it clear that De Caulerij, brimming with energy and self-confidence, was in the prime of life. The same applies to the young painter, who produced an extraordinarily expressive portrait of his subject. QB

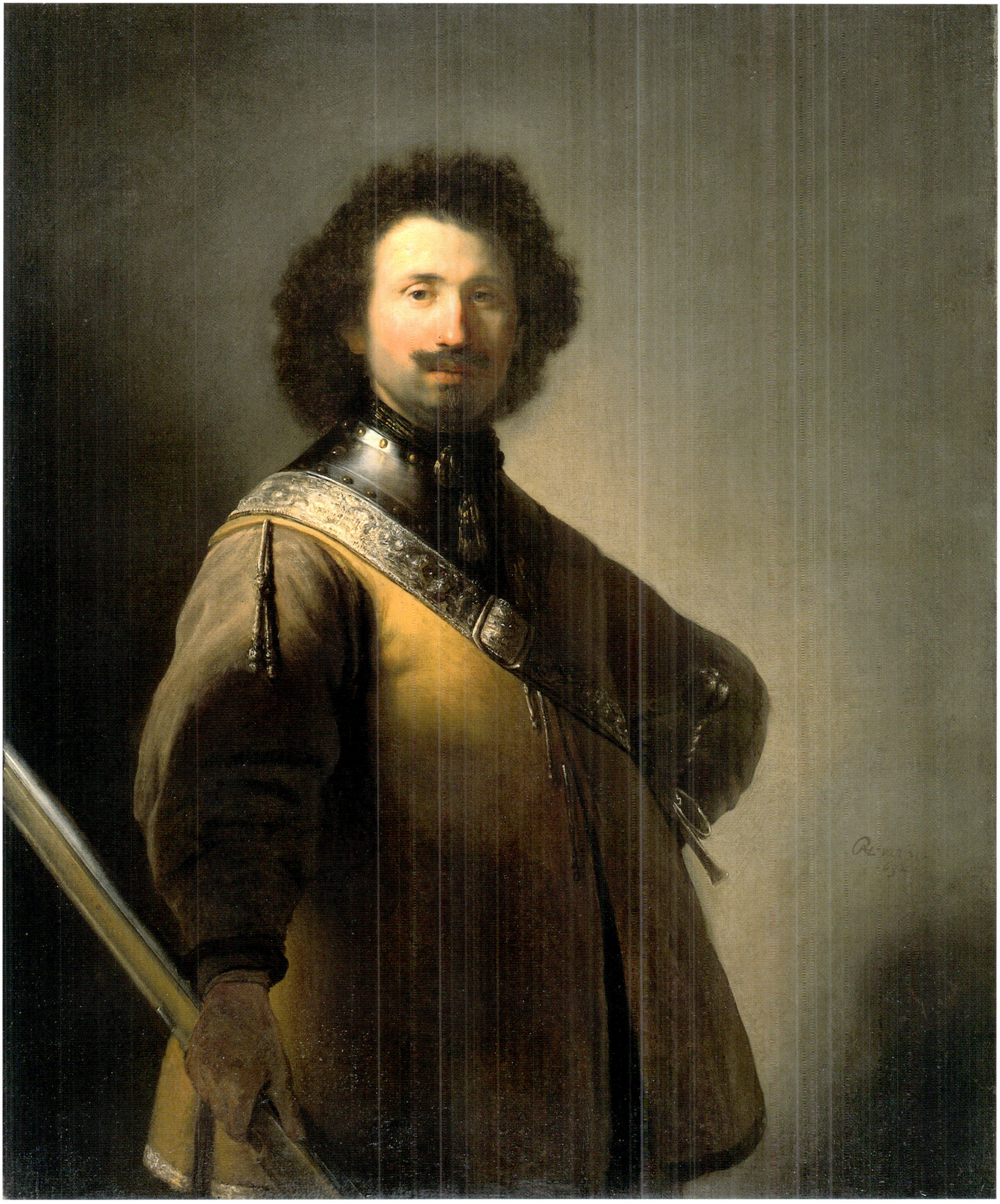

Rembrandt

Leiden 1606–1669 Amsterdam

52

Portrait of Aeltje Uylenburgh, 1632

Oil on panel (oval), 74 x 56 cm
At upper right: RHL *van Ryn* / *1632* (RHL in ligature); at upper left: *Æ 62*
Private collection (on loan to the Mauritshuis, The Hague)
The Hague only

This painting from 1632 is not only characteristic of portraits Rembrandt made in his first year in Amsterdam, but also provides insight into his personal life: it has been recently discovered that Rembrandt depicted here someone to whom he would soon become related. Jaap van der Veen has identified the woman – who according to an inscription was 62 years of age when this portrait was painted – as Aeltje Pietersdr Uylenburgh (1570?–1644),[1] wife of the Reformed Church minister Johannes Sylvius (1564–1638). The couple witnessed the baptism of several of Rembrandt's children.[2] Aeltje belonged to Rembrandt's circle of intimates. She was a cousin not only of the Amsterdam art dealer Hendrick Uylenburgh, in whose house Rembrandt was living at the time, but also of the far younger Saskia Uylenburgh, whom the painter married in 1634.

A will dating from 1681 drawn up on behalf of Cornelis Sylvius, the son of Aeltje and Johannes, includes descriptions of portraits of the couple by Rembrandt.[3] The painting of Sylvius has probably been lost, but we know his facial features from works including two etchings by Rembrandt, one of which was made in 1633.[4] The format of Sylvius's portrait, made to be hung to the left of Aeltje's, can be inferred from another work by Rembrandt dated 1632, which is painted on an oval panel of the same dimensions.[5] In this portrait, the sitter is represented – like Aeltje – to the waist, and gazes directly at the viewer (fig. 52a).

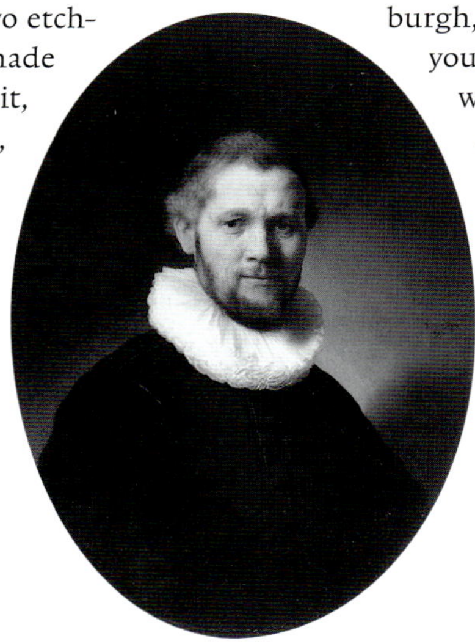

52a. Rembrandt, *Portrait of a 40-Year-Old Man*, 1632. Oil on panel (oval), 74 x 55 cm. The Metropolitan Museum of Art, New York

For many years the *Portrait of Aeltje Uylenburgh* was not exhibited in public. When members of the Rembrandt Research Project studied it in 1971, a thick layer of yellowed varnish covered the painting. Not until the portrait was cleaned and restored in 2000 did the beautiful execution and superb state of preservation become apparent. The woman's clothing has been painted in varied hues of black and grey; her face is depicted in minute detail, down to the wrinkles in the soft skin around her mouth and eyes. The face appears lifelike thanks to an ingenious combination of opaque and translucent layers of paint, and derives added vitality from a short line of white under the right eye. This remarkable face is framed by the white cap and collar with subtle reflections of the light and set against a virtually plain background. Rembrandt evidently had some difficulty deciding how to position the seated woman, but he decided against including the back of a chair, as he had done in earlier works.[6] We know from X-ray analysis that he twice reworked the contours of the figure; the woman's left shoulder was initially higher.[7]

Since 2005 Aeltje's portrait has hung in the Mauritshuis alongside Rembrandt's *Anatomy Lesson of Dr Nicolaes Tulp* (cat. 53), which also dates from 1632, the year the artist turned 26. At the end of 1631 he had moved from his hometown of Leiden to Amsterdam, where he built up a special relationship with the Uylenburgh family. He took lodgings with Hendrick Uylenburgh, who ran a thriving art gallery in which young painters were trained.[8] Rembrandt worked there mainly on portrait commissions for prominent townspeople, such as merchants, senior officials and Church ministers, but he also produced the painting discussed here as well as portraying other members of the family. QB

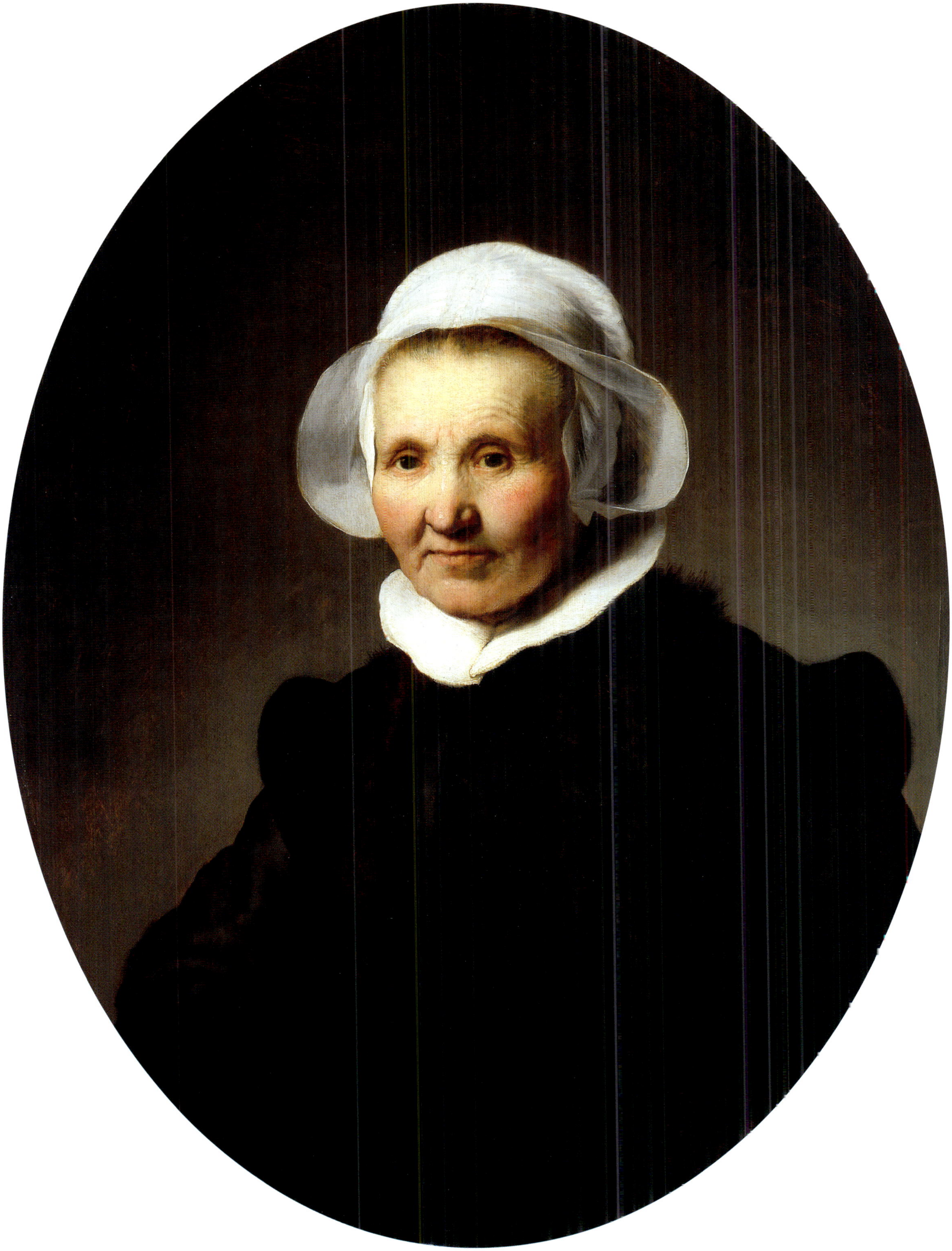

Rembrandt

Leiden 1606–1669 Amsterdam

53

The Anatomy Lesson of Dr Nicolaes Tulp, 1632

Oil on canvas, 169 x 217 cm
At upper centre: *Rembrandt. f*[t]*: 1632*
Royal Picture Gallery Mauritshuis, The Hague

The Anatomy Lesson of Dr *Nicolaes Tulp* is one of Rembrandt's most impressive group portraits. The most important commission he had received to date, it was the 25-year-old's first group portrait. It gave him a unique opportunity to display his talents as a portraitist to the art lovers of Amsterdam.

Anatomy pieces are specific to the northern Netherlands, and now one must visit a Dutch museum to see one. As early as 1555, the surgeons' guild (the body that represented physicians) began organising anatomy demonstrations in Amsterdam.[1] The *prælector anatomiæ* (reader in anatomy) dissected the body of an executed criminal and lectured to an audience of fellow physicians and members of the public, who were charged an entrance fee. The lessons lasted several days and were conducted in the winter to slow the cadaver's decomposition. Every few years an anatomy piece would be ordered to commemorate such a demonstration, generally following the appointment of a new praelector or the admission of new guild members. Nicolaes Tulp (1593–1674) served as praelector from 1628 to 1650, during which time he gave nine public lessons.[2] In 1632 he had himself immortalised together with several guild members (for a second portrait of Tulp, see cat. 46). The body made available to them that year was that of Adriaen Adriaensz, also known as Aris Kindt, an inveterate criminal who had been hanged in Amsterdam on 31 January 1632.[3]

The members of the surgeons' guild in Amsterdam had commissioned portraits of themselves with some regularity since the early seventeenth century. By 1632 the guild-hall boasted three anatomy pieces, dating from 1603 (p. 172, fig. 45a), 1619 (cat. 45) and 1625.[4] Compared to these rather stiffly arranged group portraits, Rembrandt's composition is extremely dynamic and innovative.[5] It is the first painting in which we see a praelector actually performing a dissection. Rembrandt has positioned the body diagonally across the picture plane with an open anatomy book at its feet. Rejecting the customary, somewhat static grouping of the surgeons standing behind one another in rows, he arranged his subjects in a pyramidal configuration, with the instructor, Tulp, dominating the right half of the painting and the other physicians filling the left. While Tulp's prominence leaves us in no doubt as to his overriding importance in the portrait, the hierarchy among the other surgeons is more difficult to make out.

Another original element in Rembrandt's composition is his decision to avoid having all of his subjects look straight out of the picture. Instead, he focused the gaze of each man on a different point either within or outside the image – the partly dissected arm, the anatomy book, Tulp or the viewer – which results in a far livelier painting. The man immediately behind the cadaver craning his neck forwards adds movement to the composition and subtly emphasises the physicians' concentrated attention. The bright shaft of light illuminating the group enhances the dynamism of the scene.

Rembrandt's fabulous technique is displayed to best advantage here, and it was indeed this painting that firmly established his reputation as a portraitist. The manner in which he played with the thickness and transparency of the paint, applying it quite thinly in the portraits positioned towards the background and thickly in those at the front, is truly masterful.[6] The glitter of light on the impastoed paint surface brings these latter sections forward, enhancing the illusion of depth. Since the clothing of the men situated towards the background is painted in less saturated hues, these sections appear to be further away.

Nicolaes Tulp's prominent position, emphasised by the small niche crowned by scalloped moulding behind him, makes his importance immediately apparent to the viewer. He is also the only figure wearing a hat. The surgeon at the top of the pyramidal group, Frans van Loenen, initially also had a hat, but later on – at Tulp's request? – Rembrandt painted it out. A vague shadow around his head bears witness to this intervention. We know the identity of the other figures thanks to inscriptions and numbers added in the eighteenth century.

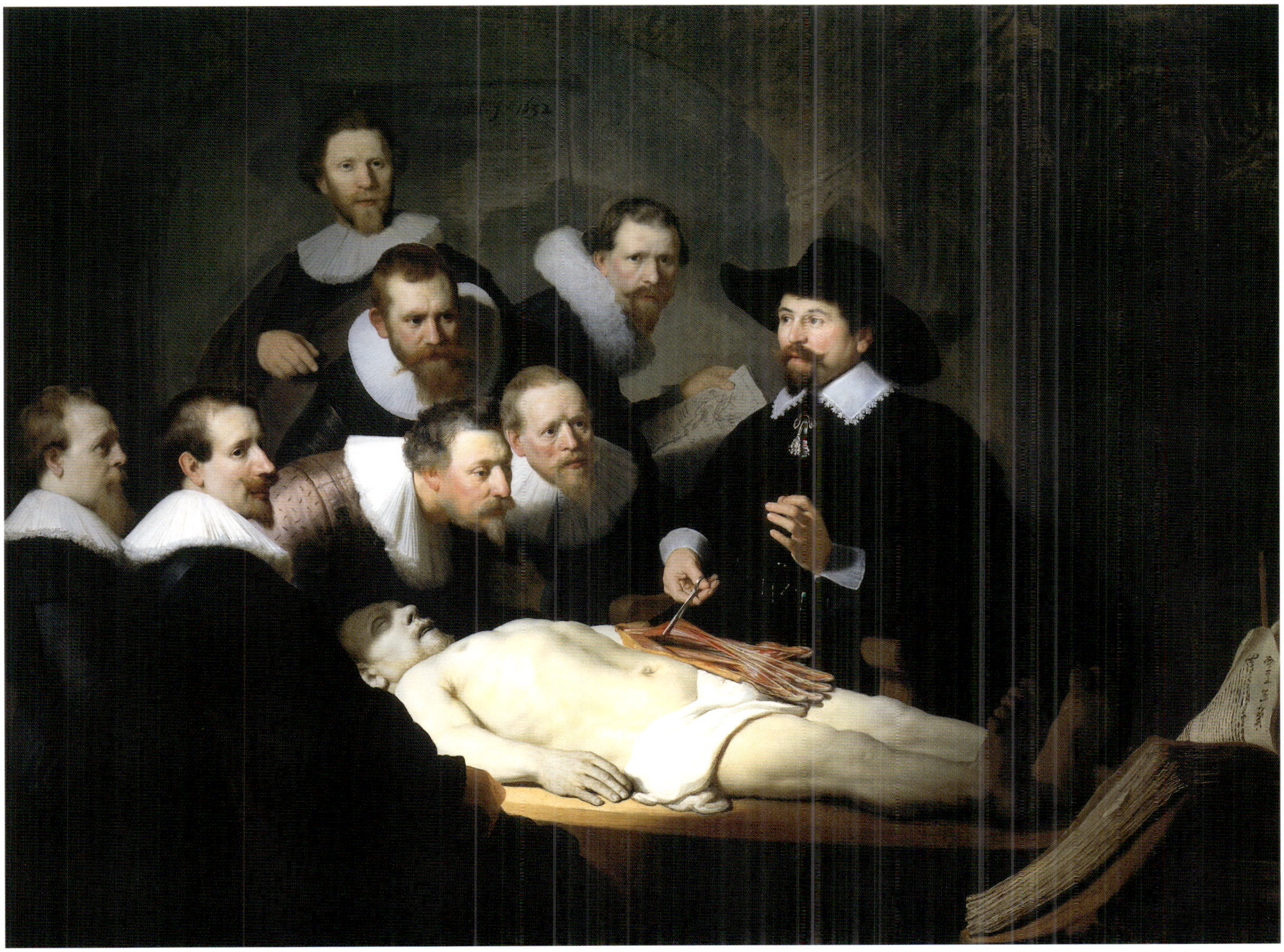

One of the surgeons is holding a sheet of paper, on which Rembrandt has painted two studies of an arm; in the early eighteenth century, the names of all eight surgeons were inscribed here. The corresponding numbers beside each figure, still visible today, were added at the same time. The names on the drawing were heavily touched up during restoration in 1951, but these retouches were removed during the most recent restoration in 1997–8, and today they are barely legible.[7] Seated to the left of the body is the head of the guild, Adriaen Slabbraen (about 1600–1661); behind him stands Jacob Colevelt (about 1595–1649). The man bending over in the purple cloak is the deputy head of the guild, Jacob de Wit (1581–1654), with Matthijs Calkoen (1591–1653) to his right. At the top we see Frans van Loenen (1592–1662); in front of him is Jacob Block (1601–1664). The man holding the sheet of paper is Hartman Hartmansz (1591–1659).[8] All the sitters contributed to the cost of the painting, which explains why there is no sign of the dozens of other spectators who would normally have been present at an anatomy lesson.

In this lesson Tulp demonstrates the workings of the hand: with his forceps he lifts the muscles and tendons connecting the forearm to the flexors and tensors of the fingers: with his left hand he gestures to reinforce the object of the demonstration.[9] For a praelector to be shown starting the dissection by opening up an arm and a hand was contrary to actual practice. In reality, anatomy lessons commenced with the dissection of the abdominal cavity, so that the perishable organs could be removed first.[10] Here, the aim was evidently to omit anything that might distract the viewer's attention from Tulp's demonstration. It is tempting to conjecture that Tulp may have sought to emulate his illustrious predecessor, Andreas Vesalius (1514–1564): the frontispiece of Vesalius's standard textbook on human anatomy shows a portrait of the famous Flemish anatomist holding up a dissected arm (fig. 53a). Vesalius describes the arm as the physician's most important instrument.[11] Rembrandt probably based his rendering of Kindt's forearm on an limb that had already been dissected, possibly by Tulp himself.[12]

Aris Kindt's other hand is also noteworthy: it exhibits a slight discoloration relative to the rest of the body and X-ray examination has revealed that Rembrandt originally painted a stump here.[13] It seems that the criminal Kindt had already lost his right hand in punishment for an earlier transgression – but this stump in the foreground was probably altered as it attracted too much attention. Since the upper paint layers have become more transparent over the centuries the hand is now a slightly different colour from the rest of the arm, but the fact that Rembrandt initially painted a stump suggests that he was actually present at Tulp's lesson.[14]

When Rembrandt painted *The Anatomy Lesson of Dr Nicolaes Tulp*, public dissections were performed in the weighing-house or *De Waag*, once part of Amsterdam's city wall named St Anthony's Gate (fig. 53b), where the surgeons had had an anatomy theatre built to resemble the larger *Theatrum anatomicum* in Leiden. The guild-hall in this building remained in use even after a new anatomy theatre was installed in the Kleine Vleeshal (small meat market) on Nes in 1639.[15] Rembrandt produced another anatomy piece for the surgeons' guild, depicting a strongly foreshortened body, in 1656.[16] Fire destroyed all but a fragment of this ambitious painting, as a result of which the fame of the painting discussed here grew to mythical proportions. *The Anatomy Lesson of Dr Nicolaes Tulp* remained in Amsterdam until 1828, when it was transferred to the Mauritshuis in The Hague.[17] QB

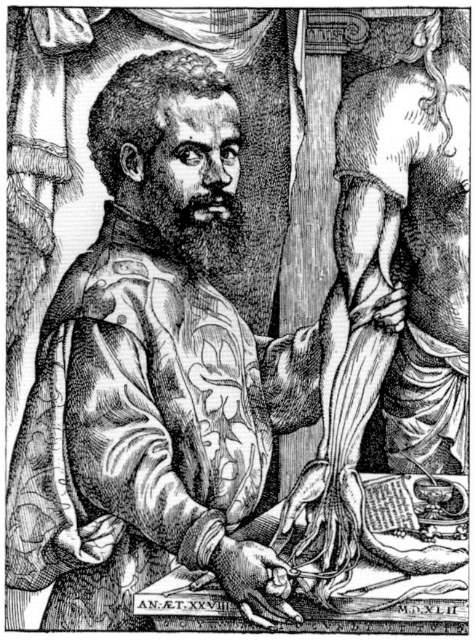

53a. After Johann von Kalkar, *Portrait of Andreas Vesalius*, 1542. Woodcut, 20 x 15 cm. From A. Vesalius, *De humani corporis fabrica libri septem*, Basel 1543

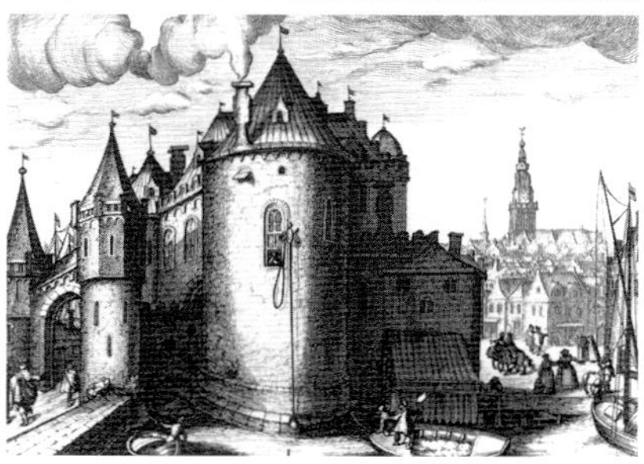

53b. Nicolaes Visscher after Simon de Vries, *The Weighing-House in Amsterdam*, before 1619. Etching, 17 x 21 cm. Amsterdams Historisch Museum, Amsterdam

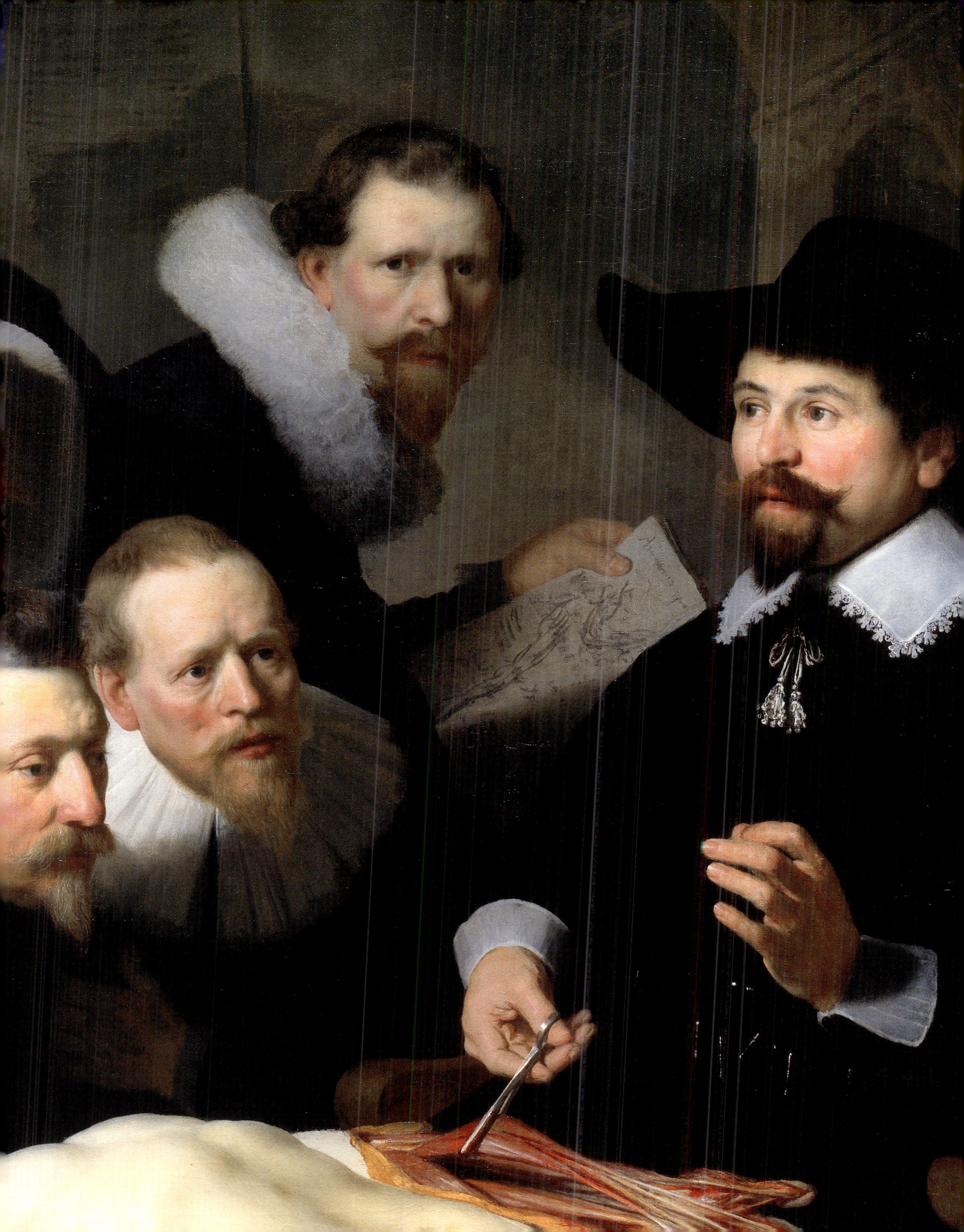

Rembrandt

Leiden 1606–1669 Amsterdam

54

Double Portrait of Jan Rijcksen and Griet Jans, 1633

Oil on canvas (cut down along the upper edge),[1] 111 x 166 cm
On the sheet of paper: *Rembrandt. f: / 1633.*
The Royal Collection, London

As in the *Anatomy Lesson of* Dr Nicolaes *Tulp* (cat. 53) of the previous year, Rembrandt sought to make this double portrait as lively as possible. It is one of the very few portraits by this artist in which the figures are placed in an elaborately described interior.[2] The elderly Jan Rijcksen (about 1561–1637), a ships' architect, is seated in his study surrounded by numerous allusions to his profession, including a design for a ships' keel with two profile sketches of a hull lying prominently on the table. Rijcksen is holding a pair of dividers, and on the table is an instrument that shipbuilders used to determine the measurements of the garboard strakes (the first wide planks laid next to the ship's keel).[3] Beside this instrument are an inkpot, a few books and papers with writing, including a curled sheet displaying the design of another ship. Rijcksen's wife, Griet Jans (died about 1653), has disturbed him at work. With her hand still on the door-handle – as if she is just entering the room – she gives him a letter, bending over his chair to do so. Her arms are stretched out wide as she performs this action, as a result of which her body takes up more than half of the image. Her hands and those of her husband are placed along an imaginary diagonal line that extends from lower left to upper right. The light entering the room from the window subtly illuminates the key elements of the portrait: the design on the table, and the faces and hands, which contrast superbly with the dark clothing and background. The man looks up from his work rather absent-mindedly and even, perhaps, with a hint of irritation, while the woman appears conscious of the fact that she has disturbed him and must beat a hasty retreat. Her mouth is open, as if she is speaking.

The couple's old-fashioned, rather modest dress emphasises their advanced years, since in the seventeenth century elderly persons tended to dress according to the fashion prevalent in their youth.[4] Rijcksen wears a doublet with a simple flat ruff, Jans a black skirt and a short coat trimmed with brown fur. She also sports large vertical shoulder-wings or *bragoenen* (see cat. 8). Over her coat she wears a black apron with a brown leather pouch, possibly a purse. The black garments are depicted in wonderfully nuanced shades, as are the other parts of the image, which apart from the green tablecloth is made up of predominantly brown and grey hues. Large sections of the image are painted in quite broad brushstrokes, appropriate to the portrait's format and the distance from which it should be viewed. The faces, on the other hand, are more meticulously worked up. Through the skilful manipulation of light and shadow, Rembrandt created a painting with enormous depth; its three-dimensionality is enhanced by the dark shadow cast by the woman on the light-brown door. Since the painting has been cut down by at least 15 centimetres along the upper edge, the effect of depth created by the sombre background – where we can barely discern a niche in the wainscotting with a bottle and a book – and the open door must once have been even greater.[5]

The unusual composition is unique in the portraiture of the Northern Netherlands in the 1630s. A fleeting moment, such as the delivery of a letter, had never been depicted to such grand effect before. This highly expressive scene gives the impression of having been conceived as a history painting, Rembrandt's favourite genre: in depicting a story from the Bible, classical mythology or history, it was the choice of the correct dramatic moment that determined whether the image was convincing. The motif of delivering a letter was introduced in Amsterdam by Thomas de Keyser, whose 1627 portrait of Constantijn Huygens shows the secretary accepting a missive from the hands of a messenger or clerk (cat. 34). While the latter work is executed in a relatively small format – one of De Keyser's trademarks – Rembrandt chose to depict life-sized figures. The most important difference between the two portraits is that De Keyser clearly has his figures assume a pose, making their attitudes appear almost frozen, while Rembrandt allows the viewer to witness an active gesture that seems to be taking place in the here and now.[6] As a result, he produced a wonderfully expressive image of incomparable vitality. Comparison of this double portrait to other paintings

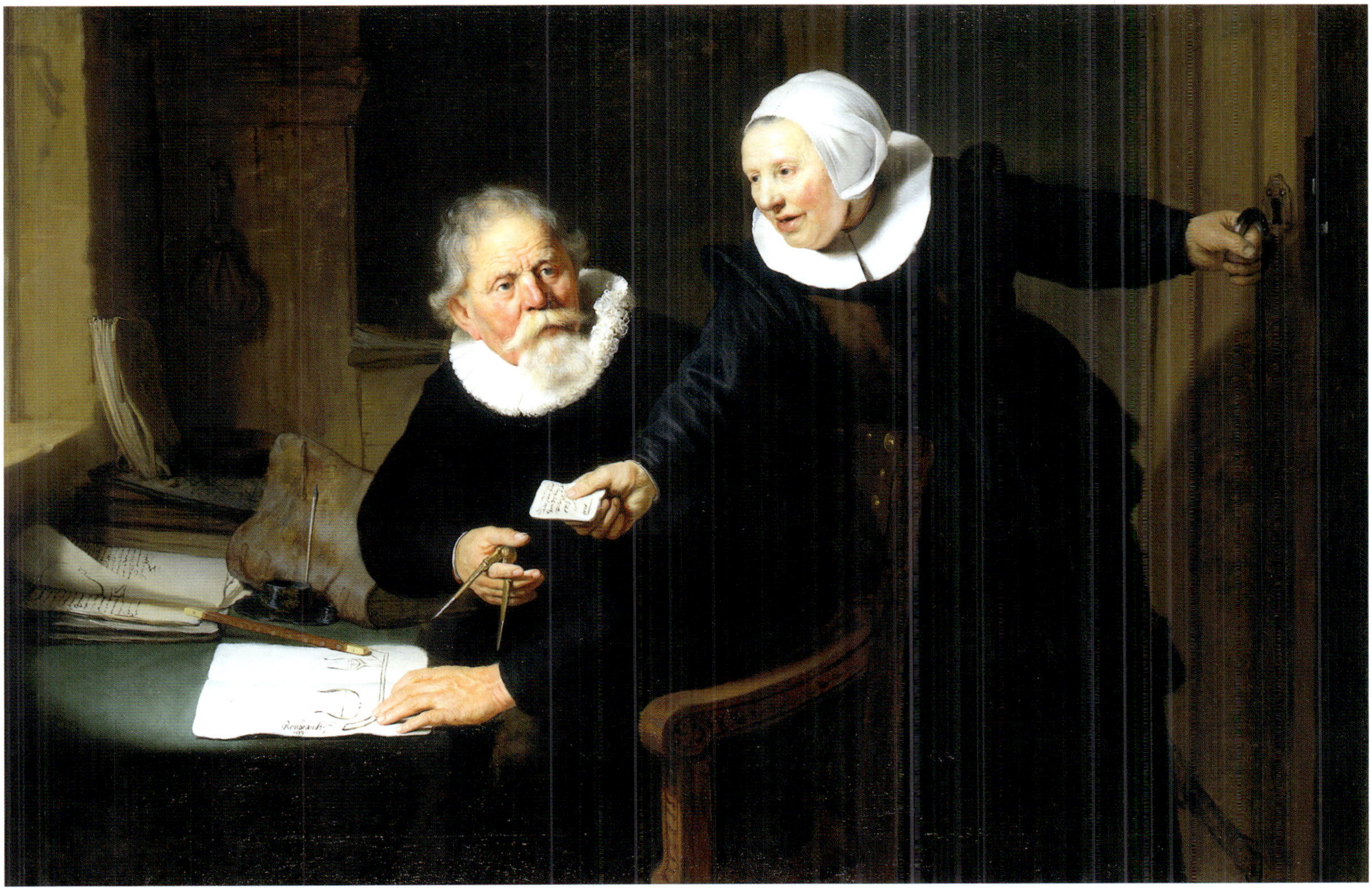

that include letters in the action – a motif used extensively by genre painters of the seventeenth-century Northern Netherlands,[7] including Johannes Vermeer – also highlights Rembrandt's immense skill.

Eight years later, in 1641, Rembrandt painted a second double portrait with figures in an interior, the *Double Portrait of Cornelis Anslo and Aeltje Gerritsdr Schouten* (fig. 54a).[8] This painting too shows a married couple depicted life-sized in an apparently everyday situation, although the action is less dynamic. From Anslo's hand gesture and open mouth we can conclude that he is speaking. His wife sits beside him in his study, listening in rapt attention to what her husband, a well-known minister, has to say. While Rembrandt chose a fairly low view for the later portrait, so that we look up at the figures, here he adopts a higher vantage point, so that the drawing on the table is clearly visible.

The *Double Portrait of Jan Rijcksen and Griet Jans* – popularly known as *The Shipbuilder and his Wife* – is one of Rembrandt's best-documented works. The name on the letter in the woman's hands has been deciphered as 'the [honourable] Jan Rykensz' ('Den [eersame] Jan Rykensz'), giving with certainty the identities of the man and his wife. Rijcksen, who had shares in the Dutch East Indies Company (VOC), was working as ship's architect for this internationally active company in 1620. Griet Jans, who became his wife in 1585, was very familiar with this profession since she came from a family of ship builders.[9] Twenty-six years after it was made the portrait was listed in an inventory drawn up after the death of the couple's eldest son, Cornelis Jansz Rijcks. In this document, dated 7 November 1659, it is described as 'a painting of the father and mother of the deceased, painted by Rembrandt'.[10] The painting probably passed by inheritance to his niece, Griet Willemsdr van Muy(d)en, the sitters' granddaughter, who died in 1672. Exactly when the painting passed out of the family's hands is unknown, but it turns up again in 1800 in the celebrated collection of Jan Gildemeester (1744–1799). Shortly afterwards, in 1811, the painting was acquired in London for the Prince of Wales, later King George IV (1762–1830; reigned 1820–30), when it was the most expensive painting this avid collector ever purchased.[11] Today it is one of the highlights of the Queen's Gallery in Buckingham Palace. QB

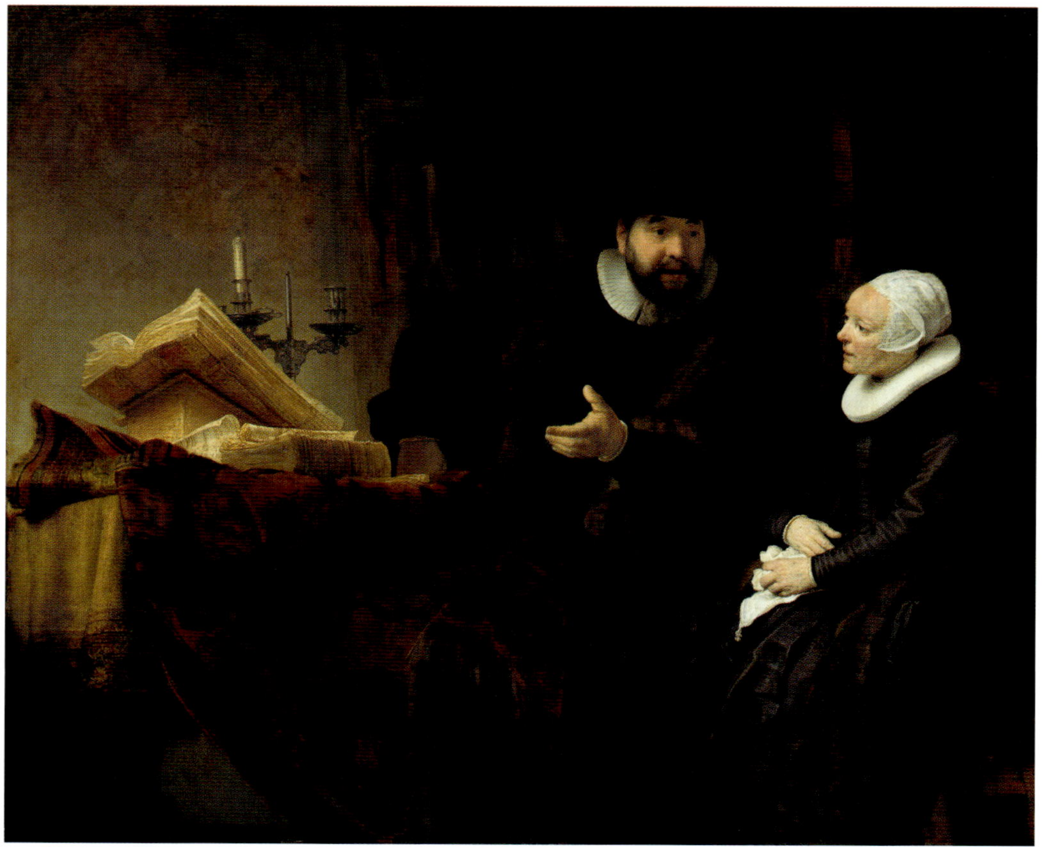

54a.
Rembrandt,
Double Portrait of Cornelis Anslo and Aeltje Gerritsdr Schouten, 1641.
Oil on canvas,
176 x 210 cm.
Gemäldegalerie,
Staatliche Museen,
Berlin

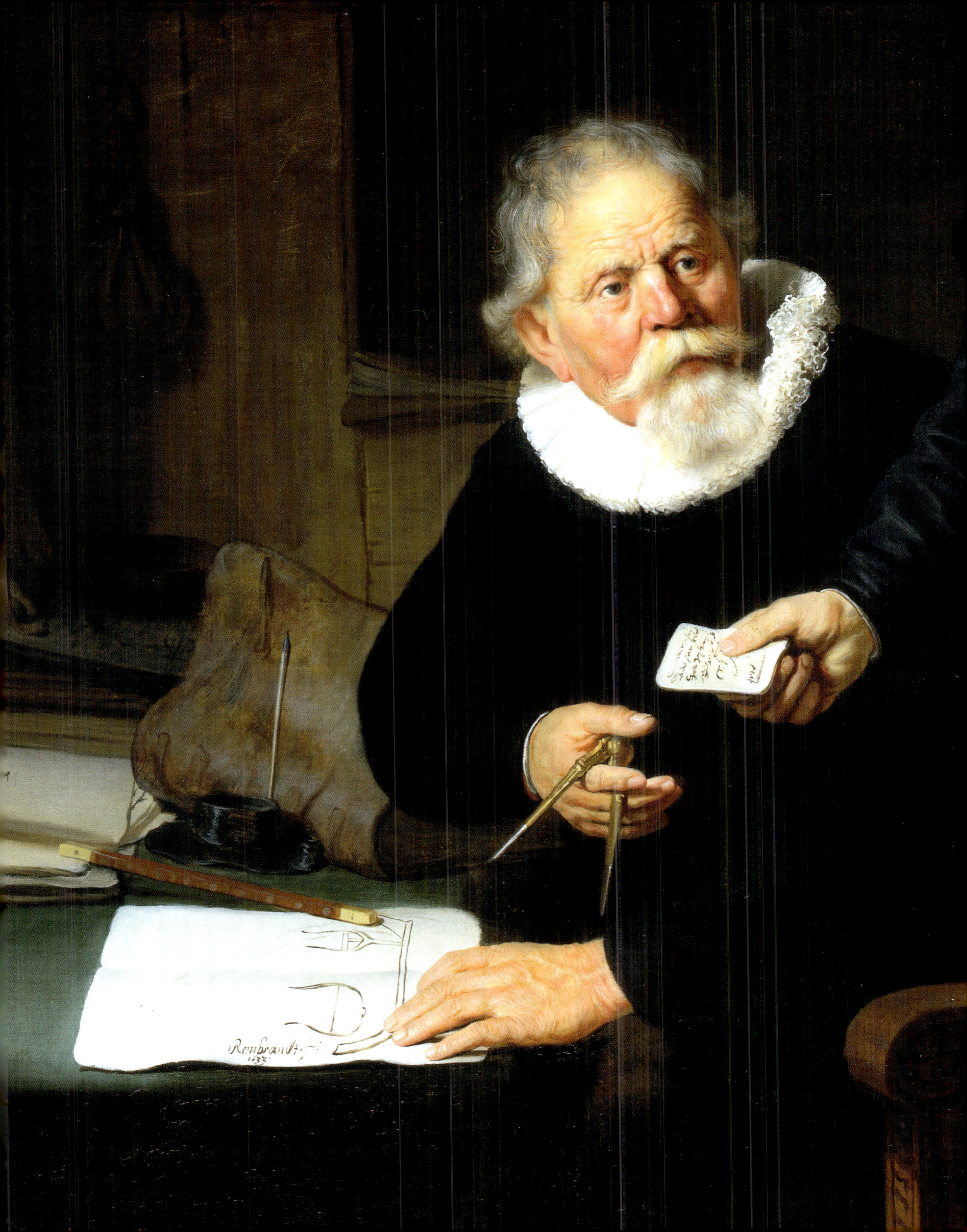
Rembrandt. f.
1633.

Rembrandt

Leiden 1606–1669 Amsterdam

55

Portrait of Aechje Claesdr, 1634

Oil on oak (oval), 71.1 x 55.9 cm
Right centre: *Rembrandt. f / 1634*; inscribed left centre: *Æ. SVE. 83*
The National Gallery, London
London only

Rembrandt's first oval portraits date from his earliest years in Amsterdam; the shape was fashionable in the city at that time. Indeed, this portrait is quite typical of the many bust-length portraits the artist painted during his first years in the capital. But Rembrandt's distinctive technique has transformed a fairly routine portrait into an extraordinary likeness. The loose modelling and broad application of paint represent a significant change in style from his more tightly painted portraits of only a year or two earlier, such as the *Portrait of Aeltje Uylenburgh* of 1632 (cat. 52).[1] The master's lively brushwork brilliantly evokes the ageing features of the sitter's face. The paint is applied in a fluid manner and the brushstrokes are short and curved and clearly done very rapidly, wet-in-wet. A highly conscious use of impasto in the lights and highlights gives liveliness and sparkle to the features; half-tones and shadows, more thinly and smoothly painted, seem to recede. Yet the very darkest shadows at the nose, mouth and under the chin are applied in thick dark paint.

On the basis of a drawing in the British Museum by Jan Stolker (1724–1785) after a lost copy of Rembrandt's painting by Hendrik van Limborch (1681–1759), the sitter was once thought to be Françoise van Wassenhove, widow of the Remonstrant preacher Eduard Poppius.[2] However, Françoise van Wassenhove was only around 60 years old in 1634. Stolker omitted this almost certainly incorrect identification from the mezzotint he made from the drawing. He gave the mezzotint the title 'Avia', literally 'grandmother' but here presumably intended to signify merely 'old woman'.[3] Because of this title, however, Gustav Waagen erroneously referred to the sitter as the painter's grandmother.[4] More recently it has been possible to identify the sitter as the 83-year-old Aechje Claesdr (1551–about 1635), widow of the Rotterdam brewer Jan Pesser (d. 1619).[5]

The Pessers were among the leading families of Rotterdam's Remonstrant community. In the year of Jan's death the Synod of Dort banned the Remonstrants and persecuted many of their preachers. Two of Aechje's sons-in-law were Remonstrant preachers and she hid one of them, Hendrick Niellius (d. 1621), in her house. The Pessers escaped persecution. In 1634 Rembrandt came to Rotterdam to paint not only Aechje's portrait but also those of her son Dirck Jansz Pesser (1587–1651), and his wife Haesje van Cleyburgh (1583–1641; fig. 55a).[6] It has been suggested that the famous preacher Johannes Wttenbogaert (1557–1644), whose portrait Rembrandt had painted in 1633,[7] and who was living in Rotterdam at that time, introduced the painter to the Pesser family.[8]

The sitter's dress is not dissimilar to that worn by Aeltje Uylenburgh (cat. 52) and Griet Jans (cat. 54). Over a simple black bodice with small buttons Aechje Claesdr wears a sleeveless coat called a *gramgat* with facings that are made of a shiny material and large shoulder wings. Around her neck she wears a modest pleated ruff and over her coat she has tied an apron. Her headdress consists of two pieces. One cap fits tightly around the head, on top of which she wears a broader white cap that flares over the ears and is held in place with three gold pins. Typically for a woman of Aechje's age, she wears modest clothes that reflect the fashion of her youth. This attitude can also be observed in the portraits of Aeltje Uylenburgh and Margaretha de Geer (cat. 59). AR

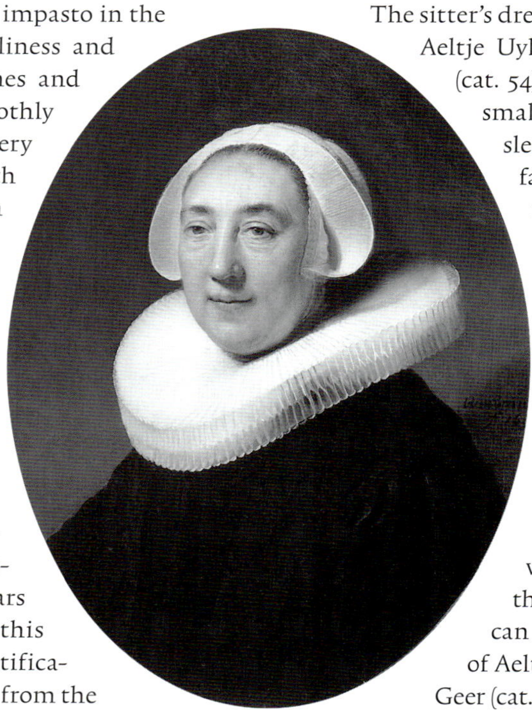

55a. Rembrandt, *Portrait of Haesje van Cleyburgh*, 1634. Oil on canvas (oval), 69 x 53 cm. Rijksmuseum, Amsterdam

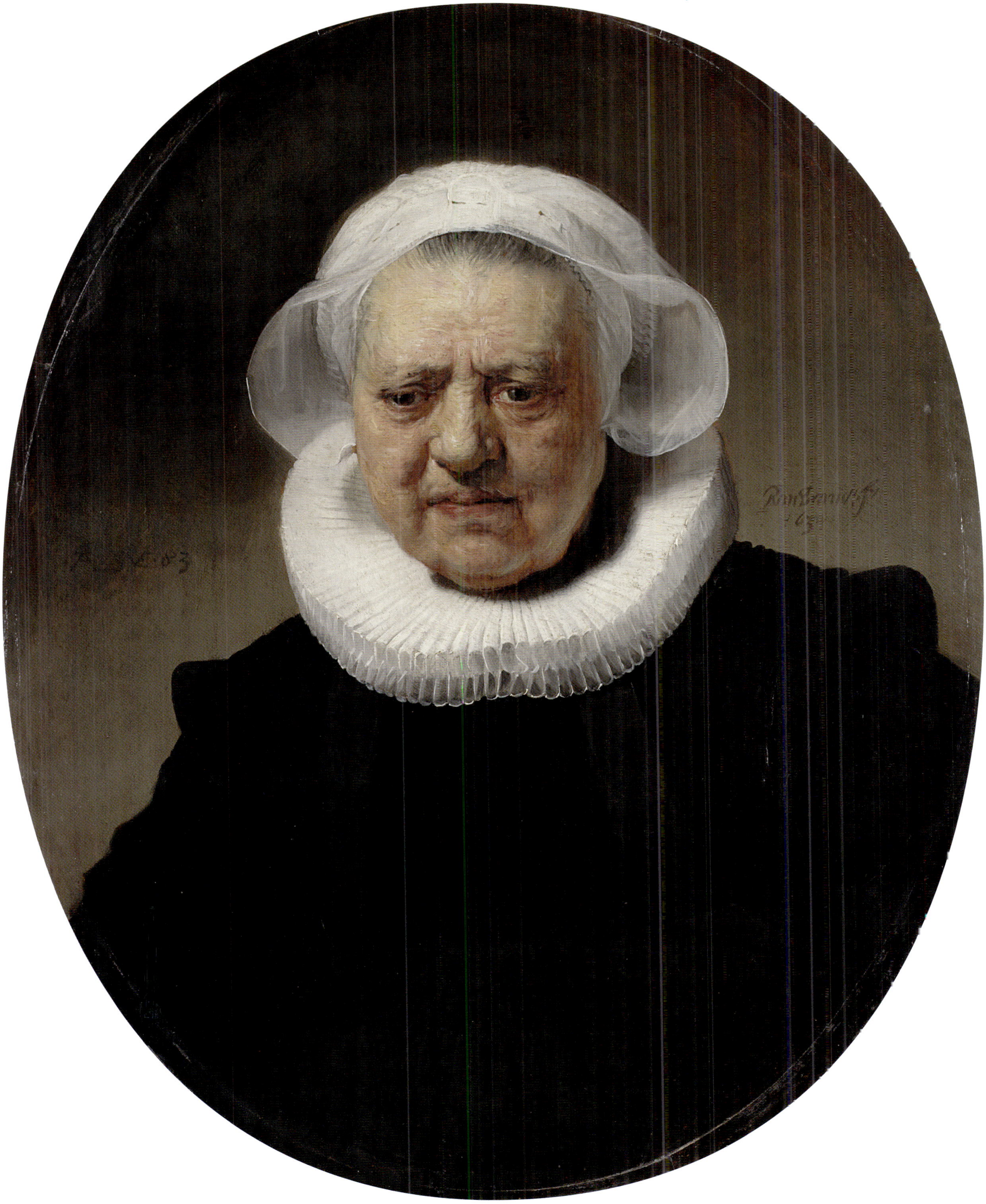

Rembrandt

Leiden 1606–1669 Amsterdam

56

Portrait of Andries de Graeff, 1639

Oil on canvas, 200 x 125 cm
At lower left: *Rembrandt fv. 1639*
Gemäldegalerie Alte Meister, Staatliche Museen, Kassel
The Hague only

Life-sized, full-length portraits are rare in Rembrandt's portrait œuvre. As far as we know, the artist painted only three: the companion-pieces depicting Maerten Soolmans and his wife Oopjen Coppit from 1634 (p. 177, figs 47–8a-b) and this portrait, executed in 1639. The choice of such a monumental format, which resulted in an extremely imposing portrait, must have been the client's decision.

The work probably depicts Andries de Graeff (1611–1679), a member of a prominent Amsterdam family who served as burgomaster of the city several times between 1657 and 1671.[1] De Graeff was 28 years of age in 1639, which seems compatible with the age of sitter, but more important for the identification is a document from 1659, in which the art dealer Hendrick Uylenburgh (see p. 186) states that in 1642 he was a member of a committee asked to mediate and advise in a dispute between De Graeff and Rembrandt.[2] The dispute concerned the value of a painting De Graeff had commissioned from the artist. Its price was eventually set at 500 guilders, which would have been a reasonable sum of money for a monumental portrait of this kind.[3] A second, corroborating piece of evidence is the portrait's provenance. After De Graeff's death, the painting passed down by inheritance within the family until 1752. That same year, the portrait was acquired for the collection of Wilhelm VIII, Landgrave of Hessen-Kassel. In 1989, the members of the Rembrandt Research Project rejected the identification as Andries de Graeff, based on a comparison of the facial features of the man in this portrait with other – but much later – portraits of the Amsterdam burgher (see p. 17, fig. 1). As an alternative identification, the researchers suggested the Amsterdam regent Cornelisz Jansz Witsen. Notwithstanding the debate triggered by this suggestion, the arguments for the De Graeff identification appear unassailable.[4]

De Graeff's casual pose is noteworthy: with his entire weight resting on his left leg, he holds his right leg slightly bent and leans his right arm on a pedestal. This position derives from the classical *contrapposto* pose, and gives the portrait a certain elegance and panache. It automatically invites comparison with Frans Hals's *Portrait of Willem van Heythuysen*, painted in about 1625 (cat. 18). Both these life-sized portraits depict self-assured gentlemen who demanded portraits with an air of grandeur, by the most prominent portraitist in their respective cities. Hals chose to convey his sitter's energetic personality, while Rembrandt kept his portrait more subdued.

De Graeff wears a fashionable suit in a French cut. The long doublet has an extremely high waist, and is trimmed with black horizontal braiding. He wears a black woollen cloak with black velvet facings, and his garters are edged with black lace trim. The hat, the brim of which is turned up, is also black. Striking for a man of such high standing is the absence of white lace on the flat collar (which is otherwise highly fashionable); there are also no cuffs. One explanation could be that the man is depicted in mourning. Besides the requirement to wear black, it was also forbidden to wear white lace in the 12 months following the death of a spouse or a parent. This could corroborate the identification of the man as De Graeff, since his father, Jacob de Graeff, had died on 4 October 1638 – his son would therefore have worn mourning for most of 1639. It is also possible that Andries may have posed for Rembrandt rather earlier, in the final months of 1638. The brown glove lying on the ground is also striking.[5] The glove, as well as the flamboyant cloak draped partly over the pedestal, the shirt glimpsed through the unbuttoned doublet, and the wrinkled stockings, reflect a more casual style of dress that became fashionable around 1639. PP / MdW

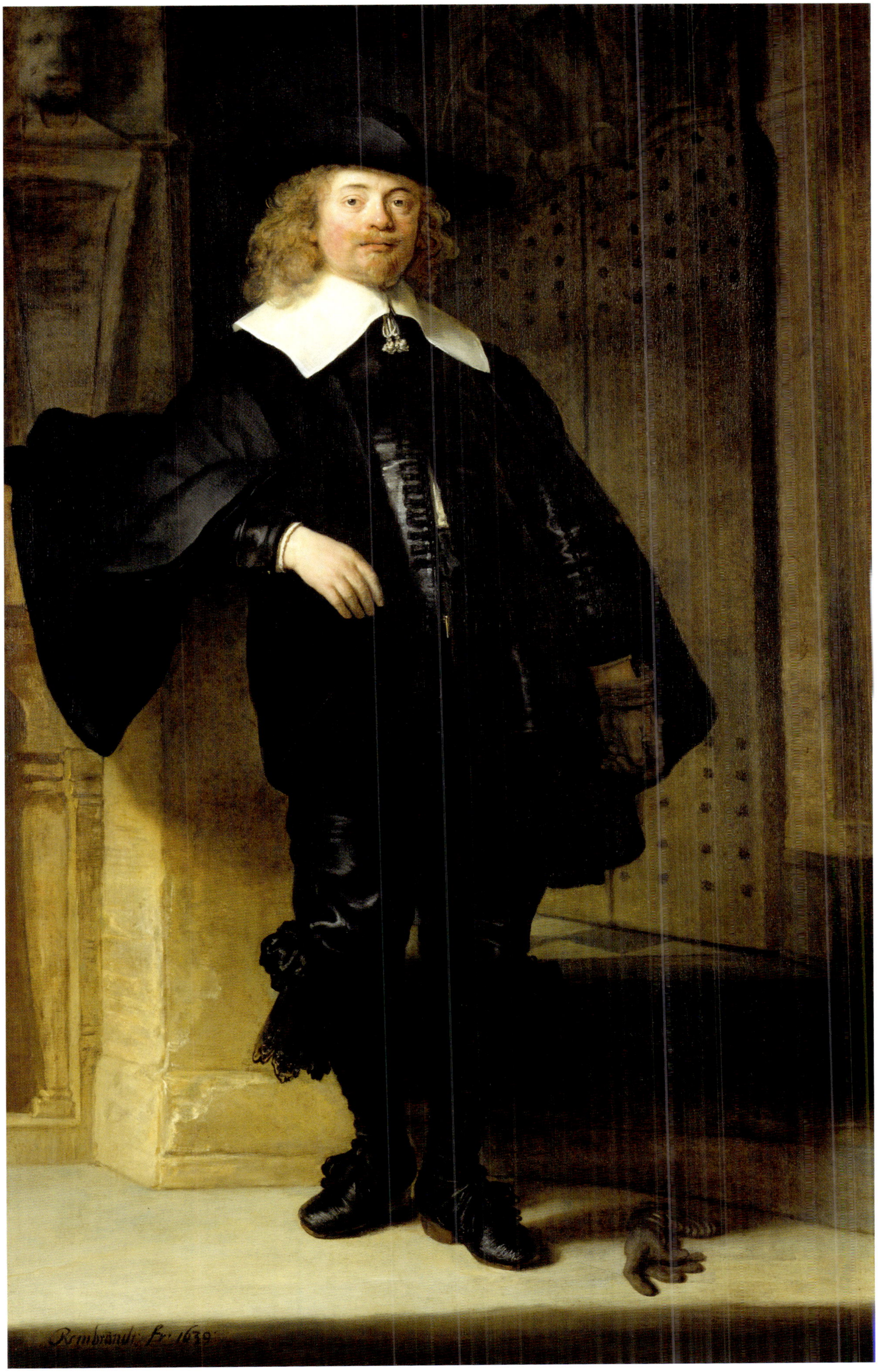
Rembrandt: fe: 1639:

Rembrandt

Leiden 1606–1669 Amsterdam

57

Portrait of Jan Six, 1654

Canvas, 112 x 102 cm
Six Collection, Amsterdam
The Hague only

If there is one Rembrandt portrait described in art literature solely in terms of superlatives, it is this portrayal of Jan Six (1618–1700). The exquisite brushwork – unerring and extremely loose – is most striking in the gold braid trimming the red cloak, executed in wide brushstrokes, but the cuffs and gloves too are painted almost nonchalantly, in a manner recalling the best work of Frans Hals (cats 14–27).[1] The superb condition of the portrait is also exceptional, due in part to the fact that it has been in the same family for over 350 years. In addition, Six's informal pose plays an essential role in our response to this painting; Rembrandt has immortalised him putting on his gloves, giving the portrait the air of capturing a brief moment in time. The cloak draped loosely over one shoulder enhances this fleeting quality, while Six's direct gaze adds immediacy to the portrait. Finally, our knowledge of the sitter, and about his relationship with the painter, give this painting an extra dimension.

We know that it was made in 1654 from a brief Latin poem written by Six. The capitalised letters in the text make up the year 1654: 'AonIDas tenerIs qVI sVM VeneratVs ab annIs TaLIs ego IanVs SIXIVs ora tVLI. Op myn schildery'. Freely translated, the poem reads: 'Such a face had I, Jan Six, who since boyhood have revered the Aeonian goddesses [the Muses]'.[2] Jan Six was born in Amsterdam, the youngest son of Jean Six and Anna Wijmer. His father died two months before his birth, having made a fortune in the silk and cloth industry and Jan's mother, whose portrait Rembrandt made in 1641 (Six Collection, Amsterdam),[3] took over the family business and ran it with a firm hand. The income generated by this business and by investments in real estate made the Six family one of Amsterdam's wealthiest.

In 1634 Jan Six enrolled at the University of Leiden, where he studied law as part of a solid education. From 1641–3 he completed a 'grand tour' of Italy, at the end of which his portrait was made by Gerard ter Borch.[4] After returning to Amsterdam he dedicated himself to his studies, wrote poetry and built up a large art collection and library. He took no part in the family business, which was run by his eldest brother Pieter after their mother's death in 1654.[5] From 1656 onwards Jan was a member of Amsterdam's city council, and in 1691 he was appointed burgomaster. Many years earlier, on 20 July 1655, he was married, in Amsterdam, to Margaretha Tulp (1634–1709), the daughter of the well-known physician Nicolaes Tulp (see cats 46, 53). A year after Rembrandt executed the present portrait, Govert Flinck depicted Margaretha (cat. 13). Flinck's portrait is over 20 cm taller than the painting described here, so it cannot have been intended as a companion-piece.

Rembrandt evidently knew Six quite well; indeed the two men were on quite friendly terms. The painter made the title print for Six's play *Medea* in 1648.[6] In 1652, Six purchased three paintings Rembrandt had made many years before.[7] That same year, Rembrandt contributed two drawings to the loose-leaf *album amicorum* for Six.[8] A year later, Six extended a loan to the artist.[9] But the earliest record of the bond between artist and patron is a portrait of Six Rembrandt etched in 1647 (fig. 57a),[10] seven years before the painting discussed here. Six's interests are communicated by this etching, a full-length image of the still-young man, leaning against a windowsill in the daylight, reading a manuscript. The documents on the chair in the foreground, the painting on the wall, and the sword and shoulder-strap allude to different aspects of Six's life: his interest in scholarship, his art collection, and his membership in the civic guard. This careful selection of details was doubtless made in consultation with Six himself.

In the present painting, all incidental staffage has been omitted. Nothing appears to refer explicitly to the sitter's character or social background; it is as if painter and subject alike were concerned exclusively with the artistic result. But this very objective may provide the key to a better understanding of the image. The apparent nonchalance conveyed both in Rembrandt's manner of painting and in Six's pose was certainly not a concept unfamiliar to the latter. One of his favourite authors, the Italian Baldassare Castiglione, states in his popular

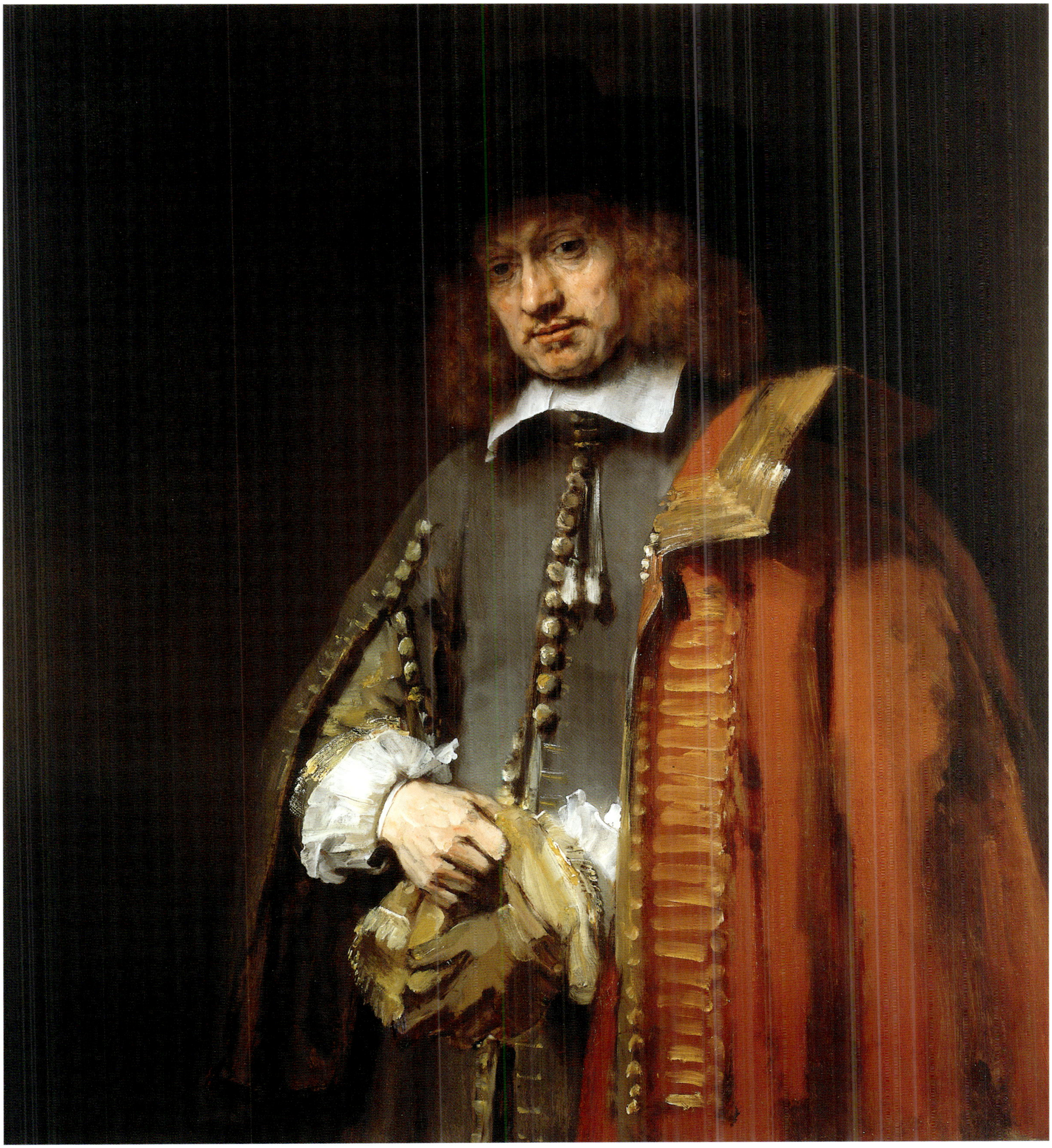

1528 handbook *Il Cortegiano* ('The Courtier') that the ideal courtier possesses the gift of *sprezzatura*.[11] This is defined as a kind of studied nonchalance, the ability to speak and act without apparent effort.[12] Six's library contained several editions of Castiglione's book.[13] His admiration for the author was indeed widely known, since the first Dutch edition of *Il Cortegiano*, entitled *De Volmaeckte Hovelinck* (1662), bore a dedication to him.[14] The decision to have his portrait made while performing an everyday activity such as putting on his gloves, creating the impression, in his gaze and pose, that the painter had caught him unawares, may be construed entirely in the spirit of *sprezzatura*. The question of whether Rembrandt too was inspired by Castiglione, either directly or through Six, is harder to answer. In *De Volmaeckte Hovelinck*, *sprezzatura* is translated, on the basis of a parallel drawn by Castiglione himself between the courtier's demeanour and the artist's technique, as *lossigheyt* [looseness]. This has prompted some art historians to posit a link between Castiglione and Rembrandt's decidedly loose style of painting in this portrait. It has rightly been observed, however, that this cannot be the sole explanation for the portrait's appearance, since such stylistic tendencies appear in the work of Rembrandt and certain other painters long before 1650.[15]

A man such as Jan Six would certainly have thought carefully about his portrait. He had a passion for art and literature, and arranged his life around his interests. In this respect too, he resembles Castiglione's ideal of the perfect courtier: an art lover who knows his languages, is erudite and dedicates his life to study, but who is at the same time a man of the world, a gentleman, who also concerns himself with more external and active pursuits, being a fine soldier and horseman, for instance. An essential element in Castiglione's description is striking a balance between the spiritual and the active life, the *vita contemplativa* and the *vita activa*.[16]

Recent research into Six's clothing has added considerably to our understanding of this painting.[17] Around 1650, it was customary for men portrayed in a public role – whether that of administrator, cleric or merchant – to be dressed soberly in black. The striking red of Six's French cloak is therefore an emphatic sign that he is depicted here as a private individual. The long grey coat beneath it, the sleeves of which can be fastened along their length with the gold-coloured buttons, is a riding outfit or *kazak*, which is worn over an ochre doublet. The *kazak's* knee-length cut and thick wool fabric provided good protection while travelling or riding (for riding clothes, see also cats 20 and 34). In 1651 Six had acquired the country estate of Elsbroeck, near Hillegom, which had stables. There he pursued the outdoor activities typical of the landed nobility, such as riding and hunting, and the choice of outfit for this portrait probably refers to horseriding as an upper-class leisure pursuit. These were interests, which – again according to Castiglione's model – were part of the life of a perfect gentleman, but they were also extolled by contemporary authors such as Constantijn Huygens (see cat. 34) in his ode to country life, *Hofwijck* (1651). The simplicity of this apparel, which is primarily practical and moreover worn here in a casual manner, also presents Six as a man who accords priority to the spiritual (rather than material) aspects of life.

In this portrait, Rembrandt created a magnificent work of art. As a portrait it is highly successful, and from an artistic point of view it is unquestionably one of the best examples of Rembrandt's artistry; it displays several fundamental aspects of Jan Six's personality in a highly effective, yet understated, manner. PP

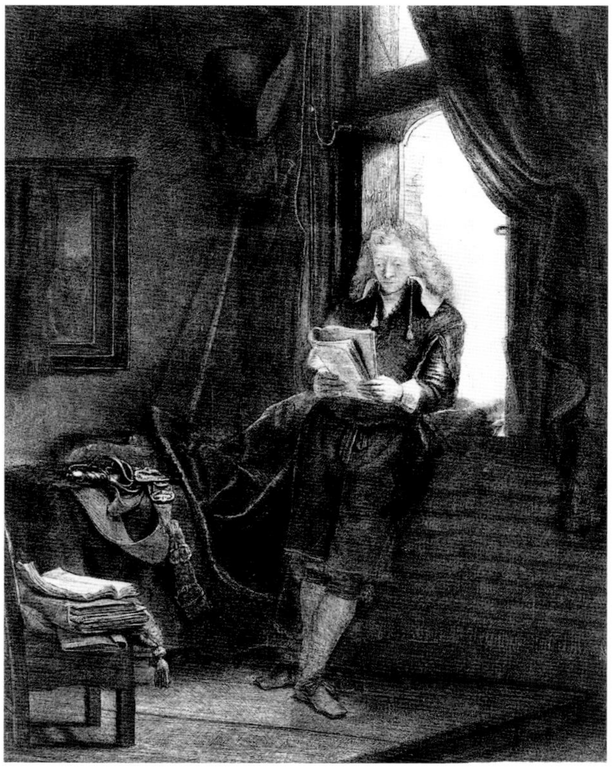

57a.
Rembrandt,
Portrait of Jan Six, 1647.
Etching, 24 x 19 cm.
Six Collection,
Amsterdam

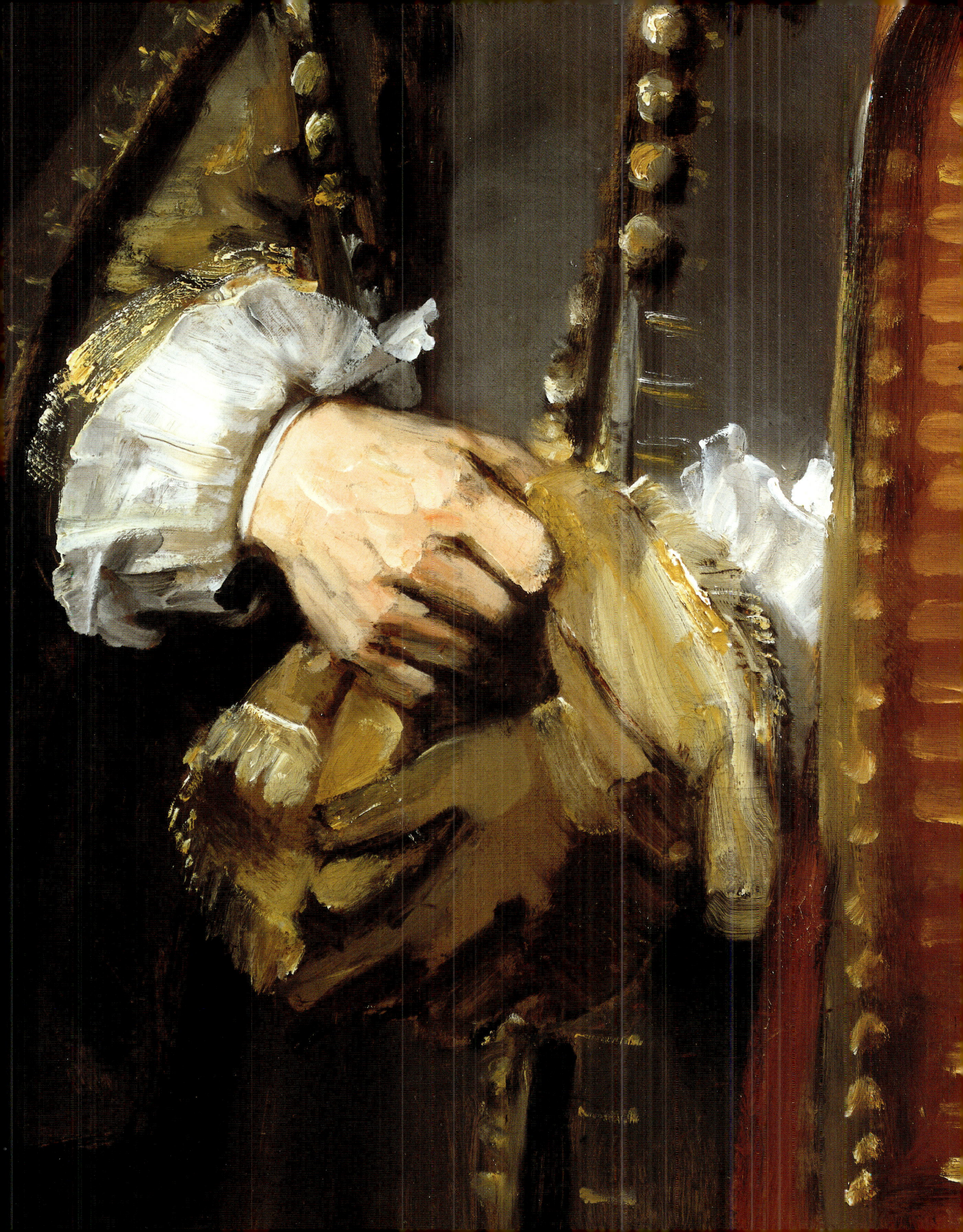

Rembrandt

Leiden 1606–1669 Amsterdam

58 | 59

Portrait of Jacob Trip, about 1661

Oil on canvas, 130.5 x 97 cm
At right: *Rembr[andt]*
The National Gallery, London

Portrait of Margaretha de Geer, about 1661

Oil on canvas, 130.5 x 97 cm
The National Gallery, London

These portraits of Jacob Trip (about 1576–1661) and Margaretha de Geer (1583–1672), painted in about 1661, attest to Rembrandt's enduring popularity as a portrait painter in Amsterdam in the last decade of his life. Jacob Trip was an immensely wealthy Dordrecht merchant.[1] He was the son of the shipowner Jacob Jansz Trip (1530–1589) who lived in Zaltbommel, a small town between Dordrecht and Nijmegen. When Jacob was still a child the family moved to the city of Dordrecht, which was then the Netherlands' largest trading port. As a merchant Jacob dealt in iron from Liège, as well as in coal, cloth, timber and salt.

Margaretha de Geer (1583–1672), daughter of the merchant Louis de Geer, was born in Liège. Her family left the Southern Netherlands in 1595, possibly for religious reasons, and settled first in Aachen and then in Dordrecht. She married Jacob Trip in 1603 and the couple had 12 children, five of whom were still living in 1660.[2] Margaretha's marriage to Jacob Trip may have been prompted by the two families' business connections. She was the sister of the wealthy and powerful industrialist Louis de Geer (1587–1652), who had established himself in Sweden, in mining and as an arms manufacturer and dealer.[3] Louis frequently worked with Jacob's brother Elias (about 1569/70–1636) who moved his business to Amsterdam in 1614, and after 1626 Jacob played a key role in that enterprise. Two of Jacob and Margaretha's sons, Louis (1605–1684) and Hendrick (1607–1666), worked with their uncle in Sweden and eventually became successful arms dealers based in Amsterdam. Their immense fortune enabled them to commission the building of the Trippenhuis, a palatial house on Kloveniersburgwal with a richly decorated façade, which was built for them by the classical architect Justus Vingboons (1620/1–1698) between 1660 and 1662.[4] Despite the formal appearance of the two portraits, the sitters are dressed in remarkably informal clothes. Jacob wears a white nightcap and a simple scarf around his neck instead of a formal collar. He is wrapped in a cloak and holds a cane in his left hand. Margaretha appears at first glance to be wearing a traditional *vlieger* overdress (see p. 67), but in fact this is not the case. The wide fur-lined black gown with the sleeves that have slashes at the elbows to put one's arms through (the lower halves of the sleeves hang down on either side of the chair) rather appears to be a night robe. Furthermore, she wears simple cuffs without any lace, and a large set ruff that was fashionable in the 1620s and 1630s. Her black peaked cap came into fashion around 1640. It was evidently not unusual for elderly people to wear this type of nightwear around the house during the day in the seventeenth century.

Interestingly, Margaretha's attire seems to contrast sharply with the almost regal image she projects. Rather than turning towards the portrait of her husband as is traditional – the 'time-honoured heraldic half-turn'[5] – she has been placed frontally, fixing the viewer with a steady gaze. This pose gives her the appearance of an enthroned ruler rather than that of the traditional – more subservient – female pendant to a male portrait.[6] This may be because she was actually a widow by the time the pictures were painted. Dudok van Heel has argued that these portraits of Jacob and Margaretha Trip were commissioned from Rembrandt by their two sons, presumably to hang in the Trippenhuis.[7] A date of about 1661 is likely on stylistic grounds and Jacob Trip died in Dordrecht in May 1661; it is unclear whether or not the portrait was begun before his death. Because of the marked difference in attitude between the two pictures it seems quite possible that the portraits were painted after Jacob's death, and that his picture was made not from life but from another portrait. The white handkerchief that Margaretha holds in her right hand could lend credence to this theory. While Mennonite women considered such handkerchiefs a sign of old-fashioned, and therefore dependable, stylishness, there is also a tradition in which handkerchiefs denote the grief and emotional fortitude of a recently bereaved person.[8] Whatever the case may be, the picture emphatically expresses the gravitas and authority of the matriarch of one of the wealthiest and most influential families in the seventeenth-century Netherlands.

It has often been remarked that in paired portraits by Rembrandt, the male portrait is of higher quality: here it is not a matter of quality, but of complexity. Clearly the portrait of Jacob Trip was executed rapidly and easily, in a more economical and direct style. The portrait of Margaretha is much more carefully worked, partly fluid and partly dabbed with drier paint covering the underlayers with repeated reworking. One is easy and straightforward, the other more careful, painstaking and laboured. These differences are explained if we accept that Jacob Trip was painted from another portrait – Rembrandt was simply reproducing an image, not responding to a real face as he was when he painted Margaretha.

Jacob and his wife spent their lives in Dordrecht and their likenesses were regularly recorded by local Dordrecht artists. There is one set of portraits by Aelbert Cuyp from 1652,[9] and eight by, or after, Nicolaes Maes were made between 1657 and 1669 (figs 58–9a-b),[10] but the most likely prototype for Rembrandt's portrait of Jacob Trip would seem to be a portrait from 1651 by Jacob Gerritsz Cuyp.[11] Rembrandt had worked for the Trip family before, having painted both Aletta Adriaensdr (1591?–1656), widow of Jacob's brother Elias, and her daughter Maria Trip (1619–1683; p. 70, fig. 65) in 1639.[12] The Trip family was one of the richest in Holland, and these large-scale formal portraits, quite possibly destined for the grandest private residence in Amsterdam built in the newest classical style, were a major commission for the painter. AR

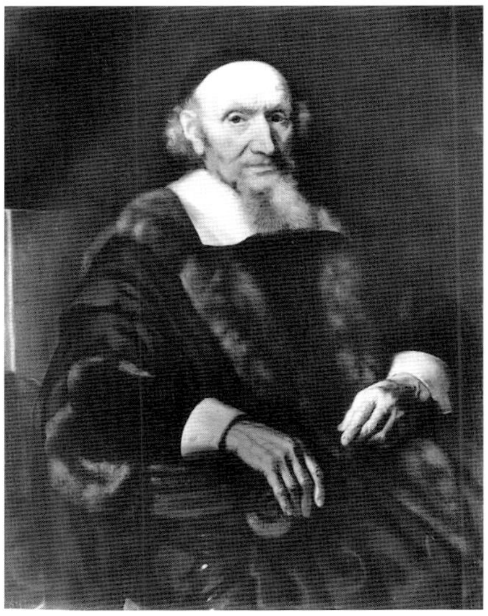

58–9a.
Nicolaes Maes,
Portrait of Jacob Trip,
about 1660–1.
Oil on canvas,
88 x 68 cm.
Szépművészéti
Muzeum, Budapest

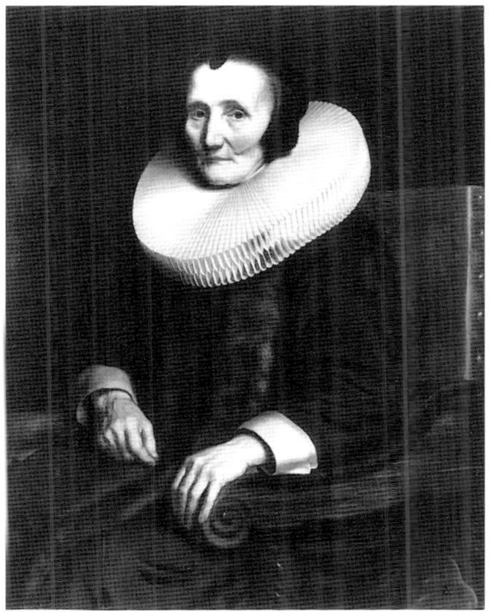

58–9b.
Nicolaes Maes,
Portrait of Margaretha de Geer, about 1660–1.
Oil on canvas,
88 x 68 cm.
Szépművészéti
Muzeum, Budapest

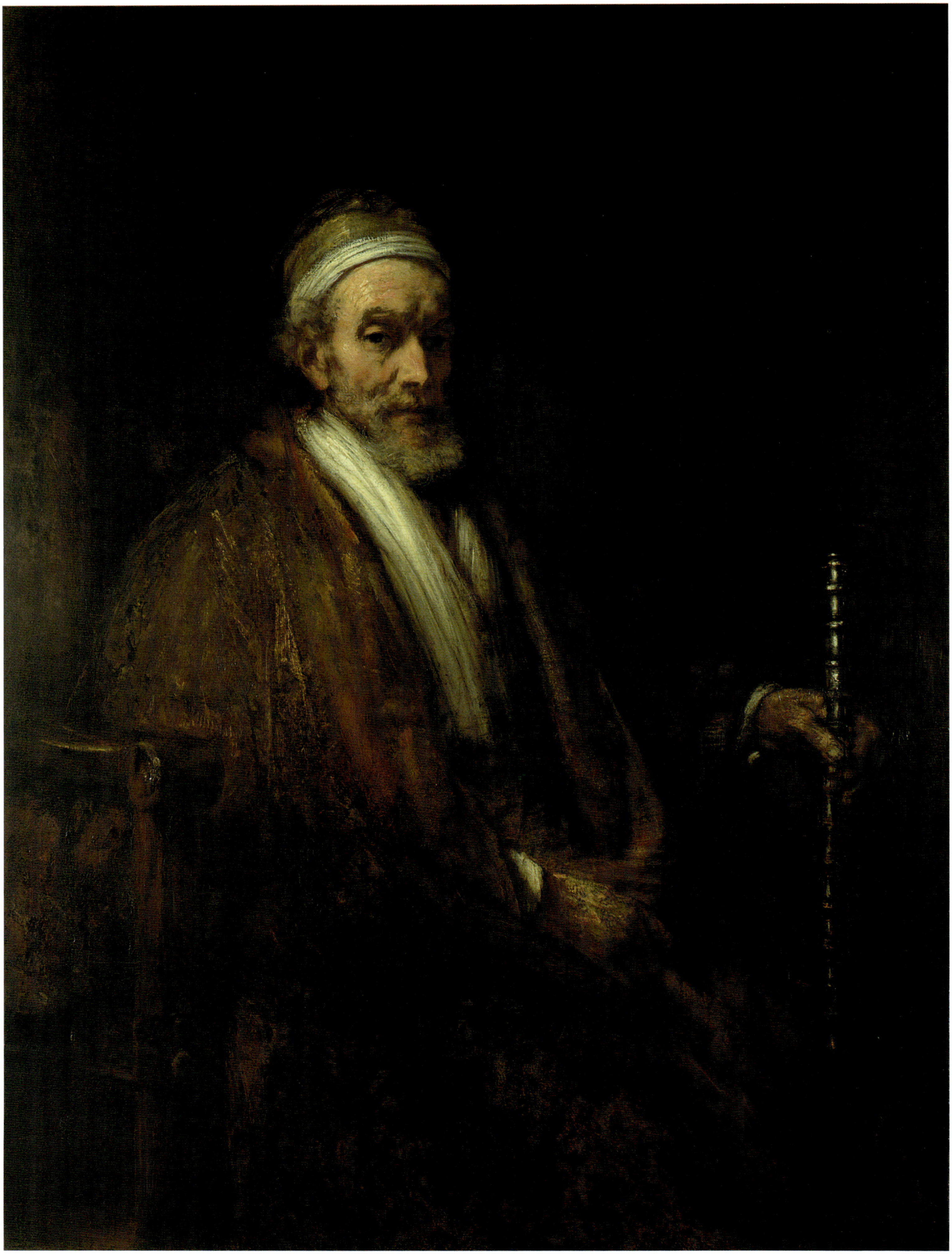

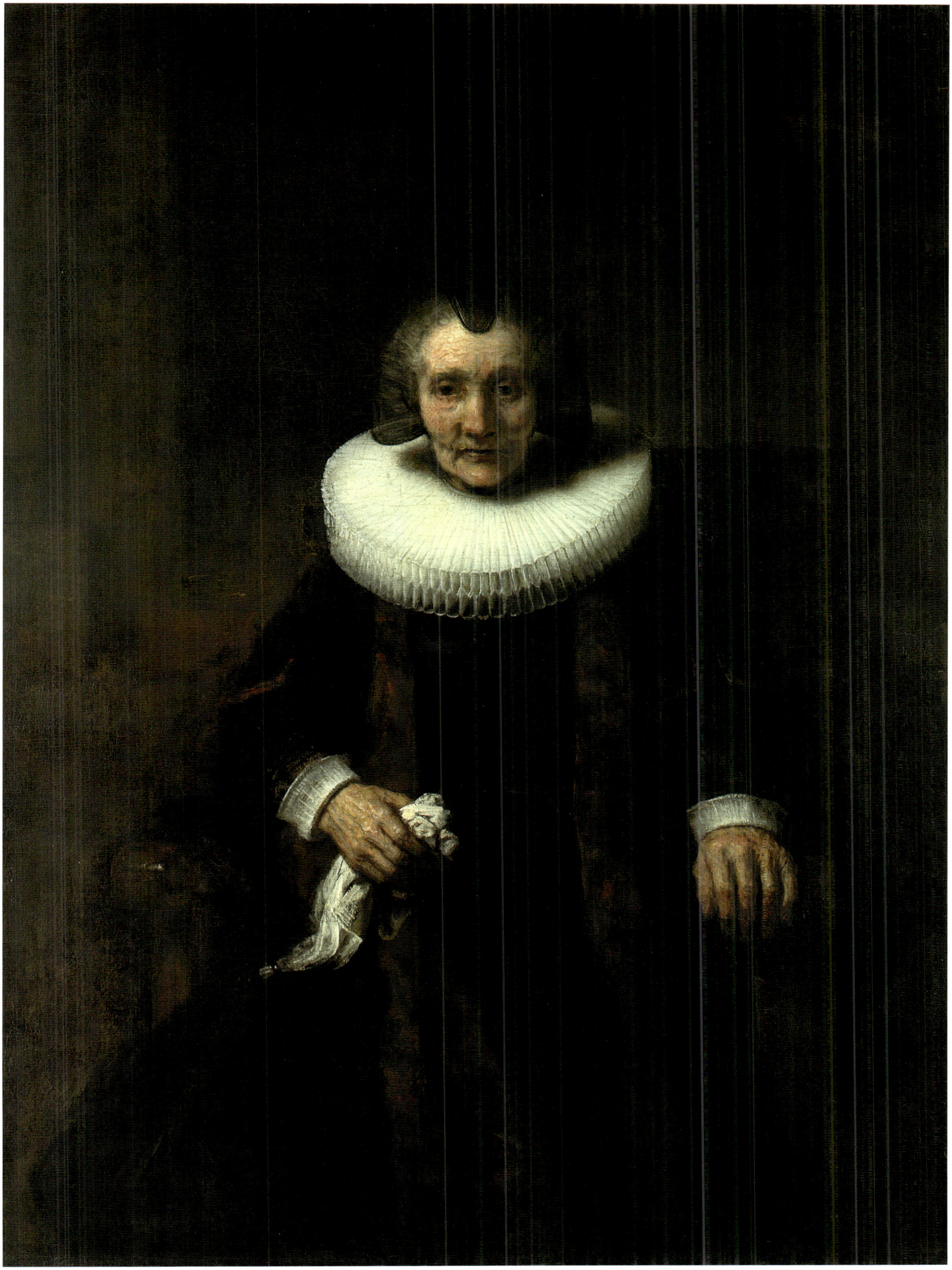

Rembrandt

Leiden 1606–1669 Amsterdam

60

Portrait of the Syndics of the Clothmakers' Guild ('De Staalmeesters'), 1662

Oil on canvas, 192 x 279 cm
On the rug: *Rembrandt f. 1662*; at right on the wall, probably not autograph: *Rembrandt f. 1661*
Rijksmuseum, Amsterdam
London only

This impressive painting from 1662 is Rembrandt's final group portrait, made 30 years after his first, *The Anatomy Lesson of Dr Nicolaes Tulp* (cat. 53). Together with *'The Night Watch'* (1642; p. 32, fig. 22), these are among Rembrandt's best-known works and some of the most famous group portraits in Northern Netherlandish painting.[1] While in the earlier painting Tulp's prominent position makes it clear that he is the most important person in the portrait, here the respective ranks of the five syndics of the clothmakers' guild in Amsterdam are more difficult to ascertain. The men gathered around the carpet-covered table are dressed in black, and all wear their hats. The sixth figure standing behind them, a servant, is the only one to sport a cap.[2] Syndics monitored the quality of dyed woollen cloth. To ensure that Amsterdam's guild members produced and traded only cloth of the highest quality, samples were checked by the syndics and furnished with a seal if the desired standard was met. The painting's Dutch title, 'De Staalmeesters', comes from the word for fabric sample, *staal*. The book lying on the table is not a book of samples, however, as was previously thought, but a ledger or book of accounts.[3]

The scale of the painting and figures – shown larger than life – has a powerful impact on viewers, but Rembrandt's composition, which ultimately derives from the regent pieces of Cornelis van der Voort (see p. 29, fig. 18), also draws our attention.[4] Rembrandt has subtly suggested movement by depicting the second man from the left just as he is seating himself to join the group – disrupting the horizontal arrangement of his fellows, and imparting a certain tension to the painting. The composition is further invigorated by the fact that four of the men gaze at the viewer directly, as if they have been disturbed at work. The figures' gestures also provide lively accents. The inherent energy might suggest that *Portrait of the Syndics of the Clothmakers' Guild* was executed with great ease, but in fact X-radiographs display many minor and more substantial alterations that Rembrandt made while painting.[5] The man beginning to sit down, for instance, was initially depicted standing. Further, the artist was initially unsure as to where to place the servant, who, as the lowest in rank, must not be too conspicuous; he initially stood on the far right. The different compositional stages can be followed not only from the X-radiographs, but also from three drawings preserved in Amsterdam, Berlin (fig. 60a) and Rotterdam, the only surviving preliminary drawings for one of Rembrandt's group portraits.[6] These are not portrait studies, but rather sketches in which the painter – who had already started on the painting some time earlier – experimented with his sitters' poses and with the play of light in the left half of the scene. He had great difficulty finding a satisfactory solution for this part of the painting, especially for the second and third figures from the left, and eventually opted for a composition in which he manipulated perspective to suit his purpose.[7] To ensure that everyone was clearly visible in the painting without detracting from the liveliness of the composition, he placed the syndics' president (situated directly behind the account book) at one end of the table. Since space had to be created for the man who is sitting down, the syndic on the far left was painted at some distance from the table. To keep him in the group despite this placement, Rembrandt deliberately placed his chair too high in the picture plane. The other two syndics are seated at the longer side of the table, to the president's right. Rembrandt placed the servant in at least four different places on the right of the composition, but he was painted finally behind the president, so high up as to defy the laws of perspective. However, since he was now in the background, his face could be shown smaller than those of the officials.

This latter alteration probably met one of his clients' most important conditions. As in the case of Rembrandt's 1632 anatomy piece, the composition of which was evidently decided in consultation with Tulp (see cat. 53), we can assume that clients and artist conferred

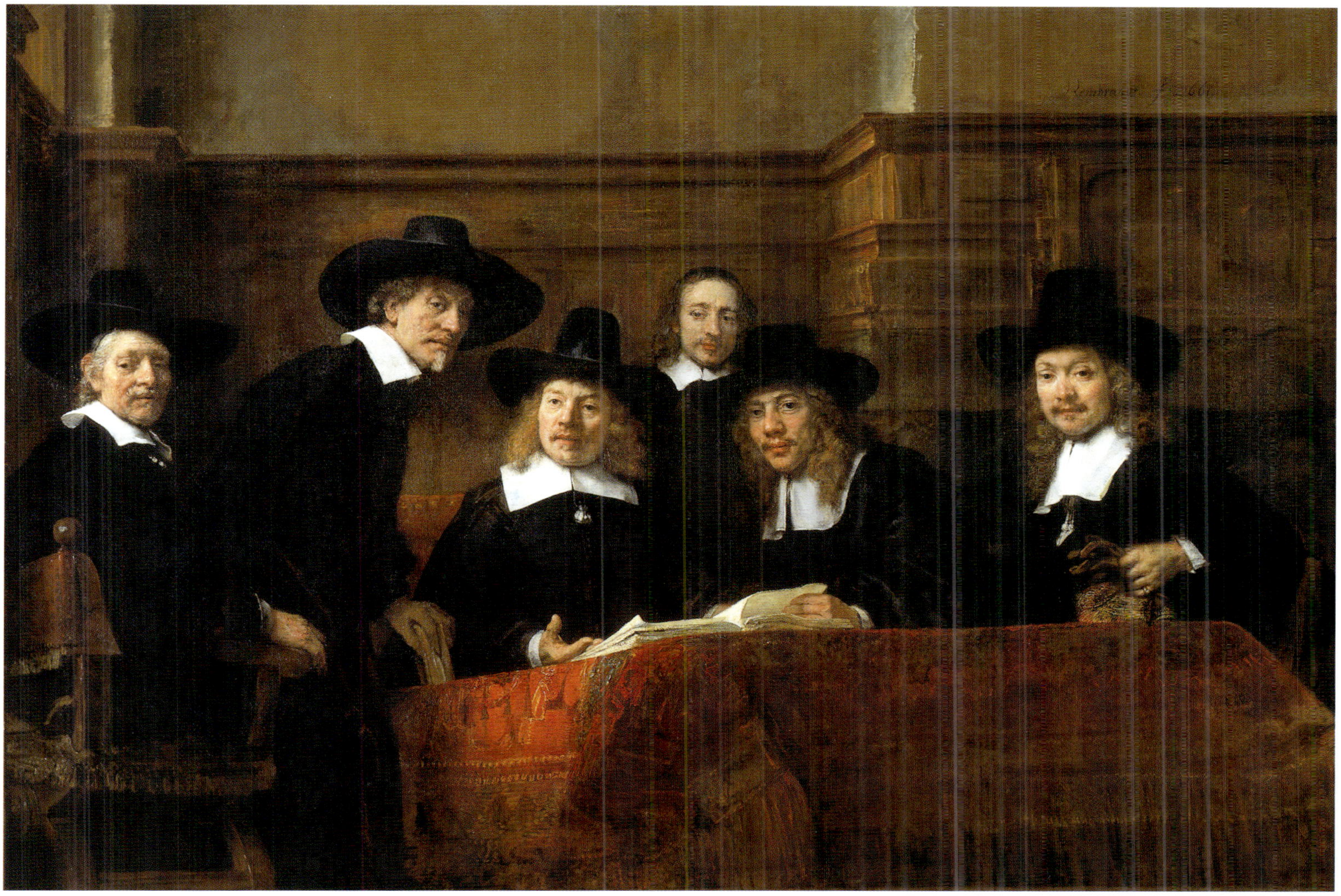

about the painting. Perhaps the portrait acquired a more profound significance as a result: on the mantelpiece in the room we can make out a picture showing one or more towers with beacons. This painting-within-a-painting very probably symbolises reliability and vigilance, concepts relevant to the syndics' work.[8] At upper right, on the wall above the fireplace, the inscription 'Rembrandt f. 1661' can be read. This was probably added after discoloration of the original signature, 'Rembrandt f. 1662', had rendered it illegible. The letters and figures of the original signature are inscribed on the rug in dots, giving the effect of having been part of the knotted fabric.[9]

It is generally assumed that the men depicted are the syndics appointed by the burgomasters of Amsterdam on Good Friday 1661, for a period of 12 months. The post of syndic was an honorary, unsalaried position, which only wealthy men could afford to accept. The first three men, from left to right, are traditionally identified as Jacob van Loon (1595–1674), Volckert Jansz (1605/10–1681) and Willem van Doeyenburg (about 1616–1687), while the servant is identified as Frans Bel (1629–1701). The identification of the two syndics on the right is less certain; they are probably Jochem de Neve (1629–1681) and on the far right Aernout van der Mye (about 1625–1681).[10] Since the syndics were of different religious denominations, Rembrandt's painting is generally regarded as epitomising the tolerance of Amsterdam society around 1660.[11] We may assume that the men commissioned the portrait because their term of office had almost expired.[12]

To fulfil their duties, the syndics met three times a week in the Staalhof, the headquarters of the clothmakers' guild in Staalstraat, Amsterdam – a building that still stands today. The painting must have hung relatively high on the wall of the syndics' office there, judging by the low vantage point that Rembrandt adopted: the viewer is not level with the men but looks up at them, such that the entire undersides of their wide-brimmed hats are visible. Whether the wooden panelling in the background corresponded to the room's actual walls, as has often been suggested, can no longer be ascertained, since nothing remains of the original interior of the Staalhof.[13] Whatever the case may be, the play of light suggests that Rembrandt took account of a window to the left of the painting's intended location. There was probably little available space left in the room, its walls being covered with portraits of previous syndics. These other pieces have vanished without a trace, with the exception of the painting made by Pieter Pietersz in 1599, the earliest known regent piece (p. 22, fig. 7).[14]

Portrait of the Syndics of the Clothmakers' Guild provides a unique demonstration of Rembrandt's capabilities in his final years. Unlike the refined brushwork of his earlier anatomy piece from 1632, his style of painting here is extremely loose. This expressive technique is one of the main factors underlying the painting's fame. In his inimitable way Rembrandt elaborated some sections more than others, making the textures of the different materials particularly convincing.[15] For the rug, Rembrandt used a palette knife to apply the thick layers of paint and here especially he introduced a striking distinction between light and dark areas: most of the rug is in shadow, while a portion on the left is bathed in light. The striking radiance of this illuminated section – the deep red glazing imparts colour to the entire image – is the result of a white ground applied locally precisely for this purpose.[16] While the red pigment has retained its colour, the darker portion of the rug has faded somewhat.[17] The vigorously painted faces and hands are extremely lifelike, in spite of the loose style of painting. The same applies to portraits that Rembrandt produced a few years later, such as his *Portrait of an Elderly Man* from 1667 (cat. 61). The quality of the faces probably explains why the syndics chose to give their commission to Rembrandt. In the 1660s, however, the majority of clients in Amsterdam preferred a more refined style of painting, such as that of Bartholomeus van der Helst (cats 29–30).

For many years, Rembrandt's painting was rather hidden away in the Staalhof. The earliest printed reference to it was as late as 1765.[18] That year, the writer Jan Wagenaar, who specialised in the history of Amsterdam, described the various paintings displayed in the regents' room of the Staalhof: 'In this room hang six paintings of syndics from the sixteenth and seventeenth centuries. In each one, five syndics are depicted seated, while the Staalhof's servant is shown standing'.[19] In 1771 the group portrait was transferred to the gallery of the town hall. It subsequently came to the Rijksmuseum, on loan from the city of Amsterdam. QB

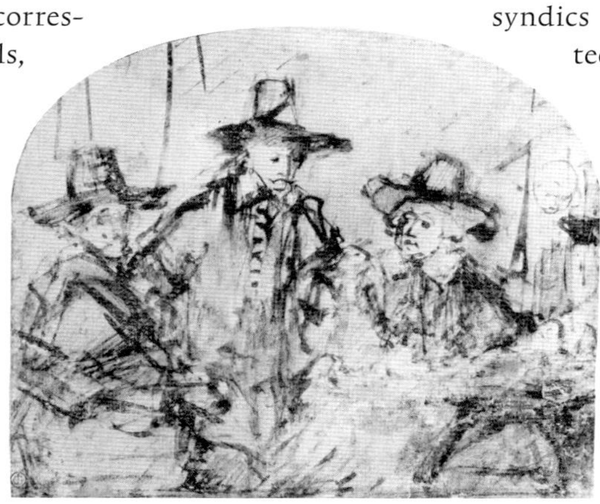

60a.
Rembrandt,
Preliminary study for the left section of 'The Syndics of the Clothmakers' Guild',
about 1662. Pen in brown ink, wash, with white body colour (rounded top, probably a fragment), 17 × 21 cm.
Kupferstichkabinett, Staatliche Museen, Berlin

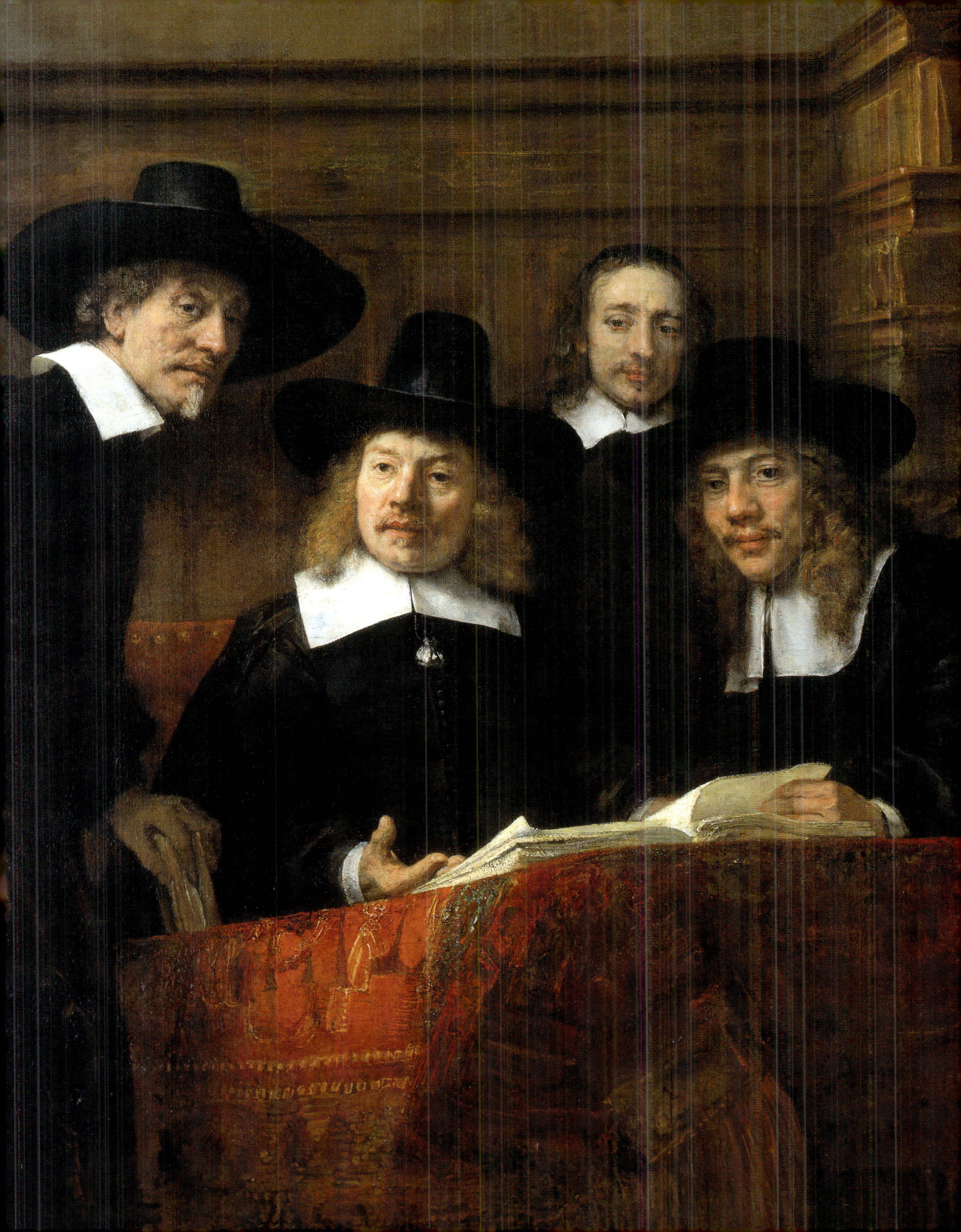

Rembrandt

Leiden 1606–1669 Amsterdam

61

Portrait of an Elderly Man, 1667

Oil on canvas, 82 x 68 cm
At left: *Rembrandt / f. 1667*
Royal Picture Gallery Mauritshuis, The Hague

This *Portrait of an Elderly Man* is one of the most informal portraits Rembrandt ever made: an elderly man slumped in an armchair, with an almost tangible physical presence. The man appears to be entirely unconscious of the fact that the painter is observing him, and the casualness of the portrait – in this respect it is a worthy successor to Rembrandt's *Portrait of Jan Six* from 1654 (cat. 57) – is enhanced by the man's lopsided hat and his nonchalantly open collar. His black coat is unbuttoned at the bottom, a detail the painter accentuated with a single bold white brushstroke.

The close framing of the figure is crucial to Rembrandt's evocative portrayal of the corpulent man. His stoutness is emphasised not only by his round face and double chin, but also by the chair that seems barely able to contain him. Like Rembrandt's other paintings from the 1660s, this image shows convincingly that the artist did not suffer any artistic decline at the end of his career: he produced this portrait in 1667, just two years before his death. After a second portrait of a man painted later that year, in which the face is elaborated in more detail and the clothing is more formal,[1] he made three self-portraits, all of which date from 1669, the year of his death.[2]

Rembrandt achieved an unprecedented degree of expressiveness in the final years of his life. This powerful, yet at the same time almost playful, portrait is representative of his late style, which is characterised by contrasting execution in different parts of the composition.[3] The varied painting styles here are extraordinarily effective: when one views the portrait from a certain distance, one is struck by its perfect balance. As in his *Syndics of the Clothmakers' Guild* from 1662 (cat. 60), Rembrandt depicted the face with immense care. It is constructed of numerous small areas of paint, modelled not only with brushstrokes, but also with a palette knife and the back end of the brush. The face seems almost to have been moulded in three dimensions. Other details – most notably the hands and cuffs – have been set down robustly with vigorous strokes: a single movement suggests each of the collar's ribbons. In the thinly painted dark clothing he scratched through the wet paint to reveal the brown ground. This ground layer, which has also been allowed to glimmer through in other parts of the painting – the hair, collar and cuffs, for instance – plays an important role in the overall tonality of the image as the collar and cuffs form white accents in the dark image. Though the portrait is quite sketchlike in parts, the artist's signature shows that he regarded it as finished. It exemplifies Rembrandt's motto that 'a piece is finished if the master has achieved his intention in it', as posthumously recorded by his biographer, Arnold Houbraken.[4] Rembrandt's loose manner of painting recalls the late work of his older contemporary Frans Hals (cat. 27).[5]

The subjects of Rembrandt's late portraits can seldom be identified – the pendants depicting Jacob Trip and his wife (cats 58–9) and the portrait of Gerard de Lairesse being exceptions to this rule.[6] The informality of the current work argues against the historical identification of the sitter as 'Admiral Tromp' – whether the naval hero Maarten (1598–1653) or Cornelis (1625–1691) Tromp – and in any case, the face does not resemble either of these men. Given the casualness of the portrait, it is more likely to represent someone in Rembrandt's circle of intimates – one recent proposal being Lodewijck van Ludick (about 1606/7–1669).[7] A merchant and art dealer, of whom no portraits are known, Van Ludick valued Rembrandt's art collections following the artist's declaration of bankruptcy in 1659, and was was a close acquaintance. In addition, a document dating from 1662 records that Rembrandt had promised to make a portrait of Van Ludick, who was one of his creditors.[8] After Van Ludick too fell prey to financial difficulties, he moved, like Rembrandt, to Rozengracht. QB

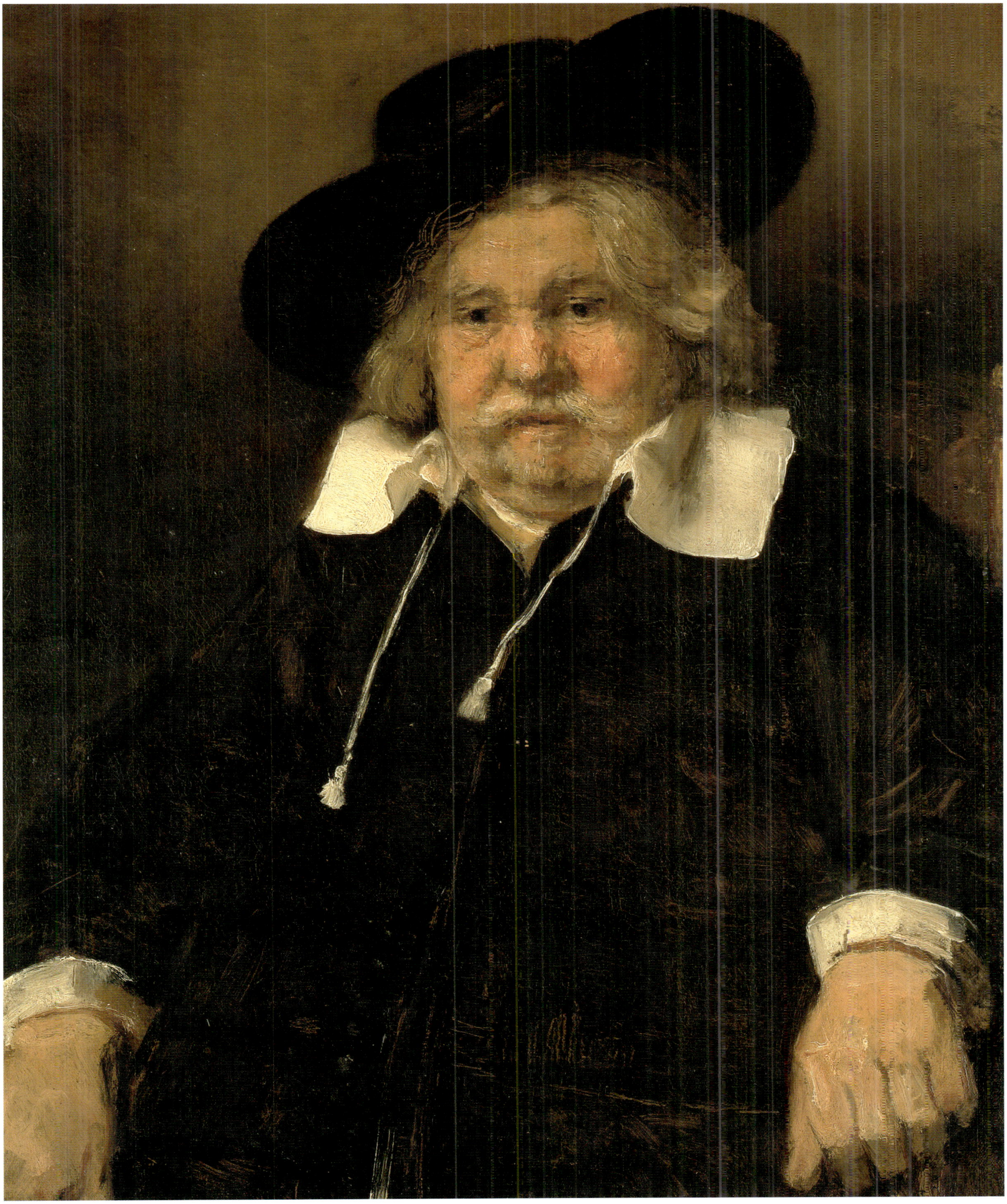

Jan Steen

Leiden 1626–1679 Leiden

62

Portrait of Bernardina van Raesfelt, 1660

Oil on canvas, 107 x 81 cm
On the wooden timbering: *JSteen. / 1660* (JS in ligature)
Royal Picture Gallery Mauritshuis, The Hague

In this highly original portrait of a young girl, Jan Steen shows himself to be a natural – if unconventional – storyteller. The extraordinary level of detail in this painting adds greatly to its appeal; indeed the colourful collection of birds has earned this work the alternative title of *The Poultry-Yard*. The little girl is shown in an enclosed courtyard with a surprising view of a castle on the horizon; she is surrounded by animals and flanked by two men who look at her with tender smiles. The picture is a combination of a portrait, genre scene, landscape and animal piece. The contrast between this lively scene and a traditional child's portrait such as Govert Flinck's subdued painting of a girl standing beside a high-chair in an unadorned interior dominated by greys and browns (fig. 62a), made only 20 years previously, is spectacular.[1] Steen made several highly original portraits including his *Portrait of Adolf Croeser and his Daughter Catharina* from 1655 (fig. 62b), which depicts a well-to-do gentleman of Delft and his daughter with a beggar-woman and her small son, and the *Double Portrait of the Baker Arend Oostwaert and his Wife Catharina Keyzerswaert* from about 1658 (Rijksmuseum, Amsterdam), which shows a couple selling bread from a display outside their bakery.[2] In these remarkable works Steen included everyday actions, clearly drawing from his background as a genre painter. Although he did not often make more traditional portraits, Steen's portrayals of the Haarlem brewer Gerrit Schouten, his wife and his parents, are more traditional in their composition and accoutrements.[3]

The building in the background of Steen's portrait is no random element of the setting. It can be identified, on the basis of an old drawing made after 1647, as Oud-Teylingen Castle, also known as Lokhorst.[4] The drawing shows Lokhorst before the expansion of the main building, whereas Steen's painting depicts it afterwards. The castle no longer exists, but it stood near Warmond just outside Leiden, where the artist was living when he painted this scene in 1660. Although the background architecture is identifiable, the stage-like foreground with wide stone steps is evidently a figment of Steen's imagination.[5]

The girl depicted here is Bernardina Margriet van Raesfelt (1649–1681), the daughter of Wennemar van Raesfelt and Jurriana van Bronckhorst. She lived at Lokhorst from 1657–63, and married Gerard van Wassenaer-Alckemade in 1674. The identification can be inferred from the building and the two coats of arms above the archway. They are those of Nicolaas van Mathenesse and Geertrui van Lokhorst,[6] the parents of Cornelis van Mathenesse, the former owner of Lokhorst Castle who died childless in 1640. His widow, Anna van den Bongard, took a second husband, Johan van Raesfelt, in 1653, before he was murdered in 1657. Johan's brother was Wennemar van Raesfelt, who died the year before, and the childless Anna adopted his daughter Bernardina – after the death of her second husband, the two moved to Lokhorst. Under the terms of her first marriage, Anna enjoyed the usufruct of the castle until her death in 1663. It is logical to conclude from the view of the castle in the background that Jan Steen has depicted Bernardina van Raesfelt at about ten years of age, and that the painting was made for her adoptive mother.[7] The portrait was one of the most important commissions that Steen ever received.

As a genre painter *pur sang*, Jan Steen emphasised the narrative elements of this ambitious image: this is not just a portrait of a young girl posing in front of the house where she lived. Bernardina has deposited her straw hat beside her on the step, and is demurely seated with one hand on her breast. In other hand she holds a bowl of milk, just filled by the balding servant, for a lamb. A small greyhound seems to be lapping up a little spilled milk, and there is another lapdog lying behind Bernardina. In the earlier *Portrait of Adolf Croeser and his Daughter Catharina*, which also features a young girl at its centre, Steen drew a deliberate contrast between rich and poor by juxtaposing the figures of the fashionably dressed father and daughter with the beggar-woman and her son.[8] Perhaps the same applies here. The opulently dressed girl wears a spotless white jacket and apron over

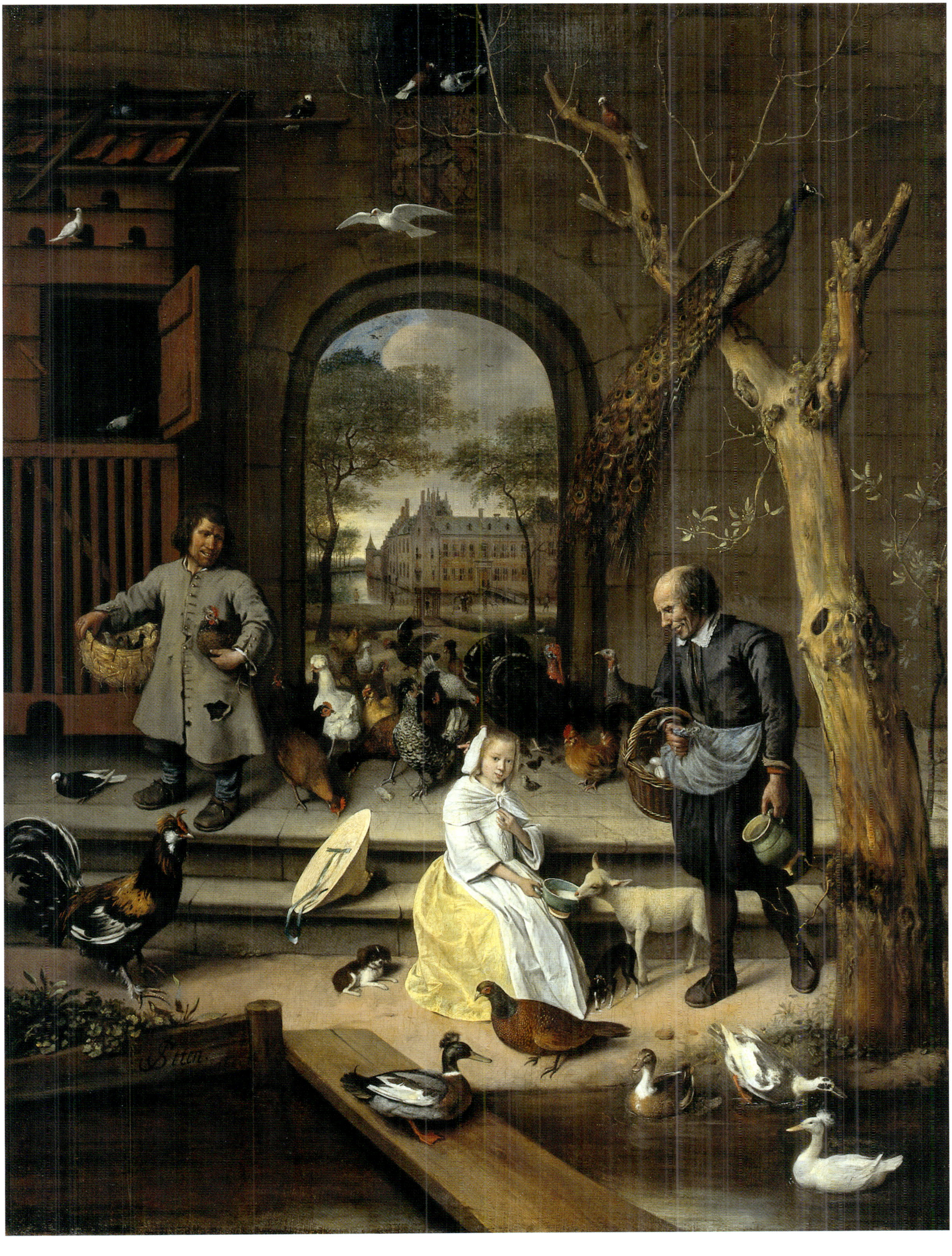

62a.
Govert Flinck,
Girl by a High-Chair,
1640. Oil on canvas,
114 x 87 cm.
Mauritshuis,
The Hague

62b.
Jan Steen,
Portrait of Adolf Croeser and his Daughter Catharina, 1655. Oil on canvas, 83 x 69 cm.
Rijksmuseum,
Amsterdam

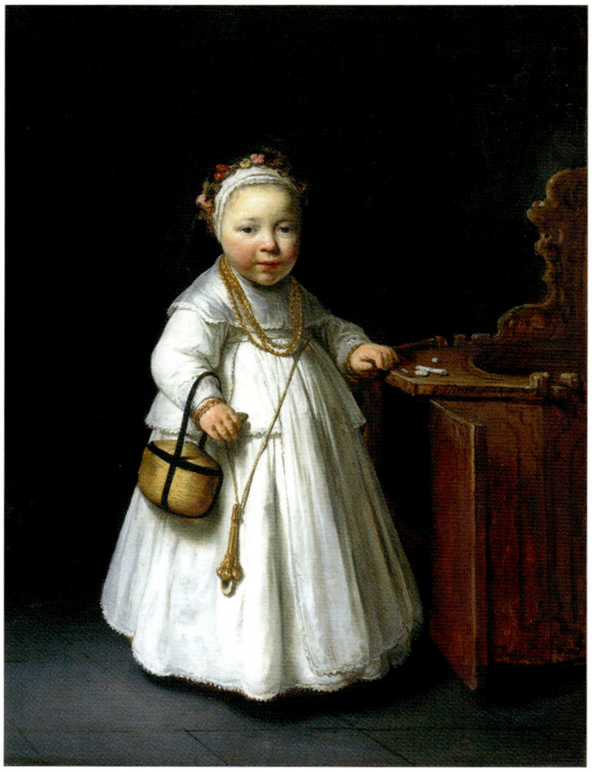

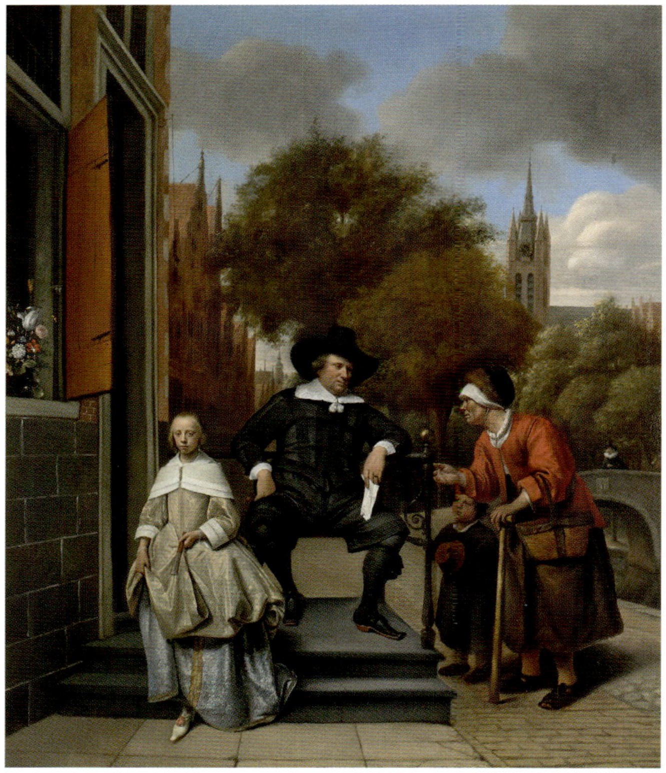

a yellow satin skirt, contrasting with the simple servants in their shabby clothes. The worn and ragged coat of the servant on the left, a dwarf, badly needs mending, and his bump-toed shoes would have been extremely old-fashioned. The second servant, who holds a basket of eggs and a milk jug, wears the blue apron that was a standard part of the apparel of domestic staff. The servants' weather-beaten faces call attention to the youth of the little girl.

Steen painted the faces with a great eye for detail. They were completed early on, after he had sketchily laid out the composition.[9] In his rendering of the diverse bird species and types of poultry – which did not necessarily belong to Lokhorst's menagerie – Steen again shows himself to be a careful observer. Besides the pigeons and the peacock in the tree, we see a turkey, a pheasant, a partridge, hens, a great many chickens and some chicks. In the water are some ornamental ducks, one of which is resting on the wooden plank placed over the water.

The poultry-yard is not without significance as a setting for this portrait: the birds and poultry are allusions to the girl's adoption. Cesare Ripa's *Iconologia*, a Dutch translation of which appeared in 1644, mentions a number of such creatures in connection with concepts such as adoption and guardianship.[10] The lamb indisputably refers to adoption too: only a lamb that has lost its mother will accept milk from a human being.[11] The prominently depicted tree is the final and perhaps most explicit allusion to Catharina's circumstances. Its bare trunk contrasts markedly with the leafy trees in the distance. In emblematic literature a dead tree denoted the inner conflict that must always be overcome to make the right decision.[12] But Steen has also painted some young shoots sprouting from the desiccated trunk, which might be construed as allusions to the subject of the portrait: as Anna van den Bongard's adopted daughter, Bernardina van Raesfelt would continue the family line.[13] QB

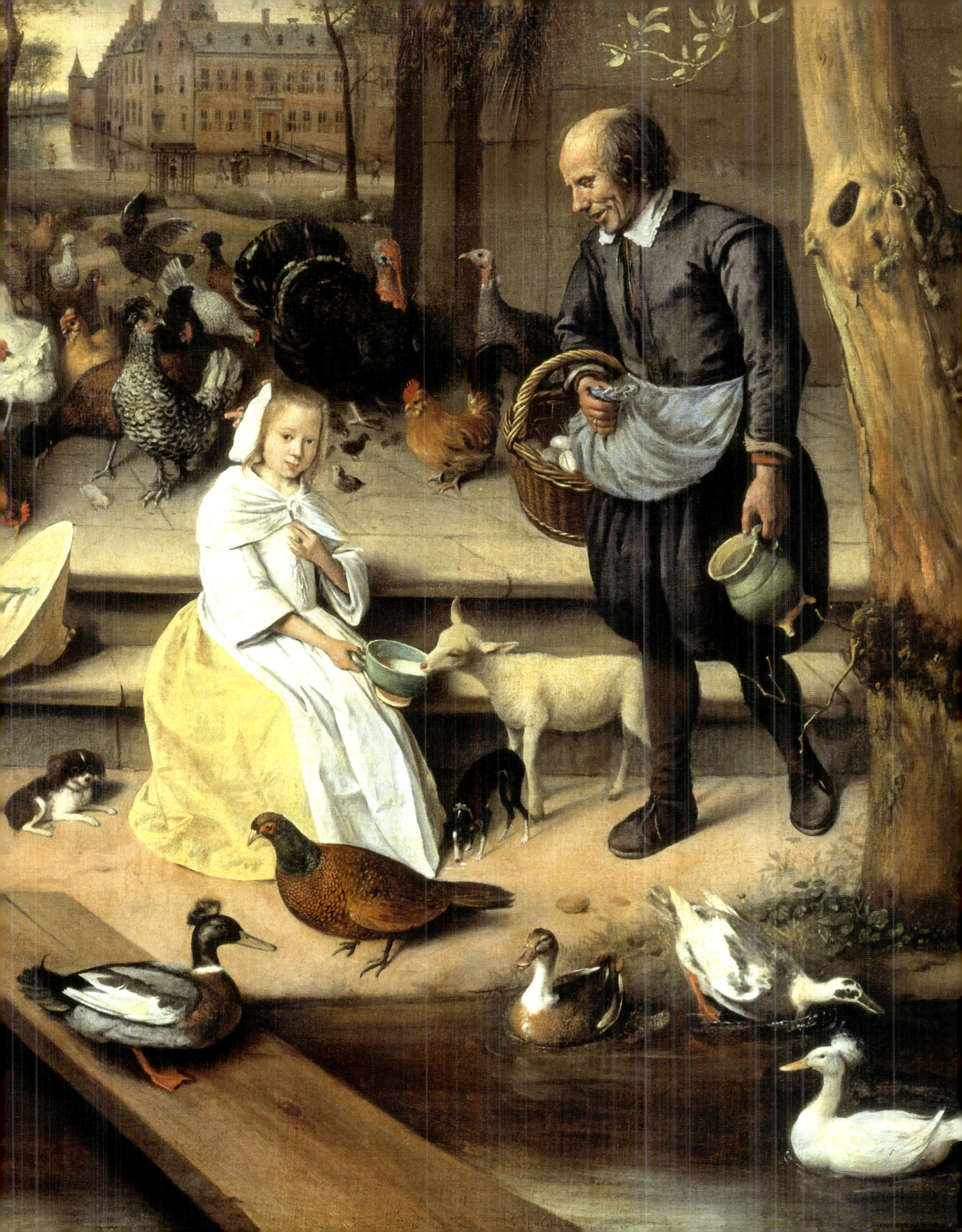

Abraham van den Tempel

Leeuwarden 1622–1672 Amsterdam

63

Double Portrait of Jan van Amstel and Anna Boxhoorn, 1671

Oil on canvas, 142 x 181 cm
On the base of the column: *AVdeTempel / 1671*
Museum Boijmans Van Beuningen, Rotterdam

In the seventeenth century the explosive increase in overseas trade held out to many young men the prospect of an attractive, lucrative career sailing the seas. Since trade routes to the east and west, as well as the far-flung Dutch colonies, had to be protected from hostile powers and pirates, the navy also had a fast-growing workforce. Jan van Amstel (1618–1669) was one of many men who spent their entire career in the navy. In the service of Amsterdam's admiralty, he took part in expeditions against privateers, the First and Second Anglo-Dutch Wars (1652–4; 1665–7) and the audacious Raid on the Medway in June 1667, which dealt the English fleet a serious blow in its own waters. Van Amstel died in 1669 of wounds sustained in a naval battle a year before.[1]

In this portrait from 1671 Van Amstel is depicted posthumously, together with his second wife, his relative Anna Boxhoorn (1642–1726), whom he married four years earlier. Abraham van den Tempel shows the couple on a bench in front of a stone parapet. They are richly dressed: Van Amstel wears a *rock*, a knee-length coat that came into fashion around 1670, supplanting the short doublet. The coat's lavish decoration includes copious amounts of silver lace and braid; the latter is also incorporated into the sword hanger, and Van Amstel's scarf and cuffs are trimmed with fashionable and expensive Italian needlepoint lace. In Anna's costume, Van den Tempel departed from reality to create a more timeless image: he omitted the customary lace around the neckline and sleeves, while the black shawl draped over her shoulders and the thin white *tour* pinned around the neckline are drawn completely from his imagination. On the other hand, Anna's coiffure, with its wide chignon and dangling curls – known as *à la Sevigné* – was the height of fashion in 1670.[2] The couple's prosperity is underscored by the presence of a young page who offers a precious chased silver dish laden with exotic produce (for the motif see also cat. 41).[3] Anna holds a fruit in her right hand – exposing the wedding ring on her thumb – while with her other hand she points to the boy. Van Amstel holds a baton in his right hand; both this and the warship visible in the right background are allusions to his rank of lieutenant-captain. Since Van den Tempel was unable to depict Jan van Amstel from life, he must have relied on an earlier portrait of him, although no such work is known today.[4]

The artist's first teacher was probably his father, the Frisian painter Lambert Jacobsz (about 1598–1636). After completing his training in Amsterdam the younger Van den Temple established himself as a painter and cloth merchant in Leiden. In 1648 he was one of the signatories of the deed establishing the city's St Luke's Guild, of which he would later be dean.[5] In Leiden he painted a number of monumental allegorical scenes, including some for the Lakenhal (Clothmakers' Hall), but after his move to Amsterdam in 1660 he specialised in portraits. He was greatly influenced by the portrait style of Bartholomeus van der Helst (cats 29–30), which was extremely popular in this period. In Van den Tempel's best portraits, such as the present work – made shortly before his death – he successfully combines a certain elegance with the aura of distinction or dignity his clients craved.[6] These qualities were valued for a long time, as is clear from this portrait's provenance. After the death of Anna Boxhoorn, 55 years after the portrait was made, the painting passed by inheritance to a relative, after which it ended up in the hands of the painter and art dealer Frans van Mieris the Younger. The latter sold it in 1745 to the Leiden collector Allard de la Court van der Voort, who owned one of the eighteenth century's most prestigious art collections. Later it was in the collection of the Amsterdam collector Johan van der Marck, and belonged to the Russian Prince Radziwill, before the newly established Museum Boijmans purchased it in 1865.[7] PP

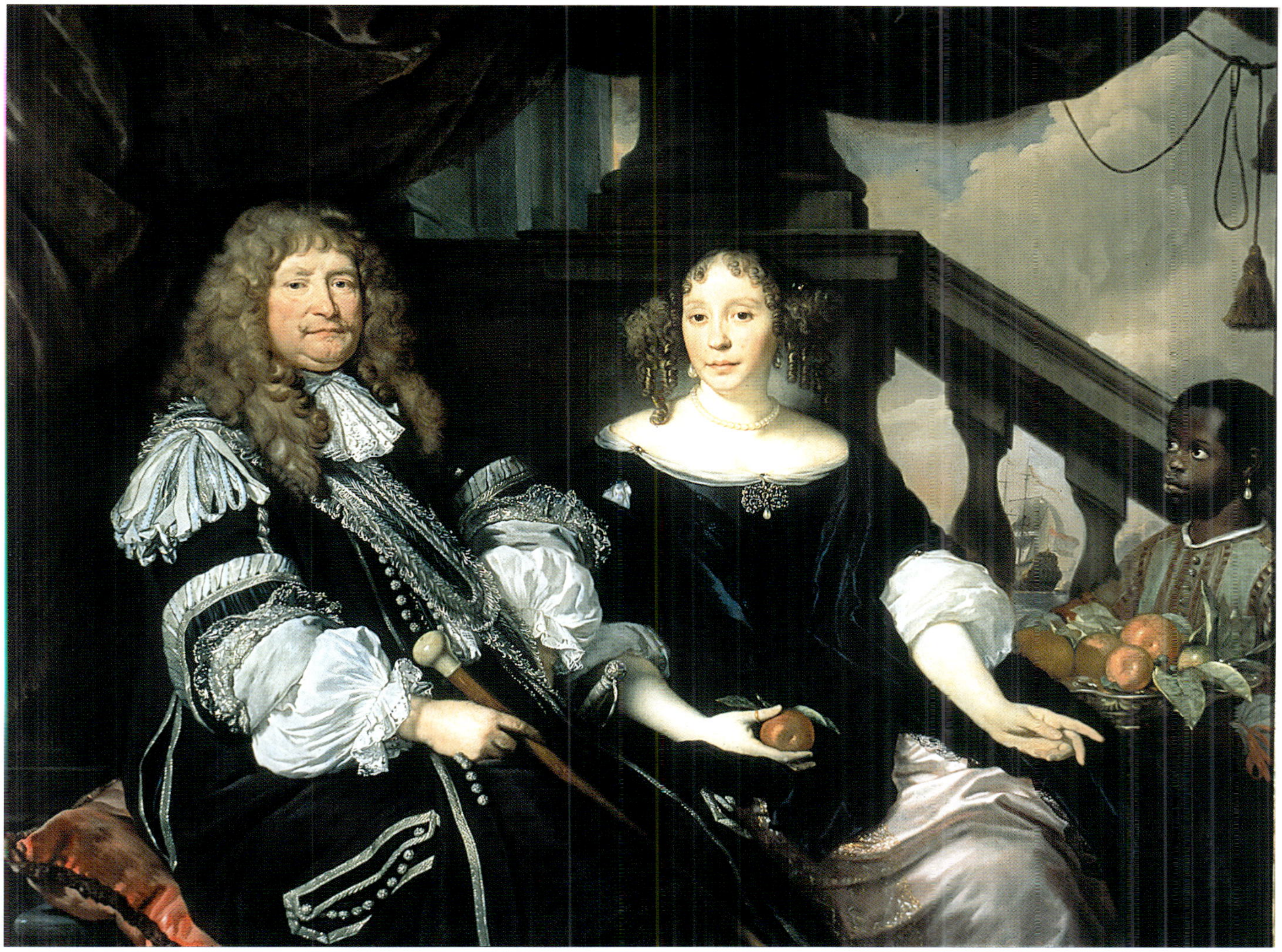

Johannes Verspronck

Haarlem 1606/9 – 1662 Haarlem

64

Portrait of Andries Stilte as a Standard Bearer, 1640

Oil on canvas (cut at left), 101.6 x 76.2 cm
At lower left: : 1640 :
National Gallery of Art, Washington, Patrons' Permanent Fund

This colourful painting by Johannes Verspronck, dating from 1640, has a singularly animated composition. The sitter's pose and clothing radiate pride in his membership in the civic guard, more so even than in the portrait of Loef Vredericx that Thomas de Keyser painted 14 years earlier (cat. 33). The painting depicts the Haarlem officer Andries Stilte (died after 1675), hand on hip, gazing straight into the viewer's eyes. This jaunty pose seems to be derived from works by Frans Hals, who was probably Verspronck's teacher.[1] The dark blue ensign, signifying Stilte's position as standard-bearer of the *Kloveniersdoelen* civic guard,[2] contrasts, like the blue sash around his waist, with the bright pink, lace-trimmed satin costume. This flamboyant and highly fashionable outfit was worn only to a banquet or some other ceremonial gathering of the guardsmen. The sword suspended from his bandolier underscores the military nature of this portrait. While guardsmen generally dressed sedately in black with white collars, standard-bearers sported more colourful attire. The brightly coloured plumes on the hat add still more colour to this already distinctive painting; even the standard's staff is wound with bright blue fabric. The standard forms a strong diagonal through the composition and originally played a more emphatic role in creating a sense of depth: on the left side of the composition, where the knob of the staff is missing, a strip of about eight centimetres has been trimmed from the canvas.

Stilte knew Verspronck because his brother Mattheus commissioned a portrait from the artist in 1636.[3] Andries Stilte, who was born and bred in Haarlem, had a particular reason for asking Verspronck to depict him as a standard-bearer in 1640. In that year he married Eva Reyniers and, as standard-bearers were required to be of good birth (the sitter's parentage being indicated here by the coat of arms at upper left) and unmarried (see pp. 120 and 148), he was automatically discharged from his office.[4] Curiously enough, he turns up as a standard-bearer again all the same, wearing the same apparel as here, in a militia piece that Pieter Soutman produced of the Kloveniers' militia around 1642, two years after Stilte's discharge.[5] At around the same time Stilte was painted by Verspronck, he ordered a second portrait from the painter (fig. 64a).[6] To some extent this second, smaller, painting can be regarded as a replica, although this time Stilte is depicted full-length in a very simple interior, and instead of a standard, he holds a walking-stick. His splendid attire is virtually identical to that in the portrait discussed here, although his hat is not plumed, and he is accompanied by a servant and a dog, giving the painting more the appearance of a genre scene than a portrait. Stilte's pose in this smaller piece – one hand on his side and the other resting on a stick – derives directly from Hals's *Portrait of Willem van Heythuysen* (cat. 18), which was made roughly 15 years earlier.

The *Portrait of Andries Stilte as a Standard Bearer* is one of the culminating achievements of Verspronck's career. The care the artist devoted to the details of the sitter's clothing is clear from certain alterations in the hat: we can see with the naked eye that he made it a little smaller on the left, and that the plumes were initially rather higher. Virtually all of Verspronck's other works show men and women in dark, relatively subdued attire.[7] This series of portraits, all of them presumably commissioned by the middle-class burghers of Haarlem, are ranked among the most austere paintings produced in the seventeenth century. Although he was a gifted portraitist, Verspronck was consistently overshadowed by Frans Hals, whose technique was more spontaneous and audacious. Nevertheless, Verspronck enjoyed a successful career in Haarlem. QB

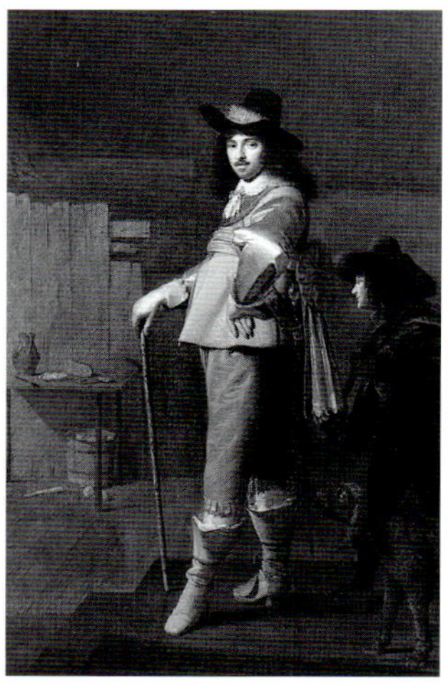

64a. Johannes Verspronck, *Portrait of Andries Stilte, with a Servant*, about 1640. Oil on canvas, 62 x 41 cm. Columbus Museum of Art, Columbus, Ohio

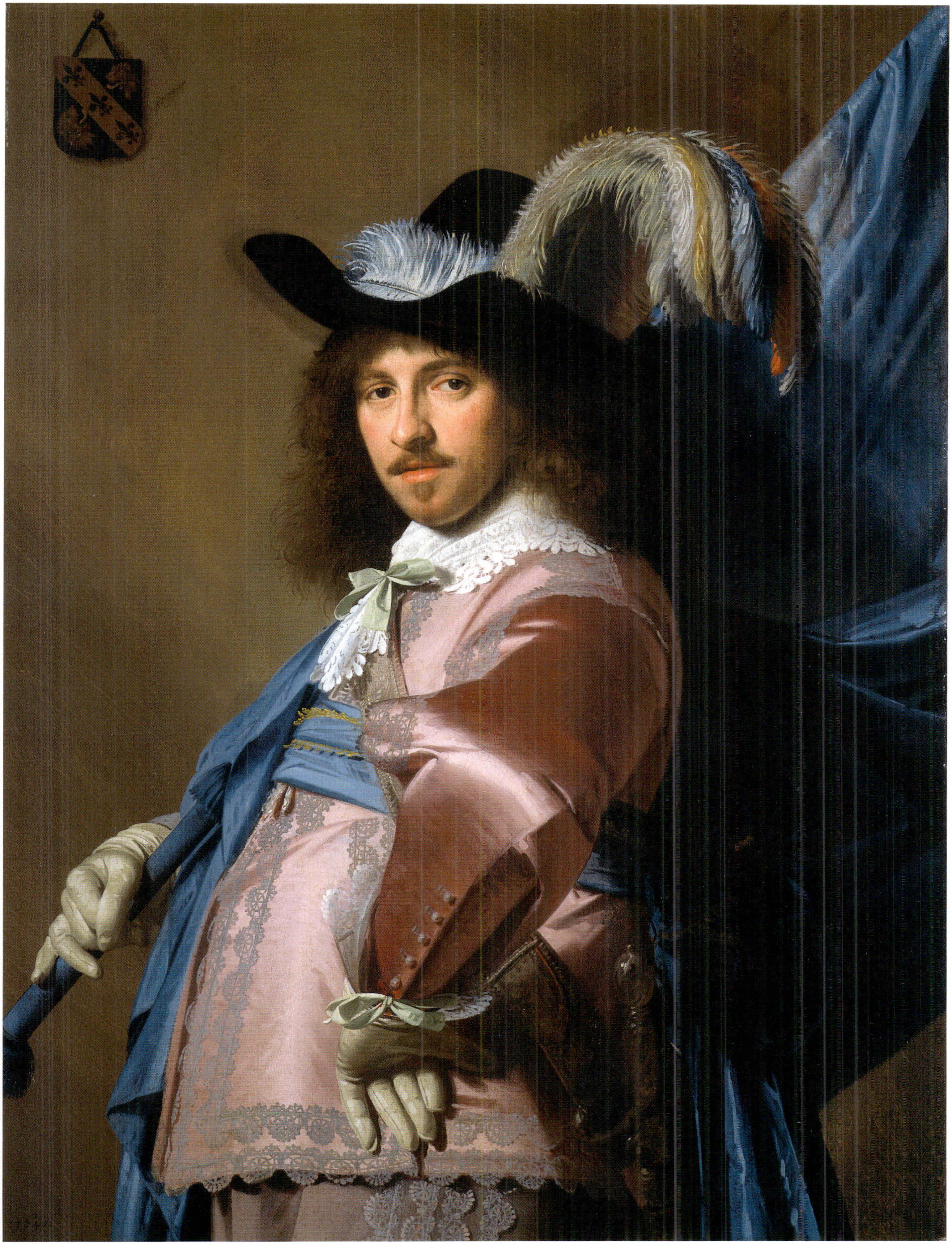

Cornelis van der Voort

Antwerp 1576–1624 Amsterdam

65

Family Group, 1620

Oil on canvas, 119 x 179 cm
At upper left: *Ætatis. Suæ.* 43. / *Anno.* 1620.;
at upper centre: *Ætatis. Suæ.* 16. *man*; at upper right: *Ætatis. Suæ.* 30.
Koninklijk Museum voor Schone Kunsten, Antwerp

Though portraits of families were certainly painted in the Northern Netherlands in the sixteenth and early seventeenth centuries, the genre did not become really popular until the 1620s.[1] This is an early example of a family portrait from the period, depicting an as-yet-unidentified 43-year-old man with his younger wife and their little son, aged 16 months. That the child is a boy is indicated partly by his hairstyle, with the little forelock protruding from a cap typically worn by boys (see also cats 8–9). Another clue is the chain the child wears diagonally over his chest – as a sash – to which his jingling bell is attached. Girls wore necklaces.[2]

The composition of the portrait is simple and well-balanced: the man stands to the left in front of a table, his right hand on his side, and holds up a pear in his left hand. The mother stands to the right and holds the child, who sits on the table. Both parents gaze at the viewer, while the child looks at the pear and reaches out for it with his right hand. The pear may have some emblematic meaning;[3] but alternatively it may be no more than an allusion to the name of the anonymous family, who probably came from Amsterdam.[4]

Until recently, the painting was attributed to the Antwerp painter Cornelis de Vos (1584/5–1651), but in 1990 Katlijne van der Stighelen omitted it from her catalogue of De Vos's portraits.[5] In 2001 the work was given, on stylistic grounds, to the Amsterdam painter Cornelis van der Voort.[6] Its addition to Van der Voort's œuvre means that the artist, who played an important role in the development of portraiture in Amsterdam with his individual portraits and regent pieces (see pp. 28–9, figs 16–18), also contributed to the modernisation of the family-groups genre. Building on simple sixteenth-century Flemish types, as seen, for example, in a family portrait from 1577 by the Antwerp painter Marten de Vos (fig. 65a),[7] Van der Voort sought to emphasise the close ties between the figures he depicted through careful orchestration of their poses and gestures. RE

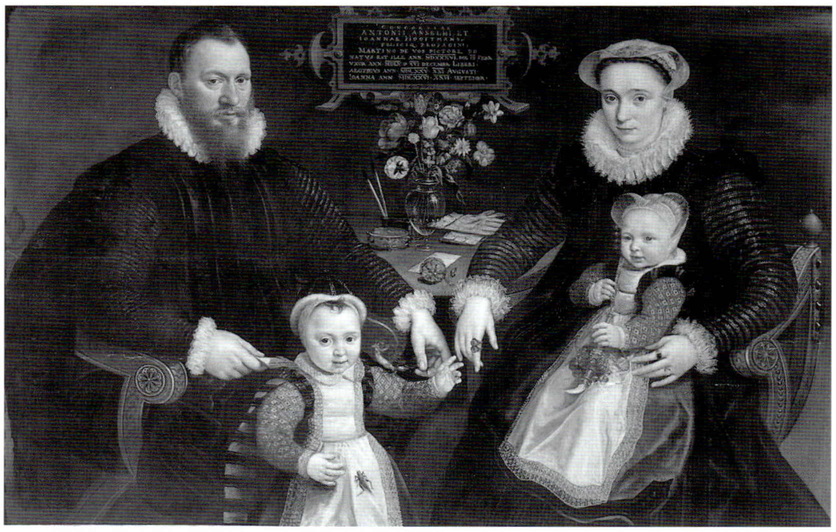

65a.
Marten de Vos,
Portrait of the Anselmo Family, 1577.
Oil on panel,
103 x 166 cm.
Koninklijke Musea
voor Schone Kunsten,
Brussels

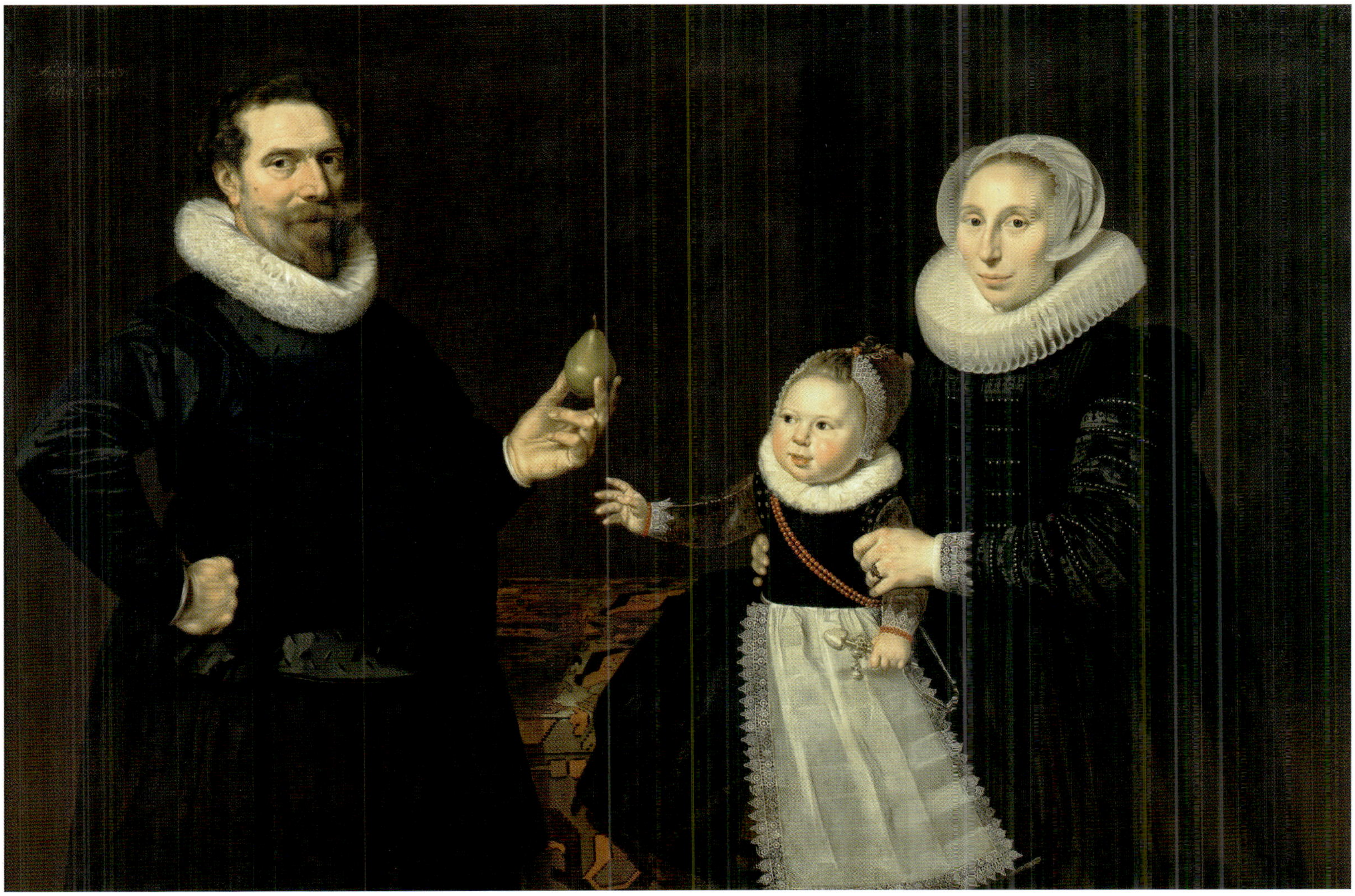

Emanuel de Witte

Alkmaar about 1617–1691/2 Amsterdam

66

Portrait of Adriana van Heusden and her Daughter at the Fishmarket in Amsterdam, about 1662

Oil on canvas, 57.1 x 64.1 cm
The National Gallery, London
London only

The booming Dutch art market of the seventeenth century forced many artists to develop a specialisation in order to retain a competitive edge over the vast number of fellow artists also trying to secure the patronage of the newly wealthy merchants and patricians. Although Emanuel de Witte started his career as a figure painter, he became one of the best known and most successful painters of real and imaginary church interiors.[1] This choice was clearly inspired by the local tradition of – and taste for – the subject in Delft, where De Witte settled in 1641. The artist continued to paint church interiors following his move to Amsterdam ten years later, and it was not until the 1660s that he again made forays into genre painting and portraiture. It was not unusual for artists specialising in other genres to paint portraits occasionally; among many others Pieter de Hooch and Jan Steen (cat. 62) both did so.[2]

At first glance, the present picture appears to be a genre scene. A woman is standing at a market stall, conversing with the fish-seller about the wares on offer. The woman is accompanied by a girl, the only figure who makes eye contact with the viewer. Although some writers have claimed an 'obvious' portrait-like character for the woman depicted as the client, the likeness is in fact quite subtly disguised.[3] She wears surprisingly mundane clothing, which a woman of her station might have worn for everyday use, but hardly for a portrait. This type of dress – the black jacket trimmed or lined with white fur, the reddish-brown skirt, the apron worn over it and the white kerchief on her head – is more commonly seen in genre scenes. De Witte painted a number of fishmarket scenes,[4] but none of these contain portraits.[5]

The identification of the housewife in the present painting as Adriana van Heusden is based on a body of circumstantial evidence relating to a complicated dispute about four pictures. In 1658 De Witte moved into the house of the Amsterdam notary Joris de Wijs, Van Heusden's husband. In exchange for all the pictures the artist painted while living at the house, he received free lodging, food and an annual stipend. Among the pictures painted by De Witte and on display in the house was a fishmarket scene with the portraits of Adriana and her daughter. When De Witte moved out in 1663, he took this picture and three others with him, evidently contravening the agreement with his landlord. The pictures were eventually sold to another party to pay off De Witte's debts to his new landlord. In 1669 Adriana's new husband, Johannes van Heden, sued for the return of the four pictures, but De Witte did not comply with the court order to give them back. It is not documented how the affair ended, but the evidence suggests that various intrigues ensued, involving further sales, blackmail and deception, culminating in the eventual return of the pictures to Adriana and her husband.[6]

This picture must be the one mentioned in this dispute. It is the only one of De Witte's fishmarket portraits to include a little girl, and it must have been painted between 1661, when the new fishmarket opened near the Haarlemmersluis in Amsterdam, and 1663, when De Witte left De Wijs's house. The sitter's costume confirms a date in the early 1660s.[7] AR

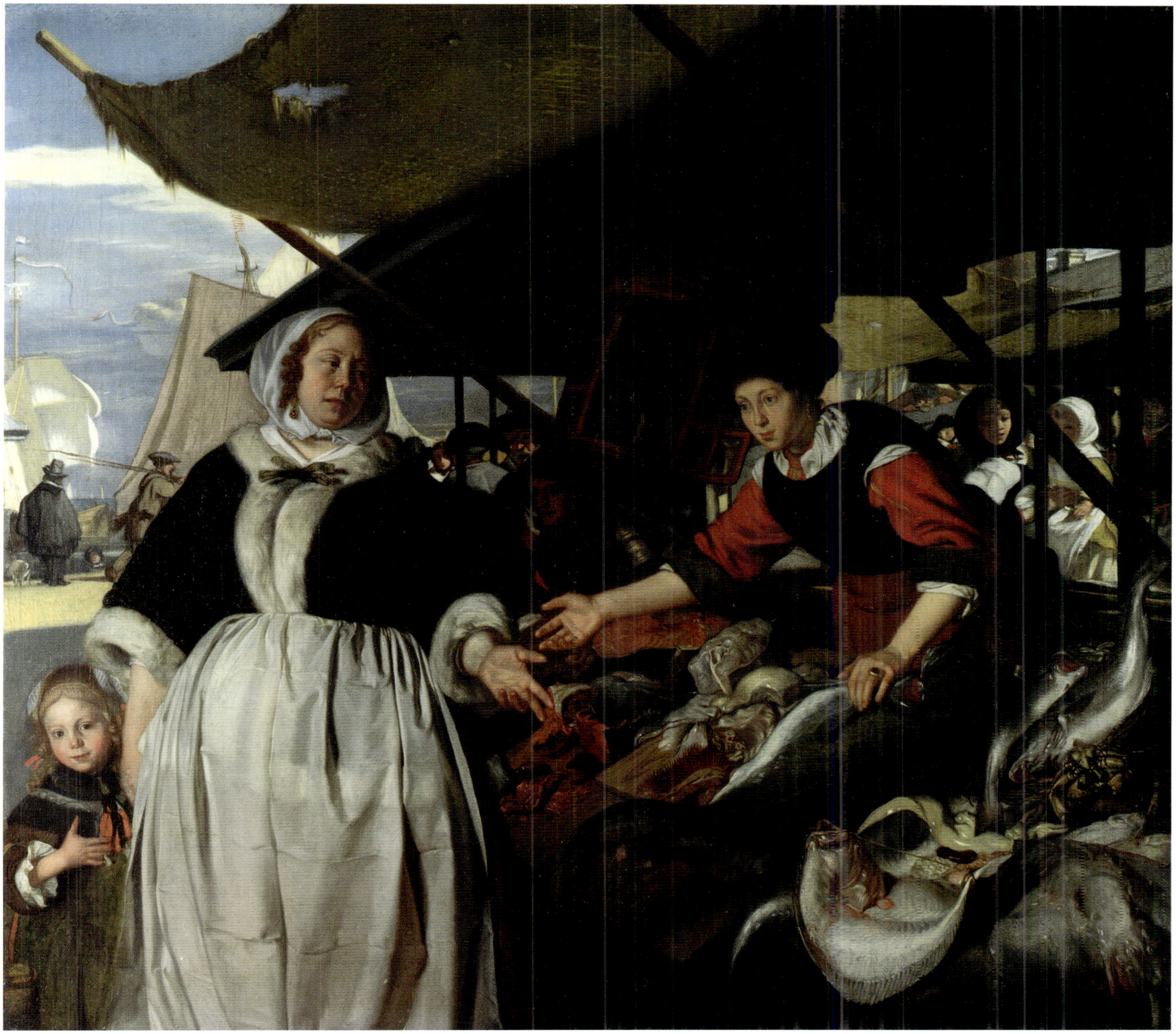

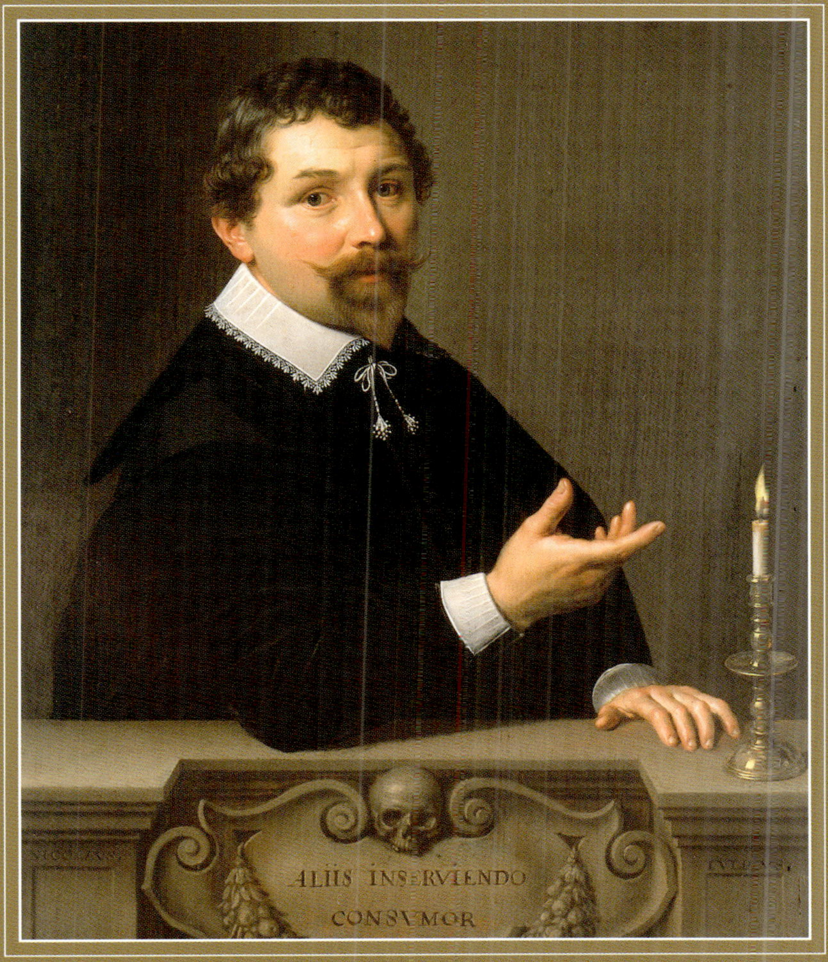
ALIIS INSERVIENDO
CONSVMOR

Notes

Portraits in the Golden Age

Rudi Ekkart

1 Bok/Schwartz (1991, p. 192), reach an estimate of between 750,000 and 1,110,000 portraits, based on the findings of a number of studies.

2 Scholten 1995.

3 Van Mander 1604, fol. 281 recto: 'sijd-wegh der Consten'.

4 See London-The Hague 1999–2000.

5 For *tronies*, see e.g. De Vries 1989; J. van der Veen in Melbourne-Canberra 1997–8, pp. 69–80; Wuestman 2006.

6 See Bibliography.

7 In this period too, a number of major monographs were published, such as those on Van der Helst (De Gelder 1921) and Moreelse (De Jonge 1938). One noteworthy exception to the lack of interest in portraits was the exhibition *Drie eeuwen portret in Nederland 1500–1800* ('Three Centuries of Portraits in the Netherlands, 1500–1800') held at the Rijksmuseum (Amsterdam 1952).

8 *Portretten van echt en trouw: Huwelijk en gezin in de Nederlandse kunst van de Gouden Eeuw*, with a catalogue by E. de Jongh (see Haarlem 1986).

9 Rosenberg/Slive/Ter Kuile 1966; Slive 1995.

10 They are the painting of Calvary with a portrait of the archdeacon and provost Hendrik van Rijn, probably painted in Utrecht, 1363 (Koninklijk Museum voor Schone Kunsten, Antwerp; see Koninklijk Museum voor Schone Kunsten 1988, p. 444, no. 519) and the *Memorial Tablet for the Lords of Montfoort*, painted for St John's Church in Linschoten, about 1380 (Rijksmuseum, Amsterdam; see Rijksmuseum 1976, p. 651, no. 831).

11 H. van Os in Rijksmuseum 2000, pp. 50–1, no. 2; Q. Buvelot in Mauritshuis 2004, p. 323, no. 831.

12 For the Northern Netherlandish portrait in the sixteenth century, see De Vries 1934; Hoogewerff 1936–47. Both books are in many respects outdated; additions and corrections can be found in numerous publications, and more information in general in Amsterdam 1986 and Amsterdam 1993–4.

13 Rijksmuseum 1976, p. 303, no. 3924.

14 Ibid., p. 302, no. C402. Two side panels were added to this painting – probably some 20 years later – with the likenesses of another 14 guardsmen.

15 Haarlem 1988, pp. 77–86.

16 Ekkart 1998a, pp. 58–83.

17 Haarlem 1988, pp. 85–8.

18 As far as we can ascertain from archival documents, old city chronicles and extant paintings, Middelburg followed in 1588, then Hoorn in 1589, Gorinchem in 1590, Delft in 1592, Alkmaar in 1593, Gouda in 1599, Rotterdam in 1604 and Leiden around 1600–5. Many other cities followed later in the seventeenth century. Militia pieces from Gorinchem constitute a separate tradition, with individual portraits of officers. The painting from Hoorn is also somewhat uncharacteristic, since it shows only two guardsmen; traditional militia pieces were not made in Hoorn until the latter half of the seventeenth century.

19 Since the masters of the mint had their own chapel, these two 'tablets' mentioned by Matthijs Balen may have been more in the nature of altarpieces.

20 Haak 1972; Rijksmuseum 1976, p. 446, no. 865.

21 Ekkart 1976.

22 We know the names of these artists from archival documents and Van Mander 1604.

23 For their work, see Frans Hals Museum 2006.

24 Ekkart 1989a; Ekkart in Lunsingh Scheurleer et al. 1986–92, vol. 6, pp. 7–12.

25 De Vries 1934, pp. 100–3; E.J. Sluijter in Delft 1981, pp. 175–6; for Delff, see also Ekkart 1989b.

26 Buijsen et al. 1998, pp. 30–2, 200–5, 230–7.

27 Ekkart in Rotterdam 1994–5, pp. 55–6.

28 Ekkart 1990a; Ekkart in Enkhuizen 1990–1; Stedelijk Museum Alkmaar 1997, pp. 29, 165–7.

29 De Meyere 1978, pp. 158–72; for Van Zijll, see F. van Kretschmar in Buurman 1986, pp. 218–19.

30 Lowenthal 1986; Centraal Museum 1999, pp. 198–201, 1551–7, 1561–70.

31 There is a survey only for portraiture in Gelderland; see Nijmegen 2002–3.

32 Wassenbergh 1967, pp. 13–22. This survey is now outdated.

33 For Van Mierevelt, see Havard 1879–81, vol. 1, pp. 11–82; Havard 1894; Bredius 1908a. Concise recent publications are Ekkart in Amsterdam 1993–4, pp. 310–11, 592–4 and in Turner 2000, pp. 213–14; and W. Liedtke in New York-London 2001, pp. 43–8. In 2007 a research project on Van Mierevelt's work is being launched in Museum Het Prinsenhof, Delft, the results of which will be presented in a publication and an exhibition.

34 See Ekkart in Haarlem 1988, p. 364, no. 184; H. Houtzager in Delft 2002–3, pp. 84–99.

35 On this artist, see Ekkart 1991; Ekkart in Buijsen et al. 1998, pp. 230–7; Ekkart in Turner 2000, pp. 265–6 (with select literature).

36 See A. van Suchtelen in Amsterdam 1993–4, no. 269; Dirkse 2001, pp. 20–2.

37 W. Kloek in Amsterdam 1993–4, p. 34.

38 See Haarlem-Antwerp 2000–1, pp. 22–3, 147–9, no. 26.

39 On Moreelse, see Domela Nieuwenhuis 2001; this monograph replaces the outdated biography by De Jonge (1938).

40 The most important literature on him consists of the now outdated articles by Jan Six: Six 1887, Six 1911 and Six 1918. A concise modern survey can be found in Amsterdam 2002–3, pp. 29–31.

41 S. Dudok van Heel in Amsterdam 2002–3, p. 46 and figs 56a-b; Dudok van Heel 2006, p. 317.

42 N. Middelkoop in Amsterdam 2002–3, no. 60.

43 For Van den Valckert, see Van Thiel 1983, pp. 128–95; for De Keyser, see Adams 1985. No survey of Pickenoy's work has been published since Six (1886, pp. 81–108).

44 For Hals, see esp. Slive 1970–4; Washington-London-Haarlem 1989–90.

45 See also Ekkart in Amsterdam 2002–3, pp. 32–8.

46 The literature on this painting is very extensive; one good study is Haverkamp-Begemann 1982.

47 On Van Santvoort, see De Roever 1889; Ekkart 1990b; Ekkart in Turner 2000, pp. 325–6; Ekkart in Haarlem-Antwerp 2000–1, pp. 158–9, 180–1, 186–9.

48 The monograph of De Gelder (1921) is now outdated. A new one by Judith van Gent is currently being prepared (see also http://home.wxs.nl/~bartholomeusvanderhelst/home.html).

49 Ekkart in Museum Boijmans Van Beuningen 1995, no. 24.

50 Bauch 1926; Sumowski 1983–95.

51 Von Moltke 1965; Sumowski 1983–95.

52 Blankert 1982; Sumowski 1983–95; Ekkart 2002.

53 Judson/Ekkart 1999.

54 Ter Kuile 1976; Ekkart in Buijsen et al. 1998, pp. 155–9 and in Turner 2000, pp. 144–5.

55 Bauer 2006.

56 Brusewicz 1978, pp. 1–49; Ekkart in Buijsen et al. 1998, pp. 212–17.

57 Ekkart in Buijsen et al. 1998, pp. 264–7.

58 See Frans Hals Museum 2006, pp. 305–11, 607–9 and pp. 273–6, 575–81, respectively.

59 Raleigh-Columbus-Manchester 2002–3; Frans Hals Museum 2006, pp. 241–5, 553–7.

60 Ekkart 1979; Frans Hals Museum 2006, pp. 323–4, 621–30.

61 Von Moltke 1938–9; Ekkart in Saur, vol. 14 (1988), pp. 31–2; J.W. von Moltke in Turner 2000, pp. 53–5; Frans Hals Museum 2006, pp. 116–20, 404–15.

62 On these and other Leiden portrait painters from this period, see Ekkart in Lunsingh Scheurleer et al. 1986–92, vol. 6, pp. 12–18. For Bailly, see Bruyn 1951, pp. 148–64, 212–27; J. Bruyn in Turner 2000, pp. 11–12.

63 On portrait painters in Delft in this period, see W. Liedtke in New York-London 2001, pp. 43–54.

64 On Rotterdam's portrait painters in this period, see Ekkart in Rotterdam 1994–5, pp. 55–61; for Cool, see Ekkart 1997, pp. 201–40.

65 Ekkart 2006.

66 Fleischer 1989; Schneeman 1932.

67 Dordrecht 2002.

68 Chong 1992; Washington-London-Amsterdam 2001–2.

69 Ekkart in Dordrecht 2002, pp. 25–7.

70 Huys Janssen 2002.

71 Ekkart in Enkhuizen 1990–1, pp. 25–32. On Ban, see also Ekkart 1991a, and on Doncker, see Laarmann 2000

72 Renckens 1948–9, pp. 165–234.

73 On Hendrick Bloemaert, see Roethlisberger 1993, pp. 437–512; on Van Bijlert, see Huys Janssen 1998.

74 On Jonson van Ceulen, see Finberg 1921–2; Ekkart in Turner 2000, pp. 176–7.

75 Gudlaugsson 1959–60; The Hague-Münster 1974; Washington-Detroit 2004–5.

76 Gudlaugsson 1959–60, no. 205; Washington-Detroit 2004–5, no. 44.

77 Wassenbergh 1967, pp. 30–40; De Vries 1982; L. de Vries in Turner 2000, pp. 114–15; E. Schavemaker in Saur, vol. 51 (2006), pp. 3–4.

78 Wassenbergh 1967, pp. 43–9

79 Stratingh 1984.

80 Nijmegen 2002–3, pp. 60–3; 71–3.

81 There is little literature on portraiture in Zeeland in this period. The most important modern contribution is a study of militia pieces in Goes: Van der Ploeg/Zonnevylle 1999 (for Eversdijck, see ibid., pp. [illegible]–20, 135–42).

82 On Van Thulden, see Den Bosch 1991–2; on De Bye, see Ekkart in Museum Boijmans Van Beuningen 1995, pp. 67–70, and in Nijmegen 2002–3, pp. 77, 124–5.

83 Wijnman 1959a. The doctoral thesis on this artist by M. Friedrich (Bonn 1993) had not yet been published.
84 Kilian 2005; Rogeaux 2002.
85 Adams 1985, no. 91; Phoenix-Kansas City-The Hague 1998–9, no. 30.
86 For a somewhat more detailed survey of Amsterdam portraiture in this period, see Amsterdam 2002–3 (with references to the literature).
87 Krempel 2000.
88 See Kilian and Sluijter in Turner 2000, pp. 228–9 and 393–4, respectively.
89 Amsterdam 2002–3, pp. 41, 262–4.
90 Ekkart in Buijsen et al. 1998, p. 215.
91 Ibid., pp. 82–5.
92 Wieseman 2002.
93 For Van Haensbergen, see C. Vermeeren in Buijsen et al. 1998, pp. 150–4. On Vollevens only brief entries in encyclopædic works have been published.
94 Von Moltke 1938–9; Frans Hals Museum 2006, pp. 116–20, 404–15.
95 Pigler 1955, pp. 169–88; Wishnevsky 1967.
96 For a survey, see Ekkart in Lunsingh Scheurleer et al. 1986–92, vol. 6a, pp. 24–35.
97 Naumann 1981; The Hague-Washington 2005–6.
98 Ekkart in Turner 1996, vol. 8, pp. 664–5; A. Rüger in New York-London 2001, pp. 352–358.
99 J. de Meyere in Zuilen 1996, pp. 36, 78–81.
100 Van Kretschmar 1970; Nijmegen 2002–3, pp. 79, 136–7, 139, 141–3.
101 L. van Dijk in Zwolle 1997, pp. 82–8, 100–21. For Ten Oever, see also Verbeek/Schotman 1957.
102 Veldman 1997.
103 Ekkart in Groenveld et al. 2003, pp. 120–3.
104 B. Brenninkmeyer-de Rooij in Paris 1986, pp. 68–72.
105 Wieseman 2002, pp. 48–51; Krempel 2000, p. 104.
106 Gaehtgens 1987.
107 For the facts of the international influence of Northern Netherlandish art, Gerson 1942 remains a seminal work.
108 The widest-ranging survey is the dictionary of English painters of the sixteenth and seventeenth centuries by Ellis Waterhouse (Waterhouse 1988).
109 For early Scottish portraiture, see Thomson 1974; Thomson in Edinburgh 1975. The beginnings of a more or less independent Irish portraiture can be located in the last quarter of the seventeenth century; one of the first exponents of this genre was the Dutch artist Gaspar Smitz (see Crookshank/Glin 2002, pp. 11–25 and Figgis/Rooney 2001, pp. 439–43).
110 For Denmark, where artists such as Pieter Isaacsz, Karel van Mander III and Abraham Wuchters played a leading role, see Eller 1971; Römelingh et al. 1984; Rodingh/Stompé 1997. For the Dutch artists in Sweden, Gerson (1942, pp. 481–95) still provides the most comprehensive survey.
111 On Von Sandrart, see Klemm 1986. On Ovens, see Schmidt 1922; Schlüter-Göttsche 1978; Sumowski 1983–95, vol. 3, pp. 2218–306, vol. 5, pp. 3113, 3295–8, vol. 6, pp. 3738, 4027–31. On Tilmann, see Beutin 1950.
112 See the literature on the various courts and individual painters. There is a survey in Georg Troescher's encyclopædic work (Troescher 1953–4).
113 For Switzerland, see Fischer et al. 1953; Schlégl 1980; Bern 1995; for Poland, see Steinborn 2004.
114 See Craven 1986; Blackburn/Piwonka 1988.

Portraiture in Practice

Rudi Ekkart

1 Ekkart in Utrecht 1991–2, p. 17.
2 See for example the series from the former Catherinakerk in Amsterdam and Laurenskerk in Stompwijk, now in Museum Catharijneconvent, Utrecht (see Catharijneconvent 2002).
3 Du Mortier 1984; Amsterdam 2002–3, pp. 88–90, nos 3a–c.
4 This is clear from a comparison of dates and marriage years. But wedding anniversaries were frequently marked by commemorative medals in the seventeenth century; see Bemolt van Loghum Slaterus 1981 and Nelemans 1968.
5 See for example the portraits made by Philips Koninck in 1656 depicting the three Van der Burch brothers from Delft (Ekkart 2006, cols 243–8).
6 Ekkart 1990b; Ekkart 2002, pp. 22–3.
7 Ekkart 2002, pp. 22–3.
8 Laarmann 2002.
9 Amsterdam 2002–3, p. 92, no. 5; Dudok van Heel 2006, pp. 351–8.
10 A clear example of a reconstructed portrait is the painting misattributed to the artist Herman van der Mast (d. 1610) depicting the so-called miracle doctor of Delft, Jacob Graswinckel (Museum Het Prinsenhof, Delft, on loan from the Netherlands Institute for Cultural Heritage, Amsterdam-Rijswijk; ICN 1992, p. 192, no. 1613). It is clear from the rendering of the facial features that the painting is based on a study of Graswinckel's body, made after his death in 1624.
11 Ekkart 1998b.
12 Haarlem-Antwerp 2000–1, pp. 292–3, no. 84.
13 One such instance involved the influential Groningen portraitist Jan Jansz 'de Stomme' (the Mute) who died in late 1656 or early 1657. Shortly before this, in 1656, the painter Hendrick Coster had moved to Groningen from Arnhem, where he had been working for many years. After Jan Jansz's death, other portraitists, including Johannes Attema of Leeuwarden and Adam Camerarius – who hailed from Groningen but had been working in Amsterdam – moved to the city to profit from the new gap in the market.
14 Ekkart in Museum Boijmans Van Beuningen 1995, pp. 67–70, no. 9; Ekkart in Nijmegen 2002–3, pp. 77, 124–6.
15 See for example the lexicon of Hague painters of the Golden

Age (in Buijsen et al. 1998, pp. 279–362), which makes it clear that it is only possible to identify one or more works for a minority of the painters listed.

16 The painting dated 1647, the landscape background of which is attributed to Salomon van Ruysdael, was at P. & D. Colnaghi Gallery, London, in 1990.

17 For Van Ostade's portraits, see Hofstede de Groot 1907–28, vol. 3, pp. 415–25, nos 874–906. Since most of these are old auction listings, it is not entirely clear which attributions are correct and whether a particular work is a portrait or a *tronie*. For Steen's portraits, see Washington-Amsterdam 1996–7, nos 7, 8, 12, 29 and 40.

18 In particular from the period 1633–7; several years later he painted a very genre-like self-portrait (see Raleigh-Columbus-Manchester 2002–3, pp. 17–18 and nos 13, 15, 24 and 30).

19 See the wager between Bartholomeus van der Helst and the apothecary Pieter Harberts on whether Pickenoy would manage to complete his militia piece for the Kloveniersdoelen before 28 July 1642 (Bredius 1895, pp. 180–1; De Gelder 1921, pp. 140–1).

20 Krempel 2000, p. 41.

21 Ekkart 1979, pp. 43, 83–90; several works that were then unknown have since been rediscovered.

22 Those who lived and died in prosperous circumstances include Van Mierevelt (see Bredius 1908, p. 15), Van Honthorst (see Braun 1966, pp. 381–3) and Verspronck (see Ekkart 1979, pp. 19–20).

23 Kam 1960.

24 Ekkart 1984.

25 Bredius 1908, pp. 1–17; Braun 1966, pp. 372–5.

26 Haverkamp-Begemann 1982, pp. 10–12, with references to a number of other prices for portraits.

27 Bredius 1908, pp. 7–14. Van Mierevelt and his assistants painted several examples of portraits of celebrities, and sold them from stock.

28 Such as Werner van de Valckert's portraits of the regents and regentesses of the Leper Asylum made in 1624 (Rijksmuseum, Amsterdam; Rijksmuseum 1976, pp. 553–4, nos 417, 419).

29 See for example the data on seventeenth-century Frisian portraits in Wassenbergh 1967.

30 See P. Noble in Mauritshuis 2004, pp. 329–30.

31 Bruyn 1979, pp. 96–115.

32 For this section, see esp. Amsterdam 1984.

33 These two virtually identical versions are both signed and dated 1635. One of them is in Stockholm (Hallwylska Museet 1997, pp. 228–9, no. 149), and the other has made frequent appearances on the art market since 1920 (most recently at Christie's, Amsterdam, 8 November 1999, no. 87). In the past it was not recognised that these are two different works, and their provenances were mixed up (see Ekkart 1979, p. 70, no. 5). It seems likely that one of the two portraits was intended for Van Herrewijn himself and the other one for his daughter Sara, who married Adriaen Ingelbrechts in 1635.

34 Van Beresteyn 1941, pp. 16–30.

35 See for example the will drawn up in 1668 by Baertjen Martens, bequeathing Rembrandt's portraits of herself and her deceased husband Herman Doomer to her son Lambert Doomer, with the proviso that he must have copies made for his sisters (see Van Eeghen 1956, pp. 133–7).

36 In the first few decades of the twentieth century, members of the Van Beresteyn family commissioned from the painter Willem Rees (1880–1962) no fewer than 55 copies of family portraits owned by others (see Van Beresteyn 1941, p. 4).

37 The artist Adriaen van Cronenburg, who worked in Friesland, signed a set of portraits of women from 1567 that are currently preserved in Madrid (see Museo del Prado 1990, pp. 265–6, 296, 728, nos 953, 955, 1068, 2785, ill.), three of the four in the form of a rebus, which later gave rise to considerable confusion: 'Aaaa V.Cronenburch' or 'Aaaa V.C.'. The first four letters should not be read as 'Anna', as has been assumed in the past, but as 'Adriaen' [Dutch 'A-drie a-en' = 'A-three-A's' – transl.].

38 Friedländer 1967–76, vol. 13, pp. 101–6.

39 Ekkart 1998a, p. 59.

40 Cornelis Ketel, on the other hand, did add his monogram to a number of individual portraits.

41 They include Gillis Hannuyts in Rotterdam and Nicolaes van der Heck in Alkmaar.

42 In the seventeenth century the 'u' was often written as a 'v', so that the inscription was frequently spelt 'ætatis svæ'.

43 Ekkart in Museum Boijmans Van Beuningen 1995, pp. 55–7.

44 One example of an original inscription incorporating the first name of the person depicted is the couplet added to the marriage portrait of Reynu Semeyns, painted by Jan Claesz in 1595 (Municipality of Enkhuizen, collection of the former Orphanage). This inscription was one of the aids used in identifying the sitter (Ekkart 1985, pp. 111–21).

45 Wassenbergh 1967, p. 36, no. 63 and fig. 89.

The Artist as Couturier: The 'Portrayal' of Clothing in the Golden Age

Marieke de Winkel

1 Van Heemskerck 1637, p. 150: 'De verscheydenheyde van drachten die sy in der selver kleedinge bespeurde: en haer dede gissen, dat se of niet van een Land, of niet van een tijdt mosten wesen'.

2 See Du Mortier 1984; Amsterdam 2002–3, pp. 88–90, nos 3a–c.

3 Another possible example is the leather buff coat belonging to the Frisian stadholder Hendrik Casimir, which is preserved in the Rijksmuseum. It may be this garment that is depicted in his portrait that was painted around 1635 by Wybrand de Geest; see Sint Nicolaas/Stevens 2006.

4 For Frans Hals, see e.g. B.M. du Mortier in Washington-London-Haarlem 1989–90, pp. 45–60. For inventories of men and

women whose portraits were painted by Rembrandt, see De Winkel 2006, pp. 15–16 and appendices I-II.

5 For this painting and its pendant, see Buijsen et al. 1998, p. 202, figs 2–3.

6 Inventory of the property of Lady Marie van Voorst van Doorwaert, 6 December 1610, Het Gelders Archief, Archief van het huis Rosendaal, no. 1068, fol. 9–12. With the exception of the linen, this inventory has been published in Van der Klooster 1980. The gown is described as 'een swart fluwele samaer, die mouwen met gout geborduyrt ende geboort rontsom met gout galon'.

7 For Dutch seventeenth-century dress terminology, see De Winkel 1995.

8 Adams 1985, vol. 3, pp. 29–30, no. 11.

9 Delft, Gemeentearchief, 72 (Weeskamer), nos 999–1000.

10 De Winkel 1995. Young girls often wore the skirt of the *bouwen* tucked up all around. In English the *bouwen* was referred to as 'Dutch' or as a 'round gown'. Besides the *vlieger* and the *bouwen*, women also sometimes wore a cymar or *tabbaard* (gown). A cymar, like a *vlieger*, was a mantle-like overgown, but with sleeves (fig. 2). A *tabbaard* was a gown with an entirely different structure. It had a bodice stiffened with whalebone, fastened at the back, and a skirt section that was open at the front (a *tabbaard* for men, it should be noted, was something completely different: it was a warm housecoat). Although in the first half of the century the women's *tabbaard* was worn only on highly formal occasions (see cat. 32); after 1650 it gradually replaced the overgowns referred to above (fig. 3a and cats 29, 63).

11 Rodriguez 1634.

12 Westerbaen 1624: 'soo proper en soo ranck [zijn] als sy steecken in de bouwen, Kleyn van eeten en van dranck. Sullen dickwils als se komen In de ruyme Vlieger-kleen Slechts van Slemp en smeeren droomen, En waerom? Sy zijn gevreen' ('Though slender and polite / While wearing virgin's draperies [*bouwen*] / And small of appetite, / When dressed in the capacious things / Of women who have wedded [*vlieger*] / They dream of feasts and surfeiting / And why? They have been bedded'; lines of verse translated from the Dutch by David McKay).

13 In 1638 Jan van Teylingen made a portrait of Hillegond Conninck at 18 years of age, wearing a *bouwen* (panel, 104 x 75 cm; Westfries Museum, Hoorn).

14 Van de Wetering 1985. The maidservant stated that she had exclaimed: 'Mistress, that is a fine ruff!' At which the latter had replied: 'Yes, that is the shoemaker's ruff ... it has to be painted in his portrait' ('Vrouw, dat is een moeye kraech! daerop d'selve antwoorde: ja dat is de schoenmaeckers kraech ... daer moet hy mede wytgeschildert werde').

15 Amsterdam, Gemeentearchief, notary A. Lock, NA 2261, fol. 253–311, 20 October to 26 November 1650, fol. 271: 'dewelcke geseyt werden te sijn tot den schilder Santvoort, die den huysvrouw van den overleden uytschildert'. His wife was called Agnes de Harden. Thanks to Jaap van der Veen for drawing my attention to this rare reference.

16 Rijksmuseum, Amsterdam; see *Corpus*, vol. 2, no. A 80.

17 According to an entry in the diary of Constantijn Huygens the Younger, see Huygens 1876-88, vol. 3, p. 289: 'Zaterdag 28 november 1693 Mevrouw Voorst ... seyde dat Flinck, de schilder, een conterfeitsel van haer vader gemaeckt had, daer hij 50 mael voor geseten had'. The portrait is no longer known today.

18 Bredius 1908, p. 5: 'Een groot conterfeitsel van den voorsz. Jan Michielsz, gedaen bij Michiel van Mierevelt, doch de cleederen niet voltrocken'.

19 Campbell 1990, p. 156: 'alle syn baggen, ketenen, ende juweelen ende veel costelycke cleederen ... die denselve meester Anthoni geconterfeyt den prins van Spaegnien ende die cleederen oick die hy droech'.

20 Van Mander 1604, fol. 238v: 'om conterfeytsel cleeren te maken'.

21 Bredius 1908, p. 11: ''t Conterfeitsel van myn Heer Beveren daervan de trontgie is voldaen en by Jacob Delff de klederen syn geschildert'.

22 Houbraken 1718–21, vol. 3, p. 391: 'Adriaen van der Werf bij Eglon van der Neer zyn meester hem naderhand gebruikte in 't schilderen van kleederen in zyne penceelwerken'.

23 Van Gool 1750–1, vol. 1, p. 237: 'van der Werf schikte de klederen op den Lêman, tekende dezelfde voorts op 't paneel, en liet ze dan zynen broeder schilderen; als die zyn werk verrigt had schilderde de ridder het zo in het nat over'.

24 Kooijmans 2000, pp. 254–7.

25 For this painting, see Mauritshuis 2004, p. 297, no. 124.

26 For the significance of the colour black in seventeenth-century fashions, see Groeneweg 1995; De Winkel 2006, pp. 100–1.

27 For the history and development of lace, see Levey 1983.

28 Rijksmuseum 1976, p. 469, no. C 597; *Corpus*, vol. 3, no. A 131.

29 For Rembrandt's method of depicting lace, see E. van de Wetering in *Corpus*, vol. 2, pp. 63–76.

30 Ekkart 1979, no. 97; Frans Hals Museum 2006, p. 628, no. 473.

31 De Chantelou 1885, p. 164: 'Le Cavalier m'a prié de dire au Roi ou lui faire dire que, quand Sa Majesté viendrait, il serait bon qu'elle eût un collet au lieu d'une cravate qu'elle avait les autres fois, et de faire, s'il se pouvait, qu'il pût voir deux ou trois collets du Roi, afin de choisir celui qui conviendra mieux pour être exécuté en marbre. M'en étant allé au lever du Roi j'ai parlé pour les collets à l'égard de la cravate' (with thanks to Volker Manuth).

32 Ibid., p. 168: 'Sur les deux heures et demie, le Roi est venu avec un collet comme le Cavalier en avait fait supplier Sa Majesté'.

33 Ibid., p. 175 (21 September): 'Cependant le Cavalier à travaillé au collet du Roi. J'ai remarqué qu'encore qu'il regardât de fois à autres celui de points de Venise qui lui a été laissé, il ne l'a point imité, me disant qu'il était sans aucun dessin. Je lui ai

reparti que ce sont ouvrages de religieuses de Venise qui n'ont aucune connaissance du beau'.

34 Ibid., pp. 176–7 (22 September): 'Le Cavalier m'a dit en riant, qu'il travaillait à un ouvrage de peu de goût, qu'il faisait une chose qu'il n'eut jamais pensé de faire, qui est du point de Venise; qu'à la vérité la princesse de Rozane [Olympia Aldobrandini] et autres ont fait tout ce qu'ils ont pu pour avoir de lui un dessin de semblables choses, mais que jamais il n'en avait voulu faire et, qu'à présent, il faisait plus qu'un dessin, puisqu'il l'exécutait en marbre'.

35 Corson 1972, pp. 121–85.

36 One exception is Rembrandt's *Portrait of Oopjen Coppit* from 1634 (fig. 47-8b). The woman is depicted with a large beauty spot on her temple.

37 Pels 1682, p. 30: 'Op 't principaal valt niet zeer hoog te roemen; / Maar 's braaven meesters hand zal ligt, / De fouten dekken, die hy vindt in't aangezigt'.

38 Bauer 2006, p. 11: 'Den een gelijck Diaen ter Jacht, den ander aen fonteyn of bloemen staen: / Of op een and're wijs met sulck een swier van kleeren / 't Sy Hollants of Romeyns, gelijck zy self begeren'.

39 See Groeneweg 1997; Gordenker 2001.

40 Mauritshuis 2004, p. 295, no. 114; Bauer 2006, pp. 265–7, no. A 143.

41 *Inventaris van alle roerende goederen, Meubelen en Juwelen, van Hare doorlt. Hoocht. de vrouw Vorstinne van Simmeren, princesse Maria van Orangien, vervardigt den 29/19 Octobr. 1668* (Dessau, Landesarchiv Oranienbaum, Abteilung Dessau, A7b, no. 65), fol. 47v: 'Een grauw sijden armosijnen rijrock met goude en silverne kante geboort met goude knopen en gouden lissen' and 'een blauwe sijden veste met silverne kante en goude lissen geboort'. With thanks to Alexandra Bauer for generously sharing this source.

42 For this discrepancy, see Bauer 2006, p. 46.

43 De Chantelou 1885, p. 236 (14 October): 'M. d'Albon m'a dit que ces messieurs eussent souhaité qu'il n'y eut point eu de collet au buste. Je lui ai demandé comme ils l'eussent voulu; il a dit: "le col découvert pour être à la façon des héros". Je lui ai dit que les héros français ne devaient pas être à la romaine ou à la grecque; qu'il était bon qu'il parût dans ce buste de quelle sorte l'on était au temps qu'ils a été fait; que cela servait à l'histoire des temps'.

Provenance and selected biography and notes to catalogue works

1 Ferdinand Bol & Willem van de Velde the Younger

Portrait of Michiel de Ruyter, 1667
Royal Picture Gallery Mauritshuis, The Hague

PROVENANCE

Amsterdam Admiralty building, Oudezijds Voorburgwal, Amsterdam, 1667–1798; 's Lands Zeemagazijn, Amsterdam, 1798–after 1818; Ministry of the Navy, The Hague, after 1818–94 (until 1889 in the 'marinemodellenkamer'; from 1889 to 1894 on loan to the Rijksmuseum, Amsterdam); acquired by the Mauritshuis in exchange with the Ministry of the Navy, 1894; inv. no. 585

SELECT BIBLIOGRAPHY

Blankert 1982, pp. 62, 63, 124, no. 77; Sumowski 1983–95, vol. 1, p. 314; P. van Thiel in Amsterdam 1984, pp. 219–20, no. 54; Prud'homme van Reine 1996, pp. 188, 197, 216; B. Broos in Mauritshuis 2004, pp. 42–6, no. 5 (with full bibliography)

NOTES

1 For De Ruyter, see Prud'homme van Reine 1996; Roeper/Daalder 2007.
2 Due to its fragile condition, the frame cannot be displayed in London. Van Thiel in Amsterdam 1984, no. 54; for comparable frames, see ibid., nos 49–50, 53, 55, 59.
3 Hollstein, vol. 2, p. 248, no. 193; Schneider/Ekkart 1973, p. 150, no. 27.
4 Brandt 1687, p. 552; Broos in Mauritshuis 2004, pp. 42, 45, note 4.
5 Now in Scheepvaartmuseum, Amsterdam; see Broos in Mauritshuis 2004, p. 45, note 5.
6 Ibid., p. 42; Blankert 1982, nos 76, 78–9. These three portraits are in museums in Amsterdam, Greenwich and Hoorn.
7 Broos in Mauritshuis 2004, p. 45.
8 Blankert 1982, pp. 23–4, 75, 114–18, nos 56, 58, 59.
9 See Blankert 1982, p. 124; for another portrait by Bol to which Van de Velde contributed a background seascape, see Q. Buvelot and G. Sluiter in Mauritshuis 2004, p. 273, no. 19; Blankert 1982, no. 88.
10 Mauritshuis 2004, pp. 43, 45 and fig. 5d.
11 Broos in Mauritshuis 2004, p. 42.
12 Ibid., pp. 42–3 and figs 5b–c.
13 Previously Kunsthalle, Bremen (lost in the Second World War); Sumowski 1979–92, vol. 1, pp. 266–7, no. 121.
14 Staatliche Graphische Sammlung, Munich; ibid., pp. 268–9, no. 122.

2 Gerard ter Borch

Portrait of Caspar van Kinschot, about 1647
Private collection (on loan to the Mauritshuis, The Hague)

PROVENANCE

Van Kinschot Collection, Leiden; private collection; on loan to the Mauritshuis since 1975; inv. no. 1050

SELECT BIBLIOGRAPHY

Hofstede de Groot 1907–28, vol. 5, p. 83, no. 240; Gudlaugsson 1959–60, vol. 1, p. 59, vol. 2, p. 79, no. 51; The Hague-Münster 1974, pp. 76–7, no. 12; A. McNeil Kettering in The Hague 1998, pp. 28–9, 54, no. 11; Münster 1998–9, p. 214, no. 618; Washington-Detroit 2004–5, pp. 68–9, 198, no. 11; Q. Buvelot in Mauritshuis 2004, p. 274, no. 1050

NOTES

1 A. Wallert in Washington-Detroit 2004–5, pp. 31–41.
2 Rijksmuseum, Rijksprentenkabinet, Amsterdam; A. McNeil Kettering in Rijksmuseum 1988, vol. 1, pp. 128–9, no. Gjr 60.
3 See A. van Suchtelen in Mauritshuis 2004, pp. 51–5, no. 7, ill.
4 Copper (oval), 10 × 8 cm; Six Collection, Amsterdam; Gudlaugsson 1959–60, vol. 1, p. 212, fig. 39, vol. 2, p. 72, no. 39.
5 See A. McNeil Kettering in The Hague 1998, passim.

6 National Gallery 1991, vol. 1, pp. 34–9, no. 896; A. McNeil Kettering in Washington-Detroit 2004–5, pp. 72–4, 198–9, no. 13.
7 Gudlaugsson 1959–60, vol. 1, p. 59, vol. 2, p. 79.

3 Gerard ter Borch

Portrait of a Young Man, about 1663
The National Gallery, London

PROVENANCE

John Rushout, 2nd Baron of Northwick, probably by 1846–59 (sale Cheltenham, Thirlestane House, 26 July–24 August 1859, no. 1114, for 65 guineas to Eastlake); Sir Charles L. Eastlake, London; bought from the estate of his widow, Lady Eastlake, 1894; inv. no. NG 1399

SELECT BIBLIOGRAPHY

Hofstede de Groot 1907–28, vol. 5, pp. 99, 112, nos 307, 345; Gudlaugsson 1959–60, vol. 1, p. 140, vol. 2, pp. 189–90, no. 193; N. MacLaren & C. Brown in National Gallery 1991, vol. 1, pp. 39–40, no. 1399; McNeil Kettering 1999, pp. 46, 60; M.E. Wieseman in Washington-Detroit 2004–5, pp. 144–5, 208, no. 37, p. 148

NOTES

1 For a fuller description of the costume, see Wieseman in Washington-Detroit 2004–5, p. 144.
2 Van Diest 1673, pp. 20–1: 'gelijck oock niet lange geleden met haer lange en wijde Broecken, zijnde onder veel wijder als boven, en hangende flodderen als vrouwen rocken tot midden voor de schenen; insgelijck voor eenige jaren met haer excessive hooge piramijdse Hoeden, en lange gehoorende Schoenen: streckende alle dese misbruycken niet als tot belemmering van den mensche, en daer benevens de excessive wijde en lange kleederen oock tot groote overdaet en verquistinge'.
3 Gudlaugsson 1959–60, vol. 1, pp. 140, 337, vol. 2, p. 190, no. 194; Wieseman in Washington-Detroit 2004–5, pp. 146–8, no. 38.

4 Jan de Bray

Banquet of Mark Antony and Cleopatra: Family Portrait with Salomon de Bray and Anna Westerbaen, 1652
The Royal Collection, London

PROVENANCE

Probably purchased by King Charles II, around 1669 (see text); first listed in the inventory of Windsor Castle in 1688; inv. no. RCIN 404756

SELECT BIBLIOGRAPHY

Von Moltke 1938–9, pp. 445–7, 484, no. 183; C. Brown in London 1976, pp. 27–9, no. 17; C. White in Royal Collection 1982, pp. 28–9, no. 31; B. Broos in The Hague-San Francisco 1990–1, pp. 193–5; J. Giltaij in Rotterdam-Frankfurt am Main 1999–2000, p. 299; Edinburgh-London 2004–5, pp. [illegible]9–52; Manchester-Washington 2004–5, p. 10; De Jongh 2007; Van Suchtelen 2007

NOTES

1 Including strips added above (24 cm) and below (9 cm); the painting on these strips is not original.
2 I.Q. van Regteren Altena (in London 1946–7, p. 121, no. 363) was the first to identify them as Salomon de Bray and Westerbaen. For the biographies of father and son De Bray, see I. van Thiel-Stroman in Frans Hals Museum 2006, pp. 116–23.
3 Pliny, *Naturalis Historiae*, Book 9 119–21.
4 See De Jongh 2007.
5 With thanks to Marieke de Winkel.
6 The identities of the siblings were proposed by F.G.L.O. van Kretschmar in a letter dated 25 April 1971 to D.S. Brooke, the then director of the Currier Museum of Art (Netherlands Institute for Art History, The Hague).
7 See Van Suchtelen 2007. This figure is usually identified as Dirck de Bray (see note 6; see also Broos in The Hague-San Francisco 1990–1, p. 195 and fig. 5) The De Bray brothers and sisters were felled by the devastating plague epidemic of 1663–4; Dirck and Jan were the only siblings to survive. The identification as Jan's self-portrait is confirmed by the similarity to a painting from 1668 that is most probably a self-portrait with his wife (Speed Art Museum, Louisville, Kentucky); Von Moltke 1938–9, no. 178; Manchester-Washington 2004–5, no. 4) and his likeness in a group portrait from 1675 (Rijksmuseum, Amsterdam): Von Moltke 1938–9, no. 189).
8 See for example London-The Hague 1999–2000, no. 1.
9 With thanks to Rupert Featherstone, The Royal Collection.
10 Combined with other sources, this enables us to establish that Salomon was born in 1597. In a portrait drawing of Jan de Bray from 1657, Salomon's age is given as 60 (Kupferstichkabinett, Berlin, inv. no. 707; Von Moltke 1938–9, no. Z 66) and in Dirck de Bray's woodcut made after this drawing in 1664, Salomon's age is given as 67 (see Hollstein, vol. 3, no. 122). These two portraits suggest that he was born in 1597 or 1598, while the inscription on the painting discussed here suggests 1596 or 1597. It follows that the year of his birth was 1597.
11 'Inventory of James II's Pictures'; with thanks to Alex Buck, The Royal Collection.
12 For this painting, see Broos in The Hague-San Francisco 1990–1, pp. 191–6, no. 13; Giltaij in Rotterdam-Frankfurt am Main 1999–2000, pp. 296–9, no. 58; De Jongh 2007.
13 This identification too derives from Van Kretschmar (see note 6).

5 Jan de Bray

Double Portrait of Abraham Casteleijn and Margarieta van Bancken, 1663
Rijksmuseum, Amsterdam

PROVENANCE

Jacob Hoofman, Haarlem, purchased between 1780 and 1783 (see Van der Willigen 1828, p. 7); Maria Hoofman, Haarlem; L.J. Quarles van Ufford, Haarlem (sale Haarlem, 23–4 March 1874, no. 6, for 960 guilders to Blaauw); Q. Blaauw, Amsterdam, 1876; bequest of F.E. Blaauw, 's-Graveland to the museum, 1939; inv. no. SK-A-3280

SELECT BIBLIOGRAPHY

Van der Willigen 1828, p. 7; Von Moltke 1938–9, pp. 445, 484, no. 179; Van Hall 1958, pp. 51–4; Ekkart 1984–5; Becker/Ouwerkerk 1985, p. 234; E. de Jongh in Haarlem 1986, pp. 181–3, no. 36; W. Kloek in Rijksmuseum 2001, pp. 194–5, no. 78

NOTES

1 Panofsky 1934, pp. 117–27; De Jongh in Haarlem 1986, pp. 51–5.
2 Becker/Ouwerkerk 1985, p. 235. The printed letter A on the pedestal of the bust is a standard motif in the Coster iconography.
3 On Casteleijn and the members of his family, see NNBW, vol. 9, cols 132–40.
4 See Van Hall 1958, p. 53; see also Ekkart 1984–5, p. 15.
5 Von Moltke 1938–9, no. Z 161. A drawing after the double portrait by Jan de Bray (sale Amsterdam, Sotheby's, 18 November 1980, no. 181) depicts the present composition.
6 See Annual Report Rijksmuseum 1986, p. 18.
7 Frans Hals Museum 2006, nos 56–8, ill.

6 Jan de Bray

Double Portrait of Salomon de Bray and Anna Westerbaen, 1664?
National Gallery of Art, Washington (Gift of Joseph F. McCrindle)

PROVENANCE

Mathilde Bonaparte, Countess Demidoff, Paris (sale Paris, 17 May 1904, no. 21); Antoine, duc de Gramont, 1904–25 (sale Paris, 22 May 1925, no. 7); J. Fuller-Feder, New York, 1925–56; Mrs George Monroe Moffet, New York, 1956; Joseph F. McCrindle (on loan to the Brooklyn Art Museum, New York, 1957–81; on loan to the Princeton Art Museum, Princeton, 1981–9; on loan to the National Gallery of Art, Washington, 1999–2001); gift of Joseph F. McCrindle to the museum, 2001, inv. no. 2001.86.1

SELECT BIBLIOGRAPHY

Von Moltke 1938–9, pp. 426, 483–4, no. 177a; Van der Marel 1964, cols 14–15; B. Broos in The Hague-San Francisco 1990–1, p. 193; J. Giltaij in Rotterdam-Frankfurt am Main 1999–2000, pp. 276–9, no. 53; Manchester-Washington 2004–5, pp. 8–9, no. 2

NOTES

1 See Von Moltke 1938–9, pp. 483–4, no. 177a: 'het conterfeytsel van sijn voorn. overleden vader ende moeder staende in een stuck ende van ter seyden geschildert'; Van der Marel 1964, cols 14–15. On the basis of the resemblance to Westerbaen's facial features in this double portrait, Van der Marel identified a portrait of a woman by Jan de Bray (National Gallery, London, inv. no. NG 1423; National Gallery 1991, vol. 1, p. 54) as another portrait of the painter's mother. This portrait, dated 1657, has the inscription 'ouwt 52 jaar' (52 years of age), supporting the supposition that Westerbaen was born around 1605. It is not impossible that Jan de Bray's portrait drawing of his father, made in 1657 (Kupferstichkabinett, Berlin, inv. no. 707; Von Moltke 1938–9, no. Z 66), is related to a lost pendant of this portrait of a woman.
2 Von Moltke (1938–9, p. 426) dated the painting around 1661; W.H. Wilson (in Sarasota 1980–1, no. 13) around 1664 (followed by A. Jensen Adams in New York 1988, no. 38; B. Broos in The Hague-San Francisco 1990–1, p. 193; Manchester-Washington 2004–5, no. 4). Giltaij (in Rotterdam-Frankfurt am Main 1999–2000, no. 53) dates it around 1660.
3 Several vertical and diagonal creases in Salomon de Bray's clothing, now painted out, suggest that initially his arm was not raised. Parts of his sleeve have been painted over his wife's costume. Since space was none the less reserved for the hand and wrist, the arm appears to have been adjusted relatively early in the painting process (see the report by Carol Christensen, 3 April 2005, archives of the National Gallery of Art, Washington).
4 See Giltaij in Rotterdam-Frankfurt am Main 1999–2000, p. 278 and fig. 53b; A. Wheelock in National Gallery Washington 2005, pp. 161–6.
5 For this memorial, see Werche 2004, vol. 1, pp. 20–1, vol. 2, figs 1–2.

7 Salomon de Bray

Double Portrait of the Twins Clara and Albert de Bray, about 1646
Private collection (on loan to the National Gallery of Scotland, Edinburgh)

PROVENANCE

Sir Charles Bagot, London, 1834; Mrs Jones, London, 1910; private collection, Scotland

SELECT BIBLIOGRAPHY

Von Moltke 1938–9, p. 388, no. 95a; F. Stampfle in Paris-Antwerp-London-New York 1979–80, p. 105; J. Lloyd Williams in Edinburgh 1992, p. 69, no. 10; Amsterdam 2000, pp. 118, 351, no. 73

NOTES

1 Either separately or included in a family portrait; see J.B. Bedaux in Sliggers 1998, pp. 88–114 and Haarlem-Antwerp 2000–1, nos 19, 32, 46, 78 and 84.

2 For portraits of twins, triplets and so forth, see Laarmann 2002, pp. 32, 84–5, nos B6 and B30.

3 Von Moltke 1938–9, p. 405, no. Z 104; see Stampfle in Paris-Antwerp-London-New York 1979–80, no. 61.

4 Noord-Hollands Archief, Oud Rechterlijk Archief Haarlem, inv. no. 96.1; with thanks to Robert van Vuuren. The date of the marriage was not 11 August 1643; nor did Simon de Bray die as early as 21 September 1647 (as noted in Van der Marel 1964, col. 10).

5 Noord-Hollands Archief, DTB Haarlem, inv. no. 71, fol. 79 and 88v; with thanks to Robert van Vuuren.

6 For a biography of Salomon de Bray, see I. van Thiel-Stroman in Frans Hals Museum 2006, pp. 120–3.

7 On the drawings by the De Bray family, see Giltaij/Lammertse 2001.

8 Canvas, 26 × 34 cm; Von Moltke 1938–9, no. 95; see also Lloyd Williams in Edinburgh 1992, p. 69, note 1.

9 With thanks to Marieke de Winkel.

10 See Stampfle in Paris-Antwerp-London-New York 1979–80, p. 105.

11 See Lloyd Williams in Edinburgh 1992, p. 69.

8 Jan Claesz

Portrait of Albert Sonck and his Son Frans, 1602
Westfries Museum, Hoorn

9 Jan Claesz

Portrait of Lysbeth Walichsdr and her Daughter Elisabeth, 1602
Westfries Museum, Hoorn

PROVENANCE

Most probably through Elisabeth Albertsdr Sonck (1598–1657), married to Seyne Coninck, by descent in the Coninck, Avenhorn and VerLoren families (see Ekkart 1990a, p. 214); bequeathed to the museum by Prof. J.P. de Monté VerLoren, Zeist, 1974; inv. nos 1415–1416

SELECT BIBLIOGRAPHY

De Vries 1934, pp. 77–8; E. de Jongh in Haarlem 1986, pp. 209–11, no. 45 (as anonymous); Ekkart 1990a, pp. 194–5, 213–14, nos 9–10 (as Claesz); R. Ekkart in Enkhuizen 1990–1, pp. 18–19; Bulk 1997, pp. 69–70

NOTES

1 De Jongh (in Haarlem 1986, p. 210) saw this as a gesture denoting constancy, derived from Roman medallions.

2 For seventeenth-century children's clothing, see S. Kuus in Haarlem-Antwerp 2000–1, pp. 73-84.

3 See De Jongh in Haarlem 1986, p. 209.

4 Ekkart 1990, p. 194.

5 Ekkart 1990, pp. 180–218; Ekkart in Enkhuizen 1990–1, pp 16–20, 47–8, 51–5, 70–7.

6 Rijksmuseum 1976, p. 675, no. A 1580 (as anonymous); Ekkart 1990, pp. 194, 213, no. 8; Ekkart in Enkhuizen 1990–1, pp. 72–3, no. 27.

7 See Ekkart 1990, pp. 197–203; Haarlem-Antwerp 2000–1, nos 10, 14, 15 and figs 10a, 15a, 26.

10 Pieter Codde

Double Portrait of a Married Couple, 1634
Royal Picture Gallery Mauritshuis, The Hague

PROVENANCE

(?) Sale Cornelis Piera, Amsterdam, 7 September 1829, no. 23; Willem, count of Aldenburg Bentinck and Waldeck-Limpurg, Middachten Castle, De Steeg, before 1882–1912 (on loan to the Mauritshuis, 1900–3); Willem van Aldenburg Bentinck, De Steeg, 1912–44; A. Nijstad Gallery, Lochem, 1944; D. Katz Gallery, Dieren, 1944; Adolf Hitler, Führermuseum, Linz, 1944–5; Collecting Point, Munich, 1945–6; Dutch Art Heritage Foundation (SNK), 1946–60; transferred to the Mauritshuis, 1960; inv. no. 857

SELECT BIBLIOGRAPHY

B. Broos in Mauritshuis 1987, pp. 101–5, no. 18; B. Broos in Mauritshuis 2004, pp. 69–72, no. 11 (with full bibliography); Wheelock 2006, p. 124

NOTES

1 A comparison can be made with De Keyser's double portrait, dated 1629, of a musician and his daughter (panel, 72 × 51 cm; The Metropolitan Museum of Art, New York; Adams 1935, vol. 3, p. 53, no. 24). The figures are set against a background similar to that in Codde's painting.

2 *Corpus*, vol. 2 (1989), nos A 100–1; Mauritshuis 2004, p. 69 and figs 11a–b.

3 This may derive from portraits made in the circle of Rembrandt (see Broos in Mauritshuis 2004, p. 69).

4 Broos in Mauritshuis 1987, p. 102.

5 Broos in Mauritshuis 2004, p. 71 and fig. 11c.

6 See E. de Jongh in Haarlem 1986, p. 40; Wheelock 2006, p. 124.

7 With thanks to Marieke de Winkel.

8 See Broos in Mauritshuis 2004, pp. 69, 71; Wheelock 2006, p. 124.

9 Broos in Mauritshuis 1987, p. 104; W.J. Müller in Braunschweig 1978, p. 53.

10 The National Gallery, London; Broos in Mauritshuis 1987, p. 104 and fig. 4.

11 Jacob Gerritsz Cuyp

Portrait of Michiel Pompe van Slingelandt as a Falconer, 1649
Dordrechts Museum, Dordrecht (on loan from the Netherlands Institute for Cultural Heritage, Amsterdam/Rijswijk)

PROVENANCE

By descent in the family (see Kuiper-Ruempol/Wolleswinkel 1982); Frans de Wildt, Amsterdam, before 1867; by inheritance to the Dowager Backer-de Wildt, Amsterdam; by inheritance to Abraham Blaauw-Backer, The Hague, 1936; D. Katz Gallery, Dieren; sold to Hermann Göring, Berlin, October 1940; Netherlands Institute for Cultural Heritage, Amsterdam/Rijswijk (inv. no. 1695); on loan to the museum since 1953; inv. no. DM/953/373

SELECT BIBLIOGRAPHY

Dordrecht 1977–8, no. 8; Kuiper-Ruempol/Wolleswinkel 1982; Bedaux 1990, p. 132; Chong 1992, p. 539, no. JC 48; Dordrecht 1992, pp. 154–5, no. 30; E. de Jongh in Yamaguchi-Kumamoto-Tokyo-Rotterdam 1994–5, p. 24, no. 6; R. Ekkart in Haarlem-Antwerp 2000–1, pp. 198–200, no. 49; L. van Noortwijk in Dordrecht 2002, pp. 152–3, no. 35; A. Chong in ibid., p. 182, no. 91 (with full bibliography); R. Ekkart in ibid., pp. 37, 41

NOTES

1 Hofstede de Groot 1907–28, vol. 2, p. 41, no. 128.
2 British Museum, London; Dordrecht 1977–8, p. 38.
3 Haak 1984, p. 340, fig. 728; Dordrecht 2002, nos 27, 30 and fig. 34.
4 Kuiper-Ruempol/Wolleswinkel 1982.
5 Huyskens 1992, pp. 57–8; E. de Jongh in Yamaguchi-Kumamoto-Tokyo-Rotterdam 1994–5, p. 24.
6 See E. Gordenker in Washington-London-Amsterdam 2001–2, p. 56.
7 See e.g. Haarlem-Antwerp 2000–1, no. 73.
8 Dordrecht 2002, p. 152 and fig. 35a.
9 For these portraits, see Kuiper-Ruempol/Wolleswinkel 1982; Bauer 2006, pp. 256–8, no. A 133.

12 Gerrit Dou

Portrait of a Young Woman, about 1655?
The National Gallery, London

PROVENANCE

Robert de Saint-Victoire, Rouen (sale Paris, 26 November 1822–7 January 1823, no. 95, for 501 francs to Mme Hazard); William Beckford, Fonthill Abbey, before 1822 (sale Fonthill Abbey, 10 October 1823, no. 220, for 29 guineas to Townley); Henry Fulton, London (sale London, 20 June 1834, no. 93, for 43 guineas to Brind); Charles Brind, London (sale London, 12 May 1849, no. 47, for 46 guineas to Emery); Wynn Ellis Bequest, 1876; inv. no. NG 968

SELECT BIBLIOGRAPHY

Martin 1911, p. 81, no. 103; Hofstede de Groot 1907–28, vol. 1, p. 447, no. 364; Martin 1913, p. 51; Sumowski 1983–95, vol. 1, p. 537, no. 303; Canterbury-London 1990, p. 13, no. 14; N. MacLaren & C. Brown in National Gallery 1991, vol. 1, p. 108, no. 968; R. Baer in Washington-London-The Hague 2000–1, pp. 108–9, no. 22

NOTES

1 See Washington-London-The Hague 2000–1, nos 9, 10, 12, 13.
2 Canterbury-London 1990, p. 13, no. 14.
3 N. MacLaren in National Gallery 1960, p. 106.
4 Sumowski 1983–95, vol. 1, p. 537.
5 C. Brown in National Gallery 1991, vol. 1, p. 108.
6 Baer in Washington-London-The Hague 2000–1, p. 108.

13 Govert Flinck

Portrait of Margaretha Tulp, 1655
Gemäldegalerie Alte Meister, Staatliche Museen, Kassel
The Hague only

PROVENANCE

F.H. Wente, Amsterdam (sale Paris, 22 February 1893, no. 12); acquired from B. Houthakker Gallery, Amsterdam, 1987; inv. no. M 1987/1

SELECT BIBLIOGRAPHY

Von Moltke 1965, pp. 149–50, no. 401; Sumowski 1983–95, vol. 5, p. 3101, no. 2088; Vis 1986; E. de Jongh in Haarlem 1986, pp. 83–6, no. 8; Raupp 1986, pp. 257–8; Gemäldegalerie Kassel 1996, vol. 1, p. 17, no. GK 1062, vol. 2, fig. 130; I. Krog in Copenhagen 2006, p. 268; Kassel 2006, p. 266, no. B 51

NOTES

1 With thanks to Marieke de Winkel.
2 For the various interpretations, see De Jongh in Haarlem 1986, pp. 83–6, and the comments on them in Raupp 1986, pp. 257–8.
3 Raupp 1986, p. 258.
4 De Jongh in Haarlem 1986, p. 54.
5 De Jongh (in Haarlem 1986, p. 83) also sees here an implicit allusion to the poem *Maeghde-wapen* by Jacob Cats; Raupp 1986, pp. 257–8.
6 De Jongh 1975–6, pp. 85–97; De Jongh in Haarlem 1986, p. 84; Raupp 1986, p. 258.
7 Communicated by Marieke de Winkel, 2006.
8 Van den Vondel 1927–40, vol. 5, pp. 852–5.
9 Published in *Hollantsche Parnas* (1660); here translated from the Dutch by David McKay, The Hague; see Van den Vondel 1927–40, vol. 8, p. 217.
10 This motto derives from Virgil's *Aeneid* 1, 464 (see Vis 1986, p. 9).

14 Frans Hals

Portrait of Catharina Hooft and her Nurse, about 1620
Gemäldegalerie, Staatliche Museen, Berlin

PROVENANCE

Inventory of the estate of Catharina de Graeff, née Hooft, Huis Ilpenstein, 1691; by descent via Pieter de Graeff, Catharina's son, from 1691 (see Dudok van Heel 1975, pp. 153–6); sale Huis Ilpenstein, Amsterdam, 3 December 1872, no. 16 (to Roos for Suermondt); Barthold Suermondt, Aachen, 1872–4; acquired with the Suermondt collection for the Königliches Museum, Berlin, 1874; inv. no. 801 G

SELECT BIBLIOGRAPHY

Slive 1970–4, vol. 1, pp. 60–1; vol. 3, pp. 9–10, no. 14; Dudok van Heel 1975; Grimm 1989, p. 271, no. 5; S. Slive in Washington-London-Haarlem 1989–90, pp. 154–5, no. 9; P. van Thiel in Amsterdam 1993–4, p. 601, no. 273 (with select bibliography); J. Kelch in Gemäldegalerie 1998, pp. 238–9; J.B. Bedaux in Haarlem-Antwerp 2000–1, p. 16; S. Gatenbröcker in Braunschweig 2006, pp. 38–9, 95, no. 9

NOTES

1 See S. Gatenbröcker in Braunschweig 2006, p. 87, note 96. The motif also occurs in a German print from 1679 (see Plessen/Von Zahn 1979, fig. p. 72).
2 Dudok van Heel 1975, pp. 153–7.
3 Dekker 2000, p. 97.
4 Thus, Marieke de Winkel points out (in a written communication of 14 November 2006) that the will of Wendela Bicker included bequests to as many as three nurses (Gemeentearchief, Amsterdam, private archives of De Graeff, no. 76; file IV, port. 3, inv. no. 610, n. 31).
5 Dekker 2000, p. 97. Geertje Dircx, the dry nurse of Rembrandt's son Titus van Rijn, bequeathed virtually all her possessions to him in her will of 1648 (Strauss/van der Meulen 1979, pp. 26–262, no. 1648/2; with thanks to Marieke de Winkel).
6 Slive in Washington-London-Haarlem 1989–90, p. 154.
7 A. Willemsen in Haarlem-Antwerp 2000–1, pp. 64–5, 298; Dudok van Heel 1975, pp. 152–3, 157.
8 S. Kuus in Haarlem-Antwerp 2000–1, pp. 77–8.
9 P. van Thiel in Amsterdam 1993–4, p. 601.
10 Van Diepen/Fuhri Snethlage 1990, p. 96.

15 Frans Hals

Double Portrait of Isaac Massa and Beatrix van der Laen, about 1622
Rijksmuseum, Amsterdam

PROVENANCE

Jan Six, Amsterdam; his sale, Amsterdam, 6 April 1702 (bought back by Six's widow); by descent in the Six family; Hendrik Six van Hillegom, Amsterdam, until 1847; his sale, Amsterdam, 25 November 1851, no. 15; acquired at the sale by the Rijksmuseum and incorporated into its collection in March 1852; inv. no. SK-A-133

SELECT BIBLIOGRAPHY

De Jongh/Vinken 1961; Slive 1970–4, vol. 1, pp. 66–8, vol. 3, pp. 11–12, no. 17; E. de Jongh in Haarlem 1986, pp. 124–30, no. 20; Grimm 1989, pp. 122, 272, no. 26; S. Slive in Washington-London-Haarlem 1989–90, pp. 162–5, no. 12; J. Kiers et al. in Amsterdam 2000, pp. 32–3, 31[illegible], no. 13; G. Jansen in Rijksmuseum 2001, pp. 100–1, no. 28; K. Sidén in Stockholm 2001–2, p. 175, no. 151; J. Bikker in Rijksmuseum 2007 (forthcoming)

NOTES

1 De Jongh/Vinken 1961, pp. 146–50.
2 Slive in Washington-London-Haarlem 1989–90, p. 16[illegible].
3 Alte Pinakothek 2002, pp. 25[illegible]–5, no. 334.
4 Ibid., pp. 117–45; De Jongh in Haarlem 1986, pp. 124–30, no. 20.
5 De Jongh in Haarlem 1986, pp. 128–9.
6 Marieke de Winkel points out that unmarried women wore a closed dress with a skirt drawn up at the hip (see p. 67).
7 De Jongh in Haarlem 1986, p. [illegible]30, note 2[illegible].
8 De Jongh/Vinken 1961, p. 140.
9 Ibid., p. 119 and fig. 3; De Jongh in Haarlem 1986, p. 126 and fig. 20b.
10 De Jongh/Vinken 1961, p. 1[illegible]9
11 Slive in Washington-London-Haarlem 1989–90, p. [illegible]0; I. van Thiel-Stroman in ibid., pp. 380–1, doc. no. 29.
12 Slive 1970–4, vol. 3, nos 42, 10[illegible]; Slive in Washington-London-Haarlem 1989–90, nos 21, 43.

16 Frans Hals

Portrait of Jacob Olycan, 1625
Royal Picture Gallery Mauritshuis, The Hague

17 Frans Hals

Portrait of Aletta Hanemans, 1625
Royal Picture Gallery Mauritshuis, The Hague

PROVENANCE

Described in the inventory of the estate of Aletta Hanemans, Olycan's widow, Haarlem, 1653; via Maria van der Horn, Jacob Olycan's niece, by descent in the Van Sypesteyn family, Haarlem; put up for auction by them, Amsterdam, 15 May 1877, nos 9–10; Van Sypesteyn family, Haarlem, 1877–80; Victor de Stuers, The Hague, 1880; purchased by the State of the Netherlands for display in the Mauritshuis, The Hague, 1881; inv. nos 459–60

SELECT BIBLIOGRAPHY

Slive 1970–4, vol. 1, pp. 50, 123; vol. 3, pp. 21–2, nos 32–3;

B. Broos in Mauritshuis 1987, pp. 180–4, no. 31; Grimm 1989, pp. 178, 272–3, nos 21–2; S. Slive in Washington-London-Haarlem 1989–90, pp. 181–4, nos 18–19; B. Broos in Mauritshuis 2004, pp. 107–11, nos 22–3 (with full bibliography)

NOTES

1 Smith 1982, p. 97.
2 One hand on the side, the other holding a hat or gloves; see Slive in Washington-London-Haarlem 1989–90, p. 328.
3 See cat. 24, note 2.
4 Slive in Washington-London-Haarlem 1989–90, p. 181.
5 With thanks to Marieke de Winkel.
6 B. du Mortier in Washington-London-Haarlem 1989–90, p. 47.
7 Both Frans Hals Museum, Haarlem; ibid., nos 41–2.
8 Slive in Washington-London-Haarlem 1989–90, pp. 121, 181.
9 Ibid., pp. 121, 249.
10 Alice Tate-Harte carried out the treatment of Olycan's portrait and Sabrina Meloni that of Hanemans's portrait, 2006–7. The illustrations predate restoration.
11 A similar approach was used to obscure (but not remove) the coats of arms in the portrait of Tieleman Roosterman from 1634, which has been at the Cleveland Museum of Art since 1999 (Slive 1970–4, vol. 3, no. 93).
12 Slive 1970–4, vol. 1, pp. 123–4; P. Biesboer in Washington-London-Haarlem 1989–90, pp. 27–8; Broos in Mauritshuis 2004, pp. 110, 111, note 15; see also Biesboer 2006, pp. 13–14.
13 Du Mortier in Washington-London-Haarlem 1989–90, p. 48; Du Mortier 1984.
14 Slive 1970–4, vol. 3, no. 46; Broos in Mauritshuis 1987, p. 182.
15 Broos in Mauritshuis 2004, p. 110.

18 Frans Hals

Portrait of Willem van Heythuysen, about 1625
Alte Pinakothek, Bayerische Staatsgemäldesammlungen, Munich

PROVENANCE

Included in the inventory of the estate of Willem van Heythuysen, Haarlem, 1650; Gerrit W. van Oosten de Bruyn, Haarlem, 1789–97; his widow, Maria Croon, Haarlem, 1797–9 (sale Haarlem, 8 April 1800, no. 13); Johann I Josef von Liechtenstein, 1821; acquired from the Liechtenstein Collection by the Bayerische Staatsgemäldesammlungen, Munich, 1969; inv. no. 14101

SELECT BIBLIOGRAPHY

Slive 1970–4, vol. 1, pp. 52–4, vol. 3, pp. 20–1, no. 31; Grimm 1989, pp. 119, 272, no. 23; S. Slive in Washington-London-Haarlem 1989–90, pp. 178–80, no. 17; Biesboer 1995; M. Dekiert in Alte Pinakothek 2005, pp. 162–3

NOTES

1 Dudok van Heel in Amsterdam 2002–3, pp. 46–63; Dudok van Heel 2006, pp. 315–71.
2 See Slive 1970–4, vol. 3, p. 20.
3 Dr Pieter Biesboer drew attention to an eighteenth-century manuscript on the Roosterman family with information on the descendants of Tieleman Roosterman (written communication of 21 December 2006 to the author). This manuscript turned up unexpectedly a few years ago at A.G. van der Steur antiquarian bookshop, Haarlem. Fol. 4 notes, in relation to Alida: 'ondertrout met Willem van Heythuysen ob[iit] 6 julij 1650, sij ob[iit] onder de geboden may 1647' ('notification published of intention to marry Willem van Heythuysen, died 6 July 1650, she died during period of said notification, May 1647'); for the relationship between Hals and the Roosterman family, see Biesboer 1995, pp. 117–19 (and for Alida's year of birth see ibid., p. 125, note 29).
4 The painting dates from 1634; see Slive 1970–4, vol. 3, no. 93 (see also cats 16–17, note 11).
5 Boot 1973, pp. 420–2; Biesboer in Washington-London-Haarlem 1989–90, pp. 29, 40, note 19; Slive in ibid., pp. 178, 180 and his note 1; Biesboer 2002, pp. 115–19.
6 See previous note.
7 See Biesboer 1995, p. 119.
8 See also Grimm 1989, p. 119; Dekiert in Alte Pinakothek 2005, p. 162.
9 Boot 1973, p. 423, ill. 5; see also Biesboer 1995, pp. 117–18; Nevitt 2003, pp. 172–82.
10 Slive in Washington-London-Haarlem 1989–90, p. 180; see also Boot 1973, p. 421.
11 Biesboer 1995, p. 119.
12 For his international contacts, see Boot 1973, p. 421.
13 Spicer 1991.
14 See B. du Mortier in Washington-London-Haarlem 1989–90, pp. 54–5, 59, note 78.
15 See note 4.

19 Frans Hals

Portrait of Pieter van den Broecke, 1633
Kenwood House, London,
The Iveagh Bequest, English Heritage
London only

PROVENANCE

John W. Wilson, Neuilly-sur-Seine, before 1873 (sale Paris, 14–16 March 1881, no. 59); Eugène Secretan, Paris, 1881–9 (sale Paris, 1 July 1889, no. 123); purchased by Thomas Agnew & Sons, London, for Sir Edward C. Guinness, Bt., the later Baron, Viscount and Earl of Iveagh, Elveden Hall, Suffolk and Kenwood House, London; Iveagh Bequest, 1927

SELECT BIBLIOGRAPHY

Slive 1970–4, vol. 1, p. 117, vol. 3, p. 51, no. 84; Grimm 1989, pp. 30, 32, 138, 275, no. 58; S. Slive in Washington-London-Haarlem 1989–90, pp. 258–61, no. 44; J. Bryant in Kenwood 2003, no. 7

NOTES

1 Van Gelder 1938; for the print, see Hollstein, vol. 21, p. 213, no. 55.

2 See Slive in Washington-London-Haarlem 1989–90, pp. 258, 268, fig. 48a.

3 *Korte Historiael Ende Journaelsche Aenteyckeninghe . . . Oost-Indien*, Haarlem 1642; see La Fleur 2000.

4 See Slive in Washington-London-Haarlem 1989–90, p. 260, note 2.

5 Slive 1970–4, vol. 3, nos 83, 86.

6 The painting has been slightly reduced in size along the lower edge but probably never included the whole of Van den Broecke's hand (see Slive in Washington-London-Haarlem 1989–90, p. 260).

7 I. van Thiel-Stroman in ibid., pp. 286–7, doc. no. 62.

20 Frans Hals

Portrait of Willem van Heythuysen, about 1634–5
Private collection

PROVENANCE

Bernardus de Bosch, Amsterdam (sale Amsterdam, 10 March 1817, no. 9, for 152 guilders to Saportas); Abraham Saportas, Amsterdam (sale Amsterdam, 14 May 1832, no. 30, for 850 guilders to Van Brienen); Guillaume-Joseph, Baron van Brienen van de Grootelindt, Amsterdam; by inheritance to Guillaume T.A.M., Baron van Brienen van de Grootelindt, Amsterdam (sale Paris, 8 May 1865, no. 10, for 35,000 francs to De Rothschild); Baron James de Rothschild, Paris; Baron Gustave de Rothschild, Paris; Robert de Rothschild, Paris; Frederick Mont, New York, 1950; Otto Schuller, São Paolo, 1963

SELECT BIBLIOGRAPHY

Moes 1909, p. 47 (as Hals); Hofstede de Groot 1907–28, vol. 3, p. 58, no. 190 (as replica of painting in Brussels); Slive 1970–4, vol. 3, p. 66 (as copy); Grimm 1972, p. 203, no. A26a (as copy); N. Middelkoop in Middelkoop/Van Grevenstein 1988, pp. 94–7 (as probable original); S. Slive in Washington-London-Haarlem 1989–90, p. 276, 278, note 2 and fig. 51c (as copy after the Brussels portrait); Grimm 1989, pp. 55, 57, fig. 55e (copy or replica from Hals's studio); Biesboer 1995, p. 122

NOTES

1 Panel, 47 × 37 cm; Musées Royaux des Beaux-Arts, Brussels (Slive 1970–4, vol. 3, no. 123; Slive in Washington-London-Haarlem 1989–90, no. 51, with literature).

2 Biesboer in Washington-London-Haarlem 1989–90, p. 29.

3 'Aen Frans Hals voor 't contrefeijtsel van Heijthuijsen ƒ36.0.0'; Speet 1995, p. 29; Biesboer 1995, pp. 120–1.

4 Slive in Washington-London-Haarlem 1989–90, p. 277.

5 On 15 December 2005 the authors visited Brussels, where Liesbeth de Belie, curator, gave them an opportunity to compare the painting described here with the portrait preserved in the museum.

6 The painting from the collection of H. Bingham Mildmay of London, known as the 'Mildmay version' (Washington-London-Haarlem 1989–90, fig. 51d; Middelkoop/Van Grevenstein 1988, p. 95, fig. 39b), surfaced in 1984. In an appended report by Professor Peter Klein, the felling of the tree occured after 1599. Dr Herman Kuhn of Munich analysed the pigments. The copy on canvas (Washington-London-Haarlem 1989–90, fig. 51b) differs so markedly from authentic paintings by Hals that it has never been regarded either as a work by his hand or produced in his studio.

7 Middelkoop asserted many years ago that the portrait described here was the original (in Middelkoop/Van Grevenstein 1988, pp. 94–7).

8 A detailed report of the scientific examination is currently being prepared.

9 See E. Hendriks and K. Groen in Washington-London-Haarlem 1989–90, pp. 109–27

10 This conclusion is based on unpublished research by Bijl.

11 See Haarlem-Hamburg 2003–4, nos 10 (Fiddler) and 12.

21 Frans Hals & Pieter Codde

Officers and Other Guardsmen of the 11th District of Amsterdam under the Command of Captain Reynier Reael and Lieutenant Cornelis Blaeuw, known as 'The Meagre Company', 1633–7
Rijksmuseum, Amsterdam
London only

PROVENANCE

Commissioned by the sisters for the Voetboogdoelen (first mentioned there in 1653; see Schaep 1885, p. 134, no. 23); transferred to the Great Council or War Chamber in the town hall by 1758; on loan to the Rijksmuseum from the City of Amsterdam since 1885; inv. no. SK-C-374

SELECT BIBLIOGRAPHY

Slive 1970–4, vol. 1, pp. 126–8, vol. 3, pp. 48–50, no. 80; K. Levy-van Halm in Haarlem 1988, pp. 381–2, no. 194; Grimm 1989, pp. 71–2, 81–4, 276, no. 70; M. Bijl in Washington-London-Haarlem 1989–90, pp. 103–8; S. Slive in ibid., pp. 252–7, no. 43; Köhler/Levy-van Halm 1990, pp. 34–6; Amsterdam 2000, pp. 104–6, no. 64; B. Cornelis in Rijksmuseum 2001, pp. 126–7, no. 43; J. Bikker in Rijksmuseum 2007 (forthcoming)

NOTES

1 Moreelse's *Company of Captain Jacob Hoyngh and Lieutenant Nanningh Cloeck* (Rijksmuseum, Amsterdam, inv. no. SK-C-623) was completed in 1616 (see Rijksmuseum 1976, p. 397, no. 623).
2 For their biographies see Elias 1903–5, vol. 1, pp. 104, 262.
3 Jochems 1888, p. 35.
4 Van Eeghen 1974, p. 139.
5 For their biographies see Elias 1903–5, vol. 1, pp. 457, 543.
6 Dudok van Heel 2006, p. 116, note 182.
7 For his biography see Elias 1903–5, vol. 2, p. 649; Van Eeghen 1958. For his address in the 1630s see Dudok van Heel in Berlin-Amsterdam-London 1991–2, pp. 58–9.
8 Musées Royaux des Beaux-Arts, Brussels; Bredius/Gerson 1969, no. 218.
9 See the picture formerly attributed to Rembrandt of about 1633 in the Wallace Collection, London (J. Ingamells in Wallace Collection 1992, pp. 290–1, no. P 82) and Cornelis van Poelenburch's earlier portrait of about 1626 in the Walters Art Gallery, Baltimore (San Francisco-Baltimore-London 1997–8, no. 60).
10 See provenance.
11 For these documents and their interpretation see Bredius 1913; Slive 1970–4, vol. 1, pp. 136–7, vol. 3, pp. 49–50; Slive in Washington-London-Haarlem 1989–90, pp. 252–6; I. van Thiel-Stroman in ibid., pp. 389–91, nos 73–5, 78.
12 On the painting's composition see especially Slive in ibid., p. 252; Köhler/Levy-van Halm 1990, p. 36.
13 Frans Hals Museum, Haarlem; Slive 1970–4, vol. 2, figs 125–8, vol. 3, pp. 47–8, no. 79; K. Levy-van Halm in Frans Hals Museum 2006, pp. 482–4, no. 181.
14 See Slive 1970–4, vol. 3, p. 48.
15 Bijl in Washington-London-Haarlem 1989–90, p. 105.
16 Ibid. Codde's share in the painting was already surmised by Jan Six (see Six 1893, pp. 102–4).
17 Bijl in Washington-London-Haarlem 1989–90, p. 105.
18 Van Eeghen 1974, p. 139.
19 As pointed out by Dudok van Heel 1993, p. 19.
20 Van Dyk 1758, p. 30.
21 Quoted from Washington-London-Haarlem 1989–90, p. 252: 'dat ze alle zo dor en rank zyn, dat men ze met recht de magere Compagnie zoude kunnen noemen'.

22 Frans Hals

Portrait of Jean de la Chambre, about 1638
The National Gallery, London

PROVENANCE

Sale Amsterdam, 1 April 1883, no. 74 (for 90 guilders to Roos); C. Wertheimer Gallery, London; P. and D. Colnaghi Gallery, London; sold for £ 650 to W.C. Alexander, London, 16 March 1892; by descent to Misses Rachel F. and Jean I. Alexander, London; Alexander Gift, 1972; inv. no. NG 6411

SELECT BIBLIOGRAPHY

London 1972, no. 6411; Slive 1970–4, vol. 1, p. 127, vol. 3, p. 65, no. 122; Grimm 1989, pp. 40, 278, no. 89; S. Slive in Washington-London-Haarlem 1989–90, pp. 273–5, no. 50; N. MacLaren & C. Brown in National Gallery 1991, vol. 1, pp. 158–9, no. 6411

NOTES

1 Other examples include the portraits of Caspar Sibelius, Henrik Swalmius, René Descartes and Jacobus Revius.
2 For more information on De la Chambre and his family, see C. Brown in National Gallery 1991, vol. 1, pp. 158-9, note 1.
3 De la Chambre 1638.
4 The print is signed 'F. Hals pinxit / J.S. Hoef sculpsit'.

23 Frans Hals

The Regents of St Elisabeth's Hospital, 1641
Frans Hals Museum, Haarlem (on loan from the Elizabeth van Thüringen Fund Foundation, Haarlem)

PROVENANCE

Painted for St Elisabeth's Hospital, Haarlem; Elizabeth van Thüringen Fund Foundation, Haarlem; on loan to the museum since 1862; inv. no. I-114

SELECT BIBLIOGRAPHY

Slive 1970–4, vol. 1, pp. 153, 155–7, 158, 174, vol. 3, pp. 73–4, no. 140; Grimm 1989, pp. 156–7, 280, no. 112; S. Slive in Washington-London-Haarlem 1989–90, pp. 284–9, no. 54; P. Biesboer in Frans Hals Museum 2006, pp. 486–8, no. 183

NOTES

1 Van Thiel/De Bruyn Kops 1995, pp. 81, 189, fig. N 2.
2 Slive 1970–4, vol. 3, p. 73.
3 See Biesboer in Frans Hals Museum 2006, p. 488, note 8; no other portrait of Cousaert has been identified.
4 Van Diepen/Fuhri Snethlage 1990, p. 106.
5 Slive in Washington-London-Haarlem 1989–90, p. 98, fig. 15, pp. 285 and 288, fig. 54a; Slive 1970–4, no. 124.
6 Slive in Washington-London-Haarlem 1989–90, p. 285.
7 Middelkoop/Van Grevenstein 1988, p. 67; see also Slive in Washington-London-Haarlem 1989–90, p. 284.
8 Ekkart 1979, no. 29.
9 Amsterdam 2002–3, no. 47; Q. Buvelot and G. Sluiter in Mauritshuis 2004, p. 288, no. 78; for the print, see Hollstein, vol. 28, p. 208, no. 14. De Keyser's painting is in the Amsterdams Historisch Museum, on loan from the Mauritshuis, The Hague.
10 Slive in Washington-London-Haarlem 1989–90, p. 288 and fig. 54c.
11 Ibid., nos 85–6; Slive 1970–4, vol. 3, nos 221–2.

24 Frans Hals

Portrait of Willem Coymans, 1645
National Gallery of Art, Washington (Andrew W. Mellon Collection)

PROVENANCE

Coymans family, Haarlem; Mrs Frederick Wollaston, London; Charles Sedelmeyer Gallery, Paris, 1894; Rodolphe Kann, Paris, 1897–1905; Duveen Brothers Gallery, London & New York, 1907; Mrs Collis P. Huntington, New York; by inheritance to her son, Archer Huntington, New York, 1924; Duveen Brothers Gallery, New York; Andrew W. Mellon, Pittsburgh & Washington, 1929; transferred to the Andrew W. Mellon Educational and Charitable Trust, Pittsburgh, 1934; donated to the museum, 1937; inv. no. 1937.1.69

SELECT BIBLIOGRAPHY

Slive 1970–4, vol. 1, pp. 160, 185, vol. 3, pp. 85–6, no. 166; Grimm 1989, p. 282, no. 127; S. Slive in Washington-London-Haarlem 1989–90, pp. 304–5, no. 61; A. Wheelock in National Gallery Washington 1995, pp. 76–9

NOTES

1 Slive 1958.
2 For the four portraits, see Slive 1970–4, vol. 1, pp. 160, 184–5, vol. 3, nos 160–1, 188–9; Slive in Washington-London-Haarlem 1989–90, pp. 322–5, nos 68–9 and figs 68a–b. On the basis of the costume details, Marieke de Winkel has dated the portraits of Geraerdts and Coymans to about 1645 (in contrast to the traditional date of around 1650–2). The pendants were presumably made shortly after the couple's wedding, which took place in October 1644.
3 Slive 1970–4, vol. 3, p. 85; Wheelock in National Gallery Washington 1995, pp. 76, 78, note 3.
4 For the Coymans family, see Zandvliet 2006, pp. 165–6.
5 Wheelock in National Gallery Washington 1995, pp. 76, 78; Slive 1970–4, vol. 3, pp. 85–6; Taylor 1970.
6 I. van Thiel-Stroman in Washington-London-Haarlem 1989–90, p. 409, doc. no. 160 (24 April 1660).
7 Slive in Washington-London-Haarlem 1989–90, pp. 190, 192.

25 Frans Hals

Portrait of Jaspar Schade, about 1645
Národní Galerie, Prague

PROVENANCE

Jaspar Schade had the painting built into the reception hall of his mansion of Zandbergen, near Utrecht, around 1650; by inheritance with the house to his son, Gaspar Cornelis, 1692; by inheritance to the latter's brother-in-law, Jacob Noirot, 1701; from 1740 onwards the painting was always sold together with the house, the last time to the Beuker family, 1865; sold to Pieter Praetorius, Amsterdam, around 1870–5 John W. Wilson, Neuilly-sur-Seine, before 1873 (sale Paris, 14–16 March 1881, no. 58); Sedelmeyer Gallery, Paris, 1881; Johann II, Prince of Liechtenstein, Vienna; donated by the Prince of Liechtenstein, 1890; inv. no. 0 638

SELECT BIBLIOGRAPHY

Slive 1970–4, vol. 1, pp. 161–2, vol. 3, p. 87, no. 168; Damsté 1985; Grimm 1989, p. 281, no. 126; S. Slive in Washington-London-Haarlem 1989–90, pp. 306–8, no. 62; Amsterdam 2000, pp. 210, 344, no. 144

NOTES

1 Van Kinschot 1910–12, vol. 1, p. 324; see Slive in Washington-London-Haarlem 1989–90, pp. 306, 308, note 1 and Damsté 1985, p. 32.
2 Damsté 1985, pp. 31–32.
3 Ibid., pp. 36–7 and figs 1–2; Slive in Washington-London-Haarlem 1989–90, pp. 306–8 and fig. 62b.
4 Damsté 1985, p. 39.
5 Rijksmuseum Twenthe 1976, p. 61, nos 99–100 and figs 149–50.
6 Slive 1970–4, vol. 1, p. 162; Slive in Washington-London-Haarlem 1989–90, pp. 306 and fig. 62a.

26 Frans Hals

Portrait of a Preacher, about 1660
Private collection

PROVENANCE

Von Liphart family, until 1919 in Gutshof Raddi (Ratshof), Tartu, Estonia, subsequently in Dresden; Mr and Mrs Edward W. Bok, Philadelphia; Cary W. Bok, Philadelphia (sale London, Christie's, 25 June 1971, no. 18); Brod Gallery, London, 1971; private collection, England; again Brod Gallery, London, 1974; Robert H. Smith, Washington; Noortman Gallery, Maastricht and London; private collection, France; Noortman Master Paintings, Maastricht, 2006

SELECT BIBLIOGRAPHY

Slive 1970–4, vol. 1, p. 198, vol. 3, p. 107, no. 209; Grimm 1989, p. 283, no. 139; S. Slive in Washington-London-Haarlem 1989–90, pp. 346–7, no. 78; B. Broos in The Hague 1995–6, pp 36–7, no. 14; B. Broos in Mauritshuis 2004, p. 118, note 25

NOTES

1 Slive 1970–4, vol. 3, p. 107.
2 Amiens, Musée de Picardie; ibid., p. 110, no. 215; Slive in Washington-London-Haarlem 1989–90, pp. 352–3, no. 81.
3 Broos in Mauritshuis 2004, no. 25; Slive 1970–4, vol. 3, pp. 107–8, no. 210. See also ibid., vol. 3, pp. 106–7, no. 208.
4 Hofstede de Groot 1907–28, vol. 3, p. 79; see also Slive 1970–4, vol. 3, p. 107.

5 Ibid., pp. 107, 108; Broos in Mauritshuis 2004, p. 118, note 25.
6 See Mauritshuis 2004, p. 118 (Technique).

27 Frans Hals

Portrait of a Man, about 1660–5
Stiftung Sammlung E.G. Bührle, Zürich
The Hague only

PROVENANCE

Francis Thomas De Grey Cowper, 7th Earl Cowper and 7th Baron Lucas, Panshanger, Hertfordshire, until 1905; by inheritance to his widow, Katrine Cecilia Compton Cowper, Countess Cowper, Panshanger, until 1913; by inheritance to Lady Ethel Desborough, Panshanger, the wife of William Baron Desborough, Taplow Court, Buckinghamshire, until about 1945; N. Katz Gallery, Basel; acquired by E.G. Bührle, Zürich, 1946; Stiftung Sammlung E.G. Bührle, since 1958

SELECT BIBLIOGRAPHY

Slive 1970–4, vol. 1, p. 208, vol. 3, p. 111, no. 219; P. ten Doesschate-Chu in Basel 1987, pp. 128–9, no. 38; Grimm 1989, p. 283, no. 144; S. Slive in Washington-London-Haarlem 1989–90, p. 360; F.J. Duparc in Washington-Montreal-Yokohama-London 1990–1, pp. 40–1, 229, no. 1 (with select bibliography); Bührle Stifung 2005, pp. 111–13

NOTES

1 Slive 1970–4, vol. 3, nos 216–18, 220.
2 For the different datings of the portrait, see Ten Doesschate-Chu in Basel 1987, p. 128, note 1.
3 The records of the work's provenance do not go back far enough to provide any clues as to the sitter's identity.
4 Ibid., vol. 1, p. 208, vol. 3, no. 220; Slive in Washington-London-Haarlem 1989–90, pp. 358–60, no. 84.
5 See Slive 1970–4, vol. 1, p. 208.
6 See Broos in Mauritshuis 2004, p. 126.
7 See the full-page detail in Grimm 1989, p. 261, fig. 109.
8 Duparc in Washington-Montreal-Yokohama-London 1990–1, p. 40.

28 Adriaen Hanneman

Portrait of Henry, Duke of Gloucester, about 1653
National Gallery of Art, Washington (Andrew W. Mellon Collection)

PROVENANCE

Count Heinrich Brühl, Dresden; his heirs, 1763–9; sold with the Brühl collection in 1769 *en bloc* to Catharine II, tsarina of Russia; Hermitage, St Petersburg; sold in November 1931 to Matthiesen Gallery, Berlin, P. & D. Colnaghi & Co., London and M. Knoedler & Co., New York; Andrew W. Mellon, Pittsburgh & Washington; transferred to The Andrew W. Mellon Educational and Charitable Trust, Pittsburgh, 1932; donated to the museum, 1937; inv. no. 1937.1.51

SELECT BIBLIOGRAPHY

Ter Kuile 1976, pp. 79–80, no. 22a; A. Wheelock in National Gallery Washington 1995, pp. 92–5; R. Ekkart in Turner 2000, p. 145

NOTES

1 See Toynbee 1950; Toynbee 1958.
2 For biographical data, see Wheelock in National Gallery Washington 1995, pp. 92, 94.
3 The original is no longer known; see Ter Kuile 1976, no. 14.
4 See Wheelock in National Gallery Washington 1995, p. 94.
5 Private collection; see ibid.
6 Ekkart in Turner 2000, p. 145.
7 See Wheelock in National Gallery Washington 1995, p. 92. When the painting was sold from the renowned Hermitage collection in 1931, its attribution, with a view to fixing the asking price, was a thorny issue, and scholars were paid to corroborate the attribution to the famous master (see Walker 1974, pp. 116–18). Hanneman's portrait of Constantijn Huygens with his five children, dating from 1640 (Mauritshuis, The Hague) was also long attributed to Van Dyck (see B. Broos in Mauritshuis 2004, p. 121).
8 See Wheelock in National Gallery Washington 1995, pp. 92, 94.
9 Staring 1956, pp. 153–62; Ter Kuile 1976, p. 79. For the various insignia of the Order of the Garter, see London 2002–3, p. 230.

29 Bartholomeus van der Helst

Double Portrait of Abraham del Court and Maria de Kaersgieter, 1654
Museum Boijmans Van Beuningen, Rotterdam

PROVENANCE

Via Abraham del Court by inheritance to his younger brother, Jacob del Court, and his descendants; Mr Aelbrecht del Court van Krimpen, Haarlem; purchased from him by the museum, 1866; inv. no. 1296

SELECT BIBLIOGRAPHY

De Gelder 1921, pp. 108–9, 243–4, no. 876; E. de Jongh in Haarlem 1986, pp. 171–4, no. 33; B. Broos in The Hague-San Francisco 1990–1, pp. 307–8; J. van Gent in Museum Boijmans Van Beuningen 1995, pp. 106–8, no. 27 (with full bibliography); K. Sidén in Stockholm 2001–2, pp. 175–6, no. 152; J. van Gent in Amsterdam 2002–3, pp. 215, 281, no. 79

NOTES

1 Van Gent in Museum Boijmans Van Beuningen 1995, p. 107.

2 De Jongh in Haarlem 1986, p. 171.
3 Boot 1973, p. 423.
4 Ibid.
5 De Jongh in Haarlem 1986, p. 172.

30 Bartholomeus van der Helst

Portrait of the Regents of the Voetboogdoelen, 1656
Amsterdams Historisch Museum, Amsterdam

PROVENANCE

Voetboogdoelen, Singel, Amsterdam, 1656–83; transferred to Amsterdam town hall, 1683; on loan from the city of Amsterdam to the Rijksmuseum, Amsterdam, 1899–1975; since 1975 housed in the Amsterdams Historisch Museum; inv. no. SA 7330

SELECT BIBLIOGRAPHY

De Gelder 1921, pp. 101–3, 237, no. 841; A. Blankert in Amsterdams Historisch Museum 1979, pp. 135–6, no. 173 (with full bibliography); Haarlem 1988, pp. 100, 101, 157, 274–5, no. 89; J. van Gent in Amsterdam 2002–3, pp. 208–10, 280, no. 77

NOTES

1 De Gelder 1921, pp. 101–7, 235–7, nos 838, 840–1; Van Gent in Amsterdam 2002–3, pp. 206–10, nos 75–7; C. Tümpel in Haarlem 1988, pp. 100–1.
2 Van Gent in Amsterdam 2002–3, p. 209.
3 Ibid., pp. 208, 210.
4 L. van den Berg in Haarlem 1988, p. 157.
5 Ibid., p. 276, no. 90.
6 Rijksmuseum, Amsterdam; De Gelder 1921, pp. 230–4, no. 836; Haarlem 1988, pp. 372–3, no. 189; Rijksmuseum 2001, pp. 138–9, no. 48.
7 See C. Tümpel in Haarlem 1988, pp. 101, 103, note 75.
8 Van Gent in Amsterdam 2002–3, p. 210.

31 Gerrit van Honthorst

Portrait of King Charles I with a Letter in his Hand, 1628
National Portrait Gallery, London

PROVENANCE

Art trade, Paris, about 1950; Ulysse Moussali, Paris (sale London, Sotheby's, 24 March 1965, no. 101a, to Leggatt, dealer, for the National Portrait Gallery); acquired with the support of the National Art Collections Fund; inv. no. 4444

SELECT BIBLIOGRAPHY

Millar 1954, p. 39, note 15; Paris 1956, p. 66, no. 375; London 1964, p. 34, no. 26; Braun 1966, p. 224, no. 80; O. Millar in London 1972b, p. 54, no. 78; R. Ekkart in Judson/Ekkart 1999, pp. 27, 296, no. 415

NOTES

1 Millar 1954, p. 36.
2 Ibid., pp. 36–9; C. White in Royal Collection 1982, pp. 53–6, no. 74; Judson/Ekkart 1999, pp. 107–8, no. 92.
3 For other portraits of Charles I, see *inter alia* National Portrait Gallery 2004, p. 115.
4 First proposed by Sir Oliver Millar (Millar 1954, p. 39, note 15) C. White is somewhat more cautious concerning the connection between the two paintings (see Royal Collection 1982, p. 56).
5 See M. de Winkel in London-The Hague 1999–2000, p. 62 and figs 3–4.
6 London, Public Record Office E 101, 434/14, 435/15–16; with thanks to Marieke de Winkel for making her research data available. For Charles I's apparel, see also A. Ribeiro in London 2000, p. 67.
7 For Van Honthorst's activities for these clients, see Ekkart in Judson/Ekkart 1999, pp. 28–33.

32 Gerrit van Honthorst

Double Portrait of Frederik Hendrik and Amalia van Solms, 1637–8
Royal Picture Gallery Mauritshuis, The Hague
The Hague only

PROVENANCE

Constantijn Huygens, The Hague, until 1687; by descent through his son Constantijn Huygens II, from 1687; sold with the Huygenshuis, of which the portrait was an integral part of the structure, to Jacob Verheye van Citters, The Hague, 1787; Johannes Goldberg, The Hague, 1800–29; Huygenshuis including the portrait purchased by the State of the Netherlands, 1829; painting subsequently transferred to the Mauritshuis, 1829; inv. no. 104

SELECT BIBLIOGRAPHY

Judson/Ekkart 1999, pp. 35, 231–3, no. 295; S. Hüneke in Krefeld-Oranienburg-Apeldoorn 1999–2000, p. 115, no. 5/8 A. van Suchtelen in Mauritshuis 2004, pp. 141–4, no. 31

NOTES

1 Van Suchtelen in Mauritshuis 2004, p. 141 and fig. 31b.
2 Ibid., pp. 143–4 and fig. 31c.
3 Judson/Ekkart 1999, pp. 245–7, nos 306–8. After the stadholder's death in 1647, Amalia commissioned Van Honthorst to produce monumental paintings for the Oranjezaal, the decorations of which were dedicated to the life and work of Frederik Hendrik (ibid., pp. 149–55, nos 172–5; Buvelot 1995, pp. 132–41).
4 Judson/Ekkart 1999, p. 35.
5 Ibid., pp. 36, 231–3, nos 1–18 and figs 178–9.
6 Buvelot 1995, pp. 130–1 and figs 94–5; Van Suchtelen in Mauritshuis 2004, p. 143 and fig. 31a.

7 Buvelot 1995, pp. 129–31 and fig. 93; The Hague 1997–8, p. 45 and fig. 15.
8 Van Suchtelen in Mauritshuis 2004, pp. 143, 144, note 5.

33 Thomas de Keyser

Portrait of Loef Vredericx as Standard-Bearer, 1626
Royal Picture Gallery Mauritshuis, The Hague

PROVENANCE

Loef Vredericx, Amsterdam and Utrecht, 1626–68; imperial collections, Russia, before 1801 (as Jacob Duck; see Sokolova 2007); Hermitage, St Petersburg, until 1930; Hirschman, dealer, Berlin, 1930; Van Diemen Gallery, Amsterdam, 1930–1; acquired by the museum in 1931 with the support of the Rembrandt Society and private benefactors; inv. no. 806

SELECT BIBLIOGRAPHY

Adams 1985, vol. 1, pp. 96–7, 290, vol. 2, p. 24, no. 8, pp. 42, 110–11; R. Ekkart in Haarlem 1988, p. 387, no. 197; P. van Thiel in Berlin-Amsterdam-London 1991–2, vol. 1, p. 202; A. Müller-Schirmer in Amsterdam 2002–3, pp. 90–1, no. 4; Sokolova 2003, p. 7, note 6; B. Broos in Mauritshuis 2004, pp. 145–8, no. 32 (with full bibliography); Sokolova 2007

NOTES

1 Broos in Mauritshuis 2004, pp. 145, 147.
2 See P. van Thiel in Berlin-Amsterdam-London 1991–2, pp. 200, 202.
3 See Buijsen et al. 1998, p. 203, fig. 4 (Van der Maes) and fig. p. 318 (Van Houckgeest). See also the portrait of a standard-bearer by an anonymous Dutch painter dated 1590 in Munich (*Corpus*, vol. 3, p. 230, fig. 5).
4 Mauritshuis 2004, p. 145: 'LOEF, VREDERICX, SOON, VAN V, I. / IST GEWORDEN AN° 1626. .15. AVGVSTI'.
5 Wolleswinkel 2001.
6 Adams 1985, vol. 2, no. 17. De Keyser produced another group portrait of Amsterdam's silversmiths in 1627, which has been lost (Adams 1985, no. 18). Vredericx was not, as has been claimed, depicted in this painting (see Adams 1995, p. 30).
7 Adams 1985, nos 15–16; see also Scholten 2002.
8 In 1634 De Keyser would produce portraits of two of Loef's sisters; Adams 1985, nos 56–7; see also Mauritshuis 2004, p. 147.

34 Thomas de Keyser

Portrait of Constantijn Huygens and his (?) Clerk, 1627
The National Gallery, London

PROVENANCE

By inheritance in the family of Constantijn Huygens; Susanna Louisa Huygens, The Hague, until 1785 (not in the sale of her collection of paintings, The Hague, 22 May 1786); anonymous sale, Amsterdam, 17 April 1809, no. 45 (bought in; as kindly communicated by Ruud Priem, Nijmegen); Anna Maria Ebeling, Amsterdam, until 1812; by inheritance to her husband, Paul Hogguer, Amsterdam, until 1816 (sale Amsterdam, 18 August 1817, no. 37, for 275 guilders to Coclers); Louis-Bernard Coclers, dealer, Amsterdam; John Webb Gallery, London (sale London, 30–1 May 1821, no. 145); Richard Simmons, 1821–47; bequeathed by him to the museum in 1847; inv. no. NG 212

SELECT BIBLIOGRAPHY

Adams 1985, vol. 1, pp. 96–7, 117–48, vol. 3, pp. 32–5, no. 13 (with bibliography); N. MacLaren & C. Brown in National Gallery 1991, vol. 1, pp. 215–17, no. 212; Held 1991, pp. 655–6; P. van der Ploeg in The Hague 1997–8, pp. 160–3, no. 15; De Winkel 2006, pp. 109, 144, 294, note 84

NOTES

1 See Van Gelder 1957; Held 1991; Broekman 2005, pp. 25–32. Huygens was also included in Van Dyck's *Iconography*, a collection of portraits of important public figures (see Mauquoy-Hendrickx 1991, no. 53; G. Luijten in Antwerp-Amsterdam 1999–2000, pp. 73–4). De Keyser has depicted Huygens's coat of arms on the tapestry (for this coat of arms, the tapestry – which shows St Francis before the Sultan of Egypt – and the painting above the mantelpiece, see MacLaren & Brown in National Gallery 1991, vol. 1, pp. 215, 216; Van der Ploeg in The Hague 1997–8, p. 160).
2 See The Hague 1997–8, pp. 192–7, no. 23.
3 Van der Ploeg in ibid., p. 160.
4 See also Adams 1985, vol. 1, p. 96.
5 For this messenger or clerk, see MacLaren & Brown in National Gallery 1991, vol. 1, p. 216; Adams 1985, vol. 1, pp. 146–7. A portrait made at virtually the same time by Jan van Ravesteyn depicts a boy as a clerk, writing (p. 26, fig. 13).
6 Worp 1911–17, vol. 2, p. 213; Van der Ploeg in The Hague 1997–8, p. 161.
7 S. Groenveld in ibid., pp. 31–2.
8 Van der Ploeg in ibid., p. 160.
9 MacLaren & Brown in National Gallery 1991, vol. 1, p. 216; Van der Ploeg in The Hague 1997–8, p. 160.
10 Worp 1892–9, vol. 2, pp. 179–80: 'korts voor mijn bruyloft [is] gemaeckt'; MacLaren & Brown in National Gallery 1991, vol. 1, p. 216; Van der Ploeg in The Hague 1997–8, pp. 161, 163, note 17.
11 See De Winkel 2006, p. 294, note 85.
12 See ibid., p. 109.
13 This is clear from extant correspondence from Huygens; see note 10.
14 See De Winkel 2006, chapter 3.

35 Thomas de Keyser

Portrait of a Gentleman, 1632
Musée du Louvre, Paris

36 Thomas de Keyser

Portrait of a Lady, 1632
Gemäldegalerie, Staatliche Museen, Berlin

PROVENANCE (*Portrait of a Gentleman*)
Emile Secrétan, Paris (sale Paris, 1 July 1889, no. 128); Charles Sedelmeyer Gallery, Paris; Rodolphe Kann, Paris; bequeathed to the museum by Kann, 1905; inv. no. R.F. 1560

SELECT BIBLIOGRAPHY (*Portrait of a Gentleman*)
Oldenbourg 1911, pp. 33–4, 85, no. 104; Adams 1985, vol. 1, p. 231, vol. 3, pp. 71–2, no. 37; Ydema 1991, pp. 47, 49, 147, no. 262; J. Kelch in Gemäldegalerie 1998, p. 242; J. Kiers et al. in Amsterdam 2000, pp. 30–1

PROVENANCE (*Portrait of a Lady*)
Emile Secrétan, Paris (sale Paris, 1 July 1889, no. 129, to Kann); Rodolphe Kann, Paris, 1889–1905 (sale Paris, 6 August 1907, no. 54); Duveen Gallery, Paris & New York, 1907–about 1914; Oskar Huldschinsky, Berlin (sale Berlin, Cassirer, 10 May 1928, no. 17); Boehler & Steinmeyer Gallery, New York, 1929; Arthur Hartog, Wassenaar and New York, about 1936–55; Newhouse Galleries, New York, 1975; private collection, Washington; acquired by the museum in 1982; inv. no. 82.1

SELECT BIBLIOGRAPHY (*Portrait of a Lady*)
Oldenbourg 1911, pp. 33–4, 87, no. 111; Kelch 1982; Adams 1985, vol. 3, p. 73, no. 38; Ydema 1991, p. 147, no. 263; J. Kelch in Gemäldegalerie 1998, pp. 242–3; J. Kiers et al. in Amsterdam 2000, pp. 30–1, 322, no. 12

NOTES
1 Oldenbourg 1921, pp. 33, 79, no. 64; Adams 1985, vol. 3, pp. 68–70, no. 36; Q. Buvelot and G. Sluiter in Mauritshuis 2004, p. 287, no. 77.
2 Ydema 1991, pp. 46–7, figs 37–8; pp. 49, 147, nos 262–3.
3 Amsterdam 2000, p. 31.
4 The signature and date on the man's portrait are no longer visible; see Adams 1985, vol. 3, p. 71, note 1; Louvre 1979, p. 80.
5 Du Mortier 1984; Du Mortier 1989; Du Mortier in Rijksmuseum 2001, pp. 90–1.
6 Adams 1985, vol. 1, pp. 79, 85; A. Jensen Adams in Turner 2000, p. 180.
7 Amsterdam 1952, nos 79–80; see Amsterdam 2000, no. 12; only the Berlin painting was shown in this exhibition.

37 Nicolaes Maes

Family Portrait, about 1676
Courtesy of Konrad O. Bernheimer of P. & D. Colnaghi, London, and Richard Green, London

PROVENANCE
Sir Francis Cook, 1st Baronet, Doughty House, Richmond, Surrey; in 1901 by inheritance to his son, Sir Frederick Lucas Cook, 2nd Baronet, Richmond; in 1920 by inheritance to his son, Herbert Cook, 3rd Baronet, Richmond, until 1939; in 1939 by inheritance to his son, Sir Francis Cook, 4th Baronet, Richmond and later Jersey, until 1978; private collection; P. & D. Colnaghi, London, and Richard Green, London

SELECT BIBLIOGRAPHY
Cook 1914, vol. 2, p. 53, no. 278; Hofstede de Groot 1907–28, vol. 6, pp. 603–4, no. 556; Sumowski 1983–95, vol. 3, p. 2037, no. 1444; L. Krempel in London 2007, pp. 26–9, no. 5

NOTES
1 Houbraken 1718–21, vol. 2, p. 275.
2 Dr L. Krempel wrote some observations about the painting that were published in 2006 at www.richard-green.com; this text has since been published in London 2007, pp. 26–9, no. 5.
3 E. de Jongh in Haarlem 1986, p. 172.
4 See previous note.
5 The painting's dimensions were consistently given, wrongly, as 54 x 68 cm; see bibliography.
6 On the critical regard in which portraiture was held, see Houbraken 1718–21, vol. 2, pp. 274, 276; Haak 1984, p. 58.
7 Oil on canvas, 112 x 155 cm. North Carolina Museum of Art, Raleigh, NC; Haak 1984, p. 100, fig. 173; Sumowski 1983–95, vol. 3, no. 1440; other earlier family groups by Maes also appear rather stiff; see ibid., nos 1438–9.
8 Krempel dated the painting to about 1675–6 (see note 2); the hairstyles were dated by Marieke de Winkel.

38 Nicolaes Maes

Portrait of Cornelis Munter, 1679
Amsterdams Historisch Museum, Amsterdam

PROVENANCE
Gift of C.E. Heynsius to the city of Amsterdam, 1876; inv. no. SA 946

SELECT BIBLIOGRAPHY
Hofstede de Groot 1907–28, vol. 6, p. 539, no. 216; A. Blankert in Amsterdams Historisch Museum 1979, p. 197, no. 257 (with bibliography of earlier literature); Krempel 2000, pp. 105–6, 324, no. A 21C; N. Middelkoop in Amsterdam 2002–3, pp. 107, 272, no. 13

NOTES

1 In 1672 Netscher made a comparable portrait of the Amsterdam collector Abraham van Lennep (Q. Buvelot in The Hague 2002, no. 22; Wieseman 2002, no. 114).
2 K. Ottenheym in Amsterdam 1995, pp. 189–99.
3 Blankert in Amsterdams Historisch Museum 1979, p. 197.
4 Scheltema 1879, p. 28, no. 73.
5 De Vries 1876, quoted by Blankert in Amsterdams Historisch Museum 1979, p. 197.
6 Commelin 1694, vol. 1, p. 287; quoted by Blankert in Amsterdams Historisch Museum 1979, p. 197.
7 Two oval portraits by Maes, until 1954 on loan to the Centraal Museum in Utrecht, have been identified as Munster and his wife, however, on the basis of an old inscription (Centraal Museum 1952, p. 384, nos 1133–4; see also Moes 1897–1905, vol. 2, p. 122, no. 5222/2). With thanks to Lea van der Vinde, who drew attention to these portraits.
8 Krempel 2000, p. 106 and fig. 213.
9 N. Middelkoop in Amsterdam 2002–3, p. 107.

39 Michiel van Mierevelt

Portrait of Maurits, Prince of Orange-Nassau, 1607
Museum Het Prinsenhof, Delft

PROVENANCE

Delft town hall; transferred to the museum in 1988; inv. no. PDS 68b

SELECT BIBLIOGRAPHY

De Wit 1958, pp. 31–2; Ekkart 1971, pp. 41–2; R. Ekkart in Amsterdam 1993–4, p. 593; W. Liedtke in New York-London 2001, pp. 311–13, no. 43; Verhave 2006

NOTES

1 Verhave 2006, pp. 12–13. This text makes grateful use of Johanneke Verhave master's thesis, completed in July 2006, Stichting Restauratie Atelier Limburg. This study, which is now being revised, contains a rich quantity of research material amassed by Verhave and Anita Jansen in the context of the portrait's restoration, completed in 2006, which was carried out in the studio of A. Boersma-Pappenheim.
2 Ibid., p. 12, note 30.
3 *Icones Leidenses* 1973, no. 49.
4 Upper House, The Hague, dated 1607, panel, 110 × 81 cm. A second version of the painting discussed here, painted not on a panel but on canvas, is also in Museum Het Prinsenhof (111 × 88 cm; inv. no. PDS 70; Braunschweig 2000, pp. 115–19, no. 33).
5 Hollstein 90.
6 Verhave 2006, pp. 29–31.
7 William of Orange, his sons Filips and Frederik Hendrik and Willem Lodewijk van Nassau, Stadholder of Friesland.
8 They were portraits of the Stadholder of Friesland, Ernst Casimir, and Frederick V, the 'Winter King' and his wife, Elisabeth Stuart, daughter of King Kames I of England (see Verhave 2006, p. 14).
9 Ekkart 1971, p. 37; Verhave 2006, pp. 13–15.

40 Frans van Mieris the Elder

Portrait of Florentius Schuyl, 1666
Royal Picture Gallery Mauritshuis, The Hague

PROVENANCE

Sale Amsterdam, 25 September 1743, no. 4; Govert van Slingelandt, The Hague, in or before 1752–67; his widow, Agatha Huydecoper, The Hague, 1767–8 (Van Slingelandt sale, The Hague, 18 May 1768, no. 15; the entire collection sold to William V); Stadholder William V, The Hague, 1768–95; seized by the French, transferred to the Musée Napoléon (Musée du Louvre), Paris, 1795–1815; Royal Picture Gallery, housed in the Gallery of William V, The Hague, 1816; transferred to the Mauritshuis, 1822; inv. no. 107

SELECT BIBLIOGRAPHY

Naumann 1981, vol. 1, pp. 69–70, 136–7; vol. 2, pp. 79–80, no. 63; R. Ekkart in Lunsingh Scheurleer et al. 1986–92, vol. 6a, p. 25; A. van Suchtelen in Mauritshuis 2004, pp. 164–7, no. 36; Q. Buvelot in The Hague-Washington 2005–6, pp. 175–7, 229, no. 37

NOTES

1 See Buvelot in The Hague-Washington 2005–6, p. 18.
2 Hoet/Terwesten 1752–70, vol. 2, p. 404.
3 Lindeboom 1974.
4 Van Suchtelen in Mauritshuis 2004, p. 166.
5 Ibid.
6 The Hague, Mauritshuis; ibid., no. 46.

41 Jan Mijtens

Portrait of Willem van den Kerckhoven and his Family, 1652 and 1655
Haags Historisch Museum, The Hague

PROVENANCE

By inheritance in the Van den Kerckhoven family until 1870; bequeathed to the Gemeentemuseum, The Hague, 1870; since 1991 in the Haags Historisch Museum, The Hague; inv. no. 12-1870

SELECT BIBLIOGRAPHY

De Jongh 1975–6, pp. 90–2; E. de Jongh in Haarlem 1986, pp. 231–5, no. 52; R. Ekkart in Buijsen et al. 1998, p. 209; R. Ekkart in Haarlem-Antwerp 2000–1, pp. 221–3, no. 58; Hänsel 2004, pp. 238–9; Bauer 2006, pp. 56, 251–3, no. A 129

NOTES

1 For Mijtens's œuvre, see R. Ekkart in Buijsen et al. 1998, pp. 208–10; Bauer 2006.
2 The sitters' identification is based on a manuscript, now lost, which was part of the estate in 1870; for biographical particulars, see Hofstede de Groot 1915–16, p. 169; Ekkart in Haarlem-Antwerp 2000–1, p. 222; Bauer 2006, p. 252.
3 Otte 1987, pp. 6–10.
4 It is not certain that the frame dates from 1652.
5 For the most detailed interpretation, see De Jongh in Haarlem 1986, pp. 231–5.
6 J. B. Bedaux in Haarlem-Antwerp 2000–1, pp. 240–2, 256–7.

42 Jan Miense Molenaer

Portrait of the Painter's Family, about 1635

Frans Hals Museum, Haarlem (on loan from the Netherlands Institute for Cultural Heritage, Amsterdam/Rijswijk)

PROVENANCE

Count Józef Potocki, Paris, until 1922; Joulin, dealer, Paris; Fritz Mannheimer, Amsterdam, until 1939; sold to be incorporated into the so-called Führermuseum, Linz, 1941; Dutch Art Heritage Foundation (SNK), 1946; Netherlands Institute for Cultural Heritage, Amsterdam/Rijswijk; on loan to the museum since 1952; inv. no. OS 75-332

SELECT BIBLIOGRAPHY

E. de Jongh in Haarlem 1986, pp. 280–4, no. 69; Weller 1992, pp. 16–23; Laarmann 1998, p. 33; D. Weller in Raleigh-Columbus-Manchester 2002–3, pp. 2–4, 134, 137; C. von Bogendorf Rupprath in Haarlem-Hamburg 2003–4, pp. 160–3, no. 34; N. Köhler in Frans Hals Museum 2006, pp. 555–7, no. 325 (with full bibliography)

NOTES

1 Another early example is Molenaer's portrait of the Ruychaver-Van der Laen family, also made around 1635 (Amsterdam, Museum Van Loon; see The Hague-San Francisco 1990–1, p. 347, fig. 1; Laarmann 1998, fig. 62).
2 Weller 1992, pp. 16–23; Weller in Raleigh-Columbus-Manchester 2002–3, pp. 2–4; Von Bogendorf Rupprath in Haarlem-Hamburg 2003–4, pp. 160, 163, note 11.
3 See Von Bogendorf Rupprath in Haarlem-Hamburg 2003–4, p. 163, note 4.
4 De Jongh in Amsterdam 1976, pp. 183–4 and fig. 45a; De Jongh in Haarlem 1986, p. 282.
5 De Jongh in Haarlem 1986, p. 283. Other figurative pieces by Molenaer also allude to moderation (see Van Thiel 1967–8; The Hague-San Francisco 1990–1, no. 45; Raleigh-Columbus-Manchester 2002–3, no. 13).
6 De Jongh in Amsterdam 1976, p. 184.
7 De Jongh in Haarlem 1986, p. 283.
8 Hinz 1973, pp. 209–10; De Jongh in Haarlem 1986, pp. 280, 283.
9 De Jongh in Amsterdam 1976, p. 184; De Jongh in Haarlem 1986, p. 280.
10 See Von Bogendorf Rupprath in Haarlem-Hamburg 2003–4, p. 163, note 4.

43 Paulus Moreelse

Portrait of Sophia Hedwig, Countess of Nassau-Dietz, as Charity, with her Children, 1621

Paleis Het Loo Nationaal Museum, Apeldoorn

PROVENANCE

By inheritance via the sitter, probably to Willem Frederik of Nassau-Dietz, stadholder's court, Leeuwarden; by inheritance in 1664 to his widow, Albertine Agnes of Orange-Nassau, Leeuwarden; bequeathed by her to her granddaughter, Albertine Johannette of Saxony-Eisenach, 1696; Carl Triepel, Munich (sale Munich, 28 September 1874, no. 45); Paul Delaroff, St Petersburg (on loan to Stedelijk Museum De Lakenhal, Leiden, 1908–14; sale Paris, 23–4 April 1914, no. 167); possibly private collection, Limoges, 1938; G. Stephanovitch, Dijon, 1958; anonymous sale, Paris, 17 June 1977, no. 148; Hoogsteder Gallery, The Hague, 1977; acquired by the museum in 1977; inv. no. RL 451

SELECT BIBLIOGRAPHY

De Jonge 1938, pp. 23–4, 64–5, no. 60; Drossaers/Lunsingh Scheurleer 1974–6, vol. 2, p. 40, no. 201, p. 109, no. 806, p. 208, no. 67; Haak 1984, p. 99; E. de Jongh in Haarlem 1986, pp. 312–15, no. 78; Domela Nieuwenhuis 2001, pp. 416–19, no. SAP 59

NOTES

1 Their grandson Johan Willem Friso (1687–1711), Stadholder of Friesland, inherited all the rights, titles and property of the Stadholder-King William III on the latter's death in 1702.
2 In 1611, for instance, he executed an official full-length portrait of Sophia Hedwig, which was incorporated in the English Royal Collections at an early stage (see Royal Collection 1982, pp. 81–2, no. 118).
3 The full inscription reads: 'CHARITAS no. 154 Sophia Hedwich Geb. H[erzogin]. V[on]. B[raunschweig]. G[räfin]. Z[u]. N[assau]. Henrich G[raf]. Z[u]. N[assau]. Willem Fr[ederik] G[raf]. Z[u]. N[assau]. M[aurits]. G[raf]. Z[u]. N[assau].'; see Domela Nieuwenhuis 2001, p. 419.
4 Drossaers/Lunsingh Scheurleer 1974–6, vol. 2, p. 40, no. 201: 'Een Caritas van H.F.G.'. These initials refer to Sophia Hedwig; see Domela Nieuwenhuis 2001, p. 418.
5 For a detailed account of the development of this tradition, see De Jongh in Haarlem 1986, pp. 312–15; see also Hall 1979, p. 64.
6 De Jongh in Haarlem 1986, p. 312.
7 Ibid., p. 314.

44 Caspar Netscher

Portrait of a Lady, 1683
The National Gallery, London

PROVENANCE

Private collection, London; acquired in 1860 or 1865 by the father of J.J. Humphrey Johnstone; in the latter's collection, Palazzo Contarini dal Zaffo, Venice; presented by J. J. Humphrey Johnstone on the occasion of the King George V's Silver Jubilee, 1935; inv. no. NG 4790

SELECT BIBLIOGRAPHY

C. Brown in London 1976, p. 65, no. 76; N. MacLaren & C. Brown in National Gallery 1991, vol. 1, pp. 286–7, no. 4790; Wieseman 2002, pp. 312–13, no. 217

NOTES

1 The relief is also depicted in Netscher's *Portrait of a Woman* in the Kunstmuseum, Basel, dated 1681 (Wieseman 2002, pp. 301–2, no. 198, repr.).
2 Ibid., pp. 311–12, no. 216.
3 MacLaren & Brown in National Gallery 1991, vol. 1, p. 286; Wieseman 2002, p. 313.

45 Nicolaes Eliasz Pickenoy

The Osteology Lesson of Dr Sebastiaen Egbertsz, 1619
Amsterdams Historisch Museum, Amsterdam

PROVENANCE

Surgeons' guild, Sint-Anthoniswaag, Amsterdam, 1619–1798; after the dissolution of the surgeons' guild in 1798 transferred to the Committee of Medical Supervision, Waaggebouw, Amsterdam, 1798–1862; sold together with other documents belonging to the guild to the art dealer Schouten, 1862; purchased by a 'Committee of Art Lovers, Artists and Physicians' and donated to the city of Amsterdam, 1864; on loan to the Rijksmuseum, Amsterdam, 1885–1975; inv. no. SA 7352

SELECT BIBLIOGRAPHY

A. Blankert in Amsterdams Historisch Museum 1979, pp. 160–2, no. 210 (as Thomas de Keyser; with bibliography); Van Thiel 1983, pp. 169–71 (as Werner van den Valckert); Adams 1985, vol. 1, pp. 46–59, vol. 3, pp. 4–12, no. 1 (as Thomas de Keyser); R. Ekkart in Amsterdam 1993–4, pp. 595–6, no. 268 (as Pickenoy); N. Middelkoop in The Hague 1998–9, pp. 13–14 (as Thomas de Keyser); A.J. Adams in Turner 2000, p. 180; N. Middelkoop in Amsterdam 2002–3, pp. 172–3, 277–8, no. 54 (as Pickenoy)

NOTES

1 Middelkoop in Amsterdam 2002–3, pp. 170–2, no. 53.
2 Middelkoop in The Hague 1998–9, pp. 9–38; Middelkoop and J. Jurjens in Delft 2002–3, pp. 55–83; Middelkoop in Amsterdam 2002–3, pp. 168–79.
3 Ibid., pp. 172, 277, note 3.
4 The names are listed in the upper left corner, with the corresponding numbers being inscribed beside the figures; for the names of those depicted, see ibid., p. 173, nos 1–6.
5 Ekkart in Amsterdam 1993–4, pp. 595–6, no. 268 (as Pickenoy); this attribution has since been adopted by Middelkoop in Amsterdam 2002–3, p. 173 and Adams in Turner 2000, p. 180.
6 Amsterdams Historisch Museum, Amsterdam; see Blankert in Amsterdams Historisch Museum 1979, pp. 103–4, no. 138. This painting was partly burned in 1723; see the reconstruction by Middelkoop in The Hague 1998–9, pp. 14–16, figs 8 and 10.

46 Nicolaes Eliasz Pickenoy

Portrait of Dr Nicolaes Tulp, about 1633–4
Six Collection, Amsterdam
The Hague only

PROVENANCE

By inheritance via Nicolaes Tulp to his son Diederick Tulp in 1674; via Anna Elisabeth van den Bempden, one of Tulp's descendants and from 1728 the wife of Jan Six (1668–1750), by inheritance in the Six family; under the ownership of the Six Foundation from 1922, inv. no. 00030

SELECT BIBLIOGRAPHY

Vosmaer 1868, pp. 23, 279; Amsterdam 1875, p. 48, no. 550; Six 1886, pp. 81–2, 88, 95–6; Amsterdam 1900, p. 10, no. 30; Moes 1897–1905, vol. 2, p. 485, no. 8113/3; Heckscher 1958, pp. 120, 177–8, note 231; Lipp/Gruber 1959, pp. 10–13, 44–5; Graf 1969, p. 199; Hecht 1980, pp. 27–8; Schupbach 1982, pp. 28–9, 43; Dudok van Heel et al. 1991, pp. 111, 164, 166–7; The Hague 1998–9, pp. 24, 75

NOTES

1 As mentioned by Six 1886, p. 95; see also note 3.
2 See Moes 1897–1905, vol. 2, p. 485, nos 8113/1–10; Dudok van Heel et al. 1991.
3 On the basis of the age reference on the painting of Tulp, who was born on 9 October 1593, the painting can be dated to the end of 1633 or 1634 (see also note 1).
4 See Amsterdams Historisch Museum 1979, pp. 103–4, no. 138; The Hague 1998–9, pp. 14–15 and fig. 8.
5 Tulp ed. 1991, p. 282. The little girl suffered from an abscess caused by a rib undergoing mortification, which would claim her life at an early age.
6 Dudok van Heel et al. 1991, p. 166.
7 Ibid., p. 111.
8 See the family tree in ibid., p. 85.

9 On the motto see Graf 1969.
10 Hecht 1980, pp. 27–8.
11 See Lipp/Gruber 1959.
12 The Hague 1997–8, pp. 76–8; for the Dutch edition of the books published in Latin, see Tulp ed. 1991.
13 See e.g. Delft 2002–3, figs 50, 83 and 90.
14 H. Houtzager in ibid., p. 90.

47 Nicolaes Eliasz Pickenoy

Portrait of Cornelis de Graeff, 1636
Gemäldegalerie, Staatliche Museen, Berlin
London only

48 Nicolaes Eliasz Pickenoy

Portrait of Catharina Hooft, 1636
Gemäldegalerie, Staatliche Museen, Berlin
London only

PROVENANCE

Inventory of the estate of Catharina de Graeff, née Hooft, Huis Ilpenstein, 1691; by descent in the family via Pieter de Graeff, Catharina's son, from 1691; sale Huis Ilpenstein, Amsterdam, 3 December 1872, nos 33–4, as 'Theodoor de Keyser' (to Roos for Suermondt); Barthold Suermondt, Aachen, 1872–4; acquired with the Suermondt Collection for the Königliches Museum, Berlin, 1874; inv. nos 753 A–B

SELECT BIBLIOGRAPHY

I. Geismeier in Gemäldegalerie 1998, pp. 246–7; S.A.C. Dudok van Heel in Amsterdam 2002–3, pp. 50, 118–19, nos 21a–b; Dudok van Heel 2006, pp. 336–7, 345–9

NOTES

1 Scheepvaartmuseum, Amsterdam; E. de Jongh in Haarlem 1986, pp. 137–40, no. 23; Prud'homme van Reine et al. 1992, pp. 786–7, nos I-15/16.
2 The date 1636, inscribed on old labels on the back of the portraits, is probably based on information known within the family.
3 Private collection, Canada; Amsterdam 2002–3, p. 54, figs 68a–b; Dudok van Heel 2006, figs 153–4.
4 Dudok van Heel in Amsterdam 2002–3, pp. 46–63; Dudok van Heel 2006, pp. 315–71.
5 Dudok van Heel in Amsterdam 2002–3, p. 56, nos 1–10; Dudok van Heel 2006, p. 345.
6 Town hall, Delft; Amsterdam 2002–3, pp. 50–1, figs 61a–b, 63a–b; Dudok van Heel 2006, figs 163–4, 177, 179. The whereabouts of the portraits of Overlander and Hooft that are attributed to Van der Voort are unknown.
7 Staatliche Kunstsammlungen, Kassel; Amsterdam 2002–3, p. 55, fig. 69; Dudok van Heel 2006, fig. 145.
8 Private collection; Amsterdam 2002–3, p. 51, figs 62a–b; Dudok van Heel 2006, figs 161–2.
9 Formerly Johnny van Haeften Gallery, London; Amsterdam 2002–3, p. 47, figs 56a–b; Dudok van Heel 2006, figs 155–6.
10 Dudok van Heel in Amsterdam 2002–3, p. 50; Dudok van Heel 2006, p. 337. Interestingly, in the portrait of De Graeff painted in 1633 to mark his first marriage (see note 1), this physical deformity was corrected.
11 Dudok van Heel in Amsterdam 2002–3, p. 50; *Corpus*, vol. 2 (1986), nos A 100–1.

49 Jan van Ravesteyn

Portrait of Hugo Grotius, 1599
Frits Lugt Collection, Institut Néerlandais, Paris

PROVENANCE

Moritz Binder, Berlin (acquired from the Eckhart Collection); Frits Lugt, Maartensdijk and Paris, acquired on 2 March 1918; inv. no. 175

SELECT BIBLIOGRAPHY

S. Nihom-Nijstad in Paris 1983, pp. 110–12, no. 57; A. van Suchtelen in Amsterdam 1993–4, pp. 399–400, no. 54; W.T. Kloek in ibid., p. 31; H. Buijs in The Hague 2002, pp. 146–9, no. 26 (with literature)

NOTES

1 Amsterdam 1993–4.
2 Van Beresteyn 1929, no. 5; Buijs in The Hague 2002, p. 149 and fig. 26c. For remarks supplemental to Van Beresteyn 1929, see Ekkart 2005.
3 Van Suchtelen in Amsterdam 1993–4, p. 400. For Pietersz, see also Mauritshuis 2004, no. 44; see also Bruyn 1990.
4 Van Suchtelen 1997; Q. Buvelot and G. Sluiter in Mauritshuis 2004, pp. 300–1, ill.
5 Buijs in The Hague 2002, pp. 149, 215–16, note 17.
6 See The Hague 2002, p. 215, note 6 (with references to the literature).
7 M. Schapelhouman in Amsterdam 1993–4, no. 53 Filedt Kok/Leesberg 2000, vol. 2, no. 246; The Hague 2002, figs 26a–26b.
8 Buijsen et al. 1998, pp. 230–7; G. Sluiter in Mauritshuis 2004, no. 45.

50 Jan van Ravesteyn

The Officers and Guardsmen of the Orange Company of The Hague on the Steps of the Town Hall, 1616
Haags Historisch Museum, The Hague
The Hague only

PROVENANCE

Sint-Sebastiaansdoelen, Korte Vijverberg, The Hague; transferred after 1772 to the town hall, The Hague; Gemeentemuseum, The Hague; since 1991 in the Haags Historisch Museum; inv. no. SCH-0000-0024

SELECT BIBLIOGRAPHY

Van Gool 1750–1, vol. 1, p. 17; Vosmaer 1860, p. 202; The Hague 1870, pp. 8–9, no. 13; Bredius 1881, pp. 306–7; Lafenestre/Richtenberger 1898, p. 133, no. 177; Servaas van Rooyen 1909, pp. 19–21, 25, 28, no. 8; R. Ekkart in Haarlem 1988, pp. 132–3; R. Ekkart & C. Vermeeren in Buijsen et al. 1998, pp. 66, 69, 232–3

NOTES

1 See Van Lit/Pluijmen 1989, pp. 8–47.
2 See P. Knevel in Haarlem 1988, p. 40.
3 *The Hague Magistracy Receiving the Officers of the St Sebastian Civic Guard*, 1618; *The Hague Magistracy Deliberating about the Renovation of the Headquarters of the St Sebastian Civic Guard*, 1636; *Six Officers of the White Ensign*, 1638. In 1612 Van Ravesteyn made a group portrait of the officers of St George's Company (all in Haags Historisch Museum, The Hague); see Buijsen et al. 1998, p. 65, fig. 10; pp. 68–9, figs 13–14; pp. 234–5, fig. 5.
4 Self-portraits are quite common in militia pieces; see Ekkart in Haarlem 1988, p. 134, fig. 109.
5 Lafenestre/Richtenberger 1898, p. 133; see Vosmaer 1860, p. 202 and The Hague 1870, pp. 8–9. The self-portrait corresponds to the portrait that Anthony van Dyck made of Van Ravesteyn around 1631–2 (see Barnes et al. 2004, pp. 370–1, fig. III.160).
6 Martin 1923–4, pp. 193, 195, 197.
7 The columns on the steps are no longer present; see Dumas 1991, pp. 531–5.
8 Stedelijk Museum Het Prinsenhof, Delft; Haarlem 1988, p. 364, no. 184.
9 As late as 1772, when an inventory was drawn up of the company's property, it hung 'above the mantelpiece'; see Bredius 1881, p. 306.
10 He is again depicted as captain of the Orange Company in the painting from 1618; see Martin 1923–4, pp. 194, 197.
11 The Orange Company's new ensign was depicted in this pose in 1617 by Evert van der Maes (see Buijsen et al. 1998, p. 203, fig. 4).

51 Rembrandt

Portrait of Joris de Caulerij, 1632
Fine Arts Museums of San Francisco (Roscoe and Margaret Oakes Collection)

PROVENANCE

Bequeathed by Joris de Caulerij to his daughter, Josina de Caulerij, The Hague, 1661; by inheritance to her daughter, Sara de Caulerij, The Hague, 1712; by inheritance to her relative, George van der Poel, The Hague, 1722–50; possibly sale Frankfurt am Main, 29 October 1770, no. 70 and sale Georg Bögner, Frankfurt am Main, 28 September 1778, no. 55; Stortenbeker collection, The Hague, 1867; J.H.J. Quarles van Ufford, The Hague, 1881–90; Abraham Preyer, dealer, Amsterdam, 1890; sold to Charles T. Yerkes, Chicago, 1890–1905 (sale New York, 5–8 April 1910, no. 84); Jacques Seligmann Gallery, Paris and New York, 1910–15; G. Rasmussen, Chicago, 1924; John Levy Gallery, New York, 1937; Edwin D. Levinson, New York, 1937–54; by inheritance to his daughters, Edna and Evelyn Levinson, New York, 1954–5; Knoedler and Co., New York, 1955; Roscoe and Margaret Oakes, San Francisco, 1955; on loan to the M.H. de Young Memorial Museum (since 1972 Fine Arts Museums of San Francisco), 1955; gift from the couple to the museum, 1966; inv. no. 66.31

SELECT BIBLIOGRAPHY

Bredius/Gerson 1969, no. 170; *Corpus*, vol. 2, pp. 199–205, no. A 53; B. Broos in The Hague-San Francisco 1990–1, pp. 369–75, no. 50 (with full bibliography); T. Dibbits in Amsterdam 2006, pp. 94–5, no. 20; J. van der Veen in London-Amsterdam 2006, pp. 135–6

NOTES

1 S. Dudok van Heel in Vienna 2004, p. 17.
2 For biographical particulars, see Broos in The Hague-San Francisco 1990–1, pp. 370–5.
3 Bredius 1893, p. 128; Strauss/Van der Meulen 1979, pp. 313–15, no. 1654/9; see also Van der Veen in London-Amsterdam 2006, p. 135.
4 Strauss/Van der Meulen 1979, p. 490, no. 1661/7; *Corpus*, vol. 2, pp. 204–5.
5 A portrait of a man by Van Uyttenbrouck from 1633 is believed to be a portrait of De Caulerij in his youth (see *Corpus*, vol. 2, p. 204 and fig. 5; Broos in The Hague-San Francisco 1990–1, p. 372 and fig. 2).
6 Bredius 1893, p. 128; Strauss/Van der Meulen 1979, p. 490, no. 1661/7; Broos in The Hague-San Francisco 1990–1, pp. 373, 375, note 19.
7 Schwartz 1984, p. 69; C. Vermeeren in Buijsen et al. 1998, p. 70; for the paintings that Rembrandt made for the court, see The Hague 1997–8, nos 21–3.
8 Van der Veen in London-Amsterdam 2006, pp. 135–6. The portrait of De Caulerij's son was probably not made until after 1654.
9 See The Hague 1997–8, nos 5, 17.
10 Such as *Man in Oriental Costume*, also from 1632 (The Metropolitan Museum of Art, New York); *Corpus*, vol. 2, p. 204.
11 Dibbits in Amsterdam 2006, p. 94.

52 **Rembrandt**

Portrait of Aeltje Uylenburgh, 1632

Private collection (on loan to the Mauritshuis, The Hague)

The Hague only

PROVENANCE

Probably by inheritance to Cornelis Sylvius, Amsterdam, 1644 (see text); William Coesvelt, London; put up for auction in London, 2 May 1828, no. 37 (not sold); John Smith, dealer, London; sold by him to Albertus Brondgeest, Amsterdam, 1835; Baron Alphonse de Rothschild, Paris, until 1905; by inheritance to Baron Edouard de Rothschild, Paris, until 1949; by inheritance to Baroness Bathsheva de Rothschild, Tel Aviv (sale London, Christie's, 13 December 2000, no. 52); Noortman Master Paintings, Maastricht, 2000–5; private collection; on loan to the Mauritshuis, The Hague, since 2005

SELECT BIBLIOGRAPHY

Bredius/Gerson 1969, no. 333; *Corpus*, vol. 2, no. A 63; J. van der Veen in sale catalogue London, Christie's, 13 December 2000, pp. 132–7, no. 52; J. Lloyd Williams in Edinburgh-London 2001, pp. 86–7, no. 18; M. Westermann in Newark-Denver 2001–2, p. 181, no. 56a; J. Giltaij in Frankfurt am Main 2003, pp. 76–9, no. 12; M. Bisanz-Prakken in Vienna 2004, pp. 192–3, no. 80; Buvelot 2005; E. Schavemaker in Noortman 2005, pp. 320–3, no. 95; Dudok van Heel 2006, p. 257; London-Amsterdam 2006, pp. 139–40 and fig. 81

NOTES

1 Sale catalogue London, Christie's, 13 December 2000, pp. 132–7, no. 52; Edinburgh-London 2001, p. 86.
2 For the relations between Sylvius, Aeltje Uylenburgh and Rembrandt, see Strauss/Van der Meulen 1979, pp. 107, 110, 124, 155, 209, 250–2.
3 'Twee contrefeytsels van zijn heer testateurs vader en moeder saliger door Rembran[d]t van Rijn geschildert'; see note 1.
4 Bartsch 266, 280.
5 Bredius/Gerson 1969, no. 160; *Corpus*, vol. 2, no. A 59. For the presumed pendant to this painting, see ibid., no. A 62.
6 See *Corpus*, vol. 2, no. A 55; Edinburgh-London 2001, no. 17.
7 Frankfurt am Main 2003, p. 76.
8 London-Amsterdam 2006.

53 **Rembrandt**

The Anatomy Lesson of Dr Nicolaes Tulp, 1632

Royal Picture Gallery Mauritshuis, The Hague

PROVENANCE

Surgeons' guild, Sint-Anthoniswaag, Amsterdam, 1632–1798; after the dissolution of the surgeons' guild in 1798 transferred to the Surgeons' Widows' Fund, Sint-Anthoniswaag, Amsterdam, 1798–1828; the public sale of the painting by the Surgeons' Widows' Fund planned for 4 August 1828 was prohibited by Royal Decree of 19 July 1828; acquired by the State of the Netherlands and transferred to the Mauritshuis by order of King William I, 1828; inv. no. 146

SELECT BIBLIOGRAPHY

Bredius/Gerson 1969, no. 403; Schupbach 1982; *Corpus*, vol. 2 (1986), pp. 172–89, no. A 51; B. Broos in Mauritshuis 1987, pp. 277–88, no. 48; N. Middelkoop et al. in The Hague 1998–9; B. Broos in Mauritshuis 2004, pp. 205–10, no. 47 (with full bibliography); McNeil Kettering 2006, pp. 12–19; Runia/Van Suchtelen 2006, pp. 40–7

NOTES

1 Middelkoop in The Hague 1998–9, p. 9.
2 See ibid., pp. 75–8; Dudok van Heel et al. 1991, pp. 41–115.
3 Broos in Mauritshuis 2004, pp. 208, 209 note 27.
4 Middelkoop in The Hague 1998–9, pp. 9–38 and figs 1, 7–8.
5 See ibid., p. 20.
6 P. Noble and J. Wadum in ibid., p. 67.
7 Ibid., p. 56 and fig. 12, pp. 62–3 and fig. 26;
8 Broos in Mauritshuis 2004, pp. 207–8 and fig. 47c.
9 Middelkoop in The Hague 1998–9, p. 21.
10 Ibid., p. 20.
11 Ibid., p. 22; Heckscher 1958, pp. 65–76.
12 The Hague 1998–9, p. 21.
13 Ibid., pp. 68–9 and figs 38–9.
14 Noble and Wadum in ibid., p. 68.
15 Middelkoop in ibid., p. 24.
16 Ibid., pp. 25–6 and figs 16–18; Berlin-Amsterdam-London 1991–2, no. 44; Bredius/Gerson 1969, no. 414.
17 Broos in The Hague 1998–9, pp. 43–5.

54 **Rembrandt**

Double Portrait of Jan Rijcksen and Griet Jans, 1633

The Royal Collection, London

PROVENANCE

By inheritance via the sitters to their son, Cornelis Jansz Rijcks (described in his probate inventory, 7 November 1659); in 1659 probably by inheritance to his niece, Griet Willemsdr van Muy(d)en, the sitters' granddaughter, who died in 1672; Jan Gildemeester, Amsterdam (sale Amsterdam, 11–13 June 1800, no. 180, for 8050 guilders to Jan Spaan); Pieter, Baron de Smeth van Alphen, Amsterdam (sale Amsterdam, 1–2 August 1810, no. 82, for 16,500 guilders to Lafontaine); Lafontaine Gallery (put up for auction in London, Christie's, 12 June 1811, no. 63); sold before the auction for 5,000 guineas to Lord Yarmouth for the Prince of Wales, who would become King George IV, June 1811; London, Buckingham Palace; inv. no. RCIN 405533

SELECT BIBLIOGRAPHY

Bredius/Gerson 1969, no. 408; C. White in Royal Collection 1982, pp. 104–5, no. 160; *Corpus*, vol. 2, pp. 367–7, no. A 77

NOTES

1 See Münz 1947; White in Royal Collection 1982, p. 105; *Corpus*, vol. 2, pp. 367, 372–3, 376, 377; Van de Wetering 1997, p. 115, figs 144–5. From the absence of cusping along the top of the painting we may infer that the painting was cut down along the upper edge.

2 A double portrait that Rembrandt painted before 1640 of Jan Pietersz Bruyningh and his wife, mentioned in archival documents, has been lost (see Strauss/Van der Meulen 1979, p. 669, no. 1647/1a; P. van Thiel in Berlin-Amsterdam-London 1991–2, p. 224). The composition of this painting is not known.

3 Amsterdam 1969, p. 34; White in Royal Collection 1982, p. 104.

4 With thanks to Marieke de Winkel for providing this detail.

5 See Münz 1947, p. 253; *Corpus*, vol. 2, p. 372.

6 See J.B. Bedaux in Amsterdam 2002–3, pp. 70, 72.

7 See Dublin-Greenwich 2003–4.

8 Bredius/Gerson 1969, no. 409; *Corpus*, vol. 3, no. A 143; P. van Thiel in Berlin-Amsterdam-London 1991–2, no. 33 (with bibliography); J. Kelch in Gemäldegalerie 1998, pp. 252–5.

9 See Van Eeghen 1970. For Rijcksen, see also Parthesius 2007, pp. 62–3.

10 Bredius 1908b, p. 224: '[E]en schilderije van des overledens vader en moeder geschildert door Rembrant'; Strauss/Van der Meulen 1979, p. 440, no. 1659/10; *Corpus*, vol. 2, pp. 373–4.

11 C. Lloyd in Royal Collection 1999, p. 54; C. Lloyd in Edinburgh-London 2004–5, p. 35.

55 Rembrandt

Portrait of Aechje Claesdr, 1634
The National Gallery, London

PROVENANCE

Probably sale Klaas van Winkel et al., Rotterdam, 20–1 October 1791, no. 6; Cornelis Roos, dealer, Amsterdam, 1814; chevalier Sébastien Erard, Passy, near Paris (sale Paris, 7–14 August 1832, no. 121, for 4,000 francs; sale London, 22 June 1833, no. 16, bought for 210 guineas); William Wells of Redleaf, London, by 1835 (sale London, 12–13 May 1848, no. 115, for £252 to Eastlake); Sir Charles L. Eastlake, London; purchased from his widow, Lady Eastlake, 1867; inv. no. NG 775

SELECT BIBLIOGRAPHY

Bredius/Gerson 1969, no. 343; *Corpus*, vol. 2 (1986), pp. 571–7, no. A 104; D. Bomford et al. in London 1988–9, pp. 48–51, no. 3; N. MacLaren & C. Brown in National Gallery 1991, vol. 1, pp. 341–3, no. 775; P. van Thiel in Berlin-Amsterdam-London 1991–2, vol. 1, pp. 176–7, no. 19; Dudok van Heel 1992; Giltaij 1992; Dudok van Heel 1994, p. 337; B. Schnackenburg in Kassel-Amsterdam 2001–2, pp. 380–1, no. 83; E. de la Fuente Pedersen in Copenhagen 2006, pp 182–3, no. 7; Schwartz 2006, p. 90, fig. 161; Bomford et al. 2006, pp. 70–4, no. 3

NOTES

1 *Corpus*, vol. 2 (1986), no. A 52.

2 Berlin-Amsterdam-London 1991–2, vol. 1, p. 176.

3 Sepia and wash drawing, see Hind 1915–31, vol. 4, pp. 173–4, no. 3; for the print see Charrington 1923, no. 165; also in *Corpus*, vol. 2, 1986, pp. 576–7, no. A 104, and Wuestman 2006, p. 69 and fig. 14.

4 Waagen 1854, vol. 3, p. 311.

5 Dudok van Heel 1992; Dudok van Heel 1994, p. 337.

6 *Corpus*, vol. 2 (1986), nos A 102–3. The portrait of Pesser is in the Los Angeles County Museum of Art.

7 Rijksmuseum, Amsterdam; ibid, no. A 80; see also Amsterdam 2000, no. 59.

8 Dudok van Heel 1992, p. 15; Schnackenburg in Kassel-Amsterdam 2001–2, p. 380.

56 Rembrandt

Portrait of Andries de Graeff, 1639
Gemäldegalerie Alte Meister, Staatliche Museen, Kassel
The Hague only

PROVENANCE

Gerhard Morell, dealer, Hamburg; acquired from him by Landgrave Wilhelm VIII of Hessen-Kassel, 11 March 1752; seized by Jerôme Bonaparte, brother of Napoleon I, 1806; returned to Kassel in 1814; inv. no. GK 239

SELECT BIBLIOGRAPHY

Bredius/Gerson 1969, no. 216; Dudok van Heel 1969; *Corpus*, vol. 3 (1989), pp. 297–304, no. A 129; P. van Thiel in Berlin-Amsterdam-London 1991–2, pp. 210–11, no. 29; B. Schnackenburg in Gemäldegalerie Kassel 1996, vol. 1, pp. 232 and 241, no. GK 239; S. Dudok van Heel in Amsterdam 2002–3, pp. 54–5; J. Giltaij in Frankfurt am Main 2003, pp. 134–7, no. 27; B.W. Lindemann in Berlin 2006, pp. 294–5, no. 28; G. Weber in Kassel 2006, pp. 195–201, no. 27

NOTES

1 First published by S. Dudok van Heel; see Dudok van Heel 1969.

2 Strauss/Van der Meulen 1979, p. 451, no. 1659/21.

3 *Corpus*, vol 3, p. 302.

4 See ibid., pp. 302–4; Giltaij in Frankfurt am Main 2003, pp. 134–7; Weber in Kassel 2006, pp. 195–210.

5 For the possible significance of the glove, see Van Thiel in Berlin-Amsterdam-London 1991–2, p. 210; Giltaij in Frankfurt am Main 2003, p. 134; Lindemann in Berlin 2006, p. 294.

57 Rembrandt

Portrait of Jan Six, 1654
Six Collection, Amsterdam
The Hague only

PROVENANCE

Jan Six, Amsterdam, 1654; by direct inheritance in the Six family; under the ownership of the Six Foundation from 1922, inv. no. 00070

SELECT BIBLIOGRAPHY

Bredius/Gerson 1969, no. 276; Haak 1984, pp. 354–5; De Jongh 1985, pp. 65–8; Freedman 1985, pp. 89–105; Smith 1988; Schama 1999, pp. 572–81; Berger 2000, pp. 108–9, 309–15; Six 2001, pp. 25, 27; De Winkel 2006, pp. 92–132

NOTES

1 Haak 1969, p. 247.
2 Pandora Album, Six Collection, Amsterdam, fol. 410; see Strauss/Van der Meulen 1979, p. 322, no. 1654/21; De Winkel 2006, p. 98.
3 On the family business, see Zandvliet 2006, pp. 290–2; for the portrait of Wijmer that has recently been reattributed to Rembrandt and his studio, see Bredius/Gerson 1969, no. 358; *Corpus*, vol. 3, no. C 113.
4 See cat. 2, note 4.
5 For more biographical information and a survey of the literature on this subject, see De Winkel 2006, pp. 94–5 and 289–90, notes 6–20.
6 De Winkel 2006, pp. 97, 290, note 23.
7 Strauss/Van der Meulen 1979, p. 289, no. 1652/7.
8 De Winkel 2006, p. 97.
9 Ibid., p. 302, no. 1653/11.
10 See M. Royalton-Kisch in Amsterdam-London 2000–1, pp. 235–43, no. 57.
11 Castiglione 1528.
12 For this term see Smith 1988, pp. 44–5; De Winkel 2006, pp. 122–30.
13 De Winkel 2006, pp. 120, 298, note 150.
14 Published by Lambert van den Bosch, Amsterdam, 1662. For the commission, see De Winkel 2006, pp. 120, 298, note 151 In 1651 Six published *Zede-Wetten*, a series of short poems which are likewise imbued with these views; see De Winkel 2006, pp. 120, 298, note 149.
15 Van de Wetering 1997, p. 162.
16 Freedman 1985, p. 101.
17 De Winkel 2006, pp. 92–132; this chapter is entitled 'A gentleman in a grey riding coat'.

58 Rembrandt

Portrait of Jacob Trip, about 1661
The National Gallery, London

59 Rembrandt

Portrait of Margaretha de Geer, about 1661
The National Gallery, London

PROVENANCE

Both paintings were possibly in the possession of the family of Baptist Lee (1690–1768) in the eighteenth century; the Lee family property was inherited by Sir William Fowle Middelton-Fowle, 2nd Baronet, by 1837; by inheritance to his nephew, Sir George Nathaniel Broke-Middelton, Baronet; thence to his great-niece, Lady de Saumarez, 1887; purchased from Lady de Saumarez, 1899 (with the aid of gifts from J.P. Heseltine and Alfred C. Rothschild); inv. nos NG 1674–1675

SELECT BIBLIOGRAPHY

Bredius/Gerson 1969, no. 314; Dudok van Heel 1979, pp. 14–26; Meischke/Reeser 1983; D. Bomford et al. in London 1988–9, pp. 120–5, no. 16; N. MacLaren & C. Brown in National Gallery 1991, vol. 1, pp. 350–3, nos 1674–5; J. Lloyd Williams in Edinburgh-London 2001, pp. 234–5, no. 137; Schwartz 2006, pp. 183–4; Bomford et al. 2006, pp. 166–77, nos 17–18

NOTES

1 His date of birth is uncertain; see Dudok van Heel 1979, p. 15 and B. Broos in Mauritshuis 2004, p. 149 and note 5.
2 Broos in Mauritshuis 2004, p. 149.
3 For more on Louis de Geer, see Dahlgren 1923; Van der Ham 2005.
4 For more on the Trip family see Klein 1965; on the Trippenhuis, see Meischke/Reeser 1983.
5 Dickey 1995, p. 354; quoted in Edinburgh-London 2001, p. 234.
6 Lloyd Williams in Edinburgh-London 2001, p. 234.
7 Dudok van Heel 1979, pp. 19–26.
8 Dickey 1995, pp. 354–5.
9 See National Gallery 1991, vol. 1, p. 351, note 5.
10 See ibid., p. 351, note 6; Lloyd Williams in Edinburgh-London 2001, p. 234 and note 5.
11 Private collection, New York; see National Gallery 1991, vol. 1, p. 351, note 4, for a further pair of portraits by Jacob Cuyp.
12 See *Corpus*, vol. 3 (1989), nos A 131–2; Lloyd Williams in Edinburgh-London 2001, no. 35.

60 Rembrandt

Portrait of the Syndics of the Clothmakers' Guild ('De Staalmeesters'), 1662
Rijksmuseum, Amsterdam
London only

PROVENANCE

Hung in the Staalhof, Staalstraat, Amsterdam, in 1662; transferred to the gallery of the town hall, Amsterdam, 1771; Koninklijk Museum, Amsterdam, 1815; in the Rijksmuseum since 1885, on loan from the city of Amsterdam; inv. no. SK-C-6

SELECT BIBLIOGRAPHY

Van Schendel 1956; Van de Waal 1956; Van Eeghen 1957; Van Eeghen 1958a; Bredius/Gerson 1969, no. 415; C. Brown in Berlin-Amsterdam-London 1991–2, pp. 278–83, no. 48; Amsterdam 2000, pp. 213–14, 310, no. 147; W. Kloek in Rijksmuseum 2001, pp. 200–1, no. 81; McNeil Kettering 2006, pp. 37–43

NOTES

1 See Riegl 1931; for a discussion of these three works, see McNeil Kettering 2006.
2 According to common etiquette around 1660, members of the lower classes were required to remove their hats in the presence of their superiors (see cat. 34 and De Winkel 2006, pp. 160, 307, note 96). See also Van Schendel 1956, p. 7, note 6.
3 Gerson 1968, p. 504; Brown in Berlin-Amsterdam-London 1991–2, p. 278.
4 See Van de Waal 1956, p. 72.
5 See Van Schendel 1956; see also Brown in Berlin-Amsterdam-London 1991–2, p. 282 and fig. 48d.
6 Benesch 1973, vol. 5, pp. 314–15, nos 1178–80 and figs 1476–8; see Van Schendel 1956, figs 3–5 and Brown in Berlin-Amsterdam-London 1991–2, figs 48a–c.
7 See also Van de Wetering 1997, p. 256.
8 Van de Waal 1956, pp. 98–100 and figs 22–3; see also De Jongh 1967, pp. 63–4 and figs 47–8.
9 Brown in Berlin-Amsterdam-London 1991–2, p. 283, note 1; see also Van Eeghen 1957, p. 69.
10 Six 1896; further elaborated by Van Eeghen 1957, pp. 70–80 and Van Eeghen 1958a.
11 Van Eeghen 1957, p. 80. Jansz's religion can be deduced from his clothing and hairstyle: he is the only one of the group to have short hair and he has no cuffs, as was customary among Mennonites.
12 Van Eeghen 1957, p. 69; Brown in Berlin-Amsterdam-London 1991–2, p. 278.
13 See Van de Waal 1956, p. 65, fig. 1, p. 67, note 11; Schwartz 2006, p. 176, fig. 300.
14 See Six 1896, p. 65 and Kloek in Rijksmuseum 2001, p. 200. According to McNeil Kettering (2006, p. 38), however, this painting hung in a different room of the building.
15 See Van de Wetering 1997, figs 240–2, 252–3, 299.
16 See ibid., pp. 241, 259.
17 Ibid., p. 258.
18 For the legends that later developed around the scene in this painting, see Van de Waal 1956; see also J.B. Bedaux in Amsterdam 2002–3, pp. 75–9.
19 Wagenaar 1760–68, vol. 2 (1765), p. 42: 'In dit vertrek hangen zes schilderyen van waardyns der zestiende en zeventiende eeuwe. In ieder deezer stukken, zyn vyf Waardyns, zittende, en de knegt van 't Staalhof staande, verbeeld'; Six 1896, p. 65.

61 Rembrandt

Portrait of an Elderly Man, 1667
Royal Picture Gallery Mauritshuis, The Hague

PROVENANCE

Probably Sir John Rawdon, London, 1744; Robert Bragge, dealer, London; Sampson Gideon, Belvedere House, Erith, Kent, 1761; by inheritance to Sir Francis Edward Fremantle, 1919; sold to Agnew's, London; Lord Cowdray, 1919; The Trustees of the Cowdray Estate; acquired by the Mauritshuis in 1999 with the support of the Friends of the Mauritshuis Foundation, Ministry of Education, Culture and Science, the National Art Collections Fund, the Sponsor Lottery, the VSB Fund for The Hague and environs, the Rembrandt Society, the Prince Bernhard Culture Fund, the ING Group, Prof. A.C.R. Dreesmann, the Dr Hendrik Muller National Fund and private benefactors; inv. no. 1118

SELECT BIBLIOGRAPHY

Bredius/Gerson 1969, no. 323A; C. Brown in Berlin-Amsterdam-London 1991–2, vol. 1, p. 288; Van de Wetering 1997, pp. 205–7; A. Blankert and M. Blokhuis in Melbourne-Canberra 1997–8, pp. 183–7, no. 28; F. Duparc in Mauritshuis 2004, pp. 215–20, no. 49 (with full bibliography); Copenhagen 2006, pp. 65, 66, 67 and fig. 5

NOTES

1 Canvas, 109 × 93 cm; National Gallery of Victoria, Melbourne (Bredius/Gerson 1969, no. 323; Melbourne-Canberra 1997–8, no. 27).
2 *Corpus*, vol. 4, nos 27–9; London-The Hague 1999–2000, nos 84–6.
3 See Van de Wetering 1997, pp. 205–7 and figs 267–9.
4 E. van de Wetering in London-The Hague 1999–2000, p. 35; Houbraken 1718–21, vol. 1, p. 269: 'dat een stuk voldaan is als de meester zyn voornemen daar in bereikt heeft'.
5 Hals too portrayed men wearing a lopsided hat; see Slive 1970–4, vol. 3, nos 217–18, 221.
6 For the portrait of De Lairesse, see Bredius/Gerson 1969, no. 321; New York 1995–6, vol. 2, no. 19.
7 Duparc in Mauritshuis 2004, p. 219.
8 Strauss/Van der Meulen 1979, p. 499, no. 1662/6; Mauritshuis 2004, p. 220, note 33.

62 Jan Steen

Portrait of Bernardina van Raesfelt, 1660

Royal Picture Gallery Mauritshuis, The Hague

PROVENANCE

Anna van den Bongard, Lokhorst Castle, until 1663; Bernardina van Raesfelt, Warmond House and Meerenburgh House, Lisse, until 1681; by inheritance to her son Thomas Walraven van Wassenaer-Alckemade, Meerenburgh House, Lisse, 1681–1726; heirs of Van Wassenaer (sold through the dealer Philip van der Schleij to Stadholder William V, 18 January 1769); Stadholder William V, The Hague, 1769–95; seized by the French, transferred to the Musée Napoléon (Musée du Louvre), Paris, 1795–1815; Royal Picture Gallery, housed in the Picture Gallery of Prince William V, The Hague, 1816; transferred to the Mauritshuis, 1822; inv. no. 166

SELECT BIBLIOGRAPHY

De Vries 1977, pp. 39, 47–8, 128–9, note 76, p. 160, no. 79; Braun 1980, pp. 16, 31–2, 83, 100–1, no. 113; B. Broos in Paris 1986, pp. 318–22, no. 46; B. Broos in Mauritshuis 1987, pp. 350–4, no. 58; W. Kloek in Washington-Amsterdam 1996–7, pp. 135–8, no. 12; B. Broos in Mauritshuis 2004, pp. 248–52, no. 56 (with full bibliography)

NOTES

1 Broos in Mauritshuis 2004, no. 18.
2 Washington-Amsterdam 1996–7, nos 7, 8. For the new identification of the portrait from 1655, see Grijzenhout/Van Sas 2006.
3 Ibid., nos 29A–B and p. 193, figs 1–2.
4 Fockema Andreae et al. 1974, pp. 79–80; see also Van der Wyck/Niemeijer 1989, p. 130, fig. 111. The drawing is after a composition by Roelant Roghman.
5 For the arch-shaped entrance, Steen may have drawn inspiration from the building with an archway near the castle; see Kloek in Washington-Amsterdam 1996–7, p. 136 and fig. 2.
6 The Hague 1958–9, no. 13; De Vries 1967, p. 61a; De Vries 1976, p. 128, note 76; Broos in Mauritshuis 2004, pp. 249, 250.
7 Kloek in Washington-Amsterdam 1996–7, p. 135; Broos in Mauritshuis 2004, pp. 249–50.
8 See H.P. Chapman in Washington-Amsterdam 1996–7, pp. 119, 121.
9 In the men's faces, the brownish-black underdrawing has been left visible in parts of the shaded areas.
10 Ripa 1644, pp. 16 (adoption: crested birds), 98 (unity: a nest of chicks), 185 (benevolence: hen), 558, 560 (guardianship: pigeon and hen). These passages had already been linked to the painting by De Vries (1976, p. 28; 1977, pp. 47, 128–9, note 76); see also Broos in Mauritshuis 1987, pp. 353–4.
11 See Dominicus 1997, p. 25.
12 Mauritshuis 2004, p. 251 and fig. 56d; Kloek in Washington-Amsterdam 1996–7, p. 138, note 10.
13 De Vries 1976, p. 28; De Vries 1977, p. 47.

63 Abraham van den Tempel

Double Portrait of Jan van Amstel and Anna Boxhoorn, 1671

Museum Boijmans Van Beuningen, Rotterdam

PROVENANCE

Bequeathed by Anna Boxhoorn in 1726 to Maria van der Dussen, the granddaughter of her elder sister Mariken; the dealer Frans van Mieris the Younger, Leiden; sold by him in 1745 to Allard de la Court van der Voort, Leiden, 1745–55; by inheritance to Catharina Backer, the widow of De la Court van der Voort, Leiden, 1755–66 (sale Leiden, 8 September 1766, no. 6, to Van der Marck); Johan van der Marck, Amsterdam, 1766–70 (sale Amsterdam, 25 August 1773, no. 318, to Yver); Pieter Yver, dealer, Amsterdam; Prince Sigismond Radziwill, Russia (sale Paris, Drouot, 23 May 1865, no. 83, to Museum Boijmans); inv. no. 1352

SELECT BIBLIOGRAPHY

Wijnman 1959a, pp. 80–2; Wijnman 1959b; Lunsingh Scheurleer et al. 1986–92, vol. 2 (1987), pp. 349, 375, 450, no. 84; R. Ekkart in Museum Boijmans Van Beuningen 1995, pp. 188–9, no. 67; L. Wagenaar in Amsterdam 2002–3, pp. 216, 281, no. 30

NOTES

1 For Van Amstel's life, see Wijnman 1959b; Van der Velden 1997; Wagenaar in Amsterdam 2002–3, pp. 216, 281.
2 With thanks to Marieke de Winkel.
3 For black pages in paintings, see Otte 1987.
4 Ekkart in Museum Boijmans Van Beuningen 1995, p. 189. Portraits of Van Amstel and his wife made by Van den Tempel (current whereabouts unknown) were sold at auction in The Hague in 1807; see Wijnman 1959b, p. 106 and Amsterdam 2002–3, p. 281, note 1.
5 C. Vogelaar in Rotterdam–Frankfurt am Main 1999–2000, pp. 254, 258.
6 Ekkart in Museum Boijmans Van Beuningen 1995, p. 189.
7 Ibid.

64 Johannes Verspronck

Portrait of Andries Stilte as a Standard-Bearer, 1640

National Gallery of Art, Washington (Patrons' Permanent Fund)

PROVENANCE

Possibly Six Collection, Amsterdam; by inheritance to the Bijnen family, Breda (on loan to the Mauritshuis, The Hague, 1917–23, inv. no. 753); Jacques Goudstikker Gallery, Amsterdam; Catarina von Pannwitz, Bennebroek (Friedländer/Von Falke 1925–6, vol. 1, pp. 11–12, no. 54); private collection, Germany and New York; Otto Naumann Ltd., New York; Mr & Mrs Michal Hornstein, Montreal, 1988; sale New York, Sotheby's, 30 January 1998, no. 69; Bob P. Haboldt & Co., New

York; acquired by the museum, Patrons' Permanent Fund, 2 May 1998; inv. no. 1998.13.1

SELECT BIBLIOGRAPHY

Martin 1918, p. 216; Yapou 1976, pp. 42–3; Ekkart 1979, pp. 39, 40, 71, 78, no. 19; P.C. Sutton in The Hague-San Francisco 1990–1, p. 118; New York 1995, p. 8 and fig. 1; sale catalogue New York, Sotheby's, 30 January 1998, pp. 134–7, no. 69; Van der Ploeg 2000, pp. 12–13; L. Pearson Russell in Washington 2000–1, unnumbered

NOTES

1 See for example the standard-bearer on the far right in Hals's earliest known militia piece from 1616 (Frans Hals Museum, Haarlem); Slive 1970–4, no. 7; Haarlem 1988, no. 22.
2 In Haarlem, the kloveniers were known as *cluveniers* (see Haarlem 1988, p. 22).
3 Museu Nacional, Havanna; Ekkart 1979, p. 71, no. 6.
4 Ibid., pp. 40, 78.
5 Frans Hals Museum, Haarlem; ibid.
6 Columbus Museum of Art, Columbus, Ohio, inv. no. 81.003; ibid., p. 82, no. 26, ill.
7 With the exception of the 1641 portrait of a girl in Rijksmuseum, Amsterdam (ibid., no. 33).

65 Cornelis van der Voort

Family Group, 1620
Koninklijk Museum voor Schone Kunsten, Antwerp

PROVENANCE

Sale Munich, Helbing, 12 October 1909, no. 62; sale Löwe, Cologne, Lempertz, 5–6 November 1929, no. 439; A. Roeckerath, Cologne (sale Cologne, Lempertz, 18–20 October 1934, no. 51; gift of Artibus Patriae, 1935; inv. no. 996

SELECT BIBLIOGRAPHY

Greindl 1944, pp. 58, 126–7 and fig. 60 (as Cornelis de Vos); Hulst 1960, no. 1; Koninklijk Museum voor Schone Kunsten 1988, p. 401, no. 996; R. Ekkart in Stockholm 2001–2, p. 50 (as Van der Voort); R. Ekkart in Amsterdam 2002–3, p. 30 and fig. 31

NOTES

1 Laarmann 2002, pp. 11–14.
2 S. Kuus in Haarlem-Antwerp 2000–1, p. 79.
3 Examples in the literature include comparisons between ripe pears, representing maturity, and pears that are still green, denoting youth (see Cats 1618, no. XI). Here, the fruit could thus serve to emphasise the difference between the father's maturity and his small son's tender age.
4 Research has been conducted to ascertain whether the persons depicted correspond to members of the Van der Perre family of Amsterdam or to other families with names resembling 'pear', but without producing any results as yet.
5 Van der Stighelen 1990.
6 Ekkart in Stockholm 2001–2, p. 50. See for example the undated portraits of an unknown married couple (formerly in the Demidoff Collection, Florence; sale Brussels, 16 December 1929, no. 97; sale New York, Parke-Bernet, 26 May 1943, nos 77–8; Bernt 1969–70, nos 1331–2, ill.) and the likewise undated portrait of a young woman in the Sinebrychoff Taidemuseo, Helsinki (Helsinki 1994–5, p. 69, no. 34, ill.).
7 Koninklijke Musea 1984, p. 318, no. 3689, ill.; Zweite 1980, pp. 322–3, no. 113, fig. 142.

66 Emanuel de Witte

Portrait of Adriana van Heusden and her Daughter at the Fishmarket in Amsterdam, about 1662
The National Gallery, London

PROVENANCE

Probably painted for Joris de Wijs, Amsterdam; Laurens Mauritsz Doucy, by about 1664–5; sold by his son to Johannes Collaert, Amsterdam, 1667; this painting or a closely related composition in sale Prince de Conti, Paris, 8 April–6 June 1777, no. 334 and sale Paris, 15 March 1779, no. 139, for 122 francs to Dusquenoy (as Metsu); Pierre-Louis-Casimir Dusquesnoy de Moussy, Paris (sale Paris, 1–3 March 1803, no. 1, as J. Berckheyde, but with 'GM' signature); Thomas Henry, Paris (sale Paris, 23–5 May 1836, no. 52, as attributed to Pieter de Hooch, for 900 francs; probably also in [Louis Thielens of Brussels] sale, Paris, 27 March 1841, no. 26, for 800 francs); Charles Scarisbrick, London (sale London, 11 May 1861, no. 211, for 52 guineas to Seguier); said to have been in the Watson Taylor Collection at Erlestoke Park, near Devizes, from 1863, as Jan Steen (sale Erlestoke Park, November 1919, as Steen, for £1,600); Agnew's, London; purchased, 1922; inv. no. NG 3682

SELECT BIBLIOGRAPHY

Brière-Misme 1923, pp. 137, 148–50; Manke 1963, pp. 124–5, no. 222a; N. MacLaren & C. Brown in National Gallery 1991, vol. 1, pp. 489–92, no. 3682; Franits 1993, pp. 92, 95 and fig. 75; R. Ekkart in Amsterdam 2002–3, p. 38

NOTES

1 For detailed information on De Witte as a painter of church interiors, see Liedtke 1982; Liedtke in New York-London 2001, pp. 107–11; ibid., nos 91–3.
2 For a portrait by De Hooch, see New York-London 2001, no. 27.
3 Brière-Misme 1923, p. 148: 'Elle décèle, comme l'enfant qu'elle tient par la main, le caractère indéniable d'un portrait'; National Gallery 1991, vol. 1, p. 490: 'The housewife buying fish is obviously a portrait'.

4 Manke 1963, nos 221–31.

5 The figures on a painting dated 1672 in Museum Boijmans Van Beuningen, Rotterdam (ibid., no. 223) were wrongly considered as portraits; see F. Lammertse in Museum Boijmans Van Beuningen 1998, p. 202; E. de Jongh in Utrecht 2004, p. 345.

6 For a more comprehensive account of the story, see Brière-Misme 1923, pp. 148–50; National Gallery 1991, vol. 1, pp. 489–90.

7 There has been some discussion about the picture's attribution and as to whether it is the original, since another version, signed and dated 1662, came to light in 1923. Hofstede de Groot (1907–28, vol. 1, p. 554, no. 284) had listed the painting still within the section on Pieter de Hooch, and Manke (1963, p. 124, no. 222a and fig. 51) believed that the latter picture was the original and the present one the copy. It is now accepted, however, that the National Gallery's picture is the superior one and that the figures are indeed by De Witte (see National Gallery 1991, vol. 1, p. 490).

Bibliography

A

Adams 1985
A. Jensen Adams, *The Paintings of Thomas de Keyser (1596/7–1667): A Study of Portraiture in Seventeenth-Century Amsterdam* (diss.), 4 vols, Cambridge, Massachusetts 1985

Adams 1995
A. Jensen Adams, 'Thomas de Keyser's *Portrait of Six Gold- and Silver-smiths of 1627*: Friendship Portrait and Posthumous Tribute to Andries Fredericsz', in *Shop Talk: Studies in Honour of Seymour Slive*, ed. C.P. Schneider, Cambridge, Massachusetts 1995, pp. 28–32

Alte Pinakothek 2002
K. Renger, C. Denk, *Flämische Malerei des Barock in der Alten Pinakothek*, Munich-Cologne 2002

Alte Pinakothek 2005
M. Dekiert et al., *Alte Pinakothek: Ausgewählte Werke*, Munich-Cologne 2005

Amsterdam 1879
Catalogus der Vondel-Tentoonstelling, exh. cat., Arti et Amicitiæ, Amsterdam 1879

Amsterdam 1900
Catalogus der verzameling schilderijen en familieportretten van de heeren Jhr. P.H. Six van Vromade, Jhr. Dr. J. Six en Jhr. W. Six, exh. cat., Stedelijk Museum, Amsterdam 1900

Amsterdam 1952
J. Bruyn et al., *Drie eeuwen portret in Nederland 1500–1800*, exh. cat., Rijksmuseum, Amsterdam 1952

Amsterdam 1969
Rembrandt 1669/1969, exh. cat., ed. P.J.J. van Thiel, Rijksmuseum, Amsterdam 1969

Amsterdam 1976
E. de Jongh et al., *Tot lering en vermaak: Betekenissen van Hollandse genrevoorstellingen uit de zeventiende eeuw*, exh. cat., Rijksmuseum, Amsterdam 1976

Amsterdam 1984
P.J.J. van Thiel, C.J. de Bruyn Kops, *Prijst de lijst: De Hollandse schilderijlijst in de zeventiende eeuw*, exh. cat., Rijksmuseum, Amsterdam 1984 (see also Van Thiel/De Bruyn Kops 1995)

Amsterdam 1986
Art before the Iconoclasm: Northern Netherlandish Art 1525–1580, exh. cat., eds J.P. Filedt Kok, W. Halsema-Kubes, W.T. Kloek, Rijksmuseum, Amsterdam 1986

Amsterdam 1993–4
Dawn of the Golden Age: Northern Netherlandish art 1580–1620, exh. cat., eds G. Luijten, A. van Suchtelen, R. Baarsen et al., Rijksmuseum, Amsterdam 1993–4

Amsterdam 1995
K. Ottenheym, Q. Buvelot et al., *Jacob van Campen: Het klassieke ideaal in de Gouden Eeuw*, exh. cat., Koninklijk Paleis, Amsterdam 1995

Amsterdam 2000
The Glory of the Golden Age: Dutch Art of the 17th Century: Paintings, Sculpture and Decorative Art, exh. cat., eds B. Cornelis, J.P. Filedt Kok, Rijksmuseum, Amsterdam 2000

Amsterdam 2002–3
Kopstukken: Amsterdammers geportretteerd 1600–1800, exh. cat., ed. N. Middelkoop, Amsterdams Historisch Museum, Amsterdam 2002–3

Amsterdam 2006
D. Bull et al., *Rembrandt Caravaggio*, exh. cat., Van Gogh Museum, Amsterdam 2006

Amsterdam-London 2000–1
E. Hinterding, G. Luijten, M. Royalton-Kisch, *Rembrandt the Printmaker*, exh. cat., Rijksmuseum, Amsterdam, British Museum, London 2000–1

Amsterdams Historisch Museum 1979
A. Blankert, with contributions by R. Ruurs, *Amsterdams Historisch Museum: Schilderijen daterend van voor 1800. Voorlopige catalogus*, Amsterdam 1979

Antwerp-Amsterdam 1999–2000
C. Depauw, G. Luijten et al., *Antoon van Dyck en de prentkunst*, exh. cat., Museum Plantin-Moretus, Antwerp, Rijksmuseum, Amsterdam 1999–2000

B

Barnes et al. 2004
S.J. Barnes et al., *Van Dyck: A Complete Catalogue of the Paintings*, New Haven-London 2004

Bartsch 1803–21
A. [von] Bartsch, *Le peintre graveur*, 21 vols, Vienna 1803–21

Basel 1987
P. ten Doesschate-Chu, P.H. Boerlin et al., *Im Lichte Hollands: Holländische Malerei des 17. Jahrhunderts aus der Sammlungen des Fürsten von Liechtenstein und aus Schweizer Besitz*, exh. cat., Kunstmuseum, Basel 1987

Bauch 1926
K. Bauch, *Jacob Adriaensz. Backer: Ein Rembrandtschüler aus Friesland*, Berlin 1926

Bauer 2006
A.N. Bauer, *Jan Mijtens (1613/14–1670): Leben und Werk*, Petersberg 2006

Becker/Ouwerkerk 1985
J. Becker, A. Ouwerkerk, '"De eer des vaderlands handhaven": Costerbeelden als argumenten in de strijd', *Oud Holland* 99 (1985), pp. 229–70

Bedaux 1990
J.B. Bedaux, *The reality of symbols: Studies in the iconology of Netherlandish art, 1400–1800*, The Hague-Maarssen 1990

Bemolt van Loghum Slaterus 1981
A.J. Bemolt van Loghum Slaterus, *Nederlandse familiepenningen tot 1813*, Zutphen 1981

Benesch 1973
O. Benesch, *The Drawings of Rembrandt: Complete Edition*, 6 vols, London 1973

Van Beresteyn 1929
E.A. van Beresteyn, *Iconographie van Hugo Grotius*, The Hague 1929

Van Beresteyn 1941
E.A. van Beresteyn, *Genealogie van het geslacht Van Beresteyn*, The Hague 1941

Berger 2000
H. Berger, *Fictions of the Pose: Rembrandt Against the Italian Renaissance*, Stanford, California 2000

Berlin 2006
E. van de Wetering et al., *Rembrandt: Genie auf der Suche*, exh. cat., Gemäldegalerie, Berlin 2006

Berlin-Amsterdam-London 1991–2
Rembrandt: The Master & His Workshop, exh. cat., eds C. Brown, J. Kelch, P.J.J. van Thiel, 2 vols, Altes Museum, Berlin, Rijksmuseum, Amsterdam, National Gallery, London 1991–2

Bern 1995
G. Herzog, E. Ryter, J. Strübin Rindisbacher, *Im Schatten des Goldenen Zeitalters: Künstler und Auftraggeber im bernischen 17. Jahrhundert*, exh. cat., 2 vols, Kunstmuseum, Bern 1995

Bernt 1969–70
W. Bernt, *Die niederländischen Maler des 17. Jahrhunderts*, 3 vols, Munich 1969–70

Beutin 1950
L. Beutin, *Simon Peter Tilmann 1601–1668: Ein bremisch-niederländischer Maler*, Bremen 1950

Biesboer 1995
P. Biesboer, 'Willem van Heythuysen en zijn twee portretten', in *Hart voor Haarlem: Liber Amicorum voor Jaap Temminck*, ed. H. Brokken et al., Haarlem 1995, pp. 113–26

Biesboer 2002
P. Biesboer, *Collections of Paintings in Haarlem 1572–1745*, Los Angeles 2002

Biesboer 2006
P. Biesboer, 'Pieter Jacobsz. Olycan: A Portrait and Burgomaster Revealed', in P. Biesboer, M. Bijl, *A Portrait of Pieter Jacobsz. Olycan: Frans Hals Re-discovered*, Zürich 2006, pp. 8–16

Blackburn/Piwonka 1988
R.H. Blackburn, R. Piwonka et al., *Remembrance of patria: Dutch arts and culture in colonial America, 1609–1776*, Albany 1988

Blankert 1982
A. Blankert, *Ferdinand Bol 1616–1680: Rembrandt's Pupil*, Doornspijk 1982

Bok/Schwartz 1991
M.J. Bok, G. Schwartz, 'Schilderen in opdracht in Holland in de 17e eeuw', *Holland: Regionaal-historisch tijdschrift* 23 (1991), pp. 183–95

Bomford et al. 2006
D. Bomford et al., *Art in the Making: Rembrandt*, London 2006. See also London 1988–9

Boot 1973
M. Boot, 'Über Willem van Heythuysen, seinen Nachlaß und die symbolische Bedeutung des Porträts von Frans Hals in München', *Pantheon* 31 (1973), pp. 420–4

Den Bosch 1991–2
A. Roy, *Theodoor van Thulden: Een Zuidnederlandse barokschilder ('s-Hertogenbosch 1606–1669)*, Zwolle 1991–2

Brandt 1687
G. Brandt, *Het leven en bedryf van den Heere Michiel de Ruiter*, Amsterdam 1687

Braun 1966
H. Braun, *Gerard und Willem van Honthorst* (diss.), Göttingen 1966

Braun 1980
K. Braun, *Alle tot nu toe bekende schilderijen van Jan Steen*, Rotterdam 1980

Braunschweig 1978
E. de Jongh et al., *Die Sprache der Bilder: Realität und Bedeutung in der niederländischen Malerei des 17. Jahrhunderts*, exh. cat., Herzog Anton Ulrich-Museum, Braunschweig 1978

Braunschweig 2006
S. Gatenbröcker, *Familienglück: Rembrandt und sein Braunschweiger Meisterwerk*, Herzog Anton Ulrich-Museum, Braunschweig 2006

Bredius 1881
A. Bredius, 'De kunstschatten der voormalige Haagsche schutterij', *Nederlandsche Kunstbode* 39 (1881), pp. 305–9

Bredius 1893
A. Bredius, 'De portretten van Joris de Caullery', *Oud Holland* 11 (1893), pp. 127–8

Bredius 1895
A. Bredius, 'Een acte over het schuttersstuk van 1642 door Nicolaes Elias', *Oud Holland* 13 (1895), pp. 180–1

Bredius 1908a
A. Bredius, 'Michiel Jansz van Mierevelt: Eene nalezing', *Oud Holland* 26 (1908), pp. 1–17

Bredius 1908b
A. Bredius, 'Rembrandtiana', *Oud Holland* 26 (1908), pp. 219–24

Bredius 1913
A. Bredius, 'De geschiedenis van een schutterstuk', *Oud Holland* 31 (1913), pp. 81–4

Bredius/Gerson 1969
A. Bredius, revised by H. Gerson, *Rembrandt: The Complete Edition of the Paintings*, London 1969

Brière-Misme 1923
C. [Brière-]Misme, 'Un petit maître hollandais Emmanuel de Witte', *Gazette des Beaux-Arts* 65 (1923), no. 7, pp. 137–56

Broekman 2005
I. Broekman, *De rol van de schilderkunst in het leven van Constantijn Huygens (1596–1687)*, Hilversum 2005

Brusewicz 1978
L. Brusewicz, 'The paintings by Pieter Nason in Polish collections', *Bulletin du Musée National de Varsovie* 19 (1978), nos 1–2, pp. 1–49

Bruyn 1951
J. Bruyn, 'David Bailly: "Fort bon peintre en pourtraicts et en vie coye"', *Oud Holland* 66 (1951), pp. 148–64, 212–27

Bruyn 1979
J. Bruyn, 'Een onderzoek naar 17de-eeuwse schilderijformaten, voornamelijk in Noord-Nederland', *Oud Holland* 93 (1979), pp. 96–115

Bruyn 1999
J. Bruyn, 'Een portret van Pieter Aertsen en de Amsterdamse portretschilderkunst 1550–1600 met een postscriptum over Huybrecht Beuckelaer (alias Hubbert/Hubbard)', *Oud Holland* 113 (1999), pp. 107–35

Bührle Stiftung 2005
L. Gloor, M. Goldin, *Stiftung Sammlung E.G. Bührle Zürich: Katalog I*, Zürich 2005

Buijsen et al. 1998
E. Buijsen et al., *Haagse schilders in de Gouden Eeuw: Het Hoogsteder Lexicon van alle schilders werkzaam in Den Haag 1600–1700*, The Hague-Zwolle 1998

Bulk 1997
A.M.W. Bulk-Bunschoten, 'De Hoornse wetsverzetting in 1618', *Jaarboek Centraal Bureau voor Genealogie* 51 (1991), pp. 50–98

Buurman 1986
Ammersoyen: Bijdragen tot de geschiedenis van het kasteel, de heerlijkheid en de heren van Ammersoyen, ed. D.J.G. Buurman, Zutphen 1986

Buvelot 1995
Q. Buvelot, 'Ontwerpen voor geschilderde decoratieprogramma's', in Amsterdam 1995, pp. 120–53

Buvelot 2005
Q. Buvelot, 'On Rembrandt's "Portrait of Aeltje Uylenburgh"', *Mauritshuis in focus* 18 (2005), no. 3, pp. 22–6

Buvelot/Sluiter 2004
Q. Buvelot, G. Sluiter, 'Portraits in the Mauritshuis: A Summary Catalogue', in Mauritshuis 2004, pp. 269–324

C

Campbell 1990
L. Campbell, *Renaissance Portraits: European Portrait-Painting in the 14th, 15th, and 16th Centuries*, New Haven-London 1990

Canterbury-London 1990
National Gallery Master Paintings from the Collection of Wynn Ellis of Whitstable, exh. cat., Royal Museum and Art Gallery, Canterbury, National Gallery, London 1990

Castiglione 1528
B. Castiglione, *Il Libro del Cortegiano*, Venice 1528

Catharijneconvent 2002
J. Dijkstra, P.P.W.M. Dirkse, A.E.A.M. Smits, *De schilderijen van Museum Catharijneconvent*, Utrecht-Zwolle 2002

Cats 1618
J. Cats, *Silenus Alcibiadis, sive Proteus, vitae humanae ideam*, Middelburg 1618

Centraal Museum 1952
C.H. de Jonge, *Centraal Museum Utrecht: Catalogus der schilderijen*, Utrecht 1952

Centraal Museum 1999
L.M. Helmus, *Centraal Museum: Schilderkunst tot 1850*, 2 vols, Utrecht 1999

De la Chambre 1638
J. de la Chambre, *Verscheyden geschriften, geschreven ende int koper gesneden, door Jean de la Chambre, liefhebber ende beminder der pennen*, Haarlem 1638

De Chantelou 1885
P.F. de Chantelou, *Journal du voyage du cavalier Bernin en France*, Paris 1885

Charrington 1923
J. Charrington, *A catalogue of the mezzotints after, or said to be after, Rembrandt*, Cambridge 1923

Chong 1992
A.D. Chong, *Aelbert Cuyp and the meaning of landscape* (diss.), New York 1992

Commelin 1694
C. Commelin, *Beschryvinge van Amsterdam … tot den jare 1691*, 2 vols, Amsterdam 1694

Cook 1914
J.O. Kronig, *A Catalogue of the Paintings at Doughty House, Richmond, and Elsewhere in the Collection of Sir Frederick Cook Bt., vol. II, Dutch and Flemish Schools*, London 1914

Copenhagen 2006
L. Bøgh Rønberg et al., *Rembrandt: The Master and his Workshop*, Statens Museum for Kunst, Copenhagen 2006

Corpus
J. Bruyn, B. Haak, S.H. Levie, P.J.J. van Thiel, E. van de Wetering, *A Corpus of Rembrandt Paintings*, 4 vols, Amsterdam-Dordrecht 1982–2005

Corson 1972
R. Corson, *Fashions in Makeup from Ancient to Modern*, London 1972

Craven 1986
W. Craven, *Colonial american portraiture: The economic, religious, social, cultural, philosophical, scientific and aesthetic foundations*, Cambridge 1986

Crookshank/Glin 2002
A. Crookshank, D.F., Knight of Glin, *The Painters of Ireland 1600–1940*, New Haven-London 2002

D

Dahlgren 1923
E.W. Dahlgren, *Louis de Geer 1587–1652: Hans lifn och verk*, 2 vols, Uppsala 1923

Damsté 1985
P.H. Damsté, 'De geschiedenis van het portret van Jaspar Schade door Frans Hals', *Oud Holland* 99 (1985), pp. 30–42

Dekker 2000
R. Dekker, *Childhood, Memory and Autobiography in Holland: From the Golden Age to Romanticism*, New York 2000

Delft 1981
De stad Delft: Cultuur en maatschappij van 1572 tot 1667, exh. cat., eds I.V.T. Spaander, R.-A. Leeuw, Museum Het Prinsenhof, Delft 1981

Delft 2002–3
De snijkunst verbeeld: Delftse anatomische lessen nader belicht, exh. cat., eds H. Houtzager, M. Jonker, Museum Het Prinsenhof, Delft 2002–3

Den Bosch
See Den Bosch

Dickey 1995
S.S. Dickey, '"Met een wenende ziel … doch droge ogen": Women Holding Handkerchiefs in Seventeenth-Century Dutch Portraits', *Nederlands Kunsthistorisch Jaarboek* 46 (1995), pp. 333–67

Van Diepen/Fuhri Snethlage 1990
A. van Diepen, H. Fuhri Snethlage, *Haarlem en Hals*, Zwolle 1990

Van Diest 1673
S. van Diest, *Theologische en politijcke Bedenckingen, over den bedroefden toestant der Vereenighde Nederlanden*, Amsterdam 1673

Dirkse 2001
P. Dirkse, *Begijnen, pastoors en predikanten: Religie en kunst in de Gouden Eeuw*, Leiden 2001

Domela Nieuwenhuis 2001
E.N. Domela Nieuwenhuis, *Paulus Moreelse (1571–1638)* (diss.), 2 vols, Leiden 2001

Dominicus 1997
M. Dominicus-van Soest, *Eten van Steen*, The Hague 1997

Dordrecht 1977–8
J.G. van Gelder et al., *Aelbert Cuyp en zijn familie: Schilders te Dordrecht*, exh. cat., Dordrechts Museum, Dordrecht 1977–8

Dordrecht 1992
De Zichtbaere Werelt: Schilderkunst uit de Gouden Eeuw in Hollands oudste stad, exh. cat., eds P. Marijnissen et al., Dordrechts Museum, Dordrecht 1992

Dordrecht 2002
S. Paarlberg et al., *Jacob Gerritsz. Cuyp (1594–1652)*, exh. cat., Dordrechts Museum, Dordrecht 2002

Drossaers/Lunsingh Scheurleer 1974–6
S.W.A. Drossaers, T.H. Lunsingh Scheurleer, *Inventarissen van de inboedels in de verblijven van de Oranjes en daarmede gelijk te stellen stukken*, 3 vols, The Hague 1974–6

Dublin-Greenwich 2003–4
P. Sutton et al., *Love letters: Dutch genre paintings in the Age of Vermeer*, exh. cat., National Gallery of Ireland, Dublin, Bruce Museum, Greenwich, Connecticut 2003–4

Dudok van Heel 1969
S.A.C. Dudok van Heel, 'Het maecenaat De Graeff en Rembrandt', *Maandblad Amstelodamum* 56 (1969), pp. 150–5
Dudok van Heel 1975
S.A.C. Dudok van Heel, 'Een minne met een kindje door Frans Hals', *Jaarboek Centraal Bureau voor Genealogie* 29 (1975), pp. 146–59
Dudok van Heel 1979
S.A.C. Dudok van Heel, 'Het maecenaat Trip, opdrachten aan Ferdinand Bol en Rembrandt van Rijn', *Kroniek van het Rembrandthuis* 31 (1979), pp. 14–26
Dudok van Heel 1992
S.A.C. Dudok van Heel, 'Enkele Observaties bij het portret van een 83-jarige dame uit 1634 door Rembrandt', *Jaarboek Amstelodamum* 79 (1992), pp. 6–15
Dudok van Heel 1993
S.A.C. Dudok van Heel, 'Rembrandt en de vaandrigs van de Amsterdamse schutterij: Diende Rembrandts "vaandeldrager" uit 1636 als "modello"', *Kroniek van het Rembrandthuis* (1993), pp. 15–23
Dudok van Heel 1994
S.A.C. Dudok van Heel, 'De remonstrantse wereld van Rembrandts opdrachtgever Abraham Anthoniszn Recht', *Bulletin van het Rijksmuseum* 42 (1994), pp. 334–46
Dudok van Heel 2006
S.A.C. Dudok van Heel, *De jonge Rembrandt onder tijdgenoten: Godsdienst en schilderkunst in Leiden en Amsterdam* (*Nijmeegse Kunsthistorische Studies*, vol. 14), Nijmegen 2006
Dudok van Heel et al. 1991
S.A.C. Dudok van Heel et al., *Nicolaes Tulp: The life and work of an Amsterdam physician and magistrate in the 17th century*, Amsterdam 1991
Dumas 1991
C. Dumas, *Haagse stadsgezichten 1550–1800: Topografische schilderijen van het Haags Historisch Museum*, Zwolle 1991
Van Dyk 1758
J. van Dyk, *Kunst- en historiekundige beschryving en aanmerkingen van alle de schilderyen op het stadhuis te Amsterdam*, Amsterdam 1758

E

Edinburgh 1975
D. Thomson, *Painting in Scotland 1570–1650*, exh. cat., The Scottish National Portrait Gallery, Edinburgh 1975
Edinburgh 1992
J. Lloyd Williams, *Dutch Art and Scotland: A reflection of taste*, exh. cat., The Scottish National Portrait Gallery, Edinburgh 1992
Edinburgh-London 2001
J. Lloyd Williams et al., *Rembrandt's women*, exh. cat., The Scottish National Portrait Gallery, Edinburgh, Royal Academy of Arts, London 2001
Edinburgh-London 2004–5
C. Lloyd, *Enchanting the Eye: Dutch Paintings of the Golden Age*, exh. cat., The Queen's Gallery, Holyroodhouse Palace, Edinburgh, The Queen's Gallery, Buckingham Palace, London 2004–5
Van Eeghen 1956
I.H. van Eeghen, 'Baertjen Martens en Herman Doomer', *Maandblad Amstelodamum* 43 (1956), pp. 133–7
Van Eeghen 1957
I.H. van Eeghen, 'De Staalmeesters', *Jaarboek Amstelodamum* 49 (1957), pp. 65–80
Van Eeghen 1958a
I.H. van Eeghen, 'De Staalmeesters', *Oud Holland* 73 (1958), pp. 80–4
Van Eeghen 1958b
I.H. van Eeghen, *Een Amsterdamse burgemeesterstersdochter van Rembrandt in Buckingham Palace*, Amsterdam 1958
Van Eeghen 1970
I.H. van Eeghen, 'Jan Rijcksen en Griet Jans', *Amstelodamum* 57 (1970), pp. 121–7
Van Eeghen 1974
I.H. van Eeghen, 'Pieter Codde en Frans Hals', *Amstelodamum* 61 (1974), pp. 137–41
Ekkart 1971
R. Ekkart, *De oranjeportretten in het Stadhuis van Kampen*, Kampen 1971
Ekkart 1976
R. Ekkart, 'Het portret van een Amsterdamse uitgever en zijn gezin', *Oud Holland* 90 (1976), pp. 15–20
Ekkart 1979
R. Ekkart, *Johannes Cornelisz. Verspronck*, Haarlem 1979
Ekkart 1984
R. Ekkart, 'Het portret van de familie Meerman door Pieter van Slingelandt', in *De Arte et Libris: Festschrift Erasmus 1934–4*, ed A. Horodisch, Amsterdam 1984, pp. 69–75
Ekkart 1984–5
R. Ekkart, 'Het portret van Abraham Casteleyn en zijn vrouw', *De Boekenwereld: Tijdschrift voor boek en prent* 1 (1984–5), no. 15, pp. 13–15
Ekkart 1985
R.E.O. Ekkart, 'Portretten van de vrouw van Jan Huygen van Linschoten en van haar afstammelingen', *Jaarboek Centraal Bureau voor Genealogie* 39 (1985), pp. 111–21
Ekkart 1989a
R. Ekkart, 'Jan Cornelisz. van 't Woudt als portretschilder', *Oud Holland* 103 (1989), pp. 223–42
Ekkart 1989b
R. Ekkart, 'Een tekening door Jacob Delff de Oude', *Bulletin van het Rijksmuseum* 37 (1989), pp. 322–8
Ekkart 1990a
R. Ekkart 'De Enkhuizer schilder Jan Claesz.', *Oud Holland* 104 (1990), pp. 180–218
Ekkart 1990b
R. Ekkart, 'Vijf kinderportretten door Dirck Santvoort', *Oud Holland* 104 (1990), pp. 249–55
Ekkart 1991a
R. Ekkart, 'Gerbrand Ban', *Bulletin van het Rijksmuseum* 39 (1991), pp. 426–34
Ekkart 1991b
R. Ekkart, 'The portraits of "The Vrijdags van Vollenhoven Family" by Jan Anthonisz. van Ravesteyn', *Mercury* (1991), no. 12, pp. 3–16
Ekkart 1997
R. Ekkart, 'De Rotterdamse portrettist Jan Daemen Cool (ca. 1589–1660)', *Oud Holland* 111 (1997), pp. 201–40
Ekkart 1998a
R. Ekkart, *Isaac Claesz. van Swanenburg 1537–1614: Leids schilder en burgemeester*, Zwolle 1998
Ekkart 1998b
R. Ekkart, 'De ontwikkeling van het Nederlandse doodsportret in de 16de en 17de eeuw', in Sliggers 1998, pp. 64–84
Ekkart 2002
R. Ekkart, '*A portrait historié* with Venus, Paris and Cupid: Ferdinand Bol and the patronage of the Spiegel family', *Simiolus* 29 (2002), pp. 14–41
Ekkart 2005
R. Ekkart, 'Hugo de Groot in Parijs geportretteerd', *De Nederlandsche Leeuw* 122 (2005), cols 133–6
Ekkart 2006a
R.E.O. Ekkart, 'Drie broers Van der Burch geportretteerd door Philips Koninck', *De Nederlandsche Leeuw* 123 (2006), cols 243–8
Ekkart 2006b
R.E.O. Ekkart, 'Abraham de Vries: Een Hol-

landse portrettist in Frankrijk en de Zuidelijke Nederlanden', in *Munuscula Amicorum: Contributions on Rubens and his Colleagues in Honour of Hans Vlieghe*, ed. K. van der Stighelen, Turnhout 2006, pp. 549–64

Elias 1903–5
J.E. Elias, *De vroedschap van Amsterdam 1578–1795*, 2 vols, Haarlem 1903–5

Eller 1971
P. Eller, *Kongelige portraetmalere i Danmark 1630–82: En undersögelse af kilderne til Karel van Manders og Abraham Wuchters' virksomhed*, Copenhagen 1971

Enkhuizen 1990–1
R. Ekkart, met G. Reichwein, *Portret van Enkhuizen in de Gouden Eeuw*, exh. cat., Zuiderzeemuseum, Enkhuizen 1990–1

F

Figgis/Rooney 2001
N. Figgis, E. Mayes, B. Rooney, *Irish paintings in the National Gallery of Ireland*, Dublin 2002

Filedt Kok/Leesberg 2000
J.P. Filedt Kok, M. Leesberg, *The De Gheyn family (The New Hollstein Dutch & Flemish etchings, engravings and woodcuts 1450–1700, 2 vols)*, Rotterdam 2000

Finberg 1921–2
A.J. Finberg, 'A Chronological List of Portraits by Cornelius Johnson', *Walpole Society* 10 (1921–2), pp. 1–37

Fischer et al. 1953
M. Fischer et al., *Zürcher Bildnisse aus fünf Jahrhunderte*, Zürich 1953

Fleischer 1989
R.E. Fleischer, *Ludolf de Jongh (1616–1679): Painter of Rotterdam*, Doornspijk 1989

La Fleur 2000
J.D. la Fleur, *Pieter Van Den Broecke's Journal of Voyages to Cape Verde, Guinea and Angola (1605–1612)*, London 2000

Fockema Andreae et al. 1974
S.J. Fockema Andreae et al., *Kastelen, ridderhofsteden en buitenplaatsen in Rijnland*, Arnhem 1974

Franits 1993
W.E. Franits, *Paragons of Virtue: Women and Domesticity in Seventeenth-Century Dutch Art*, Cambridge 1993

Frankfurt am Main 2003
J. Giltaij, *Rembrandt, Rembrandt*, exh. cat., Städelsches Kunstinstitut und Städtische Galerie, Frankfurt am Main 2003

Frans Hals Museum 2006
Painting in Haarlem 1500–1850: The collection of the Frans Hals Museum, ed. N. Köhler et al., Gent 2006

Freedman 1985
L. Freedman, 'Rembrandt's Portrait of Jan Six', *Artibus et Historiae* 12 (1985), pp. 89–105

Friedländer 1967–76
M.J. Friedlander, *Early Netherlandish Painting*, 14 vols, Leiden-Brussels 1967–76

Friedländer/Von Falke 1925–6
M.J. Friedländer, O. von Falke, *Die Kunstsammlung Von Pannwitz*, 2 vols, Munich 1925–6

G

Gaehtgens 1987
B. Gaehtgens, *Adriaen van der Werff 1659–1722*, Munich 1987

De Gelder 1921
J.J. de Gelder, *Bartholomeus van der Helst: Een studie van zijn werk, zijn levensgeschiedenis, een beschrijvende catalogus van zijn oeuvre, een register en 41 afbeeldingen naar schilderijen*, Rotterdam 1921

Van Gelder 1938
J.G. van Gelder, 'Dateering van Frans Hals' portret van P. v. d. Broecke', *Oud Holland* 55 (1938), p. 154

Van Gelder 1957
H.E. van Gelder, *Ikonografie van Constantijn Huygens en de zijnen*, The Hague 1957

Gemäldegalerie 1998
H. Bock et al., *Gemäldegalerie Berlin: 200 Meisterwerke*, Berlin 1998

Gemäldegalerie Kassel 1996
B. Schnackenburg, *Staatliche Museen Kassel, Gemäldegalerie Alte Meister: Gesamtkatalog*, 2 vols, Mainz 1996

Gerson 1942
H. Gerson, *Ausbreitung und Nachwirkung der holländischen Malerei des 17. Jahrhunderts*, Haarlem 1942

Gerson 1968
H. Gerson, *Rembrandt: Paintings*, Amsterdam 1968

Giltaij 1992
J. Giltaij, 'De Grafsteen van Haesje', *Kroniek van het Rembrandthuis* 1 (1992), pp. 10–12

Giltaij/Lammertse 2001
J. Giltaij, F. Lammertse, 'Maintaining a studio archive: Drawn copies by the De Braij Family', *Master Drawings* 39 (2001), pp. 367–94

Van Gool 1750–1
J. van Gool, *De Nieuwe Schouburg der Nederlantsche kunstschilders en schilderessen*, 2 vols, The Hague 1750–1

Gordenker 2001
E.E.S. Gordenker, *Van Dyck and the Representation of Dress in Seventeenth-Century Portraiture*, Turnhout 2001

Graf 1969
F. Graf, 'Aliis inserviendo consumor: Zur Entwicklung einer lateinischen Sentens', *Arcadia* 4 (1969), pp. 199–201

Greindl 1944
E. Greindl, *Corneille de Vos*, Strassbourg 1944

Grijzenhout/Van Sas 2006
F. Grijzenhout, N. van Sas, *De burger van Delft: Een schilderij van Jan Steen*, Amsterdam 2006

Grimm 1972
C. Grimm, *Frans Hals: Entwicklung, Werkanalyse, Gesamtkatalog*, Berlin 1972

Grimm 1989
C. Grimm, *Frans Hals: Das Gesamtwerk*, Stuttgart-Zürich 1989

Groeneweg 1995
I. Groeneweg, 'Regenten in het zwart: Vroom en deftig?', *Nederlands Kunsthistorisch Jaarboek* 46 (1995), pp. 199–251

Groeneweg 1997
I. Groeneweg, 'Portretkostuums: Kanttekeningen bij een 18e-eeuws Nederlands vrouwenportret in "antique kleding"', *Kostuum jaarboek* (1997), pp. 5–23

Groenveld et al. 2003
Nassau uit de schaduw van Oranje, eds S. Groenveld, J.J. Huizinga, Y.B. Kuiper, Franeker 2003

Gudlaugsson 1959–60
S.J. Gudlaugsson, *Gerard ter Borch*, 2 vols, The Hague 1959–60

H

Haak 1969
B. Haak, *Rembrandt: Zijn leven, zijn werk, zijn tijd*, Amsterdam 1969

Haak 1972
B. Haak, *Regenten en regentessen, overlieden en chirurgijns: Amsterdamse groepportretten van 1600 tot 1835*, Amsterdam 1972

Haak 1984
B. Haak, *The Golden Age: Dutch Painters of the seventeenth century*, London 1984

Haarlem 1986
E. de Jongh, *Portretten van echt en trouw: Huwelijk en gezin in de Nederlandse kunst van de zeventiende eeuw*, exh. cat., Frans Hals Museum, Haarlem 1986

Haarlem 1988
Schutters in Holland: Kracht en zenuwen van de stad, exh. cat., eds M. Carrasso, J. Levy-van Halm, Frans Hals Museum, Haarlem 1988

Haarlem-Antwerp 2000–1
Kinderen op hun mooist: Het kinderportret in de Nederlanden 1500–1700, exh. cat., eds J.B. Bedaux, R. Ekkart, Frans Hals Museum, Haarlem, Koninklijk Museum voor Schone Kunsten, Antwerp 2000–1

Haarlem-Hamburg 2003–4
Satire en vermaak: Schilderkunst in de 17e eeuw. Het genrestuk van Frans Hals en zijn tijdgenoten 1610–1670, exh. cat., eds P. Biesboer, M. Sitt, Frans Hals Museum, Haarlem, Hamburger Kunsthalle, Hamburg 2003–4

The Hague 1870
Katalogus der Schilderijen op het Raadhuis te 's Gravenhage, The Hague 1870

The Hague 1958–9
P.N.H. Domela Nieuwenhuis, A. van Duinkerken, A.B. de Vries, *Jan Steen*, exh. cat., Mauritshuis, The Hague 1958–9

The Hague 1995–6
B. Broos, Q. Buvelot, F.J. Duparc, P. van der Ploeg, C. Vermeeren, *The Amateur's Cabinet: Seventeenth-Century Dutch Masterpieces from Dutch Private Collections*, exh. cat., Mauritshuis, The Hague 1995–6

The Hague 1997–8
P. van der Ploeg, C. Vermeeren et al., *Princely Patrons: The Collection of Frederick Henry of Orange and Amalia of Solms in The Hague*, exh. cat., Mauritshuis, The Hague 1997–8

The Hague 1998
A. McNeil Kettering, *Gerard ter Borch and the Treaty of Münster*, exh. cat., Mauritshuis, The Hague 1998

The Hague 1998–9
N. Middelkoop, P. Noble, J. Wadum, B. Broos, *Rembrandt under the Scalpel: The Anatomy Lesson of Dr Nicolaes Tulp Dissected*, exh. cat., Mauritshuis, The Hague 1998–9

The Hague 2002
Q. Buvelot, H. Buijs, with E. Reitsma, *A Choice Collection: Seventeenth-Century Dutch Paintings from the Frits Lugt Collection*, exh. cat., Mauritshuis, The Hague 2002

The Hague-Münster 1974
H.R. Hoetink, G. Langemeijer, P. Pieper et al., *Gerard Ter Borch Zwolle 1617 Deventer 1681*, exh. cat., Mauritshuis, The Hague, Landesmuseum für Kunst und Kulturgeschichte, Münster 1974

The Hague-San Francisco 1990–1
B. Broos et al., *Great Dutch Paintings from America*, exh. cat., Mauritshuis, The Hague, The Fine Arts Museums, San Francisco 1990–1

The Hague-Washington 2005–6
Q. Buvelot et al., *Frans van Mieris 1635–1681*, exh. cat., Mauritshuis, The Hague, National Gallery of Art, Washington 2005–6

Van Hall 1958
H. van Hall, 'Mededelingen van het Rijksbureau voor Kunsthistorische Documentatie VIII: Portret van een Blaeu of van Abraham Casteleyn?', *Oud Holland* 73 (1958), pp. 51–4

Hall 1979
J. Hall, *Dictionary of Subjects & Symbols in Art*, New York 1979

Hallwylska Museet 1997
E.H. Cassel-Pihl et al., *Hallwylska målerisammlingen*, Stockholm 1997

Van der Ham 2005
G. van der Ham, 'Het schilderij en de werkelijkheid', *Bulletin van het Rijksmuseum* 53 (2005), pp. 68–73

Hänsel 2004
S. Hänsel, 'Wohlerzogene Kinder sind schöne Juwelen - Familie, Kinder und Erziehung auf niederländischen Familienporträts des 17. Jahrhunderts', *Zeitschrift für Kunstgeschichte* 67 (2004), no. 2, pp. 225–55

Havard 1879–81
H. Havard, *L'art et les artistes hollandais*, 4 vols, Paris 1879–81

Havard 1894
H. Havard, *Michiel van Mierevelt et son gendre*, Paris 1894

Haverkamp-Begemann 1982
E. Haverkamp-Begemann, *Rembrandt: 'The Nightwatch'*, Princeton, New Jersey 1982

Hecht 1980
P. Hecht, 'Candlelight and dirty fingers, or Royal virtue in disguise: Some thoughts on Weyerman and Godfried Schalcken', *Simiolus* 11 (1980), pp. 23–38

Heckscher 1958
W.S. Heckscher, *Rembrandt's Anatomy of Dr. Nicolaas Tulp: An Iconological Study*, New York 1958

Van Heemskerck 1637
J. van Heemskerck, *Batavische Arcadia*, Amsterdam 1637

Held 1991
J. Held, 'Constantijn Huygens and Susanna van Baerle: A Hitherto Unknown Portrait', *The Art Bulletin* 73 (1991), no. 4, pp. 633–58 (see also 'Postscript' in *The Art Bulletin* 74 (1992), no. 1, p. 173)

Helsinki 1994–5
The Beer King of Helsinki, the Czarina's Personal Physician and Dutch Old Masters: Dutch & Flemish Paintings from the Paul & Fanny Sinebrychoff and Carl von Haartman Collections, exh. cat., Museum of Foreign Art Sinebrychoff, Helsinki 1994–5

Hind 1915–32
A.M. Hind, *Catalogue of Drawings by Dutch and Flemish Artists preserved in the Department of Prints and Drawings in the British Museum*, 5 vols, London 1915–32

Hinz 1973
B. Hinz, 'Das Familienbildnis des J.M. Molenaer in Haarlem', *Städel-Jahrbuch* 4 (1973), pp. 207–16

Hoet/Terwesten 1752–70
G. Hoet, P. Terwesten, *Catalogus of naamlyst van schilderyen, met derzelver pryzen*, 3 vols, The Hague 1752–70

Hofstede de Groot 1907–28
C. Hofstede de Groot, *Beschreibendes und kritisches Verzeichnis der Werke der hervorragendsten Holländischen Maler des XVII. Jahrhunderts*, 10 vols, Esslingen a.N.-Paris 1907–28

Hollstein
F.W.H. Hollstein, *Dutch and Flemish Etchings, Engravings and Woodcuts, ca. 1450–1700*, Amsterdam 1949–

Hoogewerff 1936–47
G.J. Hoogewerff, *De Noord-Nederlandsche schilderkunst*, 5 vols, The Hague 1936–47

Houbraken 1718–21
A. Houbraken, *De groote schouburgh der Nederlantsche konstschilders en schilderessen*, 3 vols, Amsterdam 1718–21 (second edition, The Hague 1753)

Hulst 1960
H.J. Ronday et al., *Cornelis de Vos en Paulus de Vos: Schilders van Hulst*, exh. cat., Stadhuis, Hulst 1960

Huygens 1876–88
C. Huygens II, *Journaal van Constantijn Huygens de Zoon van 21 October 1688 tot 2 Sept. 1696*, 3 vols, Utrecht 1876–88

Huys Janssen 1998
P. Huys Janssen, *Jan van Bijlert 1597/8–1671: Catalogue Raisonné*, Amsterdam 1998

Huys Janssen 2002
P. Huys Janssen, *Caesar van Everdingen*

1616/17–1678: Monograph and Catalogue Raisonné, Doornspijk 2002

Huyskens 1992
W. Huyskens, *De vrije vogelvlugt: Kunst en valkerij: Motief, portret, gedicht*, Zutphen 1992

I

ICN 1992
E. de Heer et al., *Rijksdienst Beeldende Kunst / The Netherlands Office for Fine Arts The Hague. Old Master Paintings: An Illustrated Summary Catalogue*, Instituut Collectie Nederland, Zwolle-The Hague 1992

Icones Leidenses 1973
Icones Leidenses: De portretverzameling van de Rijksuniversiteit te Leiden, Leiden 1973

J

Jaarverslag Rijksmuseum 1986
S.H. Levie, 'Rijksmuseum Amsterdam', *Nederlandse Rijksmusea in 1986*, vol. 108, The Hague 1987, pp. 7–69

Jochems 1888
J.A. Jochems, *Amsterdams oude burgervendels (Schutterij) 1580–1795: Met historische aanteekeningen*, Amsterdam 1888

De Jonge 1938
C.H. de Jonge, *Paulus Moreelse: Portret- en genreschilder te Utrecht 1571–1638*, Assen 1938

De Jongh 1967
E. de Jongh, *Zinne- en minnebeelden in de schilderkunst van de zeventiende eeuw*, s.l. 1967

De Jongh 1975–6
E. de Jongh, 'Pearls of virtue and pearls of vice', *Simiolus* 8 (1975–6), pp. 69–97

De Jongh 1985
E. de Jongh, '[Review of Haak 1984]', *Simiolus* 15 (1985), pp. 65–8

De Jongh 2007
E. de Jongh, 'Een versluierd groepsportret', *Kunstschrift* 51 (2007), no. 1, pp. 26–32

De Jongh/Vinken 1961
E. de Jongh, P.J. Vinken, 'Frans Hals als voortzetter van een emblematische traditie: Bij het huwelijksportret van Isaac Massa en Beatrix van der Laen', *Oud Holland* 76 (1961), pp. 117–52

Judson/Ekkart 1999
J.R. Judson, R.E.O. Ekkart, *Gerrit van Honthorst*, Doornspijk 1999

K

Kam 1960
J.G. Kam, 'Jan Adam Kruseman Jzn. en zijn catalogus van portretten', *Jaarboek Amstelodamum* 52 (1960), pp. 144–72

Kassel 2006
G.J.M. Weber et al., *Rembrandt-Bilder: Die historische Sammlung der Kasseler Gemäldegalerie*, exh. cat., Gemäldegalerie, Kassel 2006

Kassel-Amsterdam 2001–2
E. van de Wetering et al., *The mystery of the young Rembrandt*, exh. cat., Gemäldegalerie, Kassel, Museum Het Rembrandthuis, Amsterdam 2001–2

Kelch 1982
J. Kelch, 'Eine Neuerwerbung der Gemäldegalerie: Thomas de Keyser, Bildnis einer Dame', *Berliner Museen* 26 (1982), pp. 6–7

Kenwood 2003
J. Bryant, *Kenwood: Paintings in the Iveagh Bequest*, New Haven-London 2003

Kilian 2005
J.M. Kilian, *The paintings of Karel Du Jardin 1626–1678: Catalogue raisonné*, Amsterdam 2005

Van Kinschot 1910–12
C.P.L. van Kinschot, *Genealogie van het Geslacht Van Schooten, later genoemd: (van) Schoyte (België) en Van Kinschot (België en Nederland)*, 3 vols, Leiden 1910–12

Klein 1965
P.W. Klein, *De Trippen in de 17de eeuw: Een studie over het ondernemersgedrag op de Hollandse stapelmarkt*, Assen 1965

Klemm 1986
C. Klemm, *Joachim von Sandrart: Kunst-Werke und Lebens-Lauf*, Berlin 1986

Van der Klooster 1980
L.J. van der Klooster, 'De juwelen en de kleding van Maria van Voorst van Doorwerth', *Nederlands Kunsthistorisch Jaarboek* 31 (1980), pp. 50–64

Köhler/Levy-van Halm 1990
N. Köhler, K. Levy-van Halm, *Frans Hals: Schuttersstukken*, Maarssen-The Hague 1990

Koninklijke Musea 1984
H. Pauwels et al., *Koninklijke Musea voor Schone Kunsten van België, Departement Oude Kunst: Inventariscatalogus van de oude schilderkunst*, Brussels 1984

Koninklijk Museum voor Schone Kunsten 1988
E. Vandamme et al., *Catalogus Schilderkunst Oude Meesters*, Antwerp 1988

Kooijmans 2000
L. Kooijmans, *Liefde in opdracht: Het hofleven van Willem Frederik van Nassau*, Amsterdam 2000

Krefeld-Oranienburg-Apeldoorn 1999–2000
Onder den Oranje boom: Niederländische Kunst und Kultur im 17. und 18. Jahrhunderts an deutschen Fürstenhöfen, exh. cat., ed. T. Hoeps, 2 vols, Kaiser-Wilhelm-Museum, Krefeld, Schloß Oranienburg, Oranienburg, Paleis Het Loo Nationaal Museum, Apeldoorn 1999–2000

Krempel 2000
L. Krempel, *Studien zu den datierten Gemälden des Nicolaes Maes (1634–1693)*, Petersburg 2000

Van Kretschmar 1970
F.G.L.O. van Kretschmar, 'Nog een weinig bekend portrettist: Gerrit Alberts "pourtraitschilder te Nijmegen"', *Nederlands Kunsthistorisch Jaarboek* 21 (1970), pp. 97–139

Ter Kuile 1976
O. ter Kuile, *Adriaen Hanneman 1604–1671: Een Haags portretschilder*, Alphen aan den Rijn 1976

Kuiper-Ruempol/Wolleswinkel 1982
A. Kuiper-Ruempol, E. Wolleswinkel, 'J.G. Cuyps "Jongen met valk" geïdentificeerd als 6-jarige Michiel Pompe van Slingelandt', *Bulletin Dordrechts Museum* 7 (1982), nos 3–4, n.p.

L

Laarmann 1998
F.K. Laarmann, 'Familieportret met blokfluiten', *Kunstschrift* 42 (1998), no. 6, pp. 32–6

Laarmann 2000
F.K. Laarmann, 'Herman Meindertsz. Doncker: Ein origineller Künstler zweiten Ranges', *Oud Holland* 114 (2000), pp. 7–52

Laarmann 2002
F.K. Laarmann, *Families in beeld: De ontwikkeling van het Noord-Nederlandse familieportret in de eerste helft van de zeventiende eeuw*, Hilversum 2002

Lafenestre/Richtenberger 1898
G. Lafenestre, E. Richtenberger, *La Peinture en Europe: La Hollande*, Paris [1898]

Levey 1983
S.M. Levey, *Lace: A History*, London 1983

Liedtke 1982
W. Liedtke, *Architectural Painting in Delft*, Doornspijk 1982

Lindeboom 1974
G.A. Lindeboom, *Florentius Schuyl (1619–1669) en zijn betekenis voor het Cartesianisme in de geneeskunde*, The Hague 1974

Lipp/Gruber 1959
A. Lipp, G. Gruber, 'Die Kerze als Symbol des Arzttums', *Nova Acta Leopoldina* 21 (1959), pp. 5–51

Van Lit/Pluijmen 1989
R. van Lit, E. Pluijmen, *Sint Sebastiaansdoelen: Haags Historisch Museum*, Zwolle-The Hague 1989

London 1946–7
I.Q. van Regteren Altena, *The King's Pictures*, exh. cat., Royal Academy of Arts, London 1946–7

London 1964
The Orange and the Rose: Holland and Britain in the Age of Observation, 1600–1750, exh. cat., Victoria and Albert Museum, London 1964

London 1972a
The Alexander Gift, exh. cat.,National Gallery, London 1972

London 1972b
O. Millar, *The Age of Charles I: Painting in England 1620–1649*, exh. cat., Tate Gallery, London 1972

London 1976
C. Brown, *Art in Seventeenth Century Holland*, National Gallery, London 1976

London 1988–9
D. Bomford, C. Brown, A. Roy, *Art in the Making: Rembrandt*, exh. cat., National Gallery, London 1988–9. See also Bomford et al. 2006

London 1999
C. Wright, *The Cabinet Picture: Dutch and Flemish Masters of the Seventeenth Century*, exh. cat., Richard Green Fine Old Master Paintings London 1999

London 2000
A. Ribeiro et al., *The Gallery of Fashion*, exh. cat., National Portrait Gallery, London 2000

London 2002–3
Royal Treasures: A Golden Jubilee Celebration, exh. cat., ed. J. Roberts, The Queen's Gallery, London 2002–3

London 2007
Old Master Paintings, exh. cat., Colnaghi's, London 2007

London-Amsterdam 2006
F. Lammertse, J. van der Veen, *Rembrandt & Co: Dealing in Masterpieces / Uylenburgh en zoon: Kunst en commercie van Rembrandt tot De Lairesse 1625–1675*, exh. cat., Dulwich Picture Gallery, London, Museum Het Rembrandthuis, Amsterdam 2006

London-The Hague 1999–2000
Rembrandt by Himself, exh. cat., eds C. White, Q. Buvelot, National Gallery, London, Mauritshuis, The Hague 1999–2000

Louvre 1979
A. Bréjon de Lavergnée, J. Foucart, N. Reynaud, *Catalogue sommaire illustré des peintures du Musée du Louvre*, vol. 1, *Ecoles flamande et hollandaise*, Paris 1979

Lowenthal 1986
A.W. Lowenthal, *Joachim Wtewael and Dutch mannerism*, Doornspijk 1986

Lunsingh Scheurleer et al. 1986–92
T.H. Lunsingh Scheurleer, C.W. Fock, A.J. van Dissel, *Het Rapenburg: Geschiedenis van een Leidse gracht*, 10 vols and index, Leiden 1986–92

M

Manchester-Washington 2004–5
P. Avery et al., *Jan de Bray and the Classical Tradition*, exh. cat., Currier Museum of Art, Manchester, National Gallery of Art, Washington 2004–5

Van Mander 1604
K. van Mander, *Het Schilder-Boeck*, Haarlem 1604

Manke 1963
I. Manke, *Emanuel de Witte*, Amsterdam 1963

Van der Marel 1964
A. van der Marel, 'De kunstschilders de Bray en hun familie', *De Nederlandsche Leeuw* 81 (1964), cols 6–26

Martin 1911
W. Martin, *Gerard Dou: Sa vie et son œuvre*, Paris 1911

Martin 1913
W. Martin, *Gerard Dou: Des Meisters Gemälde*, Stuttgart 1913

Martin 1918
W. Martin, 'Aanwinsten van het Mauritshuis', *Bulletin Nederlandschen Oudheidkundigen Bond* 11 (1918), pp. 214–18

Martin 1923–4
W. Martin, 'Jan van Ravesteyn's "Magistraat en Schutters", 1618, en het ontwerp daarvoor', *Oud Holland* 41 (1923–4), pp. 193–8

Mauquoy-Hendrickx 1991
M. Mauquoy-Hendrickx, *L'iconographie d'Antoine van Dyck*, 2 vols, Brussels 1991

Mauritshuis 1987
B. Broos, *Meesterwerken in het Mauritshuis*, The Hague 1987

Mauritshuis 2004
B. Broos, A. van Suchtelen, with contributions by Q. Buvelot, G. Sluiter, P. Noble, P. van der Ploeg, H. Vlieghe and F. Duparc, with an introductory essay by R. Ekkart, *Portraits in the Mauritshuis, 1430–1790*, The Hague-Zwolle 2004

McNeil Kettering 1999
A. McNeil Kettering, 'Gerard ter Borch's portraits for the Deventer elite', *Simiolus* 27 (1999), pp. 46–69

McNeil Kettering 2006
A. McNeil Kettering, *Rembrandts groepsportretten*, Zwolle 2006

Meischke/Reeser 1983
Het Trippenhuis te Amsterdam, eds R. Meischke, H.E. Reeser, Amsterdam 1983

Melbourne-Canberra 1997–8
A. Blankert et al., *Rembrandt: A Genius and his Impact*, exh. cat., National Gallery of Victoria, Melbourne, National Gallery of Australia, Canberra 1997–8

De Meyere 1978
J.A.L. de Meyere, 'Utrechtse schilderkunst in de tweede helft van de 16de eeuw', *Jaarboek Oud-Utrecht* (1978), pp. 106–91

Middelkoop/Van Grevenstein 1988
N. Middelkoop, A. van Grevenstein, *Frans Hals: Leven, werk en restauratie*, Amsterdam 1988

Millar 1954
O. Millar, 'Charles I, Honthorst and Van Dyck', *The Burlington Magazine* 96 (1954), pp. 36–42

Moes 1897–1905
E.W. Moes, *Iconographia Batava*, 2 vols, Amsterdam 1897–1905

Moes 1909
E.W. Moes, *Frans Hals: Sa vie et son œuvre*, Brussels 1909

Von Moltke 1938–9
J.W. von Moltke, 'Salomon de Bray', 'Jan de Bray', *Marburger Jahrbuch für Kunstwissenschaft* 11–12 (1938–9), pp. 309–420, 421–523

Von Moltke 1965
J.W. von Moltke, *Govaert Flinck 1615–1660*, Amsterdam 1965

Du Mortier 1984
B.M. du Mortier, 'De handschoen in de huwelijkssymboliek van de zeventiende eeuw', *Bulletin van het Rijksmuseum* 32 (1984), pp. 189–201

Du Mortier 1989
B.M. du Mortier, 'Een paar geborduurde handschoenen, Nederland, ca. 1622', *Bulletin van het Rijksmuseum* 37 (1989), pp. 204–5

Münster 1998–9
1648: Krieg und Frieden in Europa / War and Peace in Europe, exh. cat., eds K. Bussmann, H. Schilling, Westfälisches Landesmuseum

für Kunst und Kulturgeschichte, Münster 1998–9

Münz 1947
L. Münz, 'The original shape of Rembrandt's *Shipbuilder and his wife*', *The Burlington Magazine* 89 (1947), pp. 253–4

Museo del Prado 1990
A.E. Pérez Sánchez et al., *Museo del Prado: Inventario general de pinturas I: La colección Real*, Madrid 1990

Museum Boijmans Van Beuningen 1995
R.E.O. Ekkart, with contributions by J. van Gent, *Nederlandse portretten uit de 17e eeuw / Dutch Portraits from the Seventeenth Century*, Rotterdam 1995

Museum Boijmans Van Beuningen 1998
F. Lammertse, *Dutch Genre Paintings of the 17th Century: Collection of the Museum Boijmans Van Beuningen*, Rotterdam 1998

N

National Gallery 1960
N. MacLaren, *The Dutch School: 1600–1900*, London 1960

National Gallery 1991
N. MacLaren, revised by C. Brown, *The Dutch School: 1600–1900*, 2 vols, London 1991

National Gallery Washington 1995
A. Wheelock, *Dutch Paintings of the Seventeenth Century: The Collections of the National Gallery of Art*, Washington 1995

National Gallery Washington 2005
A. Wheelock, *Flemish Paintings of the Seventeenth Century: The Collections of the National Gallery of Art*, Washington 2005

National Portrait Gallery 2004
Complete Illustrated Catalogue: National Portrait Gallery, London, eds D. Saywell, J. Simon, London 2004

Naumann 1981
O. Naumann, *Frans van Mieris the Elder (1635–1681)*, 2 vols, Doornspijk 1981

Nelemans 1968
F.A. Nelemans, 'De penningen ter herinnering aan de viering van 11 gouden bruiloften in de families Van Loon en Graswinckel', *Jaarboek Centraal Bureau voor Genealogie* 22 (1968), pp. 181–203

Nevitt 2003
H.R. Nevitt, *Art and the Culture of Love in Seventeenth-Century Holland*, Cambridge 2003

Newark-Denver 2001–2
M. Westermann et al., *Art & Home: Dutch Interiors in the Age of Rembrandt*, exh. cat., The Newark Museum, Newark, Denver Art Museum, Denver 2001–2

New York 1988
A. Jensen Adams, *Dutch and Flemish Paintings from New York Private Collections*, exh. cat., National Academy of Design, New York 1988

New York 1995
Inaugural Exhibition of Old Master Paintings, exh. cat., Otto Naumann Ltd., New York 1995

New York 1995–6
W. Liedtke et al., *Rembrandt / Not Rembrandt*, exh. cat., 2 vols, The Metropolitan Museum of Art, New York 1995–6

New York-London 2001
W.A. Liedtke, M.C. Plomp, A. Rüger et al., *Vermeer and the Delft School*, exh. cat., The Metropolitan Museum of Art, New York, National Gallery, London 2001

Nijmegen 2002–3
Gelderse gezichten: Drie eeuwen portretkunst in Gelderland 1550–1850, exh. cat., eds J.C. Bierens de Haan, R. Ekkart, Museum Het Valkhof, Nijmegen 2002–3

NNBW
Nieuw Nederlandsch biografisch woordenboek, eds P.C. Molhuysen, P.J. Blok, 10 vols, Leiden 1911–37

Noortman 2005
E. Schavemaker, *One Hundred Master Paintings: Noortman Master Paintings*, Maastricht 2005

O

Oldenbourg 1911
R. Oldenbourg, *Thomas de Keysers tätigkeit als Maler: Ein Beitrag zur Geschichte des höllandischen Porträts*, Leipzig 1911

Otte 1987
M. Otte, '"Somtijds een Moor": De neger als bijfiguur op Nederlandse portretten in de zeventiende en achttiende eeuw', *Kunstlicht* 8 (1987), pp. 6–10

P

Panofsky 1934
E. Panofsky, 'Jan van Eyck's Arnolfini Portrait', *The Burlington Magazine* 64 (1934), pp. 117–27

Paris 1956
M. Bernard, N. Gand de Vernon, *France-Écosse*, exh. cat., Archives Nationales, Paris 1956

Paris 1983
S. Nihom-Nijstad, *Reflets du Siècle d'Or: Tableaux hollandais du dix-septieme siècle, Collection Frits Lugt, Fondation Custodia*, exh. cat., Institut Néerlandais, Paris 1983

Paris 1986
B. Broos et al., *De Rembrandt à Vermeer: Les Peintres hollandais au Mauritshuis à La Haye*, exh. cat., Grand Palais, Paris 1986

Paris-Antwerp-London-New York 1979–80
F. Stampfle, *De eeuw van Rubens en Rembrandt: 17e-eeuwse Vlaamse en Hollandse tekeningen uit de Pierpont Morgan Library te New York*, exh. cat., Institut Néerlandais, Paris, Koninklijk Museum voor Schone Kunsten, Antwerp, British Museum, London, Pierpont Morgan Library, New York 1979–80

Parthesius 2007
R. Parthesius, *Dutch Ships in Tropical Waters: The Development of the Dutch East India Company (VOC) Shipping Network in Asia 1595–1660*, Amsterdam 2007

Pels 1682
A. Pels, *De schilder door liefde*, Amsterdam 1682

Phoenix-Kansas City-The Hague 1998–9
M.K. Komanecky et al., *Copper as Canvas: Two Centuries of Masterpiece Paintings on Copper 1575–1775*, exh. cat., Phoenix Art Museum, Phoenix, The Nelson-Atkins Museum of Art, Kansas City, Mauritshuis, The Hague 1998–9

Pigler 1955
A. Pigler, 'Gruppenbildnisse mit historisch verkleideten Figuren und ein Hauptwerk des Joannes van Noordt', *Acta Historiae Artium* 2 (1955), nos 3–4, pp. 169–88

Plessen/Von Zahn 1979
M.-L. Plessen, P. von Zahn, *Zwei Jahrtausende Kindheit*, Cologne 1979

Van der Ploeg 2000
P. van der Ploeg, 'Face to Face in the Mauritshuis', *Mauritshuis in focus* 13 (2000), no. 2, pp. 10–21

Van der Ploeg/Zonnevylle 1999
F. van der Ploeg, C.E. Zonnevylle-Heyning, *'Brave koppen en gladde aengesigten': De Goese schutters en hun schilders: C.W. Eversdijck, W.C. Eversdijck en P. Peuteman*, Middelburg 1999

Prud'homme van Reine 1996
R.B. Prud'homme van Reine, *Rechterhand van Nederland: Biografie van Michiel Adriaenszoon de Ruyter*, Amsterdam 1996

Prud'homme van Reine et al. 1992
R.B. Prud'homme van Reine et al., *Ter navol-*

ging: Maritieme kunst en curiosa uit de Kweekschool voor de Zeevaart, Amsterdam 1992

R

Raleigh-Columbus-Manchester 2002–3
D.P. Weller et al., *Jan Miense Molenaer: Painter of the Dutch Golden Age*, exh. cat., North Carolina Museum of Art, Raleigh, Indianapolis Museum of Art, Columbus, The Currier Museum of Art, Manchester 2002–3

Raupp 1986
H.J. Raupp, '[Review of Haarlem 1986]', *Simiolus* 16 (1986), pp. 254–62

Renckens 1948–9
B.J.A. Renckens, 'De Hoornse portretschilder Jan Albertsz. Rotius', *Nederlands Kunsthistorisch Jaarboek* 2 (1948–9), pp. 165–234

Riegl 1931
A. Riegl, *Das holländische Gruppenporträt*, Vienna 1931

Rijksmuseum 1976
P.J.J. van Thiel et al., *All the Paintings of the Rijksmuseum in Amsterdam*, Amsterdam 1976

Rijksmuseum 1988
A. McNeil Kettering, *Drawings from the Ter Borch studio estate*, 2 vols, Amsterdam 1988

Rijksmuseum 2000
H. van Os, J.P. Filedt Kok, G. Luijten et al., *Nederlandse kunst in het Rijksmuseum 1400–1600*, Zwolle-Amsterdam 2000

Rijksmuseum 2001
J.P. Filedt Kok, R. Baarsen, B. Cornelis et al., *Nederlandse kunst in het Rijksmuseum 1600–1700*, Zwolle-Amsterdam 2001

Rijksmuseum 2007
Dutch Paintings of the Seventeenth Century in the Rijksmuseum. Volume I: Artists born c.1570–1600, ed. J. Bikker, Amsterdam 2007 (forthcoming)

Rijksmuseum Twenthe 1976
O. ter Kuile, *Rijksmuseum Twenthe Enschede: Catalogus van de schilderijen*, Enschede 1976

Ripa 1644
C. Ripa, *Iconologia of uytbeeldinghe des verstands*, ed. D. Pers, Amsterdam 1644 (facsimile edition, Soest 1971)

Roding/Stompé 1997
J. Roding, M. Stompé, *Pieter Isaacsz (1569–1625): Een Nederlandse schilder, kunsthandelaar en diplomaat aan het Deense hof*, Hilversum 1997

Rodriguez 1634
J.F. Rodriguez, *Nievwen dictionaris om te leeren de Nederlandtsche ende Spaensche talen*, Antwerp 1634

Roeper/Daalder 2007
Michiel de Ruyter: Het levensverhaal van de zeeheld, opgetekend door zijn tijdgenoot Gerard Brandt, eds V. Roeper, R. Daalder, Amsterdam 2007

Roethlisberger 1993
M.G. Roethlisberger, with contributions by M.J. Bok, *Abraham Bloemaert and his sons: Paintings and prints*, 2 vols, Doornspijk 1993

De Roever 1889
N. de Roever, 'Pieter Aertsz., gezegd Lange Pier, vermaard schilder', *Oud Holland* 7 (1889), pp. 1–38

Rogeaux 2002
N. Rogeaux, 'Wallerant Vaillant (1623–1677), portraitiste hollandais', *Revue du Nord* 84 (2002), pp. 25–49

Römelingh et al. 1984
J. Römelingh et al., *Art in Denmark 1600–1650* (*Leids Kunsthistorisch Jaarboek*, 1983), Delft 1984

Rosenberg/Slive/Ter Kuile 1966
J. Rosenberg, S. Slive, E.H. ter Kuile, *Dutch Art and Architecture 1600 to 1800*, Harmondsworth 1966

Rotterdam 1994–5
N. Schadee et al., *Rotterdamse meesters uit de Gouden Eeuw*, exh. cat., Historisch Museum, Rotterdam 1994–5

Rotterdam-Frankfurt am Main 1999–2000
A. Blankert, J. Giltaij, F. Lammertse et al., *Hollands classicisme in de zeventiende-eeuwse schilderkunst*, exh. cat., Museum Boijmans Van Beuningen, Rotterdam, Städelsches Kunstinstitut und Städtische Galerie, Frankfurt am Main 1999–2000

Royal Collection 1982
C. White, *The Dutch Pictures in the Collection of Her Majesty the Queen*, Cambridge 1982

Royal Collection 1999
C. Lloyd, *The Paintings in the Royal Collection: A Thematic Exploration*, London 1999

Runia/Van Suchtelen 2006
E. Runia, A. van Suchtelen, *Rembrandt in the Mauritshuis*, The Hague-Zwolle 2006

S

San Francisco-Baltimore-London 1997–8
J. Spicer, L. Federle Orr et al., *Masters of Light: Dutch Painters in Utrecht during the Golden Age*, exh. cat., The Fine Arts Museums, San Francisco, The Walters Art Gallery, Baltimore, National Gallery, London 1997–8

Sarasota 1980–1
W.H. Wilson, *The Golden Age: Dutch Seventeenth Century Portraiture*, exh. cat., The John and Mable Ringling Museum of Art, Sarasota 1980–1

Saur
Allgemeines Künstlerlexikon: Die bildenden Künstler aller Zeiten und Völker, Munich 1992–

Schaep 1885
G. Schaep, 'De schilderijen in de drie doelens te Amsterdam, 1653', in P. Scheltema, *Aemstel's Oudheid of gedenkwaardigheden van Amsterdam*, vol. 7, Amsterdam 1885, pp. 121–41

Schama 1999
S. Schama, *Rembrandt's Eyes*, New York 1999

Scheltema 1879
P. Scheltema, *Historische beschrijving der schilderijen van het stadhuis te Amsterdam*, Amsterdam 1879

Van Schendel 1956
A. van Schendel, 'De schimmen van de Staalmeesters: Een röntgenologisch onderzoek', *Oud Holland* 71 (1956), pp. 1–23

Schlégl 1980
I. Schlégl, *Samuel Hofmann (um 1595–1649)*, Zürich 1980

Schlüter-Göttsche 1978
G. Schlüter-Göttsche, *Jürgen Ovens: Ein schleswig-holsteinscher Barockmaler*, Heide in Holstein 1978

Schmidt 1922
H. Schmidt, *Jürgen Ovens: Sein Leben und seine Werke: Ein Beitrag zur Geschichte der niederländischen Malerei im XVII. Jahrhundert*, Kiel 1922

Schneeman 1982
L.T. Schneeman, *Hendrick Martensz. Sorgh: A painter of Rotterdam with catalogue raisonné* (diss.), Pennsylvania 1982

Schneider/Ekkart 1973
H. Schneider, with a supplement by R.E.C. Ekkart, *Jan Lievens: Sein Leben und seine Werke*, Amsterdam 1973 (ed. princ. 1932)

Scholten 1995
F. Scholten, *Gebeeldhouwde portretten*, Amsterdam 1995

Scholten 2002
F. Scholten, 'Onbekend portret van een zilversmid', *Kunstschrift* 46 (2002), no. 4, pp. 50–1

Schupbach 1982
W. Schupbach, *The Paradox of Rembrandt's Anatomy of Dr. Tulp*, (Medical History supplement no. 2), London 1982

Schwartz 1984
G. Schwartz, *Rembrandt: Zijn leven, zijn schilderijen*, Maarssen 1984 (also in English edition)

Schwartz 2006
G. Schwartz, *De grote Rembrandt*, Zwolle 2006
Servaas van Rooyen 1909
A.J. Servaas van Rooyen, *De kunstschatten der schutterij*, Amsterdam 1909
Sint Nicolaas/Stevens 2006
E. Sint Nicolaas, H. Stevens, 'Kolders: Van modieus militair kledingstuk tot slagveldreliek', *Bulletin van het Rijksmuseum* 54 (2006), pp. 266–89
Six 1886
J. Six, 'Nicolaes Eliasz Pickenoy', *Oud Holland* 4 (1886), pp. 81–108
Six 1887
J. Six, 'Cornelis van der Voort: Een eerste poging tot het terugvinden van zijn werk als portretschilder', *Oud Holland* 5 (1887), pp. 1–22
Six 1893
J. Six, 'Opmerkingen omtrent eenige meesterwerken in 's Rijks Museum', *Oud Holland* 11 (1893), pp. 96–104
Six 1896
J. Six, 'De namen der staalmeesters', *Oud Holland* 14 (1897), pp. 65–7
Six 1911
J. Six, 'Cornelis van der Voort', *Oud Holland* 29 (1911), pp. 129–33
Six 1918
J. Six, 'Het monogram van Cornelis van der Voort', *Oud Holland* 36 (1918), pp. 243–6
Six 2001
V. Bush et al., *The House of Six*, Amsterdam 2001
Sliggers 1998
Naar het lijk: Het Nederlandse doodsportret 1500-heden, ed. B.C. Sliggers, Haarlem 1998
Slive 1958
S. Slive, 'Frans Hals' Portrait of Joseph Coymans', *Wadsworth Atheneum Bulletin* (Winter 1958), pp. 12–23
Slive 1970–4
S. Slive, *Frans Hals*, 3 vols, London 1970–4
Slive 1995
S. Slive, *Dutch Painting 1600–1800*, New Haven-London 1995
Smith 1982
D.R. Smith, *Masks of Wedlock: Seventeenth-Century Dutch Marriage Portraiture*, Ann Arbor, Michigan 1982
Smith 1988
D.R. Smith, '"I Janus": Privacy and the Gentlemanly Ideal in Rembrandt's Portraits of Jan Six', *Art History* 11 (1988), no. 1, pp. 42–63
Sokolova 2003
I. Sokolova, 'Jacob Duck's *Guardroom*: A painter's forgotten masterpiece', *Apollo* (February 2003), pp. 3–7
Sokolova 2007
I. Sokolova, 'The Russian past of Loef Vredericx', *Mauritshuis in focus* 20 (2007), no. 1, pp. 8–18
Speet 1995
B.J.M. Speet, *Hofje van Heythuysen*, Haarlem 1995
Spicer 1991
J. Spicer, 'The Renaissance Elbow', in *A Cultural History of Gesture: From Antiquity to the Present Day*, eds J. Bremmer, H. Roodenburg, Cambridge-Oxford 1991, pp. 84–128
Staring 1956
A. Staring, 'Willem II of Willem III of wie?', *Oud Holland* 71 (1956), pp. 153–62
Stedelijk Museum Alkmaar 1997
De zestiende- en zeventiende-eeuwse schilderijen van het Stedelijk Museum Alkmaar: Collectie catalogus, ed. S. de Vries, Alkmaar 1997
Steinborn 2004
B. Steinborn, *Malarz Daniel Schultz: Gdańszczanin w Służbie Królów Polskich*, Warsaw 2004
Van der Stighelen 1990
K. Van der Stighelen, *De portretten van Cornelis de Vos (1584/5–1651): Een kritische catalogus*, Brussels 1990
Stockholm 2001–2
G. Cavalli-Björkman et al., *Face to Face: Portraits from Five Centuries*, exh. cat., Nationalmuseum, Stockholm 2001–2
Stratingh 1984
J. Stratingh, *J.J. de Stomme: Een 17e-eeuws schilder in Groningen*, Groningen 1984
Strauss/Van der Meulen 1979
W. Strauss, M. van der Meulen, *The Rembrandt Documents*, New York 1979
Van Suchtelen 1997
A. van Suchtelen, 'Twee portretten van Pieter Pietersz herenigd in het Mauritshuis', in *Album discipulorum J.R.J. van Asperen de Boer*, Zwolle 1997, pp. 203–10
Van Suchtelen 2007
A. van Suchtelen, 'Nieuwe gezichten in oude taferelen', *Kunstschrift* 51 (2007), no. 1, pp. 33–5
Sumowski 1979–92
W. Sumowski, *Drawings of the Rembrandt School*, 10 vols, New York 1979–92
Sumowski 1983–95
W. Sumowski, *Gemälde der Rembrandt-Schüler*, 6 vols, Landau-Pfalz 1983–95]

T

Taylor 1970
K.V.H. Taylor, 'A Note on the Identity of a Member of the Coymans Family by Frans Hals', *National Gallery of Art: Report and Studies in the History of Art 1969*, Washington 1970, pp. 106–8
The Hague
See *The Hague*
Van Thiel 1967–8
P.J.J. van Thiel, 'Marriage symbolism in a musical party by Jan Miense Molenaer', *Simiolus* 2 (1967–8), pp. 90–9
Van Thiel 1983
P.J.J. van Thiel, 'Werner Jacobsz. van den Valckert', *Oud Holland* 97 (1983), pp. 128–95
Van Thiel/De Bruyn Kops 1995
P.J.J. van Thiel, C.J. de Bruyn Kops, *Framing in the Golden Age: Picture and frame in 17th-century Holland*, Amsterdam-Zwolle 1995
Thomson 1974
D. Thomson, *The Life and Art of George Jamesone*, Oxford 1974
Toynbee 1950
M.R. Toynbee, 'Adriaen Hanneman and the English Court in Exile', *The Burlington Magazine* 92 (1950), pp. 73–80
Toynbee 1958
M.R. Toynbee, 'Adriaen Hanneman and the English Court in Exile: A Further Note', *The Burlington Magazine* 100 (1958), pp. 249–50
Troescher 1953–4
G. Troescher, *Kunst- und Künstlerwanderungen in Mitteleuropa 800–1800*, 2 vols, Baden-Baden 1953–4
Tulp ed. 1991
N. Tulp, *Genees insighten*, Amsterdam 1991 (facsimile of manuscript datable to 1655)
Turner 1996
The Dictionary of Art, ed. J. Turner, 34 vols, London-New York 1996
Turner 2000
The Grove Dictionary of Art: From Rembrandt to Vermeer: 17th-century Dutch Artists, ed J. Turner, London 2000

U

Utrecht 1991–2
R. Ekkart et al., *Knappe Koppen: Vier eeuwen*

Nederlands professorenportret, exh. cat., Centraal Museum & Universiteitsmuseum, Utrecht 1991–2

Utrecht 2004

Vis: Stillevens van Hollandse en Vlaamse meesters 1550–1700, exh. cat., ed. L.M. Helmus, Centraal Museum, Utrecht 2004

V

Van der Velden 1997

B. van der Velden, *'t Tydtverdryf van Jan van Amstel*, Schijndel 1997

Veldman 1997

F.J. Veldman, L. Veldman-Planten, *Hermannus Collenius 1650–1723*, Groningen 1997

Verbeek/Schotman 1957

J. Verbeek, J.W. Schotman, *Hendrick ten Oever: Een vergeten Overijssels meester uit de zeventiende eeuw*, Zwolle 1957

Verhave 2006

J. Verhave, *'De Maiesteyt sijns aensichts': Michiel van Mierevelt schildert prins Maurits*, unpublished thesis, Maastricht-Amsterdam 2006

Vienna 2004

M. Bisanz-Prakken et al., *Rembrandt*, exh. cat., Albertina, Vienna 2004

Vis 1986

D. Vis, *Een jonge vrouw geschilderd door Govert Flinck 1655*, Amsterdam 1986

Vondel 1927–40

J.F.M. Sterck et al., *De werken van Vondel*, 10 vols, Amsterdam 1927–40

Vosmaer 1860

C. Vosmaer, 'De schilderijen in het Raadhuis te 's Gravenhage', *De Nederlandsche Spectator* 26 (1860), pp. 201–4

Vosmaer 1868

C. Vosmaer, *Rembrandt Harmens van Rijn: Sa vie et ses œuvres*, The Hague 1868

De Vries 1876

A.D. de Vries, 'De schilderkunst op de historische tentoonstelling te Amsterdam', *De Gids* 14 (1876), pp. 556–7

De Vries 1934

A.B. de Vries, *Het Noord-Nederlandsch portret in de tweede helft van de 16e eeuw*, Amsterdam 1934

De Vries 1967

A.B. de Vries, 'De Hoenderhof', *Openbaar Kunstbezit* 11 (1967), pp. 61a-b

De Vries 1976

L. de Vries, *Jan Steen: De schilderende Uilenspiegel* (diss.), Amsterdam 1976

De Vries 1977

L. de Vries, *Jan Steen 'de kluchtschilder'*, Groningen 1977

De Vries 1982

L. de Vries, *Wybrand de Geest: 'De Friessche Adelaar': Portretschilder in Leeuwarden 1592–c. 1661: Met een catalogus van zijn werk in het Fries Museum*, Leeuwarden 1982

De Vries 1989

L. de Vries, 'Tronies and other single figured Netherlandish paintings', *Nederlands Kunsthistorisch Jaarboek* 8 (1989), pp. 185–202

W

Waagen 1854

G.F. Waagen, *Treasures of Art in Great Britain*, 3 vols, London 1854

Van de Waal 1956

H. van de Waal, 'De Staalmeesters en hun legende', *Oud Holland* 71 (1956), pp. 61–107

Wagenaar 1760–8

J. Wagenaar, *Amsterdam in zyne Opkomst, Aanwas, Geschiedenissen, Voorregten, Koophandel, Gebouwen, Kerkestaat, Schoolen, Schutterye, Gilden en Regeeringe*, 13 vols, Amsterdam 1760–8

Walker 1974

J. Walker, *Self-Portrait with Donors: Confessions of an Art Collector*, Boston-Toronto 1974

Wallace Collection 1992

J. Ingamells, *The Wallace Collection: Catalogue of Pictures, vol. IV: Dutch and Flemish*, London 1992

Washington 2000–1

Art for the Nation: Collecting for a New Century, National Gallery of Art, Washington 2000–1

Washington-Amsterdam 1996–7

H. Perry Chapman, W.T. Kloek, A.K. Wheelock et al., *Jan Steen: Painter and Storyteller*, exh. cat., National Gallery of Art, Washington, Rijksmuseum, Amsterdam 1996–7

Washington-Detroit 2004–5

A.K. Wheelock et al., *Gerard ter Borch*, exh. cat., National Gallery of Art, Washington, The Detroit Institute of Arts, Detroit 2004–5

Washington-London-Amsterdam 2001–2

A.K. Wheelock et al., *Aelbert Cuyp*, exh. cat., National Gallery of Art, Washington, National Gallery, London, Rijksmuseum, Amsterdam 2001–2

Washington-London-Haarlem 1989–90

S. Slive et al., *Frans Hals*, exh. cat., National Gallery of Art, Washington, Royal Academy of Arts, London, Frans Hals Museum, Haarlem 1989–90

Washington-London-The Hague 2000–1

R. Baer et al., *Gerrit Dou 1613–1675: Master Painter in the Age of Rembrandt*, exh. cat., National Gallery of Art, Washington, Dulwich Picture Gallery, London, Mauritshuis, The Hague 2000–1

Washington-Montreal-Yokohama-London 1990–1

The Passionate Eye: Impressionist and Other Master Paintings from the Collection of Emil G. Bührle, Zürich, exh. cat., National Gallery of Art, Washington, Museum of Fine Arts, Montreal, Museum of Art, Yokohama, Royal Academy of Arts, London 1990–1

Wassenbergh 1967

A. Wassenbergh, *De portretkunst in Friesland in de zeventiende eeuw*, Lochem 1967

Waterhouse 1988

E. Waterhouse, *The Dictionary of 16th & 17th Century British Painters*, Woodbridge 1988

Weller 1992

D.P. Weller, *Jan Miense Molenaer (c. 1609/10–1668): The Life and Art of a Seventeenth-Century Dutch Painter* (diss.), Maryland 1992

Werche 2004

B. Werche, *Hendrick van Balen (1575–1632): Ein Antwerpener Kabinettmaler der Rubenszeit*, 2 vols, Turnhout 2004

Westerbaen 1624

J. Westerbaen, *Sic Soleo Amicos: Satyra ofte 't Nood-saeckelick Mal*, The Hague 1624

Van de Wetering 1985

E. van de Wetering, 'Verpostzegelde kant', in *Kant: Verslag textiedag 25 april 1985* [Museum Boijmans Van Beuningen], Rotterdam 1985, pp. 75–7

Van de Wetering 1997

E. van de Wetering, *Rembrandt: The Painter at Work*, Amsterdam 1997

Wheelock 2006

A. Wheelock, '[Review of Mauritshuis 2004]', *The Burlington Magazine* 148 (2006), pp. 123–4

Wieseman 2002

M.E. Wieseman, *Caspar Netscher and Late Seventeenth-Century Dutch Painting*, Doornspijk 2002

Wijnman 1959a

H.F. Wijnman, 'De schilder Abraham van den Tempel', *Uit de kring van Rembrandt en Vondel: Verzamelde studies over hun leven en omgeving*, Amsterdam 1959, pp. 39–93

Wijnman 1959b
H.F. Wijnman, 'Abraham van den Tempel's portretgroep van de zeekapitein Jan van Amstel en zijn vrouw Anna Boxhoorn', *Bulletin Museum Boymans-van Beuningen* 10 (1959), no. 1, pp. 97–109
Van der Willigen 1828
A. van der Willigen, *Catalogus der schilderijen van Mejuffrouw Hoofman*, Manuscript 1828, Rijksbureau voor Kunsthistorische Documentatie
De Winkel 1995
M. de Winkel, *Terminology of Dress: The Netherlands 1610–1710* (diss.), Courtauld Institute, London 1995
De Winkel 2006
M. de Winkel, *Fashion and Fancy: Dress and Meaning in Rembrandt's Paintings*, Amsterdam 2006
Wishnevsky 1967
R. Wishnevsky, *Studien zum "portrait historé" in den Niederlanden*, Munich 1967
De Wit 1958
C. de Wit, 'De ikonographie van Prins Maurits', *Mededelingen Gemeentemuseum Den Haag* 13 (1958), pp. 15–37
Wolleswinkel 2001
E.J. Wolleswinkel, 'De schoonfamilie van de (portret)schilder Thomas de Keyser', *De Nederlandsche Leeuw* 118 (2001), cols 309–27
Worp 1892–9
J.A. Worp, *De gedichten van Constantijn Huygens naar zijn handschrift uitgegeven*, 9 vols, Groningen 1892–9
Worp 1911–17
J.A. Worp, *De briefwisseling van Constantijn Huygens (1608–1687)*, 6 vols, The Hague 1911–17
Wuestman 2006
G. Wuestman, 'Withered Nell or Rembrandt's aunt?: Prints of tronies and their titles', *Simiolus* 32 (2006), pp. 58–77
Van der Wyck/Niemeijer 1989
H.W.M. van der Wyck, J.W. Niemeijer, *De kasteeltekeningen van Roelant Roghman*, vol. 1, Alphen aan den Rijn 1989

Y

Yamaguchi-Kumamoto-Tokyo-Rotterdam 1994–5
E. de Jongh et al., *Faces of the Golden Age: Seventeenth-Century Dutch Portraits*, exh. cat., Prefectural Museum of Art, Yamaguchi, Prefectural Museum of Art, Kumamoto, Station Gallery, Tokyo, Kunsthal, Rotterdam 1994–5
Yapou 1976
Y. Yapou, 'Portraiture and Genre in a Painting Restored to Jan Verspronck', *The Israel Museum News* 11 (1976), pp. 41–6
Ydema 1991
O. Ydema, *Carpets and their Datings in Netherlandish Paintings 1540–1700*, Zutphen 1991

Z

Zandvliet 2006
K. Zandvliet, *De 250 rijksten van de Gouden Eeuw*, Amsterdam 2006
Zuylen 1996
Op stand aan de wand: Vijf eeuwen familieportretten in Slot Zuylen, eds J. de Meyere, A. van der Goes, Maarssen 1996
Zweite 1980
A. Zweite, *Marten de Vos als Maler*, Berlin 1980
Zwolle 1997
J. Streng, L. van Dijk, *Zwolle in de Gouden Eeuw: cultuur en schilderkunst*, exh., cat., Stedelijk Museum, Zwolle 1997

Further reading

- A. Riegl, *Das holländische Gruppenporträt*, Vienna 1931
- A.B. de Vries, *Het Noord-Nederlandsch portret in de tweede helft van de 16e eeuw*, Amsterdam 1934
- J. Bruyn et al., *Drie eeuwen portret in Nederland 1500–1800*, exh. cat., Rijksmuseum, Amsterdam 1952
- A. Wassenbergh, *De portretkunst in Friesland in de zeventiende eeuw*, Lochem 1967
- R. Wishnevsky, *Studien zum "portrait historié" in den Niederlanden*, Munich 1967
- R. Ekkart, *De oranjeportretten in het Stadhuis van Kampen*, Kampen 1971
- B. Haak, *Regenten en regentessen, overlieden en chirurgijns: Amsterdamse groepportretten van 1600 tot 1835*, Amsterdam 1972
- C. Dumas, *In het zadel: Het Nederlands ruiterportret van 1550 tot 1900*, exh. cat., Fries Museum, Leeuwarden, Noordbrabants Museum, Den Bosch, Provinciaal Museum van Drenthe, Assen 1979–80
- D.R. Smith, *Masks of Wedlock: Seventeenth-Century Dutch Marriage Portraiture*, Ann Arbor, Michigan 1982
- B. Haak, *The Golden Age: Dutch Painters of the seventeenth century*, London 1984
- E. de Jongh, *Portretten van echt en trouw: Huwelijk en gezin in de Nederlandse kunst van de zeventiende eeuw*, exh. cat., Frans Hals Museum, Haarlem 1986
- *Kunst voor de beeldenstorm: Noordnederlandse kunst 1525–1580*, exh. cat., eds J.P. Filedt Kok, W. Halsema-Kubes, W.T. Kloek, Rijksmuseum, Amsterdam 1986
- *Schutters in Holland: Kracht en zenuwen van de stad*, exh. cat., eds M. Carrasso, J. Levy-van Halm, Frans Hals Museum, Haarlem 1988
- R. Ekkart et al., *Knappe Koppen: Vier eeuwen Nederlands professorenportret*, exh. cat., Centraal Museum & Universiteitsmuseum, Utrecht 1991–2
- *Dawn of the Golden Age: Northern Netherlandish art 1580–1620*, exh. cat., eds G. Luijten, A. van Suchtelen, R. Baarsen et al., Rijksmuseum, Amsterdam 1993–4
- E. de Jongh et al., *Faces of the Golden Age: Seventeenth-Century Dutch Portraits*, exh. cat., Prefectural Museum of Art, Yamaguchi, Prefectural Museum of Art, Kumamoto, Station Gallery, Tokyo, Kunsthal, Rotterdam 1994–5
- N. Schadee et al. *Rotterdamse meesters uit de Gouden Eeuw*, exh. cat. Historisch Museum, Rotterdam 1994–5
- S. Slive, *Dutch Painting 1600–1800*, New Haven-London 1995
- R. Ekkart, with contributions by J. van Gent, *Nederlandse portretten uit de 17e eeuw / Dutch Portraits from the Seventeenth Century*, Rotterdam 1995
- *Beeld en zelfbeeld in de Nederlandse kunst, 1550–1750* (*Nederlands Kunsthistorisch Jaarboek*, vol. 46), ed. R. Falkenburg et al., Zwolle 1995
- P.J.J. van Thiel, C.J. de Bruyn Kops, *Framing in the Golden Age: Picture and frame in 17th century Holland*, Zwolle 1995 (focusing on original frames, with discussions of many portraits)
- R. Ekkart, *Portrettisten en portretten: Studies over portretkunst in Holland, 1575–1650*, Amsterdam 1997
- E. Buijsen et al., *Haagse schilders in de Gouden Eeuw: Het Hoogsteder Lexicon van alle schilders werkzaam in Den Haag 1600–1700*, The Hague-Zwolle 1998
- *Naar het lijk: Het Nederlandse doodsportret 1500–heden*, ed. B.C. Sliggers, Haarlem 1998
- N. Middelkoop, P. Noble, J. Wadum, B. Broos, *Rembrandt under the Scalpel: The Anatomy Lesson of Dr Nicolaes Tulp Dissected*, exh. cat., Mauritshuis, The Hague 1998–9
- J. Luckhardt et al., *Der Krieg als Person: Herzog Christian der Jüngere im Bildnis von Paulus Moreelse*, exh. cat., Herzog Anton Ulrich-Museum, Braunschweig 2000
- *Pride and Joy: Children's Portraits in the Netherlands 1500–1700*, eds J.B. Bedaux, R. Ekkart, Frans Hals Museum, Haarlem, Koninklijk Museum voor Schone Kunsten, Antwerp 2000–1
- F.K. Laarmann, *Families in beeld: De ontwikkeling van het Noord-Nederlandse familieportret in de eerste helft van de zeventiende eeuw*, Hilversum 2002
- *Kopstukken: Amsterdammers geportretteerd 1600–1800*, exh. cat., ed. N. Middelkoop, Amsterdams Historisch Museum, Amsterdam 2002–3
- *Gelderse gezichten: Drie eeuwen portretkunst in Gelderland 1550–1850*, exh. cat., eds J.C. Bierens de Haan, R. Ekkart, Museum Het Valkhof, Nijmegen 2002–3
- *De snijkunst verbeeld: Delftse anatomische lessen nader belicht*, exh., cat., eds H. Houtzager, M. Jonker, Museum Het Prinsenhof, Delft 2002–3
- B. Broos, A. van Suchtelen, with contributions by Q. Buvelot, G. Sluiter, P. Noble, P. van der Ploeg, H. Vlieghe and F. Duparc, with an introductory essay by R. Ekkart, *Portraits in the Mauritshuis 1430–1790*, The Hague-Zwolle 2004

Index

Photographic credits

Figure numbers preceeding a letter refer to comparatives to the appropriate catalogue entry.

Amsterdam

- Amsterdams Historisch Museum: cats 30, 38 and 45; figs 18, 46, 45a, 53b
  Museum Van Loon: fig. 24
- Rijksmuseum: cats 5, 15, 21 and 60; figs 1, 3–5, 7, 22, 25–6, 33–4, 38, 44, 47, 49, 59–61, 65, 8–9a, 19a, 23a, 55a, 57a and 62b
- Six Collection © Six Art Promotion bv: cats 46 and 57

Amsterdam & Rijswijk

- Netherlands Institute for Cultural Heritage (Instituut Collectie Nederland): cats 11 and 42

Antwerp

- Koninklijk Museum van Schone Kunsten © Reproductiefonds: cat. 65; fig. 19
- Sint-Jacobskerk: fig. 6a

Apeldoorn

- Paleis Het Loo Nationaal Museum: cat. 43; fig. 64

Berlin

- Gemäldegalerie, Staatliche Museen © Bildarchiv Preussischer Kulturbesitz Berlin: cats 14, 36, 47 and 48; figs 9 and 54a

Budapest

- Szépmüvészéti Muzeum: figs 58–9a and b

Boston

- Museum of Fine Arts, Gift of Mrs. Antonie Lilienfeld in memory of Dr. Leon Lilienfeld, 1966: fig. 27a

Brussels

- Koninklijke Musea voor Schone Kunsten (photo: KIK / IRPA, Brussels): fig. 65a

Cleveland, Ohio

- The Cleveland Museum of Art, The Elisabeth Severance Prentiss Collection: fig. 3a

Columbus, Ohio

- Columbus Museum of Art: fig. 64a

Delft

- Museum Het Prinsenhof © Gemeente Musea Delft, photographer Tom Haartsen: cat. 39 and fig. 11

Dordrecht

- Dordrechts Museum: cat. 11

Edinburgh

- National Gallery of Scotland: cat. 7

Enschede

- Rijksmuseum Twenthe: fig. 25a

Geneva

- Musée d'Art et d'Histoire: fig. 13

Haarlem

- Frans Hals Museum: cats 23 and 42; figs 21, 32, 66, 16–17a and 23b

The Hague

- Haags Historisch Museum, photographer Rob Mostert, Rijswijk: cats 41 and 50
- Netherlands Institute for Art History (Rijksbureau voor Kunsthistorische Documentatie): figs 16–17, 39, 51 and 56
- Royal Picture Gallery Mauritshuis: cats 1–2, 10, 16–17, 32–3, 40, 52–3, 61 and 62; figs 2–3, 8, 48–9, 52–3, 64, 68, 26a, 35–6a, 49a and 62a

Hartford, Connecticut

Wadsworth Atheneum, The Ella Gallup Sumner and Mary Catlin Sumner Collection Fund: figs 40–1

Hoorn

- Westfries Museum: cats 8–9

Kassel

- Gemäldegalerie Alte Meister, Staatliche Museen: cats 13 and 56

Leeuwarden

- Fries Museum: fig. 57

Leiden

- Stedelijk Museum De Lakenhal: fig. 6
- Universiteitsbibliotheek: fig. 39a

London

- © The National Gallery © Trustees of the National Gallery: cats 3, 12, 22, 34, 44, 55, 58–9, 66 and fig. 2a
- National Portrait Gallery: cat. 31
- Kenwood House © English Heritage Photo Library: cat. 19
- The Royal Collection © 2007 Her Majesty Queen Elizabeth II: cats 4, 54; fig. 31a

Manchester, New Hampshire

- Currier Museum of Art: fig. 4a

Munich

- Alte Pinakothek, Bayerische Staatsgemäldesammlungen © Artothek: cat. 18 and fig. 15a

New York

- The Metropolitan Museum of Art: figs 36–7, 11a, 52a
- The Morgan Library & Museum: fig. 7a

Oud-Zuylen

- Slot Zuylen: fig. 42

Paris

- Institut Néerlandais, Frits Lugt Collection: cat. 49; fig. 5a
- Musée du Louvre (Photo: Réunion des Musées Nationaux, G. Blot & R.J. Ojeda): cat. 35; fig. 54

Prague

- Národní Galerie: cat. 25

Raleigh, North Carolina

- North Carolina Museum of Art: figs 27–8

Rotterdam

- Museum Boijmans Van Beuningen: cats 29, 63; figs 10, 23, 50

Saint-Omer

- Musée Sandelin et Musée Henri Dupuis: fig. 62

San Francisco, California

- Fine Arts Museums of San Francisco, Photo Services Department: cat. 51

St. Petersburg

- State Hermitage Museum: fig. 44a

Stockholm

- Hallwylska Museet: fig. 55

Utrecht

- Centraal Museum: figs 14–15, 31 and 35
- Museum Catharijneconvent: fig. 12

Versailles

- Musée National de Versailles: fig. 67

Voorschoten

- Duivenvoorde Castle: fig. 58

Washington

- National Gallery of Art: cats 6, 24, 28 and 64

Winterthur

- Rathaus, Museum Briner und Kern: figs 29 and 30

Zurich

- Stiftung Sammlung E.G. Bührle: cat. 27

Private collections

- Cats 2, 7, 20, 26, 37 and 52; figs 1[illegible], 16–17, 20, 39, 43, 45, 48, 51, 56, 65, 47–8a and b

Credits

Essays
Rudi Ekkart
Marieke de Winkel

Catalogue
Quentin Buvelot

with contributions by
- Axel Rüger
  Cats 3, 12, 22, 44, 55, 58–9 and 66
- Peter van der Ploeg
  Cats 13, 31, 41, 43, 56, 57 and 63
- Rudi Ekkart
  Cats 8-9, 39, 45, 47-8 and 65
- Ariane van Suchtelen
  Cats 4–7
- Lea van der Vinde
  Cats 46 and 50
- Marieke de Winkel
  Cat. 57
- Jonathan Bikker
  Cat. 21
- Martin Bijl &
  Pieter Biesboer
  Cat. 20

Compilation and editing
Quentin Buvelot

Translation
Beverly Jackson, Amsterdam

Copy-editing
Quentin Buvelot, Marjorie E. Wieseman and Tom Windross

Picture Research
Lea van der Vinde

Design and layout
DeLeeuwDesigner(s), The Hague

Production
Royal Picture Gallery Mauritshuis, The Hague, and National Gallery Company Limited

Publishing
Waanders Publishers, Zwolle

Print
Waanders Printers, Zwolle

HB ISBN 978 1 85709 362 9
525084
PB ISBN 978 1 85709 354 4
525081

British Library Cataloguing-in-Publication Data
A catalogue record is available from the British Library